*State Party Profiles*

# State Party Profiles

## A 50-STATE GUIDE TO DEVELOPMENT, ORGANIZATION, AND RESOURCES

*Edited by*

ANDREW M. APPLETON, *Washington State University*

AND

DANIEL S. WARD, *Rice University*

*With a Foreword by*

SAMUEL C. PATTERSON, *Ohio State University*

Published in cooperation with the Ray C. Bliss
Institute of Applied Politics, University of Akron

CQ CONGRESSIONAL QUARTERLY INC.
Washington, D.C.

*For our parents
and for Amy and Jim*

Printed in the United States of America

Cover design: Rich Pottern

LIBRARY OF CONGRESS CATALOGING-IN-PUBLICATION DATA

State party profiles : a 50-state guide to development, organization,
    and resources / edited by Andrew M. Appleton and Daniel S. Ward ;
    with a foreword by Samuel C. Patterson.
        p.   cm.
    Published in cooperation with the Ray C.Bliss Institute of
Applied Politics, University of Akron.
    Includes bibliographical references and index.
    ISBN 1-56802-150-X (hardcover : alk. paper)
    1. Political Parties—United States—States.   I. Appleton, Andrew
M.   II. Ward, Daniel S.
JK2261.S83   1997                          96-25500
324.273—dc20

# Contents

# About the Editors

Andrew M. Appleton received a Ph.D. in political science from New York University and currently is assistant professor at Washington State University, where he is also associate director of the Division of Governmental Studies and Services. His research and teaching interests lie in the areas of political behavior and comparative politics. He has published in several professional journals, including *Comparative Politics, West European Politics*, and *Party Politics*. He is coauthor of *Party Politics* (forthcoming).

Daniel S. Ward received a Ph.D. in political science from New York University and currently is assistant professor at Rice University. His major research focus is on political institutions, particularly parties and legislatures. He has published articles in numerous professional journals, including *Journal of Politics, Comparative Politics, Party Politics, Legislative Studies Quarterly*, and *Electoral Studies*. He is coauthor of *Party Politics* (forthcoming).

# Contributors

JOSEPH A. AISTRUP   *Asociate professor of political science and assistant director of the Docking Institute of Public Affairs, Fort Hays State University*
Kansas (coauthor)

ANDREW M. APPLETON   *Assistant professor of political science, Washington State University*
Washington (coauthor)

SUSAN A. BANDUCCI   *Assistant professor of political science, Oregon State University*
Oregon (coauthor)

MARK BANNISTER   *Director, the Docking Institute of Public Affairs, Fort Hays State University*
Kansas (coauthor)

W. JAY BARTH   *Assistant professor of politics, Hendrix College*
Arkansas (coauthor)

ROBERT C. BENEDICT   *Associate professor of political science, University of Utah*
Utah

DAVID R. BERMAN   *Professor of political science, Arizona State University*
Arizona

DIANE D. BLAIR   *Professor of political science, University of Arkansas*
Arkansas (coauthor)

DAVID BREAUX   *Associate professor of political science, Mississippi State University*
Mississippi (coauthor)

ROBERT J. BRESLER   *Professor of public policy, Pennsylvania State University at Harrisburg*
Pennsylvania (coauthor)

DAVID M. BRODSKY   *U. C. Foundation Professor of Political Science, University of Tennessee at Chattanooga*
Tennessee

JERRY CALVERT,   *Professor of political science, Montana State University*
Montana

JOHN A. CLARK   *Assistant professor of political science, University of Georgia*
Georgia

ALAN L. CLEM   *Professor of political science (emeritus), University of South Dakota*
South Dakota

ELMER E. CORNWELL JR.   *Professor of political science, Brown University*
Rhode Island

PATRICK R. COTTER   *Associate professor of political science, University of Alabama*
Alabama

ANNEKA DePOORTER   *Graduate student in political science, Washington State University*
Washington (coauthor)

BOB EGBERT   *Associate professor of political science, Plymouth State College*
New Hampshire (coauthor)

MICHELLE ANNE FISTEK   *Associate professor of political science, Plymouth State College*
New Hampshire (coauthor)

CRAIG GRAU   *Associate professor of political science, University of Minnesota at Duluth*
Minnesota

JOHN C. GREEN   *Professor of political science and director of the Ray C. Bliss Institute of Applied Politics, University of Akron*
Ohio (coauthor)

PAUL M. GREEN   *Director, Institute for Public Policy, Governors State University*
Illinois

MICHAEL K. GUSMANO   *Robert Wood Johnson Foundation Health Policy Scholar, Institution for Social and Public Policy Studies, Yale University*
Maryland (coauthor)

DAVID J. HADLEY   *Dean of students and professor of political science, Wabash College*
Indiana

JON F. HALE   *Analyst, Morningstar, Chicago,*
Oklahoma (coauthor)

ALLAN HAMMOCK   *Chair and associate professor of political science, West Virginia University*
West Virginia

KEVIN R. HARDWICK   *Associate professor of political science, Canisius College*
New York (coauthor)

MICHAEL V. HASELSWERDT   *Associate professor of political science, Canisius College*
New York (coauthor)

PAUL S. HERRNSON   *Professor of government and politics, University of Maryland*
Maryland (coauthor)

ERIC B. HERZIK   *Associate professor of political science, University of Nevada at Reno*
Nevada (coauthor)

SAMUEL B. HOFF   *Professor of political science, Delaware State University*
Delaware

MALCOLM E. JEWELL   *Professor of political science (emeritus), University of Kentucky*
Connecticut (coauthor) and Kentucky (coauthor)

JEFFREY A. KARP   *Visiting assistant professor of politics and government, University of Puget Sound, Washington State*
Oregon (coauthor)

STEPHEN T. KEAN   *Instructor and graduate student in political science, University of Oklahoma*
Oklahoma (coauthor)

ANNE E. KELLEY   *Associate professor of political science (emeritus), University of South Florida*
Florida

ANNE FEDER LEE   *Freelance writer*
Hawaii

ROBERT D. LOEVY   *Professor of political science, Colorado College*
Colorado

G. TERRY MADONNA   *Professor of political science and director of the Center for Politics and Public Affairs, Millersville University*
Pennsylvania (coauthor)

JOHN MCGLENNON   *Chair and professor of government, College of William and Mary*
Virginia

JEROME M. MILEUR   *Professor of political science, University of Massachusetts at Amherst,*
Massachusetts

PENNY M. MILLER   *Associate professor of political science, University of Kentucky*
Kentucky (coauthor)

SARAH M. MOREHOUSE   *Professor of political science (emeritus), University of Connecticut*
Connecticut (coauthor)

GARRISON NELSON   *Professor of political science, University of Vermont*
Vermont

LLOYD OMDAHL   *Professor of political science (emeritus), University of North Dakota*
North Dakota

JOEL PADDOCK   *Associate professor of political science, Southwest Missouri State University,*
Missouri

KENNETH T. PALMER   *Professor of political science, University of Maine*
Maine

T. WAYNE PARENT   *Associate professor of political science, Louisiana State University*
Louisiana

BRIAN D. POSLER   *Visiting assistant professor of political science, University of Texas at Tyler*
Texas (coauthor)

CHARLES PRYSBY   *Professor of political science, University of North Carolina at Greensboro*
North Carolina

CARL M. RHODES    *Graduate student in political science, Rice University*
New Mexico

BARBARA G. SALMORE    *Associate dean of the College of Liberal Arts and professor of political science, Drew University*
New Jersey (coauthor)

STEPHEN A. SALMORE    *Professor of political science, the Eagleton Institute of Politics, Rutgers University*
New Jersey (coauthor)

STEPHEN SHAFFER    *Professor of political science, Mississippi State University*
Mississippi (coauthor)

DANIEL M. SHEA    *Assistant professor of political science and research fellow of the Ray C. Bliss Institute of Applied Politics, University of Akron*
Ohio (coauthor)

CARL E. SHEPRO    *Associate professor of political science, University of Alaska at Anchorage*
Alaska

ROBERT F. SITTIG    *Professor of political science, University of Nebraska at Lincoln*
Nebraska

ANDREW SKALABAN    *Assistant professor of political science, University of California at Davis*
California

ROBERT P. STEED    *Professor of political science, the Citadel*
South Carolina

BARBARA TRISH    *Assistant professor of political science, Grinnell College*
Iowa

OLIVER WALTER    *Dean of arts and sciences and professor of political science, University of Wyoming*
Wyoming

DANIEL S. WARD    *Assistant professor of political science, Rice University*
Texas (coauthor)

DAVID G. WEGGE    *Professor of political science, St. Norbert College*
Wisconsin

CAROL S. WEISSERT    *Associate professor of political science, Michigan State University*
Michigan

ALLEN R. WILCOX    *Professor of political science, University of Nevada at Reno*
Nevada (coauthor)

THOMAS WILSON    *Graduate student in political science, University of Mississippi*
Mississippi (coauthor)

STEPHANIE L. WITT    *Chair and associate professor of political science, Boise State University*
Idaho

# Foreword

There surely are peculiar myths about the role of political parties in American politics and especially about the standing of organized political parties in the states. One myth draws on the muckraking vein in American political history, conjuring the image of party political machines and bosses. The historical litany of city party bosses stretches from William M. "Boss" Tweed's control of the New York City Democrats meeting in Tammany Hall, to Thomas J. Pendergast's sway over the Democratic machine in Kansas City, to Edward H. "Boss" Crump of Memphis, to Cincinnati Republican boss George B. "Old Boy" Cox, to Mayor Richard J. Daley of Chicago. The litany of state party organization bosses stretches from Boies "Big Grizzly" Penrose of Pennsylvania to Huey P. "the Kingfish" Long of Louisiana. The mythology alleges that state parties, like these political machines, exert undue influence over political affairs.

The more prevalent mythology of recent experience is that the state parties have been displaced by the national party organizations because of the rise of political action committees, the centrality of electronic media in modern politics, or simply the decay and decline of state organizations. Far from propounding the image that state parties control political affairs, the mythology of decline alleges that the parties have decomposed so pervasively that they no longer can be counted as substantial or important actors in electoral politics.

The truth of the matter lies somewhere between these extremes. State political parties certainly are not dead. There is too much anecdotal evidence of party consequentiality and too convincing empirical evidence of party organizational strength to accept the doctrine of party irrelevance, incapacity, or ineptitude.

The myths and misconceptions about the status of the state political parties are fed by ignorance, neglect, and a paucity of systematic information. Recently, whenever scholars have looked for evidence of state party strength and vitality, they have found a considerable amount of both. But the state parties are numerous and diverse, and systematic data collection has been spotty and peripatetic.

Monitoring the development and performance of the state parties will be assisted measurably by *State Party Profiles: A 50-State Guide to Development, Organization, and Resources*. In these chapters, editors Andrew M. Appleton and Daniel S. Ward have assembled a guide to crucial sources of data and a rich trove of information about the political background of the parties and party development in each of the fifty states. Each chapter provides a very fecund profile of the condition of the parties in the state and a veritable gold mine of information about the archival resources in the state upon which analysis in depth and over time can proceed. This compilation is a valuable, indeed an indispensable, reference source for the study of political parties in the United States. It will help to continue the important process of demythologizing our state parties and both encourage and abet the systematic study of party organizational politics in the states.

This collection of historical and archival guidelines underscores the diversity of the state party systems and adumbrates some of the crucial effects of time and circumstance on party change. The collection sheds light on the adaptation of the state parties to the political and technological realities of modern political life, and in particular to the inexorable polarization of politics in America over the past three decades. And we learn of the continuing importance of state party leadership, not in the heavy-handed manner of the machine bosses of an earlier era but in the capacity of leaders to practice effective management of organizations and symbols. Finally, this foray into the putative archival materials available for scholarly research exposes the remarkable resources available and brings into bold relief the hills and valleys of the archival record. We are brought to appreciate what more can be learned about state parties from archival material and where the historical records, because they are skimpy or nonexistent, will not allow scholars to accumulate a full portfolio of diachronic data for every state.

Those of us who study state party politics can rightfully feel indebted to this assemblage of authors and their editors for compiling this valuable historical and archival information for each of the American states. And we may hope that this effort is only a beginning—that it will stimulate and foster developmental and comparative research that will give the study of subnational party systems and their role in national party politics its proper place in the sun.

*Samuel C. Patterson*
*Ohio State University*

# Preface

*State Party Profiles* brings together previously disparate information on state Democratic and Republican parties. This work, in fifty alphabetical profiles written by experts on the politics of each state, is intended to serve several purposes for those interested in state politics and political parties. First, it provides a unique historical accounting of the development of the two-party system at the state level. Although the principal focus of the profiles is on the modern era (since 1960), many of the contributors have provided a deeper historical perspective as well. Second, it lays out the contours of contemporary party politics in the states, emphasizing the official state party organizations, their structures, activities, and leadership. Finally, a major contribution of the volume is that it catalogs the primary research resources available on the one hundred state parties. Through surveys, interviews, and site visits, the contributors have documented virtually all the original material on state parties, noting the location, contents, and accessibility of each source. By combining these elements, *State Party Profiles* offers as complete a portrait of state party politics as can be found on a library's or scholar's shelves today.

The book's genesis was a conference paper on subnational parties, first presented in 1991, which we published in *Comparative Politics* two years later. One of the central arguments of that article was that party organizational change is a result of changes in the competitive environment of those organizations. Because of a dearth of organizational data, we limited the empirical analysis to the competition side of the equation. Our attempts to locate organizational data sufficient for longitudinal analysis led us to conduct several case studies using state party archives and to conduct a survey of all one hundred state parties and the official archive or library of each state. What we discovered was both encouraging and disheartening.

We were encouraged because there appeared to be a vast amount of original data on state political parties available for analysis, but it remained largely untapped. Unfortunately, much of the data was uncataloged, locked away in storage, and otherwise out of the easy reach of scholars. Moreover, it was clear that few parties viewed their historical records as valuable documents that should be part of the public record, and so the existing archives were vulnerable. *State Party Profiles* began as an effort to have scholars with intimate knowledge of the politics of each state review the existing records and report on their condition. Needless to say, the volume has grown into something considerably more extensive and valuable.

Once the task of locating interested scholars in each state was completed (on which more below), we set out to produce a work that would contain useful comparative information, while at the same time would allow each state expert to elucidate the most important aspects of that state's party politics. The result, we believe, is an unparalleled compilation of state party histories in combination with information on resources available for research purposes. Not only will this volume tell researchers where to find primary data on state political parties (or whether, indeed, such data exist), but the state profiles themselves will become required reading on the politics of each state. The authors of each profile were asked to follow a template that, while somewhat restricting, was designed to add to the comparative utility of the volume. It will be clear to readers, however, that each author or set of authors brings unique expertise to the chapters. Some are experts on state politics (among them former candidates for public office), whereas others have more general scholarly interests that they bring to bear on their analyses. What is remarkable is the amount of information that the contributors have been able to fit into the strict word limit that we imposed on them.

## THE PLAN OF THE BOOK

In the introduction we discuss the significance of state parties as objects of systematic analysis. We highlight the central role of these organizations in contemporary politics and draw examples from the succeeding profiles to identify consistent patterns of adaptation that the state parties have exhibited during the modern era. The goal of the introduction is to offer a collective portrait of state parties today, whereas the individual state profiles describe many unique features of the fifty party systems.

Each state profile has four essential sections. The first part deals with the historical development of the two-party system. Here we are interested to detail the process by which the two major national parties of today, the Democratic and the Republican, became established within each state. The second element of each profile, though still historical, focuses more narrowly on the modern era of party development. As Cornelius Cotter, John Bibby, James Gibson, and Robert Huckshorn revealed in their Party Transformation Study more than a decade ago (1984), state and local party organizations have, on balance, become stronger and more active in the modern period than they had been before, with higher levels of institutionalization and professionalization. Where recent evidence suggests that these revitalized party organizations may have changed not just the way that they do business but also the business that they do, the contributions in this volume illustrate the forces that have shaped and molded each state party in recent years.

The third section of each state profile emphasizes the current state of affairs for each of the one hundred parties. Each profile conveys the place of the two major parties in the contemporary politics of the state by documenting the current organizational structure and the major activities of the parties and their leaders. Finally, in a fourth section every author provides a resource guide detailing the availability, contents, and condition of original party documents that may be of value for research in the state. Resource guide tables are presented for those states with substantial archival records, and more detailed descriptions of the material are included for the most comprehensive holdings. The reference list for each profile serves both as a bibliography and as a guide to the most important writings on the politics of the state. Together with the resource guide this information will offer clear direction for anyone interested in conducting research on party politics in a particular state or states.

In addition to providing the material for individual profiles, authors were asked to complete a checklist of state regulations regarding the organization of parties and the treatment of parties in the electoral process (see Appendix). We believe this is the first attempt to bring such information together in a single source since the important report a decade ago by the Advisory Commission on Intergovernmental Relations (1986). We have attempted to condense the vast array of separate state provisions into a form that allows for simple comparisons of the regulatory contexts in which the state parties operate.

Taken together, these profiles provide a unique and detailed look at state political parties, from their origins to their current status. Our intention is that readers of this volume will learn more about the collective aspects of state parties than was realistically possible in the past. Naturally, there is much more to be learned about any one state party, both the intricacies of its history and the complexity of its current operation. We hope this book will serve as a roadmap for such research.

## A NOTE ON PARTY ARCHIVES

In the resource guides, authors have noted the location of party archives, if any. Most parties report the existence of historical documents, housed at party headquarters, in a storage facility, or at a university or state library. The resource guides indicate the principal years covered by the collection along with information about the accessibility and organization of information. All information located in libraries is available for public viewing, though parties may restrict access. To view materials located at party headquarters, researchers almost always must make an appointment before access will be granted. Several parties indicated reluctance to allow any access to party documents.

Authors were asked to determine whether certain sets of documents, which we view as most informative and useful, are part of the party collections; these included executive committee minutes, correspondence, party rules, budgets, and information on the organizational structure of the party. Perhaps the most valuable documents for systematic analysis of party operations over time are executive committee minutes. Just as party platforms have been characterized as the public face of political parties, minutes record their most important internal activities. Most, if not all, of a party's actions that are of interest to scholars will be noted in committee minutes, including personnel changes, recruitment efforts, get-out-the-vote drives, financing strategies, and so forth. Moreover, internal conflicts are likely to be indicated by recorded votes on important organizational decisions. Because they are an organization's institutional memory, and because they normally are not deemed to be part of the public record, minutes may be among the most objective and reliable of all party documents. Fortunately, reports from the states indicate that minutes are among the most commonly retained records. In fact, in many cases where other items are stored haphazardly, minutes are bound and easily accessible.

Ultimately, through the efforts of individual scholars in different states, the information contained in party archives may become part of the shared data so vital to scholarly research. Through the evidence provided by contributors to this volume, that pursuit, although still painstaking, has become more feasible than in the past. Over time we hope the parties will recognize that their documents constitute the historical record of our national party system. We trust that these records will then be turned over to professional archivists for proper preservation, as all such historical collections warrant.

## ACKNOWLEDGMENTS

Any work of this magnitude inevitably is the result of a vast collective effort. First, we thank the sixty-four contributors who provided immeasurable local expertise that could never be matched by a smaller (though perhaps more manageable) group from afar. We thank them for their indulgence as the project grew and our coordination wavered. We also are indebted to Samuel C. Patterson for lending his imprimatur to our effort and launching the work so eloquently in the foreword. We are grateful to John Bibby, an early supporter of the volume who helped us in our initial search for contributors. When we had exhausted our professional contacts in our efforts to locate contributors, we were aided by two resources: the Southern Grassroots Activists Project, many of whose participants signed on to our work, and Clive Thomas, who apparently knows every living political scientist. The ongoing efforts of John Green, Dan Shea, and the Ray C. Bliss Institute of Applied Politics at the University of Akron, including their support for this project, are gratefully acknowledged. A number of graduate students assisted in preparing this manuscript, including Christine Guillory, Philip Moore, Brian Posler, and Carl Rhodes of Rice University and Thomas Morgan and Anneka DePoorter of Washington State University.

Our support at Congressional Quarterly has been extraordinary. Our acquisitions editor, Shana Wagger, bought the idea from us despite the risks involved and sold it to the powers that be at CQ. She encouraged, prodded, and advised us along the way, helping to keep a sprawling venture under control. Jerry Orvedahl, the manuscript editor for this project, was a godsend. Jerry made his way through the entire manuscript, reading with a skilled eye and editing with a talented pen (or keyboard, as the case may be). Though we have vowed never to engage in a project of this nature again, we would be delighted to work with Shana and Jerry and Congressional Quarterly in the future.

A collaboration that began with a conference paper in 1991 has now produced nearly a dozen published works, with more on the horizon. If our working relationship can survive this effort, the rest should be easy. In addition to the joint appreciation expressed above, each of us has several personal "thank yous" to offer.

Dan is indebted to a number of friends and colleagues who offered moral support during a difficult year, including Nasrin Abdolali, Chris Anderson, Cary Funk, Amy Mazur, Kathleen O'Connor, Charles Pearson, Mickey Quinones, Sherry Bennett Quinones, and (of course) Andrew. As always, he owes a professional debt to Paul Brace, Christine Harrington, Gary King, and the late Barbara Hinckley, whose special capacity to join politics and political science continues to inspire his own work. Finally, the book is dedicated to his parents, Kathleen and Dennis Ward, for their unquestioning love, support, and understanding, and to Jim Wiltfong, whose sacrifices render this dedication meager compensation. As further tribute, we spare him from reading the final product.

Andrew could not have survived without the friendship and support of Joanna Baker, Cornell Clayton, Wendy Clayton, Adam Gaines, Corinne Herbel, Yves Herbel, and "Dan from Houston." It is possible that the latter may not have survived Demon's Drop unscathed had his coauthor not had a frightening vision of all those profiles left to edit. In addition, his friends and colleagues at Canisius College and at Washington State University have been patient and understanding and have thrown dinner parties at all the right moments. Kay Lawson, John Keeler, Martin Schain, and Susan Scarrow have provided special professional advice and encouragement along the way. From his parents, Ruth and Joseph Appleton, he has received much that cannot be repaid in one sentence; he dedicates this book to them. Finally, the book is also dedicated to Amy; she must wish that she had never had such an idea!

## REFERENCES

Advisory Commission on Intergovernmental Relations. 1986. *The transformation in American politics.* Washington, D.C.: ACIR.

Cotter, Cornelius, John Bibby, James Gibson, and Robert Huckshorn. 1984. *Party organizations in American politics.* New York: Praeger.

# Introduction

At a time when American political leaders are effecting the most significant shift in policy-making powers since the New Deal, a devolution from federal to state authority, a refocusing of scholarly attention on state political institutions is in order. Moreover, the "deinstitutionalization" of state legislatures that is inherent in term limits and other reform proposals will likely enhance the importance of political parties in the representative and policy-making processes. To the casual observer, this might seem an untenable proposition; surely the state political parties cannot be prepared for increased responsibility after decades of centralization of party power in Washington and the growth of political action committees (PACs) and other institutions of political influence. But the titles of two recent essays by leading party scholars hint otherwise. In "The Persistence of State Parties" (Patterson 1993) and "State Party Organizations: Coping and Adapting" (Bibby 1994), the authors portray state parties as resilient and innovative institutions that may be prepared for their growing role in the coming decades.

*State Party Profiles* establishes the contours of contemporary state party politics by portraying the full measure of the parties' organizational strengths and weaknesses. Although the profiles document that the one hundred state parties exhibit many unique features, it is equally striking that a vast majority of the parties have had to respond to similar environmental stimuli and that many have done so in a like manner. Here we review these shared patterns of behavior. We begin by exploring the nationalization of politics, to which most, if not all, parties have had to react. We next examine the parties' principal means of response and adaptation to nationalization. Finally, we consider what may be the key variable that determines the success or failure of a party's response to its environment—organizational leadership.

## HOW NATIONALIZATION OF AMERICAN POLITICS AFFECTS STATE PARTIES

Every type of organization is designed to function in a particular kind of arena or environment. For example, businesses must compete in an economic market, whereas law firms face a formally prescribed legal system. For political parties in the United States, the most relevant arena is the electoral marketplace. Although parties compete in the legislative arena as well, in a two-party system electoral victory is paramount because legislative power is wielded by the party winning the majority of seats. In order to understand how environmental change affects party organizational performance, it is necessary to focus on changes in the electoral arena.

In the modern political era, which we define as 1960 forward, electoral politics in the United States has been shaped by many forces, but the process of nationalization may be the most far-reaching. William M. Lunch has described the nationalized political environment as one in which "to a much greater extent significant choices in American society are made directly by the national government, or at least with the approval of the national government" (1987, 3). Among the early manifestations of nationalization that shaped the electoral process were the Supreme Court's *Baker v. Carr* decision in 1962 (369 U.S. 186), the Voting Rights Act of 1965, and the emergence of the primary system as a principal means of selecting presidential and other nominees (Appleton and Ward 1993, 77–79). A less political but nevertheless important factor promoting nationalization has been the emergence of mass media and communications, especially television, as a source of political information.

The implications of nationalization for political party organizations have been profound. More than thirty years into the modern party era, a general consensus has begun to form about the state of contemporary political parties. Although an initial and persuasive argument was made that an inevitable result of nationalization was party decline (see Wattenberg 1994 for a clear presentation of the "declinist" perspective), more recent scholarship has focused on the emergence of a new kind of political party. Through sound theorizing (see especially Schlesinger 1991; Aldrich 1995) and exhaustive empirical analysis (for example, Cotter et al. 1989; Herrnson 1988) we now have a more complete understanding of modern parties, one whose evidentiary base is not confined to voting behavior. The transition from traditional party organizations as described by Mayhew (1986), which were largely autonomous and dependent on a mass base of support, to "parties in service" (Aldrich 1995), which must compete with other types of organizations for influence in the electoral and political processes, now seems nearly complete.

One of the most important results of the transition for state parties has been a convergence of structures and practices. Moreover, their convergence toward a common service-vendor model of organization and activity largely has been orchestrated by the national party organizations. Schlesinger's theory of a new American political party (1991) predicts greater cooperation among legally autonomous party units as a result of a more volatile electorate.

*Convergence.* For a substantial portion of U.S. history, politics could not be understood absent a discussion of sectionalism. Indeed, party history is replete with accounts of one-partyism in the South and political machines in the urban North. Although regional differences remain an important component of contemporary political analysis, they no longer define the structures and practices of political party organizations. Indeed, in a 1994 survey of state party chairs, we found that party leaders describe their activities in very similar ways regardless of region or party affiliation. For example, using responses to questions regarding the significance of various campaign techniques, we constructed an index of modern activities (such as polling and electronic media) and an index of traditional activities (canvassing, get-out-the-vote drives, and the like). Comparing the means of the indices across four regional categories yielded no statistically significant differences, nor did a comparison of Democrats and Republicans. In another set of questions, respondents were asked to rate the influence of four organizations—the state party, national party, candidate campaign, and independent organizations—on the outcome of gubernatorial races in their states. Again, region and party had little or no effect on leaders' responses.[1]

The 1994 survey produced just a snapshot of the postconvergence state parties rather than a comprehensive accounting of the convergence process. The state profiles herein, however, offer a more complete description of that dynamic. In state after state, party organizational development toward the service-vendor model in the modern era was shaped by events at the national level. During the critical years—the mid-1960s to the mid-1970s—

the Republican National Committee (RNC) was headed by two organizationally minded and innovative chairs, Ray C. Bliss and Bill Brock. Both contributed greatly to introducing innovations that gave rise to the "party in service" (Aldrich 1995). In contrast, the Democratic National Committee (DNC) during this period was preoccupied with questions of representation and internal democracy. Consequently, most state Republican parties were transformed into service-vendor organizations under the tutelage of the RNC before their state Democratic counterparts made the transition (notable exceptions were Hawaii and New Hampshire).

In some cases, the Republican makeover entailed not just a transformation of the state party but the very birth of such an organization. Obviously the southern states are prime examples of this latter phenomenon. The presidential campaigns of Dwight D. Eisenhower and Barry Goldwater were catalysts for most long-dormant southern Republican parties, but sustained support from the RNC and local leadership proved to be the critical factors for success. In some states outside the South—for example, Arizona—the state Republican Party evolved in an atmosphere of great independence from the RNC; there, however, the presence of Goldwater, a national figure, militated against national party involvement. Only a very few state Republican parties have operated virtually autonomously from the national party in the modern era, New Hampshire being perhaps the most obvious. It is surely no coincidence, then, that the New Hampshire Republicans have struggled to make the transition to a service-vendor type of party organization.

Obviously the experience of state Democratic parties was colored by more than just struggles over representation and internal democracy in the first decade and a half of the modern party era. Particularly in the South, but also in states such as Indiana, the Voting Rights Act of 1965 had a profound effect on state-level politics by bringing a large number of minority citizens into the electorate—and particularly into the Democratic Party. The act's influence was felt first through inevitable changes in federal elections, in which the organizational apparatus necessary to incorporate new voters was in place. Its influence was felt next within the Democratic Party over the issue of representation at national conventions (presidential nominating politics), an issue that culminated in the McGovern-Fraser reforms that are cited in so many chapters as having shaped the internal politics of state Democratic parties at that time. The turmoil created by the McGovern-Fraser reforms was not confined to southern Democratic parties; dissension surfaced in diverse states such as Arizona, Michigan, and even Hawaii. The point is made in the Texas profile but can be applied more generally that the aggregate effect of McGovern-Fraser on state Democratic parties was to shift the organizational emphasis away from the new kinds of services that the Republicans were beginning to provide. Only later, when the Republican innovations began to affect electoral outcomes in the Republicans' favor, did most state Democratic parties respond.

*Professionalization.* The convergence of parties toward the service-provider prototype, we believe, is not the result of an inevitable process of institutionalization. Instead, given that convergence has taken place in the context of nationalization, it is reasonable to conclude that the national parties have been instrumental in directing the course of change at the state level. Not only has political power been concentrated in Washington in the past three decades, but the changes that have taken place in electoral politics are relatively costly ones that are dependent on modern technologies. The comparatively wealthy national parties have been in a better position to develop, test, and improve the means of modern campaigning and then to transmit knowledge and resources down to the state level. As a result of national party assistance, the state parties have moved a considerable distance from being amateur, volunteer-based organizations toward durability and professionalism.

Naturally, the process of professionalization has not been identical for all state parties. Considering 1960 as the beginning of the modern era, we find that some organizations were starting from an already strong base, whereas others were starting virtually from nothing. But evidence from the state profiles indicates that parties from across the spectrum have moved largely in the same direction, toward professionalization.

The fundamental element of a professional party organization is money; the RNC began in the 1960s to provide cash to state parties (see, for example, Arkansas), a practice that continues today. But of more consequence, the RNC furnished the technical expertise that allowed state Republican parties to raise their own money through direct mail and tele-marketing; the Indiana Republicans took the lead, and other Republican state parties fol-lowed suit. In some cases—Maryland, for example—RNC cooperation extended to sharing its direct-mail operation with the state party; party records indicate the same was true in Arkansas.

Professionalization also occurred within state Democratic parties but rarely ahead of their Republican competitors. In many cases the Democrats continued to lag behind well into the 1990s, North Carolina being one example; in a few cases, among them Nevada and Alaska, the state Democratic parties continue to be more ad hoc and amateur than perma-nent and professional. Another generalization that can be drawn from the profiles is that state Democratic parties have, in the main, tended to place more emphasis on campaign coordination and candidate training and less on direct financial support compared with Republicans. This observation cannot be divorced from the comparative disadvantage in financial resources of state Democratic parties that is portrayed in many of the profiles.

## STATE PARTY ADAPTATION IN THE MODERN ERA

It is not our contention that state parties have changed simply because the national par-ties directed them to do so. Despite the centralization fostered by the nationalization of American politics, state parties do remain legally autonomous institutions. In fact, the 1989 Supreme Court decision in *Eu v. San Francisco County Democratic Central Committee* (489 U.S. 214), which held that rigid state control of the organization and activities of political parties was an infringement of the right of association, may have been the boldest stroke ever in favor of state party autonomy (see the Appendix for a full catalog of state regula-tions over party organizations). Moreover, it is axiomatic that organizations of all types are resistant to change. The changes undertaken by state parties were in response to threats in the parties' environments that affected their performance. In other words, parties change when they determine that their existing practices are inadequate for the environment in which they exist. Harmel and Janda (1994) came to the same conclusion; they contend that the more pronounced the parties' electoral failures the more likely the parties are to make changes in their operations.

That many parties have adapted in much the same way, that is, toward a service-vendor type of organization, is attributable to the fact that the most compelling environmental shock for a majority of parties has been nationalization. So, for example, all parties had to adjust to the realities of redistricting imposed by the Supreme Court in the early 1960s. Southern parties especially had to respond to the Civil Rights and Voting Rights Acts. In order to have their delegations recognized at the national conventions and to play a role in the presidential nomination process, state Democratic parties consistently struggled in the early 1970s with delegate-selection processes imposed by the national party. What these and other factors have done is create a more volatile electorate and increasingly competitive constituencies. In addition, changes in campaign techniques brought about by nationalization have introduced new players into the electoral arena, creating competitiveness between parties and other organizations in addition to increasing competitiveness between the two major parties.

*Adaptation to Electoral Competitiveness.* A central tenet of the "party in decline" school of thought is that as voters become more independent overall, and even partisans are less committed to their particular party, parties will suffer. But as voters were behaving in just that way (Wattenberg 1994), there was increasing evidence of continued, if not growing, state party strength (Cotter et al. 1989), strengthened national parties (Herrnson 1988), and a return to partisanship in the U.S. Congress (Rohde 1991; Ward 1993, 1994). Electoral behavior indicated that voters were willing to switch allegiance and divide their votes, so parties could no longer rely on a mass base of support from election to election. This voter volatility produced opportunities for nascent parties and a threat to dominant ones. As Schlesinger (1991) and Aldrich (1995) have argued, this situation contributed to the emergence of service-vendor parties.

The adaptation by state party organizations is most apparent in the South, where changes in competitiveness were most acute. All over the region, V. O. Key's observations about the weakness of the state Democratic Party organizations continued to hold true until well into the 1970s. In Alabama, Arkansas, Florida, Georgia, Louisiana, Mississippi, North Carolina, South Carolina, Texas, and Virginia increased party competition and newly vitalized state Republican Parties finally forced the Democrats to respond. In West Virginia—the notable exception among southern states—the continued lack of competitiveness in the early 1990s has allowed the state Democratic Party to persist in an organizationally weak mode.

Increased competitiveness was not confined to the South, however. Other state profiles provide an array of examples from other regions of the country where a vital two-party system has been a stimulus for organizational change. The Arizona Democrats have become more competitive and have built a vital party organization; the same is true of Maine Democrats in the past thirty years. In a slightly different scenario, Montana, Ohio, and Washington are states where the maintenance of competitiveness in national-level elections is cited as the reason for continued organizational efforts on the part of the state parties. The evidence from these profiles is compelling; increased party competition is a stimulus for increased party organization.

*Adaptation to Competing Organizations.* As noted above, state parties not only have to struggle to compete with the opposition party but also with new and alternative types of political organizations. These alternative organizations were themselves a result of the political processes discussed above (including nationalization and professionalization). For example, the emergence of candidate-centered campaigns and associated candidate committees may be viewed, at least in part, as a result of the implementation of direct primaries, which took the nomination process out of the hands of party activists. Campaign finance reform of the early 1970s and the related 1976 Supreme Court decision in *Buckley v. Valeo* (424 U.S. 1) at once gave rise to political action committees, while also promoting the use of individual wealth as a source of campaign funds (Sorauf 1988). Finally, in an uncertain environment some political leaders felt a need to link campaign activities with the legislative work of parties, a development that led to the emergence of legislative campaign committees, both at the national (Herrnson 1988) and state (Shea 1995) levels.

According to the "party in decline" school, the advent of so many formidable competitors in the electoral arena did not bode well for parties in the late 1970s and early 1980s. According to this view, the parties, already enervated by the loss of mass support, could be dealt a fatal blow by any threat to their place in electoral campaigning. Rather than crumble, however, both national and state parties adapted to their new environment, developing symbiotic rather than competitive relations with PACs, candidate campaign committees (CCCs), and legislative campaign committees (LCCs).

Nearly all the profiles contain evidence that state party organizations have had to confront these new competitors in the electoral arena. The outcomes, however, differ. In some cases the parties seem to have adapted quite well and have found ways to coexist productively with PACs, CCCs, and LCCs. In states as diverse as Louisiana, Idaho, and New Mexico, state parties find themselves working closely with these kinds of organizations. But in Kansas, PACs have tended to undermine the ability of the state Democratic Party to shape campaigns through the power of the purse, and they may even have contributed to increased factionalism within the party. On the other hand, the Wisconsin Republicans have used a PAC as a conduit to circumvent state public financing provisions in a fascinating example of adaptation. Generally, relations between parties and other organizations are strong where personality and leadership are strong, and relations are weak where personality and leadership are weak.

Although it does not properly constitute a change in the environment for all parties, the continued influence of elected incumbents over state parties should not be neglected. The continuum runs from those states where the party organization is part of the "governor's team" (for example, Michigan Republicans) to those where the party constitutes a negligible factor in gubernatorial politics (Louisiana Democrats). In few states are the relationships between parties and statewide elected officials smooth and unencumbered. The southern Democratic parties, prior to modern party-building efforts, were largely vehicles of personal ambition; in some cases, little has changed in that regard. Yet in other states— for example, Maryland—state parties have been challenged by the independent power base of elected officials, especially the governor. Kansas is another example; deep rifts between the Republican governor and the state party in the mid-1990s have exposed the fragile relationship that exists between party organization and party in government. Sometimes, as in the case of Michigan, an organizationally minded governor can prove an asset to the state party. But as more and more states have become truly competitive, no longer is there only one dominant party that has to chart a course in its relations with elected officials; to this extent, the environment has changed appreciably for hitherto minority parties.

## THE ROLE OF PARTY LEADERSHIP

To this point we have discussed changes made by organizations in response to environmental pressures. Of course, it is not organizations that decide to adapt or adjust their structures or behaviors but the leaders of those organizations. Despite the general patterns of change that we have described, there remains considerable variance in party behavior across the one hundred organizations discussed in this book—all amply demonstrated by the contributors. Leadership is one of the principal explanations for that variance. Individuals, often joined in committees, must make purposive decisions about the activities of their organizations. Some are more experienced or talented than others; a handful may place personal goals ahead of party goals; some party leaders are more constrained by state law, party rules, or resources than others. These and many other factors affect the ways that organizations respond to environmental pressures.

Two important developments during the modern era help us to understand the central role of party leaders in the recent history of state parties. First, in a particularly dynamic period characterized by organizational adaptation it might be argued that the most successful parties were those willing to take a chance on new ideas—that is, to innovate. Those leaders who were more comfortable falling back on familiar practices were less likely to respond swiftly to the challenges posed by modern politics. A related development that assisted state party leaders who promoted change was the centralization of power in state party organizations and in party chairs particularly. Professionalization fostered centralization by placing a paid, full-time leader at the party helm. This outcome, in turn, streamlined communications between state party leaderships and the national parties.

*Organizational Innovation.* An important choice made by many party leaders during the modern era was to innovate. In general, innovation can be a principal means of advancement for organizations of all types. As noted before, however, organizations have a built-in resistance to change, and this may be especially so for innovation, which entails new, often untested, change (Appleton and Ward forthcoming). In a period of swift and transforming technological development, however, a willingness to attempt new methods of operation was crucial for the successful adaptation of parties. This was especially so because some of the greatest threats to parties came from new organizations, which lacked the reluctance to innovate that characterizes older institutions. The national Republicans have long been recognized as more innovative than their Democratic counterparts, and they took the lead in modernization during the 1960s and 1970s under the leadership of Bliss and Brock (Bibby 1994, 37–38). State Republicans were early beneficiaries of the national party's innovation, as many of the state profiles demonstrate. In some states Democrats responded to their partisan competitors prior to national party action. In more recent years, however, the national Democrats essentially have achieved parity with the Republicans, and greater equity has been achieved at the state level as well.

From the introduction of new technologies, to alternative organizational strategies, to changing involvement in campaigns, the critical role played by party leaders is highlighted throughout this book. Naturally, the leaders' choices are limited by available resources. Whereas the Florida Republican chair carries out the work of the party with more than two dozen full-time paid staff, the Democratic chair in Nevada runs essentially a one-person operation.

But regardless of staff size and budget there are still decisions to be made in most parties about organizational priorities and the use of resources. Often change in organizational practice is preceded by a change in leadership. Party building has not been purely incremental in the modern era; as is emphasized in the Utah profile, the pace and timing of change are clearly affected by individual decisions. Whether it be Harry Hughes in Maryland, Charles Pine in Arizona, Karen Marchioro in Washington, or Lisa Walker in Mississippi, party leaders have been able to force rapid and effective change in organizational practices at the state level.

*Centralization of Party Power.* As party politics moved from mass-based support and volunteer activity toward professional, technologically oriented campaigning, strong central leadership became an asset. It is no longer viable to put together temporary organizations for an election year; instead, a vital, ongoing operation is essential. This necessity has led to a strengthening of party leadership. Another fortunate development for party leaders was the Supreme Court's decision in *Eu,* which freed state party organizations from much statutory control (see Appendix). Recent state-level campaign finance legislation seems to bode well for state party organizations as well. For example, in Washington new campaign finance regulations have made it possible for the state parties to insert themselves more inexorably into the campaign process.

Prior to the modern era, the majority of state parties seem to have been in a condition of structural and behavioral weakness vis-à-vis county organizations, where they existed. This seems especially true of northeastern states such as New York, Massachusetts, New Jersey, and New Hampshire. The same was true, for different reasons, of heavily regulated western states, such as Idaho, Washington, and Oregon. Where county parties did not really exist, neither did the state parties; this was characteristic of the South. In either condition—weak or strong county parties—professionalization in the modern era has coincided with a de facto concentration of power at the state-party level. In strong-county states, like New York, county party organizations have been particularly hard hit by the emergence of CCCs and LCCs; state party organizations, on the other hand, have developed precisely the coordinating service-oriented role that none of the county organizations is able to perform. In Washington, state party organizations have found the means to have the restrictions of state law reinterpreted in their favor (the Democratic Party taking its case all the way to the Supreme Court in *Marchioro v. Chaney* (442 U.S. 191, 1979).

Where party building took place, as in the South, it was the state party organizations that tried to build vitality at the county level. In all cases—in states of the Northeast, West, and South, in states with traditionally strong county organizations and states with traditionally weak county parties—there has been a significant accretion of power at the state level.

## CONCLUSION

In sum, the fifty state profiles in this book describe the vast changes that have swept the state parties as they organized to win elections. The nationalization of the party system is visible both in the convergence of parties toward the service-vendor model and in the professionalization of their organizations. State parties are clearly as adaptable as their national counterparts; competitive electoral arenas have been a stimulus for change in previously dominant party organizations, while continued competitiveness in others has maintained the incentives to organize. Yet parties have faced new competitors, and our contributors highlight the fragility of relations between state parties and these competing organizations, a relationship that continues to evolve. Finally, what makes state politics fascinating to many is the rich array of colorful figures who have dominated and marked the political scene in individual states. State parties are not immune from the influence of personality; the following profiles document the efforts of men and women, party leaders, who have helped shape political life in state and nation.

## NOTE

1. We conducted a pre- and postelection survey of state party chairs in 1994. These results are from the preelection phase, with a response rate of 54 percent. For further details on this survey, see Appleton and Ward 1996.

## REFERENCES

Aldrich, John. 1995. *Why parties?* Chicago: University of Chicago Press.

Appleton, Andrew M., and Daniel S. Ward. Forthcoming. Party response to environmental change: A model of organizational innovation. *Party Politics.*

___. 1996. How are we doing? State party leaders evaluate performance in the 1994 elections. In *The state of the parties: The changing role of contemporary American parties,* rev. ed., ed. D. Shea and J. Green. Lanham, Md.: Rowman and Littlefield.

___. 1993. Party transformation in France and the United States: The hierarchical effects of system change in comparative perspective. *Comparative Politics* 26, no. 3.

Bibby, John F. 1994. State party organizations: Coping and adapting. In *The parties respond,* 2d ed., ed. L. Sandy Maisel. Boulder, Colo.: Westview Press.

Cotter, Cornelius, James Gibson, John Bibby, and Robert Huckshorn. 1989. *Party organizations in American politics.* Pittsburgh: University of Pittsburgh Press.

Harmel, Robert, and Kenneth Janda. 1994. An integrated theory of party goals and party change. *Journal of Theoretical Politics* 6:259–287.

Herrnson, Paul. 1988. *Party campaigning in the 1980s.* Cambridge: Harvard University Press.

Lunch, William M. 1987. *The nationalization of American politics.* Berkeley: University of California Press.

Mayhew, David. 1986. *Placing parties in American politics: Organization, electoral settings, and government activity in the twentieth century.* Princeton: Princeton University Press.

Patterson, Samuel C. 1993. The persistence of state parties. In *The state of the states,* ed. Carl E. Van Horn. Washington, D.C.: Congressional Quarterly.

Rohde, David. 1991. *Parties and leaders in the postreform Congress.* Chicago: University of Chicago Press.

Schlesinger, Joseph. 1991. *Political parties and the winning of office.* Ann Arbor: University of Michigan Press.

Shea, Daniel. 1995. *Transforming democracy: Legislative campaign committees and political parties.* Albany: State University of New York Press.

Sorauf, Frank. 1988. *Money in American elections.* Glenview, Ill.: Scott, Foresman.

Ward, Daniel S. 1994. Alive and well in the U.S. Senate: Parties in the committee setting. *Congress and the presidency* 21, no. 2.

___. 1993. The continuing search for party influence in Congress: A view from the committees. *Legislative Studies Quarterly* 18, no. 2.

Wattenberg, Martin P. 1994. *The decline of American political parties, 1952–1992.* Cambridge: Harvard University Press.

# *Alabama*

PATRICK  R.  COTTER

## PARTY HISTORY

In the years before and immediately after the Civil War, Alabama had a competitive, though confusing, party system. As Reconstruction ended, however, Democrats began to dominate the state's electoral politics. The Democratic Party, in turn, was dominated by the "Bourbons," the state's traditional leadership group centered primarily among the large landowners residing in the Black Belt section of Alabama. The Bourbons, along with their financial and industrial "Big Mule" allies, controlled the party through their skills, considerable resources, and ability to suppress issues and groups that threatened to undermine their authority. In particular the Bourbons stressed the issue of white supremacy. By raising the prospect that "disagreements between white men might open the door for 'black government,' the Bourbons could both legitimize their authority and brand their opponents as dangerous radicals" (Rogers et al. 1994, 289).

Even the Bourbons could not suppress all challenges. In the late nineteenth century hard economic times and resentment against the self-serving policies of the Bourbons led to the emergence of a protest movement based on an alliance of small farmers and urban industrial workers. Along with what remained of the often-divided Alabama Republican Party, the Populists were a serious threat to the state's traditional leadership. Through calls for white supremacy, fraud, and considerable skill, the Bourbons were able to defeat the reform movement. They then moved to ensure that this threat would not arise again. In particular, they promulgated a new state constitution which had the effect of disenfranchising large segments of the state's black and lower income white population (Rogers et al. 1994; Key 1949).

With the defeat of the Populists, Alabama became a solidly one-party state. Throughout the first half of the twentieth century, Alabama voters faithfully supported Democratic presidential candidates and consistently elected only Democrats to congressional and state government positions. Electoral competition occurred only within the Democratic Party. Typically this competition was highly factionalized. In his midcentury study of southern politics, V. O. Key (1949, 37) noted that in Alabama,

> Political factions form and reform. Leadership in state-wide politics tends to be transient. New state-wide leaders emerge, rise to power and disappear as others take their places. Voters group themselves in one faction and then in another in the most confusing fashion. No orderly system prevails . . . for the recruitment, development and advancement of political leaders. Rather the political process appears as a free-for-all, with every man looking out for himself.

Occasionally, Alabama's Solid South politics would coalesce into bifactional competition, with more progressive voters from north and southeast Alabama aligning against the Black Belt landowners and the city Big Mules. Progressive candidates, such as Lister Hill

(U.S. House, 1923–1938; U.S. Senate, 1938–1969), John Sparkman (U.S. House, 1937–1946; U.S. Senate, 1946–1979), and two-term governor James "Big Jim" Folsom (1947–1951 and 1955–1959), frequently won these contests.

Throughout the first half of this century the Alabama Republican Party was largely irrelevant to the state's politics except as a source of federal patronage. It was also internally divided between "blacks who attributed their emancipation to the party, and hill country whites who had opposed secession and Black Belt Democratic rule of the state" (Rogers 1994, 438).

Democratic hegemony did not long exist without facing serious challenges. These challenges were caused and exacerbated by nonpolitical factors such as increasing urbanization and industrialization and the migration of blacks to the North.

One of the first political challenges to the Solid South was the 1928 presidential nomination of Al Smith. The Democratic Party's selection of an anti-Prohibition, Catholic, New Yorker caused unhappiness among what would today be called socially conservative voters (Rogers et al. 1994, 438). Franklin Roosevelt's New Deal policies further upset states' rights supporters and economic conservatives. In 1948, Alabama Democrats split over the national party's adoption of a more liberal position on civil rights issues. This led to an extended factional conflict between Loyalists and States' Righters, or Dixiecrats (Barnard 1974).

The 1952 election showed that the state's presidential politics were becoming competitive. In that year, Dwight D. Eisenhower won 35 percent of the vote in the state, compared with Thomas E. Dewey's 18 percent in 1944. Republican presidential strength increased further in 1956 (39 percent) and 1960 (41 percent).

The 1962 U.S. Senate election, in which Republican Jim Martin nearly defeated veteran New Dealer Lister Hill, signaled that Republican strength was not confined to presidential contests. The Alabama GOP achieved a major breakthrough in 1964. In that year's presidential election, Barry Goldwater won 69.5 percent of the vote. More important, more than ninety Republicans were elected to office in Alabama, including five to the U.S. Congress (Cosman 1968).

The rising prospects of the Alabama Republican Party did not last, however. In the 1966 gubernatorial election, Jim Martin was beaten badly by Lurleen Wallace, the wife of the incumbent governor, George Wallace (who was then constitutionally barred from seeking a second consecutive term). With this victory, George Wallace became the dominant political figure in the state as well as an important player on the national scene. The Alabama GOP, facing a Democratic Party headed by a social conservative who spent considerable time criticizing both the national government and the national parties, had a difficult time mounting serious campaigns within the state. As long as Wallace continued to dominate the state's politics, Alabama Republicans gained little support among voters in state and local elections. A similar handicap did not exist, however, in presidential and congressional elections. Republicans carried Alabama in five of the seven presidential elections held between 1968 and 1992. Similarly, the GOP held at least two of the state's congressional seats from 1964 to 1996.

In 1980 the GOP achieved its first major statewide victory, when Jeremiah Denton won an open U.S. Senate seat. Further GOP gains occurred in 1986, when the Democratic Party experienced a deep and rancorous split over the issue of whether Attorney General Charlie Graddick had illegally encouraged Republican primary voters to "cross over" and vote in the Democratic runoff election. This dispute involved a considerable amount of legal maneuvering, and eventually a Democratic Party hearing committee found that Graddick had violated party rules. The committee then awarded the gubernatorial nomination to the runoff loser, Lieutenant Governor Bill Baxley. Unhappiness over this decision contributed to Guy Hunt's unexpected election as the state's first Republican governor since Reconstruction (Cotter and Stovall 1987).

Hunt narrowly won reelection in 1990. In 1993 he was convicted of violating the state's ethics law and removed from office. His replacement, Democrat Jim Folsom Jr., lost the 1994 gubernatorial election by about 1 percent of the vote to Forrest Hood "Fob" James Jr., who had previously served as governor, as a Democrat, from 1979 to 1983.

In 1996 Republicans held three of the state's seven House seats. Following the 1994 election, Sen. Richard Shelby (who had defeated Denton in 1986) switched to the Republican Party. In addition to James's victory in the 1994 gubernatorial election, GOP candidates won, for the first time, several "down ticket" offices such as auditor and commissioner of agriculture. Democrats, however, continue to dominate the state legislature, holding roughly two-thirds of the seats in both the house and the senate.

## ORGANIZATIONAL DEVELOPMENT

*Democratic Party.* During the first part of the twentieth century, the Democratic Party devoted few resources, or even attention, to its formal organization. At midcentury, the emergence of the civil rights issue resulted in conflict over who controlled the Alabama Democratic Party. This battle, which had little to do with the day-to-day operation of the party, was fought between Loyalists and those (Dixiecrats, States' Righters, and Wallace supporters) who wanted to distance Alabama from the national party. With the end of the civil rights era and Wallace's withdrawal from presidential politics, this conflict subsided.

An important change which occurred within the Democratic Party, largely prompted by the 1965 Voting Rights Act, was the incorporation of the state's newly enfranchised black voters into the party. (This was less of an issue with Republicans, since few blacks supported the GOP and the party made no effort to recruit black candidates.) The change did not occur rapidly or easily. In 1966, for example, heated debates accompanied the Democratic State Executive Committee's decision to remove the slogan "White Supremacy" from underneath the party's symbol (the Democratic Rooster) on election ballots (Strong 1972, 470). As is the case nationally, the role of blacks and whites within the party remains an ongoing issue for Alabama Democrats.

The growing challenge from Republicans has also resulted in Democrats increasing their attention to building an effective organization. For example, unlike in previous years, the Democratic State Executive Committee was actively involved in electioneering in the 1966 campaign (Strong 1972, 456). Additionally, in recent years Democratic Party officials have sought to enhance party unity by urging candidates to limit the level of conflict during statewide primary campaigns. Also, after both the 1986 and 1994 elections, the party held meetings and gathered information about how to revitalize and reform itself (Gordon and Lindley 1995; Stevenson 1995).

Still, the Democratic Party has yet to develop a strong electoral organization. A survey of local party activists found Democrats to be less active in a number of election- and organization-related activities than were Republicans (Cotter, 1995). Democratic activists also see less of a change in their party's organizational capabilities in the use of computers, polls, or the mass media. Similarly, financial problems have caused the Democratic Party to close its Montgomery satellite office. In 1992 Democratic headquarters had nine employees. In 1995 it had a staff of three (Beyerle 1995).

*Republican Party.* The development of an organization has been the major change in the Alabama Republican Party in recent decades. As stated previously, the breakup of the Solid Democratic South, and the resulting rise of the Republican Party, can be traced to a variety of sources. Similarly, several events can be used to chart the course of the Republican revival. Among these, the 1952 nomination of Eisenhower is particularly important. Eisenhower attracted considerable support among Alabama voters and, perhaps more important, significantly increased the number of Alabamians involved in Republican Party activities (Rogers et al. 1994, 438; Strong 1972)

Another important event in the development of the Alabama Republican Party was the 1962 selection of John Grenier as party chair. As a result of Grenier's efforts, the party hired its first professional staff members, increased and revitalized its county organizations, and increased its fund-raising efforts. The failure of the GOP to gain significant state-level victories, however, led to financial problems, and the professional party organization was reduced in 1967. Republican growth was further inhibited during this period by ideological struggles between more moderate and less moderate conservatives within the party (Lamis 1990).

More recently, GOP organizational strength has increased. Local Republican Party activists are highly involved in a variety of party-related activities. These activists also report a considerable increase or improvement in the party's use of computers, media relations, fund raising, and candidate recruitment (Cotter 1995). The party still faces difficulties in recruitment. Also, there continues to be no Republican organization in some of the rural or traditionally Democratic areas of the state.

Recently the Alabama Republican Party, which is headquartered in Birmingham, opened a satellite office in Montgomery staffed with a political director and fundraiser. A $1.2 million budget was adopted for the 1996 election. The party hoped to present candidates for nearly all the offices up for election in 1996 (Beyerle 1995). The party is also involved in encouraging Democratic officeholders to switch to the GOP (Brumas 1995).

*Role of State Party Organizations in State Politics.* Party competition is strong in Alabama at the present time. Befitting this level of competition, party organizations, particularly on the Republican side, are increasingly involved in electoral activities. Research shows that Democratic and Republican Party activists in Alabama offer voters distinct positions on a range of political issues (Cotter 1995). Party also has an important impact on the decision making of Alabama voters (Cotter, Stovall, and Fisher 1994).

This same image of growth, activity, and importance is not seen when the operation of the Alabama state government is examined. The state government is not organized along party lines. There are no elected majority or minority leaders within the state legislature. Both Democrats and Republicans chair legislative committees. Overall, it seems that parties are labels that officeholders attach to themselves in order to win elections. These labels do not indicate any loyalty to an organization, nor do they seem to influence legislative behavior.

The weakness of parties within state government is illustrated by the ease with which Alabama officeholders shift their partisan affiliations without any apparent political costs. For example, the incumbent governor, Fob James, began his political career as a Republican. In 1978 he switched to the Democratic Party and won the gubernatorial election, campaigning as a political newcomer. In both 1986 and 1990 he unsuccessfully sought the Democratic gubernatorial nomination. In 1994 he switched again and entered the Republican primary. Similarly, the latest Democratic legislator to switch to the Republican

Party, state representative Steve Flowers, remarked that he was never "a real Democrat." The evidence supports his claim. Flowers had worked for Barry Goldwater in 1964 and attended the 1968 Republican National Convention. The reason he had run as a Democrat when first elected to the legislature in 1980 was that "just about everybody ran in the Democratic primary" *(Birmingham Post-Herald* 1995).

As their organizational capabilities increase in the future, the electoral influence of the Democratic and Republican Parties is likely to grow. This will, in turn, have some effect on the influence of parties on state government. The influence of parties on state government may remain limited, however. In its elections, Alabama uses a runoff system and has a long ballot. Institutionally, the state has a relatively weak governor and a strong interest group system. These structural characteristics encourage fragmentation within parties and independence among officeholders. Thus, even though Alabama may develop strong and competitive electoral parties, much of its politics may continue to resemble the fragmented, disjointed, and confusing pattern observed by Key a half-century ago.

## CURRENT PARTY ORGANIZATION

According to Alabama law, political parties may establish a state executive committee. They may also establish an executive committee in each county or municipality (Thomas and Stewart 1988). The size and composition of these committees are not specified by law. Thus each party is allowed to determine for itself the makeup of its executive committees. In recent years, both parties generally have selected county and state committee members through primaries rather than conventions or caucuses.

*Democratic Party.* The governing body of the Alabama Democratic Party is the State Democratic Executive Committee. The state executive committee has the authority to prescribe and enforce penalties for violation of party rules, including removal from party office and rescinding party nomination, party privilege, or committee membership. The state committee can review decisions of county committees concerning nomination to county offices and application of party rules and policies.

The State Democratic Executive Committee is composed of 210 members elected from state legislative districts. One man and one woman are elected from each district. Party rules also require that minority members be represented on the executive committee in proportion to their presence in the Democratic electorate of Alabama or in proportion to their presence in the population of Alabama, whichever is greater. Members of the state committee serve a four-year term. In addition to the popularly elected members, the state executive committee also includes national committee persons; the chair, vice chairs, secretary, and treasurer of the state committee; the governor (if a Democrat); and all Democratic members of Congress from Alabama. According to party rules, the chair and the first vice chair shall be of different sexes.

Democratic Party rules also provide for congressional district committees and county committees. Members of the county committees are elected from districts within counties for a four-year term. County committees have the responsibility for discharging Democratic Party affairs within the county, subject to the direction of the state committee. However, the different organizational levels of the Democratic Party seem to work somewhat independently of one another.

The Democratic Party generally is not split over issues or philosophical or even strategic questions. Instead, internal Democratic Party splits largely involve the question of which groups or individuals hold power. For example, the deepest and most visible recent intra-party fight involved the outcome of the 1986 gubernatorial runoff election. This conflict had little to do with policy questions, though there were issue differences between Bill Baxley and Charlie Graddick. Nor did the conflict concern the question of what was best for the Democratic Party. Instead the conflict was largely over power. Graddick's apparent runoff victory was challenged because it was a serious threat to the groups and interests, such as teachers and trial lawyers, that held power within the state government. Indeed, the outcome of the dispute seriously hurt the party.

*Republican Party.* The stated purpose of the Republican Executive Committee, the governing body of the party in Alabama, is "to build and promote the Republican Party." The committee has the power to direct, manage, and supervise the affairs and business of the Republican Party, determine party policies, issue calls and prescribe rules for conventions and primaries, settle party controversies, and give direction and assistance to Republican organizations within Alabama.

Each county in the state is represented on the committee on the basis of population (one representative for each 25,000 citizens). Primary elections are used to select committee members, except in the smallest counties. Members of the committee serve four-year terms. In addition to the elected members, the committee includes the state chair (who is elected by the committee); any vice chairs; the secretary, treasurer, and finance chair of the committee; the immediate past state chair; the chairs or presidents of the Young Republicans, College Republicans, Republican Women, and the Republican Council; and the national committee representatives. Additionally, the chair appoints ten members to the committee, with the approval of the committee. Finally, counties that have elected two or more Republicans to county or state office are entitled to a bonus member of the committee. To be eligible for the committee, an individual must be a registered voter, a resident of the county or precinct he or she represents, and "a regular financial contributor to the Republican Party of Alabama."

Party rules also provide for congressional district committees and county executive committees. The county committee and its elected chair are responsible for local candidates, the settlement of local intraparty disputes or contests for local nominations, and matters of local patronage. The GOP does not currently have separate committees in each congressional district. Instead it has three congressional organizations, each representing two or three districts. Also, the Republican Party does not yet have committees in each county. However, the number of "unorganized" counties is decreasing. Currently, Republican county committees exist in sixty-five of the state's sixty-seven counties.

As is the case with Democrats, internal divisions within the Republican Party are based primarily on questions of personal or group power rather than broader ideological conflicts. For example, despite its 1994 successes, in its spring 1995 meeting the state Republican Executive Committee voted incumbent GOP state chair Elbert Peters out of office and replaced him with Mobile County chair Roger McConnell. Peters's ouster was in part due to dissatisfaction with the operation of the party. Specifically, his opponents felt that he should have done more organizational work at the county level, and they pointed out that seven hundred Democrats won uncontested victories in 1994. However, personality differences, particularly between Peters and the party's professional staff, had an even greater role in the leadership change. Before the executive committee vote, Dixie Effinger, the party's bookkeeper and former office manager, said "If the nerd gets in again, I'm gone" (Gordon 1995).

**Table 1** Alabama Resource Guide

|  | Democrats | Republicans |
|---|---|---|
| Archive | Yes | Yes |
| Location | Alabama Democratic Party | Alabama Republican Party |
|  | 300 Massey Building | P.O. Box 320800 |
|  | Birmingham, Ala. 35203 | Birmingham, Ala. 35232-0800 |
| Dates | Late 19th century– | Unspecified |
| Finding aid | No | Yes |
| Access | Public | Public |
| Contents: |  |  |
|   Executive committee minutes | Yes | Yes |
|   Correspondence | Yes | Yes |
|   Organizational structure | Yes | Yes |
|   Budgets | Yes | Yes |
|   Rules | Yes | Yes |

## RESOURCE GUIDE

Records of the Alabama Democratic Party are found at both party headquarters in Birmingham and the State Department of Archives and History in Montgomery. The material at party headquarters is uncataloged but includes a wide variety of information on party activities. Extensive material, some of which involves party activities prior to 1900, is also found in the state archives. Additionally, the state archives contains the papers of prominent Alabama Democrats such as Jim Folsom, Sam Englehart, and Oscar Underwood. The Auburn University library also holds the papers of several important Alabama Democrats.

Materials on Republican Party activities are found at the party's headquarters in Birmingham. Additionally, Republican Party papers are housed, and cataloged, at the Auburn University library. Included in this collection are the papers of John Grenier. An extensive collection of material related to Alabama politics is also found at the Hoole Library at the University of Alabama.

Alabama party organizations have not been the focus of much scholarly research. Biographies of important Alabama politicians also have paid little attention to the state's political parties. For example, most of the research on George Wallace has focused on his presidential campaigns. The information that is available about party organization in Alabama comes largely from works that take a broader view of the state's politics.

## REFERENCES

*Asterisks denote the most important publications on Alabama party politics.*

*Barnard, William D. 1974. *Dixiecrats and Democrats: Alabama politics 1942–1950*. University, Ala.: University of Alabama Press.

Beyerle, Dana. 1995. Hunt says whoa. *Tuscaloosa News,* April 23, 8A.

*Birmingham Post-Herald.* 1995. Flowers switches to GOP. June 1, A9.

Brumas, Michael. 1995. Alabama GOP seeks Democrat converts. *Birmingham News,* April 13, 1A.

Cosman, Bernard. 1968. Deep South Republicans: Profiles and positions. In *Republican politics: The 1964 campaign and its aftermath for the party,* ed. Bernard Cosman and Robert J. Huckshorn. New York: Praeger.

Cotter, Patrick R. 1995. Alabama: Activists in a competitive age. In *Southern state party organizations and activists,* ed. Charles D. Hadley and Lewis Bowman. Westport, Conn.: Praeger.

Cotter, Patrick R., and James Glen Stovall. 1987. The 1986 election in Alabama: The beginning of the post-Wallace era. *PS* 20:655–666.

*Cotter, Patrick R., James Glen Stovall, and Samuel H. Fisher III. 1994. *Disconnected: Public opinion and politics in Alabama.* Northport, Ala.: Vision Press.

Gordon, Tom. 1995. GOP changes chairmen; Demos don't. *Birmingham News,* February 12, 23A.

Gordon, Tom, and Tom Lindley. 1995. State Democrats: Let's define stand on issues. *Birmingham News,* April 9, 17A.

*Key, V. O. 1949. *Southern politics in state and nation.* New York: Alfred A. Knopf.

Lamis, Alexander P. 1990. *The two-party South.* 2d expanded ed. New York: Oxford University Press.

*Rogers, William Warren, Robert David Ward, Leah Rawls Atkins, and Wayne Flynt. 1994. *Alabama: The history of a Deep South state.* Tuscaloosa: University of Alabama Press.

Stevenson, Tommy. 1995. Blount: State to remain two-party. *Tuscaloosa News,* April 9, 1B.

*Strong, Donald S. 1972. Alabama: Transition and alienation. In *The changing politics of the South,* ed. William C. Havard. Baton Rouge: Louisiana University Press.

*Thomas, James D., and William H. Stewart. 1988. *Alabama government and politics.* Lincoln: University of Nebraska Press.

# Alaska

CARL E. SHEPRO

When examining politics in Alaska, one finds an immediate and glaring contradiction in its electoral politics. On the one hand, Alaskans only weakly identify with political parties; in 1992 about 54 percent of the electorate was registered as either nonpartisan or independent. On the other hand, several political parties are active in the state. The 1990 gubernatorial election featured five party tickets, one more than appeared on the 1994 ballot.[1]

## PARTY HISTORY

Although political parties have been active in Alaska since 1867, they were less central to the development of government and politics than parties were in most other states. Few written records about political parties exist from the preterritorial (1867–1912) or territorial (1912–1959) periods in Alaska, and those that do suggest parties were relatively unimportant as unifying organizations. The first election for nonvoting delegates to Congress, in 1906, provides evidence of the unimportance of parties. The election included both Democratic and Republican candidates but was won by nonpartisan candidates from two mining districts in Alaska (Hulley 1953, 93–94). One Alaska historian suggests that personality rather than party was preeminent in Alaska politics during the early territorial period, citing as an example the case of Judge James Wickersham, a prominent political figure who ran for election at various times as an Independent Republican, an Insurgent Republican, a Progressive, and an independent supporter of President Woodrow Wilson. After 1916 he regularly identified himself as a Republican, to the chagrin of some members of that party (Mangusso 1978).

Other scholars see environmental factors influencing the development or lack of development of political parties, factors that include but are not limited to: elections, political institutions, statutory regulation, political culture, and the nonpolitical environment, which would include personality (Beck and Sorauf 1992, 27–31). This more inclusive perspective will provide the framework for the discussion that follows.

In Alaska, native Americans comprise nearly 15 percent of the diverse population, a higher percentage than in any other state. Alaska also has ". . . the most in and out migration of any state" (Morehouse 1994), resulting in participation by disproportionate numbers of new arrivals and withdrawal from participation by longer-term residents who are more familiar with local and state personalities and issues (Wakefield 1993). The non-native American population appears to be informed primarily by an individualistic, privatistic (Elazar 1984) political culture where the political arena is viewed as a marketplace of competition between private interests for utilitarian ends and government's role is seen as keeping the marketplace open and functioning (McBeath and Morehouse 1987, 145–160). Alaska's political culture has also been described as a frontier culture, where the symbolism and imagery of the pioneer on the fringes of modern society are seen to shape behavior rather than the more mundane notions of politics and economics (Cuba 1987, xv–xvi). The native American population appears to be informed by a more holistic political culture, based on aboriginal understandings of basic relationships between people and their environment and how behaviors are conditioned by those relationships (Demmert 1984; Shepro 1985; Jennings 1994). The political cultures help explain the weak partisan identification of the Alaska electorate.

An equally important factor explaining weak party identification is that Alaska parties operate in an institutional and political environment characterized by the reform tradition in the United States, by which government should be insulated from the "corrupting influence of politics" (Hofstadter 1955). Many states operate in a similar environment, but the parties in most of them had control of governmental institutions when the reform impulse struck and were able to adapt to and influence its direction. In Alaska, the reform movement defined the institutions and the regulatory machinery within which parties evolved (Harrison 1992), effectively constraining the ability of parties to link citizens with the government, their primary function in many, if not most, states.

Alaska political parties have also been influenced by the size of the state and isolation of its population on a regional basis. In some cases, this has led to regional competition within the parties rather than to statewide competition between them, making strong organizations difficult to achieve.

Finally, the relationships between the federal government and outside groups and interests on the one hand and Alaska governments, individuals, and groups on the other have been fertile ground for the emergence of third parties representing several points on the ideological spectrum.

## ORGANIZATIONAL DEVELOPMENT

The organizational development of Alaska's political parties occurred primarily after statehood in 1959. Their late development can be attributed in part to the constraints on local and regional self-governing institutions imposed by Congress during much of the prestatehood period (Morehouse and Fischer 1971; Morehouse, McBeath, and Leask 1984). Unlike in the contiguous states, the institutions and processes that defined and shaped Alaska political parties were established only at statehood.

*Legislative Support.* Several factors contribute to the weakness of party organizations in Alaska, among them is a lack of legislative support for parties in the electoral process

(Conlan, Martino, and Dilger 1984). Alaska does not require parties to endorse candidates prior to the general election, and with the exception of the Republican Party after implementation of its "classical closed" primary in 1992,[2] parties have seldom endorsed candidates. From 1947 to 1959 and from 1967 to 1992, Alaska was one of three states with a blanket primary, in which voters receive a ballot with all candidates for all offices to select from. (McBeath and Morehouse 1994, 214–215). An open primary was initiated between 1959 and 1967, giving voters a choice of either an all-Republican or an all-Democratic ballot during the first few years of statehood, but the Third Alaska Legislature reinstated the blanket primary to further open the nomination process. In addition, voters are not required to state a party preference when registering, and a majority of voters are registered as nonpartisan or independent.

At its state convention in 1990, the Republican Party amended its rules to allow "only registered Republicans, registered independents, and those who state no preference of party affiliation . . . to vote in the Republican primary election. . . ." (McBeath and Morehouse 1994, 214–217). The Alaska State Division of Elections refused to implement a ballot listing only Republican candidates, given the legislation noted above, and the Republican Party filed suit in U.S. district court to require compliance. The district court ruled in favor of the Republican position, and the August 1992 primary election featured two ballots, one for the Republican candidates and one listing all candidates for office. The Republican primary, although it has made Republican candidates more accountable to the party platform, has remained controversial among all voters in Alaska. In 1996 the U.S. Supreme Court ruled that Alaska's blanket primary did not violate the Republican Party's associational rights and reversed the earlier ruling by the district court. Currently, the Division of Elections is preparing to issue one ballot listing all candidates for each office being contested for the August 1996 primary, while the Republican state leadership continues to search for ways to maintain a separate ballot for Republican candidates.[3]

*Party Structure.* A second major factor that contributes to the comparative weakness of Alaska parties is their organizational structure. Most party structures reflect the organization of the electoral system, according to a noted political scientist:

> The party organizations created by the states have in common one dominant characteristic: They match the voting districts and at least some of the constituencies of the state. They form great step pyramids as they reflect the myriad, overlapping constituencies of a democracy committed to the election of vast numbers of officeholders (Sorauf 1984, 66).

A comparison of the structure of the Republican and Democratic Parties in Alaska with the "typical" party organization of most states demonstrates a major weakness of party structures in Alaska: the absence of organizational levels that mediate conflicts between local districts and that aggregate support for partisan issues prior to discussion at the state level.

The absence of county, judicial district, and city organizational structures limits administrative centralization and support for local levels, resulting in varying levels of effectiveness between district organizations.[4]

The three minor parties display a variety of organizational structures. The Green Party has the *bio-region* as its major organizational unit, an area in which socioeconomic and cultural similarities provide boundaries rather than artificially defined political subdivisions such as legislative districts (Sykes 1993). The party does not have registered voters in every legislative district, and the bio-region is viewed as both a way to attract voters and a structural foundation. The Alaska Independence Party (AIP) is a party ". . . with the pretense of being statewide"(Vogler 1993). It is a loose-knit organization that was established in 1974 primarily to support the idea of separating Alaska from the United States based upon broken federal promises made in the statehood compact (Vogler 1993). The Libertarian Party features virtually no organizational structure (Prax 1985) and has fallen from its high point of collecting 15 percent of the gubernatorial vote in 1982, to a low of about one hundred dues-paying members statewide in 1993 (Karpenski 1993).

Both major parties have provisions for an executive director and an office manager. However, neither party has filled those positions continuously. Both the Republican and Democratic state offices had paid staffs in 1985 (Quesnell 1985; Stout, 1985), but only the Democrats had both an executive director and office manager in 1995. All of the third parties maintained an office in a party member's home, and none had paid staff. The stronger position of the Democratic Party can be attributed to the election of Democrat Tony Knowles as governor in 1994, which brought about an intensive Democratic effort to strengthen the party and its role in the electoral process (Toal 1995). The Republican Party has had less money than in the past and functions with only volunteers and a half-time clerk in the office (Martens 1993).

*Economy and Population.* The state's economy and demographics are a third major influence on parties in Alaska. Within the first decade of statehood, the economic boom triggered by the flow of oil from the North Slope led to demographic changes that weakened the parties. Between the start of pipeline construction in 1974 and the peak of the oil boom in 1985, Alaska's population roughly doubled. The newer residents brought with them different economic expectations (such as government-related rather than construction-related employment) and political attitudes (they were better educated, younger, had different expectations of the political structure, and were more interest-group than party oriented) than longer-term residents (Wakefield 1993). In addition, the huge petroleum-related revenues filling state coffers meant that political parties were not necessary to link people to state or local government. Interest groups increasingly became the preferred linkage institutions, while individuals could contact their state legislator or local government official directly with demands if necessary. Although these demographic changes did not cause the decline of Alaska political parties, they definitely contributed to it (McBeath and Morehouse 1987; McBeath and Morehouse 1994; Morehouse, McBeath, and Leask 1984).

*Parties in Government.* Political parties have not figured prominently in the organization of the state legislature since 1960. Coalitions have been organized in either or both houses in two-fifths of the legislative sessions, and parties have been unable to control simultaneously both houses of the legislature and the executive branch since 1967 (McBeath and Morehouse 1994, 217).

Clearly, parties in Alaska are not strong vehicles for controlling government, linking citizens and government, organizing the electoral system, or even organizing themselves.

## CURRENT PARTY ORGANIZATION

*Democratic Party.* In the past three years the Democratic Party has undergone some revitalization, due at least in part to the emphasis placed on partisan loyalty by the incumbent governor, Tony Knowles. Democratic incumbents who encourage partisanship have strengthened the party, whereas those encouraging bipartisanship or "nonpartisan" politics have had the opposite effect.[5] Democratic Party fortunes appear to be on the rise since the election of Knowles and his maintenance of good relations with the Clinton administration. Although Democratic registration has not increased appreciably, Democrats have been able to raise more revenues than in the past. This has allowed for office staff, active candidate recruitment, and support for campaigns (Toal 1995).

Democratic Party fortunes in the 1994 election were heavily influenced by the endorsement given the Democratic gubernatorial candidate by the Alaska Federation of Natives (AFN).[6] Turnout in rural Alaska native villages was extremely high, approaching 90 percent in many places, and produced large majorities for Knowles. There is general agreement that "bush"[7] support was the deciding factor in the three-way race for governor and that a continued focus on bush issues would strengthen and maintain the party organization (Anvik 1994; Hensely 1993; Wakefield 1993).

To overcome the absence of intermediate organizational structures, the party plans to intensify outreach to the precincts, especially in the bush areas, replacing precinct organizations with district ones, and then to establish regional structures (Wakefield 1993).

*Republican Party.* The Republican Party, although experiencing an increase in registered voters, is less well organized and less able to raise money than in the past (Martens 1993). This appears to result from the emergence of three major factions within the party statewide: "old-guard" Republicans and two groups of "Christian Republicans." One faction of Christian Republicans is known as the "Prevo Conservatives," considered by most activists to be moderate on issues with the exception of abortion rights. A more militant faction of Christian conservatives is made up of followers of the older Moral Majority and supporters of Pat Robertson (Martens 1993; Collins 1993; Sturgelewski 1993). In 1988 the Christian Republicans focused their energies on capturing control of the Republican Party through the precinct caucuses. They were successful in obtaining by a narrow margin endorsement by the caucuses for Pat Robertson's presidential nomination. However, the state convention endorsed George Bush for the nomination, largely because the Prevo Conservatives supported Bush. A major split between the Christian Republicans and the old guard then developed, focused on the issue of abortion and the 1988 gubernatorial campaign of a "liberal" Republican, Arliss Sturgelewski (Sturgelewski 1993). The Christian Republicans did control the state central committee for a short period, beginning with the 1990 convention. However, the friction between the two factions of Christian Republicans led to the election of a more moderate slate of officers in 1992. The costs of these struggles for control have included:

> [diminished] influence of the Republican party on elections because the effort has been on controlling the precincts and the conventions rather than on [fund] raising ... to support the party and its candidates. New party members are not the strength of the party, because they don't participate beyond the levels urged by the pastors, i.e., the precincts and conventions (Sturgelewski 1993).

Unlike the Democratic organizational structure, in the Republican structure there appears to be a direct connection between the precinct and state levels, at least in terms of establishing party platforms and policies. The drive to establish a closed Republican primary and to make Republican candidates accountable to the party are initiatives flowing from the precinct level. In addition, the Republican organizational plan calls for a regional organization of legislative district chairs to coordinate party positions. The problem is that control of the precincts, and ultimately the ability to establish policy at the state convention, is being exercised by a minority of the registered Republican voters in the state, namely, the Christian Republican factions of the party.

Unlike the Democratic Party, the Republican Party focuses almost exclusively on urban Alaska. The major region supporting Republican candidates is the southcentral region, which includes Anchorage, with over one-half the population of the state. Although on paper the Republican constituency includes elements in the bush areas of the state, Republican candidates for statewide office seldom direct their energies and resources to the bush.

*Third or Minor Parties.* Some indication of the influence exercised by third parties in Alaska is provided by the 1990 election of Alaska Independence Party candidate Walter J. Hickel as governor. Hickel had won the office in 1966 as a Republican, and despite several attempts to reclaim the office, had failed to win another Republican primary election. In 1990 Hickel did not enter the primary election against Sturgelewski. Instead, the Alaska Independence Party candidates for governor and lieutenant governor stepped aside, allowing Hickel to create a three-way contest in the general election between himself as the AIP candidate, former Republican state senator Sturgelewski, and former Democratic mayor of Anchorage Tony Knowles. Hickel enticed "Mr. Republican" Jack Coghill to desert the Republican ticket and join the AIP ticket as the candidate for lieutenant governor, leaving Sturgelewski to scramble for a last-minute replacement as her running mate. Hickel won the 1990 election with 39 percent of the vote, with Knowles, Sturgelewski, the Green Party candidate, and a People's Party ticket following in that order. The 1994 election was similar in terms of the field, with Democrat Knowles winning by a slightly larger percentage of the vote, the Republican candidate (who had been the 1990 candidate for lieutenant governor) trailing only slightly, and Coghill, the AIP candidate, a distant third.

## CONCLUSIONS

The most obvious conclusion about Alaska's political parties is that they are weak, and probably weaker than those in any other state. One indication of their weakness is the lack of a sense of history among the "leaders" of the parties. No party maintains any semblance of archives; they all keep only those financial records required by the Alaska Public Offices Commission (APOC).[8]

The continued lack of stability in the state offices of all parties is another indication of their weakness. They continue to rely on volunteer office staff rather than full-time, paid individuals, notwithstanding the ability of the Democratic Party to pay an executive director and budget/office manager in 1994–1995. While the Republican and Democratic Parties have maintained state offices in Anchorage over the past two decades, only the Republican office has been in the same location for at least five years. All third parties maintain their offices in the homes of party leaders.

The paucity of structural components in Alaska's political party organizations makes communication between the state central committees, nominally the decision-making core of the major parties, and the precinct activists extremely difficult. The difficulty is exacerbated by the regionalism and other aspects of Alaska political culture (nonpartisanship, individualism, a propensity to support candidates rather than parties, and a tendency to rely on interest groups for access to government) that tend to weaken Alaska parties. At best, this leads to an absence of coherent and coordinated party leadership at the center of the party and leads to decisions being made at the level of individual legislative districts. At worst, it leads to the current situation in the Republican Party, where important policy decisions (such as the official position on abortion and the closing of the Republican pri-

**Table 1**  Alaska Resource Guide

| | Democrats | Republicans |
|---|---|---|
| Archive | Yes | Yes |
| Location | State Headquarters | State Headquarters |
| | P.O. Box 104199 | 1001 W. Fireweed Lane |
| | Anchorage, Alaska 99501 | Anchorage, Alaska 99503 |
| | (907) 258-3050 | (907) 276-4467 |
| Dates | 1985– | 1991– |
| Finding aid | No | No |
| Access | By appointment | By appointment |
| Contents: | | |
| Executive committee minutes | Limited | Limited |
| Correspondence | No | Limited |
| Organizational structure | Limited | Limited |
| Budgets | No | No |
| Rules | Limited | Limited |

mary) are being made by a well-organized, minority within the rank-and-file member-ship—despite attempts by the central committee to diffuse its power.

Finally, the 1990 election demonstrates the weakness of parties as unifying mechanisms. Although Hickel ran on the Alaska Independence Party ticket, his Republican affiliation was known to everyone in the electorate. His winning 39 percent of the total vote was dependent on supporters within both major parties, and most analysts agree that his can-didacy cost the Republican nominee the election. Votes were not cast on the basis of parti-san identification, but instead on identification with the individual candidate.

These tendencies, combined with the increasing reliance on interest groups as links between government and governed among the politically active segment of the Alaska pop-ulation, suggest that Alaska's political parties are not merely weak but that current efforts to resuscitate them are unlikely to succeed.

## RESOURCE GUIDE

In Alaska there is minimal accessible archival data on the state's political parties. The Democrats report having some very recent data on state conventions, rules, organizational activities, and minutes housed at party headquarters, but little that would assist with longi-tudinal or historical research on the party.

## NOTES

1. In addition to the winning Alaska Independence Party, the Alaska Democratic Party, the Republican Party of Alaska, the Green Party of Alaska, and the People's Party were on the 1990 bal-lot. All but the People's Party were on the 1994 ballot. In addition, the Libertarian Party fielded can-didates for several local and state legislative races.
2. Although the Republican Party of Alaska defines its primary as "classical closed," it is technically an open primary in which anyone registered as Republican, independent, or nonpartisan can vote.
3. Interviews with activists in all the Alaska political parties tend to support this observation, not just those with Republican leaders.
4. This observation was consistent in all interviews with activists in the Democratic and Republican Parties, those conducted in 1985 as well as those in 1993.
5. For example, Bill Sheffield, governor from 1982 to 1986, emphasized partisanship through his nom-ination of Democrats to important positions in government and in his attempts to build support

for the Alaska Democratic Party. Although his efforts led to confrontations between himself and the Republican-dominated coalitions controlling both houses of the legislature, the Democratic Party did benefit organizationally and in terms of its ability to raise funds during the Sheffield administration. Governor Sheffield was defeated in the primary election of 1986 by Steve Cowper, who adopted a more bipartisan approach upon winning the general election. But Cowper soon found himself with little support in the legislature or among the general public.

6. AFN is a political organization created during the land-claims movement in the late 1960s to present a united front to Congress and the oil industry. The 1994 endorsement of Knowles was a first ever endorsement for any political party or office by AFN.

7. Bush is a colloquialism for rural, predominately Alaska native, areas—particularly outside Anchorage and Fairbanks and in southeast Alaska.

8. When party officials were asked about records, most stated that the only repository they were aware of was the APOC, indicating a lack of knowledge about the role of that regulatory body and of party history.

**REFERENCES**

*Asterisks denote the most important publications on Alaska party politics.*

Anvik, Jane. 1994. Cochair, Anchorage Women's Political Caucus; former Anchorage Assembly member; longtime Democratic Party activist. Interview by author, Anchorage, Alaska, March 15.

Beck, Paul Allen, and Frank J. Sorauf. 1992. *Party politics in America*. 7th ed. New York: HarperCollins.

Collins, Virginia. 1993. Former state senator; 1992 Republican candidate for Congress. Interview by author, Anchorage, Alaska, June 3.

Conlan, Timothy, Ann Martino, and Robert Dilger. 1984. State parties in the 1980s: Adaptation, resurgence and continuing constraints. *Intergovernmental Perspective* 10, no. 4 (fall):13.

*Cornwall, Peter, and Gerald A. McBeath, eds. 1982. *Alaska's rural development*. Boulder, Colo.: Westview.

Cuba, Lee J. 1987. *Identity and community on the Alaskan frontier*. Philadelphia: Temple University Press.

Demmert, Dennis. 1984. Natives, non-natives view world differently. *Fairbanks Daily News-Miner*, November 11.

Elazar, Daniel J. 1984. *American federalism: A view from the states*. 3d ed. New York: Harper and Row.

*Harrison, Gordon S. 1992. *Alaska's constitution: A citizen's guide*. 3d ed. Juneau: Alaska Legislative Research Agency.

Hensely, Willie. 1993. Vice president, Northwest Arctic Native Corporation; former Democratic congressional candidate; longtime Democratic Party activist. Interview by author, Anchorage, Alaska, July 21.

Hofstadter, Richard. 1955. *The age of reform*. New York: Vintage Books.

Hulley, Clarence C. 1953. *Alaska: 1741–1953*. Portland, Ore.: Benfords and Mort.

Jennings, Michael L. 1994. One university, two universes: Alaska natives and higher education in Alaska: 1972–1985. Ph.D. diss., University of British Columbia.

Karpenski, Len. 1993. Vice chair, Alaska Libertarian Party. Interview by author, Anchorage, Alaska, February 12.

Kresge, David T., Thomas A. Morehouse, and George W. Rogers. 1971. *Issues in Alaska development*. Seattle: University of Washington Press.

Mangusso, Mary Childers. 1978. Anthony J. (Tony) Dimond: Democratic delegate to Congress. Ph.D. diss., Texas Tech University.

Martens, Pauline. 1993. Chairperson, Republican Party of Alaska. Interview by author, Anchorage, Alaska, July 26.

*McBeath, Gerald A., and Thomas A. Morehouse. 1994. *Alaska politics and government*. Lincoln: University of Nebraska Press.

*McBeath, Gerald A., and Thomas A. Morehouse, eds. 1987. *Alaska state government and politics*. Fairbanks: University of Alaska Press.

Morehouse, Thomas A. 1994. Lecture delivered for the University of Alaska Anchorage Distinguished Lecture Series. Anchorage, Alaska. April.

Morehouse, Thomas A., Gerald A. McBeath, and Linda Leask. 1984. *Alaska's urban and rural governments*. Lanham, Md.: University Press of America.

Morehouse, Thomas A., and Victor Fischer. 1971. *Borough government in Alaska*. Fairbanks: Institute of Social, Economic, and Governmental Research.

Prax, Mike. 1985. Chair, Interior Fairbanks Libertarian Party. Interview by author, Fairbanks, Alaska, October 13.

Quesnell, Paul. 1985. Executive director, Alaska Democratic Party. Interview by author, Anchorage, Alaska, February 13.

Shepro, Carl E. 1985. Culture, ideology and organization: Popular participation and political change. Ph.D. diss., University of Washington.

Sorauf, Frank. 1984. *Party politics in America*. 5th ed. Boston: Little, Brown.

Stout, Kenneth. 1985. Chair, Republican Party of Alaska. Interview by author, Anchorage, Alaska, February 12.

Sturgelewski, Arliss. 1993. Former state senator; 1990 Republican gubernatorial candidate. Interview by author, Anchorage, Alaska, June 3.

Sykes, Jim. 1993. Chair, Green Party of Alaska. Interview by author, Anchorage, Alaska, March 3.

Toal, Christopher. 1995. Executive director, Alaska Democratic Party. Interview by author, Anchorage, Alaska, May 19.

Vogler, Joe. 1993. Founder and chair, Alaska Independence Party. Interview by author, Fairbanks, Alaska, March 13.

Wakefield, Greg. 1993. Chair, Alaska Democratic Party. Interview by author, Anchorage, Alaska, July 26.

# Arizona

DAVID R. BERMAN

## PARTY HISTORY

In the early 1860s enthusiastic Democrats and Republicans were scattered throughout the recently created Arizona Territory. Up to the mid-1870s, however, leaders of the two partisan groups agreed to ignore their differences in the interests of survival from hostile Indians and territorial development. Together, they formed a nonpartisan clique called the "federal ring," which controlled territorial affairs. As Arizona began to develop, its politics became more and more partisan. Sensing they had the votes to carry the territory, Democratic leaders serving in the territorial legislature began to organize the party faithful for various territory-wide contests in the 1870s. The Arizona Democratic Party held its first territorial convention in 1874 to nominate a candidate for the position of delegate to Congress. By 1880 both the Democratic and Republican Parties were meeting in territorial conventions to nominate candidates for that office (Wagoner 1970). Throughout the remainder of the territorial period, until 1908, the congressional seat was the principal partisan contest in Arizona. Democratic candidates won eleven of the fifteen contests held from 1880 to 1908. During the same period, Democrats also usually dominated the territorial legislature.

From the framing of the state constitution in 1910 to the 1960s, the Democratic Party usually controlled Arizona politics. During the 1920s there were some signs of increased two-party competition, but Democrats still outnumbered Republicans by a two-to-one

ratio in registered voters. In the 1930s the state became even more Democratic. This resulted in large part from the severe depression and the influx into the state of Democrats from
the South. Republicans fell from 32 percent of all registered voters in 1928 to 12 percent in
1940. Over the same period, the number of registered Republicans fell from 39,000 to
21,000. Republicans did not reach 39,000 again until 1948. In the 1930s and 1940s the GOP
virtually disappeared from the state legislature and other elected positions.

The one-party Democratic regime survived, though with diminishing intensity, into the
mid-1960s. Several factors influenced the gradual loss of Democratic control. Perhaps of
prime importance was the steady migration into the state of people from small towns of
the Midwest and the East who were largely Republican by heritage. The GOP also benefited
to some extent from the conversion or partial conversion of longtime Arizona Democrats
who found the national Democratic Party too liberal. Conservative Democrats also conflicted with liberal Democrats in state politics. Liberal Democrats, many new to the state,
began to gain influence within the party as workers and candidates in the 1950s. As the
Democratic Party became more liberal, the state GOP intensified its courtship of the conservative Democrats (Berman 1992b).

By the early 1950s, around 25 percent of the voters in Arizona who identified with one of
the major parties were Republicans. This figure jumped to around 45 percent in the early
1970s. Initially, GOP success at the polls came in "top of the ticket" contests—highly visible
campaigns for the U.S. Senate or governor—where personalities and issues offset the
importance of party identification. Republican gains in the state legislature were mini-
mized by an apportionment system that discriminated against the party's growing strength
in the Phoenix area. Starting in the early 1950s, however, Republicans won enough House
seats to alter the balance of power in that body. From the early 1950s to the mid-1960s,
Republicans and conservative Democrats often organized the House on a coalition basis. A
longer lasting breakthrough for Republicans in the legislature came in 1966 when they captured both houses for the first time. This turnaround was due to a court-ordered reapportionment plan which greatly increased the representation of Republican areas.

Over the past three decades there have been swings in the political fortunes of the major
parties. Yet, although there has been considerable competitiveness and balance in the party
system, most indicators point to the long-term growth in Republican strength. Registered
Republicans have outnumbered registered Democrats since 1985 by about 3–5 percent.
Although the GOP frequently has lost the battle for governor and other statewide offices
since the 1970s, Republicans have regularly controlled the state house and have lost the senate on only a few occasions. The state has voted Republican consistently in presidential
elections since 1948.

In some respects the parties have reversed their positions of the 1950s. Democrats in
recent years, like Republicans in the 1950s, have done best in campaigns for top-of-the-tick-
et offices. In the 1950s and early 1960s a Republican governor often confronted a
Democratic or coalition legislature. The more recent pattern has been a Democratic governor trying to get along with a Republican legislature. Democrats since the 1980s, like
Republicans in the 1950s, have won statewide offices they should have lost based on party
registration and have been complaining about the way representation is structured in the
legislature. Republicans in recent years, like Democrats in the 1950s and 1960s, have had
serious intraparty disputes which threaten their cohesion. Chief among the Republican
trouble spots has been intraparty squabbling between the moderates and conservatives or,
as some view it, conservatives and ultraconservatives.

## ORGANIZATIONAL DEVELOPMENT

Historically, political party organizations in Arizona have been relatively weak. Part of this is due to the lack of attachment to the major parties in the state's formative period. Another factor was the insistence of progressive Democrats in 1910 that the state's constitution require primary elections. Before statehood, party leaders meeting in conventions controlled nominations. The primary system encouraged candidates to form independent and personalized organizations to win the nomination. The growth of personal organizations also tended to factionalize the parties, making it harder for party organizations to coordinate general election campaigns.

*Democratic Party.* The primary system was particularly hard on Democratic Party organizations. Party officials followed the spirit as well as the letter of the law and took themselves out of the nomination process and concentrated on the general election. During the long period of Democratic electoral dominance, however, the Democratic primary was often the only election that counted. When it came to patronage, Democratic officeholders tended to give whatever jobs and contracts they had to those who had helped in the all-important primary rather than to those who worked for the party in the not-very-important general election. From statehood to the 1950s the state Democratic Party struggled to be much more than a paper organization.

The direction of the state party began to change in the early 1950s in large part because of the emergence of a competitive Republican Party and the growing prominence of liberal activists within Democratic ranks. Later, national Democratic Party intervention helped prompt further changes in the direction of the party.

In the 1950s Democrats still had a large majority of the registered voters but were losing regularly to the better organized Republicans in statewide campaigns. As competition heated in the mid-1950s, party leaders decided to keep a state party headquarters open year-round. Previously, the party had opened a state office only for a five- or six-week period around election time. The organization also stepped up its activities, though funding continued to be a problem. Most of the revenue to run the state campaign came from contributions, mildly coerced, from the party's nominees for office. At times, the organization relied on the ability and willingness of the state chair to finance party activities.

State chairs in the 1960s and early 1970s sought to make the state party the center of activity, to move it in a more liberal direction, and to bring about more party discipline. They encountered considerable resistance. Democrats serving in the state legislature, for example, resented the efforts of state chairs to bring them into the process of writing a party platform, feeling that it compromised their independence, and sometimes disavowed the more liberal platform planks adopted at party conventions. In the 1960s party leaders also tried but failed to punish Democrats in the legislature who joined with Republicans in organizing the state house. Some county organizations voted to deny support to Democratic legislators who cooperated with the Republicans. Organizations in rural areas, where most of the legislators in question lived, however, took the position that legislators should be free to decide how best to represent their constituents even if this meant working in a coalition with another party. The rural county chairs also noted there wasn't much they could do about the situation—their financial support for candidates did not amount to much, and the threat of its withdrawal was not apt to scare anyone (*Tucson Daily Citizen* 1964).

Continuing on a path of reform, the state party in the early 1970s, with the encouragement of the national Democratic Party, changed how it selected delegates to the national convention, opening up the process to rank-and-file party members and reforming the process along affirmative action lines. Party leaders, including state chair Herb Ely, were committed to civil rights and became not only a part of the movement to open up the selection process but leaders in that movement.

As the party continued to lose ground, however, it began to gravitate toward a "big tent" approach—one that would make the party more acceptable to independents and conservatives—and toward a more singular focus on getting the party's nominees elected to office. The party in 1974 experienced something of a renaissance under a determined state committee and a moderate chair, Charles Pine, who placed renewed emphasis on party unity and electoral success. The party redoubled its fund-raising efforts, thus enabling it to hire its first full-time executive director. It also devoted resources, including its share of revenues from a Democratic national fund-raising telethon, to a get-out-the-vote program, and, in 1974, it successfully targeted enough seats in the state senate to give Democrats a majority in that body. The Watergate scandal greatly aided the party in its fund-raising and registration drive (Pine n.d.) The party's efforts helped produce a string of victories in the 1970s and helped stem what had looked like a strong Republican tide.

The party continued to improve its ability to raise funds, conduct get-out-the-vote drives, target legislative seats, and put together coordinated campaigns under the leadership of former governor Sam Goddard in the 1980s. The state party during this period also drew upon the technical assistance offered by the national party to modernize its operations. By the mid-1980s Arizona Democrats had begun to catch up with the state Republican Party and Democratic Party organizations elsewhere by adopting more sophisticated methods, for example, computerized lists and phone banks to find and register party members (Davis 1995).

*Republican Party.* Republicans, unlike Democrats, were initially untroubled by the constitution's direct-primary requirement. Republican leaders opposed the idea and simply ignored the law. For several years they chose their state and county nominees through a conference, a device that differed little from the old convention system. The party, however, until the 1950s was anemic when it came to getting votes. It let many legislative elections go uncontested and often did not offer a complete slate of candidates for statewide offices. Seldom successful in winning office, it survived on contributions from a few wealthy members and federal patronage during national Republican administrations.

Starting in the 1950s the state Republican organization grew rapidly in terms of funds, organization, and services to candidates. By the 1960s the organization was running smoothly with a full-time executive director and institutionalized fund-raising events. Much of the strength of the organization, however, was built on voluntary efforts at the local level aimed at registering voters and getting the party faithful out to vote on election day.

Compared with the Democratic Party, the operation of the state Republican Party over the years has been less influenced by the national party. The national party has not pressured the state party to change its method of selecting delegates to the national convention (a state convention-caucus system).[1] Nor has the state party relied greatly on the national party's help in modernizing its activities, though it has taken advantage of national funds for special projects.

From the 1950s to the mid-1970s the state Republican Party was far more unified and centrally directed than the state Democratic Party. The establishment consisted of Barry Goldwater and other prominent officeholders. Also included were state party chairs such as Harry Rosensweig, a longtime friend and political associate of Goldwater, who held the position from the mid-1960s to the mid-1970s. When the party faced an internal dispute, the establishment leaders would meet and resolve the matter. As one observer noted: "Their combined prestige and strong leadership positions were automatic 'enforcers' of the collective decision. The few who refused to abide found themselves on the outside looking through the window" (Wynn 1976). By the mid-1970s, however, this power center had largely disappeared. The party had grown larger and more diverse, and some of the former leaders were out of office, while others had become bogged down in their own problems and had lost interest in party affairs.

During the 1950s and 1960s the Republican establishment was challenged at various times by a far-right-wing group led by political figures like Evan Mecham, who found Goldwater's dedication to conservatism to be somewhat suspect (Rice 1969). Mecham, after repeated failures at gaining elective office, in 1986 finally became governor. The Mecham years were particularly difficult for Republican Party chair Burt Kruglick. Departing from the norm of neutrality in primary elections, Kruglick had endorsed Burton Barr, who ran against Mecham. After the primary, however, he worked for Mecham's election. Controversy during Mecham's brief tenure in office (cut short by impeachment and ouster in 1988) split the Republicans into warring camps. As Mecham's difficulties as governor mounted, Kruglick felt it was his duty to come to Mecham's defense, though behind the scenes he hosted several meetings at his home at which prominent party leaders encouraged Mecham to resign (Kruglick 1995).

Right-wingers continued to be influential in the party, often showing up in relatively large numbers at party meetings. In 1989 they successfully sponsored a resolution (later reversed) proclaiming the United States a "Christian nation." In 1992, at another state party meeting, the group scuttled an attempt to put the state party on record in favor of a holiday for Martin Luther King Jr. That same year, right-wing Republicans also attacked Goldwater who, by this time, had become a force for moderation within the party. They threatened to strip his name off state GOP headquarters and other buildings for what they claimed was his backing away from a 1980 pledge to oppose abortion and for endorsing a Democrat running for Congress.

## CURRENT PARTY ORGANIZATION

State law in Arizona organizes political parties in the traditional pyramidal manner. At the base are precinct committee members who are elected by party members in primary elections. As of 1994 there were 1,846 precincts in the state. The board of supervisors in each county draws the precinct boundaries. The number of committee members for each party in a precinct varies with the number of registered party members within its boundaries—each party gets at least one position and an additional committee member for each 125 voters registered with the party. In practice, only a few of the positions are filled by election. Some vacancies are filled through appointment by the county board of supervisors from a list of names suggested by the county chair, as prescribed by law. In many cases, the positions remain vacant because no one can be found to take them. The minimum duties of a precinct committee member, as spelled out in law, are to assist his or her party in voter registration and in getting out the vote on election day.

Above the precinct level, state law calls for a county committee and prescribes when it is to meet, how it is to be organized, and what officers it is to elect. The county committee, which is made up of all the precinct committee members in a county, is to meet no later than the second Saturday in January in the year following a general election to choose various county officers from among its own members. Officers to be chosen are a county chair, a first vice chair, a second vice chair, a secretary, and a treasurer. Parties are also authorized to establish legislative district committees to supervise legislative elections. The process followed is the same as that used in forming county organizations: all precinct committee members in a given legislative district must meet by a certain time to elect a chair and other officers from their membership.

The state committee of each party, by law, comprises the chairs of the several county committees plus additional members from each county organization depending on the size of its committee. The state committee must meet in the state capital by the fourth Saturday in January to elect a chair, secretary, and treasurer from its membership. State law also calls for an executive committee of the state committee which is to "consist of the elected officers of the state committee, the county chairman and first and second county vice-chairmen from each county, and three members at large from each congressional district" *(Arizona Revised Statutes* 1994). The parties are free to add other voting or ex officio members. The chair of the state committee is ex officio chair of the executive committee. Interviews conducted for this study suggest that state party chairs have had more to say than anyone about what the organization does, though most decisions have to be cleared through the executive committee and chairs have to maintain a base of support in the state committee.

In assessing the role of state party organizations, one should first note that Arizona continues to have a candidate-centered campaign system. Candidates, particularly for major offices, are still on their own financially and organizationally, in large part because they want to be. Independence gives them greater control over their campaigns. The availability of money from political action committees and other sources and easy access to the technical expertise necessary to run campaigns make independent efforts possible. Rather than relying on patronage, incumbents form winning coalitions through legislative activity and constituent service.

In spite of these developments, state party organizations are stronger in Arizona than they were in the 1960s. Since then, both state parties have enlarged their budgets, staffs, and range of candidate services. The Democratic organization has improved the most in recent years, catching up somewhat with the Republicans.[2] In the spring of 1995 Republicans had eight full-time staff persons and an operating budget of $520,000 (budgets are substantially higher in election years). Democrats in the same period had a budget of $439,000 and three full-time staff members. Not long ago, the state Democratic Party was deep in debt and had to borrow funds from the state chair to meet salary commitments.

Since the 1960s both parties have added direct mail and telephone solicitations to the more traditional fund-raising dinners and social gatherings for party activists. They have institutionalized fund raising through membership programs. A recently adopted "early voting" law has kept both parties busy at election time mailing out absentee-ballot requests to the party faithful.

In general elections, both state parties attempt to mesh their statewide generic campaigns—put together with party organizations at the county and district levels—with the campaigns of party nominees for statewide office, particularly the governor's office and the U.S. Senate. In addition, the state parties appear to have discovered a role in targeting state legislative seats they wish to take over and in coordinating campaign efforts to accomplish this objective.

**Table 1**  Arizona Resource Guide

|  | Democrats | Republicans |
|---|---|---|
| Archive | Yes | Yes |
| Location | State Party Headquarters | State Party Headquarters |
|  | 2005 N. Central Ave., Suite 310 | 3501 N. 24th St. |
|  | Phoenix, Ariz. 85004 | Phoenix, Ariz. 85016 |
|  | (602) 257-9136 | (602) 957-7770 |
| Dates | 1960–present | 1960–present |
| Finding aid | No | No |
| Access | By appointment | By appointment |
| Contents: |  |  |
| Executive committee minutes | Yes | Yes |
| Correspondence | Yes | Yes |
| Organizational structure | Yes | Yes |
| Budgets | Yes | Yes |
| Rules | Yes | Yes |

Though the two party organizations have developed in different ways, both have now largely adopted the view that their basic and almost singular goal is simply to get party nominees elected to office. With this in mind, and learning from experience, each party has made a strong effort to avoid taking stands that might limit the party's appeal in the broader electorate and to minimize friction within the party by taking a big-tent approach. Consistent with this approach, party officials generally stay out of primaries (leaving candidate endorsements to interest groups or party-like organizations with a philosophical slant) and concentrate on fund raising and generic general-election campaigns (those aimed at helping the party generally rather than specific candidates). However, problems of unity persist because of the factionalized nature of the parties.

### RESOURCE GUIDE

The best places to look for primary materials on the development of Arizona state party organizations since the 1960s are the party headquarters, both of which are located in Phoenix. Uncataloged information at Democratic headquarters includes minutes of state executive committee meetings; records of state conventions and delegates; correspondence with national and county party organizations; party rules; and records of organizational structure, procedures, party activities,, and budgetary matters. The same records are found at Republican headquarters, though those on activities and budgets are only partial.

Collections of private papers deposited by former political figures in libraries throughout the state contain additional material relating to the history and development of Arizona political party organizations. Finding aids are available for most of these collections, but researchers are likely to find that useful materials are widely scattered throughout the various collections. Two large collections at the Arizona Historical Foundation at Arizona State University, the Barry Goldwater papers and Paul Fannin papers, contain a wealth of material on the Republican Party in the 1950s, 1960s, and 1970s. The papers of Harry Rosensweig Sr., though a small collection, are also useful. In the Arizona Collection, also at Arizona State University, the large number of papers deposited by John J. Rhodes has a smattering of materials on the Arizona Republican Party. The Arizona Collection also has a variety of materials relating to the state Democratic Party in the Carl T. Hayden papers.

Special Collections, University of Arizona, has the Stewart Udall papers, which cover Arizona politics in the 1950–1974 period. The Bruce Babbitt papers at Northern Arizona University consist of material on Babbitt's terms as governor, January 1978 through January 1987. Each of the above-mentioned libraries has smaller collections under the names of particular parties or under a heading such as "Arizona campaigns and elections." Official papers of most governors are found in the Department of Library, Archives and Public Records (Phoenix). These collections have finding aids and contain materials such as governors' correspondence with party organizations.

## NOTES

1. For many years, Republicans used a state convention-caucus system. In 1995, however, the state legislature created a presidential primary, which changed the manner in which the party selected delegates.
2. In the mid-1970s, one study rated the organizational strength of the state Republican Party as "moderately strong." The state Democratic Party, on the other hand, was rated "moderately weak." The same study ranked the local Republican Party organizations as among the strongest Republican organizations in the nation (number six), whereas local Democratic Party organizations were ranked in the middle of the pack (number thirty) compared to their counterparts elsewhere (Cotter 1984).

## REFERENCES

*Asterisks denote the most important publications on Arizona party politics.*
*Arizona Revised Statutes.* 1994. Title 16, Chapter 5.
* Berman, David R. 1985. *Parties and elections in Arizona: 1863–1984.* Tempe, Ariz.: Morrison Institute, Arizona State University.
*——— 1992a. *Reformers, corporations, and the electorate: An analysis of Arizona's age of reform.* Niwot, Colo.: University of Colorado Press.
*——— 1992b. Regime and party change: The Arizona pattern. In *Party realignment in the American states,* ed. Maureen Moakley, 35–55. Columbus: Ohio State University Press.
Cotter, Cornelius P., et al. 1984. *Party organizations in American politics.* New York: Praeger.
Davis, Glen. 1995. Interview by author, May 31.
Kruglick, Burt. 1995. Interview by author, June 2.
Pine, Charles W. n.d. The Democratic Party in Arizona: Its past, present and future. Unpublished paper.
*Rice, Ross R. 1969. Arizona: Politics in transition. In *Politics in the American West,* ed. Frank Jonas, 41–72. Salt Lake City: University of Utah Press.
*Shadegg, Stephen C. 1986. *Arizona politics: The struggle to end one-party rule.* Tempe: Arizona State University.
*Tucson Daily Citizen.* 1964. Democratic 'purge' action discussed. December 18, 41.
*Wagoner, Jay J. 1970. *Arizona Territory 1863–1912: A political history.* Tucson: University of Arizona Press.
Wynn, Bernie. 1976. Little chance left to avert bloodletting in state GOP. *Arizona Republic,* January 2, B1, B5.

# Arkansas

DIANE D. BLAIR AND W. JAY BARTH

## PARTY HISTORY

The story of evolving political party organizations in Arkansas is both very simple and very complicated. It is simple in the sense that, until recently, Arkansas exemplified the truism that in the absence of competition, parties exist in name only. It is complicated in the sense that Arkansas's evolution toward a competitive party system does not appear to have followed any straightforward line of cause and effect, event and appropriate response. Opportunities for growth have been both exploited and squandered by the winners; electoral defeat has sometimes galvanized, sometimes demoralized the losers. Congruent with the intense personalism that has been one of Arkansas's strongest political traditions, party fortunes have flourished and floundered depending on the strength, skills, and agendas of their leaders. For clarity's sake, we will distinguish between the traditional period (the twentieth century until the 1960s); the emergence period (the 1960s through early 1990s), when both parties began to organize; and the present (mid-1990s).

No state has elected its officials more consistently and exclusively from the ranks of one party than has Arkansas. Arkansas was the last of the southern states to enter the Republican presidential fold (in 1972), and has yet to elect a Republican to the U.S. Senate. From statehood in 1836 to 1995, with the artificial exception of the Reconstruction period, voters have sent a total of four Republicans to serve in the U.S. House of Representatives, two of whom began service in 1992; and only two Republicans have been elected governor (Winthrop Rockefeller in 1966 and 1968, and Frank White in 1980). As recently as 1994, Republicans held only 19 of 135 seats in the state legislature, and a smattering of local offices, primarily in the Ozark uplands.

Unsurprisingly, then, throughout the traditional period, there was little reason for either political party to organize, and they did not. "Democrat" was a mere label under which candidates sought the coveted nomination that ensured victory, and Republicans existed primarily to dispense federal patronage. As one of the authors has summarized elsewhere,

> Given the absolute electoral domination of the Democrats and the complete absence of office-contesting Republicans, both political parties were highly elitist and ephemeral organizations that rarely met, neither recruited nor campaigned for candidates, took no positions, raised no funds, and played no part in persuading and mobilizing the electorate (Blair 1995, 3).

At the county level, Democrats had to be sufficiently organized to manage, staff, and pay for the primaries. Lacking this functional imperative, Republicans had few county committees or even county chairs.

Two major factors stimulated Republican electoral hopes and organizational activity in the emergence period. One was the partisan activity of Winthrop Rockefeller, who lavished millions of dollars not only on his own gubernatorial candidacies (in 1964, 1966, 1968, and

1970) but on building a Republican Party structure as well. With Rockefeller's 1970 defeat and 1973 death, and the Democrats' easy gubernatorial victories throughout the 1970s, the Republicans suffered serious financial and organizational decline. However, Republican presidential victories in Arkansas by progressively larger margins in 1980, 1984, and 1988 reinvigorated Republican aspirations and activism (Blair 1986; 1991; 1994).

The major factor stimulating Democratic organizational activity in the emergence period was the presence, and occasional success, of the Republicans, particularly Rockefeller's victories in 1966 and 1968 and Frank White's shocking upset of Bill Clinton in 1980. That Democratic presidential nominees could no longer count on carrying Arkansas without even the pretense of effort, that the general election had become increasingly problematic for even established and popular Democratic officeholders (as with Bumpers's Senate reelection bid in 1980 and Pryor's Senate reelection bid in 1984), that Republican candidacies for state legislative and county office were increasing numerically and spreading out geographically, and that all the other southern states were rapidly moving in a more Republican direction—all sent warnings to the Democratic Party that its days of easy dominance were waning.

## ORGANIZATIONAL DEVELOPMENT

Fortunately for scholars seeking to better understand the development of political parties in Arkansas, Bass and Westmoreland (1984) offer a chronology of the parties' chairs and executive directors between 1970 and 1984, a thorough overview of the parties' organizational structures, and an analysis of differences between the parties in Arkansas and variations from national patterns. They concluded that "both state parties have become institutionalized. They have attained a raison d'etre transcending personal leadership within the organization or from the statehouse" (Bass and Westmoreland, 54). Although this characterization is even more apt in 1995 than it was in 1984, the two parties have reacted differently to the past decade's changes in the state's political environment.

First, the state Republican Party has attempted to take advantage of the more Republican-receptive climate (created by Reagan's and Bush's popularity) through the active recruitment of candidates, particularly for the state legislature. In an excellent example of what Appleton and Ward (1994) term "horizontal innovation," the GOP has implemented a targeting system, which first showed success in Texas, known as Optimal Republican Voting Strength (ORVS). According to Richard Bearden (1995), the executive director of the GOP now plays a hands-on role in recruiting potential candidates, including the encouragement of party switching by Democrats, in those areas of the state that past elections indicate are prime for Republican growth. The executive director's most effective recruiting tool is a pledge of maximum party financial support to the candidates' campaigns. In contrast, state Democratic chairs have only recently begun occasional strategic recruiting.[1]

The presidency of Arkansan Bill Clinton has also been consequential for state party development, but in somewhat surprising ways. The Republican National Committee (RNC) has been more willing to give the Arkansas Republican Party funds for projects that could lead to home state "black eyes" for the president, and, according to one party official, state fund raising and candidate recruitment have been facilitated (Bearden 1995). Oddly, Clinton's presidency has not strengthened the state Democratic Party. A great deal of the state Democratic loyalists' financial and emotional energy has been directed toward

Clinton's campaigns, and a number of potential Democratic statewide and congressional candidates are presently part of the Clinton administration. And, because the Democratic National Committee (DNC) opened a satellite office in Little Rock to handle Clinton's home state political activity, very little has changed in the day-to-day operations of the state Democratic Party.

Furthermore, the Whitewater investigation has provided state Republicans an opportunity to wave the "reform" banner, which worked so successfully for them in the Rockefeller emergence period. This time, they are labeling the "Clinton-Bumpers-Pryor-Tucker Democrats" a "political machine" and urging voters to "unplug" it. Close observers of Arkansas politics are quite aware that the Arkansas Democratic Party organization more closely resembles a big, rusty combine than a hi-tech "machine," but the message resonated with voters in the successful 1993 campaign of Republican Mike Huckabee for lieutenant governor (Morris 1993).

The reform rhetoric also infused Republican advocacy of a successful (and for the "out" party highly advantageous) 1992 term limits initiative and has also surrounded a series of lawsuits aimed at bringing about changes in the Arkansas election laws that Republicans argue have created an uneven playing field (Hutchinson 1995). A 1995 ruling by the 8th U.S. Circuit Court of Appeals declaring unconstitutional the state system requiring parties to conduct and pay for their own primary elections was an important legal victory for the party. Legislation passed by the General Assembly in reaction to the ruling now assures that the state will pay for primaries, and this means voters will be able to vote in either party primary at all primary precincts.

The possible consequences of this change constantly surfaced in interviews with officials from both parties, with all officials arguing—and hoping—that the change will benefit their party in the long run. Republicans expect a dramatic increase in participation in GOP primaries since voters in rural counties will no longer have to drive long distances to cast Republican ballots, and they believe that local Republican parties that have used proceeds from fundraisers to pay for local primaries will now use those funds for local get-out-the-vote efforts (Bearden 1995; Smith 1990; Brummett 1995).

Democrats are optimistic that local activists will now shift their energy from holding elections to building parties and recruiting candidates and that the state party, which will still receive filing fees from candidates for races above the county level, will be able to pay off the state party's debt and begin to develop a candidate recruitment program and a more effective statewide get-out-the-vote campaign (Maxwell 1995). The combination of feeling threatened and having additional resources may actually make the Democrats the beneficiary of the move to state-funded primaries.

The election of several "young, Reagan disciple firebreathing conservatives" (Bearden 1995) has resulted in the rise of partisanship in the Arkansas House of Representatives. Recently, Democrats—who still hold eighty-eight of the one hundred House seats—have responded by rehabilitating the House Democratic caucus (Oman 1995). Such activity on the part of Arkansas Democrats may, as in the response to the shift to joint primaries, indicate the first awakening grumbles of a giant that has long been asleep.[2]

## CURRENT PARTY ORGANIZATION

Arkansas's two political parties, each of which maintains a single state headquarters located in Little Rock, are certainly more alike than dissimilar structurally and institutionally. For each party, a state convention composed of several hundred delegates meets in the fall of even-numbered election years to, among other formalities, elect a state party chair and members of the state committee and executive committee, the two important party organizations. The state committee of each party comprises about 350 members, and the more important executive committee has between 45 and 50 members. Although state committees do meet several times between party conventions, it is the executive committees that make major decisions about the direction the parties take and about which individuals will be hired to carry out those policies.

Executive committees meet between four and twelve times per year, with the Republican committee meeting more often than its Democratic counterpart. In most instances, the "decisions" that are made by party executive committees are simply stamps of approval on policies formulated by the party chair.[3]

Although neither party can accurately be deemed factionalized, there are hints of factionalism within both parties. Until 1980 the Republican Party divided ideologically between a moderate wing (remnants of the once dominant Rockefeller supporters) and a conservative wing consisting of younger activists. In 1980 the Reaganites took control of the party committees.[4] A recent, extensive survey of county committee activists found that 85 percent consider themselves "conservative" (Blair 1995, 11).[5]

With Clinton loyalists still occupying a majority of Democratic executive and state committee positions and Tucker appointees filling the positions of party chair and executive director, some tension exists (Maxwell 1995). A more serious source of internal division results from the fact that Democratic activists are much less united ideologically than their GOP counterparts; approximately one-third of Democrats identify themselves as liberal, moderate, and conservative, respectively (Blair 1995, 11).

Party chairs are unpaid, typically part-time officials, usually reimbursed for travel and entertainment expenses.[6] The chairs' personal leadership styles, as well as where in the state they live, affect the roles they play in the party. Asa Hutchinson, the Republican Party chair from 1990 to late 1995, and Bynum Gibson, the current Democratic chair, shared similar leadership styles (Ault 1995). Both men practice law in towns several hours from Little Rock. When he served as chair, Hutchinson was in daily contact with party headquarters but visited headquarters only about twice a month; Gibson follows the same pattern. Although the chairs are involved in decisions, they are not able to micromanage their party's operations from such a distance and instead delegate to salaried staff members. Other recent Democratic chairs have not been as "hands off" as Gibson. George Jernigan, a Little Rock lawyer and lobbyist who was party chair from 1991 to 1994, spent almost every afternoon in his party headquarters office, involving himself in both major and minor decisions (Blair 1995).

The size of the parties' paid staffs varies and is based primarily on whether or not it is an election year In general, the state GOP maintains a larger staff than the Democratic Party. As of 1995, only two paid staff members were employed by the Democratic Party—the executive director and communications director. The party hoped to add a political director and an office manager—two positions that have typically existed—by the beginning of the 1996 campaign season. The Republicans had four full-time paid staff members (executive director, finance director, director of the coordinated campaign, and office manager) and planned to add a political director and research coordinator for the 1996 campaign cycle.

A party executive director is the most important paid staff member of each party.[7] In recent years, Republican Party executive directors have had an average tenure of about two years; Democratic executive directors have served slightly longer. Particularly when the chair is not in Little Rock regularly, the executive director can gain considerable power. For a short period (1990–1991), the Democratic Party had a single chair/executive director in the form of longtime Clinton chief of staff Betsey Wright. Wright was likely the most pow-erful—and highest paid—party leader in modern Arkansas history.

The party chairs are the chief spokespersons for the party, holding press conferences and writing newspaper op-ed pieces that "cheerlead" when their party finds success, "spindoc-tor" when electoral and legislative results are disappointing, and—for the "out party" GOP chair, play "watchdog," again emphasizing the popular "reform" theme (Hutchinson 1994). Both chairs also represent their parties' interests in public policy debates. Chairs have regu-larly lobbied the legislature on election and campaign laws and spoken for their parties on proposed constitutional and statutory initiatives.

While many of their day-to-day responsibilities overlap, the party executive directors do have different foci. Because the Democratic Party has financial difficulties, the present exec-utive director focuses on fund raising.[8] The Republican Party has a paid finance director who heads up the fund-raising operation. Therefore, the GOP executive director is able to spend more energy on candidate recruitment, specifically for winnable state legislative seats.

The design of the two headquarters suggests some subtle organizational differences. Permanent offices exist in the Democratic Party headquarters for each of the party's four auxiliary organizations (Senior Democrats, Young Democrats, Democratic Women, Black Caucus) and for the Pulaski County (Little Rock) Democratic Party. At the Republican Party headquarters, no offices are maintained for the party's similar auxiliary groups. The Pulaski County Republican Party is temporarily leasing an office from the state party, but was to establish a separate headquarters early in 1996. Although the auxiliary organizations maintain autonomy in both parties, the Democrats make a greater effort to integrate the auxiliaries into the party organization as a whole. The vitality of the auxiliaries depends a great deal upon their elected leaders. All of the Democratic auxiliaries are active organiza-tions presently, whereas the Arkansas Federation of Republican Women is the only one of the five GOP auxiliaries that has remained consistently active over the past two decades (Bearden 1995; Maxwell 1995).

Both parties raise funds from a variety of sources, including direct mail and fund-raising events, but the state Republican Party is much more reliant on the national party as a source of money. In particular, grants from the RNC have provided the party's phone sys-tem, the salary for a research director in election years, and "seed money" for the training of a finance director (Bearden 1995). In contrast, although it is a beneficiary of the DNC's "Dialing for Democrats" phone solicitation campaign, the Arkansas Democratic Party does not receive significant funding directly from the national party (Maxwell 1995).

The deeper financial relationship with the national party makes the state GOP slightly less autonomous than its Democratic counterpart. While the Arkansas Democrats main-tain contact with the DNC's Southern Political Desk through regular phone calls, the state GOP is visited a number of times each year by the RNC's regional representative. Both par-ties receive daily faxes from their national organizations with the day's "talking points."

While the linkages between the national and state parties are not particularly strong, the relationships between the two state parties and their local party organizations are even weaker. The county organizations of both parties are almost entirely autonomous, aside from county party officials' membership on the state committees. Although local Democratic Party organizations typically remain more active than their Republican coun-

**Table 1** Arkansas Resource Guide

|  | Democrats | Republicans |
|---|---|---|
| Archive | Yes | Yes |
| Location | State Party Headquarters | State Party Headquarters |
|  | 1300 W. Capitol Ave. | 1201 W. 6th St. |
|  | Little Rock, Ark. 72201 | Little Rock, Ark. 72201 |
|  | (501) 374-2361 | (501) 372-7301 |
| Dates | 1920s–present | 1961–present |
| Finding aid | No | No |
| Access | By appointment | By appointment |
| Contents: |  |  |
|   Executive committee minutes | Yes | Yes |
|   Correspondence | Yes | Yes |
|   Organizational structure | Yes | Yes |
|   Budgets | No | Yes |
|   Rules | Yes | Yes |

terparts, the gap has closed in recent years. In several counties in the northwest part of the state, the local Republican Party is better organized than the Democratic Party and has taken over several county quorum courts (the county legislative body).[9] Despite these successes, the Republican lieutenant governor recently noted that GOP organizations are "fairly tepid in many counties. In fact, they expect to lose" (Huckabee 1995). Only two GOP county parties in the state maintain permanent headquarters, but a dozen or so typically open headquarters during election years.

At present, the state Democratic Party is making a conscious attempt to rehabilitate its local parties, whose activity level has largely reflected that of their chairs. As the Democratic speaker of the state house of representatives recently said, "You would be surprised how many House members tell me their county committees do nothing" (Oman 1995). On the other hand, some chairs do carry out the party-building work that the state party is attempting to make more common, a larger number of Democratic than Republican county organizations maintain permanent and election-year headquarters, and there is some evidence that the increasingly competitive nature of elections is sparking some of this new activism on the part of local Democrats.

Over the last several election cycles, both parties have established coordinated campaigns focused on get-out-the-vote efforts to benefit statewide and congressional candidates. However, an important feature of Arkansas politics is that each statewide officeholder and member of Congress maintains a personal political organization that has little linkage to the state party. One state senator recently said of Bill Clinton's field army: "Clinton had as strong a county organization as any politician, including (Orval) Faubus. His ties to those county coordinators were personal, and he nurtured those ties" (Oman 1993). The Democrats' greater success in statewide and congressional races creates a special problem for the state Democratic Party as it attempts to strengthen itself organizationally. Although Democratic candidates' organizations sometimes overlap with each other and with the county party without causing dissension, in some counties they are the basis of local factionalism.

This is not just a Democratic phenomenon. The Republican lieutenant governor and two Republican members of Congress also maintain organizations that are autonomous from the state party. Lieutenant Governor Huckabee recently noted that his personal organization is larger than the GOP organization in most Arkansas counties (Huckabee 1995). One

GOP member of Congress from a traditional Democratic district "does as little as possible" to maintain connections to the state party (Bearden 1995). So, one key reason that the state Republican Party organization has maintained more control over its internal politics than has the Democratic organization is that there have been fewer elected Republicans. Perversely, while Republicans will gladly welcome the additional electoral victories that current trends project for the future, the state Republican Party organization could be a loser in that process.

## RESOURCE GUIDE

*Democratic Party.* Except for very recent years, the records of the Arkansas Democratic Party are a mess. The party's pre-1990 records sit in unmarked file cabinets and boxes in a storage room in the party's headquarters. Some of the records go back to the 1920s, but the records become more complete about the time of Party Chair Herby Branscum's arrival in 1976. The task for scholars would be finding documents of interest in the mass of papers. Correspondence is included in the files, along with membership lists, meeting minutes, and party rules and platforms. However, the correspondence included is likely not consistent enough to allow any real tracing of the party's history. Access to these files and current files, which are well maintained, is at the discretion of the chair. Scholars would have to explain a research project in writing to the chair to gain access, which would almost always be granted. The party is much more protective of financial records. Because all the Democrats who have been governor since 1970 are still in elective office as of 1995, their personal papers, many of which will relate to state party activities, are not yet available. It might be fruitful for scholars to contact past party chairs to gain access to their correspondence files relating to the party's activities.

Two of the Democratic Party's auxiliary organizations, the Senior Democrats and the Black Caucus, have maintained good records over the years. Availability of these records, and access to the files of the other auxiliaries, would be determined by the president of each auxiliary.

Some Democratic Party county organizations in the state have fairly complete records dating back decades. The Pulaski County Democratic Party, which is housed at the state headquarters, has some of the oldest and most complete records.

*Republican Party.* Although state Republican Party records are less extensive than the Democratic records, they are much better organized. The state party newspaper, *The Arkansas Outlook,* which was created in the early 1960s, goes well beyond most party newsletters in terms of the information contained. Through the mid-1970s, the *Outlook* was published on a monthly basis and included party budget information, party rules, state committee membership lists, and overviews of conventions and committee meetings. The paper, which is available in bound volumes in the party headquarters, is an excellent guide to the activities and activists of the Arkansas GOP, at least until it began to be published only quarterly in the 1970s. Bound editions of the minutes of executive committee meetings for the modern era are also available in the headquarters. These materials, as well as some unorganized correspondence in file cabinets, are available for the use of scholars. The papers of Governor Winthrop Rockefeller, who breathed life into the state GOP in the 1960s, are available in the archives of the University of Arkansas at Little Rock.

The auxiliary groups of the Arkansas Republican Party have been less active than their Democratic counterparts. The Arkansas Federation of Republican Women is the only party auxiliary to maintain fairly complete records of its membership and activities. Access to these records could be attained only by contacting the current chair of the organization. Similarly, because many Republican county organizations have come of age only recently, the records of even the largest county party organization are quite limited.

## NOTES

1. The major exception to this hands-off attitude came in 1990 when party chair/executive director Betsey Wright personally recruited state legislative candidates and provided crucial support in a generally successful year for the party's legislative candidates (Wright 1991). Present Democratic chair Bynum Gibson has begun attempting to identify and encourage strong Democratic candidates, generally minus the financial resources offered to candidates by his GOP counterpart (Gibson 1994; Kern 1991).
2. The GOP has had active caucuses in both houses of the legislature since 1982 (Bearden 1995). Since Republican legislators are concentrated in the northwest quadrant of the state, Democratic state senator David Malone (1995) suggests that activities that the state GOP would cite as examples of a vibrant Republican caucus are, in reality, an expression of regionalism.
3. In fact, Ron Maxwell (1995), the Democratic Party communications director, could remember no instances where the executive committee overturned a proposal presented by the chair. Richard Bearden (1995), a former executive director and present coordinated campaign director of the state GOP, could only remember a single case in recent years. Although it was the exception, the disagreement was an important one. Whereas the party chair and other party officials opposed pursuing a lawsuit to overturn the state policy of having parties conduct and pay for party primaries because of the litigation's expense, the executive committee of the party insisted that the ultimately successful lawsuit be undertaken.
4. Aside from a short-lived effort by the supporters of Pat Robertson to gain power in 1988, those who gained power in 1980, and their political offspring, still control the party (Bearden 1995).
5. While not divided ideologically, the state GOP has regularly had to put energy into keeping the peace within its own ranks. Over the past decade there have been regular skirmishes over filling the positions of chair and executive director. The battle lines have generally been based on personality conflicts and old political and business grudges. Although these battles have produced occasional newspaper headlines focusing on the internal divisions, they have never developed into permanent, debilitating stand-offs.
6. The selection process for party chairs has differed significantly for the two parties in recent years. For the Democrats, who have controlled the governor's office since 1983, the party convention (or the executive committee when a vacancy occurs) officially chooses the party chair, but a chair hand-picked by the governor has always been ratified without opposition. On the other hand, Republicans have consistently had contested races for party chair. The party has been lucky in that none of these contests have led to permanent internal party divisions. To avoid such a problem, in 1990 the party elected cochairs: the just-defeated Republican candidates for governor and attorney general.
7. The salary of the executive director, which can range dramatically based on the previous experience of the individual, is set by a party's executive committee.
8. The shortfall is due to a dramatic increase in party spending during the 1990 election cycle that was not met by increases in fund raising and from the expenses incurred in conducting primary and runoff elections in a special election for lieutenant governor in 1993.
9. Although local parties were given direction in these efforts by the state party, the candidate recruitment necessary to bring about these dramatic shifts in representation was carried out by county organizations (Bearden 1995).

## REFERENCES

*Asterisks denote the most important publications on Arkansas party politics.*
Appleton, Andrew M., and Daniel S. Ward. 1994. Understanding organizational innovation and party-building. In *The state of the parties: The changing role of contemporary American parties,* ed. Daniel Shea and John Green. Lanham, Md.: Rowman and Littlefield.

Ault, Larry. 1995. New state chairman from Conway wants GOP to 'move quickly.' *Arkansas Democrat-Gazette.* December 10.

*Bass, Harold F., Jr., and Andrew Westmoreland. 1984. Parties and campaigns in contemporary Arkansas politics. *Arkansas Political Science Journal* 5:38–58.

Bearden, Richard. 1995. Interview by author, June 19. (Bearden was a former executive director of the Republican Party at the time of the interview and has since returned to that position.)

Blair, Diane D. 1986. Arkansas. In *The 1984 presidential election in the South,* ed. Robert P. Steed, Laurence W. Moreland, and Tod. A. Baker. New York: Praeger.

*———. 1988. *Arkansas politics and government: Do the people rule?* Lincoln: University of Nebraska Press.

———. 1991. Arkansas. In *The 1988 presidential election in the South,* ed. Laurence W. Moreland, Robert P. Steed, and Tod A. Baker. New York: Praeger.

———. 1994. Arkansas: Ground zero in the presidential race. In *The 1992 presidential election in the South,* ed. Tod A. Baker, Robert P. Steed, and Laurence W. Moreland. New York: Praeger.

*———. 1995. Arkansas: Emerging party organizations. In *Southern state party organizations and activists,* ed. C. D. Hadley and L. Bowman. Westport, Conn.: Praeger.

Brummett, John. 1995. Two-party progress. *Arkansas Democrat-Gazette,* March 4.

Gibson, Bynum. 1994. Class lecture, Arkansas Politics course, University of Arkansas at Fayetteville, December 2.

Huckabee, Mike. 1995. Class lecture, Arkansas Politics course, University of Arkansas at Fayetteville, April 12.

Hutchinson, Asa. 1994. Class lecture, Arkansas Politics course, University of Arkansas at Fayetteville, November 16.

———. 1995. Reform's next step. *Arkansas Democrat-Gazette,* June 23.

Kern, David F. 1991. Democrats' $59,572 ranked 2nd in gifts to lawmakers' races. *Arkansas Democrat,* September 12.

*Kielhorn, Thomas G. 1973. Party development and partisan change: An analysis of changing patterns of mass support for the parties in Arkansas. Ph.D. diss., University of Illinois.

Malone, David. 1995. Interview by author, June 16.

Maxwell, Ron. 1995. Interview by author, June 15.

Morris, Dick. 1993. GOP wins one in Arkansas. *Campaigns & Elections* (October/November):46–47.

Oman, Noel. 1993. Governor's race another "if" in Hardin's political career. *Arkanas Democrat-Gazette,* August 30.

———. 1995. House speaker says Democrats need waking up. *Arkansas Democrat-Gazette,* June 18.

*Ranchino, Jim. 1972. *Faubus to Bumpers: Arkansas votes, 1960–70.* Arkadelphia, Ark.: Action Research.

Smith, Valerie. 1990. GOP primary costly. *Arkansas Gazette,* June 14.

*Urwin, Cathy K. 1991. *Agenda for reform, Winthrop Rockefeller as governor of Arkansas, 1967–71.* Fayetteville: University of Arkansas Press.

Wright, Betsey. 1991. Activity report to state committee, September 28.

# *California*

ANDREW SKALABAN

Most scholars and observers of the political system consider California political parties to be weak (see, for example, Bell and Price 1992; Mayhew 1986; Sorauf 1984; Walters 1993). However, their opinion is not universally shared (Cotter et al. 1984; Jewell and Olson 1988). The difference between the two points of view is one of emphasis. Compared with the political parties in many other American states, the California parties have sub-stantial organizational capacity; that is, they are fairly professional and can mobilize sub-stantial resources for activities such as fund raising. Yet, by most accounts, the Republican and Democratic organizations in California have a limited ability to affect the outcome of elections.

In part the weakness of the political parties in California results from the rules under which they must operate. California is a "reform" state and has historically constrained the scope of party activities. A second part of the explanation centers on the strength of com-peting sectors of partisan political power. Business and professional organizations, ideolog-ical groups, partisan caucuses in the state legislature, shadow party organizations and clubs, and regional fund-raising centers tied to one or more politicians all compete with the state party central committees for influence. In fact, party politics in California is best described as a partisan network of groups and individuals who move in and out of the political system depending on the issue or election involved. The formal party organiza-tions are part of the network but in no way dominate it, nor could the party organizations even be considered the most important players.

### PARTY HISTORY

Political parties formed in California about the time of statehood, in 1850. The Whigs, for example, were mounting an organizational effort in the 1850s before the national Whig Party dissolved. However, the first one hundred years of statehood were dominated by the Republican Party. California had been admitted to the union as a "free" state in 1850, and the control of the Republican Party over national politics in the wake of the Civil War was mirrored at the state level. One-party dominance did not, however, imply consensus. At both ends of the one-hundred-year time line, the reform or Progressive wing of the Republican Party battled with other factions. The battles were to shape the political land-scape in California and help determine the limits of formal party organization in the state.

The latter part of the nineteenth century saw the clash of two visions for California pol-itics. One vision was of a kind of corporate/patronage-based politics typified by the politi-cal activities—such as putting politicians on the payroll in exchange for political support—of the Southern Pacific Railroad. The other vision grew out of the emerging Progressive movement in American politics. Reform-minded politicians and citizens began to get the upper hand. They made changes in the election laws, such as the introduction of a uniform ballot in 1872 and an Australian ballot (a single ballot printed by the government, rather than by the parties themselves, that listed all candidates for all offices) in 1891, that helped limit corrupt practices. But the reforms also began to limit the role of political par-ties (Cresap 1954).

The beginning of the twentieth century was the heyday for Progressive politics in America and in California. A 1906 political scandal involving San Francisco political boss Abraham Ruef and the Southern Pacific Railroad crystallized support for party reform (Cresap 1954). Progressive politicians seized the opportunity and formed the Lincoln-Roosevelt League. The leader of the league, Republican Hiram Johnson, was elected gover-nor in 1910. Under Johnson's leadership, a number of reforms that had the effect of crippling political parties were instituted. Most notable were the institution of a system of candidate cross-filing (whereby a single candidate could capture the nomination of both major parties), the redefinition of all local and judicial elections as nonpartisan, the legal separation of state and county party organizations, and the development of a system of citizen initiative and recall.

These reforms had the effects of subduing political parties and strengthening the power base of political moderates, especially Republican political moderates. Cross-over candidates could effectively eliminate the voice of a less moderate opposition party candidate by denying that candidate his or her party's nomination. That possibility served as an incentive for the political parties to nominate moderates so as to forestall cross-over candidacies. Even during the realignment of the Great Depression, Republicans generally held sway in California state politics. As testimony to the strength of the Republican center, the onset of prosperity that accompanied World War II saw the election of Earl Warren as governor—one of the last of a unique breed of California politicians who used nonpartisanship as an issue to strengthen the hold of the Republican moderates on the party and the state government. Whereas in 1946 Warren captured the nomination of both the Democratic and Republican Parties and won the general election with almost 92 percent of the vote, in 1950, running as a Republican, he faced strong Democratic opposition and won the election with only 65 percent of the vote.

The nonpartisan political climate of the state began to change in the 1950s. Taking their cues from national politics, staunch anticommunist conservative Republicans such as Richard Nixon and William Knowland began pulling the Republican Party to the right (Walters 1993). The impact of anticommunism on California politics was enhanced by population increases fueled by growth in defense-related industries and the associated spread of the Southern California suburbs into Orange County. When the system of cross-filing ended in 1959, moderates became even less attractive to the Republican Party as political candidates. At first the Democrats moved to seize the political middle, as exemplified by the gubernatorial candidacy and tenure of Pat Brown. However, the Democrats eventually moved to the left as the politics of the 1960s played themselves out in the state.

In an absolute sense, the parties entered the 1960s stronger than they had been in decades. With the end of cross-filing, it would be impossible for elections for major offices to go virtually uncontested because one candidate had captured the endorsements of both major parties. However, in a relative sense, the parties would find their power little enhanced. Other partisan institutions would rise out of the ideological struggles of the Republicans and Democrats that would sometimes compete with established party organizations. Most important, an increasingly professionalized legislature would take advantage of changes in the nature of American political campaigns—especially the movement away from a reliance on party workers and toward the use of the media and direct mail in campaigning—to establish party caucus organizations that could function independently of the state committees.

## ORGANIZATIONAL DEVELOPMENT

The elections of 1958 were among the more significant in recent American history and were particularly important in California. An economic recession, coming at a time when the Eisenhower administration appeared to have run out of energy, created a larger constituency for Democratic candidates. Even in California, Democrats won decisively: Edmund G. (Pat) Brown Sr. was elected governor, and a group of more activist Democrats won control of the legislature. Thus the elections of 1958 signaled the end of the unrivaled dominance of the Republican Party in California and the emergence of a vigorous and modernized Democratic competitor.

The advent of a new cohort in state politics had a profound effect on the political environment in California. Carmines and Stimson (1986) demonstrated how the election of a new group of legislators for economic reasons could affect other issues, such as civil rights, later on. They described this as issue evolution. A similar phenomenon happened in California, though in this case it might be more aptly termed institutional evolution. The newly elected Democrats quickly set about reforming the institutions and processes of state politics. Most notably, Jesse Unruh was elected assembly speaker in California following the 1958 elections. Unruh undertook as one of his main political objectives the professionalization of the California legislature. Professionalization in the absence of institutionalization (see Squire 1993) meant that the leadership within the legislature acquired substantial power, and the leadership's aggrandizement of power continued in subsequent years. The rise of political action committees in the 1970s and the predominance of candidate-centered media campaigns, with all that implied for personality-based politics, served to increase the importance of the legislative leadership in assembly and state senate campaigns yet further. This trend reached its apex under the assembly speakership of Willie Brown (1980–1995). Brown used the contributions generated by his office to maintain Democratic dominance of the legislature until the 1994 elections, when Brown's position as speaker and Democratic dominance were undermined by a 40–40 split in the assembly.

The ability of the assembly and senate caucuses to raise money and to spend it on campaigns, often through transfer from the leadership to candidates in contested races, further inhibited the development of strong central party organizations in California. Although the parties in California have the institutional capacity to raise and distribute money to important candidates—compared with individual campaigns or the intervention of legislative leaders—the parties are unwieldy mechanisms for distributing money. Elected officials are extremely well represented on the state central committees of both political parties. However, a variety of other individuals and groups influence party policy. Their goals may not be as pragmatic as those of the professional politicians. Moreover, representation on the state party committees of elected officials from a variety of levels of government, from holders of national office to representatives of county central committees, makes coming up with a consensus about election priorities difficult. A professionalized legislature has also led institutional donors, business or other PACs, to give money through the party leadership in the legislature rather than through the state party apparatus; that is the direct route to access and influence on policy making.

Somewhat ironically, and mostly unintentionally, the emergence of the legislative party caucuses as independent powers led to the most visible upsurge of business influence in California politics since the time prior to the Progressive era. Business groups became extremely active in funding legislative war chests. Industry's development of active and professional political organizations, rather than working behind the scenes through personal contacts, unleashed new forces in California politics: business and professional groups as initiative sponsors. One of the keystones of Progressive reforms to thwart the direct influence of industry in politics, the initiative became a vehicle for reasserting business power. The use of initiative by business has had the effect of marginalizing the parties relative to business groups.

Of course, the upswing in interest group and PAC activity in the 1970s and 1980s was not limited to business groups. Schoolteachers and trial lawyers were among the professional groups most supportive of Democratic candidates. Environmental groups became active in campaign politics and very active in the initiative process. Finally, the tax revolt movement of the late 1970s, led by Howard Jarvis and Paul Gann, though more closely identified with the Republican Party, transformed California fiscal politics through the initiative process and not through officeholders as representatives of the party. The antitax movement led and the politicians, including Democratic governor Jerry Brown, followed. Clearly, no one would mistake this as a model of responsible party government.

Over the past forty years other groups that served as adjuncts of, and sometimes outright competitors to, the regular party organizations proliferated. The ideological fragmentation of the 1950s and the upsurge of grassroots politics in the 1960s saw the development of splinter groups within the party organizations. These organizations filled roles forbidden to regular party organizations, such as making preprimary endorsements. One such group, the California Democratic Council (CDC), was set up in the 1950s to help steer the state Democratic Party to the left. Another emerged in 1976, when Tom Hayden, a former antiwar activist, set up the Campaign for Economic Democracy (CED) with a new-left political agenda. Eventually the campaign mutated into the more moderate Campaign California, which had less of a radical grassroots focus and more of an emphasis on championing high-profile issues such as the environment (Bell and Price 1992).

The state Democratic Party became home to a number of special caucuses set up to provide formal representation for women, gays, and racial and ethnic groups. They were granted special recognition by the Democratic State Central Committee through a process set up in the party bylaws.

The Republican Party also developed adjunct and special-status groups. The United Republicans of California was formed in the 1960s to serve as a home base for the arch-conservative Republican agenda. The California Republican Assembly (CRA), with roots in the immediate post-Progressive era, served as a guardian of Republican moderation until it moved toward the growing conservative majority in the party during the last couple of decades (California Center for Research and Education in Government 1975). The moderates now are best represented by the California Republican League (CRL). The CRA and CRL are guaranteed representation on the Republican State Central Committee, as are the California Republican Congress, the California Federation of Republican Women, the California Young Republicans, and the California College Republicans.

Overall, the influence of the splinter groups, especially the CDC, CRC, and CRA, has waned recently. Their incorporation into the parties has been used as an institutional vehicle for resolving and channeling conflict within the parties. In that sense, the splinter groups have helped energize the debate within the parties and have helped keep the parties in tune with important constituencies. On the other hand, they can make consensus building within the parties more cumbersome. More voices mean less cohesion; the result is very democratic but not necessarily a formula for the assertion of more power by the state party organizations.

## CURRENT PARTY ORGANIZATION

Political parties in California currently have fewer legal restrictions on their exercise of power than at any time since the Progressive era. The legal separation of county and state central committees and cross-filing are long gone. Moreover, a series of court decisions in the 1980s and early 1990s has increased the ability of the parties to make preprimary endorsements. Technological changes and organizational innovations, including such simple things as maintaining databases of active donors, have made fund raising easier and more profitable. Still, the political parties in California remain organizationally moribund.

The California political parties, by law, are headed by state central committees. The central committees are made up largely of national and state officeholders and their appointees and include at least four members selected by each county committee; central committee membership numbers more than one thousand for each party. The Republicans give past nominees seats and allow them to make appointments based on the success of their campaigns. The Democrats have something of a quota system, with some officeholders and nominees required to choose at least half of their appointees of the opposite sex. Both parties have complex rules governing membership on the central committees, but both parties rely heavily on national and state officeholders. The Democrats favor some form of affirmative action in the appointment of other members by officeholders, whereas the Republicans favor a system of incentives; that is, the better a candidate's performance, the more appointments he or she may make.

The county central committees, relatively small bodies of a few members each who are elected in party primaries, also have representation on the state central committees. Representation on the Democratic State Central Committee of county central committee appointees is proportional, with a base of four appointees and one additional appointee for each 10,000 Democrats registered in the county. The Republican county chairs get to appoint four members each to the state committee. In addition, another incentive formula exists for additional appointments based on current registration, new registrants, and party performance in national elections.

No provisions exist for the representation of local officeholders on the state committees because all local elective offices in California are nonpartisan. This is one of the legacies of the Progressive past that continues to affect the capacity of the parties to become more encompassing organizations. Many towns and cities do have vital partisan clubs, which often provide a welcome pool of volunteers for legislative or statewide campaigns. However, no provision has been made by either party for their representation on the state central committees.

A quick analysis of the incentives provided to politicians and citizens to participate in California politics reveals why the inability of the parties to mobilize more effectively for political action is at least partly structural. Politicians do not have to rely on the parties to run effective campaigns. The professionalization of the legislature, the rise of PACs and media-oriented campaigns, and the relatively freewheeling campaign finance laws in the state enable politicians to run effectively without the parties. Dianne Feinstein, for example, won the Democratic nomination for U.S. senator in 1992 without the support of the party. Nor did her insurgent candidacy preclude the party from later supporting her in the general election. In economic terms, relying on one's own campaign apparatus is more efficient than relying on the party.

Similarly, interest groups can more directly tie campaign contributions to policy outcomes by giving to politicians rather than the party. Or they can bypass the partisan system entirely and work for policy change through the initiative system in the state.

All this having been said, the parties are still necessary. Even in California, most voters still think of themselves as Republicans or Democrats and organize their political lives along those lines. That is why the parties can still raise substantial amounts of money even though attendance at county committee meetings is in decline. The California political parties may still be able to take advantage of this affective attachment by voters to increase their role in the politics of the state, but some past efforts to increase grassroots participation have not been particularly productive. Real modernization of the parties may require a rethinking of party organizational structure and a reassessment of the role of the parties in political campaigns.

Modernization of the party organizations might prove especially important now that term limits will reduce the capacity of individual legislators to amass large campaign surpluses and to wield power based on their positions as campaign money conduits. Moreover, campaign finance reform, passed before by the voters only to be overturned by the courts, may be on its way through the initiative process. Finance reform could further reduce the ability of candidates to run campaigns independent of the parties. The prognosis for campaign finance reform in the long run is quite good. The reform urge runs deep in California politics. It would be the ultimate irony of California politics if, this time, political reform were to enhance the power of political parties.

## RESOURCE GUIDE

The circumscribed role of political parties in California extends to the keeping of official party records. State information agencies have only a limited amount of official information pertaining to the Democratic and Republican Parties. The state archives in Sacramento, an agency of the secretary of state, acts as a depository for records of appointments to the state central committees and nominations as presidential electors. These records are maintained pursuant to state election law. Beyond this, the archives can offer little in the way of official party records.

The state archives, however, has other, nonofficial, materials relating to the role of parties in politics and government. For example, the archives contains collections of papers of important officeholders in the state. Included are the papers of former assembly speaker Jesse Unruh—one of the state's pivotal political figures of the twentieth century.

The state library in Sacramento and the libraries of the University of California (UC) also have scattered primary materials. The state library has the original, and the some university libraries have microfiche copies, of the California Information File. The California Information File is a catalog, of sorts, of documents and articles pertaining to important events in the state. The file contains records from the end of the nineteenth century to 1985. The state library also has some campaign materials documenting the role of parties in election politics. For example, the library contains an array of materials from the Merriam/Sinclair gubernatorial election of 1934.

For research into the early history of political parties and politics in the state, the Bancroft Library on the UC-Berkeley campus seems to have the best collection. Among its holdings are the records of a number of early party conventions.

Another good source for information on contemporary political parties is the Committee on Elections and Reapportionment in the California State Legislative Assembly. Some recent committee material will be available for purchase at the state capitol, whereas other material will be available at the archives, state library, or libraries of the UC system.

Finally, the state offices of the Democratic and Republican Parties have contemporary documents. The parties have professional staff who are busy but still accessible. They may also be of some help in locating older documents that have been stored, literally, in the garages and houses of past party officials. The best places to contact the parties are the Democratic state office in Sacramento and the Republican state office in Burbank.

REFERENCES

*Asterisks denote the most important publications on California party politics.*

*Bell, Charles G., and Charles M. Price. 1992. *California government today: Politics of reform.* 4th ed. Pacific Grove, Calif.: Brooks/Cole Publishing.

California Center for Research and Education in Government. 1975. *Almanac of state government and politics.* Sacramento: California Center for Research and Education in Government.

California Commission on Campaign Financing. 1985. *The new gold rush: Financing California's legislative campaigns.* Los Angeles: Center for Responsive Government.

California Democratic Party. 1995. *By-laws and rules of the California Democratic Party.* Photocopy.

*California Journal.* Sacramento: California Journal Press. Various issues.

*California political almanac.* Sacramento: California Journal Press. Various issues.

California Republican Party. 1994. *Standing rules and bylaws.* Photocopy.

Carmines, Edward G., and James A. Stimson. 1989. *Issue evolution: Race and the transformation of American politics.* Princeton, N.J.: Princeton University Press.

Cotter, Cornelius P., James L. Gibson, John F. Bibby, and Robert J. Huckshorn. 1984. *Party organizations in American politics.* New York: Praeger.

*Cresap, Dean R. 1954. *Party politics in the Golden State.* Los Angeles: Haynes Foundation.

Jewell, Malcolm E., and David M. Olson. 1988. *Political parties and elections in American states.* Chicago: Dorsey Press

Mayhew, David R. 1986. *Placing parties in American politics.* Princeton N.J.: Princeton University Press.

*Owens, John R., Edmond Costantini, and Louis F. Weschler. 1970. *California politics and parties.* New York: Macmillan.

Sorauf, Frank. 1984. *Party politics in America.* Boston: Little, Brown.

Squire, Peverill. 1993. The theory of legislative institutionalization and the California assembly. *Journal of Politics* 54:126–154

Walter, Dan. 1993. California: A state of change. *California political almanac.* Sacramento: California Journal Press.

# Colorado

Denver

ROBERT D. LOEVY

## PARTY HISTORY

A single sentence sums up the recent history of political parties in Colorado: Colorado is a Republican state, but the Democrats frequently win important elections there.

*Electoral History.* The Republican claim to political dominance in Colorado stems from the GOP's strong grip on the state legislature. The Republicans controlled both houses of the Colorado General Assembly for thirty-two of the thirty-six years from 1960 to 1996.

The Democrats briefly won control of the Colorado House and Senate in 1964 when incumbent Democratic president Lyndon Johnson overwhelmed Republican challenger

Barry Goldwater. The Democrats won control of just the Colorado house in 1974 when the Watergate scandal in Washington, D.C., produced a wave of Democratic victories in Colorado. In each of these cases, however, the Democrats lost their legislative majorities to the Republicans in the next general election two years later.

Since 1974, when Democrat Richard Lamm won the governor's race, the Democrats have dominated the Colorado chief executive's office. Lamm was elected to three consecutive four-year terms. His successor, former state treasurer Roy Romer, captured another three gubernatorial elections in a row for the Democrats. Romer was easily reelected in 1994 despite having a well-known opponent, former Republican state chair Bruce Benson, who raised and spent millions of dollars, much of it his own money, in the effort to unseat Romer.

When it comes to the U.S. Senate and U.S. House of Representatives, Colorado voters have divided their support between the two political parties but often have given a slight edge to the Republicans. From 1978 to 1994 Colorado consistently elected one U.S. senator from each political party. This even split was upset early in 1995 when Colorado's Ben Nighthorse Campbell, the only Native American in the U.S. Senate, switched from the Democratic to the Republican Party. His switch gave Colorado two Republican U.S. senators for the first time since 1972.

This same even split between the parties has applied to the U.S. House of Representatives. Throughout much of the 1980s the state delegation was composed of three Democrats and three Republicans. In 1992, however, Republican Scott McInnis won a formerly Democratic House seat in southern and western Colorado, thereby giving the GOP a four-to-two edge.

In presidential elections Colorado has been very much a bellwether state, but when the voting gets close Colorado tends to favor the Republicans. In 1960, when the nation gave a razor-thin victory to Democrat John F. Kennedy for president, Colorado supported Republican Richard M. Nixon. The same pattern occurred in another close election in 1976. Democrat Jimmy Carter narrowly won the presidency, but incumbent Republican Gerald Ford easily carried Colorado.

In all other presidential elections from 1960 to 1992 Colorado supported the national winner. Although Republican presidents Ronald Reagan and George Bush were unusually popular in Colorado during the 1980s, Colorado "swung with the nation" and gave a comfortable margin of victory to Democrat Bill Clinton in 1992.

*City-suburban Polarization.* Over 80 percent of Colorado's population lives on the "Front Range," an urbanized strip of rolling prairie stretching some two hundred miles from north to south at the foot of the eastern edge of the Rocky Mountains. The vast majority of Coloradans live in this fast-growing megalopolis of cities and suburbs from Fort Collins and Greeley in the north, through Denver and Colorado Springs in the middle, to Pueblo in the south.

The two political parties polarize along the same city-suburban lines in Colorado as in the nation as a whole. The base of Democratic Party strength in Colorado is Denver, where the state's African American and Hispanic voters are concentrated. Adding to the Democratic Party's urban base is the city of Pueblo, 110 miles south of Denver, which is the location of a major steel-making plant and thus a longtime bastion of labor union support.

Democrats also do well in the intellectually prominent and decidedly upscale city of Boulder, twenty miles northwest of Denver, where the state university and a number of high-tech research organizations are located.

Republican strength in Colorado is concentrated in Colorado Springs, a suburban-style city located seventy miles south of Denver at the foot of Pikes Peak. Colorado Springs is so Republican that the county in which it is located, El Paso County, voted almost two-to-one for George Bush over Bill Clinton for president in 1992.

Other small cities on the "Front Range," such as Fort Collins and Greeley north of Denver, add to the Republican base. The GOP also does well in the rural areas of Colorado, particularly in Grand Junction, a resort and fruit-growing center across the Rocky Mountains on the western edge of the state.

The swing vote in Colorado partisan politics is found in the Denver suburbs. Two counties, Jefferson County to the west of Denver and Arapahoe County to the south, contain most of the suburban population of the Denver metropolitan area. Ordinarily these two populous counties vote Republican, but they will abandon the Republican Party and vote Democratic whenever they see a Democratic candidate they like better.

Richard Lamm and Roy Romer were two Democratic governors who showed particular ability at garnering normally Republican votes in Jefferson and Arapahoe Counties. In the 1992 presidential election, Jefferson and Arapahoe Counties gave only slim majorities to Republican George Bush, thereby enabling Democrat Bill Clinton to engineer a statewide victory with a heavy Democratic vote in the cities of Denver, Pueblo, and Boulder.

## ORGANIZATIONAL DEVELOPMENT

Political party organization in Colorado is distinguished by the large and important role that rank-and-file party members play in nominating party candidates for political office.

For all elected offices, from county sheriffs to governor, Colorado uses a nominating system in which the party convention is held *prior* to the party primary election. Most candidates for elected office must first win at least 30 percent of the vote at a county or state convention before their names will be placed on the ballot in the party primary. The only exceptions to this statutory requirement are for a limited number of candidates who gather petition signatures to get on the primary ballot rather than go through the convention.

Most important, every member of a political party in Colorado may participate in the nominating process if he or she chooses to do so. Persons registered in the Democratic or Republican Party are encouraged to attend their respective neighborhood precinct caucuses in early April of each election year. At the precinct caucus the party faithful elect delegates to the county convention, which is held in May and selects nominees for county offices to go on the ballot in the August party primary.

In order to get on the August primary ballot, would-be party candidates must receive at least 30 percent of the delegate vote at the county convention. The party convention thus has the effect of limiting the number of party members who run in the primary election. Only two or three candidates are likely to qualify for the party primary. Often only one candidate gets 30 percent or more of the county convention vote. That candidate becomes, in effect, the party nominee.

The party conventions in Colorado's sixty-three counties elect delegates to the state party convention, which operates under the same procedures as the county conventions. To qualify for the August party primary, candidates for statewide office must get 30 percent or more of the delegate vote at the state convention. As a result, state conventions in Colorado can be lively, with major battles raging over who will get on the primary ballot for such important statewide offices as governor, lieutenant governor, state treasurer, and secretary of state.

There have been only two major changes in the nominating process in Colorado since 1960. In the late 1980s, the percentage of convention delegate votes required to get on the primary election ballot was raised from 20 percent to 30 percent. The purpose of this change was to make it easier for incumbent officeholders to get renominated without primary opposition. The assumption was that a popular incumbent could easily win 70 percent or more of the delegate votes and thereby keep a potential challenger from getting the 30 percent necessary to get on the ballot.

The second change altered the rules on gathering petition signatures to get on the state primary ballot without going to the state party convention. Originally, candidates were expected to petition on to the primary ballot *after* they had failed to get 30 percent of the vote at the state party convention. In the late 1980s the secretary of state moved back the deadline for filing petitions to a date preceding the state conventions, so that candidates now have to turn in their petition signatures *prior* to the state party convention.

In 1994 the eventual Republican candidate for governor, Denver millionaire oilman Bruce Benson, decided to petition on to the Republican primary ballot rather than be nominated at the state convention. Benson's primary election opponents, who had been nominated at the state convention, severely criticized Benson for bypassing the party convention process. Benson nonetheless won the August Republican primary, but he was easily defeated by incumbent Democratic governor Roy Romer in the November general election. Some observers attributed Benson's defeat partly to the fact that he had petitioned on to the primary ballot rather than put his name before the party faithful at the state convention.

A major addition to the nominating process in Colorado was the establishment of the Colorado presidential primary in 1992. Prior to that time Colorado elected its delegates to the national conventions at the state party conventions in June of each presidential year, long after the party nominees had been determined by early presidential primaries held in other states. Colorado's presidential primary is held on the first Tuesday in March, the first date allowed under national Democratic Party rules.

## CURRENT PARTY ORGANIZATION

In every voting precinct in Colorado, each of the two political parties elects two committeepersons at a precinct caucus, the same precinct caucus at which the nominating system begins. The committeepersons from all the precincts in the county meet every two years to elect a county chair, vice chair, and other county party officers.

Both the Republican and Democratic Parties in Colorado are governed by a state central committee. There are some differences in the way the central committees are elected, but mainly they are composed of the party officers (chair, vice chair, and secretary) from each of Colorado's sixty-three counties, the party's members in the state senate and the state house of representatives, and any statewide officeholders (such as governor and treasurer) from the party as well as the party's U.S. senators and U.S. representatives. Both parties also permit the state's more populous counties to elect "bonus" members to the state central committee.

The state central committee of each party chooses the state chair, state vice chair, and state secretary. The state chair is the highest and most powerful party officer in Colorado and is responsible for hiring the staff at state party headquarters. The state party chair also has much to say about how party funds are distributed to the various party candidates for office at election time.

The state chair and the state party staff have four major responsibilities: operate the state party headquarters; raise funds (so-called soft money) and allocate it to the various party candidates for office; provide "in kind" support services—such as demographic research, polling, and press releases—-to all party candidates for office; work to develop a unified party program and "message" to the voters.

*Headquarters Operations.* There is something of a contrast between Republican and Democratic headquarters operations in Colorado. For one thing, the Republicans operate out of a separate building, a small office structure located several blocks west of the state capitol in downtown Denver. The building has a large sign identifying it as Republican headquarters which is readily visible to the many commuters on Colfax Avenue, one of the major east-west traffic arteries through Denver.

The Democrats, on the other hand, have about the same amount of space as the Republicans in a suite of offices in a low-rise office building several blocks south of the capitol. The Democrats have a much smaller sign than the Republicans, and it is much less prominently displayed. The Democrats, however, have a substantially larger public meeting room than the Republicans. In the summer of 1995 the Democrats were planning to reduce their state headquarters office space, either by cutting the size of their present suite or moving to a smaller suite in the same building.

The Republicans in 1995 had a paid state staff of six persons, whereas the Democrats had only three persons on the payroll. The Democrats, however, expand the state party staff, often to as many as six-to eight-paid workers, during election times.

*Party Finance.* Both political parties in Colorado avidly raise money and channel it to political candidates. Because they use different accounting methods, it is difficult to compare the two parties directly, but most observers agree the Republicans raise and spend more than the Democrats. In the two years leading up to the November 1994 elections, the Republicans claim to have raised and spent about $2 million. They set a goal of raising $2.5 million for the two-year 1996 election cycle.

The Democrats report that the amount of money they have to spend varies with the strength of the particular candidates in a given election year. The amount of money goes up when there is a strong Democratic presidential candidate, such as Bill Clinton in 1992, or when there is a strong Democratic gubernatorial candidate, such as Roy Romer in 1994. But even in the 1992 election cycle, with a strong presidential candidate, the Democrats had a total budget of about $1.5 million, roughly a half-million dollars less than the Republicans.

*Candidate Services.* In the mid-1980s the Republican Party in Colorado greatly expanded its services to party candidates throughout the state. These services included "briefing books" for all candidates on the demographic characteristics of their election district and facts, both positive and negative, about their Democratic opponent. Candidates also were provided help in writing press releases and given advice on carrying out other routine campaign chores. Leadership training was instituted for county party officials and party candidates for office.

The Democrats admit they had to reorganize their operation in the 1980s to keep up with the Republicans. As a result, both parties now provide extensive in-kind services. The Republicans appear to be maintaining their lead in this important area. They currently mail political materials in bulk for their candidates and operate a statewide telephone bank that made over 500,000 phone calls to Republican voters just prior to the 1994 election. For the 1996 election cycle, the Republicans plan to conduct a "campaign management college" for Republican campaign managers from around the state.

The Colorado Republicans also operate what they believe is the first state party computer bulletin board in the nation. Computer users with a modem can telephone "GOP Net" in Denver and get the party calendar of events, Republican "talking points" on major issues, a review of GOP bills pending in the legislature, Republican candidate biographies, and other information.

*State Legislative Campaigns.* One of the most important activities of both state party organizations in Colorado is working to win a party majority in one or both houses of the Colorado legislature. Staff members at party headquarters in Denver carefully study past election returns, working to identify legislative seats that appear ripe to change from one political party to the other. Both political parties in Colorado rely on computers to process the election results and other demographic data that are used to identify seats that will be closely contested in the next general election.

As might be expected, both the Democratic and the Republican Parties tend to come up with identical lists of targeted legislative seats. As a result, only twelve to fifteen of the eighty or so legislative seats that are up for a vote in any one election are seriously contested by the two political parties. Once a state senate or state house seat has been targeted, however, both parties pour in extra money and, sometimes, outside political expertise in order to win.

Apparently the Republicans did an effective job of targeting in 1994, which was a big Republican year nationwide and in Colorado. The Republicans said they targeted nineteen seats in the Colorado legislature (both senate and house) and won fifteen of them.

At first glance it appears that the Republicans are better organized than the Democrats at the state level in Colorado. This may be more a difference of style and emphasis than effectiveness, however. The Republicans pour more money and effort into party activities, whereas the Democrats tend to organize more strongly around the campaigns of individual candidates, particularly those Democratic candidates who are likely winners. This candidate-centered style has served the Democrats well in Colorado, particularly when it comes to winning statewide offices such as governor and U.S. senator.

### RESOURCE GUIDE

Research on state party organizations is facilitated in Colorado by the fact that each party has a single state headquarters in Denver. The state party records that exist can be found at the respective state headquarters and are available to scholars.

*Democratic Party.* The Democrats keep a file on each county in the state. Most of these files contain records concerning county party leaders, party activists, and caucus and county convention attendees. There is also a file on each state legislative district (state senate and state house) with "opposition information" on those seats currently held by Republicans. There is an index to the files entered since 1980, but it is arranged chronologically rather than alphabetically.

There are a number of archival files that go back to the 1950s and 1960s, but they do not appear to have been preserved in any systematic way. These include minutes of meetings and party rules, platforms, and events.

The real treasure at Democratic headquarters in Colorado is the photograph files, which date back to the 1960s. There are many well-preserved photos of leading national figures in the Democratic Party campaigning in Colorado. In a number of cases national leaders are pictured with prominent Colorado Democrats of the time.

**Table 1**   Colorado Resource Guide

| | Democrats | Republicans |
|---|---|---|
| Archive | Yes | Yes |
| Location | Colorado Democratic Party | Colorado Republican Party |
| | 770 Grant Street, Suite 200 | 1275 Tremont Place |
| | Denver, Colo. 80203 | Denver, Colo. 80204 |
| Dates | 1950–present | 1960–present |
| Finding aid | Since 1980 | Recent |
| Access | By appointment | By appointment |
| Contents: | | |
|   Executive committee minutes | Yes | Yes |
|   Correspondence | Yes | Yes |
|   Organizational structure | Yes | Yes |
|   Budgets | No | 1990– |
|   Rules | Yes | Yes |

Equally impressive is the videotape collection, which includes television commercials (both Democratic and Republican) from recent statewide campaigns in Colorado. There also are a number of short promotional videos on Colorado Democratic candidates for office and a number of training and spirit-building videos put out by the Democratic National Committee and the Clinton administration. The Colorado Democrats have a much better video collection than the Republicans, but ironically, the Democrats do not have a video cassette recorder (VCR) on which to play their tapes. The Republicans have a VCR/TV monitor combined.

The Democrats also have a small audio tape collection and a drawer full of recent precinct maps. The videotapes, audio tapes, and precinct maps are all uncataloged.

The Colorado Democrats are rapidly computerizing much of the essential information for their statewide party operation. A directory of important state and county Democratic Party officials is maintained in the computer and distributed in loose-leaf form to key party workers. Also computerized is a ten-year history of regular Democratic Party caucus attendees, party activists, and party contributors.

*Republican Party.* The Republicans in Colorado keep their active files in their party headquarters building and store inactive files in the basement of an office building next door. Their basement storeroom is windowless and dank but contains an extensive collection of uncataloged materials dating back over many years.

The Republicans have extensive files on elected officials and candidates, particularly on incumbent Democratic officeholders in the state. These files contain clippings, campaign brochures, and candidate speeches and statements, among other items. There is an extensive file on Democratic president Bill Clinton, with the clippings and other data arranged by issue. There are more than five file drawers of material on incumbent Democratic governor Roy Romer.

Similar to the Democrats, the Republicans have organizational files on each of the state's sixty-three counties and one hundred legislative districts (state senate and state house). Financial records are kept for six years and are stored mainly on computer tape. Files on recent state conventions and state central committee meetings are kept in a pair of file drawers in the state chair's office. Computerized information includes selected voter files, voting results, and letters and form letters sent out from party headquarters.

## REFERENCES

*Asterisks denote the most important publications on Colorado party politics.*

*Cronin, Thomas E., and Robert D. Loevy. 1993. *Colorado politics and government: Governing the centennial state.* Lincoln: University of Nebraska Press.

Lamm, Richard D., and Duane A. Smith. 1981. *Pioneers and politicians: 10 Colorado governors in profile.* Boulder, Colo.: Pruett.

*Lorch, Robert S. 1991. *Colorado's government.* 5th ed. Niwot, Colo.: University Press of Colorado.

Martin, Curtis W., and Rudolph Gomez. 1972. *Colorado government and politics.* 3d ed. Boulder, Colo.: Pruett.

*Straayer, John A. 1990. *The Colorado General Assembly.* Niwot, Colo.: University Press of Colorado.

Ubbelohde, Carl, et al. 1988. *A Colorado history.* 6th ed. Boulder, Colo.: Pruett.

# Connecticut

SARAH M. MOREHOUSE AND
MALCOLM E. JEWELL

## PARTY HISTORY

The Republican Party dominated Connecticut from the realigning election of 1896 until the beginning of the New Deal. Republican candidates for president carried Connecticut in eight of the nine presidential elections from 1896 through 1928 (all except the three-way race in 1912). Republicans also won fifteen of the eighteen gubernatorial elections (for two-year terms) from 1896 through 1930, but only four of these victories were by more than 55 percent of the vote.

The New Deal transformed Connecticut into a closely competitive two-party state and led to Democratic gains in the large cities, particularly among ethnic groups and members of labor unions. Each party won half the presidential elections from 1932 through 1960; the Democrats controlled the governorship for eighteen of thirty years from the 1932 through the 1958 elections, although neither party won more than 56 percent of the vote until Abraham Ribicoff's Democratic landslide in 1958. The Democrats controlled the Senate over two-thirds of the time during this period, while the Republicans always won the malapportioned House.

Connecticut in the twentieth century has been characterized by strong party organizations at the state and local levels. Two state chairs dominated their party organizations for remarkably long periods of time. The Republican chair, J. Henry Roraback, served from 1912 to 1937. Lockard (1959, 245) described his rule as "virtually a benevolent dictatorship" for most of his tenure, until the Democrats grew more competitive during the Roosevelt administration. He controlled state nominating conventions, kept the support of local organizations through the judicious use of patronage, and controlled the state legislative process. He denied renomination to two successive Republican governors in the 1920s.

John Bailey chaired the state Democratic Party from 1946 until his death in 1975. Benevolent dictatorship was no longer possible, and Bailey's power depended on his skill in building alliances with city bosses, labor unions, and ethnic minorities. The party's voting strength was based primarily on the large cities, many of which had party bosses. Bailey was actively involved in the state legislative process, and he was particularly skillful and influential in recruiting strong candidates for public office and ensuring their nomination. Both Roraback and Bailey (in his early years as chair) were empowered by a nominating process that did not involve primary elections until 1955; nominations for statewide offices were made by state conventions until that time (Lockard 1959, ch. 9).

In the years since 1960 Connecticut has leaned Republican in presidential elections but has been solidly Democratic in state and congressional elections. Republicans won five of eight presidential elections from 1964 through 1992 (including five consecutive victories from 1972 through 1988). But in U.S. Senate races the only Republican to win was Lowell Weicker, a moderate who served three terms because of his ability to appeal to Democrats and independents. The Democrats held the governorship for thirty-two of thirty-six years from 1955 through 1990. In 1990 former senator Lowell Weicker was elected governor on a third-party ticket. In 1994 the voters elected John Rowland, a solid conservative and the first Republican governor in twenty-four years. Since the 1966 reapportionment, Democrats have consistently won majorities in both houses of the Connecticut legislature, except in the 1972 and 1984 elections, when the Republicans won both houses, and in the 1994 election, when the Republicans won the senate.

## ORGANIZATIONAL DEVELOPMENT

Democratic Party registration gradually increased from parity with the Republican Party (27 percent to 27 percent) in 1960 to a twelve point advantage (38 percent to 26 percent) in 1994. The proportion of registered voters who do not affiliate with any party is higher in Connecticut than in most states. It was 45 percent in 1960 and 36 percent in 1994. In the early years of the primary system contested primaries were rare, and Connecticut voters had little incentive to affiliate with a party. The increase in such contests starting in the 1970s has probably contributed to the gradual growth in the proportion of affiliated voters. There is evidence from other states that fewer voters register with a party when primary contests are infrequent (Jewell 1984, 207–208).

A more useful measure of voters' partisanship than voter registration is party identification, which is derived from public opinion surveys. By this measure there are more Democrats than Republicans in Connecticut, but the gap is narrowing. In the early 1980s the Democrats led the Republicans in party identification 36 percent to 21 percent, but by 1995 the lead had shrunk to 32 percent for the Democrats to 24 percent for the Republicans, with 39 percent of voters claiming to be independent (according to the *Hartford Courant*/Institute for Social Inquiry Connecticut Poll at the University of Connecticut, Storrs).

*Changes in the Nominating System.* Connecticut was one of the last states to adopt some form of primary election to replace conventions for nominating candidates. In 1955 the legislature adopted what is called a challenge primary. Candidates are still nominated by party conventions and caucuses, but any candidate who receives a minimum percentage of the votes at the convention or caucus may challenge the party's choice in a primary. The minimum has been lowered from 20 percent to 15 percent of the convention or caucus vote.

The adoption of the challenge primary initially had little effect because relatively few candidates challenged the party's nominee. The first contested primary for statewide office did not occur until 1970. Since then both parties have seen a gradual increase in the number of statewide primaries, although incumbent governors and U.S. senators and representatives rarely face primary challenges. There were gubernatorial primaries in one party in 1970, 1978, 1986, and 1990, and in both parties in 1994. Both parties had U.S. senatorial primaries in 1970, and the Republicans had primaries in 1980, 1992, and 1994. For the six U.S. House seats, there were five primaries in the 1970s, eleven in the 1980s, and six in the three elections from 1990 through 1994. In recent years the average number of state legislative primaries has been about twenty-five (Rose 1992, 15–16, 50).

Despite the growing number of primary challenges, most nominations made in the party conventions and caucuses still go unchallenged. This gives the Connecticut state and local political parties unusually large influence over the selection of candidates. Party discipline is relatively strong in Connecticut. Delegates to conventions and caucuses are often pressured by state and local leaders to support their candidates. Candidates who fail to win endorsement are under considerable pressure from party leaders not to challenge the endorsee.

Less than two-thirds of registered voters are affiliated with one of the parties, and a relatively low proportion of these actually vote in primaries (about 23 percent of party-affiliated voters cast primary ballots in 1994, when both parties had contested gubernatorial primaries). In 1984 Sen. Lowell Weicker persuaded the Republican Party to adopt a rule permitting unaffiliated voters to vote in the Republican primary. Weicker, an unusually liberal Republican, hoped this would make the Republican primary electorate less conservative. The legislature refused to modify the closed primary law, but the U.S. Supreme Court (in *Tashjian v. Republican Party of Connecticut*) ruled that the state legislature could not prohibit the Republican Party from admitting unaffiliated voters to its primary if it chose to do so. The Republican Party acceded to Weicker's request and opened its primary to all registered voters. After Weicker left the Republican Party to run for governor on a third-party ticket in 1990, the Republican Party once again closed its primary.

*The Role of Political Parties.* Observers of Connecticut politics have found some signs that the parties are declining in importance (Rose 1992; McKee 1983), but the evidence is mixed. Successors of veteran Democratic state chair John Bailey, since his death in 1975, have served shorter tours of duty and have had much less power. Democratic Party machines in the larger cities are better organized than in most states but are less effective than they were in the past. In 1994, for example, local party leaders were able to win convention endorsement for the gubernatorial candidate they preferred but failed to provide him with the votes needed to win the primary election.

Until the last few years, the Republican Party organization has been handicapped by its long-time minority status and by its ideological divisions. Lowell Weicker was the only Republican to win a major statewide office between 1970 and 1994, but he was out of step with increasingly conservative Republican activists. The election of John Rowland to the governorship in 1994 seems likely to strengthen the Republican Party organization as well as to give it a more conservative orientation.

The parties presumably were handicapped by the elimination of the party lever on voting machines in 1986, which was a result of a very close vote on a referendum. Ironically, Republicans had campaigned for the change even though the state was growing more Republican in presidential elections and a Republican legislative majority had been elected in 1984, aided by the coattails of Ronald Reagan's 60 percent victory in the state.

Lowell Weicker's election as governor in 1990 as the candidate of A Connecticut Party (ACP) appeared to demonstrate a lack of voter confidence in both parties. The Democratic candidate ran third with only 21 percent of the vote, barely more than the 20 percent that the Democrats needed to retain their legal status as a major party. Four years later the ACP candidate for governor got only 19 percent of the vote, though her presence in the race may have cost the Democrats the governorship. The ACP's endorsement of candidates in some congressional and legislative races provided an added measure of political influence. But A Connecticut Party was largely a personal vehicle for Lowell Weicker, and, in his absence, is likely to decline in importance. In 1994 only two thousand voters were affiliated with the ACP, about one-tenth of one percent of registered voters.

There are several signs that the major Connecticut parties are alive and well. The ability of the Democratic and Republican Parties to run candidates for most legislative seats is one good measure. In the elections from 1968 through 1988, only about 5 percent of all legislative seats were uncontested (less than 7 percent of those won by Democrats and less than 4 percent of those won by Republicans). Even though the rate from 1980 to 1988 rose to almost 10 percent, it was still a much lower percentage of uncontested races than in most states.

The state legislative parties in Connecticut are among the more cohesive in the country. Voting in the legislature on important issues often follows party lines. The caucuses lack the tight discipline imposed on the Democrats by John Bailey, but they are among only a few in the country which sometimes take binding votes, particularly on budgetary issues. The caucuses are often used by the leadership to build cohesion and mobilize votes (Jewell and Whicker 1994, 100–101). Morehouse (1992) found that, in voting on the governor's program, members' votes correlated closely with party; the governor had very strong support from his party and little support from the opposition.

Since the mid-1980s, the state senate and house legislative leaders and the caucuses of both parties have played an increasing role in raising money and providing services for the campaigns of legislative candidates. This has built party cohesion and strengthened the power of legislative leaders.

## CURRENT PARTY ORGANIZATION

Under Connecticut law, the parties have considerable organizational freedom. The one exception is the procedures governing state and local nominating conventions and challenge primaries, which are prescribed in considerable detail by state law.

Connecticut law places no limitations on the amount of money that the political party committees can contribute to statewide, state legislative, or local candidates, but there are limits on PAC and individual contributions.

Each party is governed by a state central committee consisting of seventy-two members, two from each state senatorial district. Democratic Party rules require that each senatorial district select one man and one woman. The members are elected to two-year terms by delegates from each senatorial district, who are chosen by the local parties. The state chair of the party is chosen by the members of the state central committee for a two-year term.

*Democratic Party.* Since 1975, when John Bailey's thirty-year tenure as party chair ended, Democratic chairs have served only one or two terms. Democratic governors have usually been able to determine who will chair the party. Recent Democratic governors (Ella Grasso, 1975–1980, and William O'Neill, 1980–1991) have played very active roles in the political party. Recent party chairs have not had the power or the patronage resources that Bailey had, nor have they tried to dominate the Democratic legislative caucuses. But a skillful chair has considerable opportunity to determine priorities and plan strategies and may work closely with legislators on particular issues. At present, one of the most important roles of the state chair is to serve as spokesperson for the party, responding to calls from journalists and appearing on television. This role assumes greater importance when the party does not control the governorship.

The state central committee meets six times a year and carries out much of its work through subcommittees, but it is not a particularly influential body. In 1995 the state party organization had what the chair described as a "bare bones" budget of about $450,000. In addition to the unpaid chair, the organization included an executive director, a person handling communications with the media and local parties, an accountant, and a receptionist.

Democratic Party leaders strongly favor the preprimary convention endorsement system, and four-fifths of delegates to the 1994 convention supported it in a survey. But a majority of Democratic House members tried unsuccessfully in 1995 to pass a bill that would have permitted candidates to run in the primary without getting at least minimal support at the convention. In recent years most candidates endorsed by the Democratic convention for major statewide offices have avoided a primary challenge. But there were such challenges in the 1990 and 1994 gubernatorial races, with the endorsee losing in the latter year. Carrying on the tradition of John Bailey, Democratic state chairs have attempted, with considerable success, to influence decisions of the state convention, particularly by attracting strong candidates to run and by brokering compromises at the convention.

There are no strong factions in the Democratic Party, although short-term conflicts do arise, often resulting from contested primaries. There are continuing differences between the moderate wing of the party and the liberal wing. This division was an underlying factor in the 1994 gubernatorial primary and has led to some significant leadership fights among Democratic state legislators. At the national level, Sen. Joseph Lieberman represents a much less liberal viewpoint than Sen. Christopher Dodd.

The Connecticut Democratic Party has a close relationship with, and receives considerable financial and other assistance from, the national party. This relationship has grown even closer since Senator Dodd became national party chair in 1995. Because Connecticut is usually a closely competitive state in presidential elections, and has been recently in congressional contests as well, it gets considerable attention from the national party.

Most local Democratic Party bodies are relatively well organized, and the state chair works closely with the town party chairs. Although party leaders in the largest cities lack the patronage resources that formerly permitted them to rule with an iron fist, most of them remain strong.

State and congressional candidates raise most of their own money, but the state party is sometimes able to help them get financial assistance from the national party or from sources in Connecticut. It makes lists of financial contributors readily available to Democratic candidates.

The state party chair has sometimes assisted state legislative candidates, but legislative leaders in recent years have controlled fund raising for, and campaign assistance to, Democratic legislative candidates. This development has significantly reduced the influence of the state party leadership over Democratic legislators.

*Republican Party.* The influence exerted by the chair of the Republican Party has varied in recent years depending on the political strength and skills of the person occupying the post. As the legislature and its leadership have grown more independent, the party chair's influence on the legislature has declined, although some recent party chairs have met frequently with a legislative caucus.

In 1994 the first Republican governor since 1970 chose Richard Arnold as the new party chair. During a brief term as chair, Arnold worked closely with Governor Rowland and had less responsibility to serve as a party spokesperson. Governor Rowland has shown interest in party affairs and fund raising from the start.

The chair of the Republican Party has considerable opportunity to make operational and political decisions but must get approval of the state central committee for decisions on budgetary and broad policy matters. One of the heaviest responsibilities of the party chair is making sure that adequate funds are raised to keep the organization functioning. A chair who lets the party slide into debt will have trouble staying in office. Party norms allow a chair to serve more than one two-year term.

The full-time staff of the state party includes an executive director, a finance person responsible for fund raising, and an operations director. The chair is a part-time job, though a conscientious chair finds the workload demanding. The annual budget of the state Republican Party is about $700,000.

There is considerable consensus among Republican Party leaders that the preprimary convention system should be continued without significant change. Among delegates to the 1994 Republican convention, more than 80 percent favored the endorsement system. A majority wanted to strengthen it; many suggested that the minimum convention vote required for entering a primary be restored to 20 percent from the current 15 percent. House Republicans unanimously rejected a legislative proposal to permit candidates to bypass the convention. Despite this support for the principle of endorsement, there were Republican primaries for the U.S. Senate in 1992 and 1994, and for governor in 1986 and 1994. The senatorial endorsee lost in 1992, and the gubernatorial endorsee lost in 1986.

The departure of Lowell Weicker from the Republican Party has reduced the level of factionalism in the party. In ideological terms, the party is more unified and more conservative on economic issues than in the recent past. The lack of a strong pro-life or Christian right group also reduces party factionalism.

The relationship between the state party and the national Republican Party is close. The election of a Republican governor in 1994 improved this relationship, and the closely competitive character of the state motivates the national party to provide financial assistance to Connecticut Republicans. The state and national parties trade information on their financial contributors.

The Republican Party is reasonably well organized at the town level, particularly in areas where Republicans usually win elections. One of the state chair's major responsibilities is staying in touch with the 169 town chairs.

The state party provides financial and other forms of assistance to candidates for statewide office, and to a lesser extent for congressional office. It provides lists of financial contributors to Republican candidates after the nomination process has been secured. Party rules prohibit such assistance prior to that. Party leaders and caucuses in the Connecticut legislature raise substantial sums of money which they distribute to legislative candidates. The state Republican Party is currently working closely with legislative leaders to develop a coordinated strategy for raising and allocating these funds.

### RESOURCE GUIDE

Neither political party in Connecticut maintains a well organized or comprehensive archive of party records. Both parties have some records available at state party headquarters in Hartford, covering recent years. At state Republican headquarters, the records most likely to be available are the minutes of state central committee meetings. The Democratic Party reports that, in addition to minutes of recent state committee meetings, it maintains records of some state conventions, party rules, and scattered correspondence. It is clear that neither party has made any effort to develop and maintain a systematic record of the party's activities, even for the past few years.

The political parties have not deposited records with the state archives or with any historical associations or university libraries. The Historical Manuscripts and Archives section of the University of Connecticut does have several collections of papers of prominent political figures, including members of Congress and one governor. These might contain correspondence or other records pertaining to the political parties. The Bridgeport Public Library maintains a clipping file on state and local political parties that may be useful to researchers.

**REFERENCES**

*Asterisks denote the most important publications on Connecticut party politics.*
Arnold, Richard. 1995. Chair, Connecticut Republican Party. Interview by author, July 18.
Jewell, Malcolm E. 1984. *Parties and primaries: Nominating state governors.* New York: Praeger.
Jewell, Malcolm E., and Marcia L. Whicker. 1994. *Legislative leadership in the American states.* Ann Arbor: University of Michigan Press.
*Lieberman, Joseph I. 1981. *The legacy.* Hartford, Conn.: Spoonwood Press.
*———. 1966. *The power broker.* Boston: Houghton Mifflin.
*Lockard, Duane. 1959. *New England state politics.* Princeton, N.J.: Princeton University Press, chaps. 9 and 10.
Marcus, Edward. 1995. Chair, Connecticut Democratic Party. Interview by author, July 14.
*McKee, Clyde D., Jr. 1983. Connecticut: A political system in transition. In *New England political parties,* ed. Josephine Milburn and William Doyle. Cambridge, Mass.: Schenkman.
Morehouse, Sarah M. 1992. Legislative party voting for the governor's program. Paper presented at the annual meeting of the American Political Science Association.
Noel, Don. 1995. Veteran journalist and columnist for the *Hartford Courant.* Interview by author, July 20.
Pelto, John. 1995. Former state legislator and former political director, Connecticut Democratic Party. Interview by author, July 20.
*Rose, Gary L. 1992. *Connecticut politics at the crossroads.* New York: University Press of America.

# Delaware

SAMUEL B. HOFF

Political parties have played a crucial role in the political life of Delaware, the first state to ratify the Constitution. Delaware political parties have been shaped by three factors: personalities; independence from neighboring states and the national parties; and, more recently, moderation and balance across issues and offices.

## PARTY HISTORY

The etiology of political parties in Delaware begins with the American Revolution. Harold Hancock observes the following about Delaware on the eve of independence:

> Occasionally the names of contesting parties are identified with "court" and "country" though the exact meaning of these labels is not clear. Election contests were primarily between the ins and the outs, with personalities playing an important part. Elections were sometimes decided by the voters' ties of kinship, church affiliation, and feuds (1976, 28).

As in other colonies, the "ins" and "outs" gave way to relatively stable factions over the question of independence, the role of a national government, and other colonial-era issues. The Delaware legislative factions united in December 1787 to ratify unanimously the U.S. Constitution.

During the pre–Civil War era, Delaware strongly backed Federalist and, later, Whig candidates over candidates from other parties. Between 1789 and 1828, for instance, Delaware voters elected ten Federalist and three Democratic-Republican governors. At the presidential level, state electors endorsed Federalist candidates in every election until 1820, when James Monroe outpolled John Quincy Adams (Munroe 1979; Martin 1984). When the new national party system evolved in the 1830s featuring Democrats and Whigs, Delaware voters continued their nationalist leaning, electing Whigs in three of five gubernatorial elections between 1832 and 1846, selecting Whigs in seven of ten U.S. House races from 1834 to 1853, and choosing Whig presidential candidates in four of eight races from 1832 to 1860 (Nelson 1989, 1407–1410; Martin 1984; Austin 1986). Both parties developed effective machine organizations during this period (Huckshorn 1976).

With the demise of the Whigs, Delaware parties severely fragmented. In 1854 a candidate from the American Party, Peter Foster Causey, won the governorship. Causey's third-party triumph was followed by the narrow defeat of James S. Buckmaster of the People's Party in the 1858 gubernatorial race and the victory of William Cannon of the Union Party in 1862 (Martin 1984). Delaware elected a Free Soil candidate to the U.S. House in 1854 (Austin 1986). In the 1860 presidential election, Delaware supported Southern Democratic Party candidate John Breckinridge (Munroe 1979). Delaware's split party support at that juncture mirrored the state's position on the conflicts that precipitated the Civil War: "Delaware paid homage to both sections, but gave complete allegiance to neither. In feeling the majority of the people were pro-Southern, but few were secessionist" (Hancock 1961, 179).

Events during the Civil War, including the invasion of Delaware by Union soldiers to disarm militias, the suspension of habeas corpus rights, the imprisonment of suspected southern sympathizers, and the required oaths of loyalty to the Lincoln administration, led to a three-decade domination of state politics by the Democratic Party. Not only did Delaware reject the constitutional amendments granting freedom and civil and voting rights to blacks, but it also sent a succession of Democrats to Washington who pleaded the cause of the defeated states with such consistency that Delaware came to be regarded, in political terms, as a part of what eventually would be known as the Solid South (Munroe 1979, 145).

The evidence of a Democratic dynasty in Delaware politics during the latter part of the nineteenth century, which contrasted starkly with national trends, is convincing. Between 1866 and 1896 Democrats won eight of nine gubernatorial elections and thirteen of sixteen U.S. House elections. From 1864 through 1892 Democratic candidates for president took the state in every election except 1872, when voters endorsed Ulysses Grant's reelection (Munroe 1979; Martin 1984; Austin 1986).

The party realignment of 1896 finally brought Delaware in line with national political trends. One of the major reasons for the success of the Republican Party in the state over the first third of the twentieth century was the support it received from business. The DuPont Corporation, in particular, exercised political power (Gosnell and Smolka 1976). From 1900 through 1932 Republicans won all nine gubernatorial elections. From 1898 through 1932 Republicans held the state house for twenty-six of thirty-six years. Similarly, Republicans wielded a majority in the state senate for twenty-six of thirty-six years. Republicans controlled both chambers simultaneously for eighteen years, or half of the period. In U.S. House contests between 1898 and 1932, Delaware Republicans were victorious in thirteen of eighteen. Starting with the popular election of U.S. senators in 1916, Republicans captured four of six seats through 1934. Delaware helped elect Republican presidential candidates in every election except one from 1896 to 1932, with the single exception being the 1912 endorsement of Democrat Woodrow Wilson (Munroe 1979; Martin 1984; Austin 1986).

The period from 1936 to 1996 has been one of relative equity for Delaware Democratic and Republican Parties in electing candidates to office. At the outset, "it was the reputation of Roosevelt himself and of his policies that won the support of Delaware voters, not any particular attractiveness of the local Democratic Party" (Munroe 1979, 209). Indeed, Franklin Roosevelt carried the state in 1936, 1940, and 1944. However, in the twelve ensuing presidential contests, Delaware voters backed Republican candidates in eight. Between 1936 and 1996 Republicans won nine of fifteen gubernatorial contests, Democrats took thirteen of twenty-nine U.S. House elections, and Republicans were victorious in twelve of eighteen U.S. Senate elections (Munroe 1979; Martin 1984; Austin 1986).

### ORGANIZATIONAL DEVELOPMENT

Three studies of state party competitiveness encompassing the early 1960s to the late 1980s labeled Delaware as a balanced two-party system. David Pfeiffer (1967) based his assessment on the results of all statewide general elections from 1940 through 1964. Austin Ranney (1976) came to the same conclusion after studying the popular vote for governor and average percentage of seats held by each party in the two chambers of the state legislature between 1962 and 1973. A study by Malcolm Jewell and David Olson (1988) of state party competitiveness between 1965 and 1988, using the same methodology as Ranney, also classified Delaware as a competitive two-party state. Jewell and Olson observed that, while Democrats controlled the state senate for sixteen of the twenty-four years, Republicans held a majority in the state house for fourteen of twenty-four years.

The partisan alignment in 1996 certainly is indicative of an even party competition; a Democratic governor, a Republican U.S. House member, and one U.S. senator from each party serve the state. Party control of the state legislature was split in 1996, with the Democrats holding a 12-9 edge in the senate and the Republicans possessing a 27-11 majority in the house.

The balanced nature of party representation in modern Delaware shows no signs of changing and is reflected in the parties' organizational activities. Neither party dominates the political environment, and the relationship between the parties can be summarized in three words: tradition, tolerance, and compromise.

Delaware has initiated a unique celebration of politics called *Return Day,* held in Georgetown, Sussex County, two days after the election for president and state governor. Carol Hoffecker (1988, 192) describes the festival:

A man in old-fashioned clothes and a silk hat announces the winners of the state elections from the courthouse steps. The winning and losing candidates ride together in a parade into town in horse-drawn carriages past cheering people.

As long as Delaware politicians continue to not take themselves too seriously and enjoy such bipartisan events, the parties will continue to be governed by tradition.

Although they engage in occasional acrimony, Delaware parties have displayed tolerance toward one another and toward minor parties. One measure of such respect is the ballot access granted to third parties. Delaware election law places the same requirements for ballot access on minor parties as on the Democratic and Republican Parties; they must have 191 registered party members, or 5 percent of registered voters. By mid-1996 three minor parties—the Libertarian, Natural Law, and U.S. Taxpayers Parties—had qualified for the 1996 ballot.

In presidential elections, third parties have often received a respectable percentage of votes cast in Delaware. For example, the Socialist Party had a candidate on the state ballot in every presidential election from 1912 to 1964; the Prohibition Party earned votes in nine of ten presidential elections from 1940 through 1976; and the Libertarian Party obtained a considerable number of votes in recent presidential elections (Harper 1993). Such autonomy granted to minor parties is indicative of the maturity and viability of the party system in Delaware, as is the number of state citizens registered as independents or as members of a third party (21 percent, as compared with 43 percent registered as Democrats and 36 percent registered as Republicans in 1994, according to Barone and Ujifusa [1995]).

Finally, Democrats and Republicans in Delaware have been able to compromise and reach consensus on important issues. Though some divisive issues are now being debated, including affirmative action, gun control, abortion, and same-sex marriages, Delaware's party officials and elected leaders have recognized that "when good laws are passed or needed new programs are begun, there is enough credit for both political parties" (Taylor 1996, H3).

## CURRENT PARTY ORGANIZATION

The rules of the state political parties have been revised several times. The current Democratic and Republican Party rules were enacted in 1993, within two months of one another. The Delaware Democratic Party, headquartered in Wilmington, has four political subdivisions: the city of Wilmington and the counties of New Castle, Kent, and Sussex. Each subdivision has authority to elect officers and draft operating rules, which must not conflict with state party guidelines. A state convention is mandated in May of the year following a presidential election in order to choose state committee officers, including a chair, two vice chairs (one of each gender), a secretary, and a treasurer. Each officer serves a four-year term. In addition to choosing state committee officers, the party convention elects two representatives to the Democratic National Committee and conducts other business pertinent to the party.

The state Democratic committee is formally composed of the five officers listed above, the chair of each political subdivision, five additional representatives from New Castle County, and two representatives from each of the other subdivisions. The state committee has two standing committees—Finance and Candidate Support—and meetings of the state committee are required quarterly. Among the duties of the state committee are to select the party's presidential electors and recommend a delegate selection plan for the party's national convention; the latter must be approved by the Democratic National Committee.

The state Republican Party organization is divided into seven convention districts or regions: Wilmington, Brandywine, Christiana-Mill Creek, Colonial, Newark, Kent, and Sussex. State conventions are of three types: organizational, held in odd-numbered years; general, held in even-numbered years; and special organizational. All conventions consist of 344 delegates. Whereas the organizational convention chooses state party officers and receives annual reports, the general convention endorses candidates for national and statewide posts.

The officers of the Delaware Republican Party, elected for a two-year term, include a chair, vice chair, secretary, and treasurer. The state party committee is composed of the party officers together with the chair and vice chair of each convention district; a national party committeeman and committeewoman; all Republican statewide elected officeholders; two members per representative district within each convention district; and the president or chief executive officer of the New Castle County Republican Committee, Delaware Federation of Republican Women, Young Republican Federation of Delaware, Delaware Federation of College Republicans, Republican Heritage Council, Black Republican Alliance of the State of Delaware, and other organizations as designated. The state Republican Party has just two standing committees—Rules and Finance. Like the Democratic state headquarters, the state Republican Party headquarters is in Wilmington.

Although no recent financial reports were available from the state party organizations, Federal Election Commission figures for the 1991–1992 election period show that Democrats collected $486,292 and disbursed $472,153, whereas the Republicans garnered $1,001,656 and appropriated $949,102. State Democratic Party spending ranked forty-second among the fifty states, whereas state Republican Party spending ranked twenty-seventh (Biersack 1994). Over the same period, the Center for Responsive Politics reported that the Delaware Democratic Party gave $12,800 in soft money donations to the Democratic National Committee, and the state Republican Party contributed $332,490 to the Republican National Committee. Conversely, the Democratic and Republican National Committees transferred $40,431 and $93,750 to the Delaware Democratic and Republican Parties, respectively (Goldstein 1993).

In terms of state laws overseeing political parties, Delaware has been classified as a light regulator in two different studies (Conlan et al. 1984; Advisory Commission on Intergovernmental Relations 1986). There are no state provisions limiting state or local party committee selection, composition, rules, or activities; there is no government funding of state election campaigns; and voter registration requirements are minimal.

The influence of political parties in Delaware is no doubt mitigated by the impact of major economic enterprises such as DuPont Corporation, by the part-time nature of the state legislature, and by the two-term limit for governor. Yet on February 24, 1996, state Democrats and Republicans joined together to hold Delaware's first-ever presidential primary. Bucking the national party committees, which threatened to reduce the number of delegates allotted to the state parties at the national conventions in deference to New Hampshire, Delaware officials stuck to their plan of holding the maiden presidential primary just four days after the Granite State's. Although New Hampshire's hardball tactics seemed to work prior to voting—only two presidential candidates actively campaigned in Delaware—the election was a stunning win for Steve Forbes and provided hoped-for national exposure for Delaware. The national party committees later promised that no retribution would be taken against Delaware's delegates, and both parties sent full contingents to their respective 1996 national nominating conventions. Two lessons may be drawn from the episode: state political parties, particularly when they cooperate with one another, can exert substantial influence over national party organizations; and timing, not necessarily delegate count, is the key to affecting the presidential nomination process.

## RESOURCE GUIDE

No useful original party documents have been located at either the Democratic or Republican party headquarters or the state archives.

## REFERENCES

*Asterisks denote the most important publications on Delaware party politics.*

Advisory Commission on Intergovernmental Relations. 1986. *The transformation in American politics.* Washington, D.C.: Advisory Commission on Intergovernmental Relations.

Austin, Erik. 1986. *Political facts of the United States since 1789.* New York: Columbia University Press.

Barone, Michael, and Grant Ujifusa. 1995. *The almanac of American politics 1996.* Washington, D.C.: National Journal.

Biersack, Robert. 1994. Hard facts and soft money: State party finance in the 1992 federal election. In *The state of the parties: The changing role of contemporary American parties,* ed. Daniel Shea and John Green. Lanham, Md.: Rowman and Littlefield.

Carpenter, Allan, and Carl Provorse. 1996. *The world almanac of the U.S.A.* Mahwah, N.J.: World Almanac Books.

*Christensen, Gardell Dano, and Eugenia Burney. 1974. *Colonial Delaware.* Nashville: Thomas Nelson.

Conlan, Timothy, Ann Martino, and Robert Digler. 1984. State parties in the 1980s.*Intergovernmental Perspective* 10:6–13, 23.

Goldstein, Josh. 1993. *Soft money, real dollars: Soft money and the 1992 election.* Washington, D.C.: Center for Responsive Politics.

Gossnell, Harold F., and Richard G. Smolka. 1976. *American parties and elections.* Columbus, Ohio: Charles E. Merrill.

*Hancock, Harold Bell. 1961. *Delaware during the Civil War.* Wilmington: Historical Society of Delaware.

*Hancock, Harold B. 1987. *Delaware 200 years ago: 1780–1800.* Wilmington: Middle Atlantic Press.

*———. 1976. *Liberty and independence: The Delaware state during the American Revolution.* Wilmington: Delaware American Revolution Bicentennial Commission.

Harper, Richard B. 1993. *State of Delaware 1992 general election results.* Dover: State Election Commission.

Henderson, Gordon G. 1976. *An introduction to political parties.* New York: Harper and Row.

*Hoffecker, Carol E. 1988. *Delaware, the first state.* Wilmington: Middle Atlantic Press.

Huckshorn, Robert J. 1976. *Party leadership in the states.* Amherst: University of Massachusetts Press.

Jewell, Malcolm E., and David M. Olson. 1988. *Political parties and elections in American states.* Chicago: Dorsey Press.

*Martin, Roger A. 1984. *A history of Delaware through its governors 1776–1984.* Wilmington: McClafferty Press.

*Munroe, John A. 1987. *Delaware becomes a state.* Newark: University of Delaware Press.

*———. 1979. *History of Delaware.* Newark: University of Delaware Press.

Nelson, Michael, ed. 1989. *Guide to the Presidency.* Washington, D.C.: Congressional Quarterly.

Pfeiffer, David G. 1967. The measurement of inter-party competition and systemic stability. *American Political Science Review* 61:457–467.

Ranney, Austin. 1976. Parties in state politics. In *Politics in American states: A comparative analysis,* ed. Herbert Jacob and Kenneth N. Vines. Boston: Little, Brown.

*Spruance, John S. 1955 *Delaware stays in the Union.* Newark: University of Delaware Press.

Sundquist, James L. 1973. *Dynamics of the party system.* Washington, D.C.: Brookings Institution.

Taylor, John. 1996. Delaware remains a bastion of political compromise. *Wilmington News Journal,* June 9, H3.

# *Florida*

ANNE E. KELLEY

## PARTY HISTORY

The Civil War, rapid population growth, and urbanization gave Florida parties their distinctive character.

"Organized party politics began in Florida as a prelude to the state's admission into the Union," remarked Dorothy Dodd (1980). When Florida entered the Union in 1845, Democrats and Whigs fought for control of the new state government. After a brief rule by the Whigs (1848–1852), the Democrats gained control of government. The Civil War obliterated party lines. The power struggle that ensued during the formation of the Reconstruction Constitution of 1868 brought about party organization in the modern sense. The Republican Party held the governor's office from 1868 to 1877, at which time the Democratic Party regained control of the office and of state government; the Democrats remained unchallenged until after World War II. In fact, the Republican Party legally dissolved as a result of *State el rel Merrill v Gerow* (1921). In the eyes of the law the Republican Party was dissolved because it had failed to poll more than 5 percent of the total vote in the general election. However, the party remained as a patronage organization; the so-called Post Office Republicans (Klingman 1984, 118) became distributors of appointments made by Republican presidents. After the emergence of the solid Democratic South, Republican Party members became "presidential Republicans," meaning they voted Republican in presidential elections but cast their ballots in the Democratic primaries in order to have a voice in state and local matters.

The issues of race and civil rights influenced the political parties throughout Florida history. From statehood to the Civil War, African Americans constituted nearly half of the population in Florida but were disfranchised (Tebeau 1973, 181). The constitution of 1868 permitted African Americans to vote and to hold office. But soon after Democrats won control of the governor's office in the election of 1876, they began disfranchising African Americans, who constituted the bulk of the Republican Party's political base. Poll taxes, literacy tests, multiple ballot boxes, restrictive registration, and other Jim Crow laws passed by Democrats excluded most African Americans and many lower-class whites from voting for almost a century (Gannon 1980, 30). Meanwhile, the GOP became "lily white," an image that would later hamper the party. The election of 1884 was the last in which African Americans attempted to participate in Florida politics. The 1885 Florida constitution allowed the governor to dilute the power of African American voters through his power to appoint county commissioners, who controlled local elections. By 1902 the Democratic-controlled state government had set up primary elections that were open to whites only, which virtually disfranchised Florida's African American citizens. In the 1930s a complete change occurred in the voting pattern of African Americans, when they abandoned Republicanism in favor of the Democratic New Deal, which promoted economic and social reform programs (Williamson 1976, 322).

Autonomous executive county committees led by influential county leaders were the life blood of the Democratic Party. However, rarely did party leaders exert influence beyond their own county (Williamson 1976, 36). Intraparty factionalism was traditional. Most important, neither Whigs nor Republicans nor Democrats were able to build strong permanent organizations to challenge "the courthouse gangs" in the counties.

## ORGANIZATIONAL DEVELOPMENT

Rapid population growth and patterns of migration had a profound influence on the nature of state party systems; in no state was this more true than Florida. In 1940 the state ranked twenty-seventh in population; in 1996 it ranked fourth, with more than 14 million people. In 1996 migrants constituted more than 80 percent of the total population. Even more important, the massive influx after World War II changed the character of the population. According to V. O. Key, Jr. (1949, 86), the transplanted population lacked political loyalties, traditional habits of action with respect to local personages, leaders, parties and issues. South and central Florida were inhabited by a large immigrant population from nonsouthern Republican areas. Initially, the immigrants in the immediate postwar period were white, affluent, and conservative Republicans, Northeasterners and Midwesterners, Protestants, professionals, and members of the managerial class (Huckshorn 1991, 64). Increased population expanded local markets and demands for skilled labor, which in turn lured waves of skilled laborers, technicians, New Deal Democrats, Catholics, Jews, and ethnic minorities from the North.

In the mid-1960s more conservative Republicans—wealthy, suburban retirees—moved to south and central Florida. Many of these immigrants were Republican by family tradition and preference. They had no interest in the Civil War, which the native politicians exploited to maintain their rule; nor could the race issue be used to unify them (Havard and Beth 1962, 4). Next came large numbers of Cubans fleeing Fidel Castro, who formed the nucleus of the Republican Party in Dade County, the largest county in the state. In fact, the immigrant population of the south and central Florida counties provided a sound base for an emerging Republican Party. The few immigrants who settled in rural north Florida were Democrats from adjacent southern states, who brought with them their traditional southern political attitudes. The population growth led to a state divided into a rural, agrarian north and an urban, industrial south.

In the first half of the twentieth century two-party competition had all but ceased (Bartley and Graham 1975, 81). The earliest evidence of growth and change emerged when Republican presidential candidates received substantial voter support during the late 1940s and 1950s as a result of the shifts in the demographic character of the electorate. One effect of GOP electoral success at the presidential level was the development of the party's organizational capabilities in elections. An invigorated Republican Party began competing with the Democratic Party in statewide, congressional, legislative, and local elections. GOP organizational strength contributed to the election of Republican governors in 1966 (the first since Reconstruction) and 1986 and to the election of U.S. senators in 1968, 1980, 1988, and 1994; the party also gained a majority in the Florida congressional delegation in 1990, 1992, and 1994. In 1994 the GOP also gained control of the state senate for the first time in a century and occupied one-half of the cabinet seats. The Republican Party was only four seats shy of taking control of the house of representatives after the 1994 elections. The state is now marked by vigorous two-party competition at all levels.

A final indicator of the electoral balance between the parties is the increased percentages of registered Republicans. In 1964, 70 percent of registered voters identified with the Democratic Party (Crew 1994, 58–60). By 1994, however, the Democrats and Republicans were virtually even, with 32 percent and 33 percent, respectively; independents had grown to be the largest single group (35 percent). Clearly, the Democrats have lost their dominant place in party identification. Between 1960 and 1992 GOP registration increased rapidly from 338,340 to 2,430,261, while Democratic registration increased from 1,656,023 to 3,318,565. GOP increases have come mostly within the white population.

Shifting demographic and electoral patterns led to a reapportionment of Republican Party organizational structures in the late 1960s (Havard 1972, 114–115). Until then, each state executive committee had been composed of two state committee members from each of the sixty-seven counties, regardless of party registration in the county (Klingman 1984, 159). Although the majority of registered Republicans lived in four urban counties, they were represented by only eight votes on the committee. Ten rural north Florida counties with only 103 registered Republicans controlled twenty votes. Overrepresentation of rural areas and underrepresentation of urban areas not only led to inequity in representation but also enabled the chairs and state executive committees to ignore the will of a majority of party members. In contrast to the Republican organizational overhaul, the Democratic Party merely partially reapportioned its congressional district committees.

In the early 1970s the Democrats were organizationally weak, reflecting decades of little competition from the Republicans. Democratic governor Reubin Askew (1971–1979) began to revitalize the Democratic Party organization. Under his direction a professional staff was developed to work on party organization, candidate recruitment, and party unity (Bass and DeVries 1976, 124–125). By tradition, Askew chose a personal friend, Jon Moyle, as chair of the state Democratic executive committee. Moyle led a statewide study of the delegate selection process and instituted a new plan for improving the process. He also established service centers to train a corps of workers in target counties in the use of modern technology to advance campaigning (Huckshorn 1976, 244–245). Moyle focused on party unity at the county level, resulting in more cohesion than ever before. Previously, little activity had taken place at the county level on a continuing basis.

The Republican Party organization began to change and modernize under William Murfin, who served as party chair from 1966 to 1970 (Klingman 1984, 164–167). His campaign for the post as a reform candidate revealed basic cleavages in the party. An old-guard faction was composed of the state executive committee leadership and county leaders. U.S. representative William Cramer (1955–1971), a major developer of the modern Florida GOP, led the reform group, which was composed mostly of urban public officeholders who desired more influence in the state party organization and greater participation by the Young Republicans. As chair, Murfin and his cohorts were able to prevent Gov. Claude Kirk (1967–1971) from taking control of the party organization. Intraparty factional feuding continues over control of the party organization, particularly over the chairmanship. The losers frequently are more conservative than sitting chairs and the members of the state executive committee.

The election of Claude Kirk in 1966 and U.S. senator Edward Gurney in 1968 invigorated the GOP organization. Even though all Republican gubernatorial candidates were defeated in the 1970s, the massive increase in the size of the GOP primary electorate in the decade was a compelling display of grassroots strength (Black and Black 1982, 130). Furthermore, a reapportionment of the state legislature ordered by the courts after Kirk took office provided the GOP enough seats in the legislature to sustain a vote. The court ordered a reapportionment that adhered to the principles of population equity and compactness rather than to county lines or territory. Now the GOP can be successful in local elections without a Republican presidential landslide.

## CURRENT PARTY ORGANIZATION

Two statewide studies of Democratic and Republican Party activists have revealed significant insights into party organizations (Hulbary et al. 1986, 1988, 1995; Bowman et al. 1990). The vitality of organizations was measured by how frequently party leaders (those who hold elected office within the party organization, such as the chair) communicated with each other and with party officials (those elected by party voters in the precincts). Democratic and Republican precinct committee members and county chairs reported higher levels of intraparty communication at the local level than communications with other levels of the party (Hulbary et al. 1986). Only about a third communicated frequently with state and district committee members. Both parties communicated less frequently with state party chairs and national party members; chairs rather than party members reported high levels of communication with public officials at all levels.

When county party activists were asked to assess the overall strength of their respective county organizations compared with five or ten years earlier, Republican county party activists were much more likely than their Democratic counterparts to view their party as much stronger overall and with respect to party activity, such as fund raising, campaign effectiveness, party recruitment, use of public opinion polls, and electronic data processing (Hulbary et al. 1986, 19). These findings suggest that Democrats are maintaining their organization statewide, whereas Republicans are confident of continuous party growth.

A new breed of dedicated grassroots party workers appeared on the political scene (Hulbary et al. 1995, 19–36). About half of the Democrats and Republicans surveyed by the research team indicated they were self-starters who ran for party positions "pretty much on their own." Others ran in response to some external urging, mainly from party committee members. What did they expect from such activity? The party workers designated "concern for public issues" as their most important consideration, followed by "a way to influence politics and government." The self-starters, motivated by concern for public issues and electing like-minded candidates, are hardly reflective of the patronage politics of the past.

Florida law permits Democratic and Republican Party committees to organize in each of the sixty-seven counties, in each congressional district, and statewide (Kelley 1993). Registered party members in each precinct choose in primary elections one committeeman and one committeewoman to serve on the party's county executive committee. In some counties there are numerous vacancies. If no one files for the positions, then the county executive committee may fill the vacancies from precinct lists, which include incumbents.

The statewide study of both parties' county precinct members and chairs in Florida revealed that the Democratic county organizations had a greater number of complete county organizations than the Republicans (Hulbary et al. 1988). Furthermore, 99 percent of Florida counties had a Democratic chair, whereas only 84 percent of the counties had a GOP chair. The turnover rate was fairly high among county chairs and committee members in both parties. Turnover was somewhat higher among Republican than Democratic county chairs. More than half of the party chairs were new, which suggests a lack of continuity. But organizational strength and continuity are increased by the tendency of party activists to have had long periods of political experience prior to becoming party chairs and committee members.

The county executive committees elect members to the state executive committees, which in turn elect members of the district committees and national party committees. At each level of party organization, the parties are permitted to operate a party headquarters, to advertise the general slate of party candidates, and to hold conventions. Funds for the Republican and Democratic state executive committees are provided partially by the filing fees that candidates are required to pay in order to qualify for public office (Dauer and St. Angelo 1980, 64). Fees also are used in part for soliciting private contributions to increase the party treasuries and operating expenses for the permanent party headquarters. Since political parties are not allowed to participate in party primaries, the state committee provides funds only to primary winners for use in the general election.

For a long time, the GOP state organization had portable headquarters, located in homes or businesses of state party chairs or in the hometown of state chairs (Huckshorn 1991, 66). In the 1990s the party hired a few full-time staff, usually an executive director, research director, and fundraiser. Both parties have since purchased headquarter buildings in Tallahassee, and their administrative and political staffs have been expanded. The Republicans have approximately twenty-five full-time, salaried staff members and a few part-time workers, and the Democrats have sixteen full-time and four part-time staff members. The Democrats maintain one field office; the GOP currently has two field personnel.

At the county level the two parties have year-round headquarters with full-time executive directors in a few highly urbanized counties. Most county organizations are part-time, voluntary operations without telephone listings or office space.

By 1990 the two parties had modernized and had transformed their state organizations into more effective service-vendor agencies for candidates. Both parties now concentrate on providing campaign seminars for candidates, publishing newsletters, and maintaining lists of county committee members. In addition, the state organizations are fully computerized and are able to produce automated letters, mailing lists, and fund-raising data.

The Democratic Party receives assistance from the Democratic National Committee (DNC), primarily for organization management. The DNC first began helping the Florida party by providing campaign training, resources, and services to congressional candidates. Later, DNC officials and political consultants started working with the state party to improve their technical, communications, voter registration, and fund-raising capabilities (Advisory Commission on Intergovernmental Relations 1987, 48).

The Florida GOP gets support from the Republican National Committee (RNC) in organization and electoral activities. Much of the modernization of state and county party organizations, through training to improve fund raising and candidate campaign capabilities, was undertaken under the aegis of RNC chair Ray Bliss in the late 1960s (Advisory Commission on Intergovernmental Relations 1987, 47). The RNC also increased its contributions and expenditures on behalf of congressional candidates. A staff of regional operatives helped with funds, technology development, and training in targeting, communications, and fund raising.

The relationship between the state and local levels in both party organizations centers on get-out-the-vote drives, mailing lists, and voter registration drives. The GOP provides more services, such as computer assistance and voting behavior data, to the counties than does the Democratic Party. The Republicans consistently have exceeded the Democrats in financial contributions to counties.

The study of party activists found a majority in both parties perceived factionalism as low or nonexistent; only about 25 percent reported that factionalism was high (Hulbary et al. 1986, 20). Nevertheless, partisan differences were apparent in the types of factionalism. Activists in both parties stressed "personal followings" as the major type of factionalism; Republicans stressed this type more than Democrats. The Democratic activists put more emphasis on the ideological nature of their party's factionalism. In sum, personalities as well as ideology continue to split both parties. Factions within the GOP that affect party decisions are more likely to be based on groups vying for control of the Republican Party, whereas the Democrats tend to divide along racial and urban-rural lines.

In the Sunshine State there is a strong link between Democratic governors (only two Republicans have served as governor since Reconstruction) and the chair of the state party organization. Extensive factionalism within the state organization makes it difficult for the governor to discern precise party positions on various policies. Second, governors are typically elected on the strength of their own candidate-centered organization, without party organization support; but they have traditionally appointed a personal follower to chair the state party organization. Gov. Lawton Chiles, however, was denied the appointment of his choice for party chair: Lt. Gov. Buddy MacKay. Instead, the Democratic Party organization held firm to its charter, which provided for a chair elected by the state executive committee. Frequently, though, the appointed chair serves as a personal arm of the governor and looks out for the governor's political interests. In 1995 Governor Chiles negotiated a law through the legislature that increased the voting power of the governor and other public officials from 2 to 42 percent of the total state Democratic executive committee vote. The party believed the change would bring about closer ties between the governor and the party.

State party chairs maintain regular liaison with legislators in their respective parties. Party contacts mainly involve soliciting support for substantive policy legislation, soliciting support for election law changes, and providing services such as research assistance to legislators (Huckshorn 1976, 151, 250–251).

Since the Florida legislature was dominated by the Democratic Party for decades, there was little contact between the state Republican Party and state legislators until the 1990s. Now the Republicans have 55 percent of the seats in the senate and 48 percent of the seats in the house. Considering the present party ratio, the relationship between the state GOP and the legislature likely will be closer.

Keen competition for control of the state legislature prompted the legislative party leaders to turn their attention to the election of their party members. The legislative leaders work to reelect incumbents of their own parties and target the opposition's most valuable incumbents for defeat. Democratic legislative candidates are helped through the Democratic President's Fund in the senate and the Speaker's Fund in the house. Republicans aid their members through a joint Senate-House Campaign Fund.

The cost of campaigns has skyrocketed, especially in large states such as Florida. Statewide campaigns have changed from speeches, rallies, and door-to-door canvassing to technocratic campaigns. Since Florida has eleven broadcast markets, candidates rely more on broadcast and cable television for advertising, which is the most expensive campaign technique.

Support for gubernatorial, statewide, and congressional races does not come primarily from Florida's weak state party organizations. Gubernatorial candidates plan and execute their own campaigns. Other statewide candidates also rely on their own consultants, polling and media experts, and fundraisers. The state party organizations seem to be more active in congressional and legislative contests.

Party assistance to candidates includes campaign contributions, campaign consultants, public opinion polling, voter mobilization programs, training workshops, fund-raising assistance, and maintenance of voter files. However, modern campaign technologies, political consultants, and PAC contributions have enabled the candidates to rely much less on state party organizations. PACs are one of the most influential forces in campaign finance. Thus the candidates are able to operate outside the influence of party organizations.

## RESOURCE GUIDE

The best places to begin studying political party organizations and development in Florida are the archives of the Democrats and Republicans, which are housed in buildings in Tallahassee owned by the parties. The Democratic archives date to 1988 and are accessible to the public; they are filed in boxes by year. The Republican archives date to 1970 and are accessible to the public by appointment. Both party archives contain executive committee minutes, correspondence, organizational structure information, budgets, and party rules. The Florida State Archives, however, has no records on political parties.

Useful insights into the nature of party organizations and their development may be gleaned from the public records of governors and others. Often public records contain newspaper clippings, office memoranda, and public correspondence. In contrast, private gubernatorial papers present more detailed pictures of the governors' administrative activities and relationships in Florida politics. The public records of Democratic governors William S. Jennings (1901–1905), Napoleon Bonaparte Broward (1905–1909), Albert Gilchrest (1909–1913), and Park Trammell (1913–1917) are available in the Robert Manning Strozier Library at Florida State University, Tallahassee. The private papers of Jennings, Broward, Millard Caldwell (U.S. representative, 1933–1941; governor, 1945–1949), Reubin Askew (governor, 1971–1979), and Fuller Warren (governor, 1949–1953) are in the P. K. Yonge Library of Florida History, University of Florida, Gainesville. The public papers of Spessard Holland (governor, 1941–1945; U.S. senator, 1946–1971) are in the Strozier Library. The papers of Governors LeRoy Collins (1955–1961) and Claude R. Kirk (1967–1971) and U.S. representative Sam Gibbons are in the University of South Florida library, Tampa.

The best overall collection of papers dealing with Florida politics is in the P. K. Yonge Library of Florida History, which in addition to the public and private papers mentioned above includes the papers of state legislative leaders such as Verle Pope (1949–1972) and Gene Hodges (1972–1984). Additionally, researchers might consult the papers of Manning J. Dauer, professor of political science, University of Florida, and Virgil Newton, political journalist and editor of the *Tampa Tribune*. In the Robert Strozier Library, the papers of political journalist Malcolm Johnson of the *Tallahassee Democrat* and political analyst Allen Morris may be examined.

*The Journal of the House of Representatives* and the *Journal of the Senate* are informative. Florida Statutes, 1943 to date, are necessary for understanding party organizations and development.

Newspaper coverage of state politics offers detailed information about party organizations and politics. The *Jacksonville Florida Times-Union* is the newspaper of record for the Democratic Party. The *Miami Herald, St. Petersburg Times,* and *Daytona Beach Evening*

*News* present the liberal positions, whereas the *Jacksonville Florida Times-Union, Orlando Sentinel, Tallahassee Democrat,* and *Tampa Tribune-Tampa Times* present conservative viewpoints. Finally, Allen Morris's *Florida Handbook,* published annually since 1947, is an outstanding compendium of Florida politics and government.

## REFERENCES

*Asterisks denote the most important publications on Florida party politics.*

*Advisory Commission on Intergovernmental Relations. 1987. *The transformation in American politics: Implications for federalism.* Rev. ed. Washington, D.C.: Advisory Commission on Intergovernmental Relations.

Bartley, Numan V., and H. D. Graham. 1975. *Southern politics and the second reconstruction.* Baltimore: Johns Hopkins University Press.

Bass, Jack, and Walter DeVries. 1976. *The transformation of southern politics: Social change and political consequences since 1945.* New York: Basic Books.

*Black, Merle, and Earl Black. 1982. The growth of contested Republican primaries in the American South, 1960–1980. In *Contemporary southern political attitudes and behavior,* ed. Laurence W. Moreland, Tod A. Baker, and Robert P. Steed. New York: Praeger.

Bowman, Lewis, William E. Hulbary, and Anne E. Kelley. 1990. Party sorting at the grassroots: Stable partisans and party changers among Florida's precinct officials. In *The disappearing South?* ed. Robert P. Steed, Laurence W. Moreland, and Tod A. Baker, 54–70. Tuscaloosa: University of Alabama Press.

Crew, Robert E., Jr. 1994. Political participation and policy management. In *The Florida public policy management system: Growth and reform,* ed. Richard Chackerian. Tallahassee: Florida Center for Public Management.

Dauer, Manning J., and Douglas St. Angelo. 1980. Political action: Elections, parties, and lobbies. In *Florida's politics and government,* ed. M. J. Dauer. Gainesville: University Presses of Florida.

Dodd, Dorothy. 1980. Political parties, campaigns. In *Florida handbook, 1979–80,* 17th ed., ed. Allen Morris. Tallahassee: Peninsular Publishing.

Gannon, Michael V. 1980. A history of Florida to 1900. In *Florida politics and government,* ed. Manning J. Dauer. Gainesville: University Presses of Florida.

*Havard, William C., ed. 1972. *The changing politics of the South.* Baton Rouge: Louisiana State University Press.

Havard, William C., and Loren P. Beth. 1962. *The politics of misrepresentation: The rural-urban conflict in the Florida legislature.* Baton Rouge: Louisiana State University Press.

Huckshorn, Robert J. 1976. *Party leadership in the states.* Amherst: University of Massachusetts Press.

Huckshorn, Robert J., ed. 1991. *Government and politics in Florida.* Gainesville: University Presses of Florida.

*Hulbary, William E., Anne E. Kelley, and Lewis Bowman. 1995. Florida: From freebooting to real parties. In *Southern state party organizations and activists,* ed. Charles D. Hadley and Lewis Bowman. Westport, Conn.: Praeger.

———. 1988. A political mid-elite in traditional party setting. Paper presented at the Fourteenth World Congress of the International Political Science Association, Washington, D.C.

———. 1986. *Political party precinct officials in Florida: A summary of findings.* Tampa: Department of Political Science, University of South Florida.

Kelley, Anne E. 1993. *Modern Florida government.* Rev. ed. Lanham, Md.: University Press of America.

Key, V. O., Jr. 1949. *Southern politics in state and nation.* New York: Alfred A. Knopf.

*Klingman, Peter D. 1984. *Neither dies nor surrenders: A history of the Republican Party in Florida, 1867–1970.* Gainesville: University Presses of Florida.

Lamis, Alexander P. 1984. *The two party South.* New York: Oxford University Press.

Morris, Allen. *The Florida handbook, 1947–1995.* Tallahassee: Peninsular Publishing.

Tebeau, Charlton W. 1973. *A history of Florida.* Coral Gables: University of Miami Press.

Williamson, Edward C. 1976. *Florida politics in the Gilded Age, 1877–1893.* Gainesville: University Presses of Florida.

# Georgia

JOHN A. CLARK

## PARTY HISTORY

Much has been written about southern politics since V. O. Key's (1949) seminal work, but party organizations at the state and local levels in the South have been largely ignored. A partial explanation stems from the longtime absence of a traditional organizational presence in many southern states (Mayhew 1986). Cotter and his colleagues (1984, 49–51) found that local parties in the South were, on average, weaker than those in the rest of the country as of the late 1970s. State Republican Party organizations in the South have fared somewhat better than the national average, due to a successful top-down strategy for party building in the region, but state Democratic Party organizations have lagged behind.

Georgia's political parties are excellent examples of the development of southern party organizations in recent years. Local Democratic Party organizations in Georgia ranked forty-sixth of the fifty states in the late 1970s, whereas local Republicans received the lowest ranking for either party in any state (Cotter et al. 1984, 53).[1] Both state parties, in contrast, were rated "moderately strong." The state Republican Party organization was singled out as one of the fastest growing since World War II (Cotter et al. 1984, 28–29, 90). Since then, the Republican organizational presence has trickled down to the local level in most Georgia counties (Lockerbie and Clark 1995). Electoral factors have contributed to the Republicans' dramatic change, but a focus on elections obscures much of the story. As Republican electoral success promoted organizational development, so too the organizational infrastructure contributed to further Republican victories.

*Electoral Context.* Democrats exercised unchallenged control over the political process in Georgia from the end of Reconstruction until the 1960s (Key 1949; Lamis 1990). The Democratic Party's dominance of the South arose in response to the Civil War and the Republican-led Reconstruction that followed. Opposition to punitive Reconstruction measures united white southerners of all social classes under the Democratic banner. Later, the realigning elections of the 1890s reinforced Democratic loyalties. Northern Republicans did not need the South's votes in presidential elections or in Congress, which left conservatives and progressives to fight for control of the Democratic Party and southern politics (Key 1949, 6–9; Grantham 1988). Georgia Republicans did not even nominate a candidate for governor between 1876 and 1962.

The electoral context within which Georgia's parties operate is undergoing dramatic change in the mid-1990s. There were no Republicans in the state's congressional delegation as recently as 1977-1978 and only one immediately prior to the 1992 elections (Lockerbie and Clark 1995). Shortly after the 1994 elections, in contrast, Republicans controlled eight of eleven seats in the U.S. House of Representatives and a majority of statewide elected offices. In a state that has not elected a Republican governor since Reconstruction, the rise of the GOP might be the political story of the century.

Two factors are especially important for understanding the change in party competition in Georgia. First, the decline of the Solid South as the conservative base of the Democratic Party created a window of opportunity for Republican development. Cracks in the Democratic coalition appeared shortly after Franklin D. Roosevelt combined the forces of liberal northern and conservative southern voters into the New Deal coalition. Since then, many conservative white southerners have shifted their allegiances from the Democratic Party of their ancestors to what once was the party of Lincoln (Petrocik 1987; Carmines and Stimson 1989).

The second factor that altered the partisan context in Georgia was the series of civil rights changes affecting the state's political balance. Rural hegemony over the Democratic Party was weakened when the U.S. Supreme Court ruled unconstitutional the county unit system used for Democratic Party nominations.[2] The debate over the Civil Rights Act of 1964 led Georgia voters to support Barry Goldwater in that year's presidential election, the first time a Republican had received the state's electoral college votes. The Voting Rights Act of 1965 may have been the single most important piece of civil rights legislation for party development. Its immediate backlash helped independent candidate George Wallace win the state in the 1968 presidential election and weakened the ties of many white voters to the Democratic Party. The creation of racially gerrymandered districts allowed conservative white Republicans to control eight U.S. House districts in 1995, leaving the remaining three to African American Democrats.[3]

## ORGANIZATIONAL DEVELOPMENT

Georgia was a one-party Democratic state in the first half of the century, but it was virtually a "no-party" state in terms of party organization. The Democratic dominance of elections led to a lack of organizational development in both parties until recently. Democrats operated in a system where the individual candidate came before the organization. Republicans faced a different problem in that there were simply no Republican candidates and few GOP voters to organize (Key 1949).

The presidency of Dwight Eisenhower (1953–1961) provided Georgia's Republicans with a reason to organize. Despite tepid support for Ike at the polls in both 1952 and 1956, the state party was needed to dispense the federal patronage available from a Republican administration. Attempts to foster a grassroots organization were hardly successful, and the loss of the presidency in 1960 and the death of the party's first gubernatorial candidate in 1962 were severe blows. Despite the success of Goldwater's candidacy in 1964, the state Republican Party organization remained little more than an empty shell (*Atlanta Journal* 1965). Each time the party seemed on the brink of establishing its credibility, it suffered one or more serious electoral setbacks. The Goldwater victory was followed by the unusual defeat of gubernatorial candidate Howard "Bo" Callaway two years later.[4] Five Democratic elected officials switched to the Republican Party in 1968, but none of them won subsequent election to any office. Republican president Richard Nixon won 75 percent of the Georgia vote in his bid for reelection in 1972, but the combination of Watergate and native son Jimmy Carter's 1976 election negated those gains. A newspaper report in 1977 suggested that "a lot of smart money is betting on the Georgia GOP going the way of the dinosaur" (Allen 1977, 17A).

Instead, the party continued to emphasize organizational development.[5] The party had adopted a statewide primary to nominate candidates in 1968, allowing Republican candidates to place their names on the general election ballot without gathering signatures to petition the secretary of state. A new small-donor campaign using direct mail yielded thirty-five hundred contributors in 1969. With the support of the Republican National Committee, the party expanded its efforts to train and recruit candidates, raise funds, and improve campaign technology. By the mid-1980s, the GOP had a budget of a half-million dollars and eight full-time employees. In contrast, state Democrats were saddled with a $150,000 budget, three employees, and a series of budget deficits (Bernstein 1985).

As the Republican Party established a toehold in Georgia politics, the Democrats recognized the need to create their own organizational presence. Permanent state party headquarters were set up with a full-time executive director in late 1963, partially in response to Goldwater's potential Republican presidential candidacy (*Savannah Morning News* 1963). Until the mid-1960s, most local party organizations functioned as boards of elections for Democratic primaries rather than as political organizations. "Outside of local personality cults and a few local Democratic executive committees, there has been no state-recognized organizational effort," a party official admitted in 1965 (*Savannah Morning News* 1965; see also Mayhew 1986, 115–117).

Democratic efforts to create active party organizations at the state and local level were stymied repeatedly by the electoral success of Democratic candidates. Although some advances were made under the leadership of state chair Marge Thurman (1974–1982), it took the election of Republican Mack Mattingly to the U.S. Senate in 1980 to shock the Democratic Party into action. Plans were developed to increase the party's budget, staff, and candidate support activities (McDonald and Hopkins 1983). Instead, the party had difficulty retiring its debt from the 1982 state elections, and the ambitious plans were scaled back dramatically. Substantial progress has been made since then, but the Democrats continue to lag behind the GOP in most areas of state party organization.

*Party Leadership and Factionalism.* The state Democratic Party traditionally has served the wishes of the governor, the titular head of the party. In the formerly one-party South, winning the Democratic nomination was a guarantee of general election success. Once the primary election was completed, the gubernatorial nominee assumed the mantle of party leadership. The nominee named the state chair and selected the delegates to the state convention (Kelley 1962). Until the process was challenged at the 1968 Democratic National Convention, the governor even hand-picked the state's national convention delegates.[6] The governor was limited to one four-year term from 1942 until the 1970s, when a second term was allowed. Consequently, the state party organization was perhaps more useful for patronage than for reelection politics. Though weakened in recent years, the governor continues to dominate the activities of the state party.

The Democratic Party has not been immune to factional divisions, but the governor's influence has kept most fights outside the state party organization. The splits have generally followed ideological and racial lines. Loyalty to more liberal Democratic presidential nominees has been a problem since at least 1964; in 1988, nearly a quarter of local Democratic Party officials voted for Republican George Bush (Lockerbie and Clark 1995, 140).

Lacking the stability and leadership of an elected governor, Georgia's Republicans frequently display factional rifts in their state party organization. In 1952 separate delegate slates were sent to the party's national convention. The Eisenhower slate was seated and took over the state organization, but a similar factional dispute involving some of the same leaders erupted in 1964. The Goldwater insurgents took control of the party in that year, and the infighting also split the Georgia Federation of Republican Women. The factions were based both on geography and ideology, pitting wealthy Atlanta moderates against conservatives from the rest of the state. For two years the state GOP operated dual head-quarters in Atlanta and Savannah, home of state chair and Goldwater supporter Joseph Tribble.

The emergence of Bo Callaway as a Republican leader quelled some of the bitterness within the party. As a member of Congress, gubernatorial candidate, and national commit-tee member, Callaway provided leadership and financial support for the struggling party organization in the 1960s and early 1970s. Mack Mattingly attained similar status as state chair and later as U.S. senator (1981–1987). Mattingly helped orchestrate the removal of a Reagan supporter as state chair in 1981 in favor of an individual with ties to elected officials within the state.

Factional infighting erupted again in 1988 at the Republican state convention. Supporters of television evangelist Pat Robertson disrupted the convention proceedings when some delegates from their ranks were not seated. When party regulars walked out, the Robertson supporters held a rump convention, electing their own slate of national convention dele-gates and national committee members. The dispute was not resolved until members of the national Bush and Robertson campaign organizations negotiated a settlement prior to the national convention (Abramowitz and Davis 1991). Surprisingly, evidence of this split was not apparent at subsequent party conventions. One state party official estimated that only 15 to 20 percent of the delegates to the state convention in 1995 were active supporters of the Christian Coalition, the national organization that emerged from the Robertson campaign.

## CURRENT PARTY ORGANIZATION

Strategies of party development reflect the different organizational philosophies held by the Republican and Democratic Parties in Georgia. The Republicans offer top-down lead-ership from the state party in their effort to build grassroots organizations. The Democrats, in contrast, maintain the division of authority between levels of the party. The differences between the parties grow out of differences in party culture (Freeman 1986; Klinkner 1994) and past electoral success.

In the off-year of 1995, the Georgia Republican Party employed a full-time staff of six, down from eight during the 1994 elections. The state chair established a goal of raising $3 million for the party in 1995, of which $1 million was raised prior to the state convention in June. The GOP fund-raising strategy relies equally on regular contributions (direct mail and telephone solicitation) and special events (fund-raising dinners, for example).

The Republican Party is currently organized in 140 of Georgia's 159 counties. In 1991 the state party created its "Four Star" program to encourage local party development. County organizations are awarded points for various organizational activities, with the top finish-ers receiving cash awards. Nearly all of the county organizations participated in the pro-gram in 1994. The state party also sponsors workshops and meetings for county chairs on a regular basis.

One of the obstacles to Republican development has been a lack of candidates for lower-level offices. The party organization continues to be very active in recruiting candidates. County chairs are encouraged to identify possible candidates, and recruitment is frequent-ly one of the topics at county chair meetings and other workshops. The state party works closely with Republicans in the state legislature to encourage people to run for office. The party supports candidates through training workshops, voter information, and campaign contributions when resources permit. For local candidates, monetary contributions are generally small and distributed in accordance with certain requirements regarding campaign organization.

The state chairs of both parties are selected by the respective state conventions. The Republican state convention meets in odd-numbered years, and chairs serve two-year terms. The state executive committee is responsible for filling vacancies in state offices. Republicans have not elected a governor since Reconstruction, and the conventions are held in off-years. Thus, the battle for control of the state party often plays itself out at the state convention.

For Democrats, the state convention meets in gubernatorial election years, so the chair serves a four-year term. When vacancies arise, the governor nominates a new chair subject to the approval of the state executive committee. These arrangements give the governor (or gubernatorial nominee) considerable influence over the selection process.

In the past, the state Democratic Party did the bidding of the governor. But the selection of the current executive director marked an important shift in the direction of the party leadership. Although the executive director was chosen by the governor, the decision was made in coordination with several other leading elected officials. In the face of Republican advances, these leaders saw a need to build the party for future challenges *before* they lost power. The executive director has been given considerable flexibility to raise the profile of the party and to increase its assistance to candidates.

The state Democratic Party has ongoing relations with local parties, but any intervention is likely at the initiative of the county chairs. There is frequent correspondence between levels of the party. The state party provides assistance when asked, and the state committee's attorney is available for legal advice on such matters as financial disclosure. The state party does not provide training workshops for chairs at the present time, but neither does it order their compliance with initiatives from the top.

Like many party organizations, the Georgia Democrats are continually recruiting candidates. The state party offers support to candidates only after they have paid qualifying fees to the secretary of state, thus proving the sincerity of their intent. The party focuses its efforts on candidates for the state legislature and higher offices rather than local races. The party never endorses candidates in Democratic primaries, a policy that dates back to the days when capturing the nomination was tantamount to winning the election.

## RESOURCE GUIDE

The state Democratic and Republican Parties both archive many of their official records. Unfortunately, neither party is especially willing to make them available to researchers at the present time, but party officials concede that access might be possible in certain circumstances. Many political and campaign materials are thought to be stored in the basements and attics of individual party leaders and political officials.

The Georgia Democrats keep voting returns and other recent documents relating to opposition research, finance, and delegate selection procedures at the state headquarters in Atlanta. Records going back to the 1960s are kept in a separate storage facility. A finding aid indicates that financial records dating to 1966 are stored there. The information has not been archived systematically; rather, boxes of files are periodically sent to storage when space becomes limited at the party offices. As a result, the numerous boxes of phone bank cards and voter lists are probably of limited utility to scholars.

**Table 1**  Georgia Resource Guide

|                              | Democrats                    | Republicans                       |
| ---------------------------- | ---------------------------- | --------------------------------- |
| Archive                      | Yes                          | Yes                               |
| Location                     | State Party Headquarters     | State Party Headquarters          |
|                              | 1100 Spring St., Suite 710   | 5600 Roswell Rd., Suite 200 East  |
|                              | Atlanta, Ga. 30309           | Atlanta, Ga. 30342                |
|                              | (404) 874-1996               | (404) 257-5559                    |
| Dates                        | 1960s–present                | 1965–present                      |
| Finding aid                  | Yes                          | Yes                               |
| Access                       | Permission required          | Permission required               |
| Contents:                    |                              |                                   |
|   Executive committee minutes | Yes               | Yes                               |
|   Correspondence   | Yes                          | Yes                               |
|   Organizational structure | Yes                 | Yes                               |
|   Budgets          | Yes                          | Probably                          |
|   Rules            | Yes                          | Yes                               |

The records of the Georgia Republican Party are cataloged by a private firm. The holdings date to 1965. Most of the official party records, including rules, correspondence, and the minutes of executive committee meetings, have been preserved. Budgetary information is probably included, too, according to a party official.

In addition to the parties themselves, special collections throughout the state contain some records. The Richard B. Russell Library at the University of Georgia stores the papers of many former elected officials and party officers. Among the library's Democratic holdings are the state executive committee papers from 1940–1954, information on the Democratic Charter Convention in the 1970s, and the private papers of several Democratic Party leaders. The papers of many individual members of Congress are archived there as well.

The Russell Library's Howard H. Callaway Collection includes information on the 1966 gubernatorial campaign and Callaway's service as a Republican National Committee member. Other Republican Party records are found in the papers of U.S. Senator Mack Mattingly (1981–1987) and gubernatorial candidate Rodney Cook (1978). Unfortunately, records specific to Mattingly and Cook's service as state GOP chairs in the 1970s are not available. All of the Russell Library's holdings are fully cataloged and easily accessible.

The Georgia Government Documentation Project at Georgia State University is another important resource for students of state parties and Georgia politics. An oral history collection includes more than 250 interviews with political leaders and party officials dating to the mid-1960s. Researchers are assisted by abstracts of each interview and an inventory of the entire collection. The archival collection is fully cataloged and includes the papers of Paul Coverdell from 1968 to 1989, the central period of Republican Party growth in Georgia. Coverdell, now a Republican U.S. senator, served as a state senator from 1971 to 1989 and was Republican state chair from 1985 to 1987. Other prominent holdings relate to the 1966 gubernatorial campaign of write-in candidate Ellis Arnall and legislative reapportionment in the 1980s and 1990s.

NOTES

1. As an indication of their weakness, only three-fifths of the 159 counties appear to have had a Republican chair at that time (Cotter et al. 1984, 180).

2. *Gray v. Sanders* (1963). The old system favored small, rural counties by underrepresenting more heavily populated (and generally more liberal) areas.
3. The redistricting plan developed following the 1990 census, which created three majority African American districts, was struck down by the U.S. Supreme Court on June 29, 1995 (*Miller v. Johnson*).
4. Callaway, a Republican member of Congress, received a plurality of votes in the general election, but state law required a majority to win. The Democratic state legislature awarded the governorship to the Democratic candidate, Lester Maddox (Bass and DeVries 1976, 141–144).
5. On the organizational efforts of out-parties at the national level, see Klinkner (1994) and Herrnson and Menefee-Libey (1990).
6. The slate of delegates selected by Gov. Lester Maddox in 1968 was challenged by a more integrated slate of delegates led by Julian Bond, an African American state representative. The national convention compromised by seating half of each delegation. The reforms developed by the McGovern-Fraser Commission altered the delegate selection process for subsequent elections.

## REFERENCES

*Asterisks denote the most important publications on Georgia party politics.*

*Abramowitz, Alan I., and Wendy Davis. 1991. Georgia: Ripe for the picking—presidential politics in the Peach State. In *The 1988 presidential election in the South,* ed. Laurence W. Moreland, Robert P. Steed, and Tod A. Baker. New York: Praeger.

Allen, Frederick. 1977. GOP: Going the way of the dinosaur? *Atlanta Constitution,* November 14.

*Atlanta Journal.* 1965. Building the parties. May 24.

Bass, Jack, and Walter DeVries. 1976. *The transformation of southern politics.* New York: Basic Books.

*Bernstein, Paul. 1985. The Georgia GOP comes on strong. *Atlanta Constitution,* July 23.

Carmines, Edward G., and James A. Stimson. 1989. *Issue evolution: Race and the transformation of American politics.* Princeton, N.J.: Princeton University Press.

Cotter, Cornelius P., James L. Gibson, John F. Bibby, and Robert J. Huckshorn. 1984. *Party organizations in American politics.* New York: Praeger.

*Fleischmann, Arnold, and Carol Pierannunzi. 1997. *Politics in Georgia.* Athens: University of Georgia Press, forthcoming.

Freeman, Jo. 1986. The political culture of the Democratic and Republican Parties. *Political Science Quarterly* 101:327–356.

Galloway, Jim. 1984. GOP vying to crack Democrats' control of Georgia politics. *Atlanta Constitution,* October 14.

Grantham, Dewey W. 1988. *The life and death of the Solid South: A political history.* Lexington: University Press of Kentucky.

Herrnson, Paul S., and David Menefee-Libey. 1990. The dynamics of party organizational development. *Midsouth Political Science Journal* 11:3–30.

Kelley, Wayne. 1962. Democrats once again prove full power over state party belongs to governor. *Augusta Chronicle,* October 18.

*Key, V. O., Jr. 1949. *Southern politics in state and nation.* New York: Alfred A. Knopf.

Klinkner, Philip A. 1994. *The losing parties: Out-party national committees 1956–1993.* New Haven, Conn.: Yale University Press.

*Lamis, Alexander P. 1990. *The two-party South.* 2d expanded ed. New York: Oxford University Press.

*Lockerbie, Brad, and John A. Clark. 1995. Georgia: Two-party political reality? In *Southern state party organizations and activists,* ed. Charles D. Hadley and Lewis Bowman. Westport, Conn.: Praeger.

Mayhew, David R. 1986. *Placing parties in American politics.* Princeton: Princeton University Press.

McDonald, Greg, and Sam Hopkins. 1983. Ga. demos aim for clout in choosing ticket. *Atlanta Constitution,* February 3.

Petrocik, John R. 1987. Realignment: New party coalitions and the nationalization of the South. *Journal of Politics* 49:347–375.

*Savannah Morning News.* 1965. Loyal demo groups sought. May 24.

*Savannah Morning News.* 1963. Democrats deny weakness. November 13.

Honolulu

# Hawaii

ANNE FEDER LEE

## PARTY HISTORY

Hawaii's Republican and Democratic Parties were formed shortly after Hawaii became a U.S. territory in June 1900.[1] Neither party, however, was very successful in the elections held that year. [2] A third party, the Home Rule Party, had also emerged and, appealing to native Hawaiians (who made up a majority of voters), won both a considerable majority in the territorial legislature as well as the office of delegate to Congress. [3]

The Republicans, determined to capture the native Hawaiian vote in the 1902 elections, put forth Prince Kuhio (a very popular member of the Hawaiian royal family) as a candidate for congressional delegate. This strategy, plus the electorate's dismay with a chaotic legislative session under the Home Rule majority, resulted in Kuhio's election and the election of a significant Republican majority in the territorial legislature. The Republicans' success in 1902 began a period of one-party rule lasting until just after statehood was achieved in 1959.

During most of the territorial era, Hawaii's economy was dominated by five major and interconnected corporations (referred to as the Big Five). This oligopoly, controlling the sugar industry, holding major interests in the pineapple business, and dominating transportation between the islands and the mainland, influenced almost all aspects of the islands' economy. Their support of and association with the Republican Party is quite clearly linked with Republican domination of the political scene during the territorial era.

Republicans enjoyed an active organizational structure and considerable financial support, and by the late 1940s the party claimed some twenty thousand enrolled members. Even though the Democrats maintained an organizational apparatus, they were severely hampered by factionalism and a poor financial base, and the party probably had no more than five thousand members (Tuttle 1966, 121).

World War II, however, challenged the way of life in the islands and brought significant economic, social, and political changes. New ideas and new people had an impact on the population mix as well as on attitudes. Not only did the military presence alter the economy, but mainland businesses came too, changing the business climate. Increased spending and tourism ended sugar's preeminent position in the islands' economy, and as the economy boomed, new employment opportunities appeared. A new non-Caucasian middle class, no longer satisfied with the structured society, emerged, and resentment against the plantation society, with its second-class treatment of workers (imported primarily from Japan, China, Portugal, Korea, the Philippines, and Puerto Rico) grew. Although questions arose as to the loyalty of Hawaii's Japanese population, the support of the war effort by the local Americans of Japanese ancestry and the courage of those who fought in the war dispelled notions of disloyalty. The war was a painful experience for Americans of Japanese ancestry, but it brought them new confidence, and they recognized that they could fully participate in all aspects of the society. There was at the same time a change in the perception of what a party could do, and political participation became more meaningful. Young war veterans, of various ethnic groups but primarily Americans of Japanese ancestry, returned to the islands determined to build an egalitarian, democratic society through involvement in politics. They turned to the Democratic Party and were not only welcomed but also cultivated by those who had long struggled to keep the party afloat.

Labor unions were also becoming more effective in representing the interests of sugar, pineapple, and dock workers and eventually became a formidable power. Just as the Big Five and the Republicans were politically intertwined, the labor unions, especially the International Longshoremen and Warehouse Union (ILWU), provided the power base for the Democratic Party. Even though labor union power in the state has declined since the 1970s, union support, both financially and in providing political workers, is still a key factor in Democratic Party activities.

The first signs of a reversal in GOP fortunes appeared in the elections of the mid-to late 1940s, and in 1954 Democrats won a majority of seats in both chambers of the territorial legislature for the first time. The three elections after 1954 were characterized by a high degree of party competition, but all competition disappeared in 1962, when the Democrats captured by significant margins the positions of governor and lieutenant governor, the two U.S. Senate seats, the one seat in the House of Representatives, and an increased majority in the state legislature, as well as the chief executive positions in all four counties.

Since 1962 Democrats have retained control over the state's congressional delegation and its legislative and executive branches. The same is true, although perhaps slightly less so, at the local level.[4] Thus Hawaii's political system has always been characterized by one-party dominance, first by the Republicans, then by the Democrats.[5]

The issue of statehood had not divided the parties in Hawaii since both supported it (although some individuals in each party were opposed). Once statehood was achieved, in 1959, both parties received credit for bringing it about. Both parties had had representation in the national party organizations prior to statehood, but because the territorial delegate to Congress had no vote, Hawaii's parties lacked standing. However, with statehood and with voting members of the U.S. House and Senate, their status was enhanced within the national party organizations.

Although a number of Republican leaders were important in that party's formation and long period of domination, the political figures who have become legends in Hawaii are Democrats.[6] Johnny Wilson, who founded the Democratic Party and who struggled to keep it alive, served as the mayor of Honolulu for fourteen years between 1920 and 1934 (Krauss and Wilson 1994). John Burns is singled out as the person most responsible for the revitalization of the Democratic Party after World War II. Elected governor three times (1962, 1966, 1970), Burns died during his third term in office (Fuchs 1961; Coffman 1973; Phillips 1982; Bell 1984). Wilson and Burns are legends not only because they were instrumental in bringing life to a party that has dominated politics in the state since the early 1960s but also because they consistently worked for racial and ethnic equality, not only within the party but in the islands as well.

## ORGANIZATIONAL DEVELOPMENT

The organizational development of the Republican and Democratic Parties in Hawaii since 1962 is related to their respective positions as minority and majority party.

*Candidate Recruitment.* Because of the Democratic Party's dominant position, there has been no shortage of candidates who self-select to run on the Democratic ticket, and this may explain why the party has not carried out formal programs of candidate recruitment.

In contrast to the Democrats, the Republicans have had considerable difficulty in getting candidates to run. To address the problem, the party in the 1970s instituted a policy (called "targeting") of recruiting candidates for and focusing financial support on those electoral districts where the Democratic Party was seen as vulnerable. It is not clear whether the policy contributed to the election of more Republicans than might otherwise have won. However, it is clear that the policy created bitterness within the party itself because those GOP candidates who were not getting party support felt it unfair that the party was helping some rather than all candidates. In 1991 the party chair announced a departure from the targeting policy; instead, the party began a strategy of fielding candidates in all legislative districts (Kresnak 1991). Even so, in 1992 and 1994 a significant number of Democrats, as in previous elections, ran unopposed.

*Ethnicity and Gender Equity.* One of the most important factors in party organization has been ethnicity (Boylan 1992).[7] As the Democrats moved toward political domination, they became associated with racial groups outside the old 'haole' (Caucasian) network, and much of the party's early success can be credited to its image as the party of those who did not belong to the power elite. In the early 1960s, recognizing the importance of making certain that the party organization reflected the state's diverse population, an effort was made to put forth ethnically balanced tickets. Due largely to its status as the majority party, the party has had little difficulty in attracting candidates from diverse ethnic groups.

Although it has no formal program now for the promotion of ethnically varied candidates in its organization, the Democratic Party does have an affirmative action strategy for women. In 1980 the party changed its rules to require that delegates to its biennial state convention be equally divided between men and women, and in 1990 the rules were changed again to require gender numerical equality for those elected to the state central committee. The Republicans have not adopted any gender-equality policy; however, like the Democrats, they have a nondiscrimination provision in their rules covering gender, race, and ethnicity.

*Factionalism.* Both parties have experienced a certain degree of factionalism. Factionalism within the Democratic Party has existed since the earliest days; it has been noisy and has caused serious divisions. During the latter part of the 1960s a deep factional division pitted a progressive wing (led by Tom Gill) against the old guard (led by John Burns). Their fight reached a high point in 1970 when Gill challenged incumbent governor Burns in the Democratic gubernatorial primary. Gill, whose faction supported progressive change in such areas as environmental protection, consumer protection, and development, lost to Burns.

The factional struggles within the Democratic Party continued into the early 1970s, with fights over internal rules and much rancor surrounding the selection of delegates to the 1972 national convention. Overall, the Burns faction retained power. Its success left many from the Gill faction distrustful of party politics, and some retreated from party activism as a result.

Since the mid-1980s the strength of the Burns faction has diminished, due primarily to the aging of its original members. Whereas the Democratic governor who followed Burns (George Ariyoshi, 1974–1986) was his descendant, the next two Democratic governors (John Waihee, 1986–1994, and Ben Cayetano, elected in 1994) cannot be so neatly pegged. The progressive wing, loosely associated with Jesse Jackson's Rainbow Coalition, has recently gained in strength. At the 1994 party convention, Richard Port, who belongs to this wing, won the position of party chair in a contested election but was reelected, unopposed, in 1996. The strength of the progressive wing is further illustrated by the 1996 convention's choice, in a contested election, of a Democratic national committeewoman who clearly fits into this faction and by the control that the progressives now hold over the party central committee.

The Republican Party experienced an equally bitter factional division in the late 1960s to the early 1970s, and internal conflict resurfaced in the 1980s. The early factions arose over the party's image as the party of the establishment and the plantation society of the pre–World War II era. The contest between Sam King and Hebden Porteus in the Republican gubernatorial primary of 1970 brought the split to the fore and created resentment that ran through the party well into the 1980s. Those who supported King (who won the 1970 primary but lost the general election) felt that getting individuals elected should be the most important priority of the party organization, whereas those who supported Porteus felt that ethnic diversity and getting more "locals" elected and in leadership positions was of primary importance. Although the King and Porteus factions also differed in political philosophy (with the King faction more "liberal" and the Porteus faction more "conservative"), and although the King followers thought Porteus too willing to compromise with the Democrats, the split over image was of real significance. Its importance can be understood by recognizing the party's long association with the establishment oligopoly and the plantation mentality and the rejection of that past by a large majority of Hawaiian voters after World War II. In spite of the party's claims that it is not exclusive and that it has a strong record of running candidates of varied ethnicity, the Republican Party is still today unable to overcome its long-standing negative image.

The more recent factionalism became particularly evident after the party began holding a straw poll on presidential candidates at precinct meetings in presidential election years. The intent was to steal some of the national limelight from other states; since the meetings were always held in January, Hawaii would beat even New Hampshire in announcing preferences. When the change was implemented in 1988, however, supporters of Pat Robertson came to precinct meetings in full force and at the following state convention had some success in gaining leadership positions. From the point of view of traditional Republicans, the success of Robertson's supporters was a disaster; it ended up causing disarray in the ranks and resulted in some departures from the party. For example, three incumbent GOP state legislators ran and won reelection as Democrats in that year. The traditional wing of the party was able to do away with the straw poll after 1988, and the Christian Coalition faction has since had limited success in gaining party leadership positions or elective office. The current party leadership represents the traditional wing of the party, which, compared with Republicans on the mainland, would probably be considered liberal.

*Campaigning and Party Finance.* In 1970 the parties began to introduce new campaign techniques, particularly the innovative use of television. Although the parties had begun to rely on television for campaigning in the early 1960s, the Democrats' use in 1970 of a half-hour film, suggested to them by outside consultants, revolutionized the party's use of the media. Called "To Catch a Wave," it "pulled out all the emotional stops in presenting [Governor John] Burns as the warm, open-hearted, father of modern Hawaii" (Phillips 1982, 116; see also Coffman 1973, 157–164). An estimated 80 percent of voters saw the film, and it not only helped Burns win the gubernatorial primary, but it set a precedent that both parties have followed since. The Democrats have continued to be highly successful in producing effective campaign films. Although the Republicans have attempted to follow suit, they have been less successful.

In spite of heavy reliance on the media, both parties in Hawaii continue to depend on grassroots activities. Breakfasts, stew and rice dinners, rallies, door-to-door campaigning, and sign wavers standing at busy intersections are all still important elements of party activities throughout the state.[8]

Since 1960 financial security has been a perennial problem for both parties, and fund raising has required constant attention. Republicans have relied fairly heavily on bringing well-known politicians from the mainland for fund-raising events. The Democrats, in contrast, seem to have relied more on donations by the governor and U.S. senators (from their campaign funds) as well as from a few other individuals.

For some years the Republican Party assessed a $10 membership fee. However, in late 1994 the state committee voted to eliminate dues altogether. Prior to 1994 the Democratic Party did not have a fee, but in that year it adopted an optional fee of $15 in the hope of achieving an ongoing, stable financial base. In 1994 the Democratic Party chair, Richard Port, initiated what seems to have been the first general membership fund drive, described by party activists as quite successful. Nonetheless, fund raising and party finances continue to be a pressing issue for both organizations.

Both parties continually attempt to increase their membership. In 1994 the figures were reported to be 16,800 for the Republicans and 26,800 for the Democrats (*Honolulu Star-Bulletin* 1994). The Democratic Party's much larger membership is probably due more to its recent history and status as majority party than to any formal organizational strategy.

## CURRENT PARTY ORGANIZATION

Hawaii's statutes define a political party as "an association of voters united for the purpose of promoting a common political end or carrying out a particular line of political policy" and require that a political party maintain a general organization throughout the state, including a regularly constituted central committee and a committee in all four counties. All parties must file their rules as well as the names of the officers of their central committee with the chief election officer, and they must also submit the names of their county officers to the respective county clerks.[9]

Both the Democratic and Republican Parties in Hawaii have complex bylaws detailing a wide range of organizational matters such as eligibility for membership, revocation of membership, levels of organization, election of officers, holding of conventions, and formulas for determining delegate representation at conventions. Although both parties are structured along precinct, district, county, and state levels, there are differences between them in the organizational detail. For example, Democratic Party district councils are based on the fifty-one state house districts, whereas the Republican district committees are based on the twenty-five state senate districts.

*Democratic Party.* The Democratic Party in Hawaii holds precinct, district, county, and state level organizational meetings biennially in even-numbered years. The party holds its state convention in May, over the Memorial Day weekend. The number of delegates elected by each precinct to the state convention is determined by a complex formula, but the minimum representation from each precinct is two, and the delegation elected by each precinct must be composed of equal numbers of men and women. Democratic Party rules do not specify a location for the convention. There have always been those who favor holding the convention on different islands, but since 1960 all except one have been held on the most populated island, Oahu.

The Democratic Party state central committee is made up of members elected at the convention. Five members are elected by the entire convention body: the state chair, the national committeeman and committeewoman, and one male and one female youth representative. Other members are elected according to a gender equality rule adopted in 1990: one male and one female from each of the twenty-five senatorial districts, and one male and one female representing each county.

Although the Democratic Party in Hawaii has a permanent office, it has always relied on rented space, with the result that the office has moved several times since 1960. An executive director may be appointed by the state party chair with the approval of the central committee; as of 1996 there was a three-fourths paid executive director. The four county committees have neither permanent offices nor paid staff.

Traditionally, the post of party chair has been part time, but Richard Port, first elected in 1994 and reelected in 1996, was retired and able to devote full time (unpaid) to the job. Until recently, the leadership of the Democratic Party was essentially hand-picked by the candidate running for governor. But that was not the case with the current chair, although he was not opposed by gubernatorial candidate and later governor Cayetano. It seems fair to say, based on the close relationship between past chairs and governors, that chairs have made decisions in behalf of governors, with the central committee playing an oversight role. Governors Burns, Ariyoshi, and Waihee saw themselves as strong party leaders and exercised considerable power over party matters. But there is an effort under way on the part of both the party chair and the central committee to provide more active oversight. Although it is not clear how this will turn out, there is a feeling that Governor Cayetano will be supportive of more independence for the party in its internal matters. There are also indications that he will be more independent of the party in setting public policy priorities.

County committees have been largely autonomous and have traditionally held considerable power independent of the state central committee. One reason for this balance of power is that much of the voter strength of the Democratic Party is in the rural areas of the state (for example, the neighbor islands). Another reason may be the party chair's traditional part-time attention to the party and the close ties between the chair and governor.

As mentioned earlier, candidates running under the Democratic Party label tend to be self-selected. They also have tended to be on their own with respect to establishing campaign organizations and raising funds. A priority of the current state party chair, however, is to make the party more active in working with candidates. One exception to the general rule has been gubernatorial campaigns, with which the party has always been very involved once the primary is over.

Because Hawaii is so far away from Washington, D.C., the Democratic National Committee tends not to get too involved in state party affairs, and the state party is relatively independent. On the one hand this has meant that the national party does not often intrude for fund-raising purposes. However, at the same time, it does tend to leave the party somewhat isolated. With respect to national party conventions, Hawaii's Democrats tend to get more representation than the state's population would dictate. That is due to the party's dominant status within the state; for most national conventions since 1960 the party has been able to send not only its normal complement of delegates but also the governor, the two U.S. senators, and the two members of the House of Representatives.

Perhaps because Democratic candidates have been so independent in managing their electoral campaigns, the legislative caucus has tended to ignore the state party organization when setting public policy priorities. The current party chair has set as an objective building a closer relationship with elected Democrats in the legislature.

*Republican Party.* Hawaii's Republican Party holds meetings on both an annual and a biennial basis. Precinct committees meet annually, and delegates meet in the state convention annually, but district committees and county conventions meet biennially, in odd-numbered years. In even-numbered years the state platform convention takes place and must, by party rules, be held on the island of Oahu (Honolulu). In May of odd-numbered years, the state organizational convention takes place. By rule, the organizational convention rotates between the islands of Hawaii, Kauai, and Maui. At these conventions, the state chair and officers of the state committee are elected.

Delegates to the biennial county conventions and the annual state conventions are elected at precinct meetings. Just as for their Democratic counterparts, a complex formula determines the number of delegates from each precinct; however, each precinct is guaranteed a minimum of one delegate to each convention.

Relations between the party and its elected officials are hard to gauge, in part because of the lack of Republican elected officials. Since statehood, only one Republican has been elected governor. William Quinn (1959–1962) had just completed service as the last appointed territorial governor at the time of his election in 1959. He ended up in conflict not only with the Democratic-controlled legislature but also with his own party. His relationship with the Republican Party suffered still further when he was challenged by a faction led by Republican lieutenant governor James Kealoha. The factional division was based primarily on the development of coteries around two different personalities. It appears that Kealoha felt he was not significantly appreciated for either the ethnic group he represented (native Hawaiian) or his personal capabilities. This period did not set a good precedent for relations between the party organization and its members in elected office.

For the most part, Republican gubernatorial candidates have needed to retain their own fund-raising base. It is not clear whether the election of the Republican state chair in off-election years has had any impact on the relationship between the party leadership and the party's candidate for governor. There have been times when the relationship was very close. Although it was clear in 1994 that there was tension between the chair of the state party and the gubernatorial candidate's campaign organization, the tension may have been caused more by personality conflicts that any structural aspect (Yuen 1994; Dye 1995).

On the whole, the Republican county committees have been quite weak, perhaps largely due to the fact that, in contrast to the Democrats, Republican voter strength is in the urban areas of the state rather than the rural areas. Most party matters, therefore, have been decided by the state central committee; in this regard, the Republican Party can be seen as the more centralized of the two parties. But, given the party's long-standing minority status, the state party organization cannot be seen as very powerful. There are few patronage positions to hand out, and there has always been a shortage of funds. The party often appears beleaguered and in a constant state of crisis management.

Despite the targeting strategy mentioned earlier, Republican Party candidates have generally relied more on their own campaign organizations than on the party. The party has been making efforts to become more involved. In 1994, for example, the party not only placed considerable emphasis on candidate recruitment but also became more active than ever before in providing candidate training sessions.

In the 1970s the Conference of Elected Republicans was set up to assure unity of elected Republicans and the party organization with respect to party positions. For some time it was fairly successful, but in the early 1990s it faded from the scene. In its place, the Roundtable of Elected Republicans was organized, with its primary focus on ensuring cooperation among elected Republicans. This suggests weakness in the ties between the party and its elected officials.

Hawaii's GOP, in spite of its minority status, has a close relationship with the national party organization. One illustration of their closeness is the national GOP's help over many years, much appreciated by local Republicans, in providing party VIPs for local events. Several Republicans from Hawaii have served lengthy terms on the Republican National Committee and have established long-standing relationships with members of the party hierarchy.

GOP rules specify that the party headquarters be located in Honolulu; the party has had to rely on rented space, and the office has not always been in the same location. An executive director is appointed by the state chair, with the approval of the state committee. Whereas in the past the party has been able to afford a paid executive director, as of mid-1996 it was a volunteer position.

The Republican Party has in the main been unable to play an effective role as the loyal opposition within the state political arena. The two major newspapers have repeatedly editorialized about the need for a strong second party and over the years have frequently hoped that the moment of Republican renewal was at hand. Although the Republicans currently stress organizational revitalization in order to overcome their minority status, the Democrats too are calling for renewal—to ensure that complacency with their majority status does not dull their competitive edge.

## RESOURCE GUIDE

The records of the Hawaii Democratic Party for the years 1960 through 1985 are kept at the party headquarters. Although there is no catalog per se, the papers are kept in an organized manner in file folders, so they can be characterized as semicataloged. The party is trying to form a museum of party artifacts. The records of the Hawaii Republican Party for the years 1932 through 1985 are kept at the party headquarters (although some may be in private collections).

Neither party has any collections of private papers deposited by former political figures and leaders, and neither has an official historian. Access to materials is by permission only at both the Democratic and Republican headquarters.

The Hawaii State Archives, located on the Iolani Palace grounds (Honolulu, HI 96813), was founded in 1905 and holds materials covering the period 1790 to the present. The collection includes private papers (both cataloged and uncataloged) from members of Hawaiian royalty, former political figures, and state and territorial leaders, including John Henry Wilson (mayor of Honolulu), Oren E. Long (territorial governor and U.S. senator), and John A. Burns (delegate to Congress and governor of Hawaii). Although no specific party records are deposited with the state archives, some relevant party information can be found scattered through some of these collections.

Researchers should also utilize the Hawaii Collection at Hamilton Library of the University of Hawaii at Manoa (Honolulu, HI 96822), where there is a collection of materials from government officials, writers, and scholars. A very important source of Democratic

**Table 1** Hawaii Resource Guide

|  | Democrats | Republicans |
|---|---|---|
| Archive | Yes | Yes |
| Location | Party Headquarters | Party Headquarters |
|  | 777 Kapiolani Blvd. | 50 S. Beretania, Suite 211 |
|  | Honolulu, HI 96814 | Honolulu, HI 96813 |
|  | (808) 586-2980 | (808) 526-1755 |
| Dates | 1960–1985 | 1932–1985 |
| Finding aid | No | No |
| Access | By appointment | By appointment |
| Contents: |  |  |
|   Executive committee minutes | Yes | Yes |
|   Correspondence | Yes | No |
|   Organizational structure | Yes | No |
|   Rules | Yes | Yes |
|   Budgets | Yes | Yes |

Party history is the John A. Burns Oral History Project, which includes numerous taped interviews with a wide range of individuals. The Burns project is held in the Hawaii Collection. Transcripts of some of the tapes are also available from the Hawaii State Library.

**NOTES**

1. I would like to thank the following individuals for kindly sharing their knowledge and insights: Dan Boylan, Howard Chong, Arlene Kim Ellis, Jim Hall, Betty Harris, Barbara Marumoto, Norman Meller, Richard Port, and Dan Tuttle.
2. Under the territorial government, the governor and judges were appointed by the U.S. president upon the advice and consent of the U.S. Senate. Territorial voters elected a secretary of the territory, a delegate to Congress (who had no vote there), and members of the territorial legislature. The number of legislators, originally set at twenty-five representatives and fifteen senators, was increased by Congress in 1956 to fifty-one and twenty-five, respectively. That membership size continues today in the state legislature.
3. The Home Rule Party soon vanished from the scene. Minor political parties (such as the Libertarian Party and Green Party) have fielded candidates in Hawaii but, for the most part, have never become significant factors in election outcomes. Just prior to the 1994 elections, Honolulu mayor Frank Fasi, at the time a Republican, formed the Best Party, probably so that he would not have to run in the Republican gubernatorial primary against Patricia Saiki. Saiki and Fasi split the Republican vote in the general election, and Democrat Ben Cayetano was elected governor. Fasi has been both a Democrat and a Republican and has caused controversy in both parties.
4. There are only four local governments—one for each of the four counties.
5. Since 1959, of seventy-six legislators (fifty-one house members and twenty-five senators), the highest number of Republicans to serve at one time was thirty-two, in 1959 and 1961; the lowest number was seven, in 1993. In 1995 Republicans held seven house and two senate seats.
6. Among those important to the development of the Republican Party were Samuel Wilder King (territorial delegate to Congress, 1934–1942; territorial governor appointed by President Eisenhower, 1953–1957), Joseph R. Farrington (territorial delegate to Congress, 1942–1954), Hiram Fong (U.S. senator, 1959–1976), and William Quinn (territorial governor appointed by Eisenhower, 1957–1958; first elected governor of the state, 1959–1962).
7. The most recent population breakdown in Hawaii is: Caucasian, 24.1 percent; Japanese, 20.4 percent; part Hawaiian, 18 percent; mixed non-Hawaiian, 17.5 percent; Filipino, 11.4 percent; Chinese, 4.7 percent; black, 1.5 percent; Korean, 1.1 percent; Hawaiian, 0.8 percent; Puerto Rican, 0.3 percent; Samoan, 0.3 percent (State of Hawaii 1994, 37).

8. Until recently, the placing of campaign signs in yards in Honolulu was prohibited; the prohibition may have accounted for the heavy reliance on such campaign techniques as having sign-wavers at busy intersections.
9. Hawaii Revised Statutes 11–61 through 11–65. The statutes also specify requirements for qualifying as a political party and for maintaining status as a party.

## REFERENCES

*Asterisks denote the most important publications on Hawaii party politics.*
*Bell, Roger. 1984. *Last among equals: Hawaiian statehood and American politics.* Honolulu: University of Hawaii Press.
Boylan, Dan. 1992. Blood runs thick: Ethnicity as a factor in Hawaii's politics. In *Politics and public policy in Hawaii,* ed. Zachary A. Smith and Richard C. Pratt. Albany: State University of New York Press.
*Coffman, Tom. 1973. *Catch a wave: A case study of Hawaii's new politics.* Honolulu: University Press of Hawaii.
*Daws, Gavan. 1968. *Shoal of time: A history of the Hawaiian Islands.* Honolulu: University of Hawaii Press.
Dye, Bob. 1995. Shooting themselves in the foot. *Honolulu Magazine* (May):53–55.
*Fuchs, Lawrence H. 1961. *Hawaii pono: A social history.* New York: Harcourt, Brace and World.
*Honolulu Star-Bulletin.* 1994. Comparing political party animals. *Honolulu Star-Bulletin.* December 1, A6.
*Krauss, Bob, and Johnny Wilson. 1994. *First Hawaiian Democrat.* Honolulu: University of Hawaii Press.
Kresnak, William. 1991. GOP hoping to contest all '92 races. *Honolulu Advertiser.* July 13, A5.
*Kuykendall, Ralph S., and A. Grove Day. 1961. *Hawaii: A history, from Polynesian kingdom to American statehood.* Englewood Cliffs, N.J.: Prentice-Hall.
*Meller, Norman, and Daniel W. Tuttle, Jr. 1961. Hawaii: The Aloha State. In *Western politics,* ed. Frank H. Jonas. Salt Lake City: University of Utah Press.
*Phillips, Paul C. 1982. *Hawaii's Democrats: Chasing the American dream.* Lanham, Md.: University Press of America.
State of Hawaii. 1994. *State of Hawaii data book 1993/1994.* Department of Business, Economic Development, State of Hawaii.
*Tuttle, Daniel W., Jr., ed. 1966. *Papers on Hawaiian politics, 1952–1966.* Honolulu: Department of Political Science, University of Hawaii.
*Wang, Jim. 1982. *Hawaii state and local politics.* University of Hawaii at Hilo.
Yuen, Mike. 1994. Expert: Bad advice killed Saiki's bid. *Honolulu Star-Bulletin.* December 1, A1.

# Idaho

STEPHANIE L. WITT

## PARTY HISTORY

The history of Idaho's political parties is tied to the defining characteristic of Idaho politics in general: regionalism. Carved from the Washington and Montana Territories, Idaho encompasses three distinct geographic regions separated by mountain ranges and hundreds of miles. Each region developed under unique economic and cultural influences (Moncrief

1987). The growth of the northern panhandle region was influenced by mining and timber industries, the southeast by agriculture and Mormon (Latter Day Saints) settlements, and the southwest by agriculture and commerce. Territorial politics involved factional battles, as the sparsely populated regions struggled for supremacy in the territorial legislature.

Idaho politics was dominated by Democrats even before the area's organization as a territory in 1863 through 1880; Idaho achieved statehood in 1890 (Idaho Historical Society 1961). Blank (1988) points to the importance of Confederate immigrants in creating this dominance. In 1872 the Mormon settlers in the southeast began bloc voting for the Democratic Party. In response, Republican Party activists united with northern Idaho annexationists (who wanted to be reunited with the Washington Territory) and anti-Mormons in southeast Idaho (Idaho Historical Society 1961).[1]

By 1884 anti-Mormonism and antipathy to the Mormon's bloc voting had grown to the point that the territorial legislature adopted a voter oath that effectively disenfranchised the Mormons. The oath forbade adherents to the doctrine of celestial marriage, a tenet of Mormon theology, from voting or holding office. A retroactive provision of the law made it impossible to quit the church to obtain political rights (Wells 1978). During this period, competing party organizations sprang up in the territorial counties. Parallel Democratic organizations, Mormon and non-Mormon, both attempted to elect representatives to the territorial conventions. Within several years, however, the Democratic Party abandoned the voteless Mormons (Idaho Historical Society 1961). The formal end of plural marriage and the promised end of bloc voting by the Mormons led the legislature in 1893 to repeal the voter oath and in 1895 to repeal a related ban on voting by members of an organization that supported polygamy. Thus the Mormons' political rights had been restored in full by the elections of 1896.

Anti-Mormonism resurfaced just after the turn of the century. This time, however, the anti-Mormons organized within the Democratic Party. The shift in parties occurred after a period of fluid change in political party power in Idaho. The Populists, Democrats, and Silver-Republicans all ran candidates in these early elections. Charismatic political figures switched parties to build the strongest coalitions.

Third parties organized and competed successfully after statehood. In fact, in several elections the Democratic Party came in third behind populist or progressive candidates. There were also several instances of charismatic political figures, both Democrat and Republican, taking over party organizations with their own followers or factions. This pattern would recur in modern Idaho politics during the Frank Church and Cecil Andrus years. Party organizations gained strength during a brief period (1919–1931) in which the direct primary for state offices was eliminated. The current direct primary system is open, allowing voters to choose which primary to participate in on election day.

ORGANIZATIONAL DEVELOPMENT

*Democratic Party.* The modern development of party organizations in Idaho politics is related to the power of several individuals and their power bases.[2]

The Democratic Party was strongly influenced by traditional conservatives such as Tom Boise, a northern Idaho business executive. He constructed coalitions of northern Idaho Democrats and eastern Idaho Mormons that built on the conservative agrarian foundation of the party established during the depression era. Boise never held an elective or appointive position in the Democratic Party, but his coalitions were powerful enough to control the state central committees and conventions from the 1940s until 1966 (Stapilus 1988, 86). At that point the organization created by Frank Church (a U.S. senator from 1957 to 1981) and the more liberal factions of the party—including the faction led by Cecil Andrus—wrested control from the conservative Democrats and secured the gubernatorial nomination for Andrus (Stapilus 1988). Andrus lost the 1966 general election, however.

Tom Boise's power base was the county party organizations. The 1966 reapportionment, however, created legislative districts that, for the first time, were not coterminous with county boundaries. Consequently, a new level of party organization—the legislative district party organization—was created above the county level. Andrus's supporters used these new organizations to win control of the party (Stapilus 1988). Andrus was elected governor in 1970 and later expanded his power base to include the city of Boise, which was a new development for the Democrats. Andrus was reelected three times—in 1974, 1986, and 1990. The Church and Andrus organizations were important factors in determining who had power in Democratic state politics from 1956 until 1992. The Democratic Party's reliance on their campaign organizations led to a vacuum when their combined time in Idaho politics ended with Andrus's retirement in 1992.

Staffing for the state Democratic Party fluctuated over the past few decades depending on party finances. At times, the party employed only the state party chair and a secretary; at others the party had enough funding to hire an executive director and a second secretary. Joe McCarter (1995), a party chair from the 1970s, recalled that during the late 1950s the party "went completely broke" and had to release all of its employees. The election of Cecil Andrus as governor in 1970 seems to have been the turning point in the party's fortunes. Working off of both Andrus's and Church's campaign organizations, the party developed its first pledge fund in 1970.

*Republican Party.* The Republican Party in Idaho was strongly influenced by the anti-communist movements of the 1950s. Staunchly conservative factions of the party developed, encouraged in part by the John Birch Society and the support that organization received from Latter Day Saints leader Ezra Taft Benson (an Idaho native). The central party organization was largely controlled by a small group of conservatives headed by Lloyd Adams, who played the same role in Republican politics that Tom Boise played in the Democratic Party. The conservative factions within the party were challenged by the campaign organizations of Robert Smylie, governor of Idaho from 1955 to 1967. His moderate positions were opposed by the party leadership, who backed his opponent in the 1954 primary and tried to cut off money to his campaign. Stapilus (1988, 108) reports that the Smylie network of moderate pragmatists dominated the Republican Party from 1950 to 1960. The passing of the guard in the Republican Party from the conservatives to the moderate and pragmatic Smylie was not unlike the rise of Church and Andrus in the Democratic Party.

The conservative faction of the party rebuilt its power through the work of Gwen Barnett, who served as a Republican national committee member in 1960 and 1964. Her alternative to Smylie's moderate network took control of the state convention in 1964 and endorsed Goldwater overwhelmingly. Goldwater lost in Idaho by only 1 percent in the general election (Stapilus 1988). The two factions within the party clashed again in 1966, when Smylie, entering his twelfth year as governor, asked the National Republican Coordinating Committee to condemn the John Birch Society. The society remained popular among some members of the Republican Party in Idaho, and this frontal attack further mobilized the conservatives against the moderates.

Several systemic changes weakened the power of political parties in Idaho between 1960 and 1990. First, the adoption of the merit system for state employees in 1967 drastically reduced the patronage power of county party chairs, who had enjoyed great latitude in the appointment of state employees within their counties. Second, from 1963 until 1971, statewide candidates were required to have the votes of 20 percent of the state convention delegates in order to get on the ballot. The elimination of this requirement weakened the parties' control over their nominees. Parties already had little control over many elections because all municipal elections in Idaho are nonpartisan. Finally, and perhaps most important, the implementation of the "one person one vote" principle in the 1966 reapportionment shifted the balance of power within the state from rural areas to urban areas and weakened the county party organizations as the parties created, for the first time, legislative district organizations.

## CURRENT PARTY ORGANIZATION

Idaho law prescribes the structure of the state's political parties. Each party has a state central committee comprising all legislative district chairs, all county central committee chairs, and all state committee members. The state code prescribes the makeup and selection processes for the legislative district and county central committees. State law also stipulates that each party shall meet in convention and sets the timing of these meetings. Other leadership positions within the party, however, are not specified. At times, each party has operated with and without an executive director in addition to the elected state chair.

Both of Idaho's political parties operate from headquarters in Boise, the state capital. The headquarters are located one block from one another, and their physical surroundings tell much about the relative strength and fortunes of the parties. The Republicans are housed in a newly renovated suite of offices complete with their own phone bank, fax machines, copiers, and bulk mailing operation. Although the two parties have a similar permanent staff of three, the Republicans are supplemented by a solid crew of volunteer clerical workers. The Democrats, on the other hand, are housed in the upstairs of an older home-turned-office-building. There, filing cabinets rest in the hallway close under the sloping roof, and the reception table sits crowded onto the stairway landing. The lack of space and resources drives Democratic candidates out to their own campaign headquarters during elections, whereas the Republicans can accommodate many statewide and Ada County candidates within their office space.

The differences in resources extend to the local party structures. There are several counties with no Democratic machinery. The Republicans have healthy local organizations in all forty-four Idaho counties. The geographic separation and regional differences characteristic of Idaho are reflected in the relationships between the state party headquarters and the county party organizations. With the exception of the annual state conferences, many county organizations operate independently of the state headquarters.

Both parties currently attempt "coordinated campaigns," but the strategy seems effective only for Republicans. The Republicans, utilizing the more plentiful funding of their national party, run party-sponsored commercials showcasing all of their candidates. The party also sends the candidates on statewide bus tours. The Democrats seem unable to overcome internal party differences and pool their resources in this way.

The Idaho Democratic and Republican Parties continue to suffer warring factions within their ranks. For the Democrats, the dividing lines are abortion and environmentalism. A recent party chair describes the factionalism as "wine and cheese" Democrats versus "lunch box" Democrats. The abortion issue separates the rural Democrats, predominately Mormons, from the urban liberal Democrats. Environmental issues pit urban Democrats against the labor Democrats in the logging and mining industries in the northern panhandle. The level of competition between the factions is evidenced in part by the fact that recent elections for state party chair have been decided by a one-vote margin. Traditionally, the northern part of the state has been the stronghold of the Democrats (Moncrief 1987).

The Republicans have factions within their party as well, although staff members at Republican headquarters point to the coordinated campaign efforts as a sign of party unity. Two recent electoral cycles, however, point to the growing fracture between the right-wing and moderate factions in the party. The Republican-controlled legislature had passed a model pro-life abortion law in 1989. Although the bill was vetoed by Governor Andrus, the bill's Republican sponsors suffered large losses in 1990. A determined silence on the choice issue helped the party make up for the large losses and retain control of both chambers in 1992. In 1994, however, right-wing candidates challenged several incumbent moderates in prominent state and local primaries. These divisions between the increasingly powerful right wing of the party and the moderates are likely to get worse. Moncrief (1987) points out the importance of regionalism in this factional divide: the right wing of the party tends to come from southeastern Idaho, while the moderates are based in the urban areas of the southwestern part of the state.

The state parties enjoy an informal and ongoing relationship with their members in the legislature and the governor's office, a relationship made possible by Idaho's small size. Reflecting their superior resources, the Republicans provide more information and technical support to their legislators and candidates than do the Democrats. This holds especially true in campaigns. The Democrats' smaller offices and factional differences lead Democratic candidates to run individual campaigns independent of the state party. Both state party chairs, however, have taken on the role of attacking the other party's candidates from time to time. A chief resource for the party organizations seems to be the media access given to the state chairs.

### RESOURCE GUIDE

Scholars undertaking archival research on political party organizations in Idaho will need lots of time and energy. The collections are small, uncataloged beyond a short descriptive entry, and separated by three hundred miles. The Idaho State Historical Society (450 N. 4th St., Boise, Idaho 83702; 208-334-3356) has several sets of documents from both the Democratic and Republican central committees and records from the Ada County Women's Clubs. Most of these documents pre-date 1960. A visit to the society confirmed that the collections are in a separate storage site, so advance notice of what is desired is required. The historical society does, however, have a complete set of governors' papers. Some information will be available about party activities there.

The state party headquarters have few documents available for public viewing. The Republicans have records such as convention minutes and platforms dating back to 1960. At this writing, they are in the process of sending all such materials to the University of Idaho's special collections. The University of Idaho is located in Moscow, three hundred miles from Boise, though interlibrary loan may make some of these documents available from afar. There appears to be little financial information available from either party.

**Table 1**  Idaho Resource Guide

|  | Democrats | Republicans |
|---|---|---|
| Archive | Yes | Yes |
| Location | State Party Headquarters | University of Idaho |
|  | 211 W. State St. | Special Collections, University Library |
|  | Boise, Idaho 83702 | Moscow, Idaho 83844-2350 |
|  | (208) 336-1815 | (208) 885-6534 |
| Dates | 1987–present | 1970–present |
| Finding aid | No | Yes |
| Access | By appointment | Public |
| Contents: |  |  |
| Executive committee minutes | Yes | Yes |
| Correspondence | Yes | No |
| Organizational structure | Yes | Yes |
| Budgets | Yes | No |
| Rules | Yes | Yes |

Filings with the Office of Secretary of State may give some indication of their expenditures on campaigns.

The Democrats have materials in their headquarters dating back to 1987. These include minutes of the conventions, state central committee meetings, and financial records. There are a few documents, located elsewhere in storage, that contain correspondence from the early 1980s. Aside from the much earlier records at the historical society noted above, there appears to be little available archival material on the state Democrats prior to 1980.

In addition to the governors' papers mentioned above, the papers of U.S. Senators Frank Church (D) and Len B. Jordan (R) are located at Boise State University. There is correspondence incidental to the parties in both sets of materials, but nothing comprehensive. The same is most likely true of the papers of U.S. Senator Symms (R), which are at the University of Idaho.

#### NOTES

1. The history of anti-Mormonism in Idaho is detailed in Wells (1978). Many non-Mormon settlers in southeastern Idaho objected to the Latter Day Saints' practices of collective farming and irrigation, polygamy, and insulated social and commercial communities. By allying themselves with the Republicans and the northern Idaho annexationists, the non-Mormon settlers in the southeast increased their strength in territorial politics.
2. The following descriptions of the Idaho Democratic and Republican Parties rely heavily on the works of Randy Stapilus (1988; 1990; 1994). His works include some of the few existing chronicles of party development in the modern era.

#### REFERENCES

*Asterisks denote the most important publications on Idaho party politics.*
*Blank, Robert H. 1988. *Individualism in Idaho: The territorial foundations.* Pullman: Washington State University Press.
*Idaho Historical Society. 1961. *Political party organization in Idaho, 1861–1960: A brief outline.* Idaho Historical Series, no. 4.
McCarter, Joe. 1995. Interview by author, July.
Moncrief, Gary. 1987. Idaho: The interests of sectionalism. In *Interest group politics in the American West,* ed. Ronald J. Hrebenar and Clive S. Thomas. Salt Lake City: University of Utah Press.

*Stapilus, Randy. 1988. *Paradox politics: People and power in Idaho.* Boise, Idaho: Ridenbaugh Press.
———. 1990. *The Idaho political almanac 1990.* Boise, Idaho: Ridenbaugh Press.
———. 1994. *The Idaho political almanac 1994.* Boise, Idaho: Ridenbaugh Press.
*Wells, Merle W. 1978. *Anti-Mormonism in Idaho, 1872–92.* Provo, Utah: Brigham Young University Press.
Wetherell, Jim. 1995. Interview by author, July 1.

# Illinois

PAUL M. GREEN

Illinois stretches more than four hundred miles north to south (its southernmost city, Cairo, lies farther south than Richmond, Virginia), and from its admission to the union in 1818 Illinois politics has been buffeted by dueling demographic patterns. First came the invasion of southern migrants, mainly from Kentucky and Tennessee, who brought with them their cultural traditions, their political heroes (many southern Illinois counties are named after famous men of the American South), and their faith in the Democratic Party. A few years later a trickle of migrants from the East began settling in the northern and central parts of the state. These individuals were soon joined by a rush of European immigrants who not only populated the state's rich farmland but also began congregating in the once sleepy fur-trading town on Lake Michigan called Chicago.

These settlement patterns would dictate Illinois party politics in the nineteenth century and influence party organization and competitiveness throughout most of the twentieth century. Though newcomers would eventually alter the original downstate-versus-upstate confrontations, they would never wipe out regionalism as the overriding issue in Illinois politics.

## PARTY HISTORY

*1837–1900: Alternating One-Party Rule.* Until the Civil War, downstate Illinois Democrats dominated statewide elections. Party organization in the state was loose until the mid-1830s, when a young central Illinois attorney, Stephen Douglas, convinced enough Democrats to formalize their candidate-selection procedures. Modeled after the convention that had nominated Andrew Jackson for president in 1832, the Douglas convention was a four-step process: each election district would elect delegates to a county, state, and national convention; at each convention a declaration of principles would be adopted; convention delegates would select a single candidate for each public office; the nominated candidate would receive a pledge of support from all convention delegates (Green 1980). Eventually, a fifteen-member state central committee was established to oversee convention management and party affairs, thereby creating the first modern political party in Illinois.

The main opposition to Democratic rule was the disorganized Whig Party and its successor, the Illinois Republican Party. Key to the establishment of both parties was another central Illinois lawyer, Abraham Lincoln, who would battle his Democratic counterpart, Stephen Douglas, in the 1858 Illinois U.S. Senate race and the 1860 presidential election.

Lincoln's 1860 Republican presidential nomination in Chicago magnified southern Illinois Democratic fears about the changing power structure in the state. Angered by Lincoln's antislavery position and frightened by Chicago's soaring population (more than 100,000 residents by 1860), downstate Democrats were horrified by Lincoln's election. In April 1861, following the fall of Fort Sumter, Democrats in Williamson County called a special county board meeting and voted to secede from Illinois in order to join the southern Confederacy (Dunne 1933). Cooler heads prevailed at a later meeting, thereby stopping federal troops from being sent to Williamson County. Nevertheless, the original meeting had reflected the attitude of many southern Illinoisans.

For the rest of the nineteenth century following the Civil War, Illinois Republicans dominated state politics. Chicago's massive population gains (from 100,000 in 1860 to one million in 1890) enhanced GOP statewide electoral power. Only near the end of the century did the Windy City's growing foreign-born population begin to worry Chicago and non-Chicago Republicans.

Though dissipated and disorganized, Illinois Democrats held on to their power base in southern Illinois. Between 1854 and 1870 no Republican represented any part of southern Illinois in the Illinois General Assembly, and Democrats were nearly shut out in the rest of the state except for Irish neighborhoods in Chicago.

To ease the regional stand-off, the editor of the *Chicago Tribune,* Joseph Medill, led an effort for minority party representation in the general assembly. Calling his idea "cumulative voting," Medill lobbied successfully at the 1870 Illinois constitutional convention for adoption of his plan to set up three-person legislative districts from which a party could elect only two members. This cumulative-voting system lasted until 1980, and throughout much of its 110-year history it was the main vehicle for tempering territorial regionalism and sectional politics.

*1900–1960: Chicago versus Illinois.* In the last several decades of the nineteenth century, Chicago and Cook County emerged as the new power center for Illinois Democrats. The start of the Chicago Democratic surge was marked by the mayoral election of Carter H. Harrison in 1879. Harrison and his son, Harrison II, would each be elected Chicago mayor five times between 1879 and 1915. Both were cultured, articulate, and sophisticated gentlemen who mingled politically with some of the most notorious gamblers and saloon keepers in the city (Green 1980).

Downstate Democrats were not overjoyed at the prospect of a Chicago or Cook County takeover of the party. Moreover, the party's growing ethnic composition in the Windy City and its increasingly rough and tumble politics shocked and frightened downstaters. Looking for a champion who spoke their language and supported their agrarian lifestyle, downstate Illinois Democrats turned to a Nebraskan with strong downstate Illinois roots—William Jennings Bryan. However, Bryan and downstate Democrats were unable to gain any foothold in Chicago, where conservative ethnic Democrats, mainly Irish, were struggling for control of the local party against Carter Harrison II and his multinational allies. Thus a pattern emerged that would last throughout the twentieth century—statewide and national politics for Chicago Democrats would always take a back seat to local political concerns.

Until early in the twentieth century, Illinois Republicans were far less combative than their Democratic counterparts. Strong in almost every part of the state except the south, the party of Lincoln won election after election. However, by 1904 the sheer weight of

Chicago's population (over one-third of the state's residents) led to a political showdown at the Republican state convention. In 1904 two powerful Cook County (Chicago) Republicans-Frank Lowden, Illinois national Republican committeeman and son-in-law of railroad magnate George Pullman, and Charles Deneen, Cook County states attorney—challenged incumbent governor Richard Yates for the gubernatorial nomination.

In a marathon state convention involving seventy-nine ballots over three weeks, Deneen captured the nomination (Davis 1904). Outrage and shock spread throughout non-Chicago Republican areas. Even though Deneen won the general election and became a respected statewide Republican player, downstate Republicans (those living outside Cook County), like their Democratic opponents, began to fear a Chicago takeover of their party.

Republican William Hale "Big Bill" Thompson was instrumental in the organizational development of both major parties in the twentieth century. Elected mayor of Chicago in 1915 and reelected in 1919 and 1927 (he did not run in 1923), Big Bill was a brilliant campaigner with few ethical scruples and high political ambition. Thompson was always scheming to run for statewide and even national office, and his single-minded political pursuits frightened traditional Republican voters, other GOP officeholders, and the party's principal supporter in the state—the powerful *Chicago Tribune* newspaper.

Thompson's scandal-plagued city hall administrations came at a time when progressive reforms were altering urban government elsewhere in America. Unlike Illinois Democrats, whose factionalism rested on regional, philosophical, and leadership differences, Illinois Republicans split into pro- and anti-Thompson factions.

In high-turnout presidential-election years Republican candidates did extremely well throughout the state, but in off-year and odd-year elections growing Democratic Party organizational power would often dominate. However, this pattern ended in 1931 and 1932. In 1931 Anton Cermak and his unified political machine crushed Thompson's Chicago mayoral reelection bid, and a year later Franklin Roosevelt's presidential victory swept Illinois Democrats into state and county offices.

Anton Cermak's 1931 city hall win capped the construction of the Democratic machine in Chicago and started an unbroken string of Democratic mayoral victories in the state's largest city. Cermak and his successors intertwined political and governmental processes and made them almost inseparable. Individual party members were encouraged to demonstrate loyalty to the city, loyalty to good government, and loyalty to a community, church, or constituent, but it was understood that ultimate or supreme loyalty went to the party or "machine." In setting up this complex vote juggernaut Cermak gave Illinois residents a powerful corollary to regionalism as the defining political statewide issue. To Illinois Republicans it no longer mattered what the contest was or where it took place because their top campaign strategy would be the same—to run against the "Chicago Democratic machine."

Chicago's continuing population growth made Democrats competitive in statewide races throughout the 1940s and 1950s. By 1950 Chicago residents numbered 3,620,962 and made up more than 42 percent of the statewide population; they were the main reason Democrat Harry Truman carried the state in his comeback 1948 presidential win. More than ever, Chicago was unlike the rest of Illinois—it was bigger, ethnically and racially more diverse, and far more Democratic than any other locale in the state.

Downstate legislators responded to Chicago's population and political surge by refusing to redistrict the legislative assembly. Incredibly, the Illinois state legislative map remained the same from 1901 to 1955 despite the fact that Chicago's population had more than doubled.

Just when most observers thought the duel between downstate Republicans and Chicago Democrats could not escalate any further, it did, with the emergence of Richard J. Daley. Elected Cook County Democratic Party chairman in 1953 and Chicago mayor two years later, Daley personified every fear downstaters had of the big city. Everything about "Hizonner" oozed Chicago—from his lifestyle, religion, background, and speaking voice to his unflinching faith in the Democratic Party and organization politics.

## ORGANIZATIONAL DEVELOPMENT

The presidential election of 1960 was pivotal in Illinois party history. For Democrats, especially in Chicago, it was a heroic struggle rather than just another political contest because only in John F. Kennedy's hometown of Boston was his candidacy viewed more passionately than it was in Chicago. Mayor Daley saw Kennedy as the embodiment of all the hopes, dreams, and scars of past generations of ethnic Democrats—especially the Irish. Kennedy's father, Joseph, was a longtime ally of Daley (the senior Kennedy owned the enormous Merchandise Mart building in Chicago), and in 1960 the two men worked together to energize the Chicago vote. In fact, this presidential election was unique for Daley in that it was the only time that local considerations ran second to the success of the top of the ticket.

On the Friday before the election Daley hosted Kennedy at the largest candidate rally ever held in Chicago. Before speaking to an overflow crowd at Chicago Stadium, Kennedy was honored with a parade where the spectators (Daley's ward organizations) stood four and five deep along the curb. It was the last hurrah for organizational muscle—never again would Daley or anyone else be able to muster so many people to a party function.

For the Republicans, also, 1960 was a special election year with important long-term consequences. Suburban growth had fueled a resurgence of Republican fortunes, produced new party leaders, and given the GOP a suburban-dominated party organization. Whereas many downstate Republicans had been envious of the cohesive party structure of Chicago Democrats, the new GOP suburbanites were contemptuous of traditional party politics. Many suburbanites were former Chicagoans who voted Republican as a sign of their political independence and not as new members of the party. In 1950 suburban Cook County made up 10 percent of the total state population; by 1960 its share had risen to 16 percent (Green 1982). Because of the soaring numbers in suburban Cook County and the population growth in the five emerging counties surrounding Cook known as the "collar counties" (DuPage, Kane, Lake, McHenry, and Will ), suburban Republicans were able to take control of the 1960 GOP campaign in Illinois. That Kennedy carried the state over Richard Nixon by fewer than nine thousand votes despite Daley's herculean efforts for him in Chicago (JFK's Chicago margin was 456,000 votes) was due in large part to new-found suburban Republican strength. From the breakthrough 1960 election to the present, the Illinois Republican Party has been suburban-led and suburban-driven.

The 1960 election reset statewide voting patterns in Illinois. In a typical post-1960 election (both parties nominating strong candidates and no national trend overwhelming state and local issues, such as occurred in 1964 and 1972), Democratic winning margins in Chicago were offset by GOP victory margins in the five collar counties and suburban Cook County. As a result of this standoff in the six populous northeastern counties (representing 62 to 63 percent of the total state population), downstate Illinois (the other ninety-six counties) became the deciding factor in statewide races (Colby and Green 1986).

This new electoral geography exacerbated the political imbalance between Chicago and the rest of the state by increasing the gap between primary and general-election strategies within the Democratic Party. Chicago, despite its dwindling percentage of the statewide vote, was still able to dominate Democratic primary politics because of Daley's organization. However, control of the primary meant little in the general election, when Republicans would denounce Chicago-based candidates. It is not surprising, then, that between 1964 (a nationwide Democratic landslide) and 1996 Illinois Democrats won only one gubernatorial election, and that one, the 1972 victory of Dan Walker, was due in large part to his antiorganization, non-Chicago roots. Moreover, the success in this same period of Democratic U.S. senators Adlai Stevenson III (1970–1981), Alan Dixon (1981–1993), and Paul Simon (1985–1997) was possible in large part because each man claimed his Illinois origins were located far from Chicago. Only Carol Moseley-Braun's gender-driven surprise 1992 Senate victory broke this trend. Her Chicago home gave her the votes to upset Dixon in a savage three-way Senate primary battle, and her Republican general-election opponent was unable to capitalize fully on anti-Chicago statewide feelings.

Political party organizational development in Illinois since the 1960s has been constrained by several factors. Chief among these are the decline of patronage, the struggle over internal party democracy and representation, and the continued salience of individual personality.

Patronage suffered from a series of court decisions known as the Shakman Decrees in the 1970s, which prevented political work from being a condition of hiring or firing. By limiting patronage only to exempted policy positions, the courts complicated and frustrated traditional party operations. The effect of these decisions was to remove some of the traditional mechanisms at the disposal of the political machines that had ensured their dominance. In 1990 an important case from Illinois made its way to the Supreme Court, and the Court's decision further diminished the ability of state party organizations to exert control over patronage. In 1990, in *Rutan v. Republican Party of Illinois* (110 S. Ct. 2729), the Supreme Court ruled that it is unconstitutional to hire, promote, or transfer most public employees based on their party affiliation. Along with previous court decisions and the Shakman Decrees, *Rutan* completely undercut organized party politics as practiced in Illinois.

The 1968 Chicago Democratic National Convention has become a symbol of the struggles within the Democratic Party over internal democracy and representation. Paradoxically, Mayor Daley's personal power within the Illinois party was not immediately affected by the convention; however, the wider effect of the chaos and rioting both inside and outside the hall was a surge of antiparty fervor in the state. In the aftermath of the convention, a politically independent movement was energized in Chicago and in the suburbs. The McGovern-Fraser reforms implemented by the DNC, on the other hand, did directly undermine Daley's position within the Democratic Party. At the 1972 Democratic convention in Miami, the party seated two upstart young liberal Democrats, Rev. Jesse Jackson and Chicago alderman William Singer, and ousted most of Mayor Daley's elected convention delegates from Chicago. This momentous decision resulted from the Daley organization's refusal to implement the new guidelines for delegate selection laid down by the DNC.

The ability of the state party organizations to control their electorate was severely limited in 1972 by the end of the so-called twenty-three month rule. A federal court decision invalidated an Illinois law prohibiting a voter from voting in one party's primary within twenty-three months of having voted in another party's primary. Party reformers called this decision a "sledgehammer blow to machine politics," since it opened up party primary participation to all voters. The Democratic Party experienced fallout in the 1980s from the opening up of the primary process. Two followers of extremist Lyndon LaRouche won the Democratic nominations for lieutenant governor and secretary of state. Not only did the two LaRouche followers defeat the endorsed Democratic candidates, but they forced Democratic gubernatorial nominee Adlai Stevenson III to form a third party to avoid running on the same ticket as them. The episode reveals the extent to which contested primaries have weakened the hold of parties on the candidate-recruitment process.

The third factor weakening Illinois party organizations, personality, continues to play an important role. Daley's death in 1976 ended an era of classic machine politics, where the backing of the party organization was critical for electoral success. But the importance of personality did not end with Daley's passing. In perhaps the two most exciting elections in city history, U.S. representative Harold Washington became Chicago's first African American mayor by winning the Democratic primary against incumbent mayor Jane Byrne (the city's first female mayor) and States Attorney Richard M. Daley (the late mayor's eldest son). Washington then went on to defeat Republican Bernard Epton in the mayoral general election in April 1983, in which race overwhelmed all other issues (including party) as white Democrats flocked to Epton's GOP banner. The decline of strong party machines in Illinois has not been paralleled by a decline in the salience of strong individuals.

## CURRENT PARTY ORGANIZATION

Both Illinois Republicans and Democrats maintain state party offices in Chicago and Springfield, symbolizing the regional cleavages discussed above. Each party is governed by a set of bylaws, and the leadership of each is selected by the state central committee membership by a weighted vote; the vote is based on the number of Democratic or GOP votes cast at the previous primary.

Central committee members are elected for a four-year term from each of the states' twenty congressional districts during the off-year primary. Democrats elect a man and a woman from each district, and both are allowed to cast their district's total weighted vote. Republicans elect one central committee member per district, and each district must select a deputy member of the opposite sex of the member (Illinois Republican Party 1994). Unlike the Democrats, the Republicans allow only the elected GOP committee member to cast his or her district vote.

Both state central committees have fund-raising mechanisms and they must file financial statements periodically with the Illinois State Board of Elections. However, neither party is a significant source of money in state or local elections. Democratic and Republican state central committees meet at the call of the chair. In recent years the once highly structured and organized Democratic Party has acted more like the traditionally loose and informal GOP in limiting official party endorsements. No longer does a Democratic Party endorsement mean certain primary victory—in fact, to many candidates it has become a liability.

The last bastion of strong party organization in the state rests in the Illinois General Assembly. Democratic house leader Michael Madigan and his Republican counterpart, Lee Daniels, have used their bitter personal rivalry during the past twenty years to consolidate incredible power for themselves through their various fund-raising committees. As a result most house legislative races in Illinois are not financed by the candidates but by the respective party leaders in the general assembly. The legislative leaders recognize that dollars have replaced doorknockers as the key organizational tool in Illinois politics.

Other statewide elected officials also have their own elaborate fund-raising mechanisms that obviate central committee involvement in candidate finance. To be sure, county party chairs and their local organizations remain on paper in each of the state's 102 counties, but their importance and effectiveness have been severely downgraded in recent years. Non-party-driven political fund raising and organization building have even swept up the current Chicago mayor, Richard M. Daley. Unlike his father, young Daley refuses to call himself a Democratic boss, avoids appearing before the party slatemaking committees, and accepted without comment a recently passed state law making the post of Chicago mayor officially nonpartisan.

In sum, the old-style party organization in Illinois is disintegrating. Both the tangible rewards and social joys of political participation have been undercut by the courts, changing lifestyles, new demographics and technology, and old age. Reform has won. Elective politics is now an individual rather than party-driven process. Citizens criticize government and political parties interchangeably and seek answers to complicated public issues from nonpolitical sources. Candidates with no public record or party history use their apolitical status as a weapon against more party-oriented opponents.

Illinois Democrats and Republicans and their party organizations have defended themselves against the increasingly antiparty climate and legal environment by using two of their remaining weapons—legislative control and tradition. It is still very difficult in Illinois for independent candidates or new parties to gain ballot access, and it is very unlikely that the general assembly will pass any new laws making it easier. Moreover, despite societal negativism on political activity, as evidenced by a decline in voting and disillusionment with elected officials, political parties in Illinois remain the main vehicle for running the public's business. Election night remains political party night, and though candidates may run away from party identification when campaigning, they somehow find it when governing. As one old-time Chicago pol recently told me, "Sure, some people call me a party hack and worse, but when they need something, who are they going to call—a talk show host or me?"

### RESOURCE GUIDE

Neither major political party maintains an archive—in fact, both work very hard simply to maintain offices in Springfield and Chicago.

A number of repositories in Illinois contain materials related to state party politics. The Illinois Historical Society, in Springfield, maintains early periodicals and papers on political party history as well as a manuscript collection. The Chicago Historical Society is a major source for Chicago material and has a vast photo archive and manuscript collection. The Illinois State Board of Elections, with offices in Springfield and Chicago, is a main source of information on election law, party financial reporting requirements, and election results back to 1972.

Several universities also maintain party-related materials. The University of Illinois–Urbana Institute of Government and Public Affairs, under its former director Sam Gove, collected a great deal of material on parties, politics, and legislative redistricting. The University of Illinois–Chicago maintains a growing collection of material on Chicago—especially on former mayor Richard J. Daley. The Northern Illinois University Center for Governmental Studies maintains material on suburban political developments. And the University of Chicago has vast holdings, including some manuscripts on Hyde Park party reformers.

## REFERENCES

*Asterisks denote the most important publications on Illinois party politics.*

Bogart, Ernest, and John Mathews. 1922. *The modern commonwealth, 1893–1918*. Chicago: A. C. McClurg.

*Church, Charles. 1912. *History of the Republican Party in Illinois, 1854–1912*. Rockford: Wilson Bedhers.

Colby, Peter, and Paul Green. 1986. Downstate holds the key to victory. In *Illinois elections*, ed. Paul Green, David Everson, Peter Colby, and Joan Parker. Springfield: Illinois Issues Press.

Davis, J. McCan. 1904. *The breaking of the deadlock*. Springfield: Henry Shepard.

*Dunne, Edward F. 1933. *Illinois: The heart of the nation*. 5 vols. Chicago: Lewis Publishing.

Green, Paul. 1982. Legislative redistricting in Illinois, 1871–1982. In *Redistricting an exercise in prophecy*, ed. Anna J. Merritt. Urbana, Ill.: Institute of Government and Public Affairs.

———. 1980. History of political parties in Illinois. In *Illinois: Political processes and governmental performance*, ed. Ed Crane. Dubuque: Kendall/Hunt.

*Green, Paul, David Everson, Peter Colby, and Joan Parker. 1986. *Illinois elections*. Springfield: Illinois Issues Press.

*Green, Paul, and Melvin Holli, eds. 1995. *The mayors: The Chicago political tradition*. Rev. ed. Carbondale: Southern Illinois University Press.

*Howard, Robert. 1972. *Illinois: A history of the Prairie State*. Grand Rapids: Eerdmans Publishing.

Illinois Republican Party. 1994. *Illinois Republican Party bylaws*.

*Rakove, Milton. 1975. *Don't make no waves—Don't back no losers*. Bloomington: Indiana University Press.

# Indiana

DAVID J. HADLEY

## PARTY HISTORY

Indiana's national reputation as a strongly Republican state, earned by its performance in presidential elections, contrasts sharply with the intense interparty competition that has characterized the Hoosier state through most of its history. Politics in Indiana has always been party politics conducted by and through strong organizations.

The roots of the strong organizations can be traced back to the post–Civil War years between 1872 and 1892, when the parties were so evenly divided in electoral support that every statewide election ended in a virtual photo finish. The close competition placed a premium on organizational efforts to identify every supportive voter and get each and every one to the polls. Failure of the organization in any precinct, ward, or county could result in the loss of a statewide office (Hyneman et al. 1979, 83–96). Party organization counted, was firmly established, and became an integral part of the political culture.

Since 1892 the GOP has maintained an advantage over the Democratic Party, but never with such certainty that it could forget the importance of organization and preparation for upcoming elections. Republican control of the governor's office and the state legislature would remain vulnerable, providing an incentive for those whose lives were closely tied to their party. Nor could the minority Democrats afford to forget the importance of organizing for the next election. Although they spent long periods in the minority, Democrats with some regularity scored electoral victories. The Democrats held the governor's office for eight years in the 1960s and regained the office in 1988, took control of the Indiana House following the 1990 and 1992 elections, claimed a majority of the state's congressional delegation in nine of ten elections from 1974 to 1992, and won U.S. Senate campaigns from 1958 through 1974. All these accomplishments were proof enough that Democrats could win with the right candidates and effectively organized campaigns.

Through most of this century, the competition between Democrats and Republicans aimed at winning control of public office rather than at the triumph of one set of ideas over another (Fenton 1966, ch. 4; Peirce and Keefe 1980). Thus, at least until recently, Indiana's party competition fit well Daniel Elazar's concept of individualistic political culture, with its emphasis on politics as an avenue for personal benefit and group advancement (Elazar 1984, 115). During the last fifteen years, however, the competition has tilted toward ideas, as civil service and political reforms have deprived the parties of the patronage and financial resources that had bound members' futures to party. In response to federal court decisions and developing public dissatisfaction with old ways of doing business, the extensive patronage system, mandatory contributions to the governor's party by state patronage employees, and the party-controlled auto license branch system have given way to reforms that were adopted in other states years earlier.

## ORGANIZATIONAL DEVELOPMENT

Although the basic pyramidal structure of Indiana political party organizations has remained unchanged since at least the 1940s, what happens within that structure and the interrelationships among organizational elements have been transformed by internal and external influences over the last thirty years.[1] For the most part these changes have reduced the role played by county party chairs and their organizations and shifted power toward state committees and their chairs. Among the changes that influenced this development were court-mandated reapportionment and redistricting of the state legislature and congressional districts; the replacement of convention nominations with primary elections for the selection of gubernatorial and U.S. Senate candidates; and developments in campaign techniques and technologies.

The U.S. Supreme Court's one-person, one-vote decisions (*Baker v. Carr* [1962] and *Reynolds v. Sims* [1964], among others ) in the early 1960s forced Indiana in 1965 to redistrict the state legislature for the first time since 1923. The pressure to achieve population equality, combined with the opportunity redistricting provided to construct constituencies electorally advantageous to the majority legislative party, led the General Assembly ultimately to forsake districts constructed from whole county units. Since 1970 Indiana legislative districts have been constructed of bits and pieces (wards and precincts) of four to eight counties. Under older, county-based districting plans it made sense for state legislative candidates, and even congressional candidates, to work with the small group of county organizations that comprised the district. Under recent plans, a candidate spends time more effectively constructing a single, personal organization than trying to coordinate half a dozen party chairs each of whose counties contain only a small part of the legislative district. The county chair's roles as local campaign coordinator and link between candidate and the grass roots were thus reduced. Similarly, the chair's intermediary role between voter and elected legislator diminished. At the same time that county parties' roles in legislative elections declined, legislative caucuses, working in collaboration with the state party, began to develop the service organization capacities that allowed them to provide campaign assistance to candidates.

The shift in 1976 to primary elections for selecting gubernatorial nominees removed county party organizations and their chairs from the center of the nomination process for the most important office in the state. The adoption of the primary changed the nature of the campaign for the nomination, raised its cost significantly, and placed a premium on a candidate's abilities to create a sophisticated personal organization, raise large sums of money, and appeal directly to voters through modern campaign media. County chairs lost their role in facilitating communication between candidates and convention delegates and their role as brokers in convention deal making.

The impact of these changes on Indiana party organizations has been magnified by the revolutions in campaigns themselves. One need not belabor the impact of electronic media on campaigns and the capacity they have given candidates for reaching voters directly, without party mediation. Add to this, however, the influence of computer technology and direct mail, and the potential for remaking even the sturdiest organizational arrangements emerges. The Indiana state Republican organization in the 1970s was perhaps one of the first state parties to realize the potential for developing as a provider of campaign services to candidates and local party organizations. The state committee purchased computer equipment, began compiling a central state voter data file and combining it with demographic data, developed in-house campaign consultancy capabilities, and made these resources available to local candidates and party organizations and for coordinated statewide campaigns. The Democrats followed the Republican lead in the mid-1980s, particularly after the 1988 gubernatorial election of Evan Bayh enhanced the party's ability to raise money to support technical staff.

All of the foregoing developments make Indiana parties look very ordinary, moving along with developments in other states. The Hoosier state, however, added wrinkles of its own. For example, although many of the developments pushed in the direction of stronger state chairs and more important state headquarters staffs, in 1988 the Indiana General Assembly amended the statute that regulates the selection of party leaders in such a way as to strengthen county chairs and organizations. Before the change, precinct committee persons were elected in primary elections in even-numbered years. State law prior to 1988 required that within a few weeks after the primary, the entire state party leadership, from county committee to state committee and state chair, be selected. The 1988 legislation, called by some the "County Chairmen for Life Bill," changed this schedule. Statute now provides for precinct committee persons to be elected in primary elections in nonpresidential, even-numbered years. Then, three years later, in the one year in every four when Indiana holds no elections, the county committees (all the precinct committee persons and their vice committee members) meet to select the county chair and vice chair.

Party professionals argue that this change makes it virtually impossible for a determined incumbent county chair to be deposed. By law, the county chair fills any vacancy in the county committee. It is argued that, in the three years between the election of the precinct committee persons and the election of a new county chair, any determined county chair will be able, through appointment, to ensure his or her own reelection. Supporters of the change argue, however, that the 1988 legislation protects Indiana party organizations from being taken over by narrow special interests or transient participants whose real interest is in one of the presidential candidates rather than in the party. Supporters also contend that the 1988 legislation strengthens the role of the county organization in electoral politics by requiring the county chair be selected in a year in which no November election occurs, thereby giving the chairperson more than a year to prepare to run a full-scale campaign.

Opponents of the new schedule argue that the change increases the incentive for candidates to work outside of the party organization, since it is more difficult to influence or change county leadership from above or below. They argue that the change has reduced turnover and the infusion of new blood into district and state committees. Although both sides of the argument may be supportable, a paradox remains. A change that solidified the position of incumbent county chairs at the same time may have lessened their role in statewide campaigns. Candidate-centered campaigns, unable to shape significantly party leadership at the local level, have a strong incentive to circumvent entrenched county chairs in fund raising and campaign organizing.

Other changes influencing the operation and role of parties have occurred as well. The Federal Campaign Finance Act of 1971 and its amendments encouraged the creation of political action committees, which have become predictable and lucrative sources of funds for candidates, legislative caucus campaign committees, and party organizations. In Indiana the act also worked to gut the electoral role of the parties' congressional district organizations by prohibiting any but state party organizations from raising and spending money in behalf of U.S. House candidates. District committees were left with but one real function—to elect a district chair and vice chair to serve on the state committee, which chooses the head of the state party and makes party rules.

Court decisions have been another factor influencing the parties. The courts stripped the parties of large numbers of patronage positions, while changes in public attitudes and shifts in the economy reduced the attractiveness of such positions. Finally, in 1986 the General Assembly voted to phase out the party-controlled automobile license branch system, which for fifty years had provided the state and local organizations of the governor's party with significant, dependable income as well as low-paying but numerous patronage positions throughout the state.

The decline of patronage and the disappearance of these patronage-based sources of income necessitated aggressive searches for alternative sources of funds and ways to motivate people to become involved in party and campaign activity. The leadership of both parties believes that ideas and attractive candidates are the answers. Recent state chairs in both parties speak of the importance of recruiting new blood to active roles in the party and as candidates. Indiana's senior U.S. senator, Richard Lugar, created the Lugar Leadership Program, which brings together people from across the state to discuss public issues from Republican perspectives. Even though the program is not formally a party affair, it provides a venue for identification and recruitment of potential candidates, discussion and sharing of ideas, and networking among the GOP's population base. In 1995 discussions were under way in Democratic circles to create a similar program. In addition, legislative caucuses of both parties have worked to recruit and support candidates for key races over the last two decades.

Although volunteer and candidate recruitment have long been functions associated with political parties, the focus on ideas as a mechanism for generating interest and involvement in the parties is relatively new, at least to Indiana. Indiana House Republicans gained considerable mileage in the 1994 general election and in the following General Assembly session from its Contract with Indiana, the local version of U.S. House Republicans' Contract with America. Indiana Republicans have also benefited from the presence of conservative think tanks in the state. The Indiana-based Hudson Institute contributes conservative perspectives on national issues, and the home-grown Indiana Public Policy Institute analyzes state and local issues from a right-of-center position. The recently formed Sycamore Institute will examine issues from a more Democratic perspective.

## CURRENT PARTY ORGANIZATION

Indiana political parties are statutory organizations whose basic pyramidal structure is established by state law. Primary election voters, who choose precinct committee persons, form the base. Through a series of party meetings at the county, congressional district, and state levels, party committees at each level select leadership which combines to form the organization at the next higher tier. The state committee, with its chair and headquarters staff, forms the peak of the pyramid. The state committee, acting through the chair and staff, organizes the party's convention, engages in fund raising, develops and distributes the party's campaign resources, and, to the extent possible, seeks to produce coordinated campaigns for statewide offices. It is this structure that, while basically unchanged in recent decades, has been transformed by the influences discussed above. The role and importance of the county chair have declined, and those of the state committee, the state chair, and the state headquarters staff, as developers and dispensers of modern campaign technology and know-how, have risen.

The Indiana State Democratic Party office currently includes the state chair, an administrative assistant, a political director, two persons working with the party's computer system and data files, and a receptionist. The staff located in the state headquarters grows in election years, when coordinated campaigns for statewide offices and the legislative caucus election coordinators operate from the office. Indiana Republican Party headquarters staff, traditionally larger than the state Democratic staff, in 1995 consisted of eight full-time employees and three interns. These include the chair and an assistant, a fundraiser, two staffers each in computer operations and financial records and reporting, and a receptionist.

The relative importance of the state committee and its relationship to the state chair vary, depending on whether the party holds the governor's office. Generally speaking, when the party controls the governor's office and the state chair is the governor's choice, the influence of the state committee in party decision making diminishes. Without the leadership and clout of a sitting governor, the state committee, acting through its chair and state headquarters staff, assumes responsibility for setting the party's course. The alternative to an assertive state committee is party drift or a party torn apart by contending statewide candidates and factions. All three scenarios have been experienced by both parties at some time over the last twenty-five years.

Both state party organizations in recent decades have organized and run coordinated campaigns for statewide offices. Coordinated campaigns are more successful when the party controls the governor's office. In the absence of the financial and political resources that control of the governor's office places at the disposal of the party, the state committee frequently proves too weak to manage the contending candidate factions or to bring much order to the process. The Republicans managed effective coordinated campaigns during the Otis Bowen and Robert Orr governorships (1972 through 1984 elections). After being out of power for four years, however, the Indiana GOP fell into disarray during the 1992 campaign. Democrats in 1992, on the other hand, with a sitting governor, managed a coordinated campaign unimaginable just eight years before. It is ironic to note that the party found itself in a position to run a successful coordinated campaign in 1992 under Bayh, who had himself run candidate-centered campaigns for secretary of state and then for governor.

Both parties in Indiana have had to contend with a variety of factions and divisions over time. The major division within the Republican Party today is between a strong religious right, on the one hand, and economically conservative, but socially more moderate, business Republicans on the other. The religious right has not taken control of the party organization, but it has established itself as a force to be reckoned with in the legislative arena and at election time. A Marion County (Indianapolis)/non-Marion County split also has been evident in recent years. The more moderate business faction, which is strongest in the Indianapolis metro area, currently holds the upper hand within the state organization.

Democrats, on the other hand, must manage the division between traditional labor groups, which are strong in the industrial (steel and automobile-related manufacturing) counties in northern and east central Indiana, and historically conservative elements of the party, located chiefly in southern Indiana. Today's Indiana Democratic Party also contains personal factions linked to Governor Bayh, Representative Lee Hamilton, Lt. Governor Frank O'Bannon, and perhaps others. Since the Democrats regained control of the governor's office in 1989, however, the state Democratic headquarters has followed the governor's directions for the party.

At the state government institutional level, Indiana political parties reflect the tensions seen elsewhere between the executive and legislature. Governor Bayh's relationships with General Assembly Democrats are illustrative. After gaining the governor's office for the first time in twenty years, expectations ran high among legislative Democrats. Bayh, however, determined to change the way Indiana voters view Democratic administrations, committed his administration to not raising state taxes. During a period of economic stagnation, Bayh's position left little room for meeting Democratic legislators' demands to turn state programs in new directions. Senate Democrats, lacking a majority in their chamber at any time during the Bayh administration, had little incentive to work closely with the governor and frequently made public their differences with him. House Democrats, on the other hand, who at first shared control of the lower chamber with the Republicans (a 50–50 split in 1989–1990) and then for four years held a majority, were a formidable group whose support the governor worked hard to sustain. Each side brought resources to the table, however, and through negotiations outside the public view, the governor and the House Democrats generally traveled a common path.

In the electoral arena the gubernatorial-controlled state Democratic Party and the Democratic legislative caucuses have maintained an alliance, if not closely integrated their organizations. The caucus-paid legislative campaign coordinators operate from state party headquarters, where they have access to party voter files from which to develop mailing and contributor lists. Questions about the size and allocation of state party contributions to legislative campaigns strain the alliance, as caucus leaderships and the governor's state chair differ over how best to use the available resources.

Indiana political parties have been and continue to be viable and adaptable organizations. They were forged in the intense competition that characterized the state in the final decades of the last century. They molded and remolded themselves through much of the twentieth century. If the last two decades are any indication, they will continue as major, although changing, organizational actors in Hoosier politics well into the new millennium.

## RESOURCE GUIDE

Indiana political parties have not maintained party archives systematically. Materials that do exist, except for those records that state or federal law requires to be kept, are viewed either as confidential property of the party or confidential property of the state chair.

Party records apparently reflect the fortunes and the foibles of the state parties and their personnel. Former state chairs of both parties recall records being thrown away when financial misfortunes led to relocation of headquarters to less spacious quarters. State chairs' correspondence records frequently exited state headquarters when party leadership changed. And, with the exception of those records that by state or federal law must be kept (campaign finance reports, for example), existing archival material reflects idiosyncratic decisions made by state party personnel. The state chair determines access to these records. Although both parties keep state committee meeting minutes, some leadership correspondence, and annual budgets, neither current state chair would grant access to these materials for research purposes. Party budgets are considered the most confidential documents and would not be made available to researchers or the public. Indeed, one recent state chair said a party's budget records probably would leave with an outgoing chair.

State party rules and convention rules are public documents, but neither party maintains a systematic record of past rules. The current chairs reported that party files might contain rules for the most recent convention or two, but they doubted the existence of more extensive files. One recent Democratic chair reported the state office could not produce a full collection of state platforms for the modern era from its files. Meticulously kept, however, are the financial reports required by the Federal Election Campaign Act and state law. These records are available through the Indiana Election Commission.

## NOTE

1. I am indebted to many Indiana public and party officials for the material that follows. Over the past fifteen years, Republican and Democratic Party officials, legislators, gubernatorial staff members, governors, other executive officeholders, and lobbyists and interest group representatives have given me interviews as I have sought to understand Indiana party politics. For the most recent round of interviews for this chapter, I thank Ann Delaney and John Livengood, former Democratic state chairs; Gordon Durnil, former Republican state chair; Michael McDaniel and Joseph Andrew, current GOP and Democratic state chairs, respectively; John Sweezey, Marion County Republican chair; Jim Knoop, a Republican campaign consultant and former executive assistant to Gov. Robert Orr; and Brian Williams, former Democratic state political director. For a complete list of others participating in earlier interviews, contact the author.

## REFERENCES

*Asterisks denote the most important publications on Indiana party politics.*

Dailey, J. Roberts, with Floyd A. Creech. 1988. *Mr. Speaker: Inside six sessions of the Indiana House of Representatives.* Muncie, Ind.: Fox Ridge Publications.

Elazar, Daniel J. 1984. *American federalism: A view from the states.* 3d ed. New York: Harper and Row.

*Fenton, John H. 1966. *Midwest politics.* New York: Holt, Rinehart and Winston.

*Hadley, David J. 1993. Interest groups in Indiana: Groups in a changing party environment. In *Interest group politics in the midwestern states,* ed. Clive Thomas and Ronald Hrebenar. Ames: Iowa State University Press.

*Harmon, Robert B. 1990. *Government and politics in Indiana: A selected guide to information sources.* Monticello, Ill.: Vance Bibliographies.

*Hojnacki, William P., and Raymond H. Scheele. 1983. *Politics and public policy in Indiana: Prospects for change in state and local government.* Dubuque, Iowa: Kendall Hunt.

*Hyneman, Charles S., C. Richard Hofstetter, and Patrick F. O'Connor. 1979. *Voting in Indiana: A century of persistence and change.* Bloomington: Indiana University Press.

Kessler, James B., ed. 1979. *Empirical studies of Indiana politics.* Bloomington: Indiana University Press.

*Madison, James H. 1986. *The Indiana way: A state history.* Bloomington: Indiana University Press.

Peirce, Neal R., and John Keefe. 1980. *The Great Lakes states: People, politics, and power in the five Great Lakes states.* New York: Norton.

Vandermeer, Phillip R. 1985. *The Hoosier politician: Officeholding and political culture in Indiana, 1886–1920.* Champaign: University of Illinois Press.

Watt, William J. 1981. *Bowen: The years as governor.* Indianapolis: Bierce Associates.

Welsh, Matthew E. 1981. *View from the statehouse: Recollections and reflections, 1961–1965.* Indianapolis: Indiana Historical Bureau.

# Iowa

BARBARA TRISH

## PARTY HISTORY

Although the parties in Iowa have never been as strong as their patronage-based counterparts in other states, they have been important in shaping Iowa politics. By the time Iowa entered the Union in 1846, the Democrats and Whigs, who had dominated territory politics, were exhibiting certain characteristics—including factionalism, strong grass roots, and effective management—that prevail in the present-day Democratic and Republican Parties.

Factionalism was inherent in the state Republican Party, which organized in 1856. Founded on the basis of antislavery sentiment, the Republican Party drew in dissidents from many groups. Disgruntled Whigs took their place under the Republican umbrella with such factions as antiforeign Know-Nothings and foreign-born Iowans.[1]

Despite these early intraparty debates and later urban-rural fissures, Republicans established dominance in Iowa politics. The party's gubernatorial candidates won forty-four of the forty-nine biennial elections from 1858 to 1955, most by substantial margins. An urban-rural conflict marked the Iowa GOP long after the Democrats nationwide had secured urban support. The "Republican tradition" in Iowa helped the GOP recapture urban elements after they strayed briefly in the 1930s.[2]

Competition between the Republican and Democratic Parties has intensified since the 1950s. Jewell and Olson (1988) classify the state as "competitive two party" in the period 1965–1988. The revival of the Democratic Party in Iowa coincided with the election in 1962 of Democratic governor Harold Hughes to the first of three consecutive terms. A popular explanation for the Democratic success is that by the 1950s the party had effectively responded to the post–World War II urbanization and industrialization of the state.[3] Despite Democratic gains, the Republicans continued to dominate state politics. They have held the governor's office since 1969 and as of 1995 held the lower chamber of the

Iowa General Assembly, one U.S. Senate seat, and the entire U.S. House delegation from the state. And the GOP has continued its historical dominance of presidential general election politics.

The parties in Iowa have always had a grassroots focus. In the beginning, according to Gannaway,

> [the Democratic and Republican] parties held within their ranks practically all the people of the State. The voters in each party were in a real sense members of its organization. There was no organization apart from the great mass of voters. In fact it was their organization, and theirs alone (1903, 31).

Although Gannaway also noted that the parties had moved away from this mass-based organization by the turn-of-the century, relative to other states, Iowa's grassroots quality has persisted. It does, though, take a unique form. In Iowa, the parties have taken a "managed-grassroots" approach to organization. To a large extent this is due to the reliance on and importance of the caucus system in Iowa party politics.

The caucus system, which the parties in Iowa still employ in presidential nomination activities, has always been a key part of state politics. In the 1800s caucuses were used both to conduct party business and to select nominees for all levels of elective office. The "caucus was a closely managed and too often a manipulated event" (English 1948, 256). As described by English and recounted by Winebrenner (1983), the nineteenth-century caucus could be cleverly orchestrated.

> A typical ruse to attract voters from a regularly called party caucus was to organize a competing event. In a north Iowa county the "fortunate" burning of an old shed in the outskirts of a small town at exactly the advertised hour of the holding of the caucus attracted nine-tenths of the people of the village. ... In the meantime, those in the "know" assembled at the caucus. (257)

Grassroots politics, ironically, opened the door for effective management.

Flagrant abuses of the caucus system motivated progressive sentiment at the turn of the twentieth century. The caucus tradition succumbed when in 1907 the state adopted a direct primary system for nominating the parties' candidates for "offices filled by direct popular vote" (Winebrenner 1983, 620). Tradition ultimately prevailed, however, when the legislature repealed a provision for a presidential primary after just one experiment in 1916. [4]

Several individuals have affected in a notable way the unique quality of parties and the context of politics in the state. For instance, Gov. James W. Grimes engineered the birth of the Republican Party in Iowa by drawing in and appeasing a diverse lot. Grimes, a turncoat Whig who had served as the state executive from 1854 to 1858, marshaled the varied elements of antislavery sentiment into the new state party organization. The Democratic Party, which had experienced only brief success, and that early in its history, was reborn under Governor Hughes, who served from 1963 to 1969. Under Hughes's leadership—and with the efforts in the 1970s of John Culver and Dick Clark, both of whom would serve in the U.S. Senate—the Democratic Party became competitive and organizationally strong. [5]

State party chairs have also influenced party politics. The introduction of a full-time party chair has been a recent development. Democrat Eric Tabor set the precedent when elected to that position in 1993. Chairs have also affected organizational development, although indirectly, by fighting to maintain Iowa's early presidential caucus date. Democrat David Nagle, who served in the 1980s, staved off incursions by other states and the

Democratic National Committee (DNC) regarding the timing of the Iowa caucuses. In 1995 GOP chair Brian Kennedy fought the same battle with Louisiana to maintain Iowa's first-in-the-nation status and lost.

## ORGANIZATIONAL DEVELOPMENT

Iowa's use of the presidential caucus, as well as its status since 1972 as the first in the nation, have fortified party organizations in the state. The caucuses have also reinforced some of the early qualities of the parties, especially their grassroots structure and factional nature.

Democratic rule changes precipitated by the 1968 Democratic nomination race and the chaotic national convention in Chicago made delegate selection in state party contests, both caucuses and primaries, more important. But the Iowa presidential caucuses took on added importance in 1972 when the Iowa Democratic Party, which traditionally had held its precinct caucuses in the middle of the nomination season, moved them to January 24 of that year. The effect, if not the intent, of the early precinct caucus date was to enhance the importance of the event. National attention, for the first time in presidential nomination politics, focused on Iowa.

Increased attention to the contest in Iowa encourages Iowans to participate. Party estimates put 1972 participation in the Democratic caucuses at 60,000 people, an increase of 22,000 from 1968 (Winebrenner 1983, 629). On the surface, this simply means that there are more people involved in nomination politics. But attendance takes on added significance from the perspective of the party organizations. The caucuses serve as the state parties' basic organizational tool; they are the means by which activists are channeled into the party organizations. As such, increased caucus attendance means a larger pool of activists for the parties.

The tie between the parties in Iowa and nomination politics was strengthened by the politics of 1976. Advisers to then Democratic-hopeful Jimmy Carter envisioned Iowa as a "golden opportunity" for their candidate. Carter campaigned in the state earlier than the rest of the field and developed a strong organization. Capitalizing on the attention Iowa had received in 1972, the state party organized a "dry run" caucus and a straw poll in the late summer of 1975. When Carter polled first, albeit not by a lot, national media attention followed (Witcover 1977). When Carter also prevailed in the real caucuses in 1976, the results helped establish the virtual unknown as a credible candidate.

The legacy of 1976 continues to influence the political parties in Iowa. First, candidates for the nomination have learned that while winning in Iowa will not guarantee nomination, it does pay to organize in Iowa and to campaign there early and frequently. These tactics help get supporters—who are also would-be party activists—to the caucus. This reinforces the managed grassroots quality of the Iowa parties. Second, the national media treat Iowa, like New Hampshire, its counterpart in presidential primary politics, as a testing ground. While this may or may not help a particular candidate, it works to the advantage of the parties. They are able to exploit nomination politics for financial gain in a variety of ways.

The party organizations will frequently piggyback state party fundraisers onto appearances by major candidates. [6] The state parties can also expect to receive contributions from candidates' PACs, which are interested in generating goodwill with the state party organizations. And the parties are successful in recruiting big-name presidential candidates, even for local events in the state; hence, even minor events become good opportunities for fund raising. Finally, within the constraints of federal campaign finance laws, the parties can make money by selling their services to a candidate's nomination campaign.

Because of the benefits that they receive, the parties in Iowa have fought hard to maintain their first-in-the-nation status. State law adopted in 1983 dictates that presidential caucuses will be scheduled to preserve their early position.[7] A heated debate surrounded the 1996 GOP contest and Louisiana's challenge to Iowa's early date. [8]

The state parties receive greater rewards from nomination politics when competition is high. The national media usually begin to establish a presence in Iowa about eighteen months before the caucuses if the race is competitive. Presidential hopefuls spend more time and money in the state than they would under other circumstances. And interest in the race, coupled with personal appeals by candidates or their surrogates, helps inflate attendance at the caucuses. Although still a small percentage of registered voters in Iowa, well over 100,000 might attend a party's precinct caucuses in a competitive year.

Indeed, the parties suffer when there is not a real nomination race; 1992 was difficult for both parties. Incumbent president George Bush dominated the Republican field. Democratic nomination politics, although competitive nationally, was controlled in Iowa by Tom Harkin, U.S. senator from the state. Hence, other Democratic hopefuls wrote the state off. Although Harkin's candidacy was met with enthusiasm by Iowans, it did little to help the state parties or, for that matter, the state economy, which also reaps the commercial benefits of politicking in the state.

Without question, the parties suffer financially when the race is not competitive, but other effects on the parties are less clear. There is reason to question the impact of lower attendance on the composition of the parties and their platforms. One argument suggests that regardless of attendance, politics stays the same: "The platform will be the same. The 'regulars' will still drive the process" (Kochel 1995). At the same time, the precinct caucuses provide a stepping-stone for new activists to become the "regulars."

Current factionalism within Iowa's GOP has been facilitated by inroads that new activists made in the presidential caucuses in 1988. The contemporary split within the GOP is between the religious right and mainstream Republicans. The caucuses have contributed to the organizational rise of the right and, in this sense, they have sustained the factional quality that has marked the GOP since its birth.

## CURRENT PARTY ORGANIZATION

The state parties in Iowa are centralized in Des Moines, the state capital, with power distributed between the state central committees and the state chairs. Both the Republican Party of Iowa and the Iowa Democratic Party have state chairs who, in effect, run the parties. But in both cases the chairs are technically selected by the central committees.

The Republican State Central Committee is composed of three members from each of Iowa's five congressional districts and the national committeeman and national committeewoman from Iowa. The central committee, after the biennial general election, elects the state chair and the other executive officers of the party.

The constitution of the Iowa Democratic Party specifies that the state convention, which is held in even-numbered years, is the supreme governing body of the party. When the convention is not in session, which is the vast majority of the time, the state central committee governs the party. The Democratic State Central Committee, like its GOP counterpart, includes representatives from each congressional district. The Democratic State Central Committee also includes representatives from minority groups and organizations within the party, as well as the national committeepersons. But, as with the Republican state chair, the Democratic chair and the staff that he or she selects run the state party.

The state parties in Iowa are and have been for some time professional and well managed. This description applies most accurately to their involvement in electoral politics. However, they tend not to be professional or bureaucratic in the sense that scholars of parties have come to expect.

The Iowa Democratic Party has been administered by a full-time state chair only since 1993; the Republican position is still part-time. The Democratic constitution specifies that the chair must indicate the terms of his or her service when running for election. In 1993 Eric Tabor ran and was elected on a platform that included full-time service with commensurate pay. Tabor served one two-year term. The two candidates for the seat vacated by Tabor in 1994 also proposed full-time service; the winner, Mike Peterson, has served in that capacity.

The Iowa Democratic Party is moving toward permanent professional staffing. In the past, the professional staff turned over with the state chair. Now there are approximately six professional staff members who are expected to remain across tenures of state chairs.

The activities of the state parties are oriented almost exclusively toward electoral politics. The parties identify and recruit candidates and raise funds. The party structure is used as a building block by campaign organizations. And the party organizations will frequently go to work for their candidates by attacking opponents. The concentration on electoral politics rather than party-building helps explain why Iowa's parties, though vital organizations in the state's politics, are seen by scholars as only moderately weak or moderately strong organizations. They simply do not meet the standards of either traditional patronage-based organizations or highly bureaucratized structures.[9]

The relationship between the parties in Iowa and their national counterparts is typical of that seen with other small midwestern states in that the state parties have little leverage over their national organizations. The one difference involves presidential nomination politics. The Iowa Democratic Party, in particular, has been able to hold its own in standoffs with the DNC. In 1984, for example, Democrats in Iowa aligned with those in Maine and New Hampshire to preserve the nomination schedule in a struggle against Charles Manatt and the DNC. Buell (1987, 327–328) argues that the state party was able to muster strength from its direct ties with presidential campaigns: "What candidate would risk offending potential supporters in these crucial states for the sake of national party rules?"[10] Again, Iowa's use of the caucus-convention system influences the environment in which the parties operate.

The relationship between the county and the state organizations is similarly affected. In a fashion typical of state politics, the state parties expect contributions from the counties. In return, the local parties get organizational support from the state. Indeed, the recent movement toward permanence at state Democratic headquarters has likely increased the expectations of support. But the state is also inexorably tied to the counties because the local organizations provide the building blocks for the parties' platforms and state organizations. The path to controlling the state central committees and the state conventions begins at the local level.

The present distribution of power within the state organizations reflects these dynamics; the Republican case is particularly telling. Since 1992 the religious right has controlled the Republican State Central Committee. The Christian Coalition made initial inroads at the precinct level in 1988 when supporting its founder, Pat Robertson, in the Republican precinct caucuses. Committed activists, in a matter of a few years, worked their way up through the party apparatus.

The impact of the religious right is tempered somewhat by Republican Terry Branstad, who has served as governor since 1983. Branstad is the de facto leader of the state party. Although the Republican constitution vests power in the state central committee and the state chair, the governor has been able to maintain control and to secure his choice as state chair. But Branstad's power is unchecked largely because he is suitably conservative for, although not technically part of, the religious right. They have forged a successful alliance.

Another faction within the Republican Party of Iowa comprises farmers and agribusiness. Although its importance has decreased over time, this faction remains significant. Indeed, the Farm Bureau, active particularly in state legislative politics, and the Republican Party frequently share the same policy positions.

In the Iowa Democratic Party there is presently no single base of power comparable to the religious right in the GOP. The party does have a strong nucleus of intellectual elites, many with solid ties to Iowa's academic communities, particularly the University of Iowa in Johnson County. And the Polk County Democrats from the Des Moines area have a history that includes machine politics; the organization still provides a slight blue-collar and leftist pull on the state Democratic Party.

The relationship between the state party organizations and their companions in elective office is characterized by a division of labor. Although the Republican governor leads his party, gubernatorial politics is not the same as party organizational politics. Similarly, although the interests of the legislative caucuses and the formal party organizations frequently overlap, the party caucuses in the Iowa House of Representatives and the Iowa Senate are the important partisan actors in legislative politics. The caucuses meet regularly when the legislature is in session; they even meet daily during peak periods of debate. But even though party leaders are in frequent contact with legislative leaders, the primary focus of the party organization is electoral politics.

## RESOURCE GUIDE

State Democratic and Republican Party headquarters have no archives per se. But they do have party files that scholars could gain access to. Republican records are housed in a general filing area within headquarters. The Democratic records are in the offices of individual staff members. Based on conversations with staff, it is safe to assume that the files of the Republicans would provide a stronger institutional memory. The Iowa Democratic Party is just beginning to establish permanent records.

The State Historical Society of Iowa possesses some party records. The Republican Party of Iowa donated materials from state headquarters covering a period from the 1970s to the 1980s. These materials are stored in 124 one-cubic-foot boxes. Although the contents are not cataloged, the boxes themselves are marked with handwritten labels. The labels are neither complete nor entirely accurate, but they give a sense of the contents of the box. Under the usual procedures of the historical society, staff members retrieve boxes from the archives for scholars. However, a researcher conceivably may gain access to the archives and identify the boxes to be retrieved.

The private papers of a number of individuals, containing material relating to the parties, are housed at the University of Iowa libraries in Iowa City. Various state party officials,

**Table 1**   Iowa Resource Guide

|  | Democrats | Republicans |
| --- | --- | --- |
| Archive | No | Yes |
| Location | — | State Historical Society |
|  |  | 600 East Locust |
|  |  | Des Moines,Iowa 50319 |
| Dates | — | 1970s and 1980s |
| Finding aid | — | No |
| Access | — | Public |
| Contents: |  |  |
|   Executive committee minutes | — | Some |
|   Correspondence | — | Some |
|   Organizational structure | — | Some |
|   Budgets | — | Some |

politicians, political activists, and journalists have donated their papers. These collections are indexed in *The National Union Catalog of Manuscript Collections.* Catalog indexes from 1959 through 1993 identify approximately twenty-five such collections. The material relating to the parties is contained in collections that range in size from one- to two hundred boxes. The following materials, among others, are in the holdings and relate to both parties: records of party meetings and conventions, party reports, campaign literature, convention speeches, information regarding candidates, clippings, and photos. Gubernatorial and senatorial office files on the Democratic Party are also in the collections.

In addition to the official party records, the historical society archives material that the parties submit to the state. For example, the Code of Iowa (section 43.111) mandates that the parties file copies of their constitutions and bylaws with the state commissioner of elections. Then, in accord with the *State Records Manual,* the office of the commissioner of elections deposits its records with the state archives.

The *Iowa Official Register* is another useful information source. It has been published since 1886, biennially now and for most of its history, and is available in most libraries in the state. Known widely as "The Red Book," this volume has in various editions presented information about the state parties, including the names of state party officials, central committee membership, platforms, and precinct caucus results.

The Iowa historical society has a collection of party-related items, some of which it displayed in a 1992 exhibit entitled "Winnowing the Field: Candidates, Caucuses, and Presidential Campaigns in Iowa." Included in this collection are party ballots, campaign medals and buttons, state convention badges, campaign flyers, and other political artifacts from the nineteenth-century through the present. Most of these artifacts were donated to the historical society by private individuals. As such, there is marked imbalance—in favor of Republican artifacts—in premodern materials. Most of the items are stored in drawers, and a researcher can secure access to these by working through exhibit curator Jack Lufkin. Lufkin makes a concerted effort to collect items from contemporary presidential nomination candidates in Iowa.

Scholars of Iowa parties and politics have also generated data sets that may be available for analysis. The Inter-university Consortium for Political and Social Research at the University of Michigan holds data on presidential nomination activists in Iowa for the period 1980–1992, collected by Alan I. Abramowitz, John McGlennon, Ronald B. Rapoport, and Walter J. Stone. These data are also available directly through Stone at the Social

Science Data Lab, University of Colorado. Researchers may also contact James L. Hutter at Iowa State University to discuss the feasibility of using his data set on the representative quality of 1980 convention delegates in relation to caucus attendees.

Those interested in the current parties in Iowa may look to on-line sources. The results of a 1995 survey regarding candidate support of likely 1996 Republican caucus attendees were available in 1995 under the title "The Iowa Project—1996" on the World Wide Web at the following site: *http://www.netins.net/showcase/iowaproject96*. Presently, both the Democratic and Republican state parties have homepages.

## NOTES

1. Gannaway (1903) and Hahn (1971) each document the formation and early activities of the parties in Iowa.
2. See Hahn (1971) for a discussion of this tradition and the urban-rural division in Iowa politics.
3. Ryan (1981) empirically investigates this and other explanations.
4. See Winebrenner (1983) for a thorough description of the various methods that have been used for party nomination.
5. See Larew (1980) for a complete review of the revival of the Iowa Democratic Party.
6. A 1995 straw-poll event sponsored by the Republican Party of Iowa and attended by ten candidates reportedly raised more than $250,000 for the state party (*Des Moines Register*, August 20, 1995.)
7. Section 43.4 of the Code of Iowa 1995 reads as follows: "The date shall be at least eight days earlier than the scheduled date for any meeting, caucus or primary which constitutes the first determining stage of the presidential nominating process in any other state, territory or any other group which has the authority to select delegates in the presidential nomination."
8. The 1996 schedule had Louisiana's initial nominating event, congressional district caucuses, six days before Iowa's February 12 precinct caucuses. The Republican Party of Iowa, in an effort to block the Louisiana caucuses, appealed unsuccessfully to the U.S. Department of Justice. Iowa Republicans argued that Louisiana had scheduled its caucuses in violation of the Voting Rights Act, which governs electoral activity in southern states.
9. Cotter et al. (1984) classify the Iowa Democratic Party as moderately weak and the Republican Party of Iowa as moderately strong in terms of organization in the late 1970s. In Mayhew's (1986) assessment, Iowa scores very low (one on a scale of one to five) on the measure of traditional party organization.
10. Buell (1987) provides a detailed account of the 1984 timing debate and the exemption granted to Iowa by the DNC to its Rule 10A, which establishes the basic window for Democratic nomination contests.

## REFERENCES

*Asterisks denote the most important publications on Iowa party politics.*
Buell, Emmett H., Jr. 1987. First-in-the-nation: Disputes over the timing of early Democratic presidential primaries and caucuses in 1984 and 1988. *Journal of Law and Politics* 4:311–342.
Cotter, Cornelius P., James L. Gibson, John F. Bibby, and Robert J. Huckshorn. 1984. *Party organizations in American politics.* New York: Praeger.
*Des Moines Register.* 1995. It's a tie! Voters pick Dole, Gramm. August 20, A1.
*English, Emory H. 1948. Evolution of Iowa voting practices. *Annals of Iowa* 29:249–289.
Gannaway, John W. 1903. *The development of party organization in Iowa.* Iowa City: State Historical Society of Iowa.
*Hahn, Harlan. 1971. *Urban-rural conflict: The politics of change.* Beverly Hills: Sage.
Jewell, Malcolm E., and David M. Olson. 1988. *Political parties and elections in American states.* 3d ed. Chicago: Dorsey.
Kochel, David. 1995. Executive director of the Republican Party of Iowa. Interview by author, June 8.
*Larew, James C. 1980. *A party reborn: The Democrats of Iowa, 1950–1974.* Iowa City: Iowa State Historical Society.

Mayhew, David R. 1986. *Placing parties in American politics.* Princeton, N.J.: Princeton University Press.

Ryan, Thomas G. 1981. The early years of the Iowa Democratic revival, 1950–1956. *Annals of Iowa* 46:43–63.

Schier, Steven E. 1980. *The rules and the game: Democratic National Convention delegate selection in Iowa and Wisconsin.* Washington, D.C.: University Press of America.

*Squire, Peverill, ed. 1989. *The Iowa caucuses and the presidential nominating process.* Boulder, Colo.: Westview.

*Winebrenner, Hugh. 1983. The evolution of the Iowa precinct caucuses. *Annals of Iowa* 46:618–635.

Witcover, Jules. 1977. How Carter won the first battle. *Washington Monthly,* July/August, 68–75.

# Kansas

JOSEPH A. AISTRUP AND MARK BANNISTER

## PARTY HISTORY

The history of Kansas political parties is colorful and nationally significant. Kansas political parties played major roles in defining the People's Party movement during the late 1800s and the Progressive movement that followed in the late 1890s and early 1900s (Hicks 1931; Sundquist 1983, chs. 6–8). The confluence of these two movements within the state led William Allen White to write his seminal editorial "What's the Matter with Kansas?" in which he criticized populist politics in the state.

Though Kansas has this tradition for initiating party reforms, for most of its history it has been a bastion of Republicanism. Until the late 1950s the Kansas Democratic Party was only a minor force in state-level politics. Because of its strong Republican base, Kansas has been an incubator for powerful national Republican leaders such as Charles Curtis, Alf Landon, Dwight Eisenhower, Robert Dole, and Nancy Landon Kassebaum. Despite Democratic gains since 1960, the GOP has continued to control most state elections (see Table 1). The GOP dominated the 1994 elections, sweeping all four congressional seats, the governorship, the attorney general's office, and a substantial majority of the state house of representatives.

The Republicans' base of support emanates from two geographic areas of Kansas—the western half of the state (with the exception of Ellis County) and Johnson County. The western half of Kansas is an agricultural region, and Johnson County is a wealthy suburb of Kansas City, on the eastern border of the state. Both areas have overwhelmingly white populations, minimal union membership, strong probusiness attitudes, and moderate-to-conservative social attitudes.

Though the GOP controls the state, meaningful Democratic opposition has risen in the last thirty-five years of Kansas party politics (Heil 1983, ch. 2; Loomis 1994, 18–19). The state Democratic Party began developing with the election of Democratic governor George Docking in 1956 and 1958, and its development accelerated with the four successive gubernatorial victories by his son, Robert Docking, from 1966 through 1972. The Docking family established the Democratic Party as a permanent fixture in Kansas politics by building on

**Table 1**  Republican Party Strength in Kansas

| Year | Percent voting Republican for: | | | Percent of seats controlled by GOP in: | |
|------|----------|-------------|--------------------|--------------|-------------|
|      | Governor | U.S. senator | U.S. representative | State senate | State house |
| 1960 | 56 | 55 | 83 | 80 | 66 |
| 1962 | 53 | 62 | 100 | — | 71 |
| 1964 | 51 | — | 100 | 68 | 65 |
| 1966 | 44 | 52 | 100 | — | 61 |
| 1968 | 48 | 60 | 100 | 80 | 70 |
| 1970 | 45 | — | 80 | — | 67 |
| 1972 | 37 | 71 | 80 | 68 | 64 |
| 1974 | 50 | 51 | 80 | — | 58 |
| 1976 | — | — | 60 | 53 | 48 |
| 1978 | 47 | 54 | 80 | — | 55 |
| 1980 | — | 64 | 80 | 60 | 58 |
| 1982 | 44 | — | 60 | — | 58 |
| 1984 | — | 76 | 60 | 60 | 61 |
| 1986 | 52 | 70 | 60 | — | 59 |
| 1988 | — | — | 60 | 55 | 54 |
| 1990 | 43 | 74 | 60 | — | 49 |
| 1992 | — | 63 | 50 | 65 | 53 |
| 1994 | 63 | — | 100 | — | 64 |

SOURCES: *Guide to U.S. Elections,* 3d ed. (Washington, D.C.: Congressional Quarterly, 1994); *Statistical Abstract of the United States,* 113th ed. (Washington, D.C.: Government Printing Office, 1993). Other editions used include the 87th, 91st, 97th, 101st, and 106th.

the Democrats' natural base of support in the south central part of the state around Wichita (based largely on union membership), the northeastern part of the state, principally Wyandotte County, and other semiurbanized counties like Cowley County (home of the Robert Docking family), Crawford County, and Ellis County (Heil 1983). The Democrats controlled the governorship for twenty of thirty-five years between 1960 and 1995. Other Democratic successes included gaining control of the state house in the 1976 elections and again in the 1990 elections. However, the Democrats have not won a U.S. Senate contest since the Great Depression.

## ORGANIZATIONAL DEVELOPMENT

Traditionally, the Kansas Republican Party has been the stronger of the two state organizations. In Cotter et al.'s (1984, 28–29) study of state party organizational strength for the period 1975–1980, the Kansas Republican Party ranked twenty-first, whereas the Kansas Democratic Party ranked seventieth. However, in the 1990s, the state organizations have grown closer in strength (see Table 2).

Both the Republican and Democratic Parties expend much energy on candidate-centered activities. The main difference between the two is that the Republicans stress state legislative contests, allowing their gubernatorial and congressional candidates to run self-supporting campaigns with minimal coordination by the state party. In contrast, Democrats engage in candidate-centered activities at all levels and perform many traditional organizational functions, including get-out-the-vote drives. The Kansas Democratic Party prefers to focus on what Executive Director Lynette Shaw (1995) terms "common denominator" functions—activities designed to benefit all Democratic candidates in a given geographic area.

**Table 2**  Comparison of Kansas State Party Organizational Functions

| Party organizational functions | Democratic Party | Republican Party |
|---|---|---|
| Permanent headquarters | Yes | Yes |
| Branch offices | None | None |
| Full-time professionals | Four: executive director, liaison, county outreach, fund raising | Two: executive director (currently vacant), organizational director |
| Temporary, election-year professionals | Four: coordinator of campaigns, field director, communications director, direct-mail coordinator | Two: legislative coordinator, receptionist |
| Professional contract consultants | None | Contract with consultants to coordinate direct-mail and telephone fund raising |
| Election-year budget | $556,000 | $451,000 |
| Nonelection-year budget | $200,000 | $200,000 |
| Sources of funds | Sustaining clubs, 50%; party gatherings, 10%; direct mail, 40% | Direct mail, most; telemarketing, some; party gatherings, little |
| Get-out-the-vote activities | Yes: organize and train volunteer groups in 25 counties | Yes: in targeted state legislative districts |
| Newsletter publishing | Quarterly to wide audience; monthly to county chairs | Sometimes, depending on state party chair |
| Candidate recruitment | Use county committees to set up teams to work with state legislative caucuses for recruiting state legislative and county-level candidates | Focus on state legislative candidates |
| Candidate training | Provide workshops and manuals on how to run a campaign and raise funds effectively, including direct-mail techniques | Provide campaign and fund-raising workshops for state legislative candidates |
| Candidate fund raising | Not directly | Only for targeted races |
| Candidate polling | Some multicandidate cooperative polling | Some multicandidate cooperative polling |
| Election law compliance training | No | Yes, provide seminar and assistance |
| Assistance to counties | County outreach director works with central committees to provide training manuals, help with candidate recruitment, put on precinct workshops, and develop two-year plans. Coordinate with counties for get-out-the-vote drives | Provide assistance as requested which includes fund raising, get-out-the-vote drives, and providing program information |

From the end of World War II to the late 1970s, both state organizations were largely ori-ented toward electing governors (Dreiling 1995; Bennett 1995). With gubernatorial elections occurring every two years, there was little time for the state organizations to do anything else. That both parties lacked permanent state offices reinforced this pattern of organizing every two years to nominate and run a candidate for the governorship. Focus on the gover-norship began to abate only after the two state parties established permanent headquarters in the late 1960s and early 1970s and the governorship became a four-year term in 1974. Taken together, these changes meant that the state parties had the organizational capacity and the time to pursue other activities.

*Republican Party.* The Kansas Republican Party was first to break from its gubernatorial orientation. Heated gubernatorial primaries in 1974, 1982, and 1986 contributed to the shift in organizational focus because the party could not deploy behind a gubernatorial candidate until after the August primary. Instead of expending energy on the gubernatorial level, the Republican Party focused its early election cycle efforts on lesser statewide offices, congressional elections, and state legislative contests. The party's candidate-directed activities began with swapping volunteer and contributor lists in the late 1970s, expanded to giving token monetary support to state legislative candidates in the early 1980s (Bennett 1995), and finally blossomed in the late 1980s into a concerted effort to help state legislative candidates through training seminars for rookies and vulnerable incumbents (Pishny 1995). Also, in 1988 and 1990 the state Republican organization began targeting its resources toward specific races where a Democratic incumbent was vulnerable or where there was an open seat (Pishny 1995). By 1990 state party assistance included formal education about campaign finance laws and some political polling.

Significantly, the Docking years (1967–1974) were a time of famine for Kansas Republicans. Raising the resources necessary to engage in meaningful activities for statewide candidates was difficult without a GOP governor (Bennett 1995). A couple of factors helped the party out of its hole. First, Republican Robert Bennett was elected governor in 1974, which enabled the party to leverage the governorship to raise money (Bennett 1995). Second, like most state Republican Party organizations, the Kansas party was aided by the Republican National Committee's (RNC) push to professionalize GOP state organizations in the wake of the Watergate affair (Cotter et al. 1984). In the mid-1970s, the RNC began funneling large sums of money to the Kansas Republican Party, thereby freeing state party resources for collecting and disseminating donor, volunteer, and voter lists (Bennett 1995). Also during this time, the RNC commissioned state polls to help state GOP candidates gauge the mood of the public (Bennett 1995).

By the late 1970s, Republicans possessed the resources necessary to conduct direct-mail fund-raising campaigns. A Democratic Party fund-raising letter from the early 1980s lamented that the Republicans had a ten-year lead in using computer technology (Kansas Democratic Party 1981). The development of direct mail did much to ensure a steady source of income for the party. By 1990 the Kansas Republican Party had begun to use telemarketing to enhance fund-raising efforts.

In 1995 the state Republican Party had two full-time staff members: an executive director and an organizational director. It spent about $451,000 in the 1994 election cycle (Republican State Committee 1994). In 1995 it expected to spend about $200,000 on various activities (Lintz 1995). The state Republican Party appears to be in transition from relying on paid staff to perform certain functions to contracting with consultants. For example, in 1995 the party contracted for direct-mailing and telemarketing services. Consultants allow the party to tap into a reservoir of talent without the difficulty of finding, hiring, and training people during the peak of the election cycle only to dismiss them after the election. This organizational change appears to be influenced by Senator Dole, whose support organization is sophisticated at running presidential campaigns. Key state Republican Party staff members such as Steve Brown, who was executive director from 1991 to 1995, have rotated back and forth to Dole's presidential election staff. Many of the consultants presently employed by the state party have worked for Dole's presidential campaigns.

*Democratic Party.* Until the mid-1960s the Kansas Democratic Party and its county organizations were all but meaningless. Years of Republican dominance meant that much of the Democratic Party structure existed only to dispense presidential patronage (Dreiling 1995). The party began to develop into a significant entity during Robert Docking's reign as governor. Using his connections with the state party chair, Norbert Dreiling (1966–1974), Docking used the state party in his gubernatorial election bids as a conduit between his campaign and the county organizations (Dreiling 1995). Democratic county organizations were charged with turning out the vote and performing other campaign-related activities for Docking.

In 1970 the state party headquarters became permanent and the organization started to become more professional, hiring a full-time executive secretary (a title later changed to executive director) (Bird 1995). The Kansas Democratic Party at this time was oriented toward an interesting combination of "machine politics," "retail politics," and "candidate-centered politics." Its main activities were turning out the vote for governor, campaigning for the governor, and distributing party campaign materials. The county chairs were kept active through personal contact (either by Governor Docking or Dreiling), through recommending patronage appointments, and through the granting of minor state contracts (Dreiling 1995; Bird 1995; Bennett 1995). However, during this time the state Democratic Party did not extensively recruit state legislative and county-level candidates because finding Democratic candidates in GOP-dominated areas of the state was a still difficult task for the state organization. Nor did it extensively engage in modern "wholesale" political activities, such as direct-mail fund raising, campaign advertising, or polling, though the party did engage in some of these activities to a minor degree (Dreiling 1995).

Building on the solid base of support developed during the Docking years, the state Democratic Party evolved from its focus on Democratic gubernatorial campaigns after 1972. The Democratic gubernatorial campaign of Vern Miller, who lost in 1974, was run without the aid of the state organization largely because of a rift between Miller and Governor Docking. Dreiling resigned before the 1974 election, effectively removing the Docking-built state organization as a campaign resource for Miller (Dreiling 1995; Bird 1995). Democratic governor John Carlin, who won in 1978, ran his gubernatorial campaign independently of the state organization, and some believe that he ignored the state party's input involving his administrative appointees (Bird 1995).

During the period between 1974 and 1985, the state party began diversifying its operations to include other campaign and organizational activities. In particular, the county organizations, originally formed to help elect Docking, became effective organizations for recruiting and electing state legislators and congressional candidates (Bird 1995). After the 1976 election, the Democrats had a one-seat majority in the lower state house. Though this one-seat majority was short lived, it was testimony to the effective organization that Docking had built around his gubernatorial campaigns. In 1981 state party chair Thomas Corcoran raised funds to buy computers for direct-mail fund raising (Kansas Democratic Party 1981). In 1985, under the direction of Jim Parrish, the state Democratic Party assembled manuals for candidates on how to run campaigns and win elections (Bird 1995). In the 1990s it made computer software available primarily to county-level candidates to facilitate targeted mailing and voter analysis (Bird 1995).

The state party's current activities reflect its roots as a minority party without a strong base of support in the counties. Compared to the Republicans, whose county base is more secure, the Democrats focus more on training subnational candidates and assisting county organizations with the recruitment and training of candidates. The state party does not offer to candidates assistance with election-law compliance or direct help with fund raising, although it does provide advice (see Table 2).

The state Democratic organization is permanently staffed with four full-time personnel: an executive director, liaison coordinator, county outreach coordinator, and fundraiser.

During an election year, the staff expands by four people—coordinator of campaigns, field director, communications director, and direct-mail coordinator—allowing the state organization to engage in additional campaign-related activity. During the 1994 election cycle, the Democrats spent over $556,000 on organizational and campaign-related activities (Kansas Democratic Party 1994). In 1995 about $200,000 was budgeted (Shaw 1995).

## CURRENT PARTY ORGANIZATION

Reflecting the party structure once mandated by law, both parties possess almost identical hierarchies, with a state party chair, a state party central committee, executive directors, and finally the state organization. The state party chairs have effective control of the operations of the state organizations, with the central committees providing policy direction as well as final approval for budgetary decisions. The executive directors control the daily administrative operations for their respective party organizations.

In both parties, the chair, vice chair, and other party officers are elected by party delegates to congressional district caucuses. Each county in a congressional district sends to the congressional district party caucus its chair and vice chair as well as two at-large delegates. Both parties' state central committees are composed of the elected party officers (chair and vice chair), one elected representative from each congressional district chosen at the congressional district caucus, representatives of the party's elected national officials and governor (if applicable), and representatives from youth organizations, minority groups, and other important constituencies.

*Democratic Party.* Decision making in the Kansas Democratic Party depends largely on who is in control of the governorship. In the absence of a Democratic governor, the chair exercises much control over the state party organization, naming the executive director and determining policy directives and organizational focus (within the confines of the state party platform). When there is a Democratic governor, he or she exercises much control over the state organization, effectively anointing the state party chair. During Docking's years, Dreiling was appointed by Docking, and his role was to cover the governor's back, make partisan statements that appealed to Democratic Party faithful, and rally the troops in support of the governor. Other elected officials in the state followed the lead of the governor and state party chair. This relationship between the governor and party chair differed in both of the succeeding Democratic administrations.

After Carlin was elected governor in 1978, the Kansas Democratic Party rebelled against his anointed party chair because many party faithful felt that Carlin had not used the party in his election campaign and had not consulted the party in making administrative appointments (Bird 1995). Though Carlin finally did appoint his own chair, Jim Parrish, in his second administration, the rift between the state party and the governor meant that the party did not benefit from the accelerated fund raising that usually accompanies the election of a governor.

The relationship between the governor and state party chair also changed after Democrat Joan Finney was elected governor in 1990. Though Finney successfully appointed her own state chair, John Bird, this appointment was not accomplished without a political compromise with other Democratic state leaders that enabled the existing executive director to continue in the post. This was a harbinger of a prolonged struggle between the Democratic state legislative leadership (Jerry Karr, senate minority leader, and Marvin Barkus, house speaker), the Finney administration, and the state party organization. This struggle prevented the state party from effectively recruiting and assisting state legislative candidates (Bird 1995). Though the Democrats won the governorship and lower state house in 1990, the rift within the Democratic Party contributed to the GOP's regaining control over the lower state house in 1992.

*Republican Party.* The Kansas Republican Party operates in much the same fashion as the state Democratic Party. When there is a Republican governor, the state chair is anointed by the governor. However, after the election of Republican governor Bill Graves in 1994, this tradition came to a sudden halt. The change is rooted in the rise of Christian fundamentalists in the state party. Since Pat Robinson's presidential campaign in 1988, the Christian fundamentalists have engaged in a grassroots campaign to take control of the state party. Christian fundamentalists in Wichita have been the most successful—building off the strong antiabortion activities of Operation Rescue within the city to displace longtime activists from leadership positions (Bates 1995, 1). In Johnson County, former state representative and social conservative leader Kerry Patrick has played a major role in determining Johnson County GOP activity (Gravino 1995, A1). Patrick provided a glimpse of future fundamentalist intraparty activity by challenging and losing to moderate Republican congresswoman Jan Meyers in the 1994 congressional primary. By 1995 the Christian fundamentalists had built up enough strength to control three of four state party congressional district delegations and a majority of the Republican State Central Committee (Hanna 1995).

In early 1995 socially conservative former state representative David Miller was elected state party chair without Graves's blessing. Graves and Miller have had a number of public disagreements highlighted by a battle over whether the Kansas Republican Party should write a platform for the 1996 election. In 1994 Graves used his influence to set aside the drafting of a platform, fearing a party split over abortion. Pushing a socially conservative agenda, Miller is ignoring Graves's wishes to put aside drafting a platform for the 1996 elections (Hanna 1995). When the governor was asked about the state organization's role in his possible reelection bid, he said:

> I think candidates create their own campaigns. You surround yourself with your own team of supporters and volunteers, and I guess I am not one who is overly convinced that successes at the polling place are directly attributable to the party structure. I have the organization that supported me in the primary and general elections last year (Hanna 1995).

From an analytical perspective, the rifts within both parties are significant because they may lead researchers to confuse organizational capacity with organizational strength. Researchers need to be aware that though a party organization may appear "strong" on the basis of various activities that the party pursues (capacity), conflict within the party can stifle the ability of the organization to use its capacity in an effective way.

In addition, the Christian fundamentalists' insurgency into the Kansas Republican Party is significant in light of other state GOP organizations that have come to be dominated by social conservatives (Aistrup 1995, ch. 7). If Graves is reelected despite an open rift between himself and the state organization, it would suggest that the state party is a minor player is state electoral politics. To the extent that other state organizations across the country are experiencing the same type of conflict, the outcomes of gubernatorial elections are a direct test of the influence of state party organizations and their importance in affecting election outcomes. An empirical test of this nature would shed much light on the party renewal debate in regard to the significance of these renewed party organizations.

**Table 3**  Kansas Resource Guide

| | Materials at the Kansas Historical Society | |
|---|---|---|
| | *Democrats* | *Republicans* |
| Archive | Yes | Yes |
| Location | 6425 SW 6th Ave. | 6425 SW 6th Ave. |
| | Topeka, Kan. 66615 | Topeka, Kan. 66615 |
| Dates | 1968 sporadically onward | 1885 sporadically onward |
| Finding aid | Some materials cataloged; | Some materials cataloged; |
| | most uncataloged | most uncataloged |
| Campaign finance and | Two most recent election cycles | Two most recent election cycles |
| spending records | located in the secretary of state's | located in the secretary of state's |
| | office in Topeka | office in Topeka |
| Access | Public | Public |
| Contents: | | |
|   Executive committee minutes | No | Sporadic |
|   Correspondence | 1977–1981 | Sporadic |
|   Organizational structure | 1977–1981 | Sporadic |
|   Budgets | 1977–1981 | Sporadic |
|   Rules | Sporadic | Sporadic |
| | Materials at the State Party Headquarters | |
| Location | Kansas Democratic Party | Kansas Republican Party |
| | 700 SW Jackson | 2348 SW Topeka Blvd. |
| | Topeka, Kan. 66603 | Topeka, Kan. 66611-1286 |
| | (913) 234-0425 | (913) 234-3436 |
| Dates | 1982–present (materials may be | 1980–present |
| | taken to Kansas Historical Society) | |
| Finding aid | No | No |
| Access | By appointment and permission | By appointment and permission |
| | of party staff | of party staff |
| Contents: | | |
|   Executive committee minutes | Sporadic | Yes |
|   State committee minutes | Sporadic | Yes |
|   Correspondence | Yes | Yes |
|   Organizational structure | Yes | Yes |
|   Budgets | Yes | Yes |
|   Rules | Yes | Yes |

*Party Political Action Committees.* In 1990 the state legislative leadership of both parties formed legislative party PACs (Republican House Campaign Committee, Republican Senatorial Committee, Kansans for a Democratic House, and Democratic Senatorial Committee). Control of these party PACs rests with each party's legislative leadership in each respective chamber. These PACs are active in recruiting and disbursing money to state legislative candidates. In the 1994 house elections, the Republican House Campaign Committee spent almost $80,000 (Republican House Campaign Committee 1994), while Kansans for a Democratic House spent $133,000 (Kansans for a Democratic House 1994). In 1992 Senate majority leader Paul "Bud" Burke used the Republican Senatorial Committee in combination with his "President's Club" to recruit women and minority candidates to challenge Democratic incumbents and run in open seats. His efforts were successful, as six additional Republican seats gave the GOP a 27–13 majority in the state senate.

Both state party organizations prefer to think of these legislative PACs as extensions of the party organization (Shaw 1995). The significance of the legislative PACs is that they provide the house and senate leadership of both parties with an incentive structure to enhance party discipline. To the extent that the legislative PACs push the same policy agenda as the state organizations, the legislative PACs are extensions of the state organizations. However, when the policy focus of the state organization and its respective legislative PACs diverge, the party PACs compete with the state organization. In Kansas, the Republican Senatorial Campaign Committee is at policy odds with the socially conservative Kansas Republican Party. Senate president Burke is a strong supporter of Governor Graves. On the other hand, the Republican House Campaign Committee, which is controlled by house speaker Tim Shallenburger (an ally of the social conservatives), tends to agree with the socially conservative state party. All this suggests that at the pinnacle of the GOP's efforts in Kansas to beat back two decades of Democratic gains, the Republican leadership and respective state organizations are split over social issues. The GOP split may allow the state Democrats to become strong competitors once again in Kansas.

## RESOURCE GUIDE

Kansas political parties have generally focused on the issue or need at hand. Record retention and archival creation have not been priorities for either party. At the request of the Kansas Historical Society (the official state agency that retains state records), for the last several election cycles both parties have sent campaign materials to the society for preservation. Information from earlier eras regarding state party organizations has generally not been preserved in a concerted fashion.

The historical society is also the final repository of all state-required campaign finance reports—including those of the political parties. The Kansas secretary of state retains campaign finance records for the most recent two-year cycle.

## REFERENCES

*Asterisks denote the most important publications on Kansas party politics.*
Aistrup, Joseph A. 1996. The southern strategy revisited. Lexington: University Press of Kentucky.
*Averyt, Ronald A. 1970. The minority party in an uncompetitive state: The case of Kansas. Dissertation, University of Kansas.
Bates, Michael. 1995. Abortion foes become GOP activists. *Hay Daily News,* July 10, 1, 3.
Bennett, Robert. 1995. Republican governor of Kansas, 1975–1979, and chair of Kansas Republican Party, 1982–1983. Interview by authors, July 14.
Bird, John. 1995. Executive secretary, 1970–1974, and chair, 1991–1993, of Kansas Democratic Party. Interview by Joseph A. Aistrup, July 11.
Cotter, Cornelius P., James L. Gibson, John F. Bibby, and Robert J. Huckshorn. 1984. *Party organizations in American politics.* New York: Praeger.
Dreiling, Norbert. 1995. Chair of Kansas Democratic Party, 1966–1974. Interview by authors, June 15.
Gravino, Partice. 1995. Conservatives running the show in Johnson County GOP. *Hay Daily News,* July 11, A1, A6.
Hanna, John. 1995. Graves takes aim at GOP platform. *Topeka Capital-Journal,* June 17, 5B.
Harder, Marvin A. 1959. Some aspects of Republican and Democratic Party factionalism in Kansas. Dissertation, Columbia University.
*Harder, Marvin, and Carolyn Rampey. 1972. *The Kansas legislature.* Lawrence: University Press of Kansas.
*Heil, Richard P. 1983. Indices of party strength: The case of Kansas. Dissertation, University of Kansas.

*Hicks, John D. 1931. *The populists revolt: A history of the Farmers' Alliance and the People's Party.* Lincoln: University of Nebraska Press.

Kansans for a Democratic House. 1994. Election campaign financial reports of state candidates. Report filed with Office of Secretary of State, State of Kansas.

Kansas Democratic Party. 1994. Election campaign financial reports of state candidates. Report filed with Office of Secretary of State, State of Kansas.

Kansas Democratic Party. 1981. Uncataloged party correspondence. Kansas Historical Society.

Lintz, Gilda. 1995. Organization director of state Republican Party, 1980–present. Interview by Mark Bannister, June 12.

*Loomis, Burdett A. 1994. *Time, politics, and policies.* Lawrence: University Press of Kansas.

Mayhew, David R. 1986. *Placing parties in American politics.* Princeton, N.J.: Princeton University Press.

Nugent, Walter T. K. 1963. *The tolerant populists: Kansas, populism and nativism.* Chicago: University of Chicago Press.

Pishny, Lyle D. 1995. Vice chair of Kansas Republican Party, 1989–1990. Interview by authors, July 14.

Republican House Campaign Committee. 1994. Election campaign financial reports of state candidates. Report filed with Office of Secretary of State, State of Kansas.

Republican State Committee. 1994. Election campaign financial reports of state candidates. Report filed with Office of Secretary of State, State of Kansas.

Shaw, Lynette. 1995. Executive director of Kansas Democratic Party, 1995–present. Telephone interview by Joseph A. Aistrup, June 8.

Sundquist, James L. 1983. *The dynamics of the party system.* Washington, D.C.: Brookings Institution.

# Kentucky

PENNY M. MILLER AND
MALCOLM E. JEWELL

## PARTY HISTORY

Kentucky is a border state, and its political system has been similar to that in other border states. The Civil War, which deeply divided the state and often split up families, left a legacy that helped to shape the state's political party system for nearly a hundred years. The Democratic Party dominated Kentucky politics from the end of the Civil War until the early 1890s, in large part because of the impact of the Civil War and Reconstruction. The strongest base of Republican support was in the southeastern mountains, where slaveholding had been rare, and the Republican Party also commanded a substantial minority vote in some of the larger cities.

The presidential election of 1896 drove many conservative Democrats into the Republican camp and turned Kentucky into a strong two-party state in both presidential and gubernatorial contests. From 1896 through 1928 Kentucky was one of the most competitive two-party states in the country. The Republican Party won five of nine gubernatorial elections from 1895 through 1927. At the local level, however, at least three-fourths of the counties were consistently loyal to either one party or the other in national and state elections.

The 1932 election and Franklin Roosevelt's New Deal restored the Kentucky Democratic Party to its position of dominance in national and state elections for a period of twenty years. The Republican Party remained much stronger in Kentucky, however, than in states farther south, and won at least 40 percent of the vote in every presidential and gubernatorial election from 1932 through 1951. The Republican base of support continued to be strongest in the southeastern mountains and in some of the cities. In the 1950s the Republican Party began to make progress at the presidential level, nearly winning in 1952 and carrying the state for Dwight Eisenhower in 1956.

In state politics the Republican Party was less successful. From 1931 through 1963, the Republicans won only one gubernatorial election, in 1943. The weakness of the Republican Party in gubernatorial politics made the Democratic primary more important. The Democrats used a primary in almost all elections starting in 1903, and in 1935 the state legislature made the primary mandatory for both parties for all state and local partisan elections.

From the mid–1930s to the late-1960s, the Kentucky Democratic gubernatorial primaries were dominated by two factions. One was associated with "Happy" Chandler, who was elected governor in 1935 and 1955 and who either ran or endorsed a candidate in several other gubernatorial primaries. The most prominent leader of the other faction was Earle Clements, who was elected governor in 1947 and supported candidates in other races. The Kentucky Democratic factions were based on personalities and to some extent on geography, rather than ideology or issues. The statewide factional leaders formed alliances with politicians in the county parties, many of which were also split into factions. The local factions were also based on personalities and often represented simply the "ins" and the "outs." In Jefferson County, the largest county, containing Louisville, there was a particularly strong Democratic organization, which often played a key role in the statewide factional system (Jewell and Cunningham 1968).

Of the nine presidential elections from 1960 through 1992, Republican candidates carried Kentucky in six—all except 1964, 1976, and 1992. The Republicans also won six of the twelve senatorial elections during these years. From 1966 through 1990 they consistently held two or three of the seven House seats, and in 1994 they won four of the six House seats, including the two traditionally Democratic districts in western Kentucky. Despite this success in statewide and congressional elections, the Republican Party, after electing a governor in 1967, lost seven consecutive gubernatorial races from 1971 through 1995. It has not controlled either house of the legislature since 1920, and in recent years has often held less than one-third of the membership.

### ORGANIZATIONAL DEVELOPMENT

The Republicans' mixed record of electoral success since 1960 indicates the limited effectiveness of the Republican organization. Kentucky voters are conservative enough to vote Republican frequently in presidential and congressional races. But the state Republican organization has often failed to recruit and support strong candidates for governor. Only recently has it paid attention to the task of recruiting and supporting legislative candidates outside the geographical areas of traditional Republican strength.

Democratic factions virtually disappeared in gubernatorial primaries in the 1970s, and local organizations became less powerful. Gubernatorial candidates spent less time courting state and local politicians and more time building their own campaign organizations from the large pool of Democratic Party activists scattered across the state. The candidates who succeeded in building strong statewide organizations had a significant advantage in statewide Democratic primaries.

Gubernatorial primaries were largely fought out on television. Candidates who were wealthy, like Wallace Wilkinson in 1987 and John Y. Brown in 1979, and those who were capable of raising large sums of money, like Martha Layne Collins in 1983, had a big advantage in campaigns. They were able to buy lots of time on television and hire the most skilled media specialists to design their commercials. All three ran successful races for the governorship.

### CURRENT PARTY ORGANIZATION

*Democratic Party.* Kentucky's Democratic Party is no longer seriously divided into factions, but it is still dominated by a Democratic governor. The Democrats have a large and elaborate party structure that includes party bodies at the precinct, county, legislative district, congressional district, and state levels. As of mid–1996 the Democratic State Central Committee (DSCC), the highest decision-making body, had fifty-two voting members and seven ex officio members. The DSCC membership includes three men and three women from each of the six congressional districts, elected by the congressional district conventions; three national committee members and nine members from the state at-large, elected by the state convention; the chair, vice chair, legal counsel, and treasurer; two representatives from each of the Democratic legislative caucuses; and the presidents of the Kentucky Young Democrats and the Democratic Woman's Club. All statewide Democratic constitutional officers are ex officio members of the DSCC. In reality, power resides with the governor. The nomination of a new candidate for governor (Paul Patton in 1995) results almost instantly in a reorganization of state Democratic headquarters.

Governors in Kentucky are elected to four-year terms in the years preceding presidential election years. The formal process of selecting delegates to the Democratic National Convention begins early the next year (the presidential election year) with the election of precinct leaders, and it culminates at the state convention—about six months after the governor takes office, when his or her power is usually high and the energy and will to oppose the governor are correspondingly low. In theory the state convention, and in practice the governor, selects delegates to the national convention and selects some members of the DSCC. The state convention ratifies the appointment of the party chair and vice chair (Miller and Jewell 1990). During several recent administrations, considerable turnover has occurred in the chair; over a seventeen-year period from the summer of 1979 to the summer of 1996, thirteen different persons held the position of party chair.

The Democrats have a single office, in Frankfort, the state capital. Under normal conditions their permanent staff includes an executive/political director who takes instructions from the governor (or gubernatorial nominee) a part-time party chair, an office manager who works on the party's financial reports, and a secretary/receptionist. Their phone receptionists are volunteers, and there are usually also several student interns. The state party also hires consultants, particularly to do computer work.

The state party conducts various fund-raising activities to finance its $500,000-a-year budget, though about $120,000 comes from the state government under the taxpayer check-off plan; those funds are earmarked for salaries and upkeep of state headquarters, not for support to candidates. The continuing weakness of the party, the persistent slippage of the governor's power vis-à-vis the legislature, and the campaign finance reforms enacted between 1992 and 1994 have limited large contributions to the party. Legally, individuals can contribute as much as $2,500 a year to the state party, though any amount exceeding $1,000 must be used for the party's administrative costs rather than for campaigns.

Gov. Brereton Jones (1991–1995) was committed to revitalizing state party activities. But, with the rise of candidate-run campaigns—resulting from dwindling party funds, fewer party workers, and escalating campaign costs—there has been less interaction between party organizations and the campaign organizations of local, state, and national candidates. The declining availability of patronage, which is dispensed by the governor's office, also has weakened the state Democratic Party. Nonetheless, every four years the state party headquarters still becomes "election central" for statewide nominees and helps them with fund raising.

During the Jones administration, interaction between the state party and the party's legislative leaders was limited and at times hostile. The Democrat-dominated legislature was flexing its muscles, and its leaders did not want to be associated with the state party, which they perceived as the governor's vehicle. During the last three years of the administration, although the state party spent about $200,000 on legislative races, legislators raised less than $5,000 for the financially drained state party. Still, the state party, sometimes with legislators' assistance, tries to recruit viable legislative candidates and targets certain legislative races. In the summer of 1995 the state party, along with the House Democratic leadership, held some "town meetings" with lobbyists that were actually fundraisers for House Democratic candidates. The election of Paul Patton as governor in 1995 probably will make possible closer cooperation with the legislative leadership.

In addition to providing limited fund-raising assistance (up to $300,000 in 1995 for the state campaign), the Democratic National Committee (DNC) helped the state party professionalize its operations. The DNC assisted the Kentucky party with get-out-the-vote campaigns, generic party television spots, and candidate-training workshops. For its part, state party headquarters assists national candidates during presidential campaigns. Overall, the state party interacts as much with White House political consultants as with the DNC, which is viewed as primarily a national fund-raising vehicle for the president's reelection and congressional races.

During the early-to-mid-1990s the Democratic Party had a reasonably effective organization in at least two-thirds of Kentucky's counties, with some noticeable gaps in the heavily Republican Fifth Congressional District, in the southcentral and southeastern parts of the state. The real strength in each county usually lies with the executive committee and three or four prominent members. A key figure in each county is the "contact" person, who is designated by the governor to dispense patronage. The linkages have weakened between the state organization and the organizations in major urban counties such as Jefferson and Fayette. The general changes in the nature of patronage have especially hurt these counties.

*Republican Party.* Like the Democrats, the Republicans have a large and elaborate party structure, with precinct, county, congressional district, and state levels; at its apex is a state convention whose members are chosen in a process that begins at countywide meetings of the party faithful. The Republican State Central Committee (RSCC), some of whose members are elected by the state convention, is a huge body (fluctuating between 350 and 500 members); it is much larger than the DSCC. Most of the state party's work is carried out by the RSCC's executive committee. The executive committee, in turn, is controlled by a small group headed by the elected state chair and state vice chair, who, like their Democratic counterparts, must be of opposite gender. Unlike the DSCC, the RSCC tends to reflect the regional and ideological differences within the party because there is no sitting governor to oversee its selection and to enforce some measure of homogeneity.

The Republicans have a single office, in Frankfort. Under normal conditions, the permanent staff includes an executive director, political director, finance director, and administrative assistant. Moreover, there are usually several volunteer student interns. Through direct mail, telemarketing, and fundraisers, the state Republican Party organization raises the funds necessary to finance its $550,000-a-year budget, though about $80,000 of the budget comes from the state government under the taxpayer check-off plan. There is also an ongoing membership drive; in 1994 the party picked up more than three thousand new donors, each of whom contributed, on average, $35. The Republicans have a Golden Elephant Club for donors who contribute $1,000; they expected thirty to forty new members in 1995. Some financial help comes from the Republican National Committee (RNC); in the 1995 state election campaign RNC assistance totaled $500,000.

Other ongoing activities of the state GOP include: targeting races and helping with campaigns (for example, providing limited polling, fund raising, and media aid); recruiting candidates, especially for state legislative races; assisting the various local party organizations and Republican clubs; disseminating information; and conducting voter registration drives. With the rise of candidate-run campaigns, the state party has interacted less with campaign organizations.

One of the most serious weaknesses of the Republican Party has been its failure to field candidates for a large number of local and legislative seats. Since 1988 the state party organization has developed a targeting plan to identify the legislative districts in which the party has the best chance of winning. With the help of significant state GOP and RNC financial contributions in 1994, the Republicans made net gains in each chamber of the legislature—three seats in the senate and eight in the house; the Democrats' majority shrank to four seats in the Senate, 21–17, and twenty-six seats in the House, 63–37. The state party has limited but fairly positive interactions with the legislative party organization, which anticipated having in 1996 its best chance in modern times of winning control of the state senate.

In addition to aggregating data for targeting races, the RNC assists the state party in fund-raising activities, candidate training, and improving its operations. The national Republican Party recently has played a larger role in providing services to Republican hopefuls at all levels. In 1994 national money poured into congressional races in Kentucky's First and Second Congressional Districts. In turn, the state party organization assists presidential hopefuls financially and organizationally in their bids for Kentucky votes.

The state Republican Party has tried to increase its interactions with local organizations by providing financial incentives for effective county parties. Many counties outside of the Fifth Congressional District and large metropolitan areas of the Golden Triangle— Lexington, Louisville, and metropolitan northern Kentucky (including Covington and Newport)—have party organizations that are not viable; other counties have none at all. But in the 1995 gubernatorial campaign, for the first time every county had a viable campaign organization. The entry of Pat Robertson supporters into the Fayette County party apparatus has led to more instability of leadership, as well as to factional rivalries. In the

Jefferson County party there are sharp factional divisions between the moderates (many pro-choice) and the right-wing, pro-life conservatives; this cost the party a congressional seat in 1994.

Even more than the Democratic Party, the GOP reflects Kentucky's penchant for divisiveness. The Republican members of Congress in the last two decades—Larry Hopkins, Hal Rogers, Jim Bunning, and Mitch McConnell—developed their own power bases and political fiefdoms independent of the state Republican Party. However, Sen. Mitch McConnell was extremely helpful in providing strategic plans and fund-raising assistance to the Republican candidates in their First and Second Congressional District victories in 1994. Moreover, the entire GOP congressional delegation assisted Republican nominee Forgy in 1995, recognizing that he was the best hope for the Republicans to win the gubernatorial seat since 1967. However, the capture of the state party by the Christian Right–pro-life faction backed by Forgy was a source of dissension.

Another source of dissension in the Republican Party remains the wide diversity among areas of Republican strength within the state. The social and economic interests and the issue priorities of Republican constituents in the metropolitan centers of Louisville, Lexington, and northern Kentucky are quite different from those of the Republicans in Appalachian areas.

*Recent Reforms in the Election System.* The national "motor-voter" law, which offers people who apply for government services the opportunity to register to vote, has swollen Kentucky's voter registration to a record level and shrunk the Democratic Party's historical advantage. The rolls for the November 1995 election showed 2,248,246 potential voters. That was a gain of 174,907 since January 1, the effective date of the motor-voter law, which accounted for over three-fourths of the increase. Of the new registrants, 42 percent registered as Democrats, 33 percent as Republicans, and 24 percent chose no party. That trend helped reduce Democrats' share of registration by more than two percentage points in only eleven months, to 63.4 percent of the total. It gave the Republicans 30.7 percent, for a party ratio 2.1 to 1. About ten years earlier, the Democratic advantage was almost 2.5 to 1.

Electoral politics in Kentucky has been dramatically altered by the gubernatorial succession amendment of 1992, which mandated the slating of gubernatorial/lieutenant gubernatorial candidates and mandated a runoff primary if no slate received 40 percent of the primary vote. The ability of a governor to succeed him- or herself has implications for the dominant role of the governor as party leader: the governor is no longer certain to be a lame duck after only two years in office, and he or she is better able to maintain political control of the administration and party throughout the entire four-year term. In the four Democratic gubernatorial primaries from 1979 through 1991, the number of serious candidates had averaged just over four, and the percentage for the winning candidate had ranged from 29 to 38 percent.

Also in 1992 the legislature adopted a plan for partial public financing of races for governor and lieutenant governor and imposed a $1.8 million spending limit for each participating slate in the primary and a $1.8 million limit for each slate in the general election. With the greatly reduced contribution limits—$1,000 for individuals, PACs, and political parties per slate—special interests can no longer buy undue influence in Frankfort. The new laws also enhance the role of volunteers, party stalwarts, and grassroots labor and teacher organizations in campaigns. State parties are now limited by Kentucky law to $1,000 contributions to gubernatorial slates but are unlimited in other races. The state Democratic Party, however, raised over $1.5 million in 1995 and spent much of it on television messages and get-out-the-vote efforts to help the Democratic statewide campaigns. The Republicans raised about $800,000 for similar purposes. The two national parties contributed another $800,000 to the state parties.

The first Kentucky gubernatorial primary conducted with public financing and spending limits was less corrupt and considerably cheaper than previous primaries, with more candidate debate and minimal PAC involvement. In May 1995 the three Democratic slates that accepted public financing spent a total of $5.4 million, dramatically less than the $4.5 million and $2.2 million spent by the 1987 Democratic primary winners for governor and lieutenant governor, respectively. Total spending directly by candidates for governor and lieutenant governor in the primary and general elections in 1995 was less than half that spent in 1991.

The winner of the Democratic primary got 45 percent of the vote, making a runoff unnecessary. But the race set a record for the lowest voter turnout (20.5 percent) in a gubernatorial primary since the state started keeping track of such figures. Only 24 percent of registered Democrats and 17.7 percent of registered Republicans voted. Turnout in the 1995 gubernatorial general election was above average for recent elections.

The Republican Party is resurgent in Kentucky, which may become a true two-party state in statewide as well as congressional and presidential politics. Alienated Democrats in the First and Second Congressional Districts in western Kentucky are disassociating themselves from the party and either voting Republican or not voting at all in record numbers. In 1994 almost 59 percent of voters in the six congressional races voted for Republicans, a repudiation of more than one hundred years of party loyalties and probably the start of a long-term trend rather than a temporary aberration. There are also some signs of growing Republican strength in legislative races and in some local elections. Despite the resurgence of the Republican Party, Democrat Paul Patton defeated Republican Larry Forgy in the 1995 governor's race, but only by about 20,000 votes (roughly 2 percent of the votes cast).

### RESOURCE GUIDE

Neither the Democratic nor the Republican Party has an archive of party records that is easily accessible by scholars, that is organized, or that contains a comprehensive collection of executive committee records, budgets, rules, or correspondence for any significant period of time. Scattered collections of records and campaign materials, which have been collected intermittently by a few party officials, are all that exist.

The major problem in the Democratic Party seems to be that when a Democratic governor leaves office, his or her party leaders clean house and take most of their files with them. It is possible that some former party chairs still have such records. The Democratic Party headquarters has some records of state central committee meetings dating back to the early 1980s, and it retains a handful of log books each containing party records for a four-year period, some as old as the late 1800s and some quite recent. Academic scholars may use these volumes at Democratic Party headquarters.

The Republican Party has nothing resembling a record of party activities or minutes of central committee meetings, even for recent years. Apparently, a few of the most active party leaders in recent decades have kept personal records and correspondence related to the state party organization.

Information on political parties must be gleaned from various other sources; there are no specified party archives at the Kentucky Department for Libraries and Archives. The

Kentucky Historical Society in Frankfort and the Filson Club in Louisville maintain research libraries. The Division of Special Collections and Archives at the University of Kentucky library contains more than two thousand manuscripts of both obscure and renowned Kentuckians, including governors and statespeople. Most other Kentucky universities, public as well as private, maintain primary source collections—original manuscripts and papers of notable alumni or natives of those regions.

## REFERENCES

*Asterisks denote the most important publications on Kentucky party politics.*

Blanchard, Paul. 1964. Political parties and elections in Kentucky. In *Kentucky government and politics,* ed. Joel Goldstein, 141–169. Bloomington, Ind.: College Town Press.

Jewell, Malcolm E. 1963. *Kentucky votes.* 3 vols. Lexington: University of Kentucky Press.

*Jewell, Malcolm E., and Everett W. Cunningham. 1968. *Kentucky politics.* Lexington: University of Kentucky Press.

*Jewell, Malcolm E., and Penny M. Miller. 1988. *The Kentucky legislature: Two decades of change.* Lexington: University Press of Kentucky.

Jewell, Malcolm E., and Phillip W. Roeder. 1988. Partisanship in Kentucky: 1979–1986. In *The new South's politics: Realignment and dealignment,* ed. Robert H. Swansbrough and David M. Brodsky. Columbia: University of South Carolina Press.

*Miller, Penny M. 1994. *Kentucky politics and government: Do we stand united?* Lincoln: University of Nebraska Press.

*Miller, Penny M., and Malcolm E. Jewell, 1990. *Political parties and primaries in Kentucky.* Lexington: University Press of Kentucky.

# Louisiana

## T. WAYNE PARENT

## PARTY HISTORY

The emergence of a two-party system in Louisiana has been slow even when the state is compared with the other formerly Democratic states in the Deep South. Even after the 1994 Republican sweep in the South, Democrats controlled the governorship, both U.S. Senate seats, a majority of the congressional delegation, and substantial majorities of both houses of the state legislature and other statewide elected officials. Finally, in late 1995 after two congressional Democrats had switched parties and a Republican had been elected governor, Louisiana Republicans began to experience the Republican surge that had been sweeping the South.

Louisiana requires voter registration by party, and Louisiana voters register as Democrats by a two-to-one margin. Despite this record of control by the Democrats, the Louisiana Republican Party has emerged as a viable counterpart to the Democrats and has become competitive enough to have a real chance of winning elections at every level of government in the state.

In the aftermath of the Civil War and lasting into the first half of the twentieth century, a period in which Louisiana politics was defined by Democrats Huey and Earl Long and the Democratic reformers who opposed them, Democrats dominated elections at every level in Louisiana. Their dominance was broken in 1956, when Republican Dwight D. Eisenhower overcame a 1952 loss in Louisiana to Democrat Adlai Stevenson in the race for the presidency. Then, in 1964, Republican presidential candidate Barry Goldwater's opposition to civil rights legislation carried him to victory in the state. The Goldwater victory was a breakthrough because it included poor and working-class whites as part of the Republican coalition; these voters would be critical to Republican victories that followed. In the three decades since that election, Republicans periodically have won statewide office and consistently have won seats in Congress. Although the racial issues of the 1960s gave Republicans their first major opportunities in Louisiana, two other factors allowed for more solid long-term gains (Parent 1988; Lamis 1990). The economic message of the Republicans appealed to the growing suburban white middle class in Louisiana, and the conservative social agenda articulated by the Republicans appealed to many Protestants in northern Louisiana and pro-life Catholics in southern Louisiana.

Amid the turmoil of the transition to a two-party system, Louisiana made a dramatic change in its electoral system that had enormous, if cross-cutting, political consequences. In 1975 Louisiana discarded the traditionally southern closed party primary with a run-off system for an open election system unlike any used in the fifty states. Then-governor Edwin Edwards, a Democrat concerned about the emerging Republican opposition, proposed a system that he felt would force Republicans (who normally won a place in the general election after, at most, only a token primary) to face the same intense competition and consequent financial burdens faced by Democrats who ran in a first primary, and then in a run-off primary, before reaching the general election. Edwards's proposal, which easily won approval in the Democrat-dominated legislature, requires that elections in Louisiana for all state and federal offices except U.S. president consist of a single open election in which all candidates of all parties run together; if no candidate receives a majority, the top two candidates, regardless of party affiliation, meet in a run-off. This new system removed the traditional status of party primaries. Therefore, just as it was becoming competitive, the state Republican Party found itself working outside conventional electoral rules. Despite the handicap of a new electoral system designed to hamper Republican success, a Republican won the office of governor for the first time in Louisiana history in 1979.

## ORGANIZATIONAL DEVELOPMENT

Because of the absolute dominance of the Democratic Party in state and local politics until the 1970s, the organization of the state political parties remained static for many years. By the late 1990s, however, both parties had developed organizations that performed all of the elemental functions of most other state party organizations.

*Republican Party.* A discussion of the organizational development of the Louisiana Republican Party since the 1960s is essentially a discussion of the organizational development of the party since its birth. Although there was a recognized Republican Party organization in Louisiana before that time, it had almost no impact on politics, except for its role in the national presidential nominating convention.

Eisenhower in 1952 was the first Republican presidential candidate to receive substantial support in Louisiana, and Republican efforts until then were focused almost exclusively on presidential elections (Theodoulou 1985, 89). Although the statewide organizations that supported Eisenhower for president were essentially New Orleans–based, the beginnings of the modern Republican Party, designed to promote Republicans at all levels, are traced to three men from the Shreveport area, in the opposite corner of the state. Charles Lyons, George Despot, and Tom Stagg were three Republicans who recruited candidates all over the state to run for all levels of political office (Theodoulou 1985, 91). In 1965 they founded the Republican State Central Committee and constituted its inaugural executive committee. Once the party structure was in place, Lyons resigned as chair of the committee and left the party organization with a solid structural foundation.

The growth in organization of the Republican Party followed political trends. As Stella Theodoulou notes, the Eisenhower Republicans were essentially urban fiscal conservatives; the founding trio from Shreveport were strict anti–civil rights conservatives; the post-Lyons party began moving back to an emphasis on "limited government and conservative fiscal policy" (1985, 94). When the party was dominated by urban fiscal conservatives in the 1950s, its organization was fairly stagnant. When the party was energized by the grassroots appeal of the 1960s anti–civil rights movement, it grew quickly, but mostly among rural conservatives. As the party moved beyond the anti–civil rights rhetoric, the party organization became expansive and attempted to include a wider array of the electorate. The Republican Party's electorate grew steadily, and with the watershed 1979 victory of Republican gubernatorial candidate David Treen, its permanent place as a significant political organization affecting national, state, and local elections was secured.

Since that time the party has become heavily involved at the grassroots level in recruiting candidates and helping in fund raising. With the successes of Ronald Reagan and George Bush, and despite the renegade gubernatorial candidacy of David Duke in 1991, the Republican Party made substantial organizational inroads into state and local politics, with growing numbers of the candidates it identified and supported winning elections. The substantial coordinated aid to candidates by the Republican organization has led to electoral success at the grassroots level.

One result of the electoral success has been increasing numbers of elected officials who participate in party politics after they are elected. A Republican caucus has been organized and staffed in each of the legislative chambers since the mid-1970s. Although Republican officeholders remain in the minority at most levels of government, as their numbers increase, the state party organization will likely become increasingly consequential for state politics.

*Democratic Party.* Although the first stated goal of the Louisiana Democratic Party is to assist Democratic candidates in state and local elections (Louisiana Democratic Party 1991), the actual role of the party in the electoral process historically has been minimal. The unique Louisiana election system is the major structural reason for the party's limited role in electoral politics. Before the 1970s the Republican Party threat was so minor that the Democratic Party organization did not feel pressure to become actively involved. The increased awareness of Republican strength led the Democrats in 1975 to adopt the open election system, which effectively discourages the party from taking a role in most elections. Two of the three possible outcomes of the first election in this system make party support inappropriate. Most first elections in an open-election system result in either the Democratic or Republican candidate winning outright with a majority, or two Democrats or two Republicans making the run-off. In either case, the party's role is much less relevant, since neither outcome leads to a party-versus-party run-off election. Lately, in high-profile statewide races, the third scenario has been increasingly common: the two candidates in the run-off election have been a Democrat and either a Republican or independent, in which case the Democratic Party can logically put all of its efforts into the election of its candidate.

Despite the structural hindrance, the Democratic Party has become much more active in Louisiana in the past decade than it was before. Democratic Party activists often point to two fundamental reasons for the increased role of the Democratic Party organization in Louisiana politics. The first, and most obvious, was the first systematic threat to Democratic dominance in Louisiana political history. This threat emerged in the 1960s and has increased steadily since that time. The second reason for Democratic Party organizational growth is the interest in organization shown by John Breaux, who in 1986 was the first Democratic candidate for the U.S. Senate in Louisiana to be elected in a truly competitive race with a Republican. Breaux's ability to generate interest in invigorating the party organization is almost universally mentioned as a major reason for recent party development.

The role of the Democratic Party is in a time of transformation. The party has recently formed state legislative (house and senate) Democratic campaign committees and has held training and briefing sessions for incumbent Democratic legislators. It is beginning to formulate policy statements; it offers to help candidates with campaign advertisements; and it faxes weekly updates on national political positions to candidates (Flournoy 1995). It is clearly facing the challenges posed to a once-dominant organization.

## CURRENT PARTY ORGANIZATION

Louisiana law governs the Democratic and Republican Parties differently. The law refers to parties with more than 25 percent of registered voters and those with less than 25 percent. While both parties are subject to some rules, only the Democratic Party must abide by the more particular regulations of the larger party. Republicans are not regulated as closely in terms of committee membership, elections, and vacancies. State law notwithstanding, the parties are organized in a reasonably parallel manner.

The Louisiana Democratic Party is centrally and hierarchically organized. The organizational structure is clearly defined in the *Constitution and Bylaws* (Louisiana Democratic Party 1991). The Democratic State Central Committee is the party organization at the state level, and the parish (or county) Democratic executive committees are the local organizations. All officers of the state central committee (except the legal counsel and the clerk) comprise the executive committee of the Democratic Party, which administers party functions between party elections.

The state central committee is composed of members publicly elected every four years in compliance with state law. Any registered Democrat "actually residing in and domiciled in the district in which he or she seeks election" (Louisiana Democratic Party 1991, 3) may run for membership on the state central committee or the parish executive committee.

Like the Democratic organization, the Republican organization is hierarchically arranged. A state central committee is publicly elected at the state level, while parish executive committees are elected at the local level. The state central committee elects its officers, who make up the state executive committee. Unlike the Democrats, the Republicans have a state council. This organization is the political arm of the central committee; it helps with elections and party-building activities. The state council is operated by a finance chair (appointed by the chair) and the same officers who run the state central committee. The council also includes district chairs, who are appointed by the chair to oversee Republican Party activities in their respective districts. The districts are created by the state chair with approval by the state central committee. Other members on the council are the national committee members; all statewide and federal Republican elected officials; and representatives of the state legislature, Young Republicans, College Republicans, Black Republicans, Hispanic Republicans, and Women Republicans.

The relationship of the Democratic and Republican Party organizations to their respective members in the legislature is tentative and in both parties is becoming closer. The Republican members of the Louisiana House of Representatives and Louisiana Senate are organized into caucuses that have their own staffs. This arrangement allows the legislators some degree of independence from the state central committee. However, two factors are bringing the Republican caucuses into a closer working relationship with the state organization. The first is the reputation the state organization is developing for success in aiding candidates for election and reelection. The second factor is the growing number of elected officials participating as elected members of the state party organization. Legislators are becoming more involved in the party as other state and local officials become involved. The trend in the Republican Party is clearly a slow but definite move toward closer cooperation between the legislative caucuses and the state organization.

The relationship of the Democratic Party to Democratic members of the legislature is distinctly equivocal from the point of view of legislators but is becoming more salient. The need for organized help from the Democratic Party was negligible when there was no threat from any other party. As the Republican Party grew, Democratic members of the legislature began to respond to overtures from the party organization. The party, which now offers coordinated help in fund raising and other campaign-related activities, is clearly becoming a consequential factor in the politics of its elected members in the legislature.

The relationship between the two parties and the governor has been less propitious. With the single exception of the election of Republican governor David Treen in 1979, the state Republican Party organization has been an almost negligible part of gubernatorial politics in Louisiana. In the twenty-five years since the election of Democratic governor Edwin Edwards in 1971, Louisiana has elected only four individuals as governor—Edwards (1972–1980, 1984–1988, and 1992–1996), Treen (1980–1984), Buddy Roemer (1988–1992), and Mike Foster (1996–). Edwards, a Democrat who has unquestionably been the dominant figure in Louisiana politics in this period, chose not to focus his attention on party politics or party organization building. Even though he gained his support from a classic Democratic coalition of African Americans and labor, he clearly viewed his campaigns and governance more as personal coalition building than as party politics. Roemer, elected as a Democrat, switched to the Republican Party during his term and was then defeated in his try for reelection. In his 1995 reelection bid, he chose not to seek the endorsement of the Republican Party at its convention. The past few decades of rapid party organizational development have had little connection with the office of governor.

The political leadership in the Democratic Party has been very stable for the past decade; the political leadership in the Republican Party has been much more fluid. Given the virtual abdication of party leadership by the Democratic Party's most commanding figure, four-term governor Edwin Edwards, the most forceful presence in the Louisiana Democratic Party clearly has been Democratic senator John Breaux, the highest elected official to take a genuine interest in party development. Much of the staffing, programs, and posture of the party reflects Breaux's politics of Democratic pragmatism and centrism. The continued

**Table 1**   Louisiana Resource Guide

|  | Democrats | Republicans |
|---|---|---|
| Archive | Yes | Yes |
| Location | Louisiana Democratic Party | Louisiana Republican Party |
|  | 263 3rd Street, Suite 102 | 650 North 6th Street |
|  | Baton Rouge, LA 70801 | Baton Rouge, LA 70802 |
| Dates | Recent | Recent |
| Finding aid | No | No |
| Access | By appointment | By appointment |
| Contents: |  |  |
| Executive committee minutes | Limited | Limited |
| Correspondence | Limited | Limited |
| Organizational structure | Limited | Limited |
| Budgets | Limited | Limited |
| Rules | Yes | Yes |

success of the Democratic Party in Louisiana in the face of strong Republican upheavals in the remainder of the South is at least partly due to the political strength of the Breaux faction of the party.

Power in the Republican Party, on the other hand, is not as obvious and certainly not as stable. Like most Republican state parties, the Louisiana party has an establishment, moderate wing that emphasizes fiscal conservatism over social issues and a newer faction that emphasizes "family values" and social issues such as abortion and prayer in schools. The conservative wing has been most successful in the past decade in having its candidates endorsed for political office (most notably governor) and in influencing presidential nomination politics. Its success is likely to continue, as the more moderate Republicans such as former governor Roemer ignore the party structure. The party, however, is so young that power dynamics remain volatile.

### RESOURCE GUIDE

Since the Democratic and Republican Party organizations in Louisiana have relatively short histories, important historical records are fairly limited. The records of current party functions are in both parties being organized and kept increasingly methodically. These records can be found at state party headquarters in Baton Rouge. Both parties have easily accessible charters or bylaws.

Both parties have limited cataloging of other available material. Party workers are accessible and helpful. The materials available in both cases are not comprehensive.

The three major state newspapers, the *New Orleans Times Picayune,* the *Baton Rouge Advocate,* and the *Shreveport Times* all provide extensive coverage of Louisiana politics. A particularly strong newspaper source for Louisiana politics before 1990 was the *Shreveport Journal,* which ceased publication that year.

### REFERENCES

*Asterisks denote the most important publications on Louisiana party politics.*
Flournoy, Melissa. 1995. Democratic state representative. Interview by author, May 15.
*Giles, Michael W., and Keenan Hertz. 1994. Racial threat and partisan identification. *American Political Science Review* 88 (June):317–326.
*Lamis, Alexander. 1990. *The two-party South.* New York: Oxford University Press.

Louisiana Democratic Party. 1991. *Constitution and by-laws of the Louisiana Democratic Party.* Baton Rouge: Louisiana Democratic Party.

*Mann, Robert. 1992. *Legacy to power: Senator Russell Long of Louisiana.* New York: Paragon House.

*Parent, T. Wayne. 1988. The rise and stall of Republican ascendancy in Louisiana politics. In *The South's new politics: Realignment and dealignment,* ed. Robert Swansbrough and David Brodsky. Columbia: University of South Carolina Press.

*Theodoulou, Stella Z. 1985. The Louisiana Republican Party, 1948–1984: The building of a state political party. *Tulane Studies in Political Science.* New Orleans, La.: Tulane University.

# Maine

KENNETH T. PALMER

## PARTY HISTORY

Maine has had three broad periods of political development. In the years between its entry into the Union in 1820 and 1854, the state was generally inclined to vote for Democratic candidates. This tendency reflected resistance to the Federalist voting pattern of Massachusetts, in which state Maine had been, prior to statehood, a rather rebellious northern district. In the second period, between 1854 and 1954, Maine was solidly Republican, electing Democrats to the governorship on only five occasions. Since the mid-1950s, the two parties have been competitive, with the Democrats having an edge in more recent times. Democratic governors were in office for twenty-one of forty years between 1954 and 1994. During the same period, Republicans controlled both houses of the legislature for eighteen years; Democrats had majorities in both chambers for fourteen years, including an unbroken period of dominance between 1982 and 1994. For eight years, the legislature was under divided control.

Maine voting in presidential races has followed the same trends. Between 1860 and 1960, the state voted only once for a Democratic candidate (Wilson, in 1912). However, in 1964 Maine voted for Democrat Lyndon Johnson over Republican Barry Goldwater by a wide margin and continued to support the Democratic ticket in 1968 when Maine senator Edmund S. Muskie was a vice-presidential candidate with Hubert Humphrey. In five of the past six presidential contests, the state has cast its electoral votes for the eventual winner.

Party politics in the pre-1954 Republican period generally resembled that of other rural, one-party states. A formal structure of state, county, and local committees existed, but it generally had little influence over the recruitment and election of candidates, especially candidates for state and federal office. Instead, recruitment was performed by certain interest groups, particularly the pulp and paper industry, electric power producers, and manufacturers, as well as candidates' personal organizations. Republican candidates for higher offices tended to be small-business owners, though some career paths existed within state politics. For many decades, the position of president of the state senate was considered to be the stepping-stone to the governorship.

Republican primary contests were common but centered mostly on personalities. Primary voting often resembled a "friends and neighbors" pattern, whereby candidates would have their greatest, and sometimes only, strength in their home counties. The Republican Party generally did not experience stable factions of an ideological nature. State officials elected under the party's banner were, for the most part, moderate-to-conservative politicians who had little interest in policy innovation. Maine was a poor state that provided few public services, but it was for the most part competently managed.

Republican dominance began to encounter turbulence in the early 1950s, and battles over policy became more divisive in party affairs. The Maine Republican Party experienced something of the same division that was occurring within the national party—between conservatives who wished to reject the New Deal and moderates who accepted a generally activist role for government in the management of the economy. Moderates deserted the party's gubernatorial candidate in large numbers in 1954, contributing to the election of Democrat Edmund S. Muskie, an effective and charismatic candidate. Muskie was aided by a small group of skilled Democratic politicians who were able to mount a successful campaign with very little money and almost no grassroots organization.

## ORGANIZATIONAL DEVELOPMENT

In the past thirty years, as the Democrats gained strength in Maine, the two parties seemed almost to switch organizational styles. When they began their rise in the 1950s, the Democrats had active local organizations in only a few of the larger towns and cities (Portland, Lewiston, Biddeford, Waterville), which comprised roughly one-fifth of the state's population. For the most part, these were communities with large concentrations of Franco-Americans. Power in the party resided largely with these small city machines and their legislators and a handful of state leaders such as Muskie. The state party organization focused mainly on statewide campaigns. In contrast to the isolated Democratic organizations, the Republicans had an extensive network of municipal and county party committees and officeholders throughout the state. The committees were uneven in their activities and effectiveness, but they usually were involved in the election of state senators and representatives and county officials, the vast majority of whom were Republicans. Maine has a constitutionally powerful legislature, and with the legislature safely in their hands, Republican Party officials had little need to worry about running a strong state organization.

The difference in the two party organizations at the state level was illustrated in a 1960 newspaper article about the physical locations of their respective headquarters in that campaign year: "Whereas [Republican] Gov. John H. Reed's headquarters [in Augusta] is separated by several blocks from his party's office—and the two operations are almost independent of one another—here [in the Democratic headquarters in Lewiston] the party and the gubernatorial candidate are almost one." [1]

*Democratic Party.* Beginning in the 1960s, the Democrats contested successfully more and more state legislative seats. By the 1970s they were competitive in both legislative chambers. Much of the party's increased activity was fostered by the Democratic state committee, which hired an executive director and a finance chairperson for the first time in the 1960s. The state chairmanship itself was strengthened by the recruitment to that post of politicians who would later run successfully for high office. Both William Hathaway (U.S. Senate, 1973–1979) and George Mitchell (U.S. Senate, 1980–1995) served a term as state Democratic chair.

The state Democratic Party weathered the ideological divisions that plagued the 1968 and 1972 national Democratic campaigns fairly well. The state organization helped recruit new legislators in many of the smaller towns and rural counties and, in 1974, the party gained control of the state house of representatives for the first time since 1964. During the next two decades, Democrats faced fewer internal battles in Maine than did the Republicans. However, a persistent problem for the Democratic organization was the hierarchical relationship between the state party and the national party. Maine Democrats prided themselves on local control, and they resisted the national committee's effort to set rules governing their activities.

The conflicts spanned delegate selection, the holding of party caucuses, and the level of support a presidential candidate had to achieve in the state convention to win delegates to the national convention. In anticipation of the 1980 national convention, the state party resisted a ruling of the national party that no delegate should be elected from a single-member district. The guideline was intended to ensure that men and women were equally represented at the national convention. Maine Democrats had at that time eight delegate districts, some of which elected a single member. The party, after protest, eventually conformed to the national standard. The date of Maine's Democratic caucuses for selecting delegates to its state convention was an issue in 1984. The national party wanted to establish an election calendar that would have forced Maine to hold its caucuses later than state law allowed. Maine joined with Iowa and New Hampshire to keep its earlier caucus date, but the struggle lasted for months.

In 1988 and 1992 battles occurred over delegates elected by the state convention to the national convention to represent presidential candidates who had received less than 15 percent of the votes of the state convention. The national party set the threshold at which a candidate could receive delegates at 15 percent; in Maine the threshold was zero. Due in large measure to the intervention of Sen. George Mitchell, a compromise was worked out and the state's delegation was seated at the national convention in both years despite its noncompliance with national rules. In 1995, with Mitchell no longer in office, Maine Democrats finally changed the rule to conform to the national standard.

*Republican Party.* During the past thirty years, the Republicans have had fewer problems with their national leadership than have the Democrats, but they experienced a good deal more ideological and organizational disarray within the state ranks. Much of the cause was their diminished power in a state where they had long held sway. Party leaders wanted to strengthen the state committee to provide leadership to local committees, but they could not agree on what policy slant the party should take.

A battle for control of the party machinery erupted in 1964, after Barry Goldwater won the Republican presidential nomination. The Maine party had been generally moderate in political coloration, but conservatives were growing in strength. In a battle for state committee chair in July, a few days after the Goldwater nomination, a division between moderates and conservatives was apparent. A veteran, generally moderate Republican, Roger Putnam, defeated Cyril Joly, mayor of Waterville and a strong Goldwater supporter, by a vote of 17 to 13. In an effort to reduce the impact of national influences on the state party, Republicans adopted a rule in 1965 that the state chair (who had a two-year term) should be elected in odd-numbered years.

Electorally, the Republicans fared rather poorly in the 1960s. They lost the two U.S. House seats and the governorship in 1966, and although the party did regain control of the state legislature in that year, it lost ground in the legislature in subsequent elections.

Organizationally, the party leadership steadily moved into the hands of the conservatives. Cyril Joly was elected state chair in 1967 in a bitter, four-way race, which was so heated that one county organization (Aroostook) threatened to secede from the state committee. Joly was able to persuade the group to remain in the state organization and developed enough support to win a second term unanimously in 1969. In 1971 another conservative, Charles Morehead, an Augusta attorney, won the chairmanship over two more-moderate contenders.

The chairmanship at this time was an unpaid, part-time position, and day-to-day management rested with the state committee's executive director. In 1973 an uproar occurred in the state committee when the executive director, Alex Ray, took positions on bills before the legislature and worked for a gubernatorial candidate long in advance of the party's primary, independent of any action by the committee. The committee decided to retain Ray only by a vote of 27 to 23 in a ballot that found conservatives generally supporting Ray and moderates opposing him.

Such disagreements at the state level weakened efforts by state leaders to guide the activities of municipal and county organizations during the 1970s. In 1980, for instance, the state convention rejected the recommendation of a party task force to hold all municipal caucuses, which elect delegates to the state convention, on the same day. Town Republican groups continued to decide individually on which day in February or March in even-numbered years they would hold their caucuses. (Democrats had by 1980 established a uniform caucus day for their local organizations.) As an indication of the Republicans' grassroots weakness, in 1980 the party failed to nominate candidates in 38 of the 151 House districts.

The worst debacle for the state organization seemed to come in 1982, when the party lost both houses of the legislature and the governorship. In a highly unusual move, the state's three Republican members of Congress (Sen. William Cohen, Rep. David Emery, and Rep. Olympia Snowe) wrote a joint letter to all members of the state committee urging the election of an experienced state lobbyist and veteran Republican activist, Lloyal Sewall, as state chair. The congressional delegation was alarmed that the state organization's ineptitude might begin to affect adversely their own careers, even though delegation members were generally more moderate than the state organization and mostly ran their campaigns independently of it. Sewall was elected to the position and strengthened the party in several ways. He encouraged party moderates to become involved in the work of the state committee, and he established a closer relationship with the national committee, securing greater financial and technical assistance for Republican candidates for office. In 1986 the party won the governorship for the first time since 1962.

Since the mid-1980s, moderates have generally been in control of the state party apparatus. The party included in its state platform in 1984 support of the Equal Rights Amendment and in 1988 support of a prochoice plank. The state chairmanship has been held by politicians who have had experience in running for Congress and the governorship. Conservatives have at times protested the change in the direction of the organization, but it is generally acknowledged that the move toward the political center has contributed to greater Republican electoral success, especially in gubernatorial and legislative races.

## CURRENT PARTY ORGANIZATION

Maine's political parties consist of a structure of committees.[2] The basic unit is the town or municipal committee, which is elected by the town caucus, held every two years in the late winter. The caucus is open to all members of the party who are residents of the town. In addition to selecting members of the town committee, the town caucus has traditionally selected delegates to the state convention, which meets in April or May. Because the state convention determines the composition of the delegation to the national presidential nominating convention, every four years presidential candidates invade the state and travel about the various towns trying to line up support at the municipal caucuses. Although that process has typically generated some excitement, attendance at municipal caucuses historically was quite low (about 5 percent of registered party members). The state in 1988 enacted legislation authorizing the parties to hold presidential nominating primaries if they desired, and in 1996 they did so for the first time.

Each party maintains a committee in each of the state's fourteen counties. The members are selected by the town committees and are usually drawn from town committee rosters. For instance, Democratic rules stipulate that each municipal committee chair is a member of the Democratic county committee. County committees tend to focus on getting candidates elected to positions in county government, such as sheriff, probate judge, and county commissioner.

Day-to-day leadership of the party is in the hands of the state committee, especially its executive committee. In Maine, both the Democratic and Republican state committees are large bodies. In 1995 they had 108 and 59 members, respectively. Each county has several members on the state committee (from two to five, depending on the county's population), one of whom is the chair of the county committee. In addition, the state committee includes representatives from the party contingents in the state house and the state senate as well as the governor's office (when the party holds the governorship), a representative of each member of Congress who is a member of the party, and the two members of the party's national committee. Party groups such as Republican women, college Republicans, and Maine Young Democrats also have spokespersons on their respective committees.

The representatives of the state legislative contingents, members of Congress, and party groups generally have seats on the executive committee of the state committee, which in cooperation with the state chair and the party's executive director sets the agenda for meetings. To the extent that the state party apparatus (of both parties) has significant power, it is lodged in the executive committee.

The rules governing the two parties are approved every other year, at each party's state convention. The conventions have the responsibility of setting forth the party's platform and, in presidential election years, of naming the delegation to attend the national convention. The conventions are occasions for campaigning by candidates seeking the party's nomination in the primaries, which are held in June. Convention activities and voting are usually good indicators of the party's direction and degree of unity (or discord). However, conventions do not make policy except in a very broad sense.

Major developments in the 1990s in both of Maine's parties are increased centralization and concentration of responsibility in the state party leadership. The trend toward centralization is more pronounced in the Republican Party, since it has a history of local control. With battles over control of the state committee diminishing, the Republican Party has moved forward to direct more fully the activities of local and county committees. In 1994 state party officials were able to find candidates to run in all but a handful of legislative districts. Two field directors were appointed by the state committee, and training sessions were provided for state legislative candidates. The state party appears to work very closely with the national headquarters and secures a substantial part of its budget from the national party.

Centralization has also occurred in the Democratic Party, even though Democratic officials currently view their party as the more locally oriented of the two. As the party developed a grassroots organization in the 1960s and 1970s and successfully contested legislative seats, state party officials were inclined to provide latitude for local units to manage their own affairs. The 1994 elections, however, were something of a debacle. The party lost the gubernatorial election, the U.S. Senate seat that had been held by George Mitchell, and control of the state senate, and it incurred a substantial debt. These losses helped to intensify efforts by state party officials to monitor local activities. Currently the party is considering ways to require communities that have failed to hold party caucuses (approximately 5 percent) to do so.

In both parties, relationships between the state organization and certain other institutions and groups are changing. The most interesting changes involving outside agencies appear to concern the state legislature and the national party organizations. Both the Democratic and Republican state committees and their staffs are gaining power in relation to their respective party caucuses in the legislature. Until recently, leadership groups in the legislature tended to raise more funds for candidates for the House and Senate than did the state committees. Because of state legislative term limits adopted in Maine in 1991, legislative leadership turnover is increasing, and the new leaders are less able to manage fundraising efforts. Meanwhile, the state party organizations have developed the technology to handle that responsibility better on a continuing basis than in past years. Although the trend is more pronounced in the Republican Party than in the Democratic Party, it is taking place in both.

Likewise, both state parties appear to have a closer relationship with the national parties. Conflicts of past years that impeded the building of relationships (ideological battles among Republicans, rule disputes among Democrats) have receded. Both state committees now depend heavily on the expertise and money of the national party organizations, and their association with the national parties has fostered greater centralization of party activities in the state. That process seems also to have brought the state party apparatus into closer accord with the governor's office (when the governor is of the same party) and with the campaign organizations of congressional candidates. In the 1990s Maine's state party organizations are showing a greater capacity to contribute to campaigns and to give attention to governmental management than in the past.

### RESOURCE GUIDE

The archives of the Maine Democratic Party are located in a room at the party headquarters, which is a house that the party currently rents. Most of the material goes back only to 1970, although items from the Muskie campaigns in the 1950s and 1960s are present. The material is in file folders contained in thirty to forty large cardboard boxes. The minutes of state committee meetings and the budgets of campaign years appear to be in good shape. Several of the boxes contain photographs of campaign events and posters and other advertising. A researcher would find valuable information but would have to work hard to piece it together.

The Republican Party archives are housed at the party headquarters, in a building the party owns. There are about thirty boxes of files and six file cabinets. The material goes

**Table 1**  Maine Resource Guide

|  | Democrats | Republicans |
|---|---|---|
| Archive | Yes | Yes |
| Location | Party Headquarters | Party Headquarters |
|  | 12 Spruce St., P.O. Box 5258 | 100 Water St. |
|  | Augusta, Maine 04332 | Hallowell, Maine 04347 |
|  | (207) 622-6233 | (207) 622-6247 |
| Dates | 1950s–present | 1950s–present |
| Finding aid | No | No |
| Access | By appointment | By appointment |
| Contents: |  |  |
| Executive committee minutes | Some | Some |
| Correspondence | Some | Some |
| Organizational structure | Some | Some |
| Budgets | Some | Some |
| Rules | Some | Some |

back to the mid-1950s. The budgetary information appears to be quite complete; the records and minutes of the state committee meetings are more uneven, though material includes tapes of meetings as well as written records. A researcher would find much to work with here but would need a fair amount of time to find individual items.

### NOTES

1. *Portland Press Herald,* Sept. 6, 1960. The Law and Legislative Reference Library in the Maine State Capitol contains a nearly complete file of state newspaper clippings from the mid-1950s to the present and has organized many of them chronologically into large, loose-leaf books by topic. This material is extraordinarily useful to researchers of Maine politics. Most of the discussion in this paper was drawn from books labeled "Republicans" and "Democrats," covering the period from 1960 to 1995.
2. The rules and bylaws of the two parties are available in pamphlet form at the respective state committee headquarters.

### REFERENCES

Asterisks denote the most important publications on Maine party politics.
Hayes, Kenneth P. 1983. Maine political parties. In *New England political parties,* ed. Josephine E. Milburn and William Doyle, 185–215. Cambridge, Mass.: Schenkman.
*Judd, Richard W., ed. 1995. *Maine: The Pine Tree State from prehistory to the present.* Orono: University of Maine Press.
Lockard, Duane. 1959. *New England state politics.* Princeton, N.J.: Princeton University Press.
Maisel, Louis. 1975. Party reform and political participation: The Democrats of Maine. In *The future of political parties,* ed. Louis Maisel and Paul M. Sacks. Beverly Hills, Calif.: Sage.
*Palmer, Kenneth T., G. Thomas Taylor, and Marcus A. LiBrizzi. 1992. *Maine politics and government.* Lincoln: University of Nebraska Press.

# *Maryland*

MICHAEL K. GUSMANO AND
PAUL S. HERRNSON

The Democratic Party has dominated Maryland politics for much of the state's history. The development of the state's party organizations reflects this legacy. The Democratic Party has been well organized at the local level. Its development at the state level has been hindered by divisions over issues and between party leaders and by the party's electoral success. The Republican Party has rarely been as well organized as the Democrats at the grassroots level, but it has endured less factional strife and been more successful in building a strong centralized organization at the state level. Recent developments suggest that party politics in Maryland may be experiencing significant change as elections become more competitive.

## PARTY HISTORY

Supporters of Andrew Jackson organized the first meeting of Maryland's Democratic Party in 1827. In response, anti-Jacksonian forces from the old Federalist Party formed the Whig Party. These two parties dominated Maryland politics from the 1830s to the 1850s, when slavery and secessionist politics led to the collapse of the Whig Party (Brugger 1988).

During the 1850s the American, or Know-Nothing, Party became the most important force in Maryland politics (Chapelle et al. 1986). The Know-Nothings evolved mainly from Protestant groups that opposed the influx of Catholic and Jewish immigrants into Baltimore (Brugger 1988). By 1857 the Know-Nothing Party had won control of Baltimore's city hall, amassed majorities in both chambers of the state's General Assembly, and elected one of its own to the governorship. In 1856 Maryland was the only state to cast its votes for Know-Nothing presidential candidate Millard Fillmore (Willis 1984).

Pre–Civil War politics led to the establishment of the Republican Party in Maryland. It was viewed as a radical, abolitionist party, and its presidential nominee, John Freemont, captured only 285 popular votes in Maryland in the 1856 election. Abraham Lincoln received only 2.5 percent of the state's popular vote in the following election (Willis 1984). The Democratic Party split, and its nominee, Stephen Douglas, captured only 6.6 percent of the Maryland popular vote in 1860. The main competitors were John Breckenridge and John Bell, who were nominated by the Southern Democratic Party (which had broken away from the regular Democratic Party) and the Constitutional Union Party. They received 45.9 percent and 45.1 percent of the vote, respectively.

The end of the Civil War witnessed the rapid reemergence of the Democratic Party in Maryland. By 1868 it had recaptured both houses of the General Assembly and the governor's mansion and dominated national elections in the state (Willis 1984). Democratic machines continued to dominate the state's politics from 1868 to 1918 (Callcott 1985). The Republican Party made some inroads during the Progressive Era, gaining control of the General Assembly in 1918 for the first time since Reconstruction, but it has not controlled the legislature since then (State of Maryland 1974–1975).

From 1919 to 1934 the Democratic machine of Governor Albert C. Ritchie dominated the state (Chapelle et al 1986). By opposing Franklin D. Roosevelt and his New Deal policies, Ritchie split the Democratic Party and lost his bid for a fifth term in 1934. This led to the one-term governorship of Republican Harry W. Nice.

In subsequent gubernatorial elections, Republican candidates were successful when they took more progressive positions than their Democratic opponents on social issues, particularly those involving race. As mayor of Baltimore, Theodore McKeldin built a strong base among African American voters. His popularity in the African American community allowed him to create a statewide, biracial coalition that elected him governor in 1950. Spiro Agnew took a page out of McKeldin's campaign book in 1966, defeating his opponent, George Mahoney, by staking out progressive positions on racial issues (Callcott 1985; Chapelle et al. 1986).

## ORGANIZATIONAL DEVELOPMENT

Maryland's parties experienced significant organizational development between 1960 and 1996. Until recently, most of the changes at the Democratic Party involved party rules and the representation of previously unempowered groups. The GOP has focused almost exclusively on enhancing the party's role in elections. Republican victories at the state and local level have encouraged the Democrats to begin improving their state central committee's campaign apparatus.

*Democratic Party.* The organizational strength of Maryland's Democratic Party for most of its history has been at the local rather than the state level. A variety of political clubs served as the organizational base of the Democratic Party in Baltimore City (Callcott 1985). Democratic county central committees typically dominated politics in the rest of the state. The party's state central committee, by contrast, has never been well organized. Governors typically rose through the ranks of Baltimore's political machine and used that organization to wage their election campaigns; they rewarded supporters with state and federal patronage (Callcott 1985).

The civil rights, women's, and student protest movements during the 1960s created tensions within the party. Racial issues were especially polarizing during the 1966 gubernatorial campaign, in which Democrats nominated George Mahoney (Callcott 1985). Mahoney's campaign focused on denying African Americans the right to move into the suburban neighborhoods around Baltimore and Washington, D.C. It drove liberal whites and African Americans away from the Democratic Party and contributed to the election of Spiro Agnew (Chapelle et al. 1986).

Factional tensions between party insiders and underrepresented groups reemerged in 1969, when the General Assembly selected Marvin Mandel to complete Agnew's term as governor after Agnew had been elected vice president of the United States. Mandel had risen through the ranks of the Democratic machine in Baltimore to become chair of the Ways and Means Committee in the House of Delegates, Speaker of that body, and state party chair (Brugger 1988). As governor he attempted to dominate the party apparatus in the face of national pressure to open the Democratic Party to broader participation. In an effort to defuse pressure for reform and placate the liberal wing of the party, Mandel named state senator Harry Hughes temporary chair in 1969 (Gill 1969). During Hughes's two years as chair, the party adopted its first constitution and bylaws and established its first permanent headquarters in Baltimore (Rascovar 1969).

After Mandel was indicted on bribery charges in 1975, Hughes was selected to be governor by the General Assembly. Governor Hughes opened the party to broader participation and appointed its first woman chair, Rosalie Abrams. During the Hughes administration, the party published a newsletter and conducted coordinated campaigns for state and federal candidates in 1982, 1984, and 1986 (Willis 1995).

Following the 1986 landslide victory of former Baltimore mayor William Donald Schaefer, the state party fell into a period of severe decline. Schaefer showed little interest in the party organization, counting instead on voters in Democratic-dominated Baltimore to provide him with the support he needed to be reelected. Schaefer demonstrated his lack of concern for the party by hiring Nathan Landow as party chair over the objections of many state central committee members, then firing him after a clash over who would announce Maryland's vote for the nomination at the 1992 Democratic National Convention (DeFilippo 1994). Landow was replaced by Vera Hall, a longtime party activist and Baltimore City councilwoman who had helped lead Maryland's coordinated campaign in 1992 (Smith 1994). She retired in 1994, and Harry Hughes was reappointed chair.

*Republican Party.* The Republican Party has often struggled to provide a viable alternative to the Democrats in Maryland. The GOP was badly divided over Barry Goldwater's nomination and landslide defeat in 1964. It rebounded when Agnew was elected governor in 1966 and again in 1968 when Nixon and Agnew were elected to the White House. In 1970 the party began a short-lived drive to establish precinct-level organizations around the state (Wason 1970).

The events surrounding Watergate, including Agnew's resignation and conviction, devastated the GOP and caused major strategic changes. During the 1970s and 1980s, Maryland Republicans abandoned grassroots organizing and sought to build from the top down. The state central committee focused on recruiting prominent candidates for governor and Congress rather than encouraging individuals to run for local offices (Feinstein 1982).

During this period, the state GOP used resources provided by the Republican National Committee (RNC) to initiate some organizational improvements. State GOP chair David Forward established the party's first permanent headquarters, in Annapolis. Forward's successors, Artis T. Allen (the party's first African American party chair) and Allan Levey improved the party's technical and fund-raising capacities. Under Allen, the party worked to attract minority and women voters and tapped into the RNC's computerized information and fund-raising networks (Farrell 1979). Under Levey, the state GOP's receipts jumped from $60,000 in 1978 to over $300,000 in 1980 (Kumpa 1995).

Unfortunately for the GOP, these organizational efforts failed to produce many electoral successes. Democratic electoral landslides caused divisions within the Republican Party over issues of party strategy. Levey and others favored a return to the "bottom up" approach. They sought to focus on building local Republican committees and recruiting and assisting candidates for local office. State legislative leaders preferred to continue concentrating on races that were higher up the ticket.

Tensions between moderates and conservatives also had strategic implications, making it difficult for the party to close its ranks and to attract women and minority voters (Feinstein 1982). These tensions surfaced when state chair Dan Flemming (1986–1989) used his office to promote conservative positions on social issues. Flemming's efforts antagonized party moderates and alienated many GOP supporters in the business community. By the time the state central committee dismissed him, the party was $60,000 in debt (Terhes 1995).

Joyce Terhes took over as the party's temporary chair in 1989 and was elected to a full term by the state central committee in 1990. She has played a critical role in strengthening the party's organizational apparatus. Under her stewardship the state party's budget had increased to over $800,000 by 1994. Terhes and her staff also provided record levels of campaign assistance to Republican state and local candidates. Terhes's efforts have resulted in the GOP making significant electoral progress. In 1990 the party made a net gain of 8 seats in the House of Delegates and 4 seats in the state senate. In 1994 the GOP gained an additional 16 seats in the lower chamber and 5 seats in the upper chamber, giving it control of 41 of 142 house seats and 15 of 43 senate seats. This was the largest number of Republicans in the General Assembly since 1920. Other signs of Republican progress include its winning majorities in fourteen of the state's twenty-four county councils/commissions in 1994. Moreover, Republican gubernatorial candidate Ellen Sauerbrey's 5,993-vote loss to Parris Glendening in 1994 may have ushered the state into an era of competitive two-party politics.

## CURRENT PARTY ORGANIZATION

The organization of the two political parties is governed by article 33 of the *Annotated Code of Maryland* (State of Maryland 1993). The code requires each party to have a permanent constitution and bylaws that provide for the election of a party chair and members of a state central committee. The code also regulates some internal party matters, such as requiring the state central committees to meet within forty-five days of the primary.

The two parties have very similar organizational structures. Each has a state central committee comprising the party chairs from the state's twenty-three counties and Baltimore City. The members of each county committee are elected quadrennially, in gubernatorial election years. The state central committees officially select their party's state chair and the other officers, but they merely ratify the governor's choices when a member of their party occupies the governor's mansion (Pecararo 1995).

Both parties have four full-time employees during nonelection years who design party strategy, carry out communications functions, administer the organization, organize voter files, hold fund-raising events, and carry out other important activities. During election years, the party organizations swell with more paid employees and consultants as well as volunteers and interns. In 1992 the number of paid employees at the Democratic State Central Committee ballooned to a record fifty.

Although the parties have similar structures, power within them is distributed differently. Because the Republicans have elected only five governors in the history of the state, the party chair has almost always been the GOP's major decision maker. Power in the Democratic Party, on the other hand, has usually resided with the governor. Strong party chairs, such as Hughes, have been able to amass influence and, on occasion, have even succeeded the governors who appointed them. Yet, chairs who do not follow the wishes of the governor risk being ousted.

Both parties suffer from internal divisions over national issues. The Democrats are plagued by disagreements over abortion, gun control, and programs designed to benefit city dwellers at the expense of suburban and rural residents. The redistribution of wealth from the Washington, D.C., suburbs to Baltimore is a major source of tension for Maryland Democrats. For more than three decades, moderate and conservative Republicans have been divided over social issues, especially abortion, but their minority status has helped the GOP remain more united than the Democrats.

**Table 1**  Maryland Party Receipts, 1985–1994

| Party | 1985–1986 | 1989–1990 | 1993–1994 |
|---|---|---|---|
| Democratic | $296,489 | $850,072 | $1,138,085 |
| Republican | 105,573 | 285,159 | 846,591 |

SOURCE: State Administrative Board of Elections, Campaign Fund Reports, 1985–1994.

NOTE: Figures represent total receipts from October 27 of the first year to November 16 of the second year.

Both parties raise most of their funds through dinners, events, and direct-mail and telephone solicitations (Maryland Republican Party 1994; Fisher 1995). The Democratic Party has raised more money than the Republicans in recent elections, reflecting the advantages derived from majority status (see Table 1).

The parties also receive financial and organizational assistance from their respective national committees. In 1992 the Democratic National Committee (DNC) provided $167,826 to the Maryland state party to help Bill Clinton and Al Gore, Sen. Barbara Mikulski, and congressional, state, and local candidates (Federal Election Commission 1993). The DNC also supplied Maryland with a state director to help coordinate the Clinton campaign in Maryland and a media consultant. For its 1994 election effort, the DNC provided the Maryland Democratic Party with $66,300 (Federal Election Commission 1995).

The Republican National Committee (RNC) provided the Maryland GOP with $19,000 in 1992 and $135,416 in 1994 (Federal Election Commission 1993, 1995). It also provided the state party with voter files that were used to target election precincts for campaign communications and voter mobilization efforts. One of the most successful RNC-initiated programs was the Maryland version of the Concord Conference, where GOP legislative candidates, consultants, and party staff conducted a mock campaign (Terhes 1995).

The relationships between the Democratic and Republican State Central Committees and their respective leaders in the General Assembly reflect the one-party dominance that has defined Maryland politics. The Democratic Party has a weak relationship with Democratic leadership organizations in the legislature, which were almost completely inactive until 1993, when Democrats in the House of Delegates formed the House Democratic Research Group. Moreover, Democratic leaders in the house and senate have preferred to raise money and contribute it directly to candidates rather than help raise money for the party. The historically small number of Republicans in the General Assembly have somewhat closer ties to their state central committee. However, so few Republicans held seats that the Republican minority leader in the house regularly attended Democratic leadership meetings until 1991.

Relationships between the state central committees and local party organizations and candidates are largely structured around the provision of campaign assistance. The Democratic Party in Maryland has never been extensively involved in campaigns for the state legislature or local offices because winning a Democratic primary was usually tantamount to being elected. Without competitive Republican opposition, the party had little need to encourage candidates to run or to help them wage their campaigns.

During the early 1990s the Democratic State Central Committee provided local party organizations and candidates with voter lists and volunteers. It also acted as a clearinghouse for strategic information and coordinated party and candidate activities to help minimize the duplication of efforts. The party did not give cash contributions to

Democratic officeholders or candidates. The governor, the president of the senate, and speaker of the House of Delegates have often filled this financial void by transferring funds from their campaign accounts to other candidates. In 1990, for example, Governor Schaefer transferred $163,853 from his campaign committees to ninety-eight General Assembly candidates (Common Cause of Maryland 1992). In 1994 House Speaker Casper "Cas" Taylor transferred $56,350 to twenty-six candidates (Frece 1994).[1] Senate President Thomas V. "Mike" Miller provided $48,825 to thirty incumbent senators and candidates competing for open Senate seats (Frece 1994). Although the contributions of party legislative leaders represent an important resource for Democratic candidates, they may undermine the strength of the formal party apparatus because they are distributed without party input.

The Republican State Central Committee distributes a higher volume of services to its candidates and local party committees. It is also more involved in recruiting candidates, but like its Democratic counterpart it does not distribute cash contributions. Yet, the GOP Senate-House Committee, a political action committee (PAC) created by Republican members of the General Assembly in 1979, does provide funds. The PAC contributed roughly $59,800 to Republican candidates in 1986, and $89,900 in 1990 (Common Cause of Maryland 1992). Relations between the GOP Senate-House Committee and the state central committee were strained, however, because the PAC focused most of its efforts on protecting incumbents rather than electing new legislators (Wyatt 1995). In 1994 Chairwoman Terhes persuaded the PAC to work with the state party on electing nonincumbents to the legislature. During that election, the PAC distributed $96,850 to the challenger and open-seat candidates targeted by the party (Common Cause of Maryland 1995; Wyatt 1995).

Party politics in Maryland are typical of those in most one-party states. The Democratic Party, which has traditionally dominated the state, has a legacy of decentralized power, deep factional disputes, and corruption. The Republican Party has only rarely been consequential at the state or local levels. Both parties have been influenced by national trends, becoming more participatory and more prone to divisions over social issues. Both parties' state committees also have been strengthened and modernized by the infusions of cash and organizational assistance from their national committees.

Maryland party politics began to change significantly in the early 1990s. The GOP strengthened its state and local organizations, nominated more competitive candidates, and experienced many electoral successes. The Democrats responded by selecting a former governor and party-building chair to revitalize their party organization at the state level. These developments may foreshadow the emergence of a competitive two-party system in Maryland.

### RESOURCE GUIDE

The records of the Maryland Democratic Party are poorly organized and are not housed in a single location. The Democratic Party headquarters in Baltimore has executive committee minutes and correspondence in boxes. The minutes of central committee meetings, party correspondence, and finance records are believed to be in the possession of former party chairs. Access can only be obtained by contacting them.

Most of the Maryland Republican Party records since 1960 are located at party headquarters in Annapolis. Minutes from executive committee meetings, information about rules and rules changes, correspondence to and from the state chair, executive committee reports, and party budgets are located in uncataloged office files.

**Table 2**  Maryland Resource Guide

|  | Democrats | Republicans |
|---|---|---|
| Archive | No | Yes |
| Location | — | State Party Headquarters |
|  |  | 1623 Forest Dr., Suite 400 |
|  |  | Annapolis, Md. 21403 |
| Dates | — | 1960–1985 |
| Finding aid | — | No |
| Access | — | By appointment |
| Contents: |  |  |
| Executive committee minutes | — | Yes |
| Correspondence | — | No |
| Organizational structure | — | No |
| Budgets | — | Yes |
| Rules | — | Yes |

The Maryland State Archives in Annapolis and the Enoch Pratt Free Library in Baltimore are useful sources of information. The archives houses the public papers of all Maryland governors and a complete record of party delegates to state and national party conventions. The archives also contains campaign finance data for the Democratic and Republican Parties prior to 1987. The campaign finance data from 1987 to the present are located at the State Administrative Board of Elections in Annapolis. Convenient summary figures, such as those that are available for national elections, do not exist.

The Enoch Pratt Free Library possesses articles on Maryland's political parties that were published in the *Baltimore Sun* and Baltimore's *News American* newspapers. The library has vertical files that contain articles written between 1934 and 1982. An index for *Sun* articles since 1991 is available on CD-ROM at the Pratt library (and at Hornbake Library of the University of Maryland at College Park), but there is no index for the *Sun* between 1959 and 1991.

NOTE

1. Some of this money was actually transferred to candidate slate committees. These are formed by delegates, who run in three-member districts.

REFERENCES

*Asterisks denote the most important publications on Maryland party politics.*
*Brugger, Robert J. 1988. *Maryland: A middle temperament.* Baltimore: Johns Hopkins University Press.
Callcott, George H. 1985. *Maryland & America: 1940–1980.* Baltimore: Johns Hopkins University Press.
*———. 1986. *Maryland political behavior: Four centuries of political culture.* Baltimore: Maryland Historical Society and Maryland State Archives.
*Chapelle, Suzanne, Ellery Greene, Jean Baker, Dean Esslinger, Witman Ridgway, Jean Russo, Constance Schulz, and Gregory Stiverson. 1986. *Maryland: A history of its people.* Baltimore: Johns Hopkins University Press.
Common Cause of Maryland. 1992. *Campaign money in Maryland: November 19, 1986–November 20, 1990.* Annapolis: Common Cause of Maryland.
———. 1995. *Mother's milk of Maryland politics.* Annapolis: Common Cause of Maryland.
DeFilippo, Frank A. 1994. State Democratic Party left in shambles. *Baltimore Sun,* November 17, 19A.
Farrell, John A. 1979. Revitalized state GOP sets out on the comeback trail. *News American,* July 22, 3A.
Federal Election Commission. 1993. Democrats narrow financial gap in 1991–92. Press release.

———. 1995. FEC reports on political party activity for 1993–94. Press release.

Feinstein, John. 1982. Square one for Md. GOP. *Washington Post,* December 12, B1.

Fisher, Brian. 1995. Interview by author, June 14.

Frece, John W. 1994. Md. Assembly leaders sharing election funds. *Baltimore Sun,* September 12, 1A.

Gill, Ray. 1969. Hughes is elected Democratic Party leader. *News American,* October 23, 3A.

*Kent, Frank R. 1968. *The story of Maryland politics.* Hatboro, Penn.: Tradition Press.

Kumpa, Peter J. 1995. Interview by author, May 16.

Maryland Republican Party. 1994. *1994 chairman's report.* Annapolis: Maryland Republican Party.

Pecararo, Greg. 1995. Interview by author, May 16.

Rascovar, Harry C. 1969. Democrats to set up headquarters here. *Baltimore Sun,* December 7, 34.

Smith, Fraser C. 1994. Democratic chairwoman to resign. *Baltimore Sun,* September 24, 2B.

State of Maryland. 1974–1975. *Maryland manual.* Annapolis: State of Maryland.

———. 1993. *The annotated code of the public general laws of Maryland, Vol. 3.* Charlottesville, Va.: Michie Company.

Terhes, Joyce. 1995. Interview by author, March 16.

Wason, Thomas. 1970. Maryland Republicans show new muscle. *News American,* May 30, 4A.

* Willis, John T. 1984. *Presidential elections in Maryland.* Mt. Airy, Md.: Lomond Publications.

———. 1995. Interview by author, May 24.

Wyatt, William J. 1995. Interview by author, February 28.

# Massachusetts

JEROME M. MILEUR

## PARTY HISTORY

The rhythms of Massachusetts politics are, in many ways, unlike those of the nation. The periodic realignments and changing party systems that characterize American national politics are not to be found in the history of the Bay State. There was no Jacksonian, Civil War, or Progressive realignment in Massachusetts, nor was there really a New Deal realignment, and there has been no significant conservative Republican resurgence since the 1960s. All of these periods left their marks on Massachusetts, but none was a watershed in state politics.

Historically, Bay State politics divide into three broad and somewhat overlapping eras. The first, dating from the Revolution, produced a century of one-party Federalist-Whig-Republican rule, dominated by old-stock Yankee elites from the Adamses to the Lodges and their interests from commerce to industry. The Democratic parties of Jefferson and Jackson were rarely a threat to the majority party. In the ninety-three state elections from 1797, when the Democrats first fielded a candidate for governor, to 1890 (Massachusetts had annual elections until 1920), Democrats won only ten, just two after 1842, and never controlled either branch of the state legislature.

National politics from the War of 1812 through the Jacksonian and Civil War realignments reinforced Yankee hegemony in Massachusetts, the greatest threat to which was often posed by third parties. The Free Soilers ran candidates for governor every year from 1848 to 1853, taking 20–30 percent of the vote each time, and won seats in Congress in 1848, 1850, and 1852. In 1854 the Anti-Masonic Party swept all statewide offices and won control of both houses of the state legislature. The Anti-Masons held the governorship in 1855 and 1856, elected a member of Congress in 1856, and remained a force in state politics to the end of the decade.

The second era in Massachusetts politics dates from the late nineteenth century to the end of the 1950s and is marked by the growing strength and eventual capture of the state by the Democrats. The waves of immigration, beginning before the Civil War but accelerating greatly in the final decades of the century, strengthened the Democrats in the industrial centers of the state. Irish-born Catholic Democrats won mayoral offices in Lowell (1881) and Boston (1884); others followed.

Early in the 1890s a coalition of dissident Yankees (old Mugwumps) and urban Irish Democrats enjoyed brief statewide success, winning the governorship three times, until economic recession and the national party's nomination of W. J. Bryan for president in 1896 fractured the alliance. Nonetheless, Democratic gains continued in the cities, and, when Republican regulars and progressives split in 1910, Democrats won the governorship and held it through 1914, electing the state's first Irish Catholic chief executive, David I. Walsh, in 1913. In 1912 the division in GOP ranks also enabled Woodrow Wilson, with 35 percent of the popular vote, to become the first Democrat to carry Massachusetts in a presidential election.

But 1928 was the breakthrough election for the Democrats, when the nomination of Al Smith for president—one of their "own kind" for Irish, Catholic, big city Democrats—galvanized the state's ethnic vote as no one and nothing before had. The party's presidential vote in Massachusetts almost tripled from 280,831 in 1924 to 792,758 in 1928 and made Smith the first Democrat to win a majority of the state's presidential vote. The Democrats also made major gains in the state legislature in 1928, adding twenty seats in the house and almost doubling their numbers in the senate, though Republicans retained sizable majorities in both bodies. In 1932 Franklin Roosevelt added only 7,390 votes to Smith's 1928 total, but the Democrats continued their legislative gains during the decade and elected governors in four of the decade's five elections.

In 1948 the long march for Democrats ended in triumph as they won control of state government for the first time. With Harry Truman taking 54.7 percent of the Bay State presidential vote, the largest share for a Democrat to that time, the party swept all of the constitutional (executive branch) offices. It also won a majority in the state house for the first time, with Thomas P. "Tip" O'Neill becoming the first Democratic speaker, and also tied for control of the state senate. (O'Neill 1987, ch. 3)

The Republicans recovered in 1952, winning the governorship and regaining control of the state legislature. But it was their last hurrah. The Democrats took back control of the state house in 1954 and, two years later, elected the state's first governor of Italian heritage, Foster Furcolo, and also claimed a majority of its congressional delegation. In 1958 they won a majority in the state senate for the first time and reelected John F. Kennedy to the U.S. Senate with nearly three-fourths of the popular vote. A new era of Democratic rule was at hand.

The era of one-party democracy began gloriously for Bay State Democrats in 1960, with native son John Kennedy winning the presidency. The Irish of Massachusetts had come to power in both state and nation. Edward Kennedy followed his brother to the U.S. Senate in 1962, where he has served since; he was reelected in 1994 to a sixth term. In 1964 brother Robert was elected to the U.S. Senate from New York, and two nephews were members of

Congress in the mid-1990s: Joseph, elected from Massachusetts in 1986, and Patrick, from Rhode Island in 1994. For all their national prominence, however, the Kennedys have not played a major role in state party affairs, although in the spring of 1956, to advance his bid for vice president in November, JFK did lead a fight to replace party chair William "Onions" Burke with a Kennedy man, Pat Lynch (Barbrook 1973, 115).

By 1961 the Democrats held most of the political turf in the commonwealth and, through the 1960s and 1970s, expanded their holdings against a retreating Republican Party. Other than the governorship, the Democrats have held most of the state constitutional offices most of the time since 1948. After winning full control of the state legislature in 1958, the Democrats increased their majorities in both houses to 2:1 in 1968 and to 3:1 in 1978. Except for two years in the senate in the early 1990s, the Democrats have maintained that ratio since.

Republican opposition has been erratic at best. The GOP has failed repeatedly to run candidates for even half of the state legislative seats. The governorship, however, has been a different story. When the term of Governor William Weld, elected in 1990 and reelected in 1994, expires in 1999, the GOP will have occupied the governor's office for twenty of the previous thirty-eight years. From 1961 through 1974, Republicans John Volpe and Francis Sargent served as chief executive for all but two years. In 1974 Democrat Michael Dukakis won the office, after which he and Democrat Edward King held it for sixteen years. When Dukakis declined to run in 1990, after his unsuccessful bid for president in 1988, Republican Weld won the office.

Insofar as the GOP has enjoyed success otherwise, it has been in races for major offices. Elliot Richardson was elected state attorney general in the 1960s; Edward Brooke served two terms in the U.S. Senate from 1966 to 1978; Ronald Reagan carried the state twice for president; and Joseph Malone was elected state treasurer in 1990 and reelected in 1994. Republican success in contesting these more "visible" offices led David Mayhew to suggest that Massachusetts has a system of "split-level bipartyism," in which the parties are competitive for the more prominent offices but not so competitive for all the rest (Mayhew 1968, 31–44).

Explanations for this pattern lie in Democratic Party factionalism and in the political cultures of Massachusetts. Dominated by the Irish, the Massachusetts Democratic Party has not always been hospitable to the advancement of other ethnic groups. Italians in particular have often found the GOP more rewarding to their political ambitions, as in the cases of Volpe in the 1960s and of Weld's lieutenant governor, Paul Cellucci, whose presence on the 1990 GOP ticket produced a large Republican vote for governor in Italian neighborhoods of Boston and elsewhere.

Ethnic politics defines the state's political culture. The deep cultural divide between English, Protestant, mill-owning Republicans and Irish, Catholic, working-class Democrats that shaped state politics in the late nineteenth and early twentieth centuries has yielded to a more moderate and varied political culture. Edgar Litt (1965, ch. 1) finds the explanation of state politics in the interplay of four distinct cultures: the patricians—old wealth, commercial elites, cosmopolitan; the yeomen—old stock, rural, small town, conservative; the workers—immigrant, urban, populist; and the managers—suburban, professional, reformist. The managers, many of them third- or fourth-generation Americans, are the switch hitters in state politics. Socially liberal, economically moderate, largely independent, and good government reformist, these predominantly suburban voters have become decisive in races for governor and other major offices. In 1994, for example, Republican Weld was reelected governor with 69 percent of the popular vote, while Democrat Kennedy was returned to the U.S. Senate with 57 percent of the vote, as large numbers of suburbanites split their ballots for the two offices that topped the ticket.

## ORGANIZATIONAL DEVELOPMENT

As organizations, Massachusetts political parties have never been strong. In a democracy, parties thrive on political contest and competition. Opposition that poses a continuous threat to incumbent majorities encourages strong parties; its absence does the opposite. With its history of one-party politics and with no period of genuine party competition, the Bay State has never nurtured strong parties.

The Republicans in the late nineteenth and early twentieth centuries present the state's best example of an orderly and disciplined party. Threatened by the growing numbers of immigrants, Yankee Republicans devised a party organization that systematically promoted candidates through the ranks to run for governor, raised money to finance their campaigns, and ran statewide campaigns through the party apparatus. This Republican "elevator," as it was called, survived into the 1940s but declined thereafter and was gone by the 1960s (Lockard 1959, chs. 5–6).

Massachusetts Democrats are a party of factions, whose politics has always centered more on personalities than organization. Indeed, Boston is among the eastern cities that never had a dominant party machine. John Kennedy's candidate-centered, extra-party campaign for president in 1960 mirrored Democratic politics in the Bay State. For decades the Democratic state committee has been dominated by the legislature, not the executive. Dukakis enjoyed more influence within the state party organization than most Democratic chief executives, but even during his tenure, all state party chairs were members of the legislature.

In addition to the noncompetitive nature of state politics, election reform in Massachusetts has not been conducive to strong parties. Driven by Republican desires to frustrate the growing power of immigrant Democrats, Massachusetts was in the forefront of civil service, ballot, primary, and other turn-of-the-century Progressive reforms, including the introduction of nonpartisan elections, that weakened party organizations. Since the 1960s, Democrats, with their growing middle-class constituency, have embraced many of these reforms in the name of citizen participation and a politics of diversity. The one-party character of Bay State politics yields little incentive to change the statutory environment.

## CURRENT PARTY ORGANIZATION

*Constitution of State Parties.* Party structure is simpler in Massachusetts than in other states. It consists of two levels: the state committee and the local town and ward committees. City committees are formed from ward committees and are often the more important urban party unit, especially for Democrats. State law makes no provision for county committees, an often powerful level of party organization elsewhere, nor for precinct committees, the usual grassroots level of party organization.

Members of the Democratic and Republican state, town, and ward committees are chosen quadrennially at the state's presidential primary in early March. State law provides that one man and one woman be elected for four-year terms to the party central committees from each of the state's forty senate districts. In addition, under the provisions of a party charter adopted in 1979, the Democrats elect eighty additional members to their central committee, evenly balanced by gender, at state senate district caucuses held every two years. Delegates to the district caucuses are elected at town and ward committee caucuses, which are open to registered Democrats only. Local party committees have between three and thirty-five members, depending upon local preference.

Both parties add state constitutional officers, state legislative leaders, and members of Congress to their state committees. In addition, the Democratic state committee elects about a dozen affirmative action and ten organized labor representatives as members, while Republican Party bylaws make all former state party chairs and leaders of various GOP women's, youth, and minority organizations ex officio members of the state committee. The parties differ, however, in the role given these add-on members: the Democrats give them a vote; the Republicans do not. This reflects a basic structural difference between the two state party committees.

Organizationally, the Democrats are more parliamentary in design, whereas the Republicans follow the separation-of-powers principle. The Democrats vest all power and responsibility in their state committee, which is the policy-making and administrative oversight body for the state party. The party chair and staff interact directly with all members of the state committee, and the committee is the sole governing body for the party between conventions. The Democrats have an executive committee consisting of the chair, other officers, and representatives appointed by the chair from each congressional district, all of whom are members of the state committee. The executive committee plays a steering and advisory role only and cannot bind the state party in any way.

In contrast, the Republicans separate executive and legislative functions, assigning the former to an executive committee and the latter to the state committee. Party bylaws provide for an executive committee made up of the state chair and other party officers, the members of the state committee who have been designated as regional party chairs, national committee members, state constitutional officers, and state legislative leaders, all of whom are voting members. This committee is empowered to act for the state party on matters of policy and management between meetings of the state committee, though general budgetary, oversight, and constitutional powers are reserved to the state committee.

These organizational differences reflect intraparty political differences. The Democratic structure lends the day-to-day management of the party to influence by state legislative leaders and others in Boston, while state committee meetings and party conventions are forums dominated by the party's various public policy constituencies. The Republican structure gives the leading role to party and elected officials at the state and national levels, who make policy for and manage the party, while the state committee and party conventions are arenas of "regulars," who oversee party business but for the most part ratify the actions of party leaders.

These political differences play out most clearly in the election of state party chairs. Democratic Party state chairs are commonly chosen through a process that favors "insider" politics, in which the party's legislative leaders and Boston interests have great influence. Indeed, since the 1970s, Democratic state chairs have been members of the party leadership in the state house or senate. In the GOP, the selection of state chairs is commonly a more public contest between ethnic, generational, or ideological factions within the party. In both parties, national and statewide officeholders tend to stay on the sidelines in these contests.

The election of state and local party committees at the presidential primary disconnects these levels of party from one another and from state elections. Except for Democratic state committee members chosen at senate district caucuses, there is no formal organizational link between the state and local party committees and thus no necessary internal accountability. The separation of the state primary in September from the presidential primary in March also creates a political distance between members of state and local party committees and their party candidates and campaign organizations.

To some extent, party conventions bridge these gaps. They are the governing bodies in both parties, and while not required to do so by state law, both parties call them in election years. Both parties also operate under rules that give their conventions a doorkeeping role in party nominations for state executive offices and the U.S. Senate. To qualify for primary ballots, candidates for these offices are required to obtain at least 15 percent of the convention vote for the office. These rules have led candidates for these offices in both parties to campaign more actively among town and ward committees, which are responsible for the selection of delegates to the state conventions.

Democrats and Republicans differ in their methods of picking delegates to their respective state conventions. Republicans choose their delegates at meetings of their town and ward committees, and thus almost all convention delegates are members of these committees. The Democrats select delegates at town and ward caucuses run by the local party committees but open to any registered Democrat in the town or ward. This opens their process to wider participation and leads occasionally to contested elections, as different candidates seek delegates favorable to them. Nonetheless, most delegates to Democratic state conventions are also members of local party committees.

*Operation of State Parties.* Both parties operate under a mix of state law and party bylaws or charter. By statute, party committees elect chairs and other officers following the presidential primary. Their terms of office are four years, except that Republican state chairs serve two-year terms and must stand for reelection in January following a gubernatorial election. Republican governors, upon taking office, are thus able to influence the selection of their party's state chair, whereas new Democratic governors cannot because the four-year terms of the chief executive and the party chair are not coterminous.

Relations between governors and their state parties have often been uneasy. Republican John Volpe, the first governor elected to a four-year term, seems to have had little interest in his state party, while his GOP successor, Francis Sargent, ran away from his party, appealing to Democrats and independents with the slogan "Frank Sargent doesn't dress for the party." Democrat Michael Dukakis inherited state party chairs in both 1974 and 1982 and, though he played an active role in party affairs, especially in the 1980s, was never able to have his person as chair. Democrat Edward King, a one-term governor and party outsider, never tried. Governor William Weld, first elected in 1990, has maintained an amiable working relationship with his state committee but also has kept a safe distance from internal party affairs. Even after reelection in 1994, he removed himself publicly from the selection of a new party chair.

The state chairs of both parties are chosen by their state committees and are the chief executive officers of their parties, having broad authority in the management of party affairs. The state committees also pick delegates to the national party committees. Republican Party bylaws establish eight standing committees for budget, finance, candidates, issues, public relations, registration and membership, and bylaws, as well as their executive committee. The chair appoints members of all committees, except the executive committee. The Democratic Party charter provides for a judicial council to adjudicate intraparty disputes but gives the state committee authority to establish all other committees.

Both parties maintain offices in Boston and, since the mid-1970s, have had full-time staffs and salaried chairs. In 1995, a nonelection year, the Democrats had four full-time employees: an executive director, communications director, outreach coordinator, and director of operations. The Republicans also had four full-time staff: an executive director, political director, communications specialist, and office manager. The operating budget for the Democrats in 1995 was just over $300,000; the GOP budget just over $500,000.

Both parties expand their staffs in election years, as some full-time and many part-time workers are added to provide campaign services. Both focus primarily on state legislative races, where their role is ancillary to candidate organizations but where their impact can be greatest. The Democrats work through a committee of the state party appointed to assist candidates for the legislature. Republicans designate members of the state committee as regional chairs to assist their candidates. The Democrats make no financial contributions to candidates but do provide opposition research, some polling, and advice on consultants and campaign workers, and they coordinate with labor unions and various advocacy organizations on voter registration, mobilization, and phone banks. The Republicans do give financial assistance to candidates, but only to nonincumbents. Other services are available to all their candidates: printing, mailing, phone banks, advice on consultants and campaign staff, as well as some help with polling, media, voter registration, and get-out-the-vote campaigns. Both parties also offer training for candidates and principal campaign staff.

Neither party plays a significant role in races for state executive office, but both assist as resources permit, especially in gubernatorial contests. Neither has a significant role in U.S. House or Senate races; both see their congressional party committees as responsible for these contests. As a party, the GOP seems a bit more active than the Democrats in campaigns for statewide and national office. On occasion, statewide campaigns, such as Kennedy's 1994 Senate race, can drain substantial sums of money and other resources from the state party and its other candidates.

## RESOURCE GUIDE

Neither the parties nor the state maintains an archive for party records. The Republicans have records dating to the 1970s, which are stored in boxes at state party headquarters and are not cataloged. The Democrats have records from the 1980s, but these too are boxed and not cataloged. Otherwise, party records are privately held, if they exist at all. The state archives has no materials, historical or otherwise. The John F. Kennedy Library has some Democratic National Committee materials from the 1950s and 1960s, as well as oral histories and some papers of political leaders in the commonwealth. The papers of the three Massachusetts natives who served as Speaker of the U.S. House since 1950—Joseph Martin, John W. McCormack, and Thomas P. O'Neill—are at Stonehill College, Boston University, and Boston College, respectively, while those of Michael Dukakis and others remain privately held. Party registration by town and ward, as well as state election results, are published by the Office of the Secretary of State in Public Document 43.

## REFERENCES

*Asterisks denote the most important publications on Massachusetts party politics.*
Barbrook, Alec. 1973. *God save the commonwealth: An electoral history of Massachusetts.* Amherst: University of Massachusetts Press.
*Bulger, William M. 1996. *While the Music Lasts.* Boston: Houghton-Mifflin.

*Formisano, Ronald P. 1991. *Boston against busing: Race, class, and ethnicity in the 1960s and 1970s.* Chapel Hill: University of North Carolina.

Frier, Ted, and Larry Overlan. 1992. *Time for a change: The return of the Republican Party in Massachusetts.* Boston: Davis Press.

Gaines, Richard. 1987. *Dukakis and the reform impulse.* Boston: Quinlan Press.

*Huthmacher, J. Joseph. 1959. *Massachusetts people and politics.* Cambridge: Harvard University Press.

*Litt, Edgar. 1965. *The political cultures of Massachusetts.* Cambridge: MIT Press.

Lockard, Duane. 1959. *New England state politics.* Princeton, N.J.: Princeton University Press.

Mayhew, David. 1968. Massachusetts: Split-level bipartyism. In *Party politics in the New England states,* ed. George Goodwin Jr. and Virginia Schuck. Durham: New England Center.

*O'Connor, Thomas H. 1995. *The Boston Irish: A political history.* Boston: Northeastern University Press.

O'Neill, Tip, with William Novak. 1987. *Man of the House.* New York: Random House.

# Michigan

CAROL S. WEISSERT

## PARTY HISTORY

Michigan's allegiance to the Republican Party goes back to the very founding of the party. For it was in Jackson, Michigan, on July 6, 1854, that the Grand Old Party got its name, adopted a platform, and nominated its first candidates (Browne and VerBurg 1995). Michigan residents warmly embraced the new party and its opposition to slavery and continued to support the Republicans for more than one hundred years. There were only four Democratic governors between 1900 and 1946, and three owed their victories to the popularity of Franklin Roosevelt. There were no Democrats serving in the 1925–1926 session of the legislature, and relatively few in the other sessions between 1900 and 1946. Although malapportionment continued to promote Republican dominance in the legislature, in the 1940s the migration of African Americans from the South and the rising influence of the labor unions in politics helped to end the long Republican dominance of the governor's office with the election of Democrat G. Mennen Williams as governor in 1948.

Within a few years of Williams's victory, the "long period of Republican dominance ended; spirited two-party competition had come to Michigan" (Stieber 1970, 1). Since 1951 the Democrats have had control of both houses of the legislature for six sessions (the Republicans had control of both for only seven sessions) and there were five occasions when neither party had the majority. The change was not serendipitous but was the result of a clever strategy on the part of the Michigan Democratic Party that linked labor union members with liberal intellectuals and sought to spread the liberal/labor message throughout the state (Browne and VerBurg 1995).

Since that time, both major parties have flourished, benefiting from strong grassroots organizations guided by forward-thinking leaders and, at various times, strong gubernatorial leadership as well. The Republicans dominated the governor's office over the past thirty years, with popular governors George Romney and William Milliken serving twenty consecutive years between 1963 and 1983. The Democrats were less successful in political leadership; since G. Mennen Williams, there have been only two Democratic governors. One, John Swainson, served only one two-year term in the 1960s. The other, James Blanchard, who served two terms in the 1980s, did not relish his role as party leader and provided little direct guidance to the party.

Parties in Michigan are issue-oriented, a focus forced in part by the state's near complete embrace of the merit system for state hiring in 1941, which all but eliminated the use of patronage as a party-building tool. The Democrats' issue orientation is also due in part to the decision of the Michigan Congress of Industrial Organizations (CIO) to affiliate openly and actively with the Democratic Party in 1948 (Sawyer 1960).

To understand Michigan politics, especially Democratic politics, one has to talk about labor unions. First the AFL-CIO, then the UAW (United Auto Workers), and more recently the teachers' union have played important roles in shaping and running the state Democratic Party, a party in which racial issues, inclusiveness, and urban-suburban issues have played out in a cacophony of voices over the past three decades. Democrats are noisy, said one Michigan party leader. In Michigan, party disagreements have often been aired in newspapers and courtrooms throughout the state.

## ORGANIZATIONAL DEVELOPMENT

The Democratic Party has been "reborn" at least twice in the past five decades; the Republican Party changed dramatically in the 1960s, and in the 1990s it gained a financial and emotional edge with the election of a party-oriented governor who helped garner resources and articulate clear party issues and direction.

The first Democratic rebirth occurred in the late 1940s, when the party strengthened its state central committee, carefully built county organizations, developed dependable sources of funding, and established a large pool of volunteers for electioneering—all from labor support and most from the automobile industry. "Labor was the revitalized party's nucleus and would remain so for decades" (Stieber 1970, 28). During the 1950s the Democratic Party painstakingly developed its infrastructure from the precincts to the state central committee. And the need for revitalization was great. In 1949 more than half of the state's eighty-three counties had no Democratic county committee. Two years later, all but twelve were organized (Sawyer 1960). The rebirth— orchestrated by August Scholle, president of the Michigan CIO; G. Mennen Williams; and a few others—included finding attractive candidates for statewide and local offices, integrating county and legislative committees with the state organization, and producing platforms featuring increased spending for welfare, health, and public housing.

The Republicans responded in 1961 with a plan for action, setting forth new directions in six key areas: research, education, press relations, advertising and promotion, special events, and field organization. In 1961 the staff expanded from seven employees to twenty-two, a budgetary control system was put in place, an office was set up in southeastern Michigan (a big population center that the Republicans had targeted), and a central buying agency was set up to coordinate advertising across races. The impetus for the effort was what John Gibbs, author of the reorganization plan, called "the vastly changed political conditions" of the state (1963, 1). "Republicans have failed to modify our appeal to meet the needs of a changing era," he said. "The Democratic Party in Michigan has the image of progress; the GOP is characterized as a throwback to the past" (1963, 2).

The approach to party revitalization, like the image of the Republican most associated with the era—George Romney—was quintessentially businesslike. The emphasis was on product and effective marketing. "We must sell Republicanism through the same instruments that industry sells its products," Gibbs's plan explained. "Just as industry strives for greater and greater market penetration, we must strive for greater and greater voter penetration" (1963, 4). Further, the party needed to operate full-time, not just prior to every election.

The 1961 constitutional convention helped focus the Republicans' programmatic agenda.[1] The party put out a statement of principles on the convention and held workshops for Republican candidates for the seats. The result of the election, what the party called a "stunning triumph," was Republican dominance of the convention. At the end of the year, newspapers noted the Republican resurgence as one of the biggest state news stories in 1961—bigger than the constitutional convention itself (Michigan State Central Committee 1962).

In 1962 the Republican Party launched a Neighbor-to-Neighbor drive to raise money and secure worker support for the state party at the grassroots level. For the first time, the party trained workers by television in 1962. In 1964 the party launched a recruitment drive in Wayne County, where it opened a Detroit office. The party was divided in 1964 by the selection of Barry Goldwater as presidential candidate. Romney refused to campaign for Goldwater in Michigan. In an unusual move, Romney ran campaign ads illustrating how Michiganders could split their ballot, voting for him and President Johnson. His encouragement of split-ticket voting was taken to heart by Michigan voters, who have been ticket splitters ever since. One longtime Democratic elected official called Romney's official encouragement "the beginning of the end" of party loyalty (for both parties) in Michigan.[2]

In the late 1960s the Democrats were having unity problems of their own. Some state party leaders were openly criticizing President Johnson and the Vietnam War, and the party chair stepped down, refusing to endorse the Democratic ticket of 1968. There was a schism in the party between liberals and more moderate labor leaders, and the party was on the "verge of destruction" (Buffa 1984, vi).

By 1970 both parties had wider bases than they had a decade earlier, with the Republicans making inroads in urban areas and Democrats advancing in areas outside the populous Detroit metropolitan area. Both parties relied heavily on computers to analyze voting patterns. Advertising and public relations staff sat in on strategy sessions, and polling was taken to "new heights" (Stieber 1970, 100).

For the Republicans, the 1970s were a placid period in which the party was headed by a popular governor (William Milliken) who was not active in party affairs. But the 1970s were not kind to the state Democratic Party, which ran into trouble with the national party, with its state members, and with the electorate. In 1971 a federal judge ordered that schoolchildren be bused from Detroit to suburban areas—a wildly unpopular issue initially supported by the state's Democrats. The party's resolution of support for busing became a lightning rod in the following election, and Democratic candidates, including those who had signed the document, rapidly moved away from it. But the episode was a symbol of how distant the party leaders were from their political base—the blue collar voters of the Detroit suburbs.

The state party ran into problems with the national party leadership over procedures of delegate selection in 1972. National Democratic Party provisions relating to minority participation in the delegation worried some in the Michigan party who feared that Detroit would gain strength at the expense of the suburbs and nonmetropolitan areas (Browne and

VerBurg 1995, 203). Michigan was also at odds over the timing of delegate selection. Michigan law provided that precinct delegates be selected two years before the presidential election; the new national rules specified that delegate selection was not to begin until the year of the presidential election (Browne and VerBurg 1995, 203). The new rules inadvertently favored George Wallace, the bantam segregationist governor from Alabama, who won Michigan's first presidential primary in 1972, much to the dismay of party leaders. The open Democratic primary was a draw for many voters who eschewed the less exciting Republican primary (featuring a sitting president, Richard Nixon).

It was at this low point that the second remaking of the Michigan Democratic Party occurred—once again at the instigation of labor. This time the United Auto Workers provided the impetus. As Buffa puts it, "Before 1972, the UAW acted as a participant, albeit the strongest one, in the Democratic coalition; after 1972, the UAW simply took over the leadership of the Democratic Party" (1984, viii). A UAW-supported candidate became party chair and set up a control system to whip the party back into shape. The chair, Morley Winograd, wanted to broaden the base of the party by aligning it with the political center, not the left, to which he and others thought it had drifted in the 1960s. His base, the county chairs and unions, formed a unity caucus which informally made key decisions in advance of central committee meetings. Yet it was clear that the chair was directly accountable to the UAW. As Winograd said to UAW officials in 1976, "I don't make any substantive political decision without checking with the UAW and reaching agreement." He continued that he did not want the job as state chair "without UAW support because it isn't worth having under those conditions" (Buffa 1984, 234).

But the broadening of the party base brought problems as well, namely, diminished power for Detroit's African American leadership. In 1978 Winograd headed the national commission that loosened the national Democratic Party's strict adherence to quotas for minority and women delegates to national conventions. The action was opposed by African Americans in the Michigan party, including Coleman Young, the popular and influential mayor of Detroit. Later that year, Winograd accused Young of not actively supporting the Democratic gubernatorial candidate, which led several Detroit members to boycott Democratic meetings and to schedule their own separate Jefferson-Jackson Day functions. An apology by Winograd and reinstatement of Young to his leadership position in the party ensued several months later, but the rift was widely publicized and divisive.

In 1980 national Democratic Party rules again forced changes in Michigan's elections. The national rules prohibited the seating of national delegates who were elected in open primaries. Although the Michigan Democratic Party supported a closed primary for presidential elections, the Republican governor opposed the change and the Senate concurred. The party changed to a caucus system but potentially faced embarrassment if the primary, scheduled to follow the caucuses, produced different results. The state party asked the two front-runners in the race, President Carter and Sen. Edward Kennedy, to withdraw their names from the primary race. Both did, but the Republicans had a field day highlighting the undemocratic nature of the Democratic primary. Republicans also benefited when a former state Democratic Party chair filed suit alleging that the primary was the only lawful method of delegate selection.

In an effort to achieve party accountability, the Democratic Party endorsed two key organizational changes in 1980: one change allowed the party to endorse candidates prior to the election, and the other allowed the central committee to censure party members who did not follow the party platform. In 1986 the state Democratic Party built an extensive database for use by candidates for direct-mailing and canvassing purposes. The party provided centralized phone banks, media services, telemarketing, and polling and heavily invested in get-out-the-vote efforts. In 1988 the legislature agreed on a closed presidential primary and open primaries for statewide offices. In 1992, for the first time, Michigan voters had to declare their party preferences. But in 1995 the rules changed again, as the Republican-controlled legislature passed a law mandating open presidential primaries. The change forced Michigan Democrats to return to closed caucuses in 1996.

Although labor's role in the Democratic Party is less visible and probably less dominant today than in earlier decades, it is still very strong. The UAW remains active at the local level of the party and is consulted when major policy issues arise. In recent years, the Michigan Education Association, the teachers' union, has become increasingly active in the party. Nearly half of the delegates to the 1992 Democratic National Convention were members of organized labor (Browne and VerBurg 1995, 207).[3] Browne and VerBurg (1995, 207) note that organized labor "is still the single most important element in the Democratic Party organization." However, a long-time Democratic official believes the teachers' union is not as influential in the party as its labor predecessors were and that unions are not the major players they once were.[4]

## CURRENT PARTY ORGANIZATION

The Democratic and Republican Parties in Michigan are both viewed as strong organizations. In Cotter et al.'s 1984 ranking, the state Democratic Party ranked eleventh in the country when compared with all state parties, and was the third-strongest Democratic Party. The state's Republican Party ranked twenty-second in party strength, with seventeen state Republican Party organizations ranked higher.

State law requires parties to hold a spring convention in odd years to select a state central committee, a chair, and two vice chairs. The state also requires that parties hold a convention at least sixty days before the August primary during election years. At that time, both parties select candidates for lieutenant governor, attorney general, secretary of state, state board of education, state supreme court, and the governing boards of the state's three major research institutions.

Michigan is one of a very few states in which both state and local parties are considered strong (Cotter et al. 1984). Cotter et al. ranked Michigan's local Democratic Party organizations twelfth and local Republican organizations fourteenth. According to Smith (1987), 93 percent of county Democratic and Republican organizations in Michigan have a complete set of officers, 90 percent recruit volunteer workers, and 72 percent operate under formal rules. Some 39 percent publish a newsletter, 33 percent have a regular budget, and 20 percent maintain permanent headquarters. Only 8 percent employ full-time staff. Nevertheless, these organizations are active, with 92 percent distributing literature, 86 percent arranging fund-raising events, 82 percent contributing money to candidates, 71 percent putting out press releases, 70 percent organizing telephone campaigns, 70 percent buying newspaper ads, and 35 percent conducting candidate training sessions. Smith notes that the county parties may lack the sophistication of state and national parties, but this has not dampened their enthusiasm for conducting numerous programs to get votes for their candidates.

County parties also play a major role in the activities of the state parties. Browne and VerBurg believe that Michigan parties look more hierarchical on paper than they actually are. They conclude that the "ability of the state organization to dictate policies to local organizations is limited" (1995, 208). Indeed, both parties pride themselves on their grass-roots organization and say they rely on local parties for policy guidance. Although spokespersons for both parties highlight the "bottom-up" nature of the decision making, a recent survey of Democratic activists found some dissatisfaction with top-down decisions. The new chair (appointed in 1995) is attempting to stoke grassroots efforts and to provide more assistance to county groups.

Michigan is viewed as a heavy regulator of political parties. Cotter et al. (1984) ranked Michigan in the lowest quintile in terms of supportive public policy toward parties. Yet Browne and VerBurg (1995) argue that Michigan's laws are generally supportive of parties. They point to a number of supportive state policies: candidates for all statewide offices except governor are chosen at party conventions, parties are allowed to endorse candidates in primary elections, and voters may cast a straight party ballot instead of voting for candidates individually. (Only one of these three pro-party policies was included in the Cotter index.)

The staff of the state Democratic Party is small and has gotten smaller in recent years. In contrast, the Republican staff has grown by 50 percent over the past five years. In 1990 the Michigan Democratic Party had thirteen permanent staff; in 1995 it had a staff of nine. In 1989 state Republican Party staff totaled ten in 1995 there were fifteen staffers—the largest nonelection year staff in quite some time. To a large extent the growth in staff reflects the flush nature of state Republican Party coffers. The current Republican governor, John Engler, is an active fundraiser for the party, raising millions of dollars each year. The Republicans would not release their operating budget for 1995; the Democrats reported a noncampaign budget of around $1 million.

The Democratic State Central Committee is made up of 350 members selected from six-teen districts and eighty-two counties and meets four times a year. An executive board, comprising officers and twenty members selected by the state central committee, is empowered to make policy between committee meetings. The party's main office is in the state capital; a smaller office in Detroit is opened in election years. The Republican State Central Committee has ninety-six members (six from each of sixteen congressional dis-tricts) and meets five times a year. There is no executive committee. The party's office is in the state capital; a campaign office is opened in election years in or near Detroit.

The Michigan Republican Party is currently dominated by the incumbent governor, John Engler. He is active in the party, especially in fund raising. He also sets the political agenda for the party, suggests party chairs, and helps with candidate recruitment. He is so dominant that one party staffer says, "We're part of the governor's team. This place lives and dies with John Engler."[5] Engler has been able to hold off potentially divisive elements of the party, such as the Christian Coalition and Pro Life and Michigan Right to Life groups. The state party works closely with Republican caucuses in the legislature, especial-ly since Engler has been governor. The state Democratic Party's relationship with Democratic legislative caucuses is less cordial, according to one observer who said the party and the caucuses have been "going in different directions for thirty years."[6] The disagree-ments are largely ideological in nature, with legislative members, especially senators, often more conservative than many in the Democratic Party leadership.

**Table 1**   Michigan Resource Guide

|  | Democrats | Republicans |
|---|---|---|
| Archive | Yes | Yes |
| Location | Bentley Historical Library[1] | Bentley Historical Library[1] |
|  | University of Michigan | University of Michigan |
|  | 1150 Beal Ave. | 1150 Beal Ave. |
|  | Ann Arbor, Mich. 48109-2113 | Ann Arbor, Mich. 48109-2113 |
| Dates | 1949–1991 | 1920–1979[2] |
| Finding aid | Yes | Yes |
| Access | Public | Public |
| Contents: |  |  |
| Executive committee minutes | Most years | 1962–1968 |
| Correspondence | Yes | Yes |
| Organizational structure | No | No |
| Budgets | Some years | No |
| Rules | Yes | No |

[1]   In addition to the Bentley library, the state archives contain some material from both parties, largely from the 1960s. The archives have administrative records and reports on elections from the Republican State Central Committee, 1959–1968; speeches and correspondence of Governor George Romney (1965–1969); material from the Democratic State Central Committee on the 1972 state convention, the 1972 presidential campaign and national convention, and state elections from 1969 to 1972. The archives also contain the files of James McNeely, chair of the Michigan Democratic Party, 1969–1972.
[2]   Most from the 1960s and 1970s.

## RESOURCE GUIDE

The records of both parties in Michigan are conveniently located in the Bentley Historical Library at the University of Michigan. The files are well cataloged and easy to access.

The Democratic Party files are grouped chronologically and include personal files from the state chairs from 1961 to 1991. Election/campaign files and press releases and publicity files are available for most years.

The Republican Party files contain the papers of only two party chairs, who served in the 1960s. Information on national and state party conventions is provided for various years from 1920 to 1976. Information on the state Republican Party covers the period from 1955 to 1978. The papers of two Republican governors—George Romney and William Milliken—are also in the collection. A problem with the collection is that information on state committees stops in 1978. The Republican State Central Committee, 2121 Grand River Ave., has not cataloged material from the 1980s and is generally unwilling to have researchers comb through potentially sensitive documents.

## NOTES

1. In 1961 voters approved a referendum to call a constitutional convention. George Romney, then an automobile company executive, led the effort to modernize Michigan's government structure. Partisan elections determined delegates to the convention, which proposed a new constitution that strengthened the governor's powers, required a balanced budget, and prohibited adoption of a graduated income tax. The constitution was adopted in April 1963.
2. Interview with a top Democratic official, August 9, 1995; anonymity requested.
3. A spokesperson for the Michigan Democratic Party thought this fraction was too high but did not know the correct one. Interview by author, July 10, 1995; anonymity requested.
4. Interview with a top Democratic elected official, August 7, 1995; anonymity requested.
5. Interview with top Republican staff official, July 19, 1995; anonymity requested.
6. Interview with longtime Democratic Party activist, July 26, 1995; anonymity requested.

REFERENCES

*Asterisks denote the most important publications on Michigan party politics.*

Angel, Daniel. 1974. *William G. Milliken: A touch of steel.* New York: Public Affairs Press.

*Browne, William P., and Kenneth VerBurg. 1995. *Michigan politics and government: Facing change in a complex state.* Lincoln: University of Nebraska Press.

*Buffa, Dudley W. 1984. *Union power and American democracy: The UAW and the Democratic Party.* Ann Arbor: University of Michigan Press.

Cotter, Cornelius, James L. Gibson, John Bibby, and Robert Huckshorn. 1984. *Party organizations in American politics.* New York: Praeger.

Fenton, John H. 1966. *Midwest politics.* New York: Holt, Rinehart and Winston.

Gibbs, John. 1963. *Dynamics of organization: A special report on the background problems and future development of the Republican Party of Michigan. A message from John Gibbs.* Lansing: Michigan Republican Party.

Michigan State Central Committee. 1962. *Michigan Republican Plain Talk* 1, no. 14, January 1.

Sarasohn, Stephen, and Vera H. Sarasohn. 1957. *Party patterns in Michigan.* Detroit: Wayne State University Press.

Sawyer, Robert Lee. 1960. *The Democratic State Central Committee in Michigan, 1949–1959.* Ann Arbor: University of Michigan Institute of Public Administration.

Smith, Gregg W. 1987. The effect of party organizational strength on electoral success. Paper presented at the annual meeting of the Midwest Political Science Association.

Staebler, Neil. 1991. *Out of the smoke-filled room.* Ann Arbor: Wahr Publishing.

*Stieber, Carolyn. 1970. *The politics of change in Michigan.* East Lansing: Michigan State University Press.

Young, Coleman. 1994. *Hard stuff: The autobiography of Coleman Young.* New York: Viking.

# Minnesota

CRAIG GRAU

It would not be surprising for those who think about Minnesota political parties to think of the word *different.* One of the major parties is not the Democratic Party, but the Democratic-Farmer-Labor Party. As most states voted for Republican presidents in the 1980s, Minnesota voted for Democratic candidates; and whereas most states use primaries to select their national convention delegates, caucuses are still important in Minnesota. The state, however, is not isolated from the rest of the United States. Minnesota is affected by national political trends, and famous Minnesotans—including presidential candidates Hubert Humphrey, Eugene McCarthy, and Walter Mondale—have affected the national scene. Each of these was associated with the national Democratic Party, but Republicans have a strong tradition in Minnesota as well. In addition, both parties have had to deal with a tendency toward independence from the two major parties among many in the electorate.

## PARTY HISTORY

Minnesota became a state in 1858 as political parties in the United States were undergoing transformation. The Democrats formed in 1849, and the Republicans in 1855 (Blegen 1963, 214, 216). By the time of the state constitutional convention, feelings were so partisan that delegates from the two parties met in separate rooms. Five members from each party negotiated the constitution. When the time came to sign the constitution, the two groups signed separate copies (State of Minnesota 1993, 19–20).

*Republican Dominance: 1858–1892.* The Democrats won the first election for governor and U.S. House as well as the state legislative appointments to the U.S. Senate, but the Republicans soon rebounded (State of Minnesota 1993, 165–167, 313–320; this is the principal data source for the statistics in this state profile). From 1858 to the election of 1892, Republican presidential candidates carried the state in every election. After the Democratic gubernatorial victory in 1858, Republicans carried the governorship every time as well. During these thirty-five years, Minnesota was represented in the U.S. Senate 91 percent of the time by Republicans (sixty-four years by the Republicans to six years by the Democrats). The Republicans also dominated U.S. House seats. Of Minnesotans in the U.S. House during this period, Republicans served 83 percent of the time. Interestingly, in 1890 a minor party candidate, from the Alliance Party, won a House seat. The victory was a forerunner of change.

*Increasing Competitiveness and the Rise of Independents: 1892–1944.* In the presidential election of 1892, Republican Benjamin Harrison won Minnesota's electors despite strong support for a minor-party candidate, James Weaver, of the People's Party. In the period 1892–1944, the Republicans continued to dominate but to a lesser extent. For the first forty years of this period (1892 to 1932), Republican presidential candidates carried the state in every election with the exception of 1912, when Teddy Roosevelt won as a Progressive. Roosevelt's progressive ideas appealed to Minnesota voters whether he was running as a Republican (1904) or as a Progressive (1912).

In 1932 the Democratic presidential candidate carried Minnesota for the first time in state history. Franklin Roosevelt also carried the state in 1936 and 1940, though by a smaller margin in the latter election. In other major races in the state during the period 1892–1944, the Democrats were the major opposition to the Republicans until 1916, when they were replaced in that role by the Farmer-Labor Party, which was based on an economic protest movement (Gieske 1979, viii). From 1892 until the election of 1918, Democrats held the governorship for ten of the twenty-six years. For the next twenty-six years the Farmer-Labor Party was the chief rival of the Republicans (though in one election the chief Republican rival was an independent). The Farmer-Labor candidate won the governorship in 1930, and the party controlled that office through 1938. Even the state legislature abandoned formal partisanship. Starting in the Progressive era, state legislators were elected without partisan labels.

Although its major opponent had changed, the Republican Party held the governorship 65 percent of the time (thirty-four of fifty-two years) and dominated the congressional delegation between 1892 and 1944. Of the 104 years served by U.S. senators (52 years x 2 senators), Republicans served 72 percent of those years, and nearly all the rest were served by Farmer-Laborites (a Democrat served for one and a half months). In the U.S. House, Republicans served 82 percent of the period, the Farmer-Laborites 12 percent, and the Democrats only 6 percent.

Republican Harold Stassen won the first of three consecutive gubernatorial victories in 1938. The Democrats, except for presidential elections, were faring poorly in Minnesota, and Franklin Roosevelt had received only 52 percent of the two-party vote in 1940. With opposition to the Republicans split between Democrats and the Farmer-Labor Party, some felt unity was needed (Blegen 1963, 576–577).

*Competitive Politics: 1944–Present.* In 1944 the Democratic and Farmer-Labor Parties merged into the Democratic-Farmer-Labor Party (DFL). The effect was not immediately apparent. Roosevelt's percentage of the two-party vote increased only from 52 to 53 percent. In 1948, however, the DFL candidate for the U.S. Senate, Hubert Humphrey II, became the first popularly elected Democratic senator in state history. The governor, though, was popular Republican Luther Youngdahl, who was reelected for a third term with more than 60 percent of the Republican-DFL vote in 1950. Known for his Christian principles, Youngdahl supported aid for the disadvantaged, including housing, education, and health care. He also supported curbing gambling (Blegen 1963, 552–553). In 1951 Democratic president Harry Truman appointed the liberal Republican to the federal bench (Esbjornson 1955, 230). In 1954 DFL candidate Orville Freeman won the governorship. It had been forty years since a candidate with a Democratic label had won the office. In 1958 DFL candidate Eugene McCarthy won a U.S. Senate seat, and when Hubert Humphrey became vice president in 1965, the state attorney general, DFL member Walter Mondale, was appointed to serve the last two years of Humphrey's Senate term. (Mondale would serve in the Senate until he became vice president of the United States in 1977.)

Despite the national fame of Minnesota DFL officials and the success of Democratic presidential candidates in recent years, the two major parties have been competitive. The period 1944 to 1996 has not been as dominated by one party as the other two historical periods examined. It is true that the Democrats' presidential tickets have carried the state in ten elections to the Republicans' three. It must be remembered, however, that in five of those Democratic victories, Minnesotans Hubert Humphrey and Walter Mondale were on the presidential ticket. Republicans were doing much better in other major races. During this period from 1944 to 1996, Republicans occupied the U.S. Senate seats 44 percent of the time (46 of the 104 years; 52 years x 2 Senate seats), the U.S. House 49.8 percent of the time, and the governorship 50 percent of the time.

Partisanship does not always reflect ideology. At the beginning of the 104th Congress in 1995, Minnesota's two U.S. senators were split by party and ideology, but that division was not true among the U.S. House members. In the first one hundred days of the Congress, Minnesota Democrats in the U.S. House did not always oppose Republican initiatives. For example, Democrats held a six-to-two majority in the U.S. House delegation, but only three Democrats opposed the balanced budget amendment, the line-item veto, and term limits (Congressional Quarterly 1995). These three represented Minneapolis, St. Paul, and northeastern Minnesota—including Duluth and the iron-mining communities north of it. The three DFL members who voted with the Republicans had less tenure than did the other members of the state congressional delegation; of the three, two represented rural districts, and the third represented a suburban district. In the state legislature, though, the Republicans have not controlled both houses since partisan labels were reintroduced in the mid-1970s.

The DFL-Republican competitiveness in officeholding has not eliminated independence in the electorate. In 1992, for instance, Democratic candidate Bill Clinton's percentage in the state was within 1 point of his national average, whereas Ross Perot's percentage was 5 points higher than his national average, which is indicative of Minnesota's continuing fascination with independents. By 1995 the Independence Party was a major force, and in 1996 it changed its name to the Reform Party—the party that nominated Ross Perot for president.

## ORGANIZATIONAL DEVELOPMENT

Although the structure and the functions of the DFL and Republican Parties are similar to what they were a generation ago, changes are evident. Some of the changes were caused by and occurred in coincidence with national trends. The 1968 National Democratic Convention, for example, focused on disagreements between supporters of Minnesotans Hubert Humphrey and Eugene McCarthy. To make the selection of delegates to future Democratic conventions more open, the McGovern-Fraser commission recommended changes in the delegate-selection process that the national party adopted. (George McGovern was a Democratic senator from South Dakota and the party's presidential candidate in 1972, and Don Fraser was a U.S. representative from Minnesota and later the mayor of Minneapolis.) Although many states moved to select their national delegates by primary, Minnesota stayed with a caucus/convention system, encouraging greater participation by party identifiers.

By 1976 the subcaucus had become dominant in the DFL. Attendees at caucuses, but more often at conventions on higher levels, may divide into smaller groups (subcaucuses) supporting candidates or issues. These subcaucuses then choose delegates in proportion to their numerical strength to move to the next higher convention. Logically, the most intense supporters and the least susceptible to compromise are chosen to represent each subcaucus. Even Don Fraser, who supported proportional representation, called the subcaucus "parties within our party" (quoted in Auerbach 1984, 70). A winner-take-all system, on the other hand, can result in no member of a minority faction making it to a state convention.

In deference to the popularity of presidential primaries, the Minnesota state legislature brought back the primary for 1992. The presidential primary had been used in the 1950s but was abandoned in 1959. The traditional explanation is that major party leaders were not happy with the results. Minnesota Republican favorite son Harold Stassen was hurt by the surprise victory of Dwight Eisenhower in the 1952 Republican primary. Four years later, in his bid for the Democratic presidential nomination, Estes Kefauver defeated Adlai Stevenson, who was supported by Hubert Humphrey (Auerbach 1984, 39). In 1992 the parties were to choose delegates to the national conventions in proportion to how successful candidates were in a closed primary, which is different from the open primary used in all other partisan primaries in the state (State of Minnesota 1994b, 207A.01–207A.06). The DFL Party said that it would not be bound by the primary in selecting its delegates. The Republicans, however, did choose delegates in proportion to the primary results, although the state convention delegates still decided who would represent the candidate. In fact, Harold Stassen received sufficient support to be a delegate to the Republican National Convention in 1992, but the state convention picked as a delegate a person other than Stassen. The former governor felt it was due to his support for abortion rights (Minneapolis Star Tribune 1992). This was another example supporting Malcolm E. Jewell's observation on the seriousness of issues to delegates at DFL and Republican conventions (Jewell 1984, 279). On social issues Minnesota parties have the same image as do their parent organizations nationally. After a failure to agree on primary reforms in 1995, the presidential primary was suspended for 1996 (State of Minnesota 1995c, supp., 207A.01; Star Tribune 1995).

Other national trends have also affected Minnesota parties. Watergate led to the high point of DFL strength, in 1974. As noted earlier, state legislators for sixty years had run for office without party labels but had caucused as conservatives and liberals, with the conservatives usually in the majority (Mitau 1970, 82–83). In 1974 legislators ran with party labels, and the DFL won both houses of the legislature. Wendell Anderson, the DFL member running for reelection as governor, more than doubled the vote of the Republican candidate. The Republicans had suffered a severe setback nationwide as well, and more and more voters were classifying themselves as independent (The Gallup Poll 1978, 561–562).

Minnesota Republicans in 1975 decided a major change was necessary, and they changed the name of their party to the Independent-Republican Party (Cassano 1975). Only 17 percent of the Republicans nationwide questioned by the Gallup organization felt the national Republican Party should follow the Minnesota lead (The Gallup Poll 1978, 645), but in Minnesota the Independent-Republicans achieved major successes. With the death of Humphrey in 1978 and Mondale's election as vice president in 1976, the Independent-Republicans won both Senate seats and the governorship in 1978. By the 1990s Republicanism had become more popular nationally, and although attempts to drop the word *Independent* from the party name failed in 1991 and 1993, the party dropped it in 1995 (Smith 1995). The 1994 Republican electoral successes were convincing evidence that undiluted Republicanism was popular.

Campaign finance reform, which swept the nation in the 1970s as a result of Watergate, also affected Minnesota parties. Today political action committees and public financing are more evident, as are candidate-centered campaigns and fund raising by legislative caucuses. State legislative caucuses have their own fund-raising operations. Going into 1994, for example, the two DFL legislative caucuses had six times as much cash on hand as the state central committee, and the Republican caucuses had nearly twice as much as their central committee (State of Minnesota 1995a, L 1–11). In the 1994 campaign, party contributions accounted for only 10 percent of the campaign expenditures for Minnesota state house candidates and only 1 percent of campaign expenditures of candidates for constitutional offices (State of Minnesota 1995a). Public financing also directly and indirectly goes to party candidates and accounts for a large part of the expenditures, reducing special interest competition (Coffman 1995).

Despite all of these financial competitors, parties are not impotent. Modern politics, like other selling endeavors, place a premium on mailing and telephone lists. Even though the number of activists has declined, the DFL and Republican Parties have names and addresses of tens of thousands of participants and contributors in every area of the state. Each party also has a permanent headquarters, equipped and staffed (Kunkel 1993, 119). In an era of rapid response, each party has a principal spokesperson in the Twin Cities (Minneapolis and St. Paul) for easy access to and for the media. Since the attributes and time necessary to coordinate with like-minded groups and activists as well as to keep a high media profile may be more than is possible for one person, the DFL has split the functions of spokesperson and organizational director, making the latter a paid position.

## CURRENT PARTY ORGANIZATION

The definition of a political party and certain aspects of party organizations are specified by the state of Minnesota. A distinction is made in state statutes between a "political party" and a "major political party." The former is "an association of individuals under whose name a candidate files for partisan office" (State of Minnesota 1994b, 200.02 sub. 6). A major political party is "a political party that maintains a party organization in the state, political division, or precinct in question" and presented a statewide candidate in the last election who either received votes in each county and at least 5 percent of the votes cast in the election or who presented a petition for a place on the partisan primary ballot with signatures of 5 percent of those who voted in the last statewide election (State of Minnesota 1994b, 200.02 sub. 7). In 1992 eleven candidates ran for president in Minnesota. In 1995, though, only three political parties were regarded as major: the Democratic-Farmer-Labor Party, the Republican Party, and the Independence Party; the Independence Party had a candidate for the U.S. Senate who had received the necessary number of votes in 1994 (State of Minnesota 1995b, 27–28 ). In 1996 the Independence Party changed its name to the Reform Party. By qualifying as major parties, these three parties have their names placed on tax forms for public financing by taxpayers (McGrath 1995).

Traditionally, the DFL and Republican Parties make endorsements and carry out other party functions through a caucus/convention system. State statute outlines various aspects of the caucuses and conventions, including when they are held and time frames for voting for delegates (State of Minnesota 1994b, 202A). Caucuses are held in early March of even-numbered years. At the precinct level, relatively few people gather to select party leaders for their units, discuss issues to be included in the state party platform, and select delegates to the next level of the party hierarchy.

Republicans refer to the next level as the basic political organizational unit. This may be at the county or state legislative district level. The DFL calls this level the county level, although it may be a smaller unit in more populated counties. Participants at this level discuss issues, choose party leaders, endorse candidates for offices in their geographic regions, and select delegates to the next higher level. This step is followed by conventions at the third level, the congressional district level. Here the focus is on endorsing a candidate for the U.S. House seat, although presidential delegates may be chosen as well. At the state convention the focus is on endorsements for statewide offices, the party platform, and the selection of presidential delegates in appropriate years. The DFL also chooses its state party officials at these conventions.

Between conventions a major party, as specified in statute, is generally managed by a state central committee. The central committees are large bodies of more than 325 members for the Republicans and 450 for the DFL. They include the major party officials and public officials as well. The Republican state central committee chooses its statewide party officials. The DFL state central committee chooses its statewide officials when a vacancy occurs between conventions.

By statute, the state executive committee administers the party. Among those who serve on the executive committees are the statewide elected party officers, including the national committee persons and representatives of congressional districts, and the state finance chair for the Republicans and the state head of the youth organization for the DFL. Elected DFL public officials who were endorsed by the party organization before their election are also represented. This procedure aids in bringing the party's public officials and rank-and-file activists together. The executive committees are about one-tenth the size of the central committees.

In recent years, the chair of the party has been a focal point of the organization. It is difficult, though, to find many examples of the post being used as a launching pad for a successful career in public office, as was true in 1978 and 1990 for two national committeemen. In 1995 the DFL hired an executive director, and the chair became a part-time, unpaid position (Baden 1995). The director reports to the chair but runs the state office as directed by the state executive committee. The position of executive director could become crucial in the DFL Party.

Public officials may let the activists know whom they favor to lead the party. In 1995 many Republican elected officials sided with the incumbent chair, who was opposed by a candidate of the social conservatives. The incumbent chair was narrowly reelected (Duluth News-Tribune 1995).

The caucus system has been a subject of controversy. Participation takes time, especially if one moves up the ladder of conventions. Those who are willing to take part are probably not representative of party voters. DFL state delegates appear to be more liberal than the typical DFL member, and Republican delegates tend to be more conservative than the norm. Those who attend precinct caucuses and those who set aside additional days to attend conventions on higher levels seem to be driven by an intensity not held by average voters. In addition, attendance at caucuses has been decreasing (DFLP Education Foundation 1995, 7). In presidential election years from 1972 to 1988, DFL caucus attendees numbered from 70,000 to 100,000, with the median being 72,000. For Republicans, the range was 30,000 to 60,000, with four of five being 60,000. In 1992, however, fewer than 39,000 turned out for the DFL caucuses, and only 22,000 for the Republicans. A similar decline occurred in nonpresidential years. In the period 1974–1990, DFL attendees numbered from 40,000 to 60,000, with a median of 56,000. Republican caucus attendees numbered from 15,000 to 60,000, with a median of 25,000. In 1994 the Republicans maintained their 25,000, but attendance at the DFL caucuses fell to fewer than 25,000.

Open-primary outcomes are more reflective than caucus outcomes of the electorate. A dramatic example of this was the race for governor in 1994. The Independent-Republican Party, as the Republican Party was then known, endorsed a social conservative candidate in opposition to the moderate Independent-Republican incumbent governor. The nonendorsed incumbent won the primary handily. He went on to crush the endorsed liberal DFL candidate, who had barely won nomination in the primary against two strong opponents, one of whom had been a former DFL chairperson. Similarly, in 1982 the endorsed gubernatorial candidates were defeated in primaries by candidates less reflective of party positions on controversial social issues.

The split in the Republican Party has been over social issues, primarily abortion and gay rights. Those who stress economic conservatism are at odds with those who emphasize social conservatism. As social conservatives have become more dominant, concern has grown within the party about losing large donations from fiscal conservatives (Smith 1992). Fiscal and social issues cause disagreements among DFL members as well. Some in organized labor have been upset with the party organization, which it feels emphasizes social liberalism too much, while labor's fiscal liberalism has been deserted by some DFL legislators (Parsons and McGrath 1995).

Divisiveness and the losses by party-endorsed candidates should not be overemphasized. Many endorsed candidates are not seriously opposed for their party's nomination. This has been especially true in state legislative contests (Kunkel 1988, 211).

In some ways political parties are now stronger than they were fifty years ago. They are more institutionalized and more professional than in the past, but the tasks are greater and the competition is as well. Political action committees are countered somewhat by indirect and direct public financing, but interest groups seem to have stronger identifiers and are more cohesive than the parties. Declining activist involvement is the greatest threat to Minnesota political parties. Citizen participation has been a hallmark of Minnesota parties, but competition for time in today's society has resulted in a lower proportion of citizens becoming involved. Those who are involved seem motivated by issues on which they have

**Table 1**  Minnesota Resource Guide

|  | Democratic-Farmer-Labor | Independent-Republican |
|---|---|---|
| Archive | Yes | Yes |
| Location | Research Center | Research Center |
|  | Minnesota State Historical Society | Minnesota State Historical Society |
|  | 345 Kellogg Blvd. West | 345 Kellogg Blvd. West |
|  | St. Paul, MN 55102 | St. Paul, MN 55102 |
| Dates | 1942–1984 | 1935–1988 |
| Finding aid | Yes | Yes |
| Access | Approval of party for records less than 25 years old | Approval of party for records less than 20 years old |
| Contents: |  |  |
| Executive and central committee minutes | Yes | Yes |
| Correspondence | Yes | Yes |
| Financial records | Yes | Yes |
| Chairperson's files | Yes | Yes |

more intense views than do the general public. If endorsements are overturned by primaries, there is less impetus for further involvement. Primaries without endorsements, on the other hand, hurt the less affluent candidates and participants.

Minnesota's political parties do not exist in a vacuum. National political, social, and economic forces affect them. The Watergate crisis affected Minnesota Republicans negatively, and the national Republican resurgence affected them positively. The rise of social issues, media costs, and the democratization of the nominating process have all affected Minnesota politics. The task for Minnesota party leaders is similar to that of leaders in other states: strengthen their parties so that their candidates can win elections.

## RESOURCE GUIDE

The best place to find information about political party organizations in Minnesota is the Minnesota Historical Society. Its archives include 254 boxes of material regarding the DFL state central committee. The general contents of each box are indexed. The boxes are in chronological order, so all budgets, for example, are not in one box but are scattered among several. In addition to financial records, correspondence, minutes of central and executive committees, and caucus and convention files, newspaper clippings are also archived. The period 1942–1984 is covered. The Republican Party records are divided into two groups of boxes. One group, dealing with the Republican Party from 1935 to 1977, contains 209 boxes, or 209.5 cubic feet of material. The second set deals with the Independent-Republican Party and covers mainly the period from 1975, when the party changed its name, through various years in the 1980s, and as late as 1988 for financial records. Included are general correspondence, the chairs' files, caucus and convention materials, and even audio and video tapes.

Individuals must apply through the Minnesota Historical Society to the Democratic-Farmer-Labor Party for permission to see material that is less than twenty-five years old, and to the Republican Party for material that is less than twenty years old. The applicant must explain the nature of the research. Permission will usually take less than one week to obtain.

The Democratic-Farmer-Labor Party published a history of its organization covering the first forty years of the merged party. Authored by Laura K. Auerbach (1984), it includes a history of the party complete with the major splits that developed over the years. There is also a valuable data section which includes party chairpersons and national committeemen and women during the period as well as all members elected to Congress and election results for governor. Pictures of the major persons are also included, as is a special chapter on women in the DFL.

The Republican party has recently set up a Minnesota Republican Historical Society. It is located at 444 Cedar Suite 810, St. Paul, MN 55101.

**REFERENCES**

*Asterisks denote the most important publications on Minnesota party politics.*

*Auerbach, Laura K. 1984. *Worthy to be remembered: A political history of the Minnesota Democratic-Farmer-Labor Party 1944–1984*. Minneapolis: Democratic-Farmer-Labor Party.

Baden, Patricia Lopez. 1995. State DFL chooses executive director. *Star Tribune,* July 20, 1B.

*Blegen, Theodore C. 1963. *Minnesota: A history of the state.* Minneapolis: University of Minnesota Press.

Cassano, Dennis. 1975. Minnesota GOP decides to alter name. *Minneapolis Tribune,* November 16, 1A.

Coffman, Jack B. 1995. Campaign tab on public. *Saint Paul Pioneer Press,* August 6, 1B, 8B.

Congressional Quarterly. 1995. *Congressional Quarterly Weekly Report,* January 28, 316–317; February 11, 476–477; April 1, 964–965.

Democratic-Farmer-Labor Party of Minnesota. 1992. *Constitution and bylaws of the Democratic-Farmer-Labor Party of Minnesota.* June.

DFLP Education Foundation. 1995. *Idea News* (winter). St. Paul: DFLP Education Foundation.

Duluth News-Tribune. 1995. IR chairman holds off conservative's challenge. *Duluth News-Tribune,* June 11, 1B–2B.

*Esbjornson, Robert. 1955. *A Christian in politics: Luther W. Youngdahl.* Minneapolis: T. S. Denison.

*The Gallup Poll: Public opinion 1972–1977.* 1978. Wilmington, Del.: Scholarly Resources.

*Gieske, Millard L. 1979. *Minnesota Farmer-Laborism: The third-party alternative.* Minneapolis: University of Minnesota Press.

Independent-Republicans of Minnesota. 1995. *Bylaws of the Independent-Republicans of Minnesota.* June 10.

Independent-Republicans of Minnesota. 1993. *Constitution.* September.

Jewell, Malcolm E. 1984. *Parties and primaries: Nominating state governors.* New York: Praeger.

*Kunkel, Joseph A., III. 1993. Political parties in Minnesota. In *Perspectives on Minnesota government and politics,* 3d ed., ed. Carolyn M. Shrewsbury and Homer E. Williamson. Edina, Minn.: Burgess International.

*———. 1988. Party endorsement and incumbency in Minnesota legislative nominations. *Legislative Studies Quarterly* 13 (May): 211–213.

*Lebedoff, David. 1972. *Ward number six.* New York: Charles Scribner's Sons.

*———. 1969. *The 21st ballot: A political party struggle in Minnesota.* Minneapolis: University of Minnesota Press.

McGrath, Dennis J. 1995. New party takes first step to sue state. *Minneapolis Star Tribune,* July 18, 1B–2B.

Minneapolis Star Tribune. 1992. Stassen says IR Party is out of touch. *Minneapolis Star Tribune,* June 25, state ed., 8B.

Mitau, G. Theodore. 1970. *Politics in Minnesota.* 2d rev. ed. Minneapolis: University of Minnesota Press.

Parsons, Jim, and Dennis J. McGrath. 1995. Breaking ranks, not bread: Labor boycotts DFL's Humphrey dinner. *Minneapolis Star Tribune,* May 18, 1A–2A.

*Shrewsbury, Scott, and Carolyn Shrewsbury. 1984. The organizational elite of Minnesota's political parties: Perspectives on representation. In *Perspectives on Minnesota government and politics,* 2d ed., ed. Millard L. Gieske.

Smith, Dane. 1995. IR Party: We're simply. *Minneapolis Star Tribune,* September 24, metro ed., 1A.

———. 1992. "Golden elephants" shun conservatives and IR Party coffers. *Minneapolis Star Tribune,* December 6, metro ed., 1B.

Star Tribune (Minneapolis). 1995. Undemocratic (editorial), *Star Tribune,* May 28, metro ed., 18A.

State of Minnesota. 1995a. *Campaign finance summary: 1994.* St. Paul: State of Minnesota, Ethical Practices Board.

State of Minnesota. 1995b. *Minnesota election results 1994: State primary election and state general election.* St. Paul: State of Minnesota, Secretary of State, Election Division.

State of Minnesota. 1995c. *Minnesota statutes, 1995 supplement.* St. Paul: State of Minnesota.

State of Minnesota. 1994a. *Campaign finance summary: 1993.* St. Paul: State of Minnesota, Ethical Practices Board.

State of Minnesota. 1994b. *Minnesota statutes.* St. Paul: State of Minnesota.

State of Minnesota. 1993. *The Minnesota legislative manual 1993–1994.* St. Paul: State of Minnesota, Secretary of State, Election Division.

*Valelly, Richard M. 1989. *Radicalism in the states: The Minnesota Farmer-Labor Party and the American political economy.* Chicago: University of Chicago Press.

# *Mississippi*

DAVID BREAUX, STEPHEN SHAFFER, AND THOMAS WILSON

## PARTY HISTORY

Historically, divisions grounded in social class and race have dominated Mississippi politics and have shaped competition within the dominant party and between the two major parties. Before 1860 most rural residents backed the Democratic Party of Andrew Jackson, whereas wealthy planters, urban bankers, and merchants backed the Whig Party. Racial concerns dominated the last half of the nineteenth century, as conservative Democratic whites employed fraud and violence to regain control of state government in 1876 from African Americans and Republicans. Discriminatory voting devices in the state's 1890 constitution disenfranchised African Americans, and as late as 1964 only 7 percent of voting age African Americans were registered to vote. White hostility to the party of Lincoln guaranteed a solidly Democratic state, and Democrats won every congressional election until 1964, the year of Goldwater's candidacy (Krane and Shaffer 1992).

Class differences based on economic issues reemerged at the turn of the century, and the dominant Democratic Party split into two major factions through the 1950s. Rich Delta planters led the economically conservative faction, while poor farmers in the northeast "hills" and the southern Piney Woods (who had backed the Populist movement) helped elect five "neopopulist" governors. Although they employed racist campaign rhetoric to attract white "rednecks," some neopopulist governors did enact economically progressive public policies. Both Democratic factions favored racial segregation, with the state party convention in 1948 instructing its delegates to walk out of the national convention if Truman were nominated as president. The Democratic State Executive Committee listed the States' Rights Party candidates (including Mississippi governor Fielding Wright as vice president) on the ballot as the "official" Democratic Party nominees, prompting a landslide victory (Key 1949; Krane and Allen 1980; Maisel 1991, 1075, 1235).

The electorally powerless state Republican Party organization was largely relegated after 1876 to distributing federal patronage during Republican presidential administrations and sending delegates to the national party conventions. The state Republican Party split into two factions after 1868: the "Black and Tans," who were led by noted African American lawyer Perry Howard and were recognized as the state's legitimate Republican Party by the national party in 1924; and the "Lily Whites," who organized themselves as the Independent Republican Party in 1928. After being the first to register under a 1950 state law, the Lily Whites gained state recognition as the official Republican Party of Mississippi, and with both factions backing Eisenhower, the 1956 national convention seated a unified delegation. The national party, viewing the Lily Whites as better able to attract white votes, began to channel federal patronage to them, resulting in Lily White domination of state Republican affairs by 1960 (Walton 1975, 128–137; Loewen and Sallis 1974, 237; Ginzl 1980; Hy and Saeger 1993, 219–221).

As an increasing number of African Americans registered to vote during the civil rights movement and increasingly backed the party of FDR and Kennedy, state Democrats split into two organizations. The virtually all-white "regular Democrats" controlled the state party organization, held nearly all elective offices, and backed an unpledged presidential electoral slate in 1960. Civil rights organizations, after their exclusion from the 1964 presidential delegate selection process, formed the Mississippi Freedom Democratic Party (FDP), which held county conventions in thirty-five of eighty-two counties and a state convention attended by 2,500 people. Both the FDP and the regular Democrats rejected a national convention compromise and sat out the 1964 convention. After state officials rejected FDP petitions nominating four candidates for Congress, the FDP in 1967 elected Mississippi's first African American state legislator since Reconstruction, Robert Clark (Bass and DeVries 1977, 204–206; Hy and Saeger 1993, 219–221).

Moderates loyal to the national Democratic Party gained control of the Young Democrats, and with state AFL-CIO leaders and the FDP established a "loyalists" coalition. For the first time since 1890, African Americans attended the district and state party conventions, comprising 5–15 percent of these bodies in a state with a 35 percent African American population. But at the state convention, Governor John Bell Williams opposed selecting any African Americans as at-large delegates to the national convention. Loyalists gathered evidence of "widespread irregularities" at the precinct caucus and county convention meetings dominated by the Regulars, held conventions in seventy-two counties to elect their own delegates, and had their delegates instead of the Regulars seated by the 1968 national convention. By 1972 racial moderate Bill Waller had become governor, and some Loyalists attended the Regulars' caucuses and county conventions. Again the national party seated the Loyalists instead of the Regulars, prompting Waller to offer the Loyalists 40 percent of the positions on the state and county Democratic executive committees and of the national convention delegation. The Loyalists balked, doubting that Waller's last-minute promises could be fully guaranteed, and demanded 50 percent (Hy and Saeger 1993, 224–225; Bass and DeVries 1977, 206–208; Lamis 1990, 47).

The election in 1975 of moderate Democratic governor Cliff Finch prompted the unification of the two Democratic organizations. The groups called simultaneous precinct caucuses, producing a unified delegation to the 1976 Democratic National Convention and a unified state party under the cochairmanship of African American Loyalist Aaron Henry and white Regular Tom Riddell. The party instituted a quota system that mandated an equal division of party offices by race and gender (Lamis 1990, 52).

## ORGANIZATIONAL DEVELOPMENT

*Democratic Party.* The Democratic organization, hurt by its intraparty factions, lacked a state headquarters as late as 1975. Historically dependent on the filing fees paid by candidates for office, the party in the late 1970s expanded its fund-raising ventures, participating in a "Dollars for Democrats" telephone fundraiser, and employed two staff members in a rented headquarters office. The 1980s was a period of organizational growth, and estimated annual revenue rose from approximately $30,000 in 1978 to about $100,000 in 1982 and to $200,000 by the late 1980s. The party began developing computer capabilities in 1982, hired a Ph.D. as executive director in 1983, and in 1987 purchased a house in Jackson for the state headquarters.

The biracial partnership was quite evident at the 1984 state convention, where 48 percent of the delegates were African Americans. Increased revenue boosted staffing, and by the late 1980s Democrats boasted a full-time executive director, finance coordinator, and office manager as well as a part-time secretary, with election-year additions of a field coordinator and part-time get-out-the-vote phone bank callers. In addition to voter registration and turnout drives, the state party provided its lists of party activists (caucus attendees, county committee members, and contributors) to interested candidates (Krane and Shaffer 1992, 105–108).

The state executive committee, at first responsive to Democratic governors when selecting state party chairs, by the late 1980s was asserting its independence. In 1980 the committee backed Governor (and racial liberal) William Winter's choice of a white campaign supporter and former Loyalist, Danny Cupit, despite African American opposition to Winter's move to end the cochairmanship in order to attract white voters. African Americans reluctantly acquiesced after the committee passed a bylaw requiring that the membership and chairs of all standing committees reflect the racial composition of the state. In 1981 the committee named Ed Cole, an African American and aide to Sens. John Stennis and James Eastland, as the party's vice chair. In 1984 the committee backed Governor Bill Allain's choice of campaign worker Steve Patterson, turning back a challenge by an African American former FDP leader, after Patterson successfully sought support from key African Americans. Cole's elevation by acclamation to the chair in 1987 after years of party service made him the first African American state party chair in the nation. The committee rebuffed progressive governor Ray Mabus's effort in 1988 to replace Cole with a white female supporter. The committee resented Mabus's efforts to gain personal control over the party caucuses and conventions and installed the Mabus candidate as vice chair (Handy 1984; Minor 1988; O'Keefe 1988).

Efforts to enforce Democratic Party loyalty have been uneven; self-restraint has been a greater motivator. The party's constitution requires dismissal of party officers who support another party's candidates as well as requires the appropriate party executive committee to disallow disloyal public officials from running as Democrats in future elections. Yet African American county party officials have sometimes run for local offices as independents without party retaliation. In 1984 state chair Patterson threatened party sanctions against Democratic officeholders who actively backed Ronald Reagan or GOP senator Cochran, but only one county executive committee took action against a state legislator, prompting him to run, and gain reelection, as a Republican. After African American support for an African American independent split the Democratic vote and helped elect Republican Cochran in 1978, and after white defection from Robert Clark's campaign helped elect GOP candidate Webb Franklin to Congress in 1982, state Democratic Party officials aided African American Mike Espy's successful 1986 campaign to unseat Franklin (Handy 1984; Krane and Shaffer 1992, 85–88).

*Republican Party.* The overwhelmingly white state Republican organization has exhibited a persisting ideological cleavage between its "moderate" conservative and "purist" conservative wings. With only two staff members in 1960–1961 and an annual budget of $57,000 provided by supporters in 66 percent of the state's counties, the party benefited from its Draft Goldwater movement so that in 1963–1966 its staff numbered eight and its annual budget approximated $200,000, contributed by individuals from 83 percent of the counties. It actively backed moderate Jackson businessperson Rubel Phillips for governor twice in the 1960s, establishing a campaign presence in all counties in the 1963 effort. Phillips lost to two segregationist Democrats despite a 1967 endorsement by the FDP that helped him garner about 71 percent of the African American vote in Jackson. Assisted by party-sponsored opinion polls, conservative Prentiss Walker was elected to the U.S. House in 1964 but tried unsuccessfully to "outsegregate" Eastland in a 1966 Senate race loss (Lamis 1990, 44–47).

In the mid-1960s Clarke Reed began an impressive decade-long tenure as state chair and gained national prominence as chair of the Southern Republican State Chairmen's Association. Personally a staunch conservative, Reed pragmatically pursued a more inclusive party organization. He recruited a few young African American professionals and provided African Americans with a fair share of federal patronage and a voice in party affairs that counseled moderation. Reed's tenure saw the start of TAR—Teen Age Republicans—as well as continued financial support for the Republican Women's Federation and the Young Republicans. The number of annual state executive committee meetings rose from two in the early 1960s to seven during his term, and the state party newsletter was published monthly. By 1968 the party was organized in all counties, and after the purchase of three cars in 1971, state party workers traveled widely across Mississippi. The state Republican Party provided extensive campaign assistance to candidates, such as a canvass kit and precinct organization guide, extended its candidate campaign school to municipal candidates, instituted a county leadership conference and campaign mobilization effort, and commissioned annual polls. The party's mobilization of campaign workers, canvassing efforts, and printing machine aided the elections of Thad Cochran and Trent Lott to Congress in 1972, the Nixon landslide year, and their subsequent reelection. The party benefited financially during the Nixon-Ford years from fund-raising dinners that attracted Vice President Agnew and prominent cabinet members (Witcover 1977, 443–503).

A moderating force in the GOP of the 1970s was progressive Meridian businessperson Gil Carmichael, who backed a new state constitution, openness in government, educational improvements, and the equal rights amendment. After losing a 1972 Senate race against Eastland, Carmichael gained an impressive 45 percent of the vote in the 1975 gubernatorial race, aided by four polls commissioned by the state party that identified popular themes and issues. Many Carmichael supporters joined the party organization and attended the 1976 caucuses and conventions, leading to a 16–14 split in the national delegation between moderate Ford supporters and conservative Reagan supporters. The split killed the unit rule employed since the 1940s, which had bound all delegates to vote for the candidate favored by a majority of delegates (Bass and DeVries 1977, 215–216; Witcover 1977, 443–503).

Reed was succeeded as party chair in 1976 by a young, aggressive state senator, Charles Pickering, who presided over a growing direct-mail fund-raising operation. After resigning in 1978 to wage a spirited bid for attorney general that garnered 48 percent of the vote, Pickering was succeeded by Greenville businessperson Mike Retzer. Under Retzer, the party helped elect Cochran senator, financially supported College Republican chapters, attracted presidential hopefuls to fund-raising dinners, and experienced a financial surge in 1980 as the Reagan era began. Haley Barbour, executive director of the state Republican Party during the terms of both chairs, pursued an effective "open door" policy of seeking converts in the heavily Democratic state. Barbour resigned in 1982 to give Senator Stennis his toughest challenge since 1947 (Elliott 1995).

Two energetic and capable women served as state party chair in the 1980s—Ebbie Spivey from 1982 to 1987 and Evelyn McPhail from 1987 to 1993. Both pursued a "big tent" philosophy of seeking converts to the GOP and attended meetings of normally Democratic groups, such as teachers. They stressed the benefit of a genuine two-party system in terms of heightened competition generating new ideas to move Mississippi forward. Both aggressively recruited attractive candidates, increased the number of offices contested, and continued to bring presidential candidates to party fund-raising dinners. Active campaigners for their party's candidates, Spivey and McPhail attacked national Democrats for being too liberal for most Mississippians (Lamis 1986, 58; Shaffer 1991, 97).

In 1983 the state Republicans moved into their current headquarters. In 1986 the party bought a supercomputer and promptly stored 1.7 million voter names derived from drivers' licenses. An aggressive telemarketing operation began, targeting past contributors and phone listings from more-Republican localities. With increased fund-raising activities, the annual state party budget had risen to $500,000 by the late 1980s, permitting contributions of $2,500 to each of four candidates in a given year. Aggressive recruitment of candidates—aided by the coattails of popular gubernatorial nominees like progressive Tupelo business and education leader Jack Reed in 1987 and victorious conservative businessperson Kirk Fordice in 1991—translated into party gains in the legislature (Krane and Shaffer 1992, 103–107).

## CURRENT PARTY ORGANIZATION

State law requires that each party's state executive committee determine how and when the county and state executive committees and the national convention delegates are selected. Nominees for statewide and multicounty offices are certified by their state executive committee, and county office nominees by the county executive committee. Both parties use a caucus-convention system in presidential election years for selecting party organization members and national convention delegates; the presidential primaries bind the delegates' votes.

County convention delegates (chosen by precinct caucuses) select the county executive committees, which then elect a county chair. Party rules permit thirty Democratic and thirty-six Republican county committee members. Republicans typically fill only twelve of their positions, and fifty-two of the eighty-two counties have "active" Republican organizations; Republicans are especially strong in urban areas. Although Democrats fill all thirty of their slots, many committees are active only in election years, to certify candidates (Shaffer and Breaux 1995, 166).

Congressional district conventions, attended by delegates selected by the county conventions, elect the state executive committee members. The Republican state committee consists of seven members from each of the five districts, while the Democratic committee consists of twenty members from each. The state executive committees, typically consisting of longtime party workers, independently elect the party chair after considering the views of the party's governor. The Democratic executive committee, having bucked Mabus's 1988 effort to dump Cole as party chair, replaced Cole in 1994 with another African American, state senator Johnnie Walls, after complaints by activists about the deterioration of the organization. The Republican executive committee retained highly regarded party leader McPhail after Fordice's election but had to select a replacement, businessperson Billy Powell, after McPhail's promotion to the RNC. Powell, who offered to return to his business career after Fordice in early 1995 expressed disappointment that the party continued to fail to contest enough races, agreed to remain after both Republican U.S. senators publicly praised his work (Elliott 1995).

Generally, full-time paid executive directors have supervised the day-to-day operations of the state parties, with Democrats often relying on politicos with national campaign experience. In 1989 Democrats hired Massachusetts native and Mondale campaign worker Lisa Walker, who proceeded to revitalize Young Democrats college chapters, to upgrade the party's computer equipment, and to gain a Clinton administration position after heading his state campaign. A three-year vacancy and officeholders' complaints about organizational deterioration and frequent state headquarters' closings (which made it difficult to qualify for reelection) prompted the hiring in 1995 of Alice Skelton. Skelton, a Mississippi native and Allain administration member who had been a California political consultant the previous nine years, promptly began repairing the party's public image, stressing Democratic concern with all people, "not just a select group." Republicans have also experienced staff turnover, as RNC committee member Suzanne Rogers replaced Chris Webster, who resigned in 1995 to run for secretary of state. Each party employs additional staff members whose number varies depending on funding and whether it is an election year. Both typically employ a finance director and office manager, while Republicans tend also to employ a political and communication director (Kanengiser 1989; Oeth 1995; Wagster 1995).

Both parties have organized fund-raising operations. Contributors of small sums ($10 monthly) constitute the United Republican Fund and the Yellow Dog Democrats. The annual county Democratic "beans and greens" dinners highlight prominent state elected officials as speakers; contributions are divided between the state and county parties. Both parties attract prominent national speakers for annual fundraisers, such as the Democratic Jefferson-Jackson Day dinner. Republican contributors of at least $500 annually comprise the Capital Foundation, which funds major purchases such as computers, whereas Democrats tap their master file of past contributors to finance special projects (Krane and Shaffer 1992, 105–107).

Mississippi's party organizations reflect Samuel Eldersveld's (1982, 133) notion of a "stratarchy"—rather than a hierarchy—whereby power is diffused throughout the organization. Given the unpaid nature of party work, some county committee members become relatively inactive after their elections. County chairs tend to be more experienced and motivated, taking the lead in fund raising, recruiting and organizing party workers, serving as media spokesperson for the local party, and organizing campaign events (Shaffer and Breaux 1995, 176–178).

The major factions within the contemporary parties reflect ideological differences. The Democrats exhibit greater diversity than the Republicans. A 1991 survey of county committee members and chairs across Mississippi found the GOP split 48 percent–37 percent between "somewhat" conservative and "very" conservative, while Democrats split 34–35–31, liberal to moderate to conservative. Remaining racial uneasiness within today's Democratic Party reflects ideological differences. Among the Democratic county officials polled in 1991, 55 percent of African Americans were liberal and only 17 percent conservative. Among white Democratic officials, 37 percent called themselves conservatives while 23 percent were liberal. With the sizable African American presence in the state party (African Americans comprise 33 percent of Democratic county officials), the Democratic-controlled legislature backs racial set-asides in state contracts (Shaffer and Breaux 1995, 170–176).

The personalized nature of Mississippi politics is eternally important, with each public official maintaining a personal campaign organization of friends and supporters. Public officials, reinforced by primary elections and the popular election of ten statewide officers, retain office by serving their constituents rather than being party loyalists. Although generally showing greater party loyalty than Democrats, Republicans have on occasion broken ranks. One-third of Senate Republicans in 1992 joined the successful override of a Fordice veto of a tax increase for education. Fordice's intervention in subsequent primaries to purge the "pseudo-Republicans" produced a backlash of support for them (Shaffer 1994, 68). With GOP legislative gains, Democratic house speakers and lieutenant governors have appointed some as committee chairs. Republican lieutenant governor Eddie Briggs, elected in 1991, continued this bipartisan approach, and fears among Democrats that conservative members of the party would switch parties deflated a Democratic move to form a party caucus. Fordice, angry at Briggs's lack of total support for his conservative agenda, threatened to back a conservative challenger to his renomination, prompting Briggs to threaten an independent bid for governor. Each ran for renomination to his respective office without serious opposition.

Neither party makes preprimary endorsements, and state party leaders generally urge partisans to get acquainted with everyone running for the party's nominations for offices.

### RESOURCE GUIDE

The Mississippi Department of Archives and History, located in Jackson, maintains a detailed record of the operations of the state Democratic Party from 1960 to the present. Post-1970 material is the most comprehensive. There are thirteen boxes of records, which include material on campaign filing fees, state executive committee minutes, and resolutions passed by the state and national party. A label within each box describes the contents. Also, the archives has developed a master list describing the contents of all the boxes.

Overall, the master list is a useful tool that can cut down research time, though the box labels give greater detail. Another research tool is the subject finding aid, which refers primarily to newspaper clippings. These subject files are arranged by year and are in excellent condition. Cross referencing in the subject file makes it possible to obtain material on an individual or event. Last, the archives has a card catalog for book listings, and photocopying may be done in the reference room.

The Department of Archives and History also has numerous records describing the delegate credentials battles between the state and the national Democratic Parties. Included in the archive collection is considerable correspondence between the state party leadership and key supporters. There are detailed memoranda describing party dinners, visiting political dignitaries, and party receipts and monthly expenses.

Republican Party records from 1950 to 1990 are stored meticulously in the special collections section of the Mississippi State University library in 185 boxes. The information is

**Table 1**  Mississippi Resource Guide

|  | Democrats | Republicans |
| --- | --- | --- |
| Archive | Yes | Yes |
| Location | Mississippi Department of Archives and History<br>P.O. Box 571<br>Jackson, Miss. 32905<br>(601) 359-1424 | Mississippi State University Library<br>Box 9507<br>Mississippi State, Miss. 39762<br>(601) 325-1679 |
| Dates | 1960–present | 1950–1990 |
| Finding aid | Yes | Yes |
| Access | Public | Public |
| Contents: |  |  |
| Executive committee minutes | Yes | Yes |
| Correspondence | Yes | Yes |
| Organization structure | Yes | Yes |
| Budgets | Yes | Yes |
| Rules | Yes | Yes |

sorted by subject series, according to an inventory guide, and is easily accessed and quite extensive. All records have been cataloged, and the collection is especially comprehensive from 1959 to 1983. Detailed information regarding state party budgets, income, expenditures, and staffing is provided, as well as numerous party publications and correspondence. The collection also contains information about campaigns and elections, including fundraising events, campaign aids, and polls and maintains a newspaper clipping service. For specific assistance with a search, consult the manuscripts librarian.

The state Republican Party maintains current-year records at its party headquarters, with additional information warehoused in Jackson. Given a busy staff, appointments should be arranged in advance (Mississippi Republican Party, 555 Tombigbee St., Jackson, Miss. 39201; phone 601-948-5191).

**REFERENCES**

*Asterisks denote the most important publications on Mississippi party politics.*

Bass, Jack, and Walter DeVries. 1977. *The transformation of southern politics.* New York: New American Library.

Eldersveld, Samuel J. 1982. *Political parties in American society.* New York: Basic Books.

Elliott, Jack, Jr. 1995. Recent precampaign shuffling of the Republican Party out of the ordinary. *Starkville Daily News,* February 14, 4.

*Ginzl, David J. 1980. Lily-White versus Black and Tans: Mississippi Republicans during the Hoover administration. *Journal of Mississippi History* 42:194–211.

Handy, Thomas H. 1984. Mississippi political parties, 1984 and after. Paper presented at the annual meeting of the Southern Political Science Association, Savannah, November 1–3.

*Hathorn, Billy Burton. 1985. Challenging the status quo: Rubel Lex Phillips and the Mississippi Republican Party, 1963–1967. *Journal of Mississippi History* 47:240–265.

*Hy, Ronald John, and Richard Saeger. 1993. The role and organization of political parties in Mississippi. In *Politics in Mississippi,* ed. Joseph B. Parker. Salem, Wis.: Sheffield.

Kanengiser, Andy. 1989. New executive director hired for Democrats. *Clarion-Ledger,* July 9, 1B.

Key, V. O. 1949. *Southern politics.* New York: Vintage.

*Krane, Dale, and Tip H. Allen Jr. 1980. Factional durability in Mississippi's gubernatorial elections, 1927–75. In *Party politics in the South,* ed. Robert P. Steed, Laurence W. Moreland, and Tod A. Baker. New York: Praeger.

*Krane, Dale, and Stephen D. Shaffer. 1992. *Mississippi government and politics: Modernizers versus traditionalists.* Lincoln: University of Nebraska Press.

Lamis, Alexander P. 1986. Mississippi. In *The 1984 presidential election in the South,* ed. Robert P. Steed, Laurence W. Moreland, and Tod A. Baker. New York: Praeger.

———. 1990. *The two-party South.* 2d expanded ed. New York: Oxford University Press.

Loewen, James W., and Charles Sallis. 1974. *Mississippi: Conflict and change.* New York: Pantheon.

*Lucas, Melvin Philip. 1983. *The development of the second party system in Mississippi, 1817–1846.* Dissertation, Cornell University.

*Maisel, L. Sandy. 1991. *Political parties and elections in the United States.* New York: Garland.

*McLemore, Leslie B. 1971. The Mississippi Freedom Democratic Party: A case study of grassroots politics. Ph.D. diss., University of Massachusetts.

Minor, Bill. 1988. Mabus move has party taking sides. *Clarion-Ledger/Jackson Daily News,* February 7, 3H.

Oeth, Annie. 1995. Let's put a definition with "Democratic Party." *Clarion-Ledger,* March 19, 3G.

O'Keefe, Joe. 1988. Cole retains Democratic chairmanship. *Clarion-Ledger/Jackson Daily News,* April 10, 1A.

Shaffer, Stephen D. 1991. Mississippi: Electoral conflict in a nationalized state. In *The 1988 presidential election in the South,* ed. Laurence W. Moreland, Robert P. Steed, and Tod A. Baker. New York: Praeger.

*———. 1994. Mississippi: Friends and neighbors fight the "liberal" label. In *The 1992 presidential election in the South: Current patterns of southern party and electoral politics,* ed. Robert P. Steed, Laurence W. Moreland, and Tod A Baker. Westport, Conn.: Praeger.

* Shaffer, Stephen D., and David A. Breaux. 1995. Mississippi: The "true believers" challenge the party of everyone. In *Southern party organizations and activists,* ed. Charles D. Hadley and Lewis Bowman. Westport, Conn.: Praeger.

*Simpson, William. 1982. The birth of Mississippi "loyalist Democrats," 1965–1968. *Journal of Mississippi History* 44:27–46.

Wagster, Emily. 1995. State Dems name executive director. *Clarion-Ledger,* February 28, 1B.

Walton, Hanes. 1975. *Black Republicans: The politics of the Black and Tans.* Metuchen, N.J.: Scarecrow.

Witcover, Jules. 1977. *Marathon: The pursuit of the presidency, 1972–1976.* New York: Viking Press.

# Missouri

JOEL PADDOCK

## PARTY HISTORY

Missouri, like other border states, has a history of relatively close partisan competition and persistent factionalism within the dominant Democratic Party (Fenton 1957; Mayhew 1986). Historically, the Democrats have tended to predominate in state races, but the Republicans have made substantial gains in the last twenty-five years. In presidential elections the state is considered somewhat of a bellwether. Since 1900 Missouri has voted for the winning presidential candidate in all but one election (1956).

Prior to the Civil War, Democrats won most elections, but the Whigs were usually competitive and occasionally won major offices. The central political figure in Missouri was Thomas Hart Benton (U.S. senator, 1821–1851; U.S. representative, 1853–1855), an ally of

Andrew Jackson and an instrumental figure in building the state Democratic Party around a coalition of small producers, traders, and farmers. This coalition dominated Missouri politics until the Civil War (Meyer 1982).

Sectional divisions still evident in contemporary Missouri were forged during the Civil War era. Missouri gave a plurality of its votes to Democrat Stephen Douglas in the election of 1860. The state also elected as governor Claiborne Jackson, a "Douglas Democrat" with prosouthern sympathies. Jackson supported secession, but the state legislature was split over the issue. Union troops (primarily German immigrants from St. Louis) deposed Governor Jackson and installed a pro-Union government. The state never seceded but was bitterly divided by the Civil War (see Fellman 1989). Since the Civil War the Democrats have been more successful in areas settled primarily by immigrants from southern states: the "Boot Heel" region of southeastern Missouri, the "Little Dixie" area north and west of St. Louis, and the eastern Ozarks. The Republicans have had more electoral success in areas where there was little sympathy for the Confederacy: a small region along the Missouri River west and south of St. Louis settled by pro-Union German immigrants, the farm belt counties of northwestern Missouri, and the western Ozarks, which, like most of the "upland" border South, had few slaves and was dubious of secession. The result was a competitive electoral system in which the Democrats, when they were unified, tended to predominate.

Immediately after the war, the state party system was in disarray; both parties were split into factions. With many Confederate sympathizers temporarily disenfranchised, Republicans held an advantage briefly. By 1874, however, the Democrats had reclaimed their historical ascendancy and, for the most part, dominated state politics for the rest of the century. A number of agrarian protest parties emerged between the mid-1870s and mid-1890s, but none were strong enough to win a significant number of elections (Meyer 1982).

"The political history of Missouri since 1900," John H. Fenton wrote in 1957, "has been, to a very considerable extent, the history of the rise and decline of both machines and reform movements in its two great cities" (Fenton 1957, 126). At the turn of the century, St. Louis politics was dominated by "Colonel" Ed Butler, the head of an elaborate Democratic machine that controlled both houses of the municipal assembly, the police department, and election board. However, in 1902 Joseph W. Folk, a reform-minded circuit attorney hand-picked by the machine, prosecuted Democratic leaders in St. Louis on a variety of corruption charges. The rapid demise of the Butler organization weakened the state Democratic Party. Republicans reclaimed their advantage in the state's largest city and became competitive statewide until the New Deal (Fenton 1957; Meyer 1982).

The best-known urban party machine in Missouri, Thomas J. Pendergast's organization, dominated Kansas City politics in the 1920s and 1930s. Pendergast's brother, Jim, was a major figure in the Kansas City Democratic Party as early as the 1890s, heading a faction called the Jackson Democratic Club. Upon Jim's death in 1911, Thomas Pendergast became the leader of his brother's faction, which at the time had a bitter intraparty rivalry with another faction led by Joseph B. Shannon. The factions, based largely on personal loyalties, often had violent primary contests but usually unified for the general election and divided the political patronage. By the 1920s Pendergast dominated the Kansas City organization. Because he could deliver the Kansas City vote in statewide elections, Pendergast became a major figure in the state Democratic Party (Fenton 1957; Meyer 1982). In 1939, however, Pendergast was convicted of federal income tax evasion. A reform group gained control of Kansas City politics in 1940. With the exception of a few Democratic ward organizations that controlled county and state-legislative nominations in the 1950s, the last vestiges of traditional party organization faded from Missouri with the demise of the Pendergast machine (Mayhew 1986, 100–101). There is little evidence that the state parties filled the organizational vacuum left by the decline of the urban machine.

The New Deal realignment altered but did not substantially undermine the sectional divisions forged in Missouri during the Civil War. The class-based realignment had its biggest impact on Missouri's two major cities. St. Louis, traditionally a Republican-leaning city, became strongly Democratic after 1932. And the New Deal reinforced the traditionally strong support for Democrats in Kansas City. Suburbanization after World War II followed predictable patterns: blue-collar suburbs tended to vote Democratic, and more upscale areas voted Republican. Since some of the most prosperous Kansas City suburbs were in Kansas, the suburban Republican vote was split between two states, and Democratic clout was enhanced in Kansas City, Missouri. Democrats dominated Missouri politics during the New Deal era; between 1932 and 1968 they won all but one gubernatorial election, won all but two U.S. Senate elections, and controlled both houses of the state legislature in fourteen of eighteen sessions.

## ORGANIZATIONAL DEVELOPMENT

*Republican Party.* Many observers cite John Danforth's upset of incumbent attorney general Norman Anderson in 1968 as the beginning of the modern Republican Party in Missouri. The party had not controlled the governorship and state patronage since 1945. Danforth became the first Republican to win any statewide office since 1946. Bolstered by Danforth's victory, the Missouri Republican Party emerged as an electorally viable organization, which, at various times after 1968, dominated statewide elections. Danforth's win opened the door for victories by Republicans Christopher "Kit" Bond and John Ashcroft in the 1970 and 1972 races for state auditor. Over the next twenty-five years, Danforth, Bond, and Ashcroft won four gubernatorial and six U.S. Senate elections between them and led the party to virtually unprecedented successes in other statewide races.

Prior to 1968 Missouri Republicans were ideologically factionalized and electorally demoralized, with no ideological or regional center of gravity. U.S. representative Thomas Curtis (1951–1969) of suburban St. Louis, the only Missouri Republican in the U.S. House in 1960, began trying to rebuild the Missouri GOP through a group called Missouri Republicans Unlimited (MRU), a fund-raising organization committed to raising money from the business community. At the 1960 state convention, Curtis united with state chairman H. Kenneth Wangelin (a former factional rival) and pushed for the election of MRU treasurer Frank Corley as national committeeman. Curtis's faction enjoyed widespread support in the Kansas City and St. Louis business communities (important sources of party funds) but was opposed by many in the regular party organization in St. Louis, whose leaders referred to Curtis as the new "Boss Tom" (Pendergast). MRU raised $400,000 in 1960 and targeted three U.S. House races: Curtis's suburban St. Louis district, the traditionally Republican Seventh Congressional District in southwest Missouri, and the Eleventh Congressional District in central Missouri. Republican candidates won two of the three targeted races, but both were in traditionally Republican districts. The general consensus among party leaders was that the Republican Party needed to improve its organizational capabilities in St. Louis and Kansas City. Some organizational advances were made. In 1960, for example, the St. Louis County (suburban St. Louis) Republican Party established a permanent headquarters and began publishing a party newspaper.

The Republicans' rebuilding efforts were slowed in 1964, when an ideological rift split the state convention. When state chair Lem Jones refused to seat anti-Goldwater delegates from the regular organization in St. Louis, the convention erupted. Curtis, who supported Jones and Goldwater, got into a shouting match and nearly exchanged blows with two St. Louis party leaders. The Goldwater supporters controlled the convention, but the party was seriously split. Such intraparty divisions were common in the 1960s and 1970s. A similar split emerged twelve years later, when John Danforth and Kit Bond met serious opposition for supporting Gerald Ford's presidential candidacy. These ideological rifts hindered Republican attempts to raise money and make organizational inroads in the state's two major metropolitan areas.

Perhaps the key to the Republicans' breakthrough in the late 1960s and early 1970s was their ability to recruit young, competent candidates with the ability to raise money and build sophisticated campaign organizations. The state party raised only about $300,000 in 1968, less than in 1960. However, over the next several years, Danforth, Bond, and Ashcroft proved adept at constructing well-financed personal organizations. For example, in his first race for governor in 1972, Kit Bond employed Washington political and media consultants Alan Woods and John Deardourff and had twelve full-time paid workers in his Jefferson City headquarters. The state Republican Party helped Bond raise money by coordinating a number of fund-raising dinners featuring national party figures such as Ronald Reagan and Nelson Rockefeller. In his 1986 U.S. Senate race, Bond raised more than $4 million from a variety of PACs and individuals, many from outside of Missouri. He employed the services of Baily, Deardourff, and Sipple, a Washington political consulting firm. Once again, the state party played the more passive role of funneling money and services to the Bond campaign.

Despite growing Republican electoral successes, the state party organization remained relatively weak throughout the 1970s. Although it was more successful at recruiting candidates for state legislative races, the party often lacked the funding to give these candidates much help. The national party intervened in 1978, spending more than $52,000 in Missouri, but the GOP continued to be unsuccessful in state legislative races. By most accounts, the party was successful in statewide elections largely because of well-run candidate organizations and other factors independent of party organization. In 1978, however, newly elected state chair William Macon emphasized that the party needed to become more involved in providing polling services, campaign advice, and opponents' voting records to Republican candidates (Lindeke 1978).

In the 1980s the state Republican organization experienced a modest renaissance. Under the leadership of state chair Hillard Selck, Jr., the party adopted a variety of modern electioneering techniques, including direct-mail fund raising, polling, use of computerized lists of likely Republican voters, and research on opposition candidates. By 1984 the state committee budget was about $1 million, and the committee employed a full-time staff in Jefferson City as well as a number of field organizers (Wolf 1984). In addition, intraparty ideological differences temporarily waned (Schlinkmann 1986). However, a scandal involving Republican attorney general William Webster contributed to a rejection of the party's statewide ticket in 1992, as the Democrats regained the governorship and four other statewide offices (see Leuthold 1994).

*Democratic Party.* Democratic prospects in Missouri were bright in the early 1960s. The party had controlled the governorship and state patronage since 1945. Party finances were in good shape. Democrats had a permanent though not elaborate state headquarters in

Jefferson City. Although factions often developed around competing gubernatorial candidates and there were occasional tensions between rural and urban interests, the Democrats had no serious regional or ideological divisions during this period. The party's central figure, Gov. Warren Hearnes, was first elected governor in 1964. Hearnes's choice for state party chair, Delton Houtchens, was relatively successful at raising funds for the Democratic organization. Houtchens, however, was later investigated by a federal grand jury for allegedly inducing banks to make contributions to the party in exchange for state deposits of intangible tax receipts. Allegations such as these tainted some Democratic officeholders in the late 1960s and early 1970s, providing the impetus for the initial GOP breakthroughs by Danforth and Bond.

The Democrats emerged from the 1972 election in disarray. The party lost the governorship for the first time since 1940. It was seriously split between the so-called regulars and insurgents. The regulars, such as Hearnes and Houtchens, supported Edmund Muskie for president in 1972 and were dubious of George McGovern and the intraparty reforms instigated by the 1968 national convention. The insurgents had supported Eugene McCarthy in 1968 and were more sanguine about McGovern and the push to democratize the party. Partly as the result of this split and the loss of the governorship, the party treasury dwindled. Contributions from organized labor waned. In the aftermath of the 1972 election, the Democrats reported a debt of more than $50,000.

The Democratic state committee reacted almost immediately to the Republican successes of 1970 and 1972. In July 1973 the party Ways and Means Committee recommended an ambitious fund-raising proposal; the committee saw a need to raise a minimum of $200,000, "and more like $800,000 if we are to remain a viable political force in Missouri" (Democratic state committee transcript, July 28, 1973). The committee contended that the money was needed "to staff state headquarters, establish needed voter registration drives, and to provide extensive field operations to assist Democratic candidates and local Democratic clubs" (Democratic state committee transcript, July 28, 1973). The committee recommended the party spend at least $500,000 on the 1974 elections. The Democrats established the "Committee of 10,000," which was intended to solicit sustaining contributions from all levels of the party. A portion of the contributions was funneled to the county organizations. It was hoped that contributions could be streamlined through the state organization, to prevent contributors from being solicited from a variety of sources.

The initial success of the Committee of 10,000 was modest. Shortly before the 1974 election the debt had been reduced to about $30,000 (Democratic state committee transcript, September 10, 1974). The party had funds to maintain a permanent staff but little to spend on the 1974 elections. State chair Larry Donnelly, however, remained optimistic. He proposed establishing a professional staff in Jefferson City, Kansas City, and St. Louis. The party already had hired its first executive director, in 1972. Additionally, party leaders hoped to computerize their records, employ field organizers, and maintain a permanent staff of five in their Jefferson City headquarters (Democratic state committee transcript, June 1, 1974). Over the next several years the Committee of 10,000 continued to have only modest success. The funds it raised were supplemented by national party telethons and a variety of fund-raising programs (such as "Dollars for Democrats" and "DEMPAC") coordinated by the Association of State Democratic Chairs.

During the mid- to late 1970s the Missouri Democratic organization enjoyed a period of modest resurgence. The party began publishing a regular newspaper in 1975. Previously, it had published only a one-sheet newsletter. In 1978 committee staffers conducted workshops on campaign management techniques and developed plans for statewide opinion polling, voter profile analysis, issue research, and research on Republican opponents. This was in response to a December 1977 state party subcommittee report that recommended taking a variety of steps to professionalize the organization. Still, financial woes prevented the party from fully implementing these plans. The state committee, for example, struggled to come up with $10,000 for Hearnes's losing 1978 campaign for state auditor. The lack of money forced the state committee staff to focus on a handful of marginal state legislative races. Most candidates for statewide office ran their campaigns largely independent of the state organization. For example, the party gave only logistical support (research on issues and the opponent and scheduling assistance) to Joseph Teasdale, the Democrats' successful 1976 gubernatorial candidate. Teasdale's campaign was handled by Matt Reese and Associates, a Washington consulting firm, and Teasdale campaigned as a candidate who was independent of the regular party organization.

The Democrats' electoral woes in statewide races continued in the 1980s, prompting periodic self evaluation. After the 1984 election, the organization brought in the Washington State Democratic chair to speak about the possibilities of a "party renaissance" (state Democratic Party news release, January 11, 1985). After the 1988 election, party leaders turned to Rep. Richard Gephardt to lead the effort to rebuild the party. A number of the leaders contended that the organization lacked funding, coordination, cohesiveness, and grassroots organization and that the party had never adjusted to the fact that there would not always be a Democratic governor to head the campaign (Mannies 1988). However, in the wake of the scandal involving Republican attorney general (and gubernatorial nominee) William Webster, the Democrats reclaimed the governorship and four other statewide offices in 1992.

## CURRENT PARTY ORGANIZATION

The state of Missouri heavily regulates party organizations. State law requires that each party have committees at the county, legislative district, senatorial district, circuit judicial district, congressional district, and state levels. Since the state legislature changed the comprehensive election law in 1978, the state committees have consisted of sixty-eight members: one man and one woman elected by each of the thirty-four state senatorial district committees. Prior to 1978, the state committees were selected by congressional district (three men and three women from each U.S. House district). The committees are required to meet on the second Saturday of September in Jefferson City and, with their nominees for state and federal offices, to formulate a state platform. They also are required to select a chair and vice chair (one man and one woman), and a secretary and treasurer (one man and one woman). The state chair generally has the support of the party's gubernatorial nominee. The state committees and chairs adopt party bylaws, develop fund-raising methods and means for promoting party candidates, and hire professional staff members.

Both parties have permanent headquarters in Jefferson City and full-time executive directors. The Republicans, who usually raise more money than the Democrats, generally have a larger full-time staff. Since the early 1980s the Republicans have had full-time field organizers who contribute to building local party organizations and recruit candidates (Coughlin and Hardy 1985). Both organizations provide money and assistance (such as opposition research, polling, and the coordination of state and national speakers) to their nominees, often focusing scarce resources on marginal races. In addition, the state legisla-

**Table 1**  Missouri Resource Guide

|  | Democrats | Republicans |
|---|---|---|
| Archive | Yes | No |
| Location | Western Historical Manuscripts Collection | — |
|  | 23 Ellis Library |  |
|  | University of Missouri, Columbia |  |
|  | Columbia, MO 65201 |  |
|  | (314) 882-6028 |  |
| Dates | 1965–1986[1] | — |
| Finding aids | Yes | — |
| Access | Public | — |
| Contents: |  |  |
| Executive committee minutes | Yes | — |
| Correspondence | Yes | — |
| Organizational structure | Yes | — |
| Budgets | Yes | — |
| Rules | Yes | — |

[1] Most of the material comes from the 1968–1978 period, and there is a small number of items from the late 1940s and 1950s.

tive leaderships in both parties funnel PAC money to state legislative candidates in close races, presumably in exchange for support in leadership elections.

Although there is no state law prohibiting preprimary endorsements, party rules prevent the state committees from endorsing candidates before the August primary. The parties do, however, recruit candidates and occasionally discourage others from running. They are not always successful. For example, the Democrats attempted to discourage Harriet Woods from seeking the 1982 U.S. Senate nomination by recruiting a number of alternative candidates thought to be more electable. Woods defied the party leadership, won the primary, and narrowly lost the general election to John Danforth.

Missouri has been a caucus state in presidential elections in all but one year. In 1988, presumably to aid the presidential candidacy of Richard Gephardt, the state held its only presidential primary. Missouri returned to the caucus system in 1992. Caucuses are initially held at the county, ward, or township level. The state conventions, the supreme authority in each party, select national convention delegates, presidential electors, and a national committeewoman and committeeman (Coughlin and Hardy 1985).

RESOURCE GUIDE

The Missouri Democratic Party archives are open to the public through the Western Historical Manuscripts Collection at the University of Missouri, Columbia. A finding aid provides a general guide to the contents of the fifty-one boxes of material. The bulk of the material comes from the period between the late 1960s and late 1970s. It includes an incomplete set of state committee minutes and transcripts, party budgets, bylaws, and correspondence. The collection is particularly good on the organization's response to the national party's delegate selection reforms of the early 1970s. The correspondence of Executive Director Karen Schafer and Director of Special Projects Tom Mericle in the 1970s is particularly useful to scholars interested in the party's attempts to adapt to the modern electoral system. There are only a few budgets (and virtually nothing else) prior to the 1960s, and primarily only newspaper clipping files from the 1980s. The archives are not particularly well organized. There is a lot of duplication of documents, and related materials are scattered throughout the collection.

Apparently, there has been no systematic attempt to preserve the archives of the Missouri Republican Party. State chair Tom Fowler said he knows of no collection of such documents. Repeated letters and calls to the state party executive director about the existence of Republican archives failed to get a response. The Republican resurgence in the 1970s and 1980s was described by a number of newspapers during the period. The best for state political coverage (and the ones most widely available on microfilm) are the *St. Louis Post-Dispatch* and the *Kansas City Star*. Most press accounts, however, focus more on the individual candidate organizations than on the workings of the state party. There is also virtually no coverage of the Republican resurgence in the scholarly literature. Secondary accounts of Missouri party organizations in the modern era are scant.

## REFERENCES

*Asterisks denote the most important publications on Missouri party politics.*
*Coughlin, Timothy R., and Richard J. Hardy. 1985. Political parties in Missouri. In *Missouri government and politics,* ed. Richard Hardy and Richard Dohm. Columbia: University of Missouri Press.
*Dorsett, Lyle W. 1968. *The Pendergast machine.* New York: Oxford University Press.
Fellman, Michael. 1989. *Inside war: The guerrilla conflict in Missouri during the American Civil War.* New York: Oxford University Press.
*Fenton, John. 1957. *Politics in the border states.* New Orleans: Hauser.
*Karsch, Robert F. 1978. *The government of Missouri.* 14th ed. Columbia, Mo.: Lucas Brothers Publishing.
*Leuthold, David A. 1994. *Campaign Missouri 1992.* Columbia: University of Missouri Press.
Lindeke, Fred W. 1978. Macon new GOP head; Democrats re-elect Mauer. *St. Louis Post-Dispatch,* September 13.
Mannies, Jo. 1988. Gephardt sets out on rebuilding role. *St. Louis Post-Dispatch,* November 4.
Mayhew, David. 1986. *Placing parties in American politics.* Princeton: Princeton University Press.
*Meyer, Duane. 1982. *The heritage of Missouri.* St. Louis: State Publishing.
Schlinkmann, Mark. 1986. The GOP accomplishes a remarkable reversal. *St. Louis Post-Dispatch,* November 9.
Wolf, Jacob. 1984. GOP leader plans repeat performance. *Jefferson City News and Tribune,* December 2.

# Montana

JERRY CALVERT

## PARTY HISTORY

The state of Montana has a party system characterized by a high level of competition, relative to most other states, and a weak party organizational infrastructure. The citizens of the state have a well-established tradition of bypassing the parties and their elected officials by using the initiative and referendum to enact directly statutes and constitutional amendments and, more recently, to suspend and then repeal laws enacted by the state legislature.

Both major parties are competitive in statewide and state legislative races, as reflected in the fact that between 1972 (when the current state constitution was adopted) and 1996, the governor and the majority of each house of the state legislature were of the same party for only six of the twenty-four years. The most common distribution of authority in recent years has been a governor of one party facing opposite-party control of at least one house, and sometimes both houses, of the Montana Legislative Assembly. Also, in six of the last twenty-four years, elections resulted in the parties having an equal number of legislators in one of the two legislative chambers.

Another indicator of a high level of electoral competition in Montana is found at the state legislative level. From 1974 through 1992, 29 percent of state house seats and 33 percent of senate seats were won with less than 55 percent of the popular vote. In contrast, for the U.S. House during the same period, only 16 percent of the races were won with less than 55 percent. The relatively high level of partisan competition in Montana is also reflected in the number of state legislative districts that change hands from one party to the other. From 1984 through 1992, twenty-three of fifty state senate districts (46 percent) changed party control at least once; in the state house for the same period, the figure was 65 percent (Calvert 1993). The partisan turnover rate for the U.S. House of Representatives was just 9.1 percent during the same period (Keefe and Ogul 1993).

But Montana may be evolving toward a less competitive future. The Republicans have controlled the governorship since 1988, and the current incumbent, Marc Racicot, is perhaps the most popular elected official in recent decades. Racicot is a centrist, a moderate Republican who is fiscally conservative and middle-of-the-road on social issues, and he has carefully and successfully distanced himself from the extreme conservatives in his own party.

In the legislature, the high level of competition manifest over the last two decades was not replicated in the 1994 elections. The elections were a Democratic debacle. The Republicans gained their largest majorities in the legislature in decades, winning 62 percent and 68 percent of the seats in the senate and house, respectively.

Change in each party's fortunes may also be occurring at the congressional level. In what some have called Montana's "political schizophrenia," voters have traditionally sent Democrats to Washington while voting for more conservative candidates at the state and local level (Lopach 1983). For example, from 1914 through 1988 the Republicans managed to elect only one U.S. Senate candidate, Zales Ecton (and that was only for one term). But the pattern may be changing. In 1988 a political unknown, Conrad Burns, whose only experience in elective office was serving one term as a county commissioner, bested incumbent Democrat John Melcher by a narrow majority (52 percent). Burns has since been reelected to a second term, trouncing a well-known liberal Democrat by a margin of 62 percent to 38 percent.

The relatively robust quality of partisan competition in Montana is not matched by organizational strength in Montana's state and local party organizations. James Gibson and others (1985) rate Montana's parties in the bottom third of the states in organizational strength. State party budgets, excluding election-year spending, are $200,000–$400,000 annually, and the state party staffs are usually composed of an executive director and two-to-four salaried support staff (Light 1995; Martin 1995). Because of relatively low pay and a very heavy workload, the position of executive director tends to be a revolving door; tenure beyond one or two years for any director of either party is almost unheard of.

At the county level there are no salaried employees (except during the election season), and both parties often have difficulty finding people to serve in precinct committee posts.

Finally, Montanans have a well-developed tradition of sidestepping altogether the parties and the structures of representative government by use of the initiative and referendum. Montana's constitutional system provides for the right of citizens to initiate statutes and constitutional amendments by petition; if the required number of signatures of registered voters is obtained, the issue is placed on the general-election ballot. The only topic explicitly prohibited from consideration by initiative and referendum is the appropriation of money. Montanans may also petition to place any law enacted by the legislature on the ballot for popular consideration, and if the required number of additional signatures are obtained, Montanans can force suspension of the disputed law until the voters have given their opinion. Those who oppose an enacted law can force a public vote on the issue by the direct initiative as well (Calvert 1993, 1995).

## ORGANIZATIONAL DEVELOPMENT

Montana's major parties are typical cadre organizations. They have no membership in the usual sense. Rather, they are composed of activists who occupy the chain of command from the state central committee to the precincts in the state's fifty-six counties. Part of the organizational weakness of the parties is financial. Montana's parties, in a state of just over 800,000 people, have a limited base to draw upon for contributions. As a consequence, the parties contribute little to their candidates compared with other funding sources. In congressional contests, for example, more money flows into candidates' treasuries from the national political action committees and national party campaign organizations (Magleby 1989). Candidates for state legislative and local offices are largely on their own; they self-finance their campaigns primarily by amassing small donations from friends, relatives, and local supporters (Pearson 1991).

Party organizational weakness also has a legal component. In addition to mandating the open primary (in place since 1912), Title 13 of the Montana Code Annotated spells out in detail the structure and governance of the state's parties. State law mandates how state central committee members are to be selected, prohibits elected officials from serving on state committees, requires that committees be equally divided by gender, specifies how local party committeepersons are to be selected, and mandates gender equity at the county level of the parties' governing structures, among other things. As a consequence of these rules, Montana was rated a moderate-to-heavy "regulator" of internal party organization and structure in a comprehensive study of state parties by the U.S. Advisory Commission on Intergovernmental Relations (1986).

The same survey rated Montana as generally nonsupportive of state party influence in the electoral process. State law requires the use of the direct primary to nominate all elective candidates, uses the nonpartisan ballot to elect judges and city and school board officials, allows any registered voter to vote in the primary of either party (open primary), and organizes the ballot by office rather than by party to encourage voters to split their votes between parties (U.S. Advisory Commission on Intergovernmental Relations 1986). Montana is, however, one of about two dozen states that has a "sore loser" law that prohibits the losing candidate in a party primary from subsequently filing as an independent candidate for the general election. Also, state law does not prohibit preprimary endorsement by the party organization of a preferred candidate, but neither party at the state or local level has ever tried to influence primary outcomes by preelection endorsement.

The relative weakness of party organizations in Montana is not paralleled by a lack of strength in the parties' will to govern. In the Montana Legislative Assembly, each party's legislative members routinely caucus on issues as well as on matters of internal organization and power. Though such conferences do not compel individual members to march in lockstep with their party, there is an expectation that each legislator will vote with his or her party unless a compelling reason dictates otherwise. Party leaders in the legislature exercise significant power over the fortunes of individual rank-and-file members. The house speaker and the majority party's committee on committees in the senate are selected by the party caucus, and these in turn appoint all standing committee members as well as the chairs of the committees. Legislators who stand outside the mainstream of their own party caucus will be sanctioned by loss of a committee assignment or chair or denial of a desired committee position (Lopach et al. 1983). Finally, party spirit is implicitly fostered by the high level of personnel turnover among state legislators. In an average session, almost one-quarter of the members of the state senate will be first termers, whereas in the house the proportion of newly coined state representatives has been just short of one in three. Not surprisingly, these individuals are highly dependent on their more experienced party colleagues to learn the "culture" not only of the legislative process in Montana but of the internal governing functions of the party caucuses as well. As one close observer of legislative behavior has put it: "The voting record in Montana reveals a mature and, relative to the record of many other state legislatures around the country, rather important party system. There is party consciousness at large in the Montana legislature . . ." (Bryan 1981).

## CURRENT PARTY STRUCTURE

At the base of each party is the precinct. There are more than one thousand election precincts in the state, and in theory, each of these precincts (which can vary in size from a few dozen to several hundred voters) has a designated precinct committeeman and committeewomen for the Democratic and Republican Parties. These precinct party representatives are elected for two-year terms in the state's biennial June primary and may be reelected. The qualifications are minimal; one need only be a registered voter and residing in the precinct to qualify. Neither a filing fee nor an explicit declaration of party affiliation is required to get on the ballot as a precinct candidate.

In practice, there is hardly ever any electoral competition for precinct posts in the primary. Indeed, party organizations often have difficulty finding persons willing to "volunteer" to be on the primary ballot as precinct committee candidates. This is especially true for the second party, particularly in rural counties, where the pool of voters is small to begin with. In theory, precinct persons work actively in behalf of the electioneering and organizational goals of the party; in practice it is highly probable that little sustained activity occurs or is expected, although there has been no systematic and objective examination of party organizational effort at the grassroots level in Montana.

The next unit of political organization above the precinct is the county party central committee. The party county central committee is composed of all of the party's precinct committeemen and women in the county. County committees have the authority to fill precinct positions that become vacant between elections and to appoint a candidate to represent the party on the general-election ballot should the nominee designated in the June primary leave the ticket. During elections, county committees will often support the party's slate of candidates by providing volunteers and some material aid. In counties where a party is relatively strong, temporary space may be rented to establish a county campaign headquarters.

The state central committee of each party is composed of a county committeeman and committeewoman, the county organization chair, and the county party finance chairperson from each of Montana's fifty-six counties. Elected public officials and state party organization leaders also serve on the state central committee. The authority of the central committee is exercised by the state executive committee (called the executive board by the Democrats) and is composed of the state party chair and vice chair, state national committee members, state legislative leaders, and the leaders of the youth wings of the party.

Each party selects its state chair and vice chair by majority vote of delegates at a state officers' convention held in odd-numbered years, usually in June. Persons entitled to attend and vote at these conventions are the members of the state party executive committee, all state legislators affiliated with the party, and members of the state central committee.

The executive director of the party, who is a salaried, full-time employee of the party, is appointed by the state chair, subject to approval by the state executive committee. The director serves at the pleasure of the chair.

In addition to the biennial officers' conventions, each party has a state platform convention. State platform conventions are held biennially in even-numbered years to debate and approve the party's state platform. Finally, in presidential election years each party also holds a delegate convention shortly after the June primary. The most important duties of the state delegate convention are to select the state party's delegation to the national presidential nominating convention and to select the state party's slate of presidential electors, who will cast the state's electoral votes if their presidential ticket wins the popular vote in November (Montana Republican Party 1991; Montana Democratic Party 1995).

*Party Constituencies.* In Montana the parties are clearly distinguished by the ideas they represent, the interest groups that they are allied with, and, to a lesser extent, by the voting constituencies that can be depended upon to support the party's ticket.

First, let's consider the voting constituencies. The Montana Democratic Party has always drawn its strength from somewhat disparate elements. Historically, it is strongest in the western third of the state, where its base has been the industrial working class, and unionized workers in particular, employed in mining and industrial manufacturing. The party also has had a strong base of support in the grain-growing counties of north central and northeastern Montana, called the "High Line," where the tradition of rural radicalism, first manifest by the Nonpartisan League and more recently the Montana Farmers Union, has held sway. Finally, the party has traditionally done well in urban centers like Billings, Butte, Helena, and Great Falls. The Republicans, in contrast, have been much more a rural and small town party whose strongest geographic base has been in the rural "coyote" counties in central and eastern Montana. They also do well in the middle-class suburbs surrounding urban centers like Billings and Great Falls (Waldron and Wilson 1978).

Today, in Montana these coalitions appear to be changing. For Democrats, the New Deal coalition is dead. Unions are weaker, a lot fewer people are employed in resource extraction, and there are a lot fewer family farmers. To replace these shrinking constituencies, the Democrats have done well among well-educated and urban voters, public employees, and voters with strong environmental concerns. Thus, some of the party's strong geographic bases of support are the university towns of Bozeman and Missoula.

But the replacement does not appear to be enough to ensure that Democrats will maintain parity with a surging Republican Party. For the first time in the state's history, the

Republicans appear poised to take total control of the state's congressional delegation in 1996 as well as to maintain control of the governor's mansion and the state legislature. In addition to the traditional Republican constituencies of rural and small-town voters, the party appears to be doing well among Christian fundamentalists, pro-life supporters, anti-gun control advocates, a disparate constituency of folks who oppose taxes, and disgruntled blue-collar workers in the shrinking resource industry in places like Flathead Lake. Further, the state's population, though stable in number, has witnessed significant demographic change as migrants from out of state replace in-state residents who have left. These newcomers, the largest proportion coming from California, are disproportionately older and better-off financially, and it is this type of constituency that has contributed to the growth of the Republican share of the vote in the western third of the state (Light 1995).

Second, although Montana's parties are more than the sum of the interests that support them and their candidates, they are nonetheless linked to economic and social organizations in the state. The Democrats' generally progressive stance is reinforced by ties to organized labor; state environmental lobbies; advocates for senior citizens, the poor, and women; Native Americans; and public employees, particularly in public education. The Republicans are closely allied with the chamber of commerce, the Montana Taxpayers Association, resource development interests, professional and trade associations, and small business. Finally, socially conservative groups like the Christian Coalition and antiabortion interests are closely allied to the Republican Party at the grassroots level, contributing volunteers, offering financial support, and supplying candidates for state legislative, school board, and other local offices.

*Party Nomination Procedures.* Montana adopted the primary for nominating candidates in 1912 as part of the general progressive reform effort sweeping the nation at that time. Montana also adopted a presidential primary, later abolished it, and then reinstated it in 1976 (Waldron and Wilson 1978).

Montana is one of a small number of states that has an "open" primary. In an open primary the only requirement is that the citizen be a registered voter, and those wishing to participate in the primary of either party are not required to make a public declaration of party affinity prior to voting. In nonpartisan primaries, used in Montana to nominate candidates for judicial, school board, and many local elective offices, candidates themselves may not signal a party affiliation.

State party organizations are thought to have been seriously undermined by the primary nomination device, and indeed that was the intention of the progressive reformers who championed it (Sorauf and Beck 1988). Today, state parties, unable to control formally who may run as a candidate, and in the case of open primaries, unable to condition who may vote, are sometimes saddled with candidates who are embarrassments to the party's image and who may be actively hostile to the party's program. Further, it is alleged that open primaries encourage "raiding," in which voters favoring one party vote in the other party's primary for the weakest candidate in the hopes of giving their preferred candidate an easy general-election victory. Less troubling is the fact that the party organization is dependent on the candidates who appear. One veteran Montana officeholder told this writer of filing for the first time as a candidate for the state house of representatives and then getting a call from the county chair asking: "Who are you?"

The presidential primary is held at the same time as the state primary for other offices: the first Tuesday in June in even years. The purpose of the presidential primary is to deter-

**Table 1**  Montana Resource Guide

|  | Democrats | Republicans |
| --- | --- | --- |
| Archive | Yes | Yes |
| Location | Montana Democratic Party | Montana Republican Party |
|  | P.O. Box 802 | 1419-B Helena Avenue |
|  | Helena, Mont. 59624 | Helena, Mont. 59601 |
| Dates | 1970–present | 1960–present |
| Finding aid | Yes | No |
| Access | By appointment | By appointment |
| Contents: |  |  |
| Executive committee minutes | Yes | Limited |
| Correspondence | Yes | Limited |
| Organizational structure | Yes | Limited |
| Budgets | Yes | Limited |
| Rules | Yes | Limited |

mine how many of the state party's national convention delegates each candidate will receive. In 1996 Montana Democrats will pick twenty-five national convention delegates; Montana Republicans, fourteen.

To qualify for a place on the primary ballot a presidential candidate must submit petitions signed by at least two thousand registered Montana voters. For Democrats, delegates are allocated to presidential candidates on the basis of the proportional share of the statewide vote they received. But a candidate must win a minimum of 15 percent of the statewide vote to qualify for proportional distribution. Republicans, in contrast, use a winner-take-all distribution. The candidate who has the most support wins all the delegates.

However, the Republican primary is nonbinding. Authority to elect the party's national convention delegates rests with the state delegate convention, whose members are selected before the primary. This convention is composed of delegates who are selected in April by the county central committees. Thus the Republican presidential candidate who has won the hearts and minds of the county organization officers will have won all of the state's national delegation well in advance of the June primary.

In contrast, the Democratic presidential primary is binding and more open to citizen involvement. Like Republicans, Montana Democrats formally pick their national convention delegation at a state delegate convention scheduled shortly after the June primary. But unlike the GOP, the Democrats wait until after the primary to select delegates. After the June primary, each county Democratic Party holds a delegate convention in which persons are elected as state convention delegates. The number of delegates a county sends to the state convention depends on the proportionate share of the statewide Democratic vote in the county. Any person may attend these county conventions and be elected as a county delegate. In practice, those elected are active supporters of one of the presidential candidates who is entitled (based on the June primary results) to a share of the state's national delegation. The only restriction is that national party rules require gender equity in the composition of county delegations. Once the state convention meets, any county delegate may file as a candidate to be a national convention delegate pledged to vote for the candidate of his or her choice. Thus, the state convention exercises a substantive duty to pick from among a competing number of citizen-candidates those who shall represent the state party. The state convention is also obliged to select the party's slate of presidential electors.

## RESOURCE GUIDE

Resource materials on the history of state parties in Montana are found in a limited number of sites. First, historic records of the parties, especially prior to 1960, can be found in the archives of the Montana Historical Society in Helena. For more recent years, the best place to look is in the state headquarters of the Democratic and Republican Parties, also in Helena. The state GOP has fairly complete records for 1990 to the present. Prior to that, the records are scattered, incomplete, and uncataloged. The post-1990 records are in boxes in the basement of party headquarters. State Democratic Party records are also housed in a basement, but they are well categorized, boxed, and protected. Records appear to be almost complete from 1970 onward. Both parties will permit access to these records. Giving advance notice of a site visit is recommended.

## REFERENCES

*Asterisks denote the most important publications on Montana party politics.*
Bryan, Frank. 1981. *Politics in rural states: People, parties, processes.* Boulder, Colo.: Westview Press.
*Calvert, Jerry. 1995. The popular referendum and equality of voting rights in the states. Paper presented at the annual meeting of the Western Political Science Association, Portland, Ore., March 16–18.
———. 1993. *Legislative reform and representative government in Montana.* Bozeman, Mont.: Burton K. Wheeler Center.
Gibson, James, et al. 1985. Whither the local parties? A cross-sectional and longitudinal analysis of the strength of party organizations. *American Journal of Political Science.* February: 139–159.
Keefe, William, and Morris Ogul. 1993. *The American legislative process.* 8th ed. Englewood Cliffs, N.J.: Prentice-Hall.
Light, Jack. 1995. Executive director of the Montana Republican Party. Interview by author, Helena, September 5.
*Lopach, James, et al. 1983. *We the people of Montana . . .* Missoula, Mont.: Mountain Press.
Magleby, David. 1989. More bang for the buck: Campaign spending in small state U.S. Senate elections. Paper presented at the annual meeting of the Western Political Science Association, Salt Lake City, Utah, March 30–April 1.
Martin, Brad. 1995. Executive director of the Montana Democratic Party. Interview by author, Helena, September 5.
Montana Democratic Party. 1995. *Rules of the Democratic Party of the State of Montana.* Helena: Montana Democratic Party.
Montana Republican Party. 1991. *Rules: Montana Republican Party.* Helena: Montana Republican Party.
*Office of the Secretary of State. 1989. *Title 13: Election Laws, State of Montana.* Helena: Office of the Secretary of State.
*Pearson, C. B. 1991. *Montana politics: Funding Montana's legislative races.* Helena: Montana Common Cause.
Sorauf, Frank, and Paul Beck. 1988. *Party politics in America.* 8th ed. Glenview, Ill.: Scott, Foresman.
U.S. Advisory Commission on Intergovernmental Relations. 1986. *The transformation of American politics: Implications for federalism.* Washington, D.C.: Advisory Commission on Intergovernmental Relations.
*Waldron, Ellis, and Paul Wilson. 1978. *Atlas of Montana politics, 1889–1976.* Missoula: University of Montana.

# Nebraska

ROBERT F. SITTIG

## PARTY HISTORY

Nebraska's admission to the Union in 1867 was preceded by two decades of political and partisan tumult caused by the escalating slavery issue in the nation. The early territorial governors, appointed by Democratic presidents, were able to lead local Democrats, and the party predominated during the 1840s and 1850s. The partisan climate began to change with Lincoln's election in 1860 and the appointment of the first Republican territorial governor. Passage of the Free Homestead Act in 1862 and the Union victory in the Civil War resulted in a large number of Northern veterans migrating to Nebraska to claim the free land. The war demoralized Nebraska Democrats, and once statehood was achieved, the Republican tide was strong and growing.

Republicans dominated Nebraska politics from statehood until the 1890s, when a more competitive relationship evolved. Hard economic times due to drought and restlessness by growing numbers of progressives in Republican ranks offered the Democrats as well as a third party, the Populists, electoral opportunities. Disgruntled Republicans, newly coined Populists, and Democrats employed a strategy of "fusionism"—in which they united behind a single candidate—to win major offices, especially the governorship, around the turn of the century. The Republicans made incremental gains in the early 1920s, and when they regained control of the state legislature, they eliminated fusion candidates by mandating that candidates could accept the nomination of only one political party. This legislation helped to consolidate the Republican advantage for the next couple of decades. There were, however, interludes of Democratic rule, which helped the party to maintain viability. For example, the Democrats enjoyed extended control of the Nebraska state legislature during the 1910s and occasional gubernatorial victories in the 1920s and 1930s.

In 1934 the voters initiated and adopted by a three-to-two margin a constitutional amendment calling for a single house legislature, the members of which were to be selected in nonpartisan elections. Such an amendment had been considered for a quarter-century in Nebraska and elsewhere, at the instigation of progressive reformers. Party organization and office-holding leaders at the time were opposed to the amendment, but it passed handily anyway.

The practical effect of the 1934 amendment, which took effect with the 1936 elections, was to help the majority Republican Party and to complicate the electoral landscape for the Democrats. The nonpartisan feature shielded Nebraska election outcomes from the national swing favoring the Democrats in the 1930s and 1940s and worked to the advantage of incumbents in the state legislature, the majority of whom were Republican. Although no party affiliations appear on the ballot, very rarely are independents nominated or elected despite the ease of being listed.

After nearly a century of Republican dominance punctuated by the occasional Democratic victories mentioned above, in the 1950s a shift occurred in partisan fortunes that has persisted to the present day, as complacent Republicans ended up with mediocre nominees while higher-caliber candidates sought and won Democratic nominations. Spotty Democratic wins for major offices in the mid-1950s led to frequent wins in the 1960s, and since winning the governor's office in 1970, Democrats have come to dominate U.S. Senate and gubernatorial races. And by 1995, the unofficial partisan lineup in the legislature was twenty-five Republicans, twenty-three Democrats, and one independent. The Republican Party, however, continues to control most U.S. House seats and other state administrative posts. Thus, both parties can point to electoral successes in the recent past, but given the steady Republican edge in party registrants (Democrats trailed Republicans by some 100,000 adherents in May 1996) and the recent surge by Republicans in the nation and Nebraska in the 1994 elections, the state can be best characterized as having a slight Republican tendency (Board of State Canvassers of Nebraska 1996). This assessment will be tested anew in 1996 upon the retirement of the state's senior U.S. senator, James Exon, the sole Democrat in recent years to serve a career in high elected office in Nebraska, with two terms as governor and three as a senator.

## ORGANIZATIONAL DEVELOPMENT

The party organizations in Nebraska became vibrant only in the 1950s. Before then, the state parties had no headquarters and no permanent staff, and whomever happened to be the chair of the state executive or central committee became the repository for the records of the state party. The chairs were unpaid volunteers, and their private offices—home or business—became the party headquarters. The major deviation from this pattern was the Democratic organization in Douglas County (Omaha), where the spoils and excitement of big city politics were high enough to foster ongoing machine-type local party organizations.

The major step toward permanently established state parties came in the 1960s when the Republicans hired a full-time political director and rented a headquarters in the capital, Lincoln. The Democrats took a similar step in the early 1970s, with a bit of a twist: they combined the offices of state chair and political director in the same person. For a while this was workable, but in the 1980s the Democrats separated the two positions and now have an unpaid state chair joined by a full-time salaried official to manage the day-to-day operations from a rented headquarters, also in Lincoln.

During the era of volunteer chairs, the tenure of the state party chair was, not unexpectedly, of short duration. The parties, once they began to hire permanent, salaried chairs, anticipated longer tenures, but history has shown that the hiring of full-time chairs has not affected their length of service, and frequent turnover in party chairs occurs. The same can be said of the paid executive directors, so the organizational leadership at the top of the parties lacks continuity and the benefits stemming from experience. State party chairs tend to return to private professional activities—law, business, or farming—whereas the top paid party staffers move on to more rewarding stints, often as lobbyists or campaign consultants. Thus, high turnover occurs in the upper-echelons (paid and unpaid ) of both parties in Nebraska.

The historical lack of stability and effectiveness at the top of Nebraska party organizations may explain why the top public officeholders have but limited and casual relations with their organizational counterparts. For example, when an unexpected death in 1987 caused a vacancy in the U.S. Senate, the Republican governor, Kay Orr, filled the spot without consulting the state party chair and passed over an ex-party chair as well as two sitting U.S. House Republicans. And the previous governor, Democrat Robert Kerrey, filled a top administrative elective post that had become vacant due to a resignation with a casual acquaintance who was a Republican, despite the presence of some half-dozen semiprominent Democrats who had aspirations for the post. In the backwash to this event, the state party chair resigned.

Despite the fact that party leaders in Nebraska have had little influence in the state's politics, two factors have over the years contributed to the appearance of influence. One was the presence in the 1940s and early 1950s of a preprimary endorsement law. Such laws usually reflect a dominant role of the organizational leaders in recruiting prospective candidates for major public office. But this apparently was never the case in Nebraska, and the legislature repealed the preprimary endorsement law in 1952. Another oddity not in keeping with the modest political role of state party leaders is their success in seeking election to high public office. Former state party leaders—James Exon, Democratic national committeeman, 1968–1969, and Bill Barrett, state Republican chair, 1973–1975— currently hold two of five U.S. House and Senate seats.

Harmony seems to be the watchword within both Nebraska party organizations; factional stridency is rare. Rancor might be more common if the stakes were higher, but the organizations have only a slight impact. There has been no durable factionalism since the 1950s, when moderate and conservative Republican activists sparred over gubernatorial and Senate nominations, largely because election in November of the Republican nominee was almost a certainty. The conservatives most often prevailed in these clashes. Perhaps the last such square-off came in 1964, when the Goldwater majority was unwilling to compromise over allocation of national convention delegates because Goldwater's nomination was not yet assured. On the Democratic side, organizational struggles were much less pugnacious in the 1950s and 1960s due to the party's uncompetitiveness and because those in control were able to hold off challengers who argued that the party's electoral ineffectiveness could be overcome with new leadership. Eventually, the reform element within the state Democratic Party galvanized behind a gubernatorial candidate, Frank Morrison, who won three elections and served from 1961 to 1967. Since then, the Democratic organization has been deferential to its growing number of top public officeholders, including Exon (governor, 1971–1979; U.S. senator, 1979–), Kerrey (governor, 1983–1987; U.S. senator, 1989–), Ben Nelson (governor, 1991–), and Edward Zorinsky (U.S. senator, 1976–1987).

To avoid rifts in their organizations, both parties have made concerted efforts to include top officers from every section of the state; this has blunted geographic and population disparities and resulted in special attention being paid to the low-population western region, which is euphemistically called "greater Nebraska."

Since the late 1980s disputes have become more common in Republican local and state conventions, especially over platform pronouncements regarding abortion; generally, the pro-life Christian fundamentalists have prevailed in such matters, but their influence has been less pronounced in the more broadly based nominating process.

## CURRENT PARTY ORGANIZATION

The current party organizations in Nebraska scarcely resemble their weak predecessors of the 1960s and 1970s. Both party organizations have established themselves and seem assured, based on their ability to sustain themselves over the past couple of decades, of

**Table 1** Nebraska State Party Finances, Fiscal Year 1993–1994

| | Republicans | Democrats |
|---|---|---|
| Income | | |
| Large contributions | $255,000 | $ 36,000 |
| Other contributions | 100,000 | 48,000 |
| Fund-raising events | 75,000 | 91,000 |
| Telemarketing | 200,000 | — |
| National committee | 25,000 | — |
| Miscellaneous | 15,000 | 9,000 |
| Total | $670,000 | $184,000 |
| Expenditures | | |
| Staff salary and benefits[1] | $200,000 | $ 81,000 |
| Headquarters | 115,000 | 41,000 |
| Telemarketing | 80,000 | — |
| Other fund raising | 56,000 | — |
| Newsletter | 30,000 | — |
| Events | 40,000 | 37,000 |
| Candidate support | 102,000 | — |
| Miscellaneous | 47,000 | 25,000 |
| Total | $670,000 | $184,000 |

SOURCE: Data derived from fiscal year budgets provided by state party chairs.

NOTE: Amounts are rounded, and the period covered is summarized for comparative purposes.

[1] The Republicans had seven full-time employees, and the Democrats had four.

secure, if not commanding, futures. This is more true for the Republicans than for the Democrats due to their superior financing. But even the greater resources of the state Republican Party cannot overcome the reality that party organizations everywhere in American politics have been supplanted to some extent. But despite the fact that election consultants, political action committees, and various other actors have come to the fore in electoral politics, the organizations in Nebraska are more than holding on to their slender threads of influence. A brief examination of some objective measures of party vibrancy supports this assessment.

The Republican Party holds a considerable financial lead over the Democratic Party (see Table 1), and ratios of two, three, and four to one are common on such measures as staff size, receipts and expenditures, headquarters rent, and amounts contributed to candidates. Republicans established themselves securely originally by adding sustaining memberships to their core of large corporate and individual benefactors, and more recently by implementing a costly but profitable telemarketing operation to enhance continuing donations and to uncover new sources of support. Democrats engage in similar but less productive and less comprehensive efforts.

Despite their relative disadvantage in resources, Nebraska Democrats have undertaken efforts of some significance. For example, over the past decade, in a joint state-local cooperative venture, the state party has paid for the printing of some 30,000 door hangers touting its slate of candidates in general elections and identifying all Democrats in the nonpartisan portion of primary elections; these hangers have been distributed by local volunteers in Lancaster County (Lincoln) in state and city elections and no doubt have accounted for much of the party's electoral success in the face of equal registration numbers for both parties in the county. The county Republicans are superior in financial resources, but since they lack the volunteer foot soldiers to hand-deliver their flyers, the party has to pay to mail them to Republican households in targeted high-turnout precincts. And both the Democratic and Republican Lancaster County party organizations have rented headquarters year-round and have hired permanent paid staffs; this sets Lancaster County apart from most other counties, a few of which lack even officers or a central committee.

The state Republican Party has also been persistent in its attempts to work with its elected contingent in the nonpartisan legislature. One goal of the Republican Party has been to shift the election system back to a partisan basis, but most Democrats and a few Republicans prefer the status quo, and consequently the legislature, despite coming close, has thus far failed to propose the necessary state constitutional amendment. Democratic platforms, too, have called for such a change, but the party's organizational leadership finds it difficult to persuade Democratic legislators to support the amendment. The chair of the Republican Party, elected in 1995, in addition to identifying the reintroduction of partisan elections as an important objective, has also sought to galvanize Republican legislators and staffers to oppose the public funding of state campaigns, which was adopted in a recent reform law. This chair also seeks to negate the district system for awarding presidential electoral votes, which the Democratic legislative contingent was instrumental in getting passed prior to the 1992 election.[1] These are examples of party organizational gambits and programs that one would associate with well-organized political entities, and at times the party organizations in Nebraska have qualified as such, but overall they have had only a limited and tangential role in shaping policy and directing the electoral processes in the state.

Traditionally, Nebraska public officeholders, and especially party organizational leaders, do not take sides publicly in contested primaries. This explains in part why Nebraska primaries have higher than average candidate competition and voter turnout levels. The tradition is adhered to even when the lines are clearly drawn, say, between a current or former organizational leader and an opponent with little or no standing among the party activists. Public officeholders also abide by the tradition of neutrality in primaries, but on rare occasions exceptions have occurred. In 1990, for example, the junior U.S. senator, Robert Kerrey, openly endorsed a candidate who had been his chief of staff while he was governor; Kerrey's primary endorsement no doubt made the race tighter, but his choice fell short, and the strained relationship between Kerrey and the eventual primary and general-election winner—Ben Nelson—has resulted in occasional political sniping between the two officials and their supporters.

Party leaders also tend to stay on the sidelines in the nonpartisan legislative elections unless a race evolves into a head-to-head partisan contest. When that happens, the parties offer modest amounts of in-kind aid such as mailing lists and campaign training. The party share of financing of campaigns pales in comparison with the shares interest groups and the candidates themselves contribute. In one recent election, the party's share of total campaign receipts was less than 5 percent of the average candidate's campaign chest.

A major catalyst for party building in Nebraska, especially for the Republican Party, has been funding from the national organizations. The aid has come in differing forms and amounts, ranging from cash contributions earmarked for state legislative candidates to field staffers for the general-election campaigns. The national assistance has provided an incentive for state parties to become more active on their own. For example, in 1978, the Republican National Committee provided some $30,000 to the state Republican Party to aid in state legislative races. Apparently, the national party was unconcerned about the state parties' tradition of noninvolvement and the nonpartisan nature of Nebraska legislative races. The assistance had a positive effect on Republican victories in the 1978 election, and in the years since the state party has continued the practice of directly aiding some Republican legislative candidates. Republican success stimulated the Democrats to counter with similar but less comprehensive campaign efforts in targeted state legislative races.

The relationship between the state and county party organizations is loose and tenuous. At the organizational base, county convention delegates are elected in closed primaries, and year-round precinct representatives are appointed, but, given the slim rewards for precinct service, most slots are filled in name only, and a few are vacant. The permanent state committees are similarly drawn from county delegations to the state conventions. There is little interaction between the state and local parties in the long interval between elections.

Two instances since the 1980s of state-local organizational interaction by the Republicans took a toll on the party's public image. Chairs in two counties were removed by the state party due to "indiscretion" and "insubordination." In one case, the local chair opposed his party's governor and state party platform on the siting of a low-level radioactive waste disposal facility. The other removal came after irregularities were discovered in a county chair's private financial affairs and he resisted calls from the state organization to resign. On a positive note, the state Democrats succeeded in setting up, with national help, some half-dozen sub-state headquarters in a coordinated campaign effort to bolster the ticket from top to bottom in the general election. But generally, there are only episodic dealings between the state and county levels; typically, county organizations peak in activity during the general-election campaign in support of their respective candidate slates. Additionally, the state parties conduct state conventions every two years to draft a platform, select a variety of party officers, and, in presidential election years, select national convention delegates.

On the matter of candidate recruitment the Nebraska party organizations are only tangentially involved; at the local level the party leaders are often limited to making early inquiries of incumbent officeholders regarding their intentions. If a vacancy is impending, an effort is made to inform desired prospective candidates of the opportunity and to offer them campaign training seminars if they agree to run. Caution and skill are required of party leaders when it comes to "recruiting" candidates because of the state's tradition of preprimary neutrality by organizational leaders, and this expectation is observed rigorously by state-level party activists.

In conclusion it can be said that the state party organizations in Nebraska, especially the Republican organization, have scrambled back into the picture as far as electoral and party-building activities and services go; they are a factor, but not a major one, in the swirl of politics in current times.

### RESOURCE GUIDE

The Nebraska State Historical Society maintains records from the Democratic state central committee, the Democratic Women's Group, the Young Democrats, and the Teen Democrats. The records are identified by source and date, and the historical society staff retrieves the boxed materials requested by researchers. The transfer of Democratic Party materials to the historical society since the mid-1970s has been spotty, but in the near future the party may update the society's holdings. Until such transfer takes place, recent documents can be requested or viewed at the state headquarters, 715 S. 14th St., Lincoln, Nebraska 68508, (402) 475-4584.

Nearly all the records of the state Republican Party are stored in the basement of the headquarters and are available by request or appointment. It may be that such records will

**Table 2**  Nebraska Resource Guide

|  | Democrats | Republicans |
|---|---|---|
| Archive | Yes | Yes |
| Location | State Historical Society | Party Headquarters |
|  | P.O. Box 82554 | 421 S. 9th St., #233 |
|  | Lincoln, NE 68510 | Lincoln, NE 68508 |
|  | (402) 471-3270 | (402) 475-2122 |
| Dates | 1953–1975 | ?–present |
| Finding aid | Yes | No |
| Access | Public | By appointment |
| Contents: |  |  |
| Executive committee minutes | Yes | Yes |
| Correspondence | Yes | Yes |
| Organizational structure | Yes | Yes |
| Budgets | Yes | Yes |
| Rules | Yes | Yes |

be transferred to the state historical society archives in the near future. The Republican material now in the society archives is mostly campaign literature from the 1950s and 1980s.

## NOTE

1. States since the 1840s have adhered to a winner-take-all system for awarding electoral votes to the presidential candidate who leads in the popular vote. Maine in the 1970s changed to a district awarding arrangement, and Nebraska followed suit in 1992. Neither state has as yet cast a split electoral vote.

## REFERENCES

*Asterisks denote the most important publications on Nebraska party politics.*
Board of State Canvassers of Nebraska. 1996. Lincoln: Board of State Canvassers of Nebraska.
Kolasa, Bernard. 1968. The Nebraska political system: A study in partisan politics. Ph.D. diss., University of Nebraska-Lincoln, Department of Political Science.
*Miewald, Robert D., ed. 1984. *Nebraska government and politics.* Lincoln: University of Nebraska Press.
*Olson, James C. 1966. *History of Nebraska.* Lincoln: University of Nebraska Press.
Pedersen, James, and Kenneth Wald. 1973. *Shall the people rule? A history of the Democratic Party in Nebraska politics.* Lincoln: Jacob North Publishers.

# Nevada

ERIC B. HERZIK AND ALLEN R. WILCOX

## PARTY HISTORY

The history of political parties in Nevada can be divided into five periods. For the most part, the state has produced traditional two-party electoral outcomes. Exceptions to political control by either the Democratic or Republican Party occurred in the 1890s, when the Silver Party scored a number of victories. In 1912 Theodore Roosevelt's Progressive Party and the Socialist Party both out-polled the Republicans, running close behind the Democrats (Bushnell and Driggs 1984). Since the early 1900s, various third-party candidates have run well in particular elections, but victory has remained with either Democratic or Republican candidates.

Nevada's first political period ran from statehood in 1864 to 1890. The Republican Party dominated the period, winning slightly more than 70 percent of all statewide elective offices and approximately 80 percent of state legislative seats. Republican dominance reflected the party's major role in assisting Nevada achieve statehood well before most other western territories.

The second period covered the elections of 1890 through 1906. Since silver mining was the primary industry in the state, the "free coinage" of silver dominated electoral politics. The silver mining industry had begun to decline in the 1880s, plunging Nevada into an ever-deepening economic recession. State population shrank by nearly a quarter between 1880 and 1890, and the state shifted from an urban, industrial economy with a significant immigrant population to an agrarian economy with a more nativist base. These demographic and economic changes complemented the appeals of the rising Populist Party. In 1892 the Populist Party's presidential candidate, Gen. James B. Weaver, won 67 percent of the Nevada vote. Republicans garnered 26 percent, and the Democrats trailed with a scant 7 percent (Zanjani 1979). The Populist Party, labeled the Silver Party in Nevada, initially drew votes from both the Democratic and Republican Parties, but drew more permanently and significantly from the Democrats. In part this reflected the socioeconomic and demographic changes noted above, but it also was a function of the inability of Nevada Republicans to make any headway in promoting the silver coinage issue at the national level (Glass 1969). In 1896 the Silver Party merged with the Democratic Party (becoming the Silver Democrats) and won nearly 80 percent of all state and national elections between 1896 and 1906.

A third period, lasting from 1908 through 1932, emerged with the decline of the silver issue. During this period party competition was balanced. Democrats tended to win more often at the local and state legislative levels (winning approximately 60 percent of races), whereas Republicans fared better in higher profile national and statewide elections (winning approximately 55 percent of races). The balance between the parties reflected their similar political appeals (Zanjani 1979). Both parties jockeyed for labor support with platforms stressing worker safety and fairly progressive stands on union activity as the state's industrial economy strengthened following the prolonged recession of the 1880s and 1890s.

The election of Franklin Roosevelt in 1932 marked the beginning of the fourth period, which lasted to approximately 1976. FDR's victory shifted the balance of power in party politics squarely to Democrats at nearly all electoral levels. Between 1932 and 1972 Democrats won four times as many U.S. Senate, U.S. House, and gubernatorial races as the Republicans. Republicans nearly disappeared from the state legislature, holding only four of twenty-one state senate seats as late as 1976, and never holding majorities in either house. More pointedly, Democratic Party registration hovered at about 60 percent of all registered voters and doubled Republican figures through 1968. Only in presidential races did Republicans fare well, winning half the elections held during the period (Bushnell and Driggs 1984).

A fifth period of partisan politics has emerged since 1976; it has been a period of increasing equality in the partisan balance. Nevada has tended to vote Republican in presidential races since 1968, with U.S. Senate and House races evenly split. Democrats have held the governor's office, with just a single exception, since 1971. However, partisan balance is more evident in the state legislature and in voter registration numbers. Party registration numbers are now nearly even, and control of the state senate and assembly has shifted four times since 1982. Indeed, the 1994 election left the state assembly in a 21–21 deadlock (with leadership and committee chair positions shared by the parties), the state senate under Republican control, and the governorship in the hands of a Democrat.

## ORGANIZATIONAL DEVELOPMENT

Socioeconomic, demographic, and personality factors have been the primary forces shaping Nevada party development. However, parties in Nevada have not been immune to changes wrought by major national policy and electoral trends. Shifts in partisan strength during the five historical periods discussed above were brought on by an interplay of state and national political factors. With respect to more recent changes, Democratic Party reforms made in the aftermath of the 1972 Democratic National Convention were a critical influence on party development. The "McGovern Reforms," as they are often called, greatly widened the range of participants in the Nevada Democratic Party, leading particularly to the emergence of women in positions of party leadership (Crowley 1976; Cain 1995). The Republican Party was most affected by the election of Ronald Reagan in 1980, which fueled an already growing surge in Republican Party activity within the state (McKay 1995).

Still, the organization and operation of Nevada's political parties have been affected more by events and conditions directly linked to the state. The electoral dominance of the Democratic Party from 1932 to 1976 gave it a tremendous advantage in sustaining its organization and in fielding candidates. Because they had a large number of victors at the local and state legislative levels, Democrats had an easier time than the Republicans in staffing precinct and county party positions and had a pool of candidates primed for advancement. Indeed, virtual "lines of succession" for statewide elective offices appeared on the Democratic side, whereas Republicans often scrambled to field anyone but newcomers for major statewide and national electoral positions.

The growth of the Republican Party has really occurred since 1972. It can be explained by three primary factors. Nevada has always been a conservative and highly individualistic state (Hulse 1986). Thus, there has been a widening ideological gap between the state's electorate and the policy positions of the national Democratic Party. The gap was first seen in presidential and U.S. Senate and House elections, where Nevada developed a pattern of voting Republican while voting Democratic in state and local races. Republican gains then shifted from the top of the ballot to state and local levels. Increasing membership has enabled the Republican Party to staff more easily its precinct and county chair positions. Grassroots party activity and candidate recruitment have also improved.

Nevada is also the fastest growing state in the Union. Tremendous demographic change has dramatically increased and transformed the electorate, as many new residents from traditionally Republican Southern California communities and retirees from throughout the nation have moved in. Anti-tax and spending themes have played well with new residents and have given an advantage to the Republicans (Herzik and Statham 1993).

A third factor is the emergence of modern campaign and fund-raising techniques. Use of the mass media, and particularly television, has forced a professionalization of the state's two political parties. The higher costs of modern campaigning have also forced a change from more traditional "friends and neighbors" campaigning to modern sound-stage and sound-bite electioneering. Again, the Republican Party has proven more adept at taking advantage of these changes, especially in their ability to raise money for a wide range of candidates. Coming out of a period of almost complete Democratic dominance, the two parties now compete fairly evenly in terms of candidate spending and use of the media.

## CURRENT PARTY ORGANIZATION

Political parties are broadly outlined in section 293 of the Nevada Revised Statutes but are only loosely regulated. Parties must formally register with the secretary of state's office to be placed on ballots. The statutes prescribe in great detail the regularity of and eligibility to participate in party precinct meetings. The number of delegates each precinct is entitled to send to county conventions and the number each county is entitled to send to the state convention are also set by statute, with delegate numbers based on the number of party registrants in a given area.

Both parties utilize a three-tier system of organization—precinct, county, and state. Precinct meetings, held in each general-election year, elect delegates to the county convention. County chairs are elected by delegates to the county conventions. State chairs are elected by county delegates to the state convention. Any party member may announce and run for a chair position. Neither party provides any specific support, such as salary, office space, clerical staff, or operating funds, to county or state chairs. Instead, county and state chairs must act as part-time fundraisers to support their own efforts. In 1995 the Democrats had fourteen of seventeen county chair positions staffed, whereas Republicans had staffed sixteen of seventeen. These numbers are representative of trends over the past ten years (Cain 1995; McKay 1995). Both parties report active participation across the state at the precinct level, and both maintain active organizations in the state's larger and more urbanized counties.

*Party Bylaws and Duties.* Both parties have bylaws that describe the duties of various officers and prescribe the selection of assorted committees. Both parties have a state chair, vice chair, secretary, and treasurer, all of whom are elected at the state convention for two-year terms. The most important committee for each party is the state central committee. Members of the central committee are elected for a term of two years at the state convention. Bylaws of the Nevada Democratic Party must be in accord with conditions set by the national party; the state Republican Party has no such constraint (Cain 1995; McKay 1995). Both parties strive to achieve balance for gender, race, and region in party positions, with the Democrats operating under a more formal policy for pursuing such parity.

The largest organizational difference between the two parties is that the Republican Party has a paid and full-time executive director. In the mid-1970s the Republicans established the executive director's position to sustain party operations on a day-to-day basis. In 1992 a paid political director was added. The executive director, with a paid staff and office space, has greatly assisted with party development over the past decade and is a key link between the state party, national party, and legislative caucuses.

In contrast, the Democrats have a completely ad hoc organization. The state chair receives no funding and has no paid staff unless funds are specifically raised to pay such

staff. The larger urban counties maintain formal offices, but the state chair generally operates out of his or her home and shares space in the county office.

*Delegate Selection and Primaries.* Since 1980 Nevada has used a caucus system to select
delegates to the presidential nominating conventions. Delegate slates are selected at
precinct meetings and then forwarded to county and state meetings; the final delegate slates
reflect individual candidate strength at each level of the party. However, Assembly Bill 695,
passed by the Nevada legislature in 1995, allowed parties the option of either holding a primary or maintaining the caucus system. The Republicans opted for a statewide presidential
primary, to be held in March. The Democrats opted to maintain the caucus system. The
measure also gave presidential candidates greater control over the naming of specific delegates were a primary to be held.

Candidates for state offices are selected by closed party primaries. Nevada's regular state
primary election is held on the Tuesday following the second Monday in September of
even-numbered years. Major statewide offices are elected in nonpresidential, even-numbered years.

*Party Relationships: National, Legislative, and Local.* Both parties report close working
relationships with the national party. As noted above, the Democrats are more formally
linked through various conditions established by the national party. A national committeeman and woman are selected every four years, with terms ending the day after the party's
national convention. In addition to the national committeepersons, another key link for
the national and Nevada Democrats is the party's association of state chairs. Republicans
follow the same selection process for their national committee persons. Linkage to the
national party is more informal, primarily through the individual efforts of the state and
national chairs (Cain 1995; McKay 1995).

Relationships between the state and local (county) party organizations are very dependent on the efforts of the individuals involved. Information routinely filters down from the
state party to the local parties; upward flow is far less regular. The Republicans coordinate
efforts through their executive director.

Both parties organize caucuses within the state legislature. The existence of a permanent
executive director and party staff facilitates Republican interaction between legislative and
campaign organizations. Representatives of the Republican Party Legislative Caucus meet
regularly with party officials, especially the political director. Interaction between the
Democratic Party organization and the Democratic Party Legislative Caucus is more sporadic and flows through the state chair. The quality and quantity of interaction between the
Democratic legislative caucus and state chair are thus highly dependent on the personalities of the individuals involved.

Both parties report that candidate campaign organizations are quite separate from the
party organization, although natural linkages based on access to funds and information
and mutual partisan goals provide points of contact.

Regional concerns affect nearly every aspect of Nevada politics. Both parties must balance northern and southern regional interests. Southern Nevada, which contains more
than 60 percent of the state's population, is highly urbanized, growth-oriented, and concerned with obtaining water for continued development. Northern Nevada contains more
rural and environmental interests. Northern Nevada legislators are often at odds with the
development plans of southern Nevada legislators.

The Republican Party has also faced factional infighting linked to the so-called Christian
Right. In 1988 Christian Right adherents took control of the party through an organized

grassroots campaign at the precinct level. The party as a whole, after several successful elections in the previous decade, suffered legislative and statewide losses; candidates from the moderate wing of the party, however, continued to have success. State voters also overwhelmingly endorsed a prochoice ballot initiative in November 1990. Although the Christian Right remains a key faction within the party, its recent electoral difficulties have led to greater inclusivity within the Republican Party leadership.

The parties have adapted to modern modes of campaigning and are becoming increasingly professionalized, but Nevada is still small enough that individual leaders can have a profound impact on the system. For years the Democrats benefited from the influence of former governor Grant Sawyer (1959–1967), who also was a founding partner of the state's largest and most influential law firm (Sawyer, Elliot, and King 1993). Sawyer's influence was especially apparent in fund raising and in establishing broad-based consensus within the party, even though he never served as party chair. With advancing age and health woes, Sawyer's role in the party has diminished and the party has suffered. Similarly, Nevada Republicans benefited from the prominence of state residents Frank Fahrenkopf and Paul Laxalt within the national party organization. Fahrenkopf especially, as national party chair in the early 1980s, assisted greatly in the development of the state party's professionalization and fund raising.

## RESOURCE GUIDE

Neither party maintains a systematic archive of documents. Democratic Party documents are primarily in the hands of former state chairs. Past chairs and other key party activists have files, documents, and correspondence detailing various aspects and eras of the party's activities. Republican records appear to be less extensive than the Democrats' and, similarly, are more likely to be found among activists than in a single archive. The state office does maintain key files and documents concerning voter registration, turnout, and party meetings.

Library and government archival holdings are also scant. The library at the University of Nevada has records for selected state Democratic conventions and for party-affiliated groups. The papers of key state politicians, which often have some bearing on partisan activities, are also available. The records of former governor Sawyer, including taped interviews from the Oral History Program at the University of Nevada, may be the most important of these records. The state library holds the papers of all former Nevada governors, in which correspondence relating to party activities is most likely to be found.

## REFERENCES

*Asterisks denote the most important publications on Nevada party politics.*
*Bushnell, Eleanore, and Donald W. Driggs. 1984. *The Nevada constitution.* 6th ed. Reno: University of Nevada Press.
Cain, Virginia. 1995. Chair of the state Democratic Party. Interview by author, Reno, July 28.
Crowley, Joseph N. 1976. *Democrats, delegates, and politics in Nevada.* Reno: Bureau of Governmental Research, University of Nevada.
*Edwards, Jerome E. 1982. *Pat McCarran: Political boss of Nevada.* Reno: University of Nevada Press.
*Elliot, Russell R. 1983. *History of Nevada.* 2d ed. Lincoln: University of Nebraska Press.
Glass, Mary. 1969. *Silver and politics in Nevada, 1892–1902.* Reno: University of Nevada Press.
Herzik, Eric B., and E. Robert Statham. 1993. Nevada. In *State/local budgeting issues in the western states,* ed. Carl Mott, Daniel Sloan, and Robert Huefner. Salt Lake City: University of Utah, Center for Public Policy and Administration.

*Hulse, James. 1986. *Forty years in the wilderness*. Reno: University of Nevada Press.

McKay, Brian. 1995. Former chair of the state Republican Party. Interview by author, Reno, July 31.

*Sawyer, Grant, Gary Elliot, and Robert King. 1993. *Hang tough*. Reno: University of Nevada Oral History Program.

Zanjani, Sally. 1979. A theory of critical realignment: The Nevada example, 1892–1908. *Pacific Historical Review* 48, no. 2:259–280.

# New Hampshire

## MICHELLE ANNE FISTEK AND BOB EGBERT

Political parties in New Hampshire reflect the enduring characteristics of the state: a homogeneous population, a moderately high level of economic prosperity, dominance by a narrow range of political interests, and a traditional and amateur governmental structure. New Hampshire, with a population less than 2 percent racial minority and ethnic minorities that have tended to be as conservative as the majority white population, has endured few deep and lasting cleavages among its major groups. The state has no large cities, few large employers, and no dominant industry. Interests such as railroads, newspapers, textile manufacturing, lumber, and tourism have been dominant only in alliances with one another rather than individually. The structure of government, especially the amateur nature of the 424-member legislature, has made party organization difficult. Consequently, the state has had a one-party system except during a few transitional periods. Further, dominance by a single party has made strong organization difficult for the minority party and unnecessary for the party in the majority.

### PARTY HISTORY

Several themes run through the history of New Hampshire political parties: dominance by a single party, strong party organization and party competition only during transitional periods, cycles of corruption and reform, the influence of coalitions of powerful interests, and the impact of strong personalities.

At first, New Hampshire was among the strongest of the Federalist states; the state's Puritan Congregationalism was synonymous with the Federalist Party. Most town charters required that land be set aside to build a church, the state constitution required towns to support a Congregational minister, and public office was restricted to Protestants (Heffernan and Stecker 1981, 103).

Federalists began to lose support in the Granite State when their reckless abuse of power became evident in the Union Bank fight of 1800. John Langdon, a Democratic-Republican, organized a new bank which made small loans on easy terms. The state legislature refused to charter Langdon's bank since the state owned a considerable interest in the state's only bank, the New Hampshire Bank. Langdon and the Democratic-Republicans, unable to obtain loans at the New Hampshire Bank, parlayed this into a hard-fought campaign alleging the denial of the charter was just "another piece of Federalist intolerance" (Robinson 1916, 30).

In 1806 the Democratic-Republican Party became the majority party. New Hampshire's people were ideologically much more closely aligned to the party of Jefferson, so the change is not surprising. During the transitional period after the turn of the century, the Federalists and Democratic-Republicans created permanent hierarchical organizations. The latter, still using the legislative caucus for nominations, created a "Grand Committee of Election and Correspondence" and subordinate local bodies, and the existing *New Hampshire Gazette* became the party organ. The grand committee appointed and controlled county committees, which in turn appointed and controlled town committees (Robinson 1916, 63).

Bitter conflict between the parties was in evidence when the newly empowered Democratic-Republican legislature took over Dartmouth College as a state university, revising its governance and relieving the former Federalist trustees of the property and records of the institution. Daniel Webster represented the trustees in court to reverse what Jager and Jager (1983, 58) referred to as this "novel process of creative theft." The decision against the trustees in the Supreme Court of New Hampshire was reversed by the Federalist-leaning United States Supreme Court (*Dartmouth College Case*, 4 Wheat 518 [1819]), which found the legislature's actions in violation of the impairment of contracts clause of Art. I, sec. 10.

The transfer of power from the Jeffersonian Democratic-Republicans to the Jacksonian Democrats was complete in New Hampshire by about 1835. Important political figures, of former or later national stature, behind the Democratic Party organization in the state included Isaac Hill, editor, U.S. senator, and governor; Levi Woodbury, governor, U.S. senator, secretary of the navy and the Treasury, and justice of the U.S. Supreme Court; and Franklin Pierce, U.S. senator and later president of the United States. Jacksonian Democrats brought the spirit of reform to the state, and New Hampshire became a leader in treatment of the insane, prison reform, public education, religious toleration, improved working conditions, and abolition of imprisonment for debt. The Democrats replaced "king caucus" with the state party convention and solidified their power by controlling most newspapers in the state.

The next transitional period began as the Democratic Party split into two conflicting wings in 1842. Independent Democrats, Whigs, and abolitionists combined to control the legislature in 1846. Reform efforts continued as railroads and other large interests were made subject to state regulation. The issue of slavery unified the remnants of the Whig Party, the Free Soilers, the Know Nothings, rebellious Democrats, and other smaller groups to provide the basis for the Republican Party. In 1853 Amos Tuck called a meeting at his home in Exeter, New Hampshire, where those invited claimed to have conceived and named the Republican Party (Jager and Jager 1983, 61). The Republicans elected their first governor in 1857, and in the nearly 150 years since, only five Democrats have occupied the New Hampshire executive office.

Following the Civil War, Republican hegemony supported rampant corruption and huge increases in political spending. William Chandler, former owner of the *New Hampshire Statesman* and *Concord Monitor,* while serving in the U.S. Senate chronicled the heightened role of political money at the time. He wrote that big money first appeared in 1882, when railroads began to spend "immense" amounts (Chandler 1898, 8). The state party supported candidates directly, and the state committee chair had the discretion to dispense all state party funds (Chandler 1898, 13). Some recipients signed contracts: "In consideration of one hundred dollars, I agree to vote as the maker and prior endorser [party chair, railroad, etc.]

of this draft may direct" (Chandler 1898, 15). Free railroad passes and retainers for lawyers were provided openly. By 1907 critic Frank Putnam would write that the man who really governed New Hampshire was "the president of the Boston and Maine Railroad" (Jager and Jager 1983, 61). Republican ascendance in this era did not translate into party government. There was an absence of clear party ideology and organization. Tradition, slogans, "strong personalities, enormous egos and ambitions both broad and narrow fired the political system" (Wright 1987, 53).

New Hampshire joined the progressive movement by passing legislation curbing free railroad passes in 1907. In 1909 the legislature voted to require reporting of legislative concerns and expenditures of lobbyists, to require that all public business be done in meetings open to the public, and to require use of the direct primary to nominate party candidates. Progressives were the first to understand and take advantage of the new nomination process, electing Robert Bass as governor in 1910. Under Bass, the legislature regulated utilities and monopolies and provided for child labor reform, workmen's compensation, factory inspections, and forest protection.

The feud between the Roosevelt Bull Moose Progressives and the Taft Republicans spilled into New Hampshire. As the Republicans feuded, New Hampshire Democrats organized to elect Samuel Felker governor in 1912, the Executive Council, a majority of the legislature, and a United States senator. In the first election following ratification of the 17th Amendment to the U.S. Constitution in 1913 mandating the direct election of U.S. senators, the Republicans swept back into power and have remained the dominant party since.

## ORGANIZATIONAL DEVELOPMENT

The modern era of political party development began early in New Hampshire. The parties' voters had elected delegates to the national conventions since 1913, but in 1952 the legislature created the "first in the nation" primary. In that year the state was first to combine a preference poll with the apportionment of national convention delegates, but the state also resolved to be first to hold the primary in each presidential election year. As Jager and Jager state, "the primary came to significance more by inadvertence than by design" (1983, 63). No one realized how drastic a change the combination of preference polling and delegate selection would be. The primary is a quadrennial boost to the state's economy and gives the small state a great deal of national attention. It has also proved to be a boon to New Hampshire politicians seeking positions in Washington. Republican governor Sherman Adams would be only the first to benefit, by becoming Dwight Eisenhower's powerful chief-of-staff.

Shocks to the political environment such as reapportionment and civil rights, which seriously affected the national and other state parties, have had little or no impact on the functioning of parties in New Hampshire. With no significant minority population and its early prohibition of segregation and other forms of discrimination, the state and its parties responded minimally to legislation and court decisions requiring equal protection under the laws. Reapportionment in 1965, to bring New Hampshire into line with the Supreme Court's one person, one vote decisions, did little to change the party lineup in New Hampshire's elected leaders and resulted in minor changes to district lines (Dishman and Ford 1968, 57). Even the state senate districts, formerly drawn on the basis of equal value of taxable property, needed only slight modifications.

The most significant structural changes have taken place in the Democratic Party, in response to the McGovern Commission's mandate that state Democratic Party organizations become more open to women, minorities, youth, and the poor. Democratic Party structure now includes a Platform Committee, and party rules require more local participation in the state convention. The Democratic Party constitution of 1962 had already mandated that the chair and vice chair of the state committee be of different genders "when practicable."

The early 1960s saw some strengthening of the organization of the Democratic Party. Party leaders created or reestablished committees in every county and city and in most of the larger towns (Dishman and Ford 1968, 62). Also, the new leaders in the 1960s were much more issue oriented and programmatic, which may have helped them overcome some of the party's ethnic factionalism. The party had been plagued by ethnic factionalism until this time, leading one writer in 1954 to point out that "every Democratic primary in New Hampshire is an Irish versus French-Canadian struggle" (Dishman 1954, 41). Democrats were able to unify behind their candidates with little intraparty friction during the 1960s. The revitalization of the party was helped by the increase in population, largely from more Democratic Massachusetts.

Since the 1960s voters have been willing to support Democratic candidates who are "personally appealing and not too immoderate in their political stance" (Craig and Winters 1983, 139). By the end of the 1970s New Hampshire was close to having a two-party system, but the Republican Party again tightened its electoral grip on the state with the national turn to the Republican Party during the Reagan years.

Party politics in New Hampshire are still strongly affected by personalities and by special interests, particularly by the only statewide newspaper, the *Manchester Union Leader*. It has been called the most "powerful organized political 'actor' in New Hampshire" (Craig and Winters 1983, 177). Although its influence has diminished since the 1960s and 1970s, the *Union Leader* still can play the role of "kingmaker." It tends to support the most conservative candidate, whether Democrat or Republican. It is famous for personal attacks and unflattering cartoons and pictures of its enemies. Its influence probably peaked in the 1970s during Gov. Meldrim Thomson's terms in office (1973–1979), when it was reported that Thomson made at least eleven toll calls to owner William Loeb every month (Craig and Winters 1983, 179). That it continues to be influential in Republican Party politics is suggested by its endorsement of Patrick Buchanan, the winner of the 1996 Republican presidential primary.

Many structural barriers exist to strong party organization. The large size of the legislature militates against party recruitment of candidates. It also makes party unity difficult to achieve. Few people seem to know or care what any individual legislator among its 424 members does, so many votes are cast based on friendship, as personal favors, or for other capricious reasons. There is no identifiable philosophical thread in either party: each has liberals and conservatives in its ranks. This makes strong organization very difficult. There have been some recent efforts by Democrats to support candidates who adopt the party executive committee's goals. Republican Party Chair John P. Stabile sees no reason to pursue an issue-oriented agenda, but he runs training sessions for Republican candidates which simply focus on how to win elections (Hammond 1988, 1A). Further, the traditional, conservative nature of state politics makes innovations in party organization unlikely. Even fund raising continues to be done through specific functions, rallies, door-to-door appeals, and neighbor-to-neighbor appeals.

## CURRENT PARTY ORGANIZATION

The formal structure and practices of political parties in New Hampshire have remained virtually unchanged since the 1960s. This is typical of New Hampshire government; little structural change occurs in the short term.

*Formal Structure.* New Hampshire correctly has been characterized as a "light regulator" of its political parties (Conlan and Dilger 1984). Even the requirement for recognition of a party is lax: a party must have received 3 percent of the vote in the most recent gubernatorial election (New Hampshire 1995, 652:11). Although state law requires that each party have a state committee comprising its county committees, and although it defines the membership, purpose, and meeting time of the state conventions, the parties may, by constitution or bylaws, avoid the details of such requirements (New Hampshire YEAR, 667:21,22).

Bylaws of the New Hampshire Republican State Committee, adopted January 6, 1990, and the constitution of the New Hampshire Democratic Party, adopted May 16, 1992, define the formal structure and function of the parties. State committees bear the primary responsibility for directing the affairs of the parties. The core of the state committees is the collective membership of the county committees. Officers and members of the permanent committees of the state committees may be chosen from among nonmembers of the state committee, but become members by their appointment. Democrats include some other individuals on their state committee, such as the party's nominees for national and high state offices, legislative leaders, and presidents of the Young Democrats and Democratic Women of New Hampshire.

In each party an executive committee comprising the officers of the state committee and the county chairmen act for the state committee between meetings and as otherwise assigned. The Republican executive committee also includes the mayors of the four largest cities, when they are party members. Democrats are again more inclusive, naming to the executive committee incumbents of congressional and major state offices, chairs of major permanent committees, and the party's legislative leaders. Permanent committees for advice on policy, platform, and organization support each executive committee.

The state convention determines the county committees' membership. Each party presently includes on each county committee the county's delegates to the state convention, officers of the county committee, delegates to the state convention, and additional members chosen by the party's nominees. Democrats establish a caucus in each county consisting of delegates to the state convention, all nominees of the party, and state and national committee members residing in the county.

Local party structure is defined very generally by the Democratic Party and not at all by the Republican Party. In each case, local committees are encouraged but have much latitude about their structure and activity. The Democrats provide for resolution of local disputes by the state party chair. Also, the state chair may remove for cause any local officers of the party when local committees fail to do so.

State party conventions adopt the party platform, nominate presidential electors, and govern the organization of the parties. Both parties' conventions approximate the structure suggested in state law (New Hampshire 1995, 667:21). Members include nominees for all congressional and state offices, national committee members, delegates chosen in local caucuses, and state committee members.

In a formal sense, power within the parties is dispersed widely and flows in many directions. Each level has influence over higher levels. But higher levels have some responsibility for oversight, encouragement, and instruction of subordinate committees and structures. Each level, on the other hand, has a good deal of autonomy and its own responsibilities and base of support. It seems that the New Hampshire parties are organized according to principles of "stratarchy," a structure with autonomous layers of organization, as suggested by Eldersveld (1964).

*Informal Organization and Behavior of the Parties.* In action, the parties in New Hampshire can best be described as incomplete, occasional, and highly decentralized. The Democratic Party does not compete electorally in much of the state and is not organized fully except in the state's largest cities. Both parties, at some times and in some places, fail to nominate candidates for minor offices. Although the appropriate state or county committee may nominate any party member for an office for which no candidate has filed (New Hampshire 1995, 655:32), they usually do not. In the rare case that such a nomination is made, it is usually done by the chair for the committee.

Today's Republican Party is a loose coalition of Republicans representing various ideological camps and of Democrats posing as Republicans in areas of the state inhospitable to the Democratic Party. Since parties do little recruiting of candidates, and since candidates for minor offices spend very little to campaign, there is not much need for full and active organization. Although each party provides some guidance and services to its candidates, these are modest. Each state committee maintains only a small office, an executive director, and a skeleton office staff.

The executive director of the Republican Party has recently been an important spokesperson for the party, appearing for news shows and interviews. The Democratic Party chair is usually the primary speaker for that party. In both parties, the chair is a very important and powerful figure. Article II of the Republican bylaws specifically requires that the chair be "a person of established standing in the party who has the respect and support of Republicans generally."

Most leaders of the party organizations remain aloof from factional squabbles within their party and from the competitive struggles among candidates. An exception to this general rule was the vigorous condemnation by the former Democratic Party chair, Chris Spirou, of the creation of the Democratic Leadership Council by moderate Democrats in the state *(Concord Monitor 1991, B1).* The neutrality of the party leaders is contrary to the pattern of their endorsements and campaign work within government, especially in the presidential primary races. While not unique nationally, such positioning in New Hampshire, the first primary state in the presidential nomination calendar, becomes more divisive than usual. This probably weakens the party leadership capacity of the governor and legislative leaders who openly promote presidential candidates and, indirectly, themselves.

The first in the nation status of the New Hampshire presidential primary creates stress between the national and state parties, but, more importantly, it highlights the degree of autonomy enjoyed by the state's parties. In the past, and again in 1996, the New Hampshire primary faced criticism and threats from the national and other state parties. Some states moved their primary dates forward, and national party leaders proposed a national primary or rotation of the order of states' primaries. New Hampshire and its parties have always calmly asserted that they would move the primary as far ahead as necessary to maintain its position ahead of others. Indeed, in 1996 New Hampshire Republicans garnered pledges from several Republican candidates not to campaign in any state that held its primary within one week of New Hampshire's.

RESOURCE GUIDE

Materials for the study of party organization in New Hampshire are scarce, scattered, and incomplete. There are no archives, per se. If privately held collections of organization materials exist, we have not found them. Most existing records are available in the New Hampshire State Library, the Office of the Secretary of State, and the state parties' head-quarters. The New Hampshire State Library possesses only random documents about the parties. No one type of document is part of a special collection. Extant materials are of lit-tle use in doing comparative work, even in the state. For example, the Republican platforms are available for the period 1968–1988, but those of the Democratic Party are available from 1986 to 1992. Occasional statements by the parties and party leaders are available, but they lack any pattern of content or time. No budgets, correspondence, or minutes are in the state library collection.

Records in the Office of the New Hampshire Secretary of State include reports required of political actions committees, which under the law include political parties as organiza-tions that generate and contribute money for campaigns (New Hampshire 1995, 664:6,1). Individual candidates, but not political parties, must also file records of contributions and expenditures in order to satisfy the requirements of voluntary limitations on campaign expenditures. All such records are filed for two years in the secretary of state's office in the capitol and then stored in archives.

Some limited and recent documentary materials are available in the state parties' head-quarters. All records available are accessible at the Democratic headquarters, whereas the Republicans do not provide budget records to the public. Republican records include the most recent platforms, Federal Election Commission reports and required state reports, the most recent bylaws, and a few county and town committee reports and pieces of corre-spondence. Democrats also maintain only recent records. Most Democratic records, including platforms, convention reports, committee minutes, state and federal reports, and budgets, are available for most years since the 1970s. Some types of materials—including miscellaneous correspondence, fund-raising records, county committee records, and national party materials—cover fewer than ten years.

These very limited materials do not inspire enthusiasm for research in New Hampshire party politics. In a state in which historical research is extensive in most areas, the political parties are largely ignored. In a real sense, the parties in New Hampshire have not been dri-ving forces in the state's politics. On the other hand, the state and its leaders have con-tributed significantly to the national parties, and, clearly, in some limited circumstances the parties have significantly influenced New Hampshire politics.

REFERENCES

*Asterisks denote the most important publications on New Hampshire party politics.*

Chandler, William E. 1898. The growth in the use of money in politics in New Hampshire. *Manchester Union*, Dec. 24 and 28. (A reprint, by Rumford Press, Concord, N.H., appeared in 1899.)

*Cole, Donald B. 1970. *Jacksonian democracy in New Hampshire: 1800–1851.* Cambridge, Mass.: Harvard University Press.

Conlan, T., A. Martino, and R. Dilger. 1984. State parties in the 1980s. *Intergovernmental Perspective* 10:6–13.

*Craig, Robert E., and Richard F. Winters. 1983. Party politics in New Hampshire. In *New England political parties*, ed. Josephine F. Milburn and William Doyle, 139–180. Cambridge, Mass.: Schenkman.

*Concord Monitor.* 1991. Democrats fight over splinter group. June 19, B1.

Dishman, Robert B. 1954. New Hampshire. In *Presidential nominating politics in 1952: The Northeast,* ed. Paul T. David, Malcolm Moos, and Ralph M. Goldman, 26–53. Baltimore: Johns Hopkins Press.

*Dishman, Robert B., and Joseph P. Ford. 1968. New Hampshire: Republican schisms, Democratic gains. In *Party politics in the New England states,* ed. George Goodwin Jr. and Victoria Schenck, 55–65. Durham, N.H.: New England Center for Continuing Education.

Doyle, William, and Josephine F. Milburn. 1981. Citizen participation in New England politics: Town meetings, political parties, and interest groups. In *New England politics,* ed. Josephine F. Milburn and Victoria Schuck, 33–51. Cambridge, Mass.: Schenkman.

Eldersveld, Samuel J. 1964. *Political parties: A behavioral analysis.* Chicago: Rand McNally.

*Frasier, Dudley P. n.d. The antecedents and formation of the Republican Party in New Hampshire: 1845–1860. Unpublished paper. New Hampshire State Library.

Hammond, Pat. 1988. The parties campaign differently. *New Hampshire Sunday News,* November 6, 1A.

*Heffernan, Nancy Coffey, and Ann Page Stecker. 1981. *New Hampshire: Crosscurrents in its development.* Grantham, N.H.: Tompson and Rutter.

*Jager, Ronald, and Grace Jager. 1983. *New Hampshire: An illustrated history of the Granite State.* Woodland Hills, Calif.: Windsor.

Kaplanoff, Mark P. 1968. Religion and righteousness: A study of Federalist rhetoric in the New Hampshire election of 1800. *Historical New Hampshire* 22, no. 4 (winter):3–20.

McClintock, John N. 1889. *History of New Hampshire.* Boston: BB Russell, Cornhill.

New Hampshire. 1995. *Revised statutes annotated.*

*Robinson, William A. 1916. *Jeffersonian democracy in New England.* New York: Greenwood Press.

Squires, J. Duane. 1964. *The story of New Hampshire.* Princeton, N.J.: D. Van Nostrand.

Tibbetts, Donn. 1995. GOP chief Duprey steps aside. *Manchester Union Leader,* March 28, 1A.

———. 1989. In New Hampshire politics, Republicans dominated the decade. *Manchester Union Leader,* Dec. 31, 23A.

*Wright, James. 1987. *The Progressive Yankees: Republican reformers in New Hampshire: 1906–1916.* Hanover, N.H.: University Press of New England.

# *New Jersey*

STEPHEN A. SALMORE AND

BARBARA G. SALMORE

New Jersey political parties have been fundamentally transformed over the past few decades.[1] Until the mid-1970s the state parties were dominated by strong county and local organizations that, relying on material incentives to inspire loyalty and attract workers, controlled nominations and ran campaigns for almost all municipal, county, and state offices. They were led by "bosses" who used their local power bases to dominate politics at all levels. Although politics at the state level was usually highly competitive, most counties were strongly dominated by one party. Over the last two decades, the influence of the traditional county and local organizations has dramatically declined. Political power has shifted to candidates and elected officeholders who have transformed weak state party organizations into "parties in service"; that is to say, into organizations "designed around the ambitions of office-seekers" and their candidate-centered campaigns.[2] As a result, with the exception of a few smaller, rural counties, one-party dominance of counties has given way to a more competitive politics in most areas of the state. Although remnants of the older style remain, the dramatic shift from traditional party organizations to "parties in service" took place both later and more rapidly in New Jersey than elsewhere.

## PARTY HISTORY

New Jersey parties have been strongly shaped by the geography and demography of the state. Situated between New York and Philadelphia and lacking its own large urban centers, New Jersey has been characterized by localism and strong home rule. The parties mirrored this localism, evolving early as county-based organizations. In the first half of the twentieth century, Democrats dominated in the urban, industrialized counties. The Republicans ruled in most of the more rural counties.

Reinforcing the geographic cleavages was an endemic sectarianism. By 1920 a quarter of the state population was foreign-born, and many of the immigrants were working-class Catholics who flocked to the urban counties, particularly Hudson. As a result, New Jersey's politics for one hundred years after the Civil War was competitive on a statewide basis, with the Democratic, Catholic cities arrayed against the Republican, Protestant suburban and rural areas of the state.

Although many county organizations of this era had strong leaders, the bosses of Hudson County in the north and Atlantic County in the south dominated the Democratic and Republican Parties, respectively. In Hudson, the legendary Frank ("I am the law") Hague ruled the Democratic Party from his ascension as political leader and elected local official in 1917 until his resignation in 1948. By virtue of his ability to mobilize the party faithful in Hudson County, Hague was to dominate Democratic primaries and regularly determine the outcome of gubernatorial elections. Democratic governors, nominated and elected with Hague's blessing, appointed prosecutors and judges who chose not to pursue political corruption in Hudson County vigorously. Hague was followed by John V. Kenny, who remained Hudson County's leader and mayor of Jersey City until 1971, when he drew the interest of federal prosecutors. Similarly, in Atlantic County, Republican leader Enoch "Nucky" Johnson reigned from 1909 to 1939. Brought down by an indictment for tax evasion, he was replaced by Frank S. ("Hap") Farley, who led the Atlantic Republican organization until 1971, when he also fell afoul of the law.

These leaders agreed on little but a shared antipathy to strong state government that would intrude on their local authority and a distaste for broad-based state taxes. Since for much of the first half of the twentieth century the Democrats controlled the governorship and the Republicans controlled the legislature, a pattern of mutual accommodation emerged that kept state government exceptionally weak. The Democrats had the numbers to prevail in most gubernatorial contests, particularly since turnout of suburban Republicans and independents fell off in nonpresidential years. Between 1916 and 1940 the Democrats won six of nine gubernatorial elections.[3]

The GOP, however, remained in firm and almost continuous control of both houses of a malapportioned legislature. The sixty assembly districts were apportioned by population, but each county was guaranteed at least one—benefiting the Republicans of the small rural counties. Until the 1947 constitution doubled the length of their terms, assembly members were elected annually and at large from county-based districts (tending to shut out the minority party), and most were rotated out of office after two years. Although the Democrats occasionally won brief control of the lower house, in the state senate

Republicans were virtually guaranteed majorities because that body consisted of only twenty-one members, one from each county. The senate Republicans operated under a unique system that required the Republican caucus to provide a majority of the whole senate for any measure to be released for consideration. Thus, for example, in 1950 when the Republicans occupied fourteen of the Senate's twenty-one seats, only four Republican senators representing 3 percent of the state population could hold any legislative proposal hostage. For the entire period that he served as Atlantic County leader, "Hap" Farley also controlled the senate, where he combined his vote with those of other small-county rural senators whom he dominated. In sum, none of these leaders had any interest in building either a strong state party or a strong state government, or indeed interest in much beyond maintaining their local power bases (Salmore and Salmore 1993, 28–41).

Another factor contributing to New Jersey's strong local orientation was the state's unusual mass media patterns. The state's newspapers were parochial in orientation, and the closest approximation to a statewide "quality" paper—the *Newark Daily News*—went out of business in the early 1970s as a result of a protracted strike. Until 1984 the state did not have a licensed commercial VHF television station within its borders. Thus, the entire population watched television news out of New York City and Philadelphia, and many read newspapers from those cities. Events in Trenton, much less Atlantic City or Jersey City, were of limited interest to an electorate that could more easily identify the mayor of New York City than New Jersey's governor (Salmore and Salmore 1993, 71–74).

The postwar years brought only modest changes in this localist and county-dominated system. The twenty-one-member state senate remained in place through the 1960s. Although the Democrats elected distinguished jurists to the governorship in the 1960s and early 1970s, Hudson County continued to exercise veto power over gubernatorial nominations. As late as 1973, Republican county leaders were able to deny renomination to their incumbent governor, who displeased them by calling for a statewide income tax and regionalized schools. In his analysis of traditional party organizations (which he called "TPOs") in the late 1960s, David Mayhew observed, "If the states were ranked from one to fifty according to the prominence of their TPOs, New Jersey might well rank first" (Mayhew 1986, 55).

## ORGANIZATIONAL DEVELOPMENT

During the 1970s New Jersey's traditional party organizations and their political environment were almost completely transformed in the space of a few years, and by the start of the 1990s the emergence of robust state "parties in service" was well along. To some extent, the transformation was due to demographic developments, particularly rapid population growth and even more rapid suburbanization during the previous decade. As the state's population grew, urban areas such as Hudson County declined and much of rural New Jersey was transformed into housing developments and shopping malls. Although the new suburbanites did not immediately develop more interest in state affairs, they were removed, both physically and psychologically, from the reach of traditional party organizations (Salmore and Salmore 1993, 4).

The major effects of these changes were higher levels of political independence and electoral volatility and an increased tendency for state politics to mirror national trends. Under the traditional party organizations, for example, New Jersey elected mostly Republican governors during the Roosevelt-Truman period, and had a Democratic governor in the

1950s during the Eisenhower era. However, with increased electoral volatility and independent, split-ticket voting, a Democratic governor was elected in 1961 and 1965, after President Kennedy's and President Johnson's victories; a Republican governor the year after President Nixon's first victory; a Democratic governor in 1973 after Watergate and again after President Carter's victory in 1976; and a two-term Republican governor during the Reagan era. Although Bill Clinton carried the state by a plurality—the first Democratic presidential victory in New Jersey in twenty-eight years—the Democrats' national collapse in 1994 was foreshadowed by the election of massive Republican legislative majorities in 1991 and a gubernatorial victory in 1993. Legislative majorities also now tended to move in tandem with gubernatorial outcomes.[4]

Other developments also contributed to the decline of the traditional party organizations during the 1970s. Democratic governor Brendan Byrne owed his nomination and election to party leaders of several urban counties in 1973, but they abandoned him when he sought reelection in 1977. Although the party leaders feared Byrne would be unelectable because of his successful advocacy of a statewide income tax, they could not agree on a single challenger. Byrne, faced with a number of serious primary opponents, went on television successfully to make his case to the voters. Byrne was the first gubernatorial candidate to demonstrate that television was more powerful than the county party organizations, and all subsequent statewide elections have been fought over the airwaves.

Another significant development during the 1970s was the fallout from the Watergate scandal. The national disgust with political corruption resonated especially strongly in New Jersey. In the early 1970s federal prosecutors had launched a wave of highly publicized investigations and criminal cases against a number of county party leaders. Additionally, almost every governor of both parties who served from the 1940s until 1980 suffered the embarrassment of criminal charges brought against close associates with ties to county party organizations. Thus, when Governor Byrne advocated public financing of gubernatorial elections, New Jersey became, in 1977, the first state to offer taxpayer-subsidized campaign funds to candidates for state executive. Public financing further reduced the dependence of gubernatorial candidates on county party support.

Because the lifeblood of traditional party organizations was control of offices below the statewide level, none of these developments in the 1970s proved fatal. However, the county-based party system suffered a lethal blow from the U.S. Supreme Court's "one person-one vote" decisions, *Baker v. Carr* and *Reynolds v. Sims,* in the mid-1960s. The effects of these decisions on the state legislature, legislative candidates, and thus the political parties, played out over the next decade.

State political leaders attempted both to comply with federal and state court rulings and to maintain the county-based system of legislative representation first by enlarging both houses and then by adopting a mixed system of single-member and multimember districts. These alternatives were ultimately rejected by the courts,[5] and in 1973 the present system of forty legislative districts, each including one senator and two assembly members, was adopted. About half of the new districts included portions of more than one county. The multicounty districts greatly reduced the ability of the county party organizations to control nominations and influence the behavior of legislators once elected.

An early effect of the new legislative structure was the emergence of the legislative leadership as a competitor to the county party leadership. After the 1973 elections, when the GOP was reduced to fourteen seats in the assembly, Minority Leader Tom Kean raised about $70,000 for the 1975 lower house elections, which was spent on generic newspaper advertising and targeted radio ads. When Kean was elected governor in 1981, he established the Governor's Club, which raised large sums for the legislative elections. Kean funneled the money through the Republican State Committee. Historically, the chair of the state committee was named by the gubernatorial candidate after the primary. Since the state party had few resources and little influence, the party chair was not seen as a powerful position. However, with funds raised by the incumbent governor and a staff of Kean appointees, the state party assumed a much more important and influential role.

In 1983 Kean, who was not up for reelection until 1985, directed that $600,000 of state party funds be spent on generic TV ads featuring himself, upsetting many legislators who would have preferred it to be spent on their own radio and direct-mail messages. As a result, Assembly Speaker Chuck Hardwick, in 1987, raised almost a million dollars through the Assembly Republican Majority Campaign Committee (known as ARM) for the 1987 elections, almost equaling the sums raised by the Governor's Club. In 1989 ARM spent more than $1.2 million on legislative races, and the personal political action committee of Minority Leader Chuck Haytaian contributed an additional $200,000 to ARM and to individual candidates. ARM (and its senate counterpart, SRM) hired polling, mail, and media consultants whose services were offered to candidates in targeted districts chosen by the legislative party committees (and often recruited by them as well). The state party was principally used to pass money through to legislative campaigns. The Republican county party committees, bystanders in these legislative campaigns, were reduced to impotence or to concentrating on races for county offices.

Starting a bit later, the Democrats generally followed a similar path. Assembly Speaker Alan Karcher began the Democrats' efforts by raising $125,000 for Democratic candidates in 1983. By 1987, with the Republicans in control of the lower house and the governorship, Senate president John Russo—then anticipating a run for the governorship in 1989 and determined to keep control of the upper house—established Senate Democratic Majority '87. It spent $1.7 million, almost all of it in twelve targeted districts. Most of the money was generated from the Senate President's Ball, a frank imitation of the Republican Governor's Club Ball. Majority '87 hired polling, media, and direct-mail consultants and provided central services to all of its campaigns, including statewide precinct voting analysis, opposition research, production of get-out-the-vote lists, and mailing labels.

In 1988 the Democratic State Committee assumed a larger role in campaigns when the presidential campaign of Michael Dukakis and the senatorial campaign of Frank Lautenberg raised several million dollars in "soft money" for the state party. This money was used for a coordinated election day get-out-the-vote operation designed to bring Democratic voters to the polls to vote for party candidates at all levels. In 1989 Democrats consolidated their gubernatorial and legislative fund raising in an organization called Democratic Finance '89. Gubernatorial candidate Jim Florio, limited in what he could raise and spend on his own behalf by the public financing of his own race, funneled almost $600,000 into eight targeted legislative districts before the end of October, passing the money through the Democratic State Committee. During his term in office (1990–1994), Florio continued to raise large sums of money for the state party.

Following the 1989 elections, the U.S. Postal Service questioned the way both state party committees were using the reduced "nonprofit" postal rate for which state party organizations were eligible. In violation of postal regulations, both parties permitted candidates to pay for the cost of mailings rather than use funds raised by the state party. Further, the state party committees failed to exercise editorial control over the content of the mailings. When the Postal Service sued to recover hundreds of thousands of dollars, both parties moved to comply with the law, but in somewhat different ways. The Republicans changed their corporate structure to make ARM, SRM, and the state party committee a single legal entity (while maintaining separate internal financial accounts and staffs). After 1993, with Republican Christie Whitman now governor and with Republican majorities in both houses, the combined state party and legislative campaign organizations greatly increased their fund raising. The state party leveraged its funds with the favorable postal rates to play a much more active role in assisting county and local candidates. The state party hired consultants to write direct mail—for county and municipal races as well as for the legislature—and controlled its editorial content as the law required. The result of these developments was a strong, well financed state party that played a major role in assisting Republican candidates at all levels and in providing support to elected Republican officeholders. For the Republicans, a state "party in service" had replaced the traditional county-based party system.

The Democrats simply negotiated a settlement with the Postal Service, agreeing to abide by a strict interpretation of the law without making extensive organizational changes. The favorable postal rates and continued party fund raising, however, enabled the state Democratic Party to play a more active role in providing campaign assistance to candidates. With the loss of control of both houses of the legislature in 1991 and the governor's office in 1993, the state Democratic Party was not able to match the fund-raising or campaign assistance capabilities of the Republicans.

The greater factionalism and the persistence of some relatively strong county organizations also limited the centralization of resources and authority in the state Democratic Party. Some of the stronger Democratic county organizations had transformed themselves from traditional party organizations to local "parties in service" that raised sufficient amounts of money to fund high-tech campaigns for candidates at the county and local levels. In addition, several members of Congress had established strong political operations. Within these constraints, the state party has provided extensive support in some important targeted campaigns, although in a more limited way than the state Republican Party. The present Democratic Party chair, Tom Byrne, son of former governor Brendan Byrne, was chosen because he was considered acceptable to the major party factions. He has focused much of his efforts on fund raising and organizational activities aimed at strengthening the state party's ability to provide campaign assistance to Democratic candidates.

Thus, New Jersey's state parties are well on their way to becoming effective "parties in service," run by and for candidates and officeholders. The county party leaders who ruled the state for a century or more have also transformed themselves, or have become largely irrelevant.

## CURRENT PARTY ORGANIZATION

Since 1930, Title 19 of the New Jersey State Code has served to delineate party structure.[6] However, at no time has Title 19 ever described the parties' actual structures or processes. In the era of traditional party organizations, the county parties circumvented many of its key provisions. In the "party in service" era, as a result of a number of court cases, many of the key provisions of Title 19 have been rendered unenforceable.

Title 19 outlines a hierarchical party structure of municipal, county, and organizational units. The base of the pyramid consists of two members from each municipal election district, elected in annual party primaries. The district members from each municipality meet on the first Monday after the primary to elect the municipal chair and vice chair. The following day, the district members from all municipalities in the county meet to elect the county chair and vice chair. Despite the municipal and county committees being composed of exactly the same people, Title 19 specifies no formal relationship between the municipal and county parties.

At the state level, Title 19 provides for a state committee whose members are elected every four years in the parties' gubernatorial primary and are either evenly apportioned by county (as the Republicans are, two per county) or apportioned by population (as the Democrats are). On the first Tuesday after the gubernatorial primary, the state committee members elect the state party chair and vice chair, who are not required to be members of the state committee. These officials are to serve for four years and cannot be removed by the committee during their terms. The state committees also select the two members of the national party committees.[7]

Title 19 also provides that each party must hold biannual conventions in the state capital and specifies the time and place of these meetings. Other important provisions include prohibitions on preprimary candidate endorsements (although "slating" of candidates on a single ballot line in the primary is permitted), cross-filing, and a "sore loser" provision—candidates defeated in a party primary are not permitted to run as independents in the general election.

The three levels of organization—municipal, county, and state—are in fact parallel rather than hierarchical, with few formal links. The county chairs and committee members do not have a legal role in the state committee. In 1979 two researchers observed that "since the county chairpersons have no real voice in the selection process, there is little reason for institutional loyalty to the state organization, which is often regarded as inconsequential in state politics" (Moakley and Pomper 1979, 89). Actual party procedures in the traditional party organization period deviated from Title 19's prescriptions in important ways. Most crucially, parties regularly made obvious preprimary endorsements and offered candidates other forms of support-both through ballot "slating" and through nominally extraparty organizations. These included candidate screening committees that issued endorsements and party clubs that raised money and organized workers for the primary elections. In reality, during the traditional party organization era, it was the county leaders rather than primary voters who chose gubernatorial and legislative candidates.

In 1989, just as the New Jersey parties were completing their transformation to "parties in service," the U.S. Supreme Court's *Eu v. San Francisco* decision found the California ban on preprimary endorsements an unconstitutional infringement of the first amendment rights of voters to free speech and free association.[8] The Court held that laws regulating political parties must further a "compelling state interest." Ensuring that elections are orderly, fair, and honest met this test, but dictating how a party organizes itself, conducts its affairs, and deals with intraparty factionalism did not. The *Eu* decision rendered many of the provisions of Title 19 that dealt with party organization unconstitutional and unenforceable.

Both parties responded to the *Eu* decision by making organizational changes that recognized and promoted the "party in service." Whereas New Jersey parties have chosen not to issue formal endorsements in state-level contests, many counties and municipalities have, thus rendering legal what has long been standard practice. Many counties have initiated preprimary conventions, which decide local endorsements and provide forums for statewide candidates seeking county support and a favored ballot position. Both parties have also made extensive changes in their bylaws. They have changed the term of the state chair to two years from four, emphasized the coordinated nature of fund raising and campaign activities, become more explicit about the role of the state party in providing various forms of campaign assistance, and, by omission, have relegated the county parties to a minor role. In addition, both parties now have full-time paid chairmen, executive directors, and political directors as well as paid professional and support staff.

The two-year term of the Democratic state chair now begins on January 1 following the November gubernatorial and midterm legislative elections. However, in years in which a gubernatorial term ends, the chair's term ends "between the date of the [early June] primary election and June 30"; an interim chair is appointed to serve until January 1 of the following year. This provision gives the gubernatorial nominee the ability to select the party chair. However if the gubernatorial candidate loses the election, the party chair can be replaced. The state committee chair, vice chair, secretary, and treasurer are elected by the state committee, but the state chair appoints the chair and members of the state party finance committee. He or she is also empowered to select, hire, and pay campaign consultants.

The state Democratic Party bylaws also specify a "coordinated campaign committee," appointed by the party chair. Its members are the state committee's executive director (a full-time, paid position), one representative from among the governor and the leadership of the two houses of the state legislature, all elected members of the U.S. House and Senate delegations, the county chairs, and "others designated by the chairperson." The bylaws also specify creation of a Council of County Chairpersons, but other than meeting with the state chair at least twice a year and serving on the coordinated campaign committee, this group has no responsibilities.[9]

The Republican bylaws specify that the officers of the state party committee are its chair, vice chair, secretary, and treasurer, elected by the state committee for two-year terms on the second Thursday after the party primary in odd-numbered years (that is, the year of gubernatorial and midterm legislative elections).

The bylaws also describe a "legislative steering committee," whose four permanent members are the state party chair, the senate and assembly leaders, and the (nonvoting) legal counsel to the state committee. Two "permanent and independent divisions within the Legislative Steering Committee" are the Senate Republican Majority (SRM) and Assembly Republican Majority (ARM). Each of these divisions is headed by the party's legislative leader or the leader's appointee, who are "responsible for all personnel, both paid and unpaid, of their respective divisions," and who select the staff and determine its compensation. The legislative steering committee establishes policy and collects and expends funds for legislative campaigns, with ARM and SRM maintaining separate state committee accounts. This arrangement, inspired by the need to conform to Postal Service regulations and reflecting the changed role of the party in this candidate-centered era, formalizes the merger of the state committee and the legislative leadership PACs into a unified state party.[10] Governor Whitman's selection of former assembly speaker Chuck Haytaian as party chair personifies the strong relationship between elected officials and the state party.

These new party organizational arrangements are not reflected in Title 19, which has remained unchanged since the *Eu* decision, although the arrangements clearly are affected by it. As a consequence, the state has refused to defend in court those portions of Title 19 that dictate party structure. This state of legal limbo has led to uncertainty for candidates and parties. However, with or without statutory guidance, the New Jersey Democratic and Republican Parties have transformed themselves into effective, modern, "parties in service."

**Table 1**   New Jersey Resource Guide

|  | Democrats | Republicans |
|---|---|---|
| Archive | Yes | Yes |
| Location | New Jersey Democratic State Committee | New Jersey Republican State Committee |
|  | 150 West State Street | 28 West State Street, Suite 305 |
|  | Trenton, N.J. 08608 | Trenton, N.J. 08608 |
|  | (609) 392-3367 | (609) 989-7300 |
| Dates | Since 1960s, extensive; | Since 1993, extensive; |
|  | since 1930s, partial | prior to 1993, extremely limited |
| Finding aid | No | No |
| Access | By appointment | By appointment |
| Contents: |  |  |
|   Organizational structure | Yes | Yes |
|   Executive committee minutes | Yes | Yes |
|   Correspondence | Yes | Yes |
|   Budgets | Yes | Yes |

## RESOURCE GUIDE

Both parties maintain files and records at their headquarters in Trenton. Both parties are willing to provide access to interested parties to most of their available records, but they request that prior arrangements be made before extensive searches are undertaken. They both are willing to honor requests for bylaws, press releases, platform statements, and position papers by mail or phone. The Democratic records are more complete and better organized, most chronologically in file cabinets. A fire at the Republican headquarters in the winter of 1993 destroyed much of the party's archives. The surviving files were transferred to their present location, but many remain in boxes.

State laws governing parties, elections, and campaign finance, including references to relevant court cases, are in *New Jersey Statutes Annotated: Title 19, Elections,* published and updated regularly by West Publishing Company, St. Paul, Minnesota. Reports of campaign receipts and expenditures by party organizations, leadership PACs, and campaigns are available from the New Jersey Election Law Enforcement Commission. Both the Rutgers University Library and the New Jersey State Library have extensive collections of historical documents and private papers, although the papers of recent governors are still in the former governors' possession.

## NOTES

1. This chapter draws on interviews with Garabed "Chuck" Haytaian, chairman, Republican State Committee; Gregg Edwards, Jeff Michaels, and William Ulrey, former executive directors of the Republican State Committee; Tom Byrne, chairperson, Democratic State Committee; Steve DeMicco and Deborah Lux, former executive directors of the Democratic State Committee; and Frederick Hermann, executive director of the Election Law Enforcement Commission.
2. For the definitive analysis and history of traditional party organizations, see Mayhew 1986. For the development of the concept of the party in service, see Aldrich 1995.
3. Until passage of a new state constitution in 1947, New Jersey governors served three-year terms and could not immediately succeed themselves.
4. Each governor, beginning in 1969, swept in a partisan majority in both houses with the exception of Republican Thomas H. Kean (1982–1990). Kean won by a razor-thin majority of 1,200 votes in November 1981. Republicans gained control of the assembly in his 1985 landslide victory, but because of the peculiarities of the senate election calendar, the upper house never stood for elec-

tion in a gubernatorial year until 1989, when Kean, having served two terms, was not eligible for reelection.

5. The key state court cases were *Jackman v. Bodine, Scrimminger v. Sherwin,* and *Davenport v. New Jersey Reapportionment Commission* (Friedelbaum 1975, 222–225).

6. For the actual statutes along with citations to relevant court cases see *New Jersey Statutes Annotated: Title 19 Elections* (St. Paul, Minn.: West Publishing, 1989). Annual updates have been issued through 1995.

7. Title 19 requires that all party offices, from top to bottom, be balanced by gender. This provision is still honored by both parties despite the inability of the state to enforce its terms.

8. *Eu, Secretary of State of California, et al. v. San Francisco Democratic Central Committee, et al.* 489 U.S. 214 (1989).

9. Revised By-Laws of the Democratic Party of the State of New Jersey (February 1993).

10. Constitution and By-Laws of the New Jersey Republican State Committee (March 22, 1994).

## REFERENCES

*Asterisks denote the most important publications on New Jersey party politics.*

Aldrich, John H. 1995. *Why parties? The origin and transformation of party politics in America.* Chicago: University of Chicago Press.

*Blydenburgh, John. 1975. Party organizations. In *Politics in New Jersey,* ed. Alan Rosenthal and John Blydenburgh, 110–140. New Brunswick, N.J.: Eagleton Institute of Politics, Rutgers University.

Friedelbaum, Stanley. 1975. Constitutional law and judicial policy making. In *Politics in New Jersey,* ed. Alan Rosenthal and John Blydenburgh, 206–242. New Brunswick, N.J.: Eagleton Institute of Politics, Rutgers University.

Mayhew, David R. 1986. *Placing parties in American politics.* Princeton: Princeton University Press.

McCormick, Richard P. 1975. An historical overview. In *Politics in New Jersey,* ed. Alan Rosenthal and John Blydenburgh, 1–30. New Brunswick, N.J.: Eagleton Institute of Politics, Rutgers University.

*Moakley, Maureen. 1986. Political parties. In *The political state of New Jersey,* ed. Gerald Pomper, 45–66. New Brunswick, N.J.: Rutgers University Press.

*Moakley, Maureen, and Gerald Pomper. 1979. Party organizations. In *Politics in New Jersey,* rev. ed., ed. Richard Lehne and Alan Rosenthal, 83–108. New Brunswick, N.J.: Eagleton Institute of Politics, Rutgers University.

*Salmore, Barbara G., and Stephen A. Salmore. 1993. *New Jersey politics and government: Suburban politics comes of age.* Lincoln: University of Nebraska Press.

Salmore, Stephen A. 1986. Voting, elections, and campaigns. In *The political state of New Jersey,* ed. Richard Lehne and Alan Rosenthal, 67–90. New Brunswick, N.J.: Rutgers University Press.

# New Mexico

## CARL M. RHODES

## PARTY HISTORY

Two-party competition in New Mexico is older than the state itself. By 1900, twelve years before statehood, the Democratic and Republican Parties were already engaged in a competitive relationship. Effective party organization was often the key to electoral success. The competition's evenness and vigor have waxed and waned considerably since the state's founding, but throughout much of the twentieth century, the parties and their organizations have succeeded in remaining politically conspicuous (Holmes 1967; Hain, Garcia, and St. Clair 1994).

By 1910 the Democratic and Republican Parties were maintaining an organizational presence and fielding a complete set of candidates for county and legislative office in most of the state's counties. A string of unanticipated electoral defeats between 1910 and 1924 precipitated the hiring of the Republican Party's first "party manager," Ed Safford. Safford worked diligently to bolster the party's organizational presence in the rapidly growing (and strongly Democratic) southeastern region known as Little Texas (Holmes 1967). His early recognition of the strategic importance of the state's subregions set the focus of party competition for years to come.

The Democrats actively organized in the period 1900–1930 as well. Although both parties maintained relatively strong state organizations, the Democrats were generally better organized at the local level. The Democratic counterpart to Ed Safford was Arthur Seligman, who targeted the northern region of the state for electoral and organizational development. Although the northern counties were Republican strongholds, Seligman was able to exploit factional feuds that arose in the Republican Party over contests for position and patronage (Holmes 1967).

Despite the efforts of Seligman and the Democrats, the Republicans dominated the period 1900–1930 electorally. Republican Party leaders exercised considerable influence on the content of territorial and later state legislation as well as on the internal structure of the legislature. In part, the power of state Republican Party officials was maintained by their county organizations, which limited the tenure of individual legislators by controlling the nomination process. Party officials were extremely influential with Republican governors as well, who personally consulted with them on matters of policy and appointments.

The New Deal and Republican factional infighting had made the Democrats the state's majority party by the late 1930s. Democratic governor Clyde Tingley and Party Chairman (and later governor) John Miles made effective electoral use of the Young Democrats, labor, and teacher organizations for the first time. Miles worked diligently to develop the party's ability to raise funds and continued the precedent of party influence in the legislature by placing key legislators and their constituents (as well as many county and precinct chairpersons) on the public payroll. Party business was handled through quarterly meetings with county chairpersons. Personnel, organizational problems, patronage, financing, and factions were the most common topics of conversation (Holmes 1967).

The influence of the parties on policy and officeholders was greatly reduced by the direct primary, which was adopted in 1939 and became effective with the elections of 1940. Party influence in New Mexico politics has never surpassed that of the 1920s and 1930s. New Mexico's party organizations, however, have effectively responded to their changing environment, modifying their structure and programs in order to remain an important political force.

Party politics in New Mexico has always been a strategic contest fought over several of the state's politically important subregions: the Hispanic North, Little Texas, and Bernalillo County, home of the state's largest city, Albuquerque (see Holmes 1967; Mayhew 1986; Hain, Garcia and St. Clair 1994). Traditionally, ten counties have comprised the Hispanic North, although by 1994 only five of them remained more than 55 percent Hispanic. Party politics has always been important in these counties because patronage and government jobs have been vital to the region's economic vitality. The Hispanic counties, which early in

the century were solidly Republican, have drifted steadily into the Democratic fold, return-
ing majority votes for the Democratic gubernatorial candidate since 1960.

The shift of party allegiance in the Hispanic North has been countered by the movement
of Little Texas, a six-county region in the southeastern corner of the state. Little Texas has
evolved from a one-party Democratic stronghold in the early years of statehood to a region
of two-party competitiveness. Republicans have gained ground in federal, state, and local
elections, with the region voting for the Republican gubernatorial candidate in every election since 1974.

Both of these regions have diminished in importance over the century as Bernalillo
County has grown. With over one-third of the state's voters, the county has proved vital to
Republican victories. The party has never won a statewide race without carrying the county.

Examining the state as a whole, the degree of party competition varies remarkably by
level and by office (Holmes 1967; Vigil, Olsen, and Lujan 1990; Hain, Garcia, and St. Clair
1994). New Mexico voters, although they supported Democratic presidential candidates in
the state's early years, have voted Republican in every presidential election since 1968.

At the congressional level, the Democrats controlled both U.S. Senate seats from 1930 to
1972, when Pete Domenici broke the chain of Republican losses. He was joined in 1977,
albeit briefly, by Republican Harrison Schmitt, who was defeated in 1982 by Democrat Jeff
Bingaman. In the U.S. House, Republican Manuel Lujan Jr. ended decades of Democratic
dominance in 1968. Since 1990 the Republicans have controlled two of New Mexico's three
U.S. House seats.

Democrats have dominated the modern competition for governor, holding the mansion
for all but sixteen of the years from 1949 to 1994 (although Republican Gary Johnson captured the office in the 1994 election). Democrats have dominated the state legislature as
well, holding a majority of both houses since 1933 (the only exceptions being the 1953 House
and 1985–1986 Senate). At the county level, Democratic supremacy is the rule, although in
recent years Republicans have made notable gains.

In sum, both parties now compete effectively at the federal and gubernatorial levels, but
Democrats continue to dominate the state legislature and county governments.

## ORGANIZATIONAL DEVELOPMENT

Archival data on the organizational activities of New Mexico's parties testify to their continued vitality in the modern period.[1] Although the pace of organizational activity and
innovation was far from constant during the period 1960–1980 (indeed, both parties experienced some hard times), the parties worked diligently to maintain their organizations and
at times to adapt them to a changing political environment. Both parties often focused
their attention on similar goals and problems: bolstering county and precinct organizational strength, fund raising, improving intraparty communication, and designing and
implementing effective programs to strengthen electoral performance. Despite the similar-
ity in ends, the parties often employed divergent means, in recognition of their varying
organizational assets and liabilities.

The Republicans had greater financial resources throughout the period, typically out-
spending the Democrats by a factor of one-and-a-half. Both parties spent a considerable
percentage of their resources on salaries, office support, and fund raising. To raise revenue,
both parties continued several established programs and events (often numbering about
six big fundraisers a year) as well as implemented several innovations. In the early 1970s, for

example, the Democrats established several financial clubs (such as the $100 club for those donating $100 a year, and the $1,200 club for those donating $1,200), initiated an assessment of the county organizations, and eliminated the party debt. Party officials were no doubt pleased at the latter achievement, since the party's office furniture had been impounded a year earlier.

The Republicans innovated financially as well, establishing programs from the gimmicky (donate $12 and receive a two-dollar bill; bid to play eighteen holes of golf with a senator) to the far-sighted: evidence of income from direct mail appears in the archives as early as 1976. Like the Democrats, Republicans relied heavily during this period on financial clubs. Membership in many clubs, such as the Republicans' Solomon Luna Club for those donating $1,000, entitled the donor to attend large fund-raising banquets. These events, which usually boasted a prominent keynote speaker, raised considerable revenue for the party beyond the club programs themselves.

Both parties structurally altered their organizations during the period, resulting in increasingly complex organizations. Among the more ambitious efforts of the period was the Democratic reorganization plan of the late 1960s. The plan launched a comprehensive review and evaluation of party structure and practice to generate more effective programs; the review was carried out by eight committees staffed by members of the state legislature, party officials, and party activists. The committees recommended publicizing the activities of the Democratic contingent in the legislature; feeding timely issue updates to Democratic candidates; developing campaign themes for electoral cycles; collecting and disseminating information on Republican officeholders; and improving party efforts at voter registration and precinct organization.

The Republicans, on the other hand, were seeking ways to conduct their affairs more efficiently. In the mid-1970s the party divided the unitary position of executive and financial director into two positions, the former to handle political and organizational duties, and the latter to deal solely with finance and fund raising. To routinize candidate assistance, the party created the Candidate Financial Assistance and Priority Committee, which was to prioritize and approve all candidate financial packages prior to disbursement.

Both state parties appear to have adopted a "service" orientation toward their county organizations and partisan campaigns (although they also took a somewhat paternalistic stance, frequently cajoling their county chairpersons to increase the capacities of their precinct organizations or to meet their county assessments). At times, the Democrats eschewed innovation for heightened activity, increasing the frequency with which they distributed information on party events, registration procedures, and the how-to's of county organization. Republicans appear to have placed greater emphasis on innovation: in 1973 they launched a state registration drive that included several regional seminars for county officials. By 1974 they had created and distributed handbooks on organization and public relations to all county chairpersons.

Several of the innovative Republican programs for counties were implemented in response to changes in the legal electoral environment. To address the campaign finance reforms of the 1970s, the Republicans established the Campaign Committee of New Mexico. Among other recommendations, county organizations were urged to avoid spending money on federal races directly and to work instead through the newly created committee.

Finally, both parties modified and improved their candidate services. The Democrats focused on informational mailings and seminars for legislative candidates. The Republicans initiated policy meetings with candidates, provided public relations advice and research support to incumbent legislators, established a coordination committee that held weekly meetings for all major campaigns, and, in an unprecedented move, funded statewide television ads.

## CURRENT PARTY ORGANIZATION

The Democratic and Republican Parties of New Mexico are organizationally similar (Hain, Garcia, and St. Clair 1976; 1981; Vigil, Olsen, and Lujan 1990).[2] Both are formally organized at the precinct, ward, county, and state levels. Ostensibly, both parties are represented at the county level by a chair and central committee, although a considerable disparity has existed at times between organization in theory and organization in practice. Party officers report that the difference between a vibrant and a moribund county organization is often a function of local leadership; not surprisingly, the quality of local leadership tends to be highly correlated with the underlying electoral strength the party enjoys in the area.

The Democratic Party is strongest at the county level in Bernalillo and Santa Fe, as well as throughout Little Texas. The strongest of the Republican organizations have been in Bernalillo and in the Anglo rural counties outside of Little Texas, such as Ontero, San Juan, and Los Alamos. For both parties, the effectiveness of county organizations is critical. In Ontero County, for example, an effective Republican organization has overcome Democratic advantages in voter registration to capture the county's legislative delegation.

Both parties have continued many of the county service programs previously discussed, such as organizational seminars, training programs, planning and event coordination, and press and informational assistance. At times, particular counties have been targeted for special attention. The Republican organization in Dona Ana County, the second largest county in New Mexico, was in factional disarray for several years, potentially costing the party valuable electoral turf. The state party decided to intervene, infusing guidance and resources to improve the county's organizational performance. The county eventually showed signs of improvement, culminating in Republican candidates receiving greater percentages of the vote.

At the state level, each party possesses a central committee, an executive committee, a party chair, and a small core of party officers. Major party decisions are made at the state conventions. Since the state convention is rarely in session, the state central committee is the de facto governing body. In practice, however, most power is delegated to the parties' state chairs and executive directors. Although both chairs and executive directors consult with their respective executive committees and frequently enjoy their support, responsibility for day-to-day decisions and programmatic initiatives clearly resides with the chair and executive director. This is especially true in the Republican Party, where the executive committee is appointed by the state chair and serves at his or her pleasure.

Both parties are staffed by a small core of paid, full-time professionals. The Republican Party in 1995 reported a full-time staff of three (not including the state chair, who, although he works full time, is technically a volunteer). In addition, the Republican headquarters is frequently aided by a solid core of volunteers, the size of which varies with the impending workload.

The Democrats are currently undergoing somewhat of a transformation. Three of the current five-and-a-half full-time positions were created in April 1995, when a new chair was appointed by the state central committee. The new positions include a finance director and a communications director and are evidence of the chair's desire to instill greater professionalism.

Both parties continue to innovate programmatically. Republicans recently put out a "targeting manual" to instruct county officials in the practice of analyzing electoral data so they can efficiently allocate time and resources. The state Democratic Party organization recently joined forces with the Democratic Leadership Campaign Committee, an organization based in the state legislature that seeks to recruit and train legislative candidates. Working closely with the state party, the committee has achieved considerable success in statewide fund raising. The Republican Party has long enjoyed a similar relationship with the parallel Republican legislative committee. In addition to their programmatic benefits, the committees are important links to the state legislature for both party organizations.

Party relations with the governor's office have been less consistent and have varied across both party and governor. At times, the Democratic Party has felt the relationship to be too close, as when Gov. Jerry Apodaca in 1976 imposed his choice for party chair over the objections of the state central and executive committees. This type of friction may increase in the Republican Party, now that the Democratic domination of the governor's mansion appears to be less formidable.

The Democrats and the Republicans both report highly beneficial relationships with their national party organizations. In addition to receiving daily briefings and "talking points," both parties regularly send representatives to regional and national seminars. The cross-state exchange of information at these meetings is considered especially useful. The national parties also provide fund-raising assistance. And not only do they conduct instructional seminars for state party leaders, but they also help coordinate the schedules of national political figures with local fund-raising events to maximize visibility and participation.

Both parties have continued to rely on established financial clubs and fundraisers while initiating new fund-raising efforts. The Democrats recently launched two programs, one aimed at large donors and the other aimed at broadening the party's grassroots support (the "Democratic Club" requires an initial donation of only $25). For the Republicans, the importance of direct mail and telemarketing has steadily increased since their introduction in the mid-1970s. The party now contracts with outside firms to solicit donations, although it soon hopes to have the capacity to move the direct-mail program in-house.

Historically, both parties have had their share of factional infighting (Clark and Clark 1981; Hain, Garcia, and St. Clair 1976, 1981, 1994; Holmes 1967). For the Democrats, the split has been between the liberal Hispanic counties and the conservative counties of Little Texas. Long held together by the promise of patronage, the party has found it increasingly difficult to keep both regions under the party tent. Frequently, party leaders are challenged to satisfy simultaneously the candidate and policy preferences of both regions. The party has lost several close races due to Little Texas defections from liberal nominees.

The Republicans have had to contend with ideological splits between conservatives and moderates. At times these fights have been severe: in 1976 conservative supporters of Ronald Reagan refused to seat several moderate members of New Mexico's congressional delegation at the national convention. Current divisions are mild by comparison, but the party must be continually aware of their presence.

Although both parties must attend to their internal divisions, electoral success in the future will continue to require the political support of the urban middle class, whose ever-growing numbers will determine the outcome of future elections. Organizationally, the

**Table 1**  New Mexico Resource Guide

|  | Democrats | Republicans |
|---|---|---|
| Archive | Yes | Yes |
| Location | New Mexico State Record Center and Archives 404 Montezuma St. Sante Fe, N.M. 87503 (505) 827-7332 | Center for Southwest Research Zimmerman Library University of New Mexico Albuquerque, N.M. 81171-1466 (505) 277-6451 |
| Dates | 1960–1973 | 1961–1977 |
| Finding aids | No | Yes |
| Access | Public | Public |
| Contents: |  |  |
| Executive committee minutes | Yes | Yes |
| Correspondence | Yes | Yes |
| Organizational structure | Yes | Yes |
| Budgets | Yes | Yes |
| Rules | Yes | Yes |

parties are reasonably well-positioned for the contest, with strong organizations in the counties that have significant urban centers.

### RESOURCE GUIDE

The bulk of archival materials concerning the Democratic Party of New Mexico is located at the New Mexico State Record Center and Archives. The records are most complete for the period 1960–1973 and contain a considerable sample of committee minutes and intra-party correspondence. The documents describe many aspects of party life relevant to party organization, including party programs, fundraisers, organizational structure, and pro-grammatic and organizational innovation. These documents are supplemented by the papers of Dennis Chavez (U.S. House, 1931–1935; U.S. Senate, 1935–1962), which are housed at the Center for Southwest Research at the University of New Mexico. Although not nearly as extensive as the Democratic collection at the archives, the Chavez collection does include several boxes of documents relevant to party organizational research.

The holdings of the state archives on the Republican Party are much smaller than the holdings on the Democrats. Fortunately, the papers of Republican senators Harrison Schmitt (1977–1983) and Pete Domenici (1973–), housed at the Center for Southwest Research, contain a considerable number of original party documents, including minutes, correspondence, budgets, rules, and internal memos on party organization and programs. Moreover, documents at the University of New Mexico have been cataloged and are more easily accessible than the uncataloged collection at the state archives.

Like any other source of data, archival evidence has its strengths and weaknesses. New Mexico's archival data offers the researcher information and insight unavailable elsewhere, yet the holdings are not as complete as one might like. Often we learn of a new program or change and its initial implementation, but we are unable to determine exactly how long it was maintained or the level of success it achieved. The usefulness of archival data, of course, will vary greatly by party and by state. Our experience in New Mexico suggests that a significant source of untapped information awaits the community of party organization scholars.

NOTES

1. This section draws heavily from information collected by the author at the New Mexico State Record Center and Archives, and the University of New Mexico's Center for Southwest Research.
2. This section draws heavily from interviews with New Mexico Republican Party State Chairman John Dendahl and Democratic Party Communications Director Don Brown. Their cooperation is greatly appreciated.


REFERENCES

*Asterisks denote the most important publications on New Mexico party politics.*
Clark, Cal, and Janet Clark. 1981. New Mexico: Moving in the direction of a Republican alignment. *Social Science Journal* 18:75–85.
*Hain, Paul L., F. Chris Garcia, and Gilbert K. St. Clair. 1994. *New Mexico government.* Albuquerque: University of New Mexico Press.
*———. 1981. *New Mexico government.* Albuquerque: University of New Mexico Press.
*———. 1976. *New Mexico government.* Albuquerque: University of New Mexico Press.
*Holmes, Jack E. 1967. *Politics in New Mexico.* Albuquerque: University of New Mexico Press.
*Lowitt, Richard. 1992. *Bronson M. Cutting: Progressive politician.* Albuquerque: University of New Mexico Press.
Mayhew, David R. 1986. *Placing parties in American politics.* Princeton: Princeton University Press.
*Vigil, Maurilio, Michael Olsen, and Roy Lujan. 1990. *New Mexico government and politics.* Lanham, Md.: University Press of America.

# New York

KEVIN R. HARDWICK AND
MICHAEL V. HASELSWERDT

## PARTY HISTORY

Over the years, colorful figures have been associated with New York's political parties. Three vice presidents from the state (Millard Fillmore, Chester Arthur, and Theodore Roosevelt) attained the nation's highest office following the death of a president. Another, Aaron Burr, was involved in the country's most infamous duel, in which fellow New Yorker Alexander Hamilton was killed.

In the mid-nineteenth century the current party framework began to emerge. The modern Democratic and Republican Parties were founded as a result of conflict surrounding passage of the Kansas-Nebraska Act in 1854. Following the Civil War, the Republican and Democratic Parties dominated state politics, as they have to this day.

From the outset, the Republicans were generally thought of as associated with big business, whereas the Democrats were perceived as the party of the working person. One consequence of this identification was that a disproportionate percentage of immigrants arriving in New York City in the latter half of the nineteenth and early twentieth centuries enrolled as Democrats (Markoe 1989, 67).

The Democratic dominance of the city, in turn, produced another defining feature of New York State's party politics: the upstate–New York City schism. With the tremendous growth of the city around the turn of the century, upstate residents began to fear that the city, with its large number of recent immigrants, would take control of the entire state. Therefore, upstate voters were drawn in large numbers to the Republican Party as an instrument to contain the political might of the Democrat-dominated city. Thus voters in New York have a tradition of being attracted to parties on the basis of region as much as ideology (Stonecash 1989, 44–46). This does not imply that ideology is unimportant in New York politics; however, there is a deep cleavage rooted in region and party history that cuts across ideology.

One method by which Republicans sought to circumscribe the power of the downstate Democrats was through a clause in the state constitution of 1894 that permanently established the legislative districts for both houses of the state's legislature. The malapportioned legislature that resulted from the constitutional provision benefited upstate residents, and thus Republicans dominated state politics until the U.S. Supreme Court's "one person, one vote" decisions of the early 1960s forced reapportionment (Stonecash 1994, 84–85).

Unlike in most other states, minor parties have flourished in New York. From Theodore Roosevelt's Progressive Party to today's Liberal and Conservative Parties, minor parties have played a not inconsequential role on both the state and national stage. The durable presence of the minor parties has affected competitive relations between the two major parties.

Two aspects of state election law have contributed to the organizational durability of third parties in New York. First, the law guarantees political parties that garner fifty thousand or more votes in gubernatorial elections an automatic slot on subsequent ballots. To get on the ballot initially, a new party would need to gather fifteen thousand signatures on independent nominating petitions. If the party's candidate then reached the fifty thousand vote threshold in the general election, the party would enjoy a number of benefits for the next four years. Chief among these is the right to hold publicly funded primary elections to fill its positions on the ballot for a variety of national, state, and local offices. Parties retain their position on the New York ballot until such time as their gubernatorial candidate fails to collect the required fifty thousand votes.

A second provision of state election law makes it more feasible for a minor party to collect the votes needed in a gubernatorial election to achieve official party status. This section permits parties to cross-endorse candidates for various offices, including governor. The votes that a single candidate receives on all party lines are totaled to determine the results of the election. Spitzer (1994, 106) noted that only Vermont and Connecticut have similar provisions in their election laws. In New York a minor party will ofttimes gain or retain its official status by cross endorsing the gubernatorial candidate of a major party.

Encouraged by the election law, a number of minor parties have been successful in gaining regular access to the ballot. In addition to the two major parties (Democratic and Republican), the state in 1996 recognized five minor parties: Liberal, Conservative, Right to Life, Independence, and Freedom. With the exception of the Right to Life Party, it is not uncommon for a minor party to abandon ideology in exchange for patronage when cross endorsing candidates for office. But minor parties offer a potential vehicle for a dynamic candidate. In the 1990 gubernatorial election, Conservative Herb London almost finished second, ahead of the Republican candidate. However, minor parties in New York have been less about ideas than about jobs, as they provide one more route for the channeling of influence and patronage.

## ORGANIZATIONAL DEVELOPMENT

*Democratic Party.* The modern history of the New York State Democratic Party can be divided into two segments: the period without a Democratic governor (1958–1974) and the period with a Democratic governor (1975–1994). Although the organizational dynamics in the two periods differ, in neither period has the state party been both independent from the control of powerful individuals and effective. It has, however, been resilient, which is testimony to its organizational vitality (Schlesinger 1984).

The major fault-line in the modern period has been regional, as the historical domination of the state party by New York City Democrats has been challenged by those in the suburbs and upstate. The years without a Democratic governor were characterized by rampant factionalism. Jewell and Olson called the state Democratic Party "multifactional," citing not only region but religion and the reform Democrat versus regular Democrat split as well. They went on to note that the New York Democrats displayed a pattern of interaction in which the participants remain the same but the alliances they create "shift by time and office," and the groups are so numerous that it is difficult to "cohere or dominate" (Jewell and Olson 1982, 53–60).

During the time without a Democratic governor, county leaders had fiefdoms in which they controlled campaign finances and nominations for state legislative offices. County leaders became chairs of the New York State Democratic Party and feuded with mayors of New York City and legislative leaders over the distribution of patronage and nominations for statewide office, which could result in claims for more jobs. President Kennedy even got involved in the early 1960s, funneling federal patronage through New York City mayor Robert Wagner to the detriment of state chair Michael H. Prendergast.

Given that the Democrats' disunity was based not on policies or leadership but on patronage (which without a governor was in short supply) (Roberts 1968, 6), personal charisma was seen by observers as the only hope to unify the Democrats. Robert F. Kennedy was elected to the U.S. Senate from New York in 1964 and, through both personality and considerable financial support, exerted a unifying influence. But following his assassination and the national events of 1968, the state Democratic Party was more divided than ever (Tolchin 1968, 77). When New York City mayor John Lindsay switched from Republican to Democrat in 1971, he brought a charisma to the Democratic Party that it was sorely lacking.

However, the Republicans provided the Democrats with an even greater opportunity: a national debacle with local consequences. As in the Goldwater defeat of 1964, when Kennedy became senator and the Democrats took control of the New York legislature for the first time in thirty-five years, in 1974 the Democrats benefited from the Republican problems stemming from the Watergate affair and finally elected a governor, Hugh Carey.

Despite the fact that the party won the governorship, in general, statewide candidates backed by the state Democratic Party did not do well. Indeed, Carey himself had been an insurgent, having beaten the party's endorsed candidate in the primary. By 1974 the rise of candidate-centered campaigns had begun, and they had the effect of permitting candidates more independence from the state parties. Furthermore, the state party had continually been in significant debt and could not help legislative candidates. The party's inability to help candidates financially was especially important at this time, as assembly seats had become more competitive due to the reapportionment and redistricting decisions. Incumbents of both parties in the state legislature began to utilize personal campaign organizations and to form legislature-based organizations. The Democrats formed the Democratic Assembly Campaign Committee and the Democratic Senate Campaign Committee. These developments undermined county leaders, who had parlayed their influence with state legislators into influence with the state party (Stonecash 1994, 97).

With legislative races increasingly out of its control, the state Democratic Party turned its attention to the governorship and federal offices. The debt had been eliminated by 1976, but the state legislative committees began to raise and spend more than the state party organization. The rise of candidate-centered campaigns at the statewide level meant that the county organizations were no longer courted assiduously. Although the factions did not disappear, they lost venues for their disputes.

Carey's two "appointees" as state party chair were both county leaders, as had been all previous chairs from 1958 to 1975. Carey discovered, however, that his appointees had alternative power bases, which made gubernatorial control of the party more difficult. But ultimately he exerted his control over the party, and with his reelection in 1978, the state party organization regained dominance over the county organizations.

Carey decided not to run for a third term in 1982. Instead, he and his state chair backed the endorsed Democrat, Ed Koch. However, insurgent Mario Cuomo defeated Koch in a primary and eventually became governor. The state Democratic organization then clearly became a part of Cuomo's personal political organization, as all of Cuomo's choices for state chair were loyal to him and were not county leaders.

One can conclude that the contemporary New York State Democratic Party has never been both effective and independent of strong personalities simultaneously. Without a Democratic governor, it was independent but ineffective because of factionalism. After 1974, with a Democratic governor, it was more effective, but it was effective as a part of the governor's organization, not as an independent organization. The governor's central role in the party contributed to both the rise of relatively independent state legislative party organizations and the decline in attention to the county organizations.

*Republican Party.* The Republican Party in New York State developed under the strong influence of a few powerful elected leaders. Nelson Rockefeller (governor 1959–1973), for instance, did much to shape the party in the modern era. Both his presence and his absence have had profound effects on the state's Republican organization.

During the early 1960s there was a great deal of tension between the liberal wing of the party, led by Governor Rockefeller, and party conservatives. Their running battle led to the formation of the state's Conservative Party in 1962. It was formed by a group of conservative Republicans distressed with the direction in which Rockefeller had taken the Republican Party. Through the 1960s, however, Rockefeller's control of state patronage, as well as his personal wealth, enabled him to control effectively the state committee. This is not to say, of course, that there were not battles, as indeed there were.

The liberal wing of New York's Republican Party reached its zenith with the 1966 mayoral victory of John Lindsay, a former member of Congress. In addition to Lindsay and Rockefeller, the state's senior U.S. senator, Jacob Javits, was also a liberal Republican. By 1970, however, the pendulum had swung back in the other direction as James Buckley, running on the Conservative Party ballot, defeated both incumbent Republican Charles Goodell and Democratic challenger Richard Ottinger in a contest for a U.S. Senate seat. A year later, in 1971, Mayor Lindsay, now feuding with Rockefeller and under increasing pressure from conservative Republicans, left the Republican Party to become a Democrat. In December 1973 Rockefeller resigned as governor, and in December 1974 he became vice president.

Information released during the course of his vice presidential confirmation hearings demonstrated just how important Rockefeller had been to the New York State Republican Committee. Documents revealed that from 1957 to 1974 the governor contributed $1,031,637 to the Republican state and county committees and clubs (New York Times 1974). This figure fails to reflect the additional money the party saved by not having to fund fully gubernatorial campaigns during Rockefeller's tenure as governor.

Rockefeller's abrupt departure, coupled with the lingering effects of the Supreme Court's legislative reapportionment decisions, had a profound effect on party development following the 1974 elections. By 1974 the Supreme Court's rulings from the early 1960s regarding malapportioned state legislatures had erased the Republicans' hold on both houses of the state legislature. Republican candidates found state legislative races a great deal more competitive in 1974 than they had been in the early 1960s. The absence of Rockefeller (and his money) from the statewide ticket only served to exacerbate the situation for the party's senate and assembly candidates, as the lion's share of the party's limited funds were funneled into the gubernatorial campaign of former lieutenant governor Malcolm Wilson. Not only did Wilson lose to Democrat Hugh Carey, but Republicans also lost control of the assembly. Although there were a number of reasons for the Republicans' poor showing (Watergate among them), the party's inability to replace Rockefeller's fund-raising capabilities was certainly high on the list.

The poor condition of the party did not escape the attention of Warren Anderson, the majority leader of the New York State Senate, who by default became the state's most powerful elected Republican. Following the party's 1974 losses, Anderson and his Republican colleagues in the state senate strengthened their own permanent campaign operation. The Republicans in the assembly, as well as the Democrats in both houses of the legislature, soon followed suit. Over time, Anderson's Republican Senate Campaign Committee was able to raise annually more money than the Republican State Committee. The senate campaign committee also contracted for polling and media consultants to assist the campaigns of Republican senate candidates. In addition to running their own campaigns, Republicans in the senate became the major source for Republican patronage in the state, at a time when many Republicans in Albany were looking for work. Hence, in a relatively short period of time, the concentration of Republican power in the Empire State shifted from the governor and the state committee to the Republican-controlled state senate.

The shift of power was underscored in 1980 when the chair of the state committee, Dr. Bernard Kilbourne, deemed the committee financially "bankrupt" (Lynn 1980, A1). In the same year, incumbent Republican U.S. senator Javits was defeated in a Republican primary by Alfonse D'Amato. Through the remainder of the decade, the committee continued to limp along, possessing neither the money nor the patronage of the Rockefeller era. The real sources of power in Republican politics continued to be the state senate and the state's junior senator, D'Amato. With the retirement of Anderson at the close of 1988, D'Amato's influence became even more pronounced.

Two events illustrate the power that D'Amato wields in Republican state politics. First, in 1991 William Powers, D'Amato's close friend and former aide, was elected state committee chair. His appointment effectively sealed D'Amato's grip on the state party organization. Then, as a number of Republicans lined up to challenge Mario Cuomo in the gubernatorial election in 1994, D'Amato's personal choice, state senator George Pataki, emerged as the Republican nominee. Pataki's eventual victory over Cuomo returned the executive branch of state government to Republican control for the first time in twenty years.

### CURRENT PARTY ORGANIZATION

New York State Election Law, article 2 (pages 9–18), covers party organization. The law is loose, leaving most decisions to the party itself. The party rules must be filed with appropriate boards of election. The law specifies that "a chairman, a secretary, a treasurer and such other officers as they may by their rules provide" be elected within certain time periods (art. 2-112).

*Democratic Party.* The New York State Democratic Party in the mid-1990s is in a state of transition from control by a governor, with access to all the resources that implies, to something else. Early signs suggest that the party is reverting to the factionalism that characterized it before 1974.

The electoral loss of Governor Cuomo left the party without leadership and in debt. Assembly Speaker Sheldon Silver from Manhattan has made the most visible move into the leadership vacuum. He reportedly had a strong hand in the selection of Judith Hope, longtime state party activist and fundraiser from Suffolk County, as state party chair and John Sullivan, former Oswego County party chair, as chair of the executive committee.

Although Hope and Sullivan are described as "cochairs," and although Sullivan's presence indicates a sensitivity to upstate concerns, Hope was directing day-to-day activities from a borrowed Manhattan office until September 1995. Then, with resources provided by the Democratic National Committee, the state party hired an executive director, moved into its own space, and introduced an on-line information service (Dao 1995, B6).

However, Silver was in 1995 being challenged for control of the party by the comptroller, H. Carl McCall, the only Democrat in statewide elective office, and U.S. Representative Charles E. Schumer of Brooklyn. All three were thought to be positioning themselves for a gubernatorial campaign in 1998. One consequence of the rise of competing factions is that resources could be funneled away from the party and toward the factions, making it more difficult for the state Democratic Party to retire its debt and begin to recover organizationally (Dao 1995, B1). Thus, the speed of the organizational recovery will probably depend on how much the Democratic National Committee will do for the New York state party. Help from the DNC is not improbable, since New York remains a key state in any presidential election campaign.

The 300-member Democratic State Committee is composed of a male and female from each of the state's 150 assembly districts. They meet to elect a state chair, an executive committee chair, first vice chair, up to twelve vice chairs, treasurer, assistant treasurer, secretary, assistant secretary, and sergeant-at-arms, none of whom need be members of the state committee (New York State Democratic Party 1995). There is an executive committee composed of the above officers plus the executive director, the chair of the Law Committee, the chair of the Finance Committee, the cochairs of the Policy Committee, the president of the New York State Young Democrats, two members from each of the twelve judicial districts in the state elected by the state committee members from each of the judicial districts, and eight at-large members who are elected by the entire membership of the state committee upon nomination by the state chair (New York State Democratic Party 1995). The executive committee is required to meet three times per year.

*Republican Party.* Like its Democratic counterpart, the Republican State Committee is in transition. The 1994 election produced the state's first Republican governor in twenty years. Pataki's election has had a positive impact on fund raising.

Like the Democratic state committee, the Republican state committee currently consists of three hundred members, two from each of the state's assembly districts. By party rule, one male and one female are elected from each district. The committee selects the state chair as well as male and female vice chairs. The committee employs an executive director and has staff in both its main office in Albany and its satellite office in New York City.

Although diminished by candidate-centered campaigns, county chairs still have a good deal of influence over affairs in their own counties. Their power stems in part from their role in selecting the party's nominees in special elections to fill vacancies.

As of late 1996 Senator D'Amato still exerted considerable influence over the committee. His stature as a major player in national Republican politics has made for a relatively good relationship between the state party and the Republican National Committee. The state committee's relationship with the new governor is also strong, as Pataki received its strong endorsement in 1994, and Republican county chairs campaigned hard for him.

There has been, however, some fallout from the 1994 campaign. Relations between Pataki and New York City mayor Rudolph Giuliani were strained by the mayor's endorsement of Democrat Mario Cuomo for reelection. This could lead to renewed upstate–New York City wrangling within the party. Another major development was the ouster of state senate majority leader Ralph Marino, who was slow to back Pataki and apparently paid the price when a majority of the state's Republican senators voted to replace him with Sen. Joseph Bruno. Bruno, then, joins Pataki and D'Amato as the state's most powerful Republicans. Together, these three will control the path that the party follows for the foreseeable future.

## RESOURCE GUIDE

The major New York State parties do not keep records. Both parties are required to file their rules with the State Board of Elections. Also, the state parties and the state legislative committees, as political committees, must file at least two financial disclosure forms per year. Additional financial disclosure filings may be required, depending on the campaign involvement of a party organization. Financial disclosure forms include names and addresses of those donating $100 or more in a year, transfers to and from other political committees, and expenditures. The filings are kept at the State Board of Elections for five years, after which time they are sent to the state archives. The state archives has filings from 1982 forward. If the archives receives a request a few days in advance, it will present the requested filings chronologically.

## REFERENCES

*Asterisks denote the most important publications on New York party politics.*
Dao, James. 1995. New York's Democratic depression worries the White House. *New York Times,* September 6, B6.
Jewell, Malcolm E., and David M. Olson. 1982. *American state political parties and elections.* Rev. ed. Homewood, Ill.: Dorsey Press.
Lynn, Frank. 1980. State Republican committee head reports organization is 'bankrupt.' *New York Times,* June 16, A1.
*Markoe, Karen. 1989. A short history of New York's two major parties. In *New York State today:*

*Politics, government, public policy*, 2d ed., ed. Peter W. Colby and John K. White, 61–70. Albany: State University of New York Press.

Mohr, James C. 1973. *The radical Republicans and reform in New York during Reconstruction*. Ithaca: Cornell University Press.

New York State Democratic Party. 1995. Rules of the Democratic Party of the State of New York.

*New York Times*. 1974. Summary of political contributions by Nelson A. Rockefeller: 1957–1974. November 14, A39.

Roberts, Steven. 1968. For Democrats the word is 'doldrums.' *New York Times*, November 24, p. 6.

Scarrow, Howard A. 1983. *Parties, elections, & representation in the State of New York*. New York: New York University Press.

Schlesinger, Joseph A. 1984. On the theory of party organization. *Journal of Politics* 46, no. 2 (May).

*Spitzer, Robert J. 1994. Third parties in New York State. In *Governing New York State*, 3d ed., ed. Jeffrey M. Stonecash, John K. White, and Peter W. Colby, 103–116. Albany: State University of New York Press.

*Stonecash, Jeffrey M. 1994. Political parties and partisan conflict. In *Governing New York State*, 3d ed., ed. Jeffrey M. Stonecash, John K. White, and Peter W. Colby, 83–101. Albany: State University of New York Press.

Stonecash, Jeffrey M. 1989. State-local relations: The city and upstate. In *New York State today: Politics, government, public policy*, 2d ed., ed. Peter W. Colby and John K. White, 41–49. Albany: State University of New York Press.

Tolchin, Martin. 1968. Dispirited Democrats are seeking a unifying force in state. *New York Times*, September 15, 77.

*Zimmerman, Joseph F. 1981. *The government and politics of New York State*. New York: New York University Press.

# North Carolina

CHARLES PRYSBY

## PARTY HISTORY

The Democratic Party dominated North Carolina electoral politics for the first half of the twentieth century, reflecting the prevailing pattern throughout the South during this time period.[1] Democratic presidential candidates usually carried the state, even when losing at the national level. Republicans did no better in congressional elections. It was not until 1952 that a North Carolina Republican was elected to Congress in this century. State government similarly was under complete Democratic control. Every governor during this period was a Democrat, and the state legislature was overwhelmingly Democratic as well. In 1950, for example, Republicans won only 11 of the 170 seats in the two houses of the state legislature. Republicans were strong in some counties, but they presented no serious threat throughout the state.

During the second half of the twentieth century, a two-party system developed (see Table 1). Cracks in the Democratic domination of the state appeared during the 1950s, especially in presidential contests. Dwight Eisenhower almost carried the state in 1956, winning over 49 percent of the two-party vote. Republican presidential voting did not

**Table 1**   Republican Strength in North Carolina, 1952–1994

| Year | Percent of presidential vote | Percent of gubernatorial vote | Percent of U.S. Senate vote | Percent of U.S. House delegation | Percent of state house delegation | Percent of state senate delegation |
|------|------|------|------|------|------|------|
| 1952 | 46.1 | 32.5 | — | 8.3 | 11.7 | 4.0 |
| 1954 | — | — | 34.1 | 8.3 | 8.3 | 2.0 |
| 1956 | 49.3 | 33.0 | 33.4 | 8.3 | 10.8 | 6.0 |
| 1958 | — | — | — | 8.3 | 3.3 | 2.0 |
| 1960 | 47.9 | 45.5 | 38.6 | 8.3 | 12.5 | 4.0 |
| 1962 | — | — | 39.6 | 18.2 | 17.5 | 4.0 |
| 1964 | 43.8 | 43.4 | — | 18.2 | 11.7 | 2.0 |
| 1966 | — | — | 44.4 | 27.3 | 21.7 | 14.0 |
| 1968 | 57.5[1] | 47.3 | 39.4 | 36.4 | 24.2 | 24.0 |
| 1970 | — | — | — | 36.4 | 20.0 | 14.0 |
| 1972 | 70.6 | 51.3 | 54.0 | 36.4 | 29.2 | 30.0 |
| 1974 | — | — | 37.3 | 18.2 | 7.5 | 2.0 |
| 1976 | 44.4 | 34.3 | — | 18.2 | 5.0 | 6.0 |
| 1978 | — | — | 54.5 | 18.2 | 11.7 | 12.0 |
| 1980 | 51.1 | 37.7 | 50.3 | 36.4 | 20.0 | 20.0 |
| 1982 | — | — | — | 18.2 | 15.0 | 12.0 |
| 1984 | 62.0 | 54.4 | 51.9 | 45.5 | 31.7 | 24.0 |
| 1986 | — | — | 48.2 | 27.3 | 30.0 | 20.0 |
| 1988 | 58.2 | 56.1 | — | 27.3 | 38.3 | 26.0 |
| 1990 | — | — | 52.6 | 36.4 | 30.8 | 28.0 |
| 1992 | 50.5[2] | 45.1 | 52.2 | 33.3 | 34.4 | 22.0 |
| 1994 | — | — | — | 66.7 | 55.8 | 48.0 |

SOURCES: *America Votes* (Washington, D.C.: Congressional Quarterly, 1954–1990); and *Statistical Abstract of the United States* (Washington, D.C.: Government Printing Office, 1954–1992), various editions. The 1992 and 1994 figures were provided by the North Carolina Board of Elections.

NOTE: The vote is calculated as a percentage of the two-party vote.

[1] In 1968 Republican Richard M. Nixon won the state with 40 percent of the vote; Democrat Hubert H. Humprey and American Independent George C. Wallace received 29 and 31 percent, respectively.

[2] In 1992 Republican George W. Bush won the state with 43 percent of the vote; Democrat Bill Clinton and independent Ross Perot received 43 and 14 percent, respectively.

immediately carry over to other races, even though the major state elections were held in presidential years. Following the 1956 elections, for example, the governor, both U.S. senators, ten of the eleven U.S. representatives, and over 90 percent of the state legislators were Democrats. The Republican Party did not develop into a competitive force in state politics until the late 1960s. In 1968 Republicans carried the state in the presidential election, doubled the number of their congressional seats, and made substantial gains in the state legislature. Four years later they did even better. With a popular presidential candidate, Richard Nixon, at the top of the ticket, Republicans scored historic wins. Jesse Helms became the first Republican U.S. senator and James Holshouser the first Republican governor elected in North Carolina in the twentieth century. Republicans also won four of the ten congressional seats and about one-third of the seats in the state legislature.

Republican electoral strength remained greatest at the presidential level throughout the 1970s and 1980s. Below the presidential level, Republican advances were less thorough and more uneven. U.S. Senate elections were a favorable hunting ground for Republicans; Helms retained his seat in three subsequent reelection bids, and the other seat was won by Republican John East in 1980, lost back to Democrat Terry Sanford in 1986, and recaptured by Democrat-turned-Republican Lauch Faircloth in 1992. U.S. House elections displayed a pattern of surge and decline that followed the presidential/midterm election cycle. In both

1972 and 1980, for example, Republicans won four congressional seats but lost two back in the subsequent midterm elections. It was not until 1994 that Republicans were able to win a majority of the state's congressional seats. In state elections, Jim Hunt recaptured the governorship for the Democrats in 1976 and was reelected in 1980; Republican Jim Martin then won in 1984 and 1988, followed by another Democratic victory by Hunt in 1992. Further down the ticket, Republican success was more elusive. Following Watergate, Republicans all but disappeared from the state legislature, and the party did not return to its 1972 legislative strength until 1980. The legislature remained firmly in Democratic hands until 1994, when in a major breakthrough Republicans won a majority of the seats in the state house and a near majority in the senate.

The overall pattern for the recent past clearly has been one of Republican growth. Republicans have become highly competitive not just in the races at the top of the ballot but also in races for lower-level offices. Gaining parity in the state legislature was one sign of the surge in Republican strength. The situation now is one of high competitiveness. For example, from 1972 on, neither party has been able to win more than 55 percent of the vote in a U.S. Senate election. Although gubernatorial elections have been decided by larger margins, neither party has been able to hold the governorship for more than two terms in a row over the past twenty-five years. Divided outcomes have been common in recent elections, as illustrated by the 1992 results, in which Republicans lost the governorship while Democrats lost a U.S. Senate seat. Although the electorate has moved toward the Republicans, the voters are sufficiently dealigned to create a fluid and even volatile situation. Whether a realignment will occur that establishes the Republicans as the dominant party in the state is uncertain. Much will depend on national trends and developments. Party fortunes in the state rise and fall with national trends, as the 1992 and 1994 North Carolina results clearly illustrate.

Minor parties have not played a significant role in the state's politics, and there is little reason to expect this to change. The Libertarians frequently have run candidates for office, but they usually have attracted less than 2 percent of the vote. Their best showing was in 1992, when they received about 4 percent of the gubernatorial vote and 3 percent of the U.S. senatorial vote. No other minor party has even consistently been on the ballot. It also is worth noting that independent presidential candidates have not fared well in North Carolina. Both John Anderson in 1980 and Ross Perot in 1992 did significantly worse in the state than they did nationally.

## ORGANIZATIONAL DEVELOPMENT

The development of political party organizations in North Carolina parallels the emergence of a competitive two-party system. Republican Party organizational strength naturally was weak until the party began to enjoy electoral success. The growth of Republican electoral strength over the past thirty years has been matched by increased organizational strength. Democratic Party organization also developed during this period. During the era of Democratic domination, a strong and viable state party organization was not necessary. As two-party competition emerged, it became an asset.

The strength of state party organization can be measured by examining several key indicators: headquarters, staffing, budget, and activities. Over the past three decades, both parties established more visible state headquarters that were better staffed and funded, especially in election years, and engaged in a wider range of activities. They also have attempted to establish and maintain strong county party organizations, although there naturally has been considerable variation from county to county in the vitality of the organizations for both parties. The development of party organizations has been aided by public funding. Beginning in the mid-1970s, North Carolina distributed funds collected through a voluntary tax checkoff to the state party organizations.

*Republican Party.* State Republican Party organization really began to emerge in the late 1960s. In 1965 the party moved its state headquarters from Charlotte to the capital, Raleigh, and in 1966 hired its first professional executive director. By 1972, under the chairmanship of Frank Rouse, an active state party headquarters existed. Although it consisted of a full-time staff of only three in a rented office suite, it was a permanent state party organization with a significant budget, and it was actively engaged in the 1972 campaign (Shaw 1995). This nascent organization was subsequently devastated by the Watergate scandal in 1974. The state party chair in 1975, Robert Shaw, was forced to spend extensive time raising funds to eliminate a $100,000 debt (Shaw 1995). Rebuilding the party organization took the remainder of the decade. Although one study (Cotter et al. 1984) rated the organizational strength of the party in the late 1970s as moderately strong, this seems to be an overly generous assessment. More realistically, the party organization was moderately weak at this time.

By the early 1980s a stronger state party organization existed. The party moved its state headquarters from rented quarters to a historic home that the party had purchased and renovated. Budgets expanded, activity increased, and the grassroots base was developed. A recruitment committee was formed in 1986, with a special focus on locating candidates for the state legislature (Hawke 1995). Further development of the party organization occurred in the late 1980s, under the chairmanship of Jack Hawke, who served from 1987 to 1995. The annual budget increased from $150,000 in 1980 to $1.6 million in 1988, and the staff grew to nine full-time individuals, including such positions as political director, finance director, and communications director (Hawke 1995). There also was a separate organization, Victory '88, with a sizable staff and budget, to support the 1988 campaign efforts. Even in nonpresidential election years, the state party budget was around $800,000. In 1992 the party organization remained well financed and active, with a staff of eight and a budget comparable to that of 1988, along with a Victory '92 organization to coordinate and support campaign efforts (Hawke 1995).

The increased organizational strength produced greater campaign activity. The state party engaged in a variety of efforts to help Republicans win more offices. In the successful 1994 elections, for example, the party headquarters provided substantial campaign help to candidates, including training seminars, legislative and issue research, and opposition research. The state party also helped to recruit quality candidates for targeted state legislative districts and financed direct mailings and radio advertisements in these districts (Glenn 1995).

*Democratic Party.* State Democratic Party organizational strength also increased during the 1970s and 1980s. Governor Hunt placed considerable emphasis on the party organization during his first two terms (1976–1984). Under chairpersons Betty McCain, Russell Walker, and David Price, the staff and budget for the state party organization were expanded, and the party headquarters became a more visible and active entity.

Democratic Party organizational development at the state level was similar in many ways to the Republican development described above. During the 1970s the Democrats maintained a year-round headquarters in rented quarters, just as the Republicans did. In 1980 the party purchased and renovated a historic home for its permanent state headquarters, just as the Republicans were to do a few years later. In the early 1970s the state party had a full-time staff of three or four individuals. In 1980 the staff was twice that size—plus the party had a separate organization, the Unity Campaign, to coordinate and support 1980 election efforts (Price 1995). By 1984 the party staff had grown to about twelve individuals, and another fourteen were in the Unity Campaign and the Victory Fund, another parallel campaign organization. The state party budget in 1984 was around $2 million, including the Unity Campaign and Victory Fund (Price 1995). Comparable resources were available in 1988 and 1992, although the 1988 campaign effort was hindered by poor cooperation between the national and state campaigns (Eudy 1995). Even in 1994, an off-year election with no statewide race on the ballot, the state Democratic Party had a staff of fourteen and a budget of $1.3 million (McDevitt 1995).

Differences exist in the activities of the two state parties. The Democratic Party has emphasized voter registration and get-out-the-vote activities more than the Republicans have. In 1984 extensive voter registration and get-out-the-vote efforts were mounted, including the use of a state-level phone bank to increase turnout among potential Democratic voters (Price 1995). In 1987–1988 another major effort was made to register voters, supported by a $100,000 fund solicited from PACs (Eudy 1995). Conversely, the state Democratic Party headquarters has provided less support than the state Republican Party to candidates. Although the party routinely held training seminars, provided opposition research, and so on, it appears that Democratic candidates received less assistance than did their Republican counterparts, especially when it came to state legislative elections.

*Grassroots Party Development.* Both parties have attempted to establish grassroots organizations in the counties. Strong county-level Republican organization is a recent phenomenon. Prior to the mid-1980s the party lacked much of a statewide grassroots organization, although it had been strong in selected areas, such as Mecklenburg County (which contains Charlotte, the largest city in the state). By the mid-1990s, over 90 percent of the counties had at least a minimally functioning Republican Party organization, meaning that the party held a county convention as scheduled and engaged in ongoing activity during the year (Rouse 1995). Most of the counties now establish a temporary party headquarters during election years, although very few maintain a permanent headquarters. The level of party activity varies greatly from county to county. Some have highly active organizations, which raise money, send out regular newsletters, and hold a variety of meetings and events. Others, perhaps the majority, display a more modest activity level. There are one hundred counties in the state, many of them very small, and the level of county party organization must be judged from that perspective.

Democratic county-level organization has a longer history of activity, in part because so many local officials were Democrats in earlier years. However, grassroots organization appears to have deteriorated during the 1980s and 1990s. Local fund raising and attendance at county conventions dropped, for example (Van Hecke 1995). The current state of Democratic Party county organization is roughly similar to that of the Republican Party. Few counties have a permanent headquarters; almost all establish a temporary headquarters in election years. County party activity varies greatly. Most have at least a modest level of activity; perhaps one-third could be considered highly active.

## CURRENT PARTY ORGANIZATION

North Carolina law imposes little regulation on the organizational structure of the parties, although it does significantly control their role in the electoral process, particularly concerning the nomination of candidates for office. Despite the absence of legal restrictions, the two parties have established fairly similar organizational structures that reflect the typical state, county, and precinct hierarchical model. Although the formal structures are similar, significant differences exist in important organizational aspects, such as the nature of party activists and intraparty factionalism.

*Party Structure.* Both parties have had full-time leadership in the state headquarters for some time. Democrats have either had a full-time party chair or a part-time chair with a full-time executive director. Republicans have usually, but not always, had one individual serve as both chair and executive director. Each party has a state executive committee, a body of several hundred individuals which meets infrequently. The composition of this committee differs between the two parties but in both cases includes elected officials, delegates from the county or district parties, and other state party and auxiliary group officials (North Carolina 1994, 783–842). Each party also has a smaller committee that meets more frequently: the Republican State Central Committee, a group of about thirty that meets bimonthly, and the Democratic State Executive Council, a body of about forty that meets with roughly the same frequency (North Carolina 1994, 783–842).

The county is the basic building block below the state level, although both parties also have congressional and state legislative district organizations as well, at least on paper. County organization consists of a chair and an executive committee. The Democratic county executive committees have a stronger grassroots base, since they include the chair and first vice chair of each precinct organization, along with elected officials and other party officers (North Carolina 1994, 783–842). The Republican county executive committees are elected by the county conventions, an arrangement that probably reflects the fact that counties vary greatly in Republican strength.

The differences in precinct organization also are reflected in the party rules that specify their size and composition. The Democratic precinct organizations consist of five officers plus five other active Democrats, whereas the Republican precinct organizations are simply required to have three officers (North Carolina 1994, 783–842). In recent years the Republican Party has attempted to build its precinct organizations. In 1993 the party created and distributed a precinct organizational manual; the party also held four training seminars on grassroots organizations that year (Rouse 1995). On the other hand, Democratic precinct organizational strength appears to have decayed in recent years. As a result, Democrats no longer enjoy a big advantage in grassroots organization.

Both parties hold conventions at the county, congressional district, and state levels. Republican conventions occur in odd-numbered years plus presidential election years. Democrats convene in even-numbered years. For both parties, presidential election year state conventions are important because they select the delegates to the national conventions. For Democrats, delegates are allocated to the various candidates by the presidential primaries. Republicans have not operated under the same constraint, although the delegation's first ballot at the national convention must be cast in accordance with the primary outcome. The conventions play no other role in the nomination of party candidates at any level, making them less important than conventions in some other states, such as Virginia.

*Party Activists.* Grassroots activists in the two parties differ in their participation profiles. A 1991 survey of party activists found that Democrats tend to be older and to have been involved in party activity for a longer period of time (Prysby 1995). Over 70 percent of the Democratic grassroots activists became active before 1980, compared with only 55 percent of Republicans. This is consistent with the past partisan differences in county and precinct organization.

Clear partisan differences exist in participation motives and styles. The 1991 survey of party activists revealed that purposive motives (that is, concern with issues and policy) were important for both groups, but significantly more so for Republican activists (Prysby 1995). Republican growth in the South has been based on an ideological appeal to voters, so it might be expected that purposive incentives would play a strong role in motivating individuals to be active in the party. Conversely, Democrats, as the once dominant party in the state, may have attracted more activists who simply enjoyed the excitement of being involved in politics. A related aspect is the commitment that activists have to issues. The 1991 survey of party activists found that Republicans were more purist (that is, less willing to compromise on issues and ideology to achieve electoral success) than were Democrats, a difference that seems consistent with the differences in incentive motivations discussed above. Whether Republican activists are so purist as to present a problem for the party is debatable, but there does appear to be more potential for this problem to emerge among Republicans.

*Intraparty Factionalism.* Democratic Party factionalism revolves around several factors. Ideology frequently plays an important role in intraparty divisions, since the Democrats span a broad ideological spectrum (Prysby 1995). The racial diversity of the party is significant. As in other southern states, the Democrats depend on a biracial coalition for electoral success. That coalition has the potential of being split by racially related issues. The 1991 survey of party activists found that on some issues, white Democratic activists were closer in their attitudes to Republican activists than to African American Democratic activists (Prysby 1995). Geographical differences also are important. Activists in the metropolitan counties are the most liberal, whereas eastern whites are the most conservative.

Factions reflect more than social or demographic divisions. Some are tied to individuals. As discussed earlier, Governor Hunt played a major role in improving the state party organization. However, some Democrats felt that Hunt had too much power and control over the organization. One frequently voiced complaint was that the party organization too often acted in behalf of Hunt's interests rather that the interests of Democrats in general (Effron 1995). In fact, the Hunt organization has been more than just a party faction; it has been a strong personal organization, based on key individuals in each county, that has engaged in fund raising and candidate recruitment. The success of the Hunt organization may in some years have drained contributions away from other Democratic candidates (Beyle 1995).

Republican factionalism has been more ideological in nature. The Congressional Club, an organization founded by Senator Helms in the 1970s, mastered the art of soliciting funds, which helped some Republican candidates. But the organization also created deep fissures in the party. Some Republicans felt that the club was too aggressively conservative and ideologically rigid, especially on social issues. Geography has some relationship to this division. The older and more moderate wing of the party is located primarily in the west. Eastern Republicans are clearly more conservative (Prysby 1995). Like the Hunt organization, the club is more than a party faction; it is a separate organization that engages in fund raising and candidate recruitment. However, a rift in 1994 between Helms and the club's head, Carter Wrenn, raises questions about the future role of the club.

In the 1980s religious conservatives emerged as an important force within the party, sometimes producing intense divisions over social issues, such as abortion. By the mid-

1990s, the Christian Coalition had become a very important organized force in the party, constituting the majority in many county organizations (Arrington 1995).

*Parties and Nominations.* North Carolina law substantially regulates the role of political parties in the electoral process. The most important provision is that primary elections must be held to nominate candidates. Primaries in North Carolina are held in May and are closed, and no party endorsements appear on the ballot. Current state law provides for a modified runoff primary. If no candidate receives more than 40 percent of the vote, the second-place finisher may request a runoff primary. Prior to 1989 an absolute majority was needed to avoid a possible runoff primary.

The runoff primary has been controversial in North Carolina, as in other southern states. African Americans have argued that the runoff primary makes it more difficult for African American candidates to win nomination, since white voters would unite behind the white candidate in an African American versus white runoff. In the 1982 primary for the Second Congressional District, an African American candidate led the field in the first primary with 42 percent of the vote but lost in the runoff; the case was cited repeatedly by Jesse Jackson in his quest to eliminate runoff primaries in the South (Luebke 1990, 118). These considerations led to the 1989 lowering of the threshold to 40 percent. In 1990 Harvey Gantt, an African American, led the Democratic primary for the U.S. Senate seat with 38 percent of the vote, just short of what he needed to win outright (Prysby 1996). Some observers feared that he would lose in the runoff, but he easily prevailed, in part because opponent Mike Easley did not attempt to exploit the racial issue. That outcome made the current runoff law less controversial.

Primary conflicts have been important in the Democratic Party for a long time. When Democrats dominated the state, winning the Democratic primary was tantamount to election, so competitive primaries were typical. Republican primary competitiveness is a more recent phenomenon, emerging as the Republican nomination has increased in value. Both parties have recent examples of primary divisiveness followed by general election defeat. In 1984, for example, the Democratic gubernatorial primary was an intense battle between several strong candidates. Attorney General Rufus Edmisten finally won the nomination in a runoff primary, but supporters of some of the losing candidates were lukewarm in their support for the Democratic nominee, who wound up losing to Republican Jim Martin in November. In 1986 the Republican primary for a U.S. Senate seat was a hard-fought contest between Jim Broyhill, a moderately conservative member of Congress from the western part of the state, and David Funderburk, a more extreme conservative supported by the Congressional Club. Broyhill narrowly won the nomination and then lost the general election to former governor Terry Sanford, who had united the Democratic Party behind his candidacy.

## RESOURCE GUIDE

Resource materials on the state party organizations can be found in a variety of places. Detailed information on the party rules, including the formal party structure, is in the *North Carolina Manual,* a biennial publication from the secretary of state. Regulations involving the role of parties in the electoral process are in the *Election Laws of North Carolina,* published by the State Board of Elections.

Both political parties have archival materials in their state headquarters and are willing to allow access to researchers. Items that are likely to be available include records of state con-

**Table 2**   North Carolina Resource Guide

|  | Democrats | Republicans |
|---|---|---|
| Archive | Yes | Yes |
| Location | State Party Headquarters | State Party Headquarters |
|  | 220 Hillsborough St. | 1410 Hillsborough St. |
|  | Raleigh, N.C. 27605 | Raleigh, N.C. 27605 |
|  | (919) 821-2777 | (919) 828-6423 |
| Dates | 1986–[1] | 1986–[1] |
| Finding aid | No | No |
| Access | By appointment | By appointment |
| Contents: |  |  |
| State convention records | Yes | Yes |
| Executive committee minutes | Yes | Yes |
| Correspondence | Yes | Yes |
| Organizational structure | Yes | Yes |
| Budgets | Yes | Yes |
| Rules | Yes | Yes |

[1] The information is more complete for later years.

ventions, budgets, correspondence, and records of party activities and functions. However, the party archives are not well organized and maintained, and they may be incomplete. Republicans have records for about the last ten years, but little for the period before that. These records are largely uncategorized, consisting in many cases of boxes stored in the basement. A similar situation exists in the Democratic Party. The state headquarters has considerable information in a bank of file cabinets, but it is not organized for easy searching and retrieval. Both parties are able to provide more complete and detailed information for very recent years. For historical information, the North Carolina collection in Wilson Library at the University of North Carolina at Chapel Hill has relevant materials.

### NOTE

1. Ted Arrington, Thad Beyle, Seth Effron, Ken Eudy, Tres Glenn, Jack Hawke, Wayne McDevitt, David Price, Jane Rouse, Robert Shaw, and Jim Van Hecke graciously shared their knowledge of North Carolina party politics with me. Several of these individuals also read a preliminary draft of the manuscript, and the final version benefited from their comments. Jennifer Harris provided capable research assistance at several stages in this project. I greatly appreciate the assistance of these individuals. Any errors of fact or interpretation that remain are the responsibility of the author.

### REFERENCES

*Asterisks denote the most important publications on North Carolina party politics.*
Arrington, Ted. 1995. Telephone interview by author, September 14.
Beyle, Thad. 1995. Letter to author, July 11.
Cotter, Cornelius, James L. Gibson, John F. Bibby, and Robert J. Huckshorn. 1984. *Party organizations in American politics.* New York: Praeger.
Effron, Seth. 1995. Interview by author, Raleigh, N.C., March 7.
Eudy, Kenneth. 1995. Interview by author, Raleigh, N.C., March 9.
*Fleer, Jack D. 1994. *North Carolina government and politics.* Lincoln: University of Nebraska Press.
*Fleer, Jack D., Roger C. Lowery, and Charles L. Prysby. 1988. Political change in North Carolina. In *The South's new politics: Realignment and dealignment,* ed. Robert H. Swansbrough and David M. Brodsky, 94–111. Columbia: University of South Carolina Press.

Glenn, Tres. 1995. Interview by author, Raleigh, N.C., March 21.

Hawke, Jack. 1995. Interview by author, Raleigh, N.C., March 7.

*Luebke, Paul. 1990. *Tarheel politics: Myths and realities.* Chapel Hill: University of North Carolina Press.

McDevitt, Wayne. 1995. Interview by author, Raleigh, N.C., March 21.

*North Carolina. 1994. *North Carolina manual 1993–1994.* Raleigh, N.C.: Office of the Secretary of State.

Price, David. 1995. Interview by author, Durham, N.C., March 9.

*Prysby, Charles L. 1996. The 1990 North Carolina United States Senate election. In *Race, politics, and governance in the United States,* ed. Huey L. Perry. Gainesville: University Press of Florida, forthcoming.

*———. 1995. North Carolina: Emerging two-party politics. In *Southern state party organizations and activists,* ed. Charles D. Hadley and Lewis Bowman, 37–53. Westport, Conn.: Praeger.

*———. 1994. North Carolina: Conflicting forces in a confusing year. In *The 1992 presidential election in the South: Current patterns of southern party and electoral politics,* ed. Robert P. Steed, Laurence W. Moreland, and Tod A. Baker, 139–155. Westport, Conn.: Praeger.

*———. 1991. North Carolina: The confluence of national, regional, and state forces. In *The 1988 presidential election in the South: Continuity amidst change in southern party politics,* ed. Laurence W. Moreland, Robert P. Steed, and Tod A. Baker, 185–200. New York: Praeger.

Rouse, Jane. 1995. Interview by author, Raleigh, N.C., March 21.

Shaw, Robert. 1995. Interview by author, Greensboro, N.C., March 26.

Van Hecke, James. 1995. Interview by author, Greensboro, N.C., March 16.

# North Dakota

LLOYD OMDAHL

## PARTY HISTORY

North Dakota, populated by first- and second-generation northern European immigrants, had a very limited tradition of party loyalty or affiliation when it entered the Union in 1889 (Lamar 1956, 274–284). Even though North Dakota voters demonstrated a strong affinity for the Republican Party early in balloting, their commitment was not deep. The two-to-one Republican gubernatorial victories of 1889 and 1890—the first two statewide elections—were quickly overturned by the Populists in the 1892 election, when the upstart organization won most of the statewide elective offices and captured the state's electoral votes for James B. Weaver by a scant 164 votes (Robinson 1966, 223). In the following two elections, a Fusion Party made up of Populists and Democrats gave the regular Republicans strong competition even though it lost most of the races. Except for the election of Democrat John Burke as governor by dissident reform Republicans and Democrats in 1906, 1908, and 1910, the regular Republicans dominated North Dakota politics until 1916 (Robinson 1966, 265).

The electoral reforms of the Progressive era were warmly received by North Dakotans, who were coping with machine politics under Republican Party boss Alexander McKenzie. The adoption prior to the elections of 1912 of primary elections was particularly inviting.

But the intent of the primary, to replace the boss-run conventions, was negated in North Dakota when the political parties simply moved their conventions ahead of the primaries and "endorsed" candidates for the primaries. The tradition of endorsing conventions prevails to the present day.

After 1912, challenging the regular party candidates became a new avenue of political expression for political dissidents, who were growing in number as a result of economic exploitation by out-of-state interests. Thousands of small farmers found themselves at the mercy of the banks, grain elevators, and railroads, all of which were controlled in Minneapolis and St. Paul (Tweton and Jelliff 1976, 135–138). Dominated by a laissez faire ideology and strongly influenced by the political operatives of the banking, railroad, and grain interests, McKenzie and the Republicans did little to offer political solutions to stop the exploitation.

In 1915 the cauldron of discontent boiled over when the farmers launched a membership organization called the Nonpartisan League to endorse sympathetic candidates to run against the Republicans in primary elections. Thousands of farmers flocked to the new organization that promised relief to farmers and reprisal for out-of-state exploiters. League members met in precincts to elect delegates to county league conventions, where legislative candidates were endorsed. The county conventions elected delegates to a state league convention, where state and congressional candidates were endorsed. The endorsees were free to file their nominating petitions in whichever party primary they wished, but most knew the political bent of the electorate and filed in the Republican primary, where success was likely and they felt more comfortable.

The filing of legislative, state, and congressional slates by the Nonpartisan League in 1916 launched a forty-year factional fight in the Republican Party between "establishment" Republicans, as represented by the McKenzie machine, and the NPL-structured opposition faction. The Nonpartisan League swept the 1916 and 1918 elections and controlled both houses of the legislature and the statewide elective offices by 1919. They attempted to remedy the economic ills of the farmers by creating a Bank of North Dakota to compete with private banks and a State Mill and Elevator to compete with the Minneapolis grain trade. But these political solutions were not equal to the dimensions of the problem, and disaffection and internal disagreements soon undercut the ardor of the movement. As ideological commitment to economic and social reform waned, personalities moved to the fore. Consequently, the factional fight within the Republican Party from the mid-1920s to the mid-1950s became highly personalized, with philosophical differences relatively insignificant.

Following World War II, the younger activists in the Nonpartisan League became restless as they observed the meaninglessness of the Republican Party's personality contests. At the same time, the liberal North Dakota Farmers Union, the state's largest farm organization, engaged in extensive membership-building activities. The younger league "insurgents" and the leadership of the Farmers Union arrived at a common conclusion: the North Dakota political system would become meaningful only if the Nonpartisan League filed its candidates in the Democratic primary and merged with the Democrats. Seeing the opportunity to eliminate the league, the regular Republicans made overtures to the conservatives in the league, while the insurgents and Farmers Union tugged the league to the left. The struggle concluded in 1956 when the league's conservative old guard surrendered the organization to the insurgents and the NPL convention filed its slate in the Democratic primary. Instead of fielding a competing slate, the regular Democrats endorsed the league ticket and a two-party political system in North Dakota was born (Omdahl 1961).

Though the NPL-Democratic candidates were washed overboard in the Eisenhower hurricane of 1956, the new coalition successfully elected Quentin Burdick to the U.S. House in 1958 and to the U.S. Senate in 1960. Also in 1960, Bill Guy was elected governor to begin a twenty-year era of Democratic-Nonpartisan League control of the statehouse. Even though the Democratic-Nonpartisan League had major successes in winning congressional and statewide offices, Republicans held tenaciously to control of the state legislature. Democrats have never controlled both houses simultaneously and since statehood have had a majority for only two sessions of the house (1965 and 1983) and four sessions of the senate (1985, 1987, 1989, 1991).

## ORGANIZATIONAL DEVELOPMENT

Distinctive characteristics of the party system in North Dakota can be traced to the state's political culture, which emphasizes egalitarianism and nonpartisanship. Egalitarianism was accentuated early in North Dakota by the large number of small farms and businesses that fostered individualism. Many North Dakotans, faced with the adversities of a continental climate, the challenges of frontier farming, and the isolation of distance, were forced to become strong-spirited individualists. To protect and preserve their accentuated individualism, North Dakotans nurtured a political system that facilitated the equality of all voices in public affairs.

Since partisan politics suggested a hierarchical system of power that threatened equality, and since settlers had limited partisan commitment anyway, nonpartisanship seemed to serve best the equality of influence and to prevent the artificial barrier of parties from diminishing equal opportunity. The strong current of nonpartisanship permeating the structure and process of North Dakota politics has dramatically curbed the role of parties and partisan politics in the state.

Although the open caucuses of precinct organizations invite broad participation at the grassroots level, the legislative district organization appears to be the foundation for parties in North Dakota. Even though the number of precincts has been drastically reduced over the past thirty years, both parties still have had difficulty recruiting active precinct leaders. Three-fourths of district chairs feel that less than half of their precincts have active, motivated leaders.[1]

The duties of precinct committeepersons have changed significantly over the past thirty years due to new technology and methodology that require professional skills and disciplined procedure. Thirty years ago the precinct leaders organized door-to-door voter identification programs and then managed the get-out-the-vote campaigns on election day. These duties have been taken over by district and state party organizations. Although precinct officials may be involved in the distribution of literature, more likely than not the district organization will now hire a crew or organize volunteers to make a door-to-door "drop" systematically within a span of a few hours to guarantee that the district is quickly and uniformly blanketed.

The declining reliability of precinct organizations has shifted almost all responsibility for political activity to the district level. And since the parties are organized around the legislative races, recruiting and electing legislative candidates tend to be the preoccupations at this level. The district committees or executive committees meet regularly—at least quarterly.

Recruiting candidates is not simple, because holding a seat in the state legislature does not have broad appeal to North Dakotans. The small legislative districts, each with around

12,600 residents, make campaigning manageable, but the rewards for winning are not great. Legislators are paid $90 in salary per legislative day for the seventy-odd days in session and receive $600 per month for lodging during the session. No allowance is provided for meals. Between sessions, legislators are paid $180 per month for miscellaneous expenses and, more important, receive coverage under the state medical insurance program. Because of the disruption in regular occupation for minimal compensation, many potential candidates excluded themselves from the process. Not only are the parties challenged to find candidates to run against incumbents, but they must constantly encourage their own sitting legislators to stay in the game. In the seven biennial legislative elections between 1982 and 1994, 897 legislative seats were up for election. Parties were successful in recruiting candidates for 825 seats, leaving 72 (8 percent) uncontested.

Once the candidates are recruited and endorsed by the district conventions, they are almost assured of nomination in the primary since contested primaries for legislative seats in North Dakota are rare. Of the 1,091 opportunities for primary challenges in the legislative races in the seven elections 1982–1994, only 49 challenges occurred—or 4.5 percent. Both parties experienced approximately the same number of challenges.

More than two-thirds of the district organizations help their endorsed candidates by raising money, buying advertising, and organizing mass mailings. Districts assume varying degrees of responsibility for funding campaigns, with more than half of the districts expecting candidates to raise a majority of their campaign funds. Republican district organizations have been much more supportive than Democratic organizations in terms of fund raising.

As technology and techniques have improved through the years, state and national parties have assumed greater responsibility for legislative campaigns. Development and identification of legislative issues have continued to be important state party functions, but the state parties now also assist with recruiting candidates (with a call from the governor, for example), direct mail by providing master mailing lists, advertising and literature design, polling, technical assistance, and even cash.

The extent of national participation in North Dakota legislative campaigns is undocumented and undetermined, known only to a select few in each party involved in campaign management and strategy. North Dakota's historic sensitivity to out-of-state influences makes national intervention in campaigns a political liability.

At the state level, the parties support the congressional and state ticket endorsees. Recruitment of congressional candidates is relatively easy because of the attractiveness of the offices. When it comes to campaigning, congressional candidates are not willing to entrust their elections to the ad hoc campaign crews thrown together by the party for a four-month stint at the hustings. Even though the congressional candidates want and use their own campaign staffs, they cooperate extensively with the state party headquarters in campaign coordination, issue development, and pooling resources. The North Dakota political tradition is working together.

Recruiting and electing candidates for statewide office is another matter. North Dakota places a significant recruiting and funding burden on its political system by electing eight state administrators plus three public service commissioners. Elected as a team, the governor and lieutenant governor command sufficient prestige to campaign and raise funds on their own. Even so, they require more party support than the congressional candidates, who are funded mainly from Washington, D.C., sources unless they are challengers. As for the other statewide candidates, those exercising authority affecting economic interests, such as the public service commissioners, will garner contributions, whereas others, such as the secretary of state and the state auditor, will be forced to rely on limited financial support from the state party, their friends, and their own resources.

Government employees are not a source of campaign funds in North Dakota. Even though very few employees are protected by the formal "merit" system, in practice political patronage is limited and the state's nonpartisan ethic dictates that public employees—covered or not—minimize political involvement.

A convention endorsement at the state level practically assures nomination in the ensuing primary. In the thirteen primary elections during the period 1970–1994 for all state executives, from governor to tax commissioner, 172 opportunities for primary competition drew only twenty-five challenges (14.5 percent), only five of which were successful.

## CURRENT PARTY ORGANIZATION

From a structural point of view, the nonpartisan election of county officials probably has had the most dramatic impact on the strength and importance of parties in North Dakota. Nonpartisan election of county officials has also meant nonpartisan conduct of campaigns for county offices, with candidates mobilizing their own resources and organizations for the elections. Political parties, respecting the deep nonpartisan commitment of North Dakotans, do not become involved in county elections. Because of their exclusion from county politics, parties in North Dakota do not benefit from courthouse patronage and participation in the political process. Because of this lack of a foundation, North Dakota parties are relatively anemic.

The first level of partisan electoral activity is the legislative district. Prior to the reapportionment revolution wrought by the U.S. Supreme Court's one-person, one-vote decisions of the 1960s, North Dakota parties had been organized at the county level, since state house and senate seats were assigned to counties or groups of counties. But reapportionment forced the state to disregard county boundaries. Soon the parties realized that county organizations were awkward for legislative races, so they induced the legislature to abolish county party organizations and to create more relevant legislative district organizations. The transfer was simplified by the state's use of the same districts for the election of both senators and representatives, with each district electing a senator and two house members at large.

The spirit of nonpartisanship permeates other areas of the political system. In the legislative process, in only 10–15 percent of votes does a majority of Democrats oppose a majority of Republicans. Parties caucus not so much to commit members to binding votes as to exchange information on legislation, identify leadership roles, and manage the legislative process. In the executive branch, governors strive to maintain an image of nonpartisanship in appointments by limiting patronage and touting the professional credentials of appointees. In the judicial branch, all judges are elected on the nonpartisan ballot, and the filling of vacancies by the governor is designed to neutralize partisanship.

State law governs the party organizational process, which is consummated in nonelection years to insulate it from the vagaries of election-year politics. To facilitate participation, the first level of party organization is the precinct. Precincts are mapped out by the nonpartisan city and county governing boards with the sole objective of facilitating the voting process. Rural precincts encompass several sparsely populated political subdivisions, and urban precincts consist of city blocks. With shifting population and increased election costs, the governing boards have been reducing the number of precincts. In 1960 the state had 2,300 precincts; by the mid-1990s, their number had been reduced to 740. As precincts have been abolished, so have precinct party organizations, leading to a substantial decrease in the number of precinct offices to attract interest and activity on the part of political activists. In a 1995 survey, two-thirds of the legislative district chairpersons responding felt precinct consolidation had not impaired party organization, whereas the remaining one-third felt it had weakened political parties.

After the caucus, participants elect a chairperson, they then elect for a two-year term at least one committeeperson for every 250 votes cast in the precinct for the party's candidate for president in the last election. Following the caucus, the chairperson reports the outcome of the committeeperson elections to the county auditor, who serves as the principal county elections officer in North Dakota. If a precinct fails to organize, the legislative district executive committee is empowered to make appointments.

The nonpartisan bent of the electorate has resulted in low participation in precinct organizations. When the state had 2,300 precincts, many of the precinct committee positions were vacant or filled by reluctant citizens who were drafted with the promise that they would not have any duties to perform. Even in the 1990s, with only one-third as many precincts, participation in caucuses mirrored the national trend of political disassociation by the electorate. Ninety percent of the district party chairpersons rated participation as "poor" or "very poor."

The next level of party organization, the legislative district, is reconstituted biennially within fifteen days of the precinct caucuses. Election of district officers is accomplished by the district committee, consisting of all precinct committeepersons, nominees for and members of the legislative delegation, the officers, and former members of the legislature as determined by the district committee.

At the district organizational meeting, the committee elects a slate of officers, none of whom necessarily need be precinct committeepersons; it also fills vacant precinct committee posts and chooses an executive committee of five to eighteen members. The county auditor is notified of precinct committeeperson appointments and officer elections.

According to state law, the state committee consists of the legislative district chairpersons, the two national committeepersons, and any additional persons specified by the party's bylaws. Both parties include their state party officers. Republicans have added as ex officio members the state finance chair, all Republican congressional officeholders, floor leaders of the state senate and house, elected state officeholders, the past chairperson, president of the Federation of Republican Women, chair of the Young Republicans, and chair of the College Republicans. Both state committees are charged in their respective party bylaws to conduct party business, with the Republican committee having the special authority to decide whether or not the state chair will be a full-time position.

The two party executive committees are remarkably similar. Both include the party officers, the national committeepersons, legislative floor leaders, four district chairs, and a representative of the party's elected state officials. The Republicans also include the president of the Federation of Republican Women.

The Democratic-Nonpartisan League (recognized in law only as the Democratic Party) has created an extra-legal state "policy" committee that includes all of the members of the state committee plus one additional person from each legislative district of the opposite sex of the legislative district chair, all Democratic elected state officeholders, the chair of the Young Democrats Association, and (ex officio, without a vote) all Democratic-NPL members of the state legislature and the executive director of the party. The policy committee has two significant powers: to appoint the full-time executive director of the party and to confirm the state chairperson's committee appointments.

For most of their recent history, the Republicans have opted for a full-time state chairperson, who serves as the chief executive officer of the state headquarters staff. Democrats have maintained a separation of the roles of chair and executive director.

The cultural attribute of egalitarianism constrains parties from exercising authority from the top down. Except for several full-time staffers in state offices, the parties rely on volunteers between elections. None of the legislative districts maintain offices or staff on a year-around basis. In a number of districts—mostly urban—office managers may be hired for several months during a campaign.

To finance the ongoing operations of their state headquarters, both parties look to the districts for half of their expenses by setting goals or quotas for districts. Republicans set goals on the basis of voting records in districts; Democrats ask districts to tap a certain minimum number of "Century Club" ($100) contributors. The remaining half of the headquarters' expense is met by direct solicitations and special donors. In the 1960s district quotas were much more significant in funding state operations.

State party chairs are chosen at open meetings by the district representatives with little, if any, manipulation or subterfuge. There are no wires leading to smoke-filled back rooms or external power structures dictating choices. Candidates for the state chair may be "run past" the governor for approval, but governors do not attempt to dictate choices of officers.

Since North Dakota is a small state in which political activists are familiar with one another, informal communications and personal contact are often used to develop consensus on party policies. Consequently, the processes of communication are not visible or recorded until motions are made at state committee meetings. Nevertheless, formal discussion at state meetings is kept open, and everybody who wants to be heard is given an opportunity to speak. That is symptomatic of North Dakota's egalitarianism, meaning that process is often more important than substance.

The Democrats are more decentralized than the Republicans. Whereas Republicans work with one state committee, the Democrats have two—the official state committee specified by state law and the state "policy" committee, potentially numbering from 150 to 200 members. The Democratic state chairperson serves on a volunteer basis, reserving party funds for an appointed, full-time executive director. The state Republican Party is more centralized, with a full-time state chairperson who has more authority, resources, and clout to make decisions than the Democratic counterpart. Even so, the party imposes restraints on the chair. According to Kevin Cramer, a recent Republican chairperson, "[as] long as things are going OK, the chairman has a lot of freedom. However, the state executive committee keeps close tabs on the operation." In defense of the Democratic Party's volunteer chair position, longtime Democratic chairperson George Gaukler felt that the volunteer nature of the position made it possible for a larger number of people to be available for the position.

By the mid-1990s, neither party had had a woman as state chairperson, although the number of women district chairpersons had been constantly increasing through the years. Around one-third of the district chairs in both parties were women in 1995.

Both parties have experienced the stress of accommodating conflicting ideologies. For the Republicans, the right-wing John Birch Society was disruptive in the 1960s. By the mid-1990s the religious right had not developed a track record in party politics upon which to determine the stress it may create. For the Democrats, the Vietnam War and the subsequent party reforms dominated by liberals strained relations, but identifiable factions never emerged. Neither party has experienced formal internal factions or caucuses similar to the Nonpartisan League that raised havoc for forty years in the Republican Party.

In true nonpartisan tradition, the political parties play a very limited role in government. Once elected, legislators and state officeholders become more accountable to the public than to the party, sometimes to the chagrin of party activists and ideologues. Even the party platforms adopted by the state endorsing conventions have little impact on government policy formulation. Through the years, as candidate-centered campaigns have emerged, the platforms have become shorter and more vague. As Kevin Cramer stated, "[o]fficials are more independent because voters are more independent. The parties provide the mechanism for election but offer less philosophical discipline."

Parties tend to relate informally to officeholders as support organizations, offering assistance that would help officeholders accrue electoral benefits. From time to time, a party official may attend a legislative caucus or gubernatorial press conference, not to issue mandates but to demonstrate interest and offer moral support.

As for the future of political parties in North Dakota, three-fourths of district chairpersons responding to a 1995 survey predicted that parties would be "weaker" or "the same" in twenty years. One chairperson who responded "the same" observed that they could not get any weaker.

## RESOURCE GUIDE

For a number of reasons, neither political party has a neatly organized collection of records suggested by the word "archives." First, party employees and officers have been relatively transitory, resulting in limited continuity or interest in record preservation. Second, political operatives focus their efforts primarily on current campaign and organization activities, leaving old records unused and unappreciated. Finally, both parties have been understaffed, thereby limiting the time available to integrate and rationalize records.

Because records are not neatly cataloged, researchers will require assistance in locating particular records. Advance notice of visits and interests will be required so that party personnel can locate the information requested. Most party records will be accessible, but availability will be contingent on the political operative responsible for the records at the time, the political sensitivity of the information, and the time of the request in the campaign cycle.

For the period 1980 to the present, both parties have the names of state committee members, contributors, delegates and alternates to state and national conventions, convention committee members, legislative candidates, and state candidates. They also have retained copies of correspondence with legislative candidates, state officials, state and national candidates, the national party, and legislative district party officials.

Democrats have records of income sources and expenditures back to 1980, but Republicans have such records only to 1990 due to a computer malfunction.

Both parties have minutes of state committee meetings, state conventions, and convention committees. They also have copies of party platforms, files on state convention arrangements, and collections of printed campaign materials. Some radio and television commercials have been saved.

In addition, Republicans have biographies of legislative candidates, records of state aid to legislative districts, campaign schedules of candidates, and files on get-out-the-vote efforts.

**Table 1**  North Dakota Resource Guide

|  | Democrats | Republicans |
|---|---|---|
| Archive | Yes | Yes |
| Location | 1902 East Divide | 409 W. Front St. |
|  | Bismark, ND 58501 | Bismark, ND 58504 |
|  | (701) 255-0460 | (701) 255-0030 |
| Dates | 1980– | 1980– |
| Finding aid | Yes | Yes |
| Access | By appointment | By appointment |
| Contents: |  |  |
|   Executive committee minutes | Yes | Yes |
|   Correspondence | Yes | Yes |
|   Organizational structure | Yes | Yes |
|   Budgets | Yes | Yes[1] |
|   Rules | Yes | Yes |

[1] The Republican state headquarters experienced a computer failure and lost financial records prior to 1990.

Since gubernatorial and congressional candidates organize their own files, many of their records are not captured by party headquarters. Parties have copies of party-sponsored polls but not of polls sponsored by candidate organizations.

Parties may have additional random information, some of it predating 1980. Specific inquiry will be necessary to identify this material.

### NOTE

1. Because published research on political parties is sketchy in North Dakota, the author surveyed the 102 Republican and Democratic chairpersons (or cochairpersons) in the state's 49 legislative districts. Responding were 29 of 53 Democrats and 24 of 49 Republicans.

### REFERENCES

*Asterisks denote the most important publications on North Dakota party politics.*

Baglien, David B. 1955. The McKenzie era: A political history of North Dakota from 1880 to 1920. M.A. thesis, North Dakota State University, Fargo.

Blackorby, E. C. 1938. Political factional strife in North Dakota 1920–1932. M.A. thesis, University of North Dakota, Grand Forks.

Bruce, Andrew A. 1921. *Non-Partisan League.* New York: Macmillan.

Brudvig, Glen Lowell. 1956. The Farmers Alliance and the Populist movement in North Dakota. M.A. thesis, University of North Dakota, Grand Forks.

Bureau of Governmental Affairs. 1985. A survey of public attitudes toward government in North Dakota. Special report no. 98 (February). Bureau of Governmental Affairs, University of North Dakota.

———. 1984. Survey on attitudes toward the state government. Special report no. 92 (February). Bureau of Governmental Affairs, University of North Dakota.

Dreyer, Larry. 1974. Legislator and lobbyist views of improper lobbying in North Dakota. Special report no. 40 (January). Bureau of Governmental Affairs, University of North Dakota.

Drugan, Wayne Jr. 1970. Roll call voting in the 1969 North Dakota Senate. Special report no. 15 (April). Bureau of Governmental Affairs, University of North Dakota.

Fuglesten, Harlan. 1981. Legislative reapportionment in North Dakota: From statehood to the present. Special report no. 62a (October). Bureau of Governmental Affairs, University of North Dakota.

———. 1971. Patterns of party voting in the 1971 North Dakota House of Representatives. Special report no. 26 (August). Bureau of Governmental Affairs, University of North Dakota.

Gaston, Herber. 1920. *The Nonpartisan League.* New York: Harcourt, Brace and Howe.

Goldberg, Ray. 1955. *The Nonpartisan League in North Dakota.* Fargo: Midwest Printing. (Unpublished update with Charles Press in 1962 in Chester Fritz Library, University of North Dakota, Grand Forks.)

Gust, Phillip. 1970. Survey of attitudes of party chairmen and mayors on partisan election of municipal officials. Special report no. 16 (April). Bureau of Governmental Affairs, University of North Dakota.

Harmeson, Phil. 1991. The 1988 election in North Dakota. Special report no. 164 (May). Bureau of Governmental Affairs, University of North Dakota.

———. 1987. The 1986 election in North Dakota. Special report no. 80 (June). Bureau of Governmental Affairs, University of North Dakota.

———. 1985. The 1984 election in North Dakota. Special report no. 76 (July). Bureau of Governmental Affairs, University of North Dakota.

*Howard, Thomas W., ed. 1981. *North Dakota political tradition.* Ames: Iowa State University Press. (This is a collection of seven articles, each covering a significant era of North Dakota political history.)

Kweit, Robert, Mary Kweit, and Ronald Pynn. 1982. North Dakota party activists and participation in the 1980 elections. Special report no. 67 (September). Bureau of Governmental Affairs, University of North Dakota.

Lamar, Howard Roberts. 1956. *Dakota Territory 1861–1889.* New Haven, Conn.: Yale University Press.

Lounsberry, Clement C. 1917. *History of North Dakota.* Chicago: S.J. Clarke.

Martens, Sharon Wilson. 1972. Turnover in the North Dakota state legislative assembly 1965–1971. Special report no. 31 (July). Bureau of Governmental Affairs, University of North Dakota.

*Morlan, Robert L. 1955. *Political prairie fire: The Nonpartisan League 1915–1921.* St. Paul: Minnesota Historical Society Press.

Myhre, Russell J. n.d. *How to change laws: a guide to lobbying in North Dakota.* Bismarck: United Transportation Union.

Olsen, Morgan. 1982. A study of North Dakota legislator attitudes toward lobbying and lobbying groups. Special report no. 66 (May). Bureau of Governmental Affairs, University of North Dakota.

Omdahl, Lloyd B. 1995 *Governing North Dakota 1995–97.* Grand Forks: University of North Dakota, Bureau of Governmental Affairs.

———. 1983. The 1982 election in North Dakota. Special report no. 72 (April). Bureau of Governmental Affairs, University of North Dakota.

———. 1981. The 1980 election in North Dakota. Special report no. 59 (February). Bureau of Governmental Affairs, University of North Dakota.

———. 1961. *Insurgents.* Brainerd, Minn.: Lakeland Color Press.

Omdahl, Lloyd B., et al., eds. 1993. *North Dakota votes.* Grand Forks: University of North Dakota, Bureau of Governmental Affairs.

Pedeliski, Theodore B. 1987. Interest groups in North Dakota: Constituency coupling in a moralistic political culture. Special report no. 79 (April). Bureau of Governmental Affairs, University of North Dakota.

Pynn, Ronald, Robert Kweit, and Mary Kweit. 1981. North Dakota political activists: A study of delegates to the 1980 Democratic and Republican state conventions. Special report no. 60 (March). Bureau of Governmental Affairs, University of North Dakota.

Rathke, Ann M. 1992. *Lady, if you go into politics.* Bismarck: Sweetgrass Communications.

*Robinson, Elwyn B. 1966. *History of North Dakota.* Lincoln: University of Nebraska Press.

Russell, Charles Edward. 1920. *The Non-Partisan League.* New York: Harper and Brothers.

Secretary of State. n.d. *North Dakota centennial blue book.* Bismarck: State of North Dakota.

Talbot, Ross B. 1957. North Dakota—A two-party state? *North Dakota Quarterly* 25 (fall).

Thompson, Larry. 1971. The role of the state and federal committee in North Dakota's legislative process. Special report no. 27 (September). Bureau of Governmental Affairs, University of North Dakota.

Tweton, D. Jerome, and Theodore B. Jelliff. 1976. *North Dakota.* Fargo: North Dakota Institute for Regional Studies.

Wilkins, Robert P., and Wynona Wilkins. 1977. *North Dakota: A bicentennial history.* New York: W.W. Norton.

Wright, Boyd L. 1970. Sources of legislation in the legislative assembly of North Dakota. Special report no. 20 (October). Bureau of Governmental Affairs, University of North Dakota.

Young, Allan. 1987. Changing North Dakota's primary election date 1960–1984: A partisan struggle. Special report no. 78 (March). Bureau of Governmental Affairs, University of North Dakota.

# *Ohio*

JOHN C. GREEN AND DANIEL M. SHEA

## PARTY HISTORY

Ohio is commonly described as "The Heart of It All," and this label aptly fits Buckeye State political parties. Since their founding, the Ohio Republican and Democratic Parties have closely approximated the textbook description of traditional party organizations: autonomous, hierarchical institutions maintained largely by material incentives, dedicated to nominating candidates for most public offices and securing their election (Mayhew 1986, 19–20). The Ohio party organizations have changed in tandem with the economic and political trends of the last century, so that at any one time, an observer would be hard pressed to find a better model of party organizations elsewhere in the nation.

Since the Civil War, Ohio Republicans have had one of the strongest state committees in the country, drawing on white, Anglo-Saxon Protestant farmers and the business community and buttressed by parallel county committees in rural areas and the cities of the central and southern parts of the state. The party's organizational strength helps explain why Ohio holds the record for Republican presidential nominees (and for presidents of either party). The Ohio Democratic Party, never as cohesive at the state level, has had considerable power at the local level, particularly since the New Deal. Classic city "machines" characterized the northern industrial cities such as Cleveland, Toledo, and Youngstown, where large ethnic communities and strong labor unions gave the Ohio Democrats great influence in state and national politics. The balance between the two organizations has helped place the Ohio party system among the most competitive in the country.

## ORGANIZATIONAL DEVELOPMENT

The development of Ohio parties since 1960 is characterized by three factors: continuity of the traditional forms of organization in each party, including an inverse relationship between officeholding and party strength; the decline in vitality of traditional organizations, particularly at the local level; and organizational renewal at the state level.

The pattern of Ohio party organizations in the 1990s is remarkably like that of the 1960s: a strong, sophisticated state Republican organization with ties to relatively strong local organizations in GOP areas faces a weak and disorganized state Democratic committee buoyed by relatively strong local organizations in Democratic areas. The Ohio GOP in the early 1960s was the product of Ray C. Bliss, the legendary "nuts-and-bolts" party leader from 1949 to 1965. The "Bliss model" was based on regular assistance to, and consensus building among, the county committees, candidate organizations, and business groups. This model is followed to a considerable degree by Republican chair Robert Bennett in the 1990s. In contrast, the Ohio Democrats in the early 1960s were a confederation of local parties, unions, and candidate fiefdoms, with little centralized organization except for strong personalities. The Democrats of the 1990s show much the same pattern.

The rise of candidate-centered politics and other factors—including the decline of patronage, the proliferation of interest groups, the expansion of the mass media, and the growth of the suburbs at the expense of both rural and urban populations—were hard on Ohio parties starting in the late 1960s, but there were few organizational responses until twenty years later. Two extremely popular officeholders dominated state politics during this era, to the detriment of the party organizations: Republican James Rhodes, governor for sixteen years (1963–1971 and 1975–1983), and Democrat Vernal Riffe, speaker of the General Assembly for twenty years (1975–1994). The Bliss-style Republican organization atrophied in the 1970s, during the last two Rhodes administrations, while Democratic decentralization was encouraged by the potent personal organization of Speaker Riffe. All of the foregoing factors contributed to the decline of traditional parties, while at the state level, the development of legislative campaign committees, the end of party registration, and the institution of semiopen primaries further contributed to party weakness. These changes were part of the broader national reform efforts arising first among Democratic activists and then spreading among elected officials of both parties.

The major Ohio parties did not, however, wither away. Partly due to favorable state party laws and partly due to the competitive nature of statewide and presidential elections, party organizations never completely faded from the scene. In response to their changed circumstances, the state committees began a process of party renewal in the late 1970s not unlike that which took place at the national level. The key to their renewal was providing services to candidates and developing the organizational capacity to do so.

Both state committees, as well as several of the larger county organizations, hired full-time paid staffs to provide media production support, polls, computer time, issue research, and other valuable services to their candidates. Moreover, they began to use extensive direct-mail fund raising and developed sophisticated voter registration and get-out-the-vote programs.

The Democrats made major gains in this direction under the state chairs James Ruvolo (1983–1990) and Eugene Branstool (1991–1993), who specialized in knitting together candidate organizations and local party fiefdoms to mount voter registration drives, get-out-the-vote drives, and advertising campaigns. These services were paid for by aggressive fund raising; the lack of any limits on campaign contributions allowed Speaker Riffe, the Ohio AFL-CIO, and other major organizations to make large donations to the Democratic Party.

The Republicans followed suit, building on the legacy of Ray Bliss, first under the leadership of James Tilling, secretary to the Ohio Senate (1984–1994), and then under State Chair Robert Bennett (1988–). The Ohio GOP strengthened its ties to the local committees, provided candidates with extensive in-kind contributions, and built a sophisticated headquarters organization, complete with computer technology and a competent staff. These efforts also required aggressive fund raising, and the party tapped industrialists for large donations and turned to direct mail for soliciting small donations.

Another important source of party renewal was the adoption of public financing of the party system. Since 1987 tax filers have been able to direct one dollar of their taxes to a fund that is divided among the state and county party committees. The two state committees each receive one-quarter of the funds, and the rest is spread among the counties in proportion to the fund donations that came from their county. The pool is usually about $1 million annually. In 1992 each state committee received $246,790, and the county shares ranged from $40,000 for Cuyahoga to $132 for Vinton.

Other important factors contributing to the position of parties in Ohio are their abilities to endorse candidates during primary elections and to fill legislative, county, and municipal offices when vacancies occur between elections. The number of endorsements at the county level varies widely. Some central committees, including the Cuyahoga Democratic and the Hamilton Republican committees, rarely issue formal endorsements in seriously contested primaries. Others use their power more aggressively and work hard to back up their endorsements with such support as slate mailers, financing, the use of the party's bulk-mail permit, and access to poll books. As for filling vacancies, party caucuses in the General Assembly choose replacements for vacant seats, and county central committees are empowered by state law to perform the same duty when a county or municipal post falls open. In short, Ohio's political parties have long cultivated and maintained power through grooming candidates and filling vacancies.

As for nonlegal sources of power, the provision of patronage jobs to deserving party supporters has been a trump card for county chairs. Even governors routinely defer to county chairs when dispensing state jobs and favors. Although the gradual implementation of merit-based hiring and promotion policies and the formation of public sector unions have certainly reduced the weight of this activity, it remains a common practice in the 1990s.

Although party renewal has thus far been more successful for the Republicans, both state party committees have found ways to stay competitive in a candidate-centered environment.

## CURRENT PARTY ORGANIZATION

As noted above, parties in Ohio approximate the textbook description of traditional party organizations. At the apex of the parties are the state and county committee chairs. Those seeking to discern the power structure in Ohio party politics should look first to these individuals.

Another key to understanding the weight of parties in the Buckeye State is the massive import of election law. Political parties in Ohio are heavily regulated by state law, and although the myriad rules and regulations may seem onerous—limiting much of what the parties can and cannot do—most of the laws help to preserve their duopoly of partisan power. The laws also ensure the position of state and county party committees and, of course, their chairs.

Ohio law prescribes the general organizational structure and procedures to which officially recognized parties must conform. Primary voters select their party's county central committee, which consists either of one member from each precinct or one member from each city ward and county township. Law also mandates the selection of a county executive committee, to which the central committee may delegate as much of its power as it sees fit. In practice, the executive committee assumes most real authority for party matters at the county level, with the county chair appointing and heading that body.

Primary voters also elect one man and one woman per congressional district to the state central committee for four-year terms. As with the county central committee, the state committee relinquishes most of its power to a smaller executive committee, appointed and led by the chair of the state committee. The state convention, which is held in even-numbered years, drafts a party platform and nominates presidential electors. Most of the delegates to the state convention are chosen by the county executive committees, and the remainder are included by virtue of the offices they hold. These include county central committee and executive committee chairs; state central and executive committee members; nominees for statewide, legislative, and congressional offices; and state and federal incumbents not up for election.

Each county committee is guaranteed by statute two paid members to the county board of elections, which, in turn, hires a permanent staff to register voters, maintain registration records, and establish and staff polling places. In a like manner, the law grants the two major parties formal representation on the Ohio Elections Commission — four of its five members are appointed by the state party chairs. The commission has legal authority to investigate sworn allegations of election law violations, particularly those dealing with campaign finance.

In addition to the organizations stipulated by law, numerous party auxiliaries exist. The most important are the senate and house legislative campaign committees. These bodies often work with the state committee, but generally they raise their own funds and spend them as they see fit. Their tendency to "go it alone" occasionally causes conflict between local party leaders, who wish to have their candidates supported, and the caucus leaders, who desire to fund only candidates in competitive races. Revisions in the state campaign finance laws may presage a closer relationship because the state party chairs will serve as members of the legislative caucus leadership committees. The state and county parties may also be closely associated with women's federations or youth, college, or high school organizations. Democrats have historically worked closely with labor and consumer groups, and the Republicans have had strong ties to business and manufacturing interests.

The relationship between the state party committees and the county committees might best be described as reciprocal deference. Each unit generally conducts its own activities—particularly those within its electoral sphere. There are few "commands" from the state level down to the base of the organization. Indeed, there is a long tradition in Ohio of aggressive, individualistic county party leaders. At the same time, however, each level of the party organization is aware of its place in the overall structure, and there are a number of formal and informal ties between them. Interaction between layers tends to be complementary; assistance flows in both directions.

The principal impetus for bringing the different party strata together is election activities. Various layers of the party will often work together on the same election or general activity. For example, a city committee may work with a county committee on a congressional race, or a county organization may help the state committee get out the vote.

As for the relationship between the state parties in Ohio and the national party committees, much the same can be said. Because Ohio is relatively large and competitive, the national committees are inclined to heed the wishes of state chairs. In 1992, for example, Ohio was deemed by both the DNC and the RNC to be an important swing state, thereby leading to extensive joint efforts by the national and state committees. One might go so far as to suggest that when the Ohio state party chairs come knocking, the national committees respond. To be sure, the Buckeye State gets more than its share of visits from party dignitaries and elected officials.

Finally, there exists in Ohio a high level of interaction between party and elected officials. Historically, this was due in large part to the pool of patronage slots afforded party leaders, but today it may have more to do with the campaign resources and services available from the parties. In any event, party leaders continue to have access to elected officials and may even have some, albeit limited, influence in policy decisions. Conversely, elected officials look to party leaders for advice and assistance. However, there frequently is tension between elected officials and party leaders, often to the detriment of the party organization.

### RESOURCE GUIDE

Because both state party committees in Ohio are aptly described as "professional," it is surprising that neither party has done a good job preserving party documents.

Democratic records are stored at the state committee headquarters. They consist mainly of finance information since 1983 stored on computer disk, and hard copy of executive committee minutes—also since 1983. There is some additional hard-copy material on state and national committee delegates, correspondence with the state chairs, and some notes on rule changes. Some information on party activity and issues pertaining to organizational structure may be found in the executive committee minutes. For the most part, however, it seems that as the committee made the shift from hard copy to computer records during the early 1980s, much of the information was discarded. There is no systematic effort today to archive information other than that dealing with finances.

The Democratic Party compiles its finance information on a database management system. As such, a good bit of searching can be done using the party's predetermined codes. A researcher interested in how and where the party has spent its money over the last twelve years, for example, would find this data set quite helpful. All of the hard-copy material is located in a haphazard fashion in a storage closet off of the main reception area of the headquarters. Party officials were helpful and anxious to open up records for nonpartisan-based research. But researchers should be prepared to take notes, as it is doubtful that party officials would allow computer printouts or photocopies to leave the headquarters.

Unfortunately, the Ohio Republicans have done only a modestly better job with their records. All of their material is located at the state committee headquarters. The records consist mostly of executive committee meeting minutes since 1975. Although the minutes contain some information on budgets, rule changes, party activity, and delegates to conventions, the information, like that of the Democrats, is sporadic. Moreover, there is little record of correspondence between party leaders. All of the Republican material is stored in hard copy. It is not cataloged and is located in filing cabinets in the basement of the headquarters or in the chair's office.

On a somewhat brighter side, the Republicans do have a collection of newspaper clips for the past few years and bound copies of an older weekly publication, *The Ohio Republican News,* which was published from the early 1950s to the early 1970s. A good bit of information on party activities, endorsements, and leaders can be found in here. The weekly is bound chronologically in spiral-bound notebooks. Although party officials seem helpful in aiding research efforts, the hard part of working with this information is sorting through the maze of papers. As with the Democrats, it seems doubtful the Republicans will allow extensive photocopying.

Perhaps the best place to begin a research project on Ohio parties would be the Ohio Historical Society, located at 1982 Velma Avenue, Columbus, Ohio 43211-2497. A partial list of the information stored at the society includes biographic material on nearly every prominent party leader and politician in Ohio history, including extensive information on

**Table 1**   Ohio Resource Guide

|  | Democrats | Republicans |
|---|---|---|
| Archive | Yes | Yes |
| Location | Party Headquarters | Party Headquarters |
|  | 37 W. Broad St. | 172 E. State St. |
|  | Columbus, OH 43215 | Columbus, OH 43215 |
|  | (614) 221-6563 | (614) 228-2481 |
| Dates | 1983–present | 1974–present |
| Finding aid | Computer codes | No |
| Access | By appointment | By appointment |
| Contents: |  |  |
| Executive committee minutes | Yes | Yes |
| Correspondence | Limited | No |
| Organizational structure | Limited | Limited |
| Budgets | Yes | Limited |
| Rules | Limited | Limited |

Ray C. Bliss; a massive set of correspondence among party leaders and between party leaders and politicians; speeches and public addresses from party dignitaries; some records of party activity; and information on the activities of groups associated with the parties.

## REFERENCES

*Asterisks denote the most important publications on Ohio party politics.*
*Fenton, John. 1966. *Midwest politics.* New York: Holt, Rhinehart, and Winston.
Flinn, Thomas, and Fredrick Wirt. 1965. Local party leaders: Groups of like-minded men. *Midwest Journal of Political Science* 9:77–98.
Green, John C., ed. 1994. *Politics, professionalism, and power: Modern party organization and the legacy of Ray C. Bliss.* Lanham, Md.: University Press of America.
*Lamis, Alexander P., and Mary Anne Sharkey, eds. 1994. *Ohio politics.* Kent, Ohio: Kent State University Press.
*Lieberman, Carl, ed. 1984. *Government and politics in Ohio.* Lanham, Md.: University Press of America.
Mayhew, David R. 1986. *Placing parties in American politics: Organization, electoral settings, and government activity in the twentieth century.* Princeton N.J.: Princeton University Press.

# *Oklahoma*

## JON F. HALE AND STEPHEN T. KEAN

## PARTY HISTORY

For most of the state's history, Oklahoma has been dominated by the Democratic Party. Established in the closing years of the nineteenth century, the party swept the 1907 statehood elections by exploiting widespread progressive sentiment in a state that has since become known for its conservatism. Soon after statehood, economic hardship, brought on by drought and wage stagnation, pushed many Oklahomans into the Socialist Party, which cut into Democratic strength. The Socialists won almost 20 percent of the vote for governor in 1914. With the Democratic majority diluted, the Republicans gained control of the Oklahoma House of Representatives in the 1920 elections—the GOP's only legislative majority in state history. The Great Depression, however, helped the Democrats regain dominance in the 1930s, when Oklahoma was devastated by the Dust Bowl. In the 1950s Democratic control was so thorough that nearly half the legislative seats went uncontested by Republicans. Perhaps the low point for the GOP came in 1958, when the Republican gubernatorial candidate received a mere 19 percent of the vote and lost all seventy-seven counties. From 1907 to 1975 the Republicans held an average of only 19 percent of state house seats. According to Austin Ranney's measure of interparty competition, Oklahoma was a "modified one-party Democratic state" from 1946 to 1973 (Kirkpatrick et al. 1977, 37–38).[1]

Even as the Democrats firmly controlled the congressional delegation, the state house, and the courthouses in the 1950s, Republican strength was growing at the presidential level. Dwight D. Eisenhower carried Oklahoma comfortably in 1952 and 1956, and since then Republican presidential candidates have carried the Sooner State in every election except 1964. In 1962 Henry Bellmon became the first Republican elected governor; he was succeeded by Republican Dewey Bartlett in 1966 and 1970. Bellmon was later elected governor again, in 1986. Republicans began to win more congressional seats too. First Bellmon, then Bartlett went from the governor's mansion to Washington as a U.S. senator. After the 1994 elections, the Republicans held the governorship, both U.S. Senate seats, and five of the six U.S. House seats. Having accomplished this level of success on the top of the ticket, the Republicans were poised to contest control of the state legislature with the Democrats for the first time since the 1920s.

Most Republican identifiers live in the northern half of the state; many of their forebears came to Oklahoma from GOP-dominated states in the North in the half-century following the Civil War. The middle-class and upscale populations of the two major cities, Tulsa and Oklahoma City, also became predominantly Republican between the 1950s and the 1990s. The Oklahoma Republican Party has been prone to factionalization between "money bags" and "grassroots" elements, according to one party scholar (Jones 1974, 67). The grassroots Republicans were farmers and small-town business types, and the money bags Republicans were predominantly oilmen, mostly from the two big cities. Since 1980 this factional divide has given way to one between "country club" Republicans and Christian right elements in the party. These two factions are divided over the primacy of economics or values. The task of bridging the factional conflict as well as the tasks of creating and maintaining party organization has fallen to several dominant individuals, such as Bellmon, who established the modern party organization, and to recent party chairs Tom Cole (1991–1993) and Clinton Key (1993–1995). The role of strong personalities in Oklahoma Republican politics is not new; Stephen Jones in 1974 characterized state GOP politics as largely personality-driven and dominated by a "one-man" organizational concept (Jones 1974, 65). Bellmon, Cole, and Key have been largely successful at keeping the party unified and at creating a modern party organization with the capacity to help GOP candidates get elected.

The Oklahoma Democratic Party, in contrast, has never been a particularly unified entity despite its dominance of state politics. Since the 1907 statehood election, the Democrats have been a party of candidates, often of diverse ideologies and backgrounds.[2] The traditional Democratic base is in "Little Dixie," the rural portion of the state south of Interstate 44, which runs from Miami, in the northeast corner of the state, through Tulsa and Oklahoma City, to Lawton, in the southwest corner. The politics of Little Dixie is akin to traditional southern politics—conservative but still staunchly Democratic. The liberal side of the Democratic Party is a relatively weak and loosely knit collection of minority and labor union voters in Tulsa and Oklahoma City and a few activists in Norman, the home of the University of Oklahoma. In between the liberals and conservatives are the pragmatic, moderately conservative, big-business Democrats, who finance party activities and candidates, and a dwindling base of nonunion Democrats in the cities.

Because of the party's dominance at the county level and in the state legislature, there have always been a number of forces contending for power within the party. Jones (1974, 89–90) refers to three "factions" within the party: the state legislators (who used to represent a largely rural constituency but now represent a mixture of "Little Dixie" conservatives, urban/union interests, and minority members); county commissioners (the entirely rural strength of the Democratic Party and the lone level of Oklahoma government where the Republicans have not challenged Democratic supremacy); and the "old folks" (the rural elderly). Since the days of Robert Kerr (governor from 1943 to 1947 and U.S. senator from 1949 to 1963), who exerted a major influence on the party from 1940 to his death in 1963, no one has served as a unifying force in state Democratic Party politics, and the party has remained extremely decentralized.

## ORGANIZATIONAL DEVELOPMENT

*Republican Party.* Prior to 1960, the Republican organization was limited largely to wealthy individuals in Oklahoma City and Tulsa and the conservative northwest corner of the state. Republican representation in the state legislature, as well as in the U.S. Congress, was confined to these areas, as was generally the leadership and fund raising of the party. There were only minimal efforts made outside of Republican strongholds, and, with rare exceptions, Republicans did not target Democratic seats. Many state legislative seats routinely went uncontested by the Republicans.

Since 1960 the Oklahoma Republican Party has developed into a well-organized, centralized institution that has been largely responsible for the increasing Republican success at the ballot box. After the embarrassing performances of Republican candidates in the 1950s, Henry Bellmon persuaded the state party to adopt a new strategy prior to his election as governor in 1962. "Operation Countdown," which emphasized finance, candidate recruitment, and mobilizing and registering of Republican voters, marked the beginning of a new organizational era for Republicans (Jones 1974, 79). Bellmon and his assistants traveled the state (including Little Dixie, which the Republicans had steadfastly avoided in the 1950s), setting up county organizations and signing up grassroots volunteers. His efforts created a competitive GOP in Oklahoma where it did not previously exist. Republican chairs after Bellmon slowly began to make the GOP more competitive in statewide races. It was not until the 1980s, however, that real electoral success was realized. Tom Cole, both as an influential adviser during the 1980s and as party chair from 1991 to 1993, further modernized the party, in terms of technology and fund-raising techniques. Cole also placed great emphasis on targeting seats outside traditional Republican strongholds. Clinton Key, who led the party from 1993 to 1995, had to manage conflict between the emerging factions in the Republican Party. While Key continued the efforts begun by Bellmon and Cole to develop the organization and to concentrate on fund raising, his vice chair, Quineta Wylie, took charge of the newly mobilizing grassroots element of the party. Key also brought a new focus on county-level offices, seeking, at a minimum, to recruit candidates for as many seats as possible.

Republican organizational efforts have begun to trickle down to state legislative and courthouse races. For the 1996 legislative elections, the Republican Party's primary organizational goal was to capture the state legislature. This was probably an ambitious goal, when one considers that only a decade earlier a large percentage of the seats went uncontested; however, it attests to the fact that the Republicans are beginning to make striking gains in grassroots development.

*Democratic Party.* Oklahoma's favorite son, the humorist Will Rogers, was fond of saying, "I don't belong to an organized political party; I am a Democrat." His words capture the essence of the Oklahoma Democratic Party organization. In contrast to the Republicans, the Oklahoma Democratic Party has experienced little organizational development since 1960. The state party organization remains weak, and the party as a whole remains extremely decentralized. The Democratic Party as an organization is an amalgam of local and county-level officials, who command their own campaign organizations. The state party is little more than a confederation of the Democrats active in local-level politics.

Reforms mandated by the national party over the past quarter-century have only served to reinforce the decentralized nature of the party. The Democratic central committee until 1988 included only a few state legislators, because they would have had to run against their constituents to get elected to the body. In 1987, however, the Democratic National Committee required the state to reapportion its representation and, as a consequence, the central committee was expanded to include more than 950 members, including all state legislators. Beginning with the 1990 elections, the Democratic Party in Oklahoma signed on to the coordinated campaign concept being pushed by the Democratic National Committee. Although adoption of the coordinated campaign may seem to be an organizational advancement, it has not had much of an impact. Because Oklahoma is not a priority of the national party, few resources flow to the state party. Thus the state party organization has few resources to dispense to candidates and therefore little leverage to enhance its influence on candidates.

## CURRENT PARTY ORGANIZATION

*Republican Party.* The current organization of the Republican Party is highly centralized under the authority of the state chair, who serves a two-year term and is elected during the state convention. Despite the emergence of a new group of activists around the state, the Republican state chair still directs a party that remains highly centralized in Oklahoma and Tulsa Counties. In fact, more than 43 percent of the delegates to the 1995 state convention were from these two counties.

The central committee, which includes the chair, the vice chair, and the two national committee members, is the main organizational element of the party. The central committee controls much of the party's policy agenda and strategy, but expenditures must be approved by the budget committee. The budget committee includes the four central committee members, the chairs of each of the six congressional district party organizations, and five appointees of the chair. Two of these appointees are the treasurer and the finance director. Also assisting the central committee with long-range planning is the thirty-two member executive committee, which comprises the central committee members plus the district party chairs and vice chairs, the Republican legislative leaders, and statewide officials.

Finally, the Republican State Party Committee is the broadest committee and consists of the executive committee members, four officers from each of the county party organizations, and other elected state officials.

The chair's power is reinforced by his or her ability to appoint five of the other fourteen budget committee members and the infrequency of other committee meetings (the central committee and executive committee meet only three times per year). In addition, the chair has the resources of a state headquarters (currently the Dewey Bartlett Center, a building near the state capitol which the party owns), and the services of seven full-time paid staff members.

The Republican Party has seemingly undergone major renovations in its operations in recent years. State Chair Quineta Wylie (1995–) remarked that the grassroots-oriented philosophy of Republican National Committee chair Haley Barbour has influenced the Republican hierarchy all the way down to the county level. Wylie perceives there to be a much greater degree of cooperation between the RNC and the Oklahoma party in recent years in what used to be a closed-door, elitist party. (Wylie referred to the RNC staff in Washington, D.C., before Barbour as a bunch of snobbish children of "Team 100" contributors.) A more inclusive feeling is also evident in the relationship between the state and local party organizations in Oklahoma. Although the new breed of Republicans might account for the openness at the local level, a more likely explanation of the changing relationship is the Republican Party's successes in the 1990s in state and local elections in areas outside Oklahoma City and Tulsa.

Because of Republican successes in the 1994 elections, intraparty factionalism has been muted. The party's increasing electoral successes, however, have been built on an expanding Republican coalition that has seen an influx of Christian-conservative voters from the Democratic Party and a decreasing voice for "traditional" Republican elites. In addition, the party is making strong calls (in rhetoric at least) to include a growing number of Hispanics and Asians to complement its traditional business and northern-rural constituencies. Largely because the Republicans have been a minority party for so long, today there is little legacy of personality-driven conflict. However, personal conflict may soon become inevitable now that the party, after the 1994 election, holds the governorship, both U.S. Senate seats, and five of the six congressional seats. Additionally, the party's recent success at the top of the ticket might cause what were largely uncontested Republican primaries to become heated events, especially given the party's increasingly diverse constituency.

The institutional interaction between the state party and its elected officials is virtually a new experience for the Republican Party. State Chair Wylie said that for the first time the Republicans have had to "think like a majority party." Having had only three governors, one state legislative majority, and a sprinkling of federal offices in the past century, prominent elected officials, such as Bellmon or current U.S. senator Don Nickles, have had an overwhelming influence on the state party as an institution. Their importance is now being downplayed in favor of a focus on grassroots development and candidate recruitment. The state party and the political action committees of the Republican legislative leaders are becoming much more active in seeking out challengers for legislative and county-level seats the Republicans have rarely, if ever, held. The grassroots focus resulted in the Republican Party fielding more candidates for the 1996 state legislative races than the Democrats for the first time in the state's history.

*Democratic Party.* The current outlook is considerably less optimistic for the Democratic Party. In contrast to the Republicans, the Democrats have had no paid staff—even the state chair is a voluntary position—and lease an office in Oklahoma City. It is the chair's prerog-ative, if the funds can be raised, to hire an executive director to run the day-to-day affairs of the party. In recent years, however, the party has not had the resources to fund such a posi-tion, and the chairs have served as their own executive directors. (After struggling to raise the necessary resources, the party hired Pat Hall as its first executive director in December 1995.) The Democratic organization, then, is at a distinct disadvantage, since the person who holds this position usually is a volunteer who has another full-time job and is compet-ing with a paid Republican chair and seven staff members. Furthermore, campaign tech-nologies that the Oklahoma Republicans have enjoyed for years are only just arriving at the Oklahoma Democratic Party in the mid-1990s.

The party elects its six officers at its midterm biennial convention: the chair, cochair, sec-retary, treasurer, and the national committeeman and committeewoman. These officers, because of the decentralized nature of the Democratic Party, have much more circum-scribed roles than do their Republican counterparts. Also, they have more candidates and organizational entities with which to contend.

The highest policy-making body in the Democratic Party is the executive committee, which includes the six state officers, three officers from each of the congressional districts, and a single representative each from the Democratic Women's Caucus, Young Democrats, elected state officials, state senate caucus, state house caucus, and federal officials. The exec-utive committee meets at least quarterly and is responsible for formulating party policy, hiring officials, and making large expenditures. The central committee is a rather unwieldy elected body that approves the platform and elects the officers but plays no other role in the daily functioning of the party. Finally, there is the affirmative action committee, a mixture of elected and chair-appointed Democrats who serve to ensure compliance with national party requirements.

It appears that the relationship between the national party and the Oklahoma Democratic Party is not very solid. There are limited funds flowing from national party organizations to either the state party or candidates directly. Oklahoma simply is not a priority for the national party. The 1992 presidential campaign provides an example of Oklahoma's limited importance, as the state received only a single fly-in, to Tulsa, by vice presidential candidate Al Gore, and virtually no other campaign resources. In the wake of recent election results, it is not likely that this picture will change in the near future. Furthermore, in the 1994 midterms, few resources flowed from Washington-based party committees to U.S. Senate candidate Dave McCurdy or to Democratic candidates in the Second and Fourth Congressional Districts. The Republicans gained these three traditionally Democratic seats. It also appears that the Democrats are beginning to pick up the old Republican tactic of not running aggressively in areas of opposition strength, as the Democrats in 1994 failed to field a candidate in the heavily Republican Fifth Congressional District.

The relationships among the various levels of the state organization are just as frustrat-ing to Oklahoma Democrats as is the state party's relationship to the national party organi-zation. There are so many competing tendencies and personalities within the party that there is not much that it can accomplish substantively. In fact, intraparty turmoil is often intensified during primaries when local officials, feeling they have been loyal for years, desire to run for a higher office and are told by the state party that it must remain neutral but will help out after the primary.

Intraparty factions still clearly exist within the Democratic Party. The traditionally Democratic "Little Dixie" voters of the Second, Third, and Fourth Congressional Districts are largely rural, socially conservative voters. When they are mixed with the vocal labor and minority contingents in Oklahoma City and Tulsa, it is apparent that the Oklahoma Democratic Party is much more heterogeneous than is the Republican Party.

The main problem for the Democrats is that with so many elected officials (in early 1996 they still held the state house and senate by large margins) seeking the spotlight, it is difficult for any one person to energize or direct the party in the way that Bellmon was able to do for the Republicans. When considering who leads the party, one might point to the array of prominent Democratic elected officials (including U.S. representative Bill Brewster, Attorney General Drew Edmondson, and State Treasurer Robert Butkin), rather than to state chair Betty McElderry. To limit the discussion to these four individuals, however, ignores the influence of the state legislative leaders and numerous county-level officials. Because of the large number of officials, the Democratic state chair has traditionally played a very limited role in state politics. It is also notable that the Democrats have had particularly contentious primaries, which have caused rifts, because of the large number of quality candidates that emerge. This is a problem that Oklahoma Republicans have seldom had.

The interaction among different levels of the Democratic Party, then, is very limited. Given the number of legislative and county-level officials in the Democratic Party, the state chair cannot be expected to play a leadership role in setting the party's policy or agenda. Given the current pro-Republican electoral environment, things are even more challenging for the Democratic Party chair. She is facing a Republican governor and an almost entirely Republican federal delegation, but at the same time she must try to work with Democratic state legislators who are accustomed to relying on their own resources to get reelected. At present, none of the remaining elected Democrats in the state is willing to take on the role as spokesperson of the party.

### RESOURCE GUIDE

Both Oklahoma Democratic and Republican Parties have rather limited resources on site. The on-site holdings are largely limited to committee meeting minutes (1980 to present) and statutes. In both cases, one should call with precise requests for assistance and appointments.

Other sources in the state include the Carl Albert Congressional Research Center at the University of Oklahoma, which houses the papers of Speaker Albert in addition to those of a number of other past Oklahoma members of Congress, including Lyle Boren, Ed Edmondson, Robert Kerr, and Tom Steed. Both major metropolitan daily newspapers—the *Oklahoma City Daily Oklahoman* and the *Tulsa World*—devote considerable coverage to Oklahoma politics. The *Oklahoma Observer* has the dual distinction of being the singular media outlet for liberal viewpoints in the state and of focusing entirely on state politics and policy.

### NOTES

1. Ranney rates state parties on their overall dominance within a state. A score of 1 indicates complete dominance; a score of .500 signifies a competitive two-party system. Oklahoma was found to be .8193 from 1946 to 1963. By 1973 the figure had dipped to .7297.
2. At the county level in the 1907 elections, the Democrats gained at least a plurality in sixty-two of the seventy-seven counties, which "firmly established the Democratic dominance of the courthouses" (Scales and Goble 1982, 31–32).

REFERENCES

*Asterisks denote the most important publications on Oklahoma party politics.*

Jones, Stephen. 1974. *Oklahoma politics in state and nation.* Enid, Okla.: Haymaker Press.

Kirkpatrick, Samuel A. 1978. *The legislative process in Oklahoma.* Norman: University of Oklahoma Press.

*Kirkpatrick, Samuel A., David R. Morgan, and Thomas G. Kielhorn. 1977. *The Oklahoma voter: Politics, elections, and parties in the Sooner State.* Norman: University of Oklahoma Press.

McElderry, Betty. 1995. State Democratic Party chair. Interview by author, August 13.

Morgan, Ann Hodges. 1977. *Robert S. Kerr: The Senate years.* Norman: University of Oklahoma Press.

*Morgan, David R., Robert E. England, and George G. Humphreys. 1991. *Oklahoma politics and policies: Governing the Sooner State.* Lincoln: University of Nebraska Press.

Scales, James R., and Danney Goble. 1982. *Oklahoma politics: A history.* Norman: University of Oklahoma Press.

Wylie, Quineta. 1995. State Republican Party chair. Interview by author, August 4.

# Oregon

JEFFREY A. KARP AND SUSAN A. BANDUCCI

## PARTY HISTORY

Progressive reforms, party factionalism, and, more recently, campaign finance reform have played a major role in the development of Oregon political parties. For much of state history, parties have been strictly regulated. These regulations have restricted the activities of parties and at times contributed to their divisiveness, keeping them weak. As a result, the electoral fortunes of the parties, for the most part, have been shaped by individual candidates and not by party organization.

From the 1880s to the 1950s the Republican Party was the major political force in Oregon politics. Early Republican dominance in the state was aided by the immigration of farmers from midwestern states who aligned themselves with the Republican Party after the Civil War. Between 1882 and 1910 Republicans held all statewide offices except for the election of two Democratic governors, one secretary of state, and one attorney general. From the 1920s until the 1950s the Republican Party continued to dominate the state legislature, with only a few successful challenges from the Democrats in the 1930s. During this period the Republican Party won six of nine gubernatorial contests and every U.S. Senate contest. The Republican nominee for president carried Oregon in every election from 1948 until 1964, when Lyndon Johnson carried the state. Examining the four decades between 1914 and 1954, Ranney and Kendall (1956, 158–166) classified Oregon as a "modified one-party Republican" state.

In the 1930s the New Deal realignment and an influx of people who came to work in Portland shipyards and in the forests contributed to an increase in Democratic registration (Burton 1970, 3). The electoral effect of the increase in Democratic registration was not seen until the 1950s, when a competitive Democratic Party emerged. The elections of 1954 and 1956 marked the transition from single-party control to a competitive two-party state. In 1954 Richard Neuberger became the first Democrat elected to the U.S. Senate in forty years. The Democrats also increased their representation in the legislative assembly. In 1956 Democrats experienced broader success when they took control of both houses of the legislature for the first time since 1878. They also won the governorship for the first time since 1934 and all other statewide offices except for the secretary of state. Democrats also held both U.S. Senate seats and three of the four congressional seats in 1956.

The Democrats lost the gubernatorial race in 1958 to moderate Republican Mark Hatfield. The Democrats also lost control of both U.S. Senate seats when Oregon voters elected Hatfield in 1966 and Robert Packwood in 1968. Both Republicans would serve in the Senate for three decades. However, Democrats continued to dominate state politics and held a majority of the seats in the state legislature for most of the years between 1956 and 1988.

Oregon experienced rapid growth in the 1970s with a migration of Americans who were attracted to the state's quality of life. By the late 1970s, however, recession and an ailing lumber industry had hit the state hard. The lack of economic growth weakened the Democrats' hold on Oregon politics in the late 1970s, and Oregon voters elected a conservative Republican as governor in 1978 and 1982. In the late 1980s growth returned to Oregon, and a liberal Democrat, Neil Goldschmidt, was elected governor. In the 1988 presidential election, after voting Republican in all but one of the previous nine elections, the state voted for Michael Dukakis, and it voted for Bill Clinton in 1992. The strong sense of independence among Oregon voters is evidenced by the showing in 1992 of third-party presidential candidate Ross Perot, who received 24.2 percent of the popular vote, which was a higher percentage than he received in any other state with as many electoral votes.

Consistent with the changing electoral fortunes of the Oregon parties, observers of Oregon politics have produced different estimates at different times of party competition in the state. Looking at the period from 1965 to 1988, Jewell and Olson (1988, 29) classified Oregon as a competitive two-party system. Cotter et al. (1984, 66), studying the years from 1974 to 1980, classified Oregon as "modified one-party Democratic."

In a sign of Republican reemergence, the party took control of the state house in 1990 and then took control of the senate in 1994. The Democrats, however, managed to win control of the governorship in 1990 and 1994. They also recaptured a seat in the U.S. Senate in a close election following Senator Packwood's resignation in 1995. Current voter registration favors the Democratic Party by 9 percent, but, as in most of the country, the notable trend is the increase in the proportion of voters (currently around 21 percent) who do not register with either party (Oregon Blue Book 1995–1996, 330).

## ORGANIZATIONAL DEVELOPMENT

Two factors affect the historical knowledge of the organizational development of political parties in Oregon: lack of scholarly writing and weak parties. Of course the two factors are not unrelated. Based on interviews with state and local party leaders between 1975 and 1980, Cotter, et al. ranked the state Republican Party as "moderately strong" and the state Democratic Party as "moderately weak" (1984, 28–29). They ranked the local parties of both Republicans and Democrats as moderately weak.

As in other states, the adoption of the direct primary in 1904 greatly affected party unity, as candidates for political office created personal organizations to contest nominations.

**Table 1**  Republican Strength in Oregon, 1910–1994

| Year | Percent of presidential vote[1] | Party of governor | Percent of state house delegation | Percent of state senate delegation | Voter Registration Republican | Voter Registration Democratic | Other |
|------|------|------|------|------|------|------|------|
| 1910 | — | D | 95 | 90 | 69 | 21 | 10 |
| 1912 | 42 | — | 80 | 93 | 66 | 22 | 12 |
| 1914 | — | R | 93 | 93 | 57 | 26 | 17 |
| 1916 | 51 | — | 92 | 80 | 64 | 27 | 9 |
| 1918 | — | R | 90 | 80 | 65 | 28 | 7 |
| 1920 | 64 | — | 97 | 90 | 68 | 26 | 6 |
| 1922 | — | D | 85 | 87 | 69 | 26 | 5 |
| 1924 | 68 | — | 95 | 87 | 68 | 27 | 5 |
| 1926 | — | R | 93 | 90 | 69 | 26 | 5 |
| 1928 | 65 | — | 97 | 93 | 70 | 27 | 3 |
| 1930 | — | I | 88 | 97 | 71 | 26 | 3 |
| 1932 | 39 | — | 70 | 73 | 66 | 32 | 2 |
| 1934 | — | D | 37 | 57 | 60 | 38 | 2 |
| 1936 | 32 | — | 35 | 60 | 53 | 45 | 2 |
| 1938 | — | R | 77 | 73 | 50 | 48 | 2 |
| 1940 | 46 | — | 63 | 83 | 50 | 49 | 1 |
| 1942 | — | R | 85 | 90 | 51 | 48 | 1 |
| 1944 | 48 | — | 83 | 83 | 50 | 47 | 3 |
| 1946 | — | R | 97 | 83 | 51 | 47 | 2 |
| 1948 | 52 | R | 82 | 67 | 50 | 48 | 2 |
| 1950 | — | R | 85 | 70 | 48 | 50 | 2 |
| 1952 | 61 | — | 82 | 87 | 50 | 49 | 1 |
| 1954 | — | R | 58 | 80 | 49 | 49 | 2 |
| 1956 | 55 | — | 38 | 50 | 47 | 51 | 2 |
| 1958 | — | R | 45 | 37 | 46 | 53 | 1 |
| 1960 | 53 | — | 48 | 33 | 45 | 53 | 2 |
| 1962 | — | R | 48 | 30 | 45 | 53 | 2 |
| 1964 | 36 | — | 53 | 37 | 43 | 55 | 2 |
| 1966 | — | R | 63 | 37 | 43 | 55 | 2 |
| 1968 | 53 | — | 63 | 47 | 43 | 55 | 2 |
| 1970 | — | R | 57 | 47 | 43 | 55 | 2 |
| 1972 | 55 | — | 45 | 40 | 40 | 56 | 4 |
| 1974 | — | D | 37 | 23 | 38 | 58 | 4 |
| 1976 | 50 | — | 38 | 20 | 35 | 56 | 9 |
| 1978 | — | R | 43 | 23 | 35 | 54 | 11 |
| 1980 | 56 | — | 45 | 27 | 36 | 50 | 14 |
| 1982 | — | R | 40 | 30 | 36 | 50 | 14 |
| 1984 | 56 | — | 43 | 40 | 37 | 49 | 14 |
| 1986 | — | D | 48 | 43 | 39 | 49 | 12 |
| 1988 | 48 | — | 47 | 37 | 39 | 48 | 13 |
| 1990 | — | D | 53 | 33 | 39 | 47 | 14 |
| 1992 | 43 | — | 53 | 47 | 36 | 45 | 19 |
| 1994 | — | D | 57 | 63 | 36 | 43 | 21 |

SOURCES: *The Almanac of Oregon Politics* and *Oregon Blue Book,* various editions.

[1] The vote is calculated as a percentage of the two-party vote.

Other political reforms championed by the Populists and Progressives also contributed to nonideological and weakly organized political parties. Populist William S. U'Ren, who founded the Direct Legislation League in 1898, was the moving force behind the adoption of the initiative and referendum in 1902 and the recall of public officials in 1908 (Oregon Blue Book 1995–1996, 333). The initiative, referendum, and recall came to be known as the "Oregon System."

Some of the state statutes regarding the organization and recognition of parties, such as that banning preprimary conventions in the 1960s and restricting financial help for candidates until after the primary, served to keep parties weak. Furthermore, statutes regarding the organization of parties led to conflict among party leaders. Although the national committee representatives are chosen in the primary, the rest of the party structure is hierarchical and is chosen by an unrepresentative geographical base (counties), ensuring domination by rural interests. Because they are elected by different constituencies, national committee persons and state party chairs are often in conflict.

In the 1950s an attempt was made to strengthen the organization of the Democratic Party. Howard Morgan, who was elected chair of the Democratic Party in 1952, explained the state of the Oregon Democratic Party: "[W]hen I took over the chairmanship, the party was so down flat on its back, and had been for so long, that I could do pretty much what I wanted. . . . What I basically wanted to produce was a genuine two-party state" (quoted in Hansen 1994, 271–272). With the help of Monroe Sweetland, the elected Democratic national committeeman, and Sen. Richard Neuberger (1955–1960), Morgan stepped up efforts to recruit and help Democratic candidates. Morgan and Sweetland were instrumental in recruiting Sen. Wayne Morse (1945–1969) to the Democratic Party (Hanson 1994). Senator Morse, who had resigned from the Republican Party after endorsing Adlai Stevenson in 1952, was a popular figure among Democrats and liberal Republicans (Burton 1970, 126). Morse's defection and stronger candidates, along with better organization that resulted in Democratic registration exceeding Republican registration for the first time in the state's history, contributed to the Democratic victories of 1954 and 1956 (Burton 1970, 137–138).

Although Republicans had dominated state politics prior to the 1950s, the party never possessed ideological or organizational unity (Burton 1970, 138). In the early 1960s Packwood's activities outside the formal party organization helped strengthen the moderate wing of the Republican Party (Balmer 1965, 507). Initially a Republican county chair, Packwood developed his own informal organization which worked outside the Republican Party to recruit and raise money for candidates. Out of his informal organization was born the Dorchester Conference, which organized the moderate and liberal wings of the Republican Party and became a sounding board for policy ideas. Packwood's effort to rebuild the Republican Party in Oregon along more moderate lines paid off for him in the 1968 election, when he was first elected to the U.S. Senate. Although run independently of the party organization, the Dorchester Conference continued as a tradition in Oregon Republican politics.

In 1960 the Democrats held platform conventions at the state and local levels for the first time in several years, and party officials called on officeholders to follow the party line. The state Democratic Party and the Multnomah County Democratic Party attempted to endorse candidates prior to the primary. The officeholders in each party, however, resented the parties' attempt to intrude on their domain, and the state legislature passed a statute requiring that state conventions be held after the primaries and that nominees be among the delegates to the conventions (Balmer 1963, 454).

In 1965 an attempt was made to professionalize the leadership of the state Republican Party by approving a $15,000 salary for then-chair Peter Gunnar (Hughes 1966b, A13). After drawing only three months salary, Gunnar had to contribute his own money to the party after initiating an ambitious fund-raising drive that failed and alienated conservative factions of the party (Hughes 1966a, A10). Because of funding from the state's income tax

$1 checkoff program for political parties, the Democratic Party was able in 1979 to hire its first paid permanent executive director. By that time the Republican Party had already had an executive director for several years and had even paid the state chair a salary on occasion. The Democratic Party had paid an executive director in 1969; however, the director was employed only for a year (Eals 1979, A19).

*Candidate Recruitment and Campaign Finance.* Overall, a history of weak party structure meant that when Oregon became a true two-party state, both parties still lacked the organizational structure to take an active role in politics. Swarthout (1961), characterizing the role of the Oregon political party organizations in the 1950s, wrote:

> Party funds, especially with the Democrats, are limited and used mostly to support the state organization and to campaign in a limited way for the party's whole slate. Only occasionally does a candidate depend heavily on party workers as such, and receive significant support from party coffers. The most significant party functions are those of insuring that all proper voters register and turn out to vote (259).

Interviews with staff members indicate that the role of the party in candidate recruitment and funding has not changed since the 1950s (Beckerich 1995; Ontiveros 1996). Candidate recruitment in Oregon is largely carried out by legislative party campaign committees and not political parties. These committees emerged in the early 1980s as major sources of funding for political candidates. In 1982 the Republican committee in the House contributed $18,000 to Republican candidates. Six years later the committee contributed $102,100 (Gierzynski 1992). The Democratic house caucus contributed $6,800 in 1982 and $40,100 in 1986 (Gierzynski 1992). Aside from contributing money to candidates, the legislative committees have taken on other traditional roles of parties, such as polling, consulting, advertising, and fund raising.

State laws have prohibited parties from taking a more active role in campaign funding. Party contributions are restricted prior to the primary, and funding for political candidates comes largely from personal fund raising by the candidate and not from party sources. Even more influential for political parties were the changes in campaign finance laws that resulted from the passage of a citizen initiative in 1994. Like federal campaign finance laws, these state regulations limited the amount of money that could be given to political parties, PACs, and candidates. Measure 9 of that year limited party expenditures to $25,000 for governor, $10,000 for other statewide candidates, and $5,000 for legislative candidates. Furthermore, corporations were prohibited from contributing money to any campaign or party. Even more significant, the measure limited individual contributions to political parties to $1,000.

*Factionalism within the Republican Party.* Between 1900 and World War II the Republican Party was beset by a factional dispute between conservatives and progressives, particularly in the 1930s when social and economic reforms were important issues.

Since the 1970s intraparty fighting has been carried out by the moderate wing of the Republican Party and cultural conservatives. In 1979 Walter Huss, a Baptist minister, won election as state chair; his election as chair was followed by the election of four state party chairs who represented the culturally conservative wing of the party. The religious right's control of the Republican Party made it difficult for the party to attract money from moderate Republicans. For example, after years of control by the more conservative faction, the party was in poor financial condition and without a state party headquarters for six months until the election of a moderate Republican, Craig Berkman, as chair in 1989.

The Oregon Citizen's Alliance (OCA), a religious right organization, has actively sought control of the Republican Party since the mid-1980s. The OCA originated when the religious right attempted to defeat Robert Packwood in the 1986 primary (Lunch 1995, 231). In 1990 squabbling over the Republican nomination for governor led the religious right to run Al Mobley, a member of the OCA, as an independent candidate, costing the Republicans the governorship. Mobley received 13 percent of the vote, drawing support away from Republican Dave Frohnmeyer and allowing the Democratic candidate, Barbara Roberts, to win the election with only 46 percent of the vote. In 1992 the OCA achieved greater prominence with its sponsorship of Measure 9, an antihomosexual initiative. Republican Party chair Craig Berkman denounced the measure, which led to calls for his resignation from the OCA; he later threatened to form a third party made up of moderate Republicans.

## CURRENT PARTY ORGANIZATION

Prior to 1993 the organization of political parties was dictated by state law. The law had regulated the election and terms of precinct officers, the function and organization of the central committee, and the selection of delegates to the national convention. In 1993 the Oregon legislature revised the laws governing political parties to avoid any constitutional challenge that may have resulted from the U.S. Supreme Court's decision in *Eu v. San Francisco County Democratic Central Committee* (1989), in which the Court ruled that such regulations violated the right of association. Under the new election laws, the parties were given the option of following state statutes. Despite the freedom to organize as they wish, both parties have generally followed the pre-1993 state statutes.

The Republican Party has a paid executive director who manages the daily activities of the party and two other paid positions. The Democratic Party pays an executive director and three other staff members. Budget and staff decisions are made by the administrative and executive committees of the Democratic Party and are approved by the state central committee (Ontiveros 1996). In the Republican Party, the staff and budget are largely at the discretion of the chair but must be approved by the state central committee (Beckerich 1995).

The relationship between the state party and local party organizations remains hierarchical, as neither party deviated much from the state guidelines. The relationship between the elected officials and party officials is maintained by the interaction between the legislative caucus and leaders of the party. The chair and the vice chair of the parties usually deal with elected officials. When the governor is a Democrat, two delegates from the governor's office sit on the Democratic Party central committee.

Other changes in Oregon election laws also meant changes for the parties. Whereas candidate recruitment was largely a function of the legislative caucuses, the adoption of legislative term limits in 1992 necessitated a change in the way parties recruit candidates. Local Republican Party organizations are becoming more active in recruiting candidates, compiling lists of local elected officials for the state party (Beckerich 1995). Parties also had to change funding techniques when the dollar checkoff on state income tax returns was removed in the 1980s. The Democratic Party was hurt by the change in funding. Currently, the Democratic Party holds fund-raising dinners during the year and receives money from the national party's Dollars for Democrats fundraiser.

**Table 2** Oregon Resource Guide

|  | Democrats | Republicans |
| --- | --- | --- |
| Archive | Yes | Yes |
| Location | Party Headquarters | Party Headquarters |
|  | 711 S.W. Alder Street, Suite 306 | 8196 S.W. Hall Blvd. |
|  | Portland, OR 97205 | Beaverton, OR 97005 |
|  | (503) 224-8200 | (503) 520-1996 |
| Dates | 1970–present | 1975–present |
| Finding aid | No | No |
| Access | By appointment | By appointment |
| Contents: |  |  |
| Executive committee minutes | Yes | Yes |
| Correspondence | Yes | No |
| Organizational structure | Yes | Yes |
| Budgets | Yes | Yes |
| Rules | Yes | Yes |

## RESOURCE GUIDE

Prior to the change in election laws in 1993 pertaining to the organization of political parties, parties did not need to keep records regarding organization because organization was mandated by statute. This fact, combined with weak organizational structures, meant records were not systematically archived by either party.

Republican Party records are fragmented, and there is no central storage, although the party has plans to create a resource library. Party headquarters moved with the election of new chairs, and at times the party had no office. Intraparty divisions made it difficult to keep any records in one central location. Some of the party records are stored at private residences, so it is rather difficult to determine what documents and records, if any, exist. The party has maintained its current address since July 1993. We have been told that the party has maintained minutes from executive committee meetings dating back to 1975, but it might entail some work to locate them. More recently, minutes have been recorded on tape and occasionally video, but there is no finding aid. Historical records are generally lacking; even a list of party chairs is not yet available. What is archived relates mainly to the social side of the party, including pictures and scrapbooks. Anything of public record, such as financial statements that have been turned over to the secretary of state, is not kept. The party has only recently published a newsletter on a regular basis.

The Democratic Party has most of its documents and records from the last twenty-five years at its headquarters. The Democratic Party has files dating to 1968, although they are not complete. Most of the papers are kept in boxes that are organized by date. The records include letters, correspondence, party platforms, newspaper clippings, and organizational structure and financial information. The bylaws require the party to keep executive committee minutes. These have been kept since the 1970s, although they are not systematically stored. Party records have been maintained primarily by volunteers. Different filing systems have been used over the years, which means that any researcher would have to spend some time sifting through files. The party has published a newsletter over the years, although it has been published on a regular basis (three times a year) only recently.

Additional information about the Oregon parties may be found at the Oregon State Archives and the University of Oregon Special Collections. Additionally, the Oregon Historical Society has collections that are grouped under personal names. Some Oregon political figures, such as Mark Hatfield (governor, 1959–1967; U.S. senator, 1967–1997) and Denny Smith (U.S. representative, 1981–1991), have given their personal papers to Willamette University, although they are not yet available for public viewing.

## REFERENCES

*Asterisks denote the most important publications on Oregon party politics.*

Balmer, Donald G. 1965. The 1964 election in Oregon. *Western Political Quarterly,* 502–508.

———. 1963. The 1962 election in Oregon. *Western Political Quarterly,* 453–459.

Beckerich, Marge. 1995. Executive director, Oregon Republican Party, 1993–. Interview by authors. Portland, Ore., June 26.

*Burton, Robert E. 1970. *Democrats of Oregon: The pattern of minority politics 1900–1956.* Eugene: University of Oregon Books.

Cotter, Cornelius, James L. Gibson, John F. Bibby, and Robert J. Huckshorn. 1984. *Party organizations in American politics.* New York: Praeger Publishers.

Eals, Clay. 1979. Demos appoint Jaycee as full-time executive. *Portland Oregonian,* June 3, A19.

Ferrara, Pam, and David Buchanan. 1994. *The almanac of Oregon politics.* Philomath, Ore.: Almanac of Oregon Politics.

Gierzynski, Anthony. 1992. *Legislative party campaign committees in the American states.* Lexington: University Press of Kentucky.

Hansen, Clark. 1994. The making of the modern Democratic Party in Oregon: An interview with Howard Morgan. *Oregon Historical Quarterly* (winter):368–385.

*Harmon, Robert B. 1990. *Government and politics in Oregon: A selected guide to information sources.* Monticello, Ill.: Vance Bibliographies.

Hughes, Harold. 1966a. GOP, Demos scramble to line up state chairmen for conventions. *Portland Oregonian,*July 13, A10.

———. 1966b. Hodel selected state GOP chairman. *Portland Oregonian,* July 25, A13.

Jewell, Malcolm E., and David M. Olson. 1988. *Political parties and elections in American states.* 3d ed. Chicago: Dorsey Press.

*Lunch, William M. 1995. Oregon: Identity and politics in the Northwest. *God at the grassroots,* ed. Mark Rozell and Clyde Wilcox. Lanham, Md.: Rowan and Littlefield.

Ontiveros, Amber. 1996. Director of operations, Oregon Democratic Party, 1996–. Interview by authors. Portland, Ore., August 20.

Ranney, Austin, and Willmoore Kendall. 1956. *Democracy and the American party system.* New York: Harcourt, Brace.

*Swarthout, John M. 1961. Oregon: Political experiment station. In *Western politics,* ed. Frank H. Jonas. Salt Lake City: University of Utah Press.

# *Pennsylvania*

## G. TERRY MADONNA AND ROBERT J. BRESLER

## PARTY HISTORY

In the twentieth century Pennsylvania evolved from a one-party Republican state to a competitive two-party state. From 1900 to 1934 Pennsylvania Republicans won every race for governor and U.S. senator and controlled both the state senate and house. In 1930 Democratic prospects were so grim that the party's gubernatorial nominee withdrew from the ticket to seek office as the grand exalted ruler of the Elks rather than face certain electoral defeat.

From the Civil War to the New Deal, an efficient and sophisticated Republican machine dominated Pennsylvania politics and was led by three men—Simon Cameron (1865–1887), Matthew S. Quay (1887–1904), and Boise Penrose (1904–1921). Penrose, who ran the party from the U.S. Senate, was the spokesperson for Pennsylvania corporate interests at the national level.

By their control of Harrisburg, the Republicans ensured themselves thousands of patronage jobs. The Republican state organization was buttressed by courthouse gangs that dispensed county patronage and assessed locally hired public employees a fee for their continued employment. This practice, known as "macing" in Pennsylvania parlance, was widespread and lasted into the 1960s. In addition, local political figures were known to receive kickbacks from municipal contractors responsible for the construction of sewers, roads, subways, and other public works.

The era of complete Republican dominance ended in 1934 with the election of Democrats George H. Earle as governor (1935–1939) and Joseph F. Guffey to the U.S. Senate (1935–1947). In 1936 the state went for Franklin D. Roosevelt, and the Democrats captured both houses of the state legislature. Although the state reverted to Republicanism in the 1940s, the New Deal years had fundamentally altered the politics of Pennsylvania. Catholics, Jews, African Americans, and poor voters joined with organized labor to comprise a substantial base for the Democratic Party and a significant opposition to the Republicans. Nonetheless, the Republican base, consisting of Protestants, native-born residents in the rural and suburban areas, and upper income families, still constituted a majority.

Contrary to voting trends in other northeastern cities, the trends in both Pittsburgh and Philadelphia continued to promote Republican control as late as 1951. The Republicans' success was a function of their politics and organization. As champions of the protective tariff, Pennsylvania Republicans received significant support from the manufacturing interests that formed the basis of the Pennsylvania economy—steel, oil, paint, rubber, and glass.

In the 1950s Pennsylvania emerged as a genuinely competitive two-party state. Much of this change can be attributed to the conversion of previously Republican voters (southern and Eastern Europeans and African Americans) to the Democratic Party. The Democrats expanded their geographic base from the hard-coal northeastern part of the state and the industrial southwest to Allegheny County (the Pittsburgh area) and other industrial counties of western Pennsylvania. The Democrats' widening geographic base reflected not only the impact of Roosevelt's New Deal but also the effect of Governor Earle's "little New Deal." In 1937 Earle and a Democratic-controlled general assembly passed sweeping reforms benefiting the state's labor unions. The Earle administration cemented the alliance of major industrial unions such as the United Mine Workers, the United Steel Workers, and later the merged AFL-CIO with the Democratic Party. The Democrats' success in Pittsburgh in the 1930s was a result of a strengthened labor movement, and their ascendance in Philadelphia in the 1950s can be attributed to effective attacks on corrupt Republican municipal government. By the 1960s labor was a major contributor to the party's state and local campaigns, and its leaders served on many party policy-making bodies.

Two critical elections in the 1950s solidified the Democratic gains—the 1951 Philadelphia mayoral victory of City Controller Joseph S. Clark and the 1954 gubernatorial victory of

York County state senator George Leader. Riding the issue of political corruption and campaigning as political reformers, Democrats elected not only Clark but another reformer as well, Richardson Dilworth, as Philadelphia district attorney. Dilworth later succeeded Clark as mayor. With these victories Philadelphia became a Democratic city and produced impressive vote margins for Democratic candidates running statewide. Philadelphia provided Leader with a 116,000 vote margin (he carried Pittsburgh by 88,000) in his 1954 gubernatorial victory.

## ORGANIZATIONAL DEVELOPMENT

Buoyed by John F. Kennedy's successful 1960 presidential campaign and a vigorous voter registration drive, Democratic registration at last exceeded Republican registration by election day of that year. Between 1960 and 1996 the Democrats carried the state in five presidential elections, and the Republicans in four. With the exception of Lyndon B. Johnson's (1964) and Richard M. Nixon's (1972) landslides, the margin of victory for presidential candidates in Pennsylvania during this period averaged approximately 4 percent.

Gubernatorial contests between 1954 and 1994 were equally competitive; neither party won more than two consecutive elections. Since the mid-1950s control of the two chambers of the legislature has alternated between the two major parties. Of the twenty-one legislative sessions of this period, the Republicans controlled both chambers in five sessions, the Democrats controlled both in three, and the two parties split control of the chambers in thirteen.

The establishment of a competitive party system coincided with the decline of party identification among Pennsylvania voters. Consequently, incumbency became a crucial electoral advantage, and state legislators achieved reelection with relative ease. Since most seats were safe from challenge, neither party was able to muster large majorities in either chamber. Nor were there many changes in party control. From 1980 to 1996 the Republicans controlled the state senate with the exception of one twelve-month period. The Democrats had controlled the state house since 1982 but finally lost control in the 1994 Republican tide. On election night in 1994 the Democrats actually won a majority in the state house. Soon after, however, a Democratic member switched to the Republican Party, giving it a 102–101 edge in that chamber.

Patronage historically played a major role in Pennsylvania politics, and the decline of the patronage system contributed to the general weakening of the state's political organizations. In the 1930s and 1940s approximately 35,000 jobs were at the disposal of the governor—at least nominally. In practice, however, the political bosses who controlled the party organization had considerable influence over the appointment of state employees. Until the 1970s Pennsylvania governors were limited to one term, and party leaders supported gubernatorial candidates who would follow their advice on appointments.

The election of Democrat George Leader in 1954 broke the pattern whereby Pennsylvania governors functioned more as brokers than political leaders. Leader was the first in a succession of governors to break with the process and allow the patronage system to atrophy. In 1955 the governor had more than 55,000 patronage jobs at his disposal, more than were available to any other state executive in the Union. These positions, mostly at the lower end of the salary scale, were important to local political leaders. Leader refused to remove many of the Republican appointees; did not approve many of the Democratic Party leaders' job recommendations; and extended civil service protection to almost twelve thousand heretofore patronage employees. These actions set the stage for a more strained relationship between future governors and party leaders. The party retaliated by granting Leader only lukewarm support in his failed U.S. Senate race against Republican Hugh Scott in 1958. Nonetheless, the system would never be the same.

Philadelphia business executive Milton Shapp's successful campaign for governor in 1970 dealt the death blow to patronage. Using more than $1 million of his own money, Shapp had won his first Democratic nomination in 1966 without the party's endorsement, which had been denied him. His 1966 primary campaign focused almost exclusively on the party bosses whom he accused of backroom king making. In an effective television commercial shown throughout the state, he tagged his opponent, state senator Robert P. Casey, as the candidate of the bosses. Shapp was defeated in the 1966 general election by Republican Raymond Shafer. Four years later Shapp again defeated Casey in the primary, but this time he won the general election, defeating Lt. Gov. Raymond Broderick by a half-million votes. Soon after Shapp's inauguration, a massive unionization of state government employees ended the patronage era in Pennsylvania.

The greater independence and volatility of the electorate that marked voting after 1950 was best illustrated in gubernatorial elections. Between 1954 and 1982 six of nine successful candidates were from the party without the registration advantage: Democrats George Leader (1954) and David Lawrence (1958) and Republicans William Scranton (1962), Raymond Shafer (1966), Dick Thornburgh (1978 and 1982), and Tom Ridge (1994).

Ticket splitting became habitual for Pennsylvania voters. The 1994 election, in which Republicans Tom Ridge and Rick Santorum were elected governor and senator, respectively, was the first election since 1950 in which Pennsylvania voters selected a governor and a U.S. senator of the same party. Most ticket-splitters during the 1960s came from Republican ranks, but by the early 1970s the trend was bipartisan and ticket splitting was a common practice. As the Democrats achieved a voter registration edge, Republican victories were accomplished thanks to substantial Democratic ticket splitting.

Competitive party politics evolved against the background of a declining state economy. Once the second leading manufacturing state in the nation, Pennsylvania had fallen to fifth by 1958. Committed for many decades to mass production manufacturing, Pennsylvania lagged behind other states in modernization. Unemployment in manufacturing, coal, and steel was substantially higher than the national average. The recession of 1981–1983 brought state unemployment levels to the 13–15 percent range, produced state government deficits of $300 million, and ravaged the old industrial towns of western Pennsylvania, where unemployment reached 20 percent.

The economic dislocation affected the political map. Democrats benefited from the state's economic travail in the southwestern counties of Allegheny, Washington, Greene, Westmoreland, Cambria, and Fayette as well as Beaver and Lawrence, which border Ohio. Much of central Pennsylvania was relatively untouched by the economic dislocation of the 1980s, and many of its counties were, in fact, centers of economic and population growth. They included the Philadelphia suburban counties—Delaware, Bucks, Montgomery, and Chester—and the counties of south central Pennsylvania—Lancaster, Dauphin, York, and Cumberland. These areas, largely east of the Blue Mountains, leaned Republican, whereas the economically embattled western part of the state became more Democratic.

Despite the political and economic division in Pennsylvania, the parties were not marked by sharp ideological distinctions. Republican governors were moderate and pragmatic. William Scranton (1963–1967) supported the expansion of the state's industrial authority and increased highway construction; Raymond Shafer (1967–1971) signed the most liberal public sector collective bargaining law in the nation; and Dick Thornburgh (1979–1987) proposed major initiatives to assist in the diversification of Pennsylvania's economy. Republican governor Tom Ridge, elected in 1994, was the candidate of the party's moderate wing, winning the primary over Attorney General Ernie Preate, an outspoken conservative.

Republican senators of the post-1950 era—James Duff (1951–1957), Hugh Scott (1959–1977), Richard Schweiker (1969–1981), John Heinz (1977–1991), and Arlen Specter (1981–)—identified with the moderate wing of the party. Their voting records reflected a close working relationship with labor, support for protection of the steel industry, and advocacy of civil rights. The election in 1994 to the U.S. Senate of two-term Republican representative Rick Santorum, who had campaigned unapologetically on conservative themes—the ending of abortion, support for the Republican Party's Contract with America, and opposition to gun control—was the first exception to this trend.

The most successful Pennsylvania Democratic politician of the last two decades, Gov. Robert P. Casey (1987–1995), did not match the profile of a traditional Democrat. Although a champion of liberal economic policies, Casey was a staunch supporter of the antiabortion movement and in 1989 signed a restrictive abortion control act.

Beginning in the 1970s, an era of weakened parties and moderate politics, regional voting became a more common phenomenon. Geographic residence became an important electoral ingredient; in particular, the pattern ran east-west. In the Senate election of 1974, Montgomery County Republican Richard Schweiker defeated Pittsburgh mayor Pete Flaherty by not only carrying the traditional Republican suburbs of Philadelphia but by gaining an even split in Philadelphia. In the 1976 Senate race, Pittsburgh Republican representative John Heinz was able to cut into traditional Democratic margins in western Pennsylvania to defeat Philadelphia representative William Green.

Competition and equilibrium have become the hallmarks of Pennsylvania politics. Weakened parties and the reduced partisan identification of voters contributed to an environment whereby either party in any given election was capable of emerging victorious.

## CURRENT PARTY ORGANIZATION

The Republican state committee consists of the Republican county chairs of Pennsylvania's sixty-seven counties. Other members are elected from each county at-large in the spring primary held in even-numbered years. The size of the delegation from each county is determined by the number of registered Republicans in the county. County membership in the Democratic state committee is determined by Democratic turnout in the previous gubernatorial and presidential elections. Counties gain seats on the Democratic state committee if the percentage of Democratic turnout exceeds that of the past gubernatorial and presidential election.

Elected members of the Republican state committee serve two years. The Republican state committee consists of approximately 300 members; and the Democratic state committee has 380 members. The executive offices of the Republican state committee consist of the state chair, vice chair, treasurer, assistant treasurer, and assistant secretary. The executive committee of the Democratic state committee includes the state chair, vice chair, treasurer, recording secretary, and corresponding secretary. Both the Republican state committee and the Democratic state committee have a full-time state chair, executive director, and several staff members responsible for political activity, communications, county liaison, and fund raising.

The finance committees of both parties are crucial to their fund-raising strategies and implementation. The Republican state finance committee has twenty-five members appointed by the finance chair; the Democratic state finance committee has fourteen members, also appointed by the chair.

The Republican state committee allows county parties maximum flexibility in determining local party matters, providing their decisions and activities are not inconsistent with the general rules of the state party. Local parties essentially are responsible for recruiting candidates for county offices, raising campaign funds, and operating their own headquarters.

Historically, the parties represented the divisions of the industrial era. The Pennsylvania Republican state committee through fund raising, volunteers, and personal contacts was dominated by the state's major economic interests—oil, steel, and the railroad industry. Similarly, the Democratic state committee and the labor unions were once "joined at the hip." In the postindustrial age, neither relationship is as strong. The Republican state committee now reflects a wider range of economic interests, particularly those of small- and medium-size businesses. The Republicans still represent rural and small town Pennsylvania and their values. Hence, the Christian Coalition has attempted with some success to elect its members to the Republican state committee and may now hold 25 to 30 percent of the committee seats.

The Democratic state committee has seen its relationship to Pennsylvania interest groups deteriorate. Labor has lost much of its ability to produce the vote and no longer seems as attracted to the state Democratic Party organization as it once was. Its involvement is largely with individual candidates. Similarly, liberal issue groups such as those associated with the prochoice and environmental movements have not been able to deliver votes and are less prominent in Democratic politics.

Power in the Republican state committee is brokered by the leadership. Decision making tends to be in the hands of the state chair and the national committee members and the regional caucuses. County chairs from the populous Republican counties in southeastern Pennsylvania must be accommodated. As of 1996 the Republican state leadership had a close working relationship with the state's Republican governor and legislative leadership. The Republican state committee refrains from engaging in public policy development and avoids the controversies that surround the activities of the executive and legislative branches. Its working relationship with the legislature, for example, focuses on candidate recruitment and assistance.

In the Democratic state committee, members from Philadelphia reflect the influence of powerful personalities such as Mayor Edward Rendell and state senator Vincent Fumo. The Black Caucus, of growing importance in the Pennsylvania Democratic Party, rarely speaks through a single leader, thereby weakening its own impact in the Democratic state committee. Having lost in 1994 the governor's office and the U.S. Senate seat the Democrats once controlled, the Democratic state committee is attempting to rebuild its organization and its relationship with the legislative caucus. To that end it is beginning a major push to recruit candidates and to establish a successful fund-raising strategy.

In a state as competitive, large, and complex as Pennsylvania, it has been essential that both major parties employ modern techniques of direct mail and telemarketing in their fund raising. The Republican state committee relies more heavily than its Democratic counterpart on direct-mail campaigns and maintains a comprehensive file on past donors

**Table 1**    Pennsylvania Resource Guide

|  | Democrats | Republicans |
|---|---|---|
| Archive | Yes | Yes |
| Location | Party Headquarters | Party Headquarters |
|  | 510 N. 3rd Street | 112 State Street |
|  | Harrisburg, PA 17101 | Harrisburg, PA 17101 |
|  | (717) 238-9381 | (717) 234-4901 |
|  | Fax: (717) 238-3472 | Fax: (717) 231-3828 |
| Dates | 1995– | Not available |
| Finding aid | No | No |
| Access | By appointment | By appointment |
| Contents: |  |  |
| State committee minutes | Yes | Yes |
| Correspondence | Yes | No |
| Organizational structure | Yes | Yes |
| Budgets | Yes | Yes |
| Rules | Yes | Yes |

and a list of prospective donors. The Democratic state committee relies somewhat less on direct mail, using it only in election years, and depends heavily on its telemarketing; the party calls possible donors in each quarter of the year. The Republican telemarketing effort is quite sophisticated and relies on a computer-generated, predictive-dialing system that uses a twelve-station computerized telephone bank. The Republican state committee has 80,000–100,000 names in its small-donor base. Traditional fund-raising dinners—ten to twenty a year—account for about 20 percent of the funds raised by the Republican state committee. During the 1995–1996 budget year, one-third of the money raised by the Republican state committee went to internal operations and two-thirds went to support political activities.

The Republican state committee provides direct monetary contributions to Republican candidates, mostly to those running statewide, but occasionally it contributes to state legislative candidates as well. During the 1980s assistance comes in the form of dollars, strategic and staff support, and campaign training for candidates, managers, and other campaign operatives. The Republican state committee views its mission as focusing on the base of Republican voters—those most loyal to the party. It has also been active in recruiting candidates in races it views as marginal or difficult.

By contrast, funding for the Democratic state committee was a problem during the recent administration of Governor Casey. Casey did much of his fund raising directly, preempting the Democratic state committee and weakening its access to a broad, independent funding base. Although Casey picked the chair of the Democratic state committee, he largely ignored the party on patronage matters and did not build the organization. Consequently, the Democratic state committee lost its organizational clout and its ability to deliver votes. In numerous elections the Democrats were unable to match their earlier registration percentages. Most campaigns were self-directed, and candidates expected and received little assistance from the state party.

In 1995, with no incumbent Democratic governor or U.S. senator and without control of the state legislature, Democratic state committee chair and former lieutenant governor Mark Singel was in the process of reconstructing the Democratic state committee's fund-raising potential.

## RESOURCE GUIDE

The records of both the Republican state committee and the Democratic state committee are limited in scope. They are stored in boxes at party headquarters. The Republican state committee has produced the *Pennsylvania Republican Almanac,* an extensive guide to its membership and elected government leaders. The almanac may be used as a starting point for research on contemporary Republican politics. Researchers should call party headquarters in advance and schedule an appointment to see archived materials. Neither party has indexed its material.

## REFERENCES

*Asterisks denote the most important publications on Pennsylvania party politics.*
Commonwealth of Pennsylvania. Biennial. *Pennsylvania manual.* Harrisburg: Commonwealth of Pennsylvania.
*Beers, Paul B. 1980. *Pennsylvania politics today and yesterday.* University Park: Pennsylvania State University Press.
Hicock, Eugene W., ed. 1992. *Reform of state legislatures.* Lanham, Md.: University Press of America.
*Keller, Richard C. 1982. *Pennsylvania's little New Deal.* New York: Garland Publishing.
*Klein, Philip S., and Ari Hoogenboom. 1980. *A history of Pennsylvania.* University Park: Pennsylvania State University Press.
Madonna, G. Terry, and Berwood A. Yost. 1995. *Pennsylvania votes, 1994.* Millersville, Pa.: Millersville University.
Smith, Reed M. 1963. *State government in transition: Reforms of the Leader administration.* Philadelphia: University of Pennsylvania Press.

# *Rhode Island*

ELMER E. CORNWELL JR.

## PARTY HISTORY

Rhode Island's experience with some kind of party politics extends back to the period before the Revolution. From 1760 until the war, two stable factions competed like rudimentary political parties for the executive and legislative offices made elective by the colony's liberal charter. The spoils each sought were the numerous appointive positions in the gift of the assembly majority. These positions, like latter-day patronage, were used to reward friends and build the "organization." The assembly also could and did manipulate the state property tax rate to lighten the burden on towns the majority had carried at the expense of its opponents (Lovejoy 1958).

The record does not tell us whether the factions maintained local committee structures. We do know from Noble Cunningham's research that by the Jeffersonian period there were party committee structures at various levels in many states. This was less true in New England. In Rhode Island, he writes, "a state caucus directed Republican operations. . . .

The innovation of the convention in Rhode Island in 1808 was an important exception" (Cunningham 1963, 146ff). Conventions came to supplant caucuses as nominating bodies.

During the nineteenth century and into the twentieth, the state experienced three "revolutions" which profoundly affected its parties and party competition. In combination the revolutions transformed the small, sparsely populated agrarian society of the eighteenth century into the blue-collar ethnic melting pot that Rhode Island is today.

Rhode Island claims with some justification to be the cradle of the industrial revolution in America. The Slater textile mill, established in 1790, launched an economic transformation which by the turn of the twentieth century had made the state one of the most highly industrialized in the country.

The economic transformation brought on the second—the demographic—revolution. The colony had been settled almost entirely by Anglo-Saxon Protestants. As the textile industry grew, the available labor supply from among the sons and daughters of the local farmers became inadequate. The influx of the Irish in the 1840s became a new source of supply. The Irish were followed by a major immigration of French Canadians, then Portuguese from the Azores, and, toward the end of the nineteenth century, Italians. The century of immigration transformed the state's population to one that was overwhelmingly non-Anglo-Saxon and Catholic (65 percent of the population was Catholic, making Rhode Island the most Catholic state in the Union).

Third, urbanization increased. Industrialization drew population from the rural towns into the factory centers, causing the former to shrink and the latter to grow explosively. Much of the immigrant population also flooded into the mill cities and towns, with the result that Rhode Island became one of the most highly urbanized of all the states and remains so today (Coleman 1969, ch. 6).

The stresses and strains in the social fabric produced by these enormous changes profoundly influenced and shaped parties and politics. The mill owners tended to be from the old Anglo-Saxon stock. Throughout the nineteenth century they actively recruited mill workers from Canada and elsewhere on the one hand, while on the other they ensured that the state's constitutional and legal arrangements left them in political control. Property qualifications were contrived to disfranchise most of the immigrants. The last of the property qualifications did not disappear until the 1920s. Legislative malapportionment, particularly of the state senate, ensured overrepresentation of small towns and heavy Republican majorities in the state senate.[1] The governing elite, through its chosen vehicle the Republican Party, fought reform, giving ground only gradually and grudgingly on the franchise. Little was done about malapportionment until *Baker v. Carr*. The Democrats had a natural potential majority, which grew steadily but was largely disfranchised. When the disfranchised were finally released from property restrictions, their frustrations and hostilities fueled the Democratic Party for a couple of generations and have only begun to fade appreciably in recent years.

The electoral record documents the long period of GOP dominance. Taking the seventy-four years from 1856 to 1930, the Republicans controlled the governorship for sixty-three years (sixty-five if the two terms of governors elected under the "Union" label are added). The Democrats were in office only nine years. Rhode Island voted for Republican presidential candidates in seventeen of the nineteen elections between 1856 and 1928. In 1912 the state went narrowly for Wilson, and it supported Al Smith in 1928.

The early 1930s were the watershed in the state's political history. From 1932 to 1992 Rhode Island voted Democratic for president in all but four elections (Eisenhower twice,

Nixon in 1972, and Reagan in 1984). And the Democrats held the governorship for forty-six of the sixty-six years from 1932 through 1998. A more profound change of party allegiance could hardly be imagined.

The prelude to the dramatic shift of the 1930s was the candidacy of Democrat Al Smith in 1928 and his narrow victory in Rhode Island over Hoover. Smith clearly energized the immigrants of the Rhode Island population as no one else had. Until then, their turnout had been low, and Democratic candidates generally had been unattractive. In 1932 Roosevelt carried the depression-battered state, as did Democrat Theodore Francis Green for governor. Green won again in the Democratic sweep of 1934, in which the Democrats won a solid majority in the state house and a narrow state senate majority achieved via a couple of recounts.

The Democrats in 1935 controlled both houses for the first time in decades. Following a carefully prepared script, they enacted a number of long-sought Democratic reforms, including a total restructuring of the archaic administrative branch. A modern departmental structure was established, and the party used its access to state patronage to consolidate its new majority position.[2]

Eventually, however, the Democrats' hegemony began to fray. Its basis in traditional allegiances weakened as new generations emerged for whom such ties were less compelling. Republican John Chafee's three successive victories for governor beginning in 1962 signaled a new freedom from partisan loyalties. Independent voting grew steadily in Rhode Island as elsewhere. Voters learned how to split their tickets rather than pull the master lever to vote straight party.

By the late 1980s a new preoccupation had roused the electorate: corruption, symbolized by the resignation in disgrace of two chief justices and the enforced closure of all state-chartered credit unions. Republican Edward DiPrete had been reelected to a second term in 1986 over Bruce Sundlun by a two-to-one margin only to be defeated by Sundlun by nearly three-to-one in 1990. The massiveness of the voter shift in the four years from 1986 to 1990 stemmed in part from charges of extortion and receiving kickbacks leveled against the DiPrete administration and the widespread suspicion of all politics and politicians. Voter independence has replaced party loyalty.

## ORGANIZATIONAL DEVELOPMENT

The details of party organization before the 1880s are difficult to document. Until the secret ballot and accompanying legislative regulations of parties were adopted in Rhode Island in 1889, political structures left few traces. If the state were to print all ballots (as the parties had until then), parties had to be formally defined by law and the processes for receiving nominations from them spelled out. State law still did not specify a party structural hierarchy, "though conventions or caucuses" at the state, city ward, and voting district levels were referred to in the public law of 1889.[3]

The long-standing caucus system for selecting party candidates (and the use of conventions for statewide offices) remained in effect until the adoption of the direct primary in 1947. By that time, caucus meetings at the city and ward level had been open to increasing abuse. The first reform steps were the enactment in 1902 of statutes to regulate and prescribe the conduct of city and ward caucuses. The statutes applied only to the cities but did include new language mandating the election of ward committees at the caucus and providing that the ward committees would comprise each city committee.[4]

Rhode Island was in 1947 one of the last two states to adopt the direct primary.[5] This reform caused a major change in the status of political parties. Once viewed as strictly private bodies unmentioned in law, they became subject to an increasing number of prescriptions and regulations by the state. The 1947 Rhode Island law mandated the primary as the mode of selecting all party officials below the level of the state committee.[6] Primaries sharply alter the party role in selecting nominees, which is the most important function that parties have traditionally had. The goal of the reform was to take from the party organs (committees or caucuses) and give to the rank-and-file party members that prerogative. Undoubtedly, this loss of power by the party organs explains the long resistance to the primary in Rhode Island.

The law passed in 1947 mandated a closed primary; it was designed to preserve as much power over nominations as possible for the loyal party members and the committees. It directed the party organs at each level to endorse candidates for the various nominations. These endorsees would be placed in the first column on the party primary ballot with asterisks following their names.[7] To limit primary participation to bona fide members, the law prohibited voters from participating in a party's primary within twenty-six months of having participated in a different party's primary. [8]

The most recent election law development affecting the parties was court invalidation of the twenty-six month rule. In 1978, to meet the court's concern, the Rhode Island General Assembly had to pass legislation allowing voters to cancel or change party affiliation at virtually any time they chose. The state now has, as a result, an open primary.[9] The open primary, combined with the growing tendency of voters to prefer independent status, has shrunk greatly the number of voters with any degree of stable party affiliation. Moreover, it has left the parties with steadily declining influence over nominations, especially for major offices.

As late as the 1940s and 1950s, the parties played the dominant role in recruiting candidates. The executive committee of the state committee typically presented a consensus slate to the full committee, which rarely dissented. These endorsed candidates won in the primary with no significant exceptions. In 1960 Claiborne Pell became the first unendorsed statewide candidate to win nomination. He won the U.S. Senate election in November. His unprecedented win showed others that it could be done and contributed to a trend in later primaries.

Unendorsed candidates won Democratic nominations for a large number of races, including those for the Second Congressional District in 1974; U.S. Senate (against a sitting governor) in 1976; governor in 1984; general treasurer in 1988; the Second Congressional District and governor (the endorsed candidate for governor came in third) in 1990; and governor (against a sitting governor) in 1994. Unendorsed Republican candidates won First Congressional District nominations in 1970 and 1978 and governorship nominations in 1992 and 1994. (Note that *both* candidates for governor in 1994 were unendorsed.)

In short, in a state once known for its powerful parties, control over major candidacies has steadily declined. In some recent cases it can be argued persuasively that, so hostile are voters toward what they perceive to be the machinations of parties, endorsed candidates might have been better off to decline the endorsement. The proportion of independents and crossovers voting in primaries has been increasing steadily. Between 1978 and 1995 the percent of all voters who registered as Democrats dropped from about one-third to one-quarter, the Republicans went from less than 10 percent of registered voters to the low teens, and the independents were well over half throughout.[10]

As is happening nationally, the self-starter candidate who owes little to the party organization for his or her nomination or election has become an increasingly prominent feature in Rhode Island. As a result, campaigns for congressional and statewide office are typically lone-wolf, candidate-centered affairs. Candidates must, especially to challenge incumbents, raise large sums of money to mount a credible primary campaign. The winner must then seek funds for the general election. Each candidate builds his or her own campaign organization, hires consultants, and conducts polls. A few decades ago the state parties might have organized mass rallies at which the various members of the ticket would appear or turn out the faithful to canvass. Television has largely eliminated all of this.

In the mid-1970s, Lawrence McGarry, an old-style urban "pol" out of the Providence machine, turned over the Rhode Island Democratic Party chair to Charles Reilly, a young, energetic chair with new ideas. Reilly, among other innovations, attempted to revive a coordinating campaign role for the party. A common state campaign headquarters was set up, and shared services, such as polling, were initiated. But the pressures toward campaign fragmentation were too strong, and autonomous candidacies continued.

The Republicans began to enjoy increasing success in the top offices in 1962 with the election of John Chafee to the first of three successive terms as governor. The U.S. congressional seats are now often shared by the parties, and in 1994 the GOP elected a governor and two of the other four state officers. The party's strategy has been to concentrate resources on the top of the ticket. This paid off but has left the legislature with heavy Democratic majorities. To an extent, the GOP has retained more of an electoral role than its opponents.

National issues have not greatly affected the broad stances of the parties in recent decades. The Democratic Party has remained relatively conservative on "libertarian" issues and liberal on "bread and butter" issues. The Republicans are somewhat the reverse. Since the 1930s labor has played a very large role in the Democratic Party and in its campaigns, but currently labor's role is somewhat diminished. The Republican Party finally lost its base in the rotten borough senate by the 1950s (even before the Supreme Court's decision in *Baker v. Carr* forced reapportionment).[11] It has since broadened its appeal and leadership base and gained strength, in the suburban areas in particular. Today, save for the General Assembly, the Republican Party is close to being an equal partner in a competitive two-party system.

## CURRRENT PARTY ORGANIZATION

The current organizational structure of the parties in Rhode Island is set by state law.[12] Each party is to have a state committee as its chief governing body. Individual city and town committees comprise the other major components. There are no county or regional levels of organization. In the cities there is a ward committee for each ward, and the combined memberships of these ward committees form the city committee. Towns have one town committee comprising at-large members. There are no formal party officials at the precinct level in Rhode Island (where precincts are called "voting districts"). It is probably the case that ward committees attempt to incorporate representatives of various ward neighborhoods in their membership.

In addition, there are representative and senatorial district committees.[13] The former, one each for the hundred seats in the house, have from three to five members, depending on whether the district is or is not within one city or town. The latter have from five to seven members for each of the fifty senate districts.

The members of all these committees except the state committees are chosen at the respective party primaries. The law allows each party to determine the method for selecting state committee members.[14] The Democrats choose one committeeman and one committeewoman from each of the one hundred state house districts. This has the effect of apportioning the seats quite accurately in accordance with population. It also gives a Democratic speaker and house majority leadership considerable control over the Democratic state committee because the sitting house members make efforts, usually successful, to ensure that the district committee members are their hand-picked people. Individual house members communicate leadership desires to their district state committee members, who rely on the district committee for their endorsement.

The Republican state committee membership pattern is far more complex. The local Republican committee in each city and town chooses delegates to the state body. With a few significant exceptions, each of the thirty-nine cities and towns in the state sends three delegates: usually its chair and two other individuals. Cranston, Warwick, and Providence choose eight, eight, and ten delegates, respectively. Another eight of the larger towns are allotted three or four delegates to the state committee. This allocation heavily overrepresents the (often Republican) small towns. The populations among the other twenty-eight range from 821 to well over 20,000. There are other categories of members, including twenty-three at-large members appointed by the state chair, Republican mayors and administrators of towns, and Republican legislative leaders. The intention clearly is to represent Republican strength.

State law also mandates that each party hold a state convention prior to the general election.[15] The convention membership must comprise the party's candidates in the upcoming election for all state offices (statewide, U.S. Congress, and state legislative). The sole function of the convention is to adopt the party platform. This is rarely more than a pro forma exercise since the party leaders, and the governor if of the same party, essentially write the platform. As with platforms generally in American politics, these play an almost negligible role in the ensuing campaign.

The party caucuses in the General Assembly are important elements in the overall party structures, especially of the majority party. As is true in many state legislatures, the majority party caucuses and party leadership in Rhode Island play a major role in setting agendas and managing the flow of legislation through the appointment of committee members and committee chairs, among other things. This does not mean that there are close ties or patterns of cooperation between the legislative parties and the state parties. Party ties are strong within each legislative chamber, though there is considerable interchamber rivalry. The state parties do little to try to influence the parties in the General Assembly and would not be successful if they tried. Nor do the legislative parties consult the state parties. The governor at times works closely with fellow partisans in the assembly but has very few means of exerting control or even influence over them.

In four cities and in some towns the voters approved home rule charters when that option became available in 1951, providing for nonpartisan local elections. The obvious effect of nonpartisan elections was to deprive the local party committees of their endorsing role. Even though people with partisan ties participate in these local elections, the formal party organs are left with very little to do save supporting state candidates.

Rhode Island has adopted legislation regulating both electoral expenditures and contributions.[16] The legislation has had little direct effect on the operation of the parties. Both parties for a number of years have been living hand to mouth financially. In the machine era around the turn of the century, most contributions were given to the parties and were doled out by them to favored candidates. Now, the parties struggle to maintain a small state party office. The party chairs have little importance or influence and no power, since they lack resources to distribute.

Since Rhode Island is small geographically, one central office for each party, usually in Providence, has sufficed. Generally, the GOP has had a few more staff, but neither party, especially in recent years, has had more than three or four people on salary.

Increasingly, aspirants have had to face a primary opponent. Contributions are avidly sought by aspiring candidates for state office (it costs little to run for the General Assembly) long before the primary. The parties thus find little money left among the faithful or interest groups that they can tap for operating expenses. This is another consequence of the self-starter candidate system now so prevalent. In 1994, an election year, official reports showed that the Democrats had raised about $242,000 and the Republicans, $172,000. The income tax checkoff produced approximately 20 percent of each total. The Democratic state committee ended the year owing $63,000, and the Republican committee, $28,000. These amounts are minuscule compared with the several million dollars the candidates spent in 1994.[17]

Overall, Rhode Island parties have become marginal to the political and electoral process. A sitting governor chooses the party's chair, since he wants the party on his team. This does not mean that the state committee or any other party entity exerts much influence beyond the personal advice of the chair. State party organs generally have little influence on the presidential nominating process, especially in tiny Rhode Island, now that the national convention has become so overshadowed by the presidential primaries.[18]

The state party's relationship with the local parties is largely pro forma. The state party has few resources to make available. In fact, some years ago the Democratic city and town chairs formed an association to try to exert influence on endorsements and other decisions that they felt they could not influence through the state committee. The Democratic Party in the assembly (overwhelming Democratic majorities have been the rule for decades) is no more inclined to pay attention to the state party than is the governor. In both cases there is little incentive to do so.

In sum, with political independence the order of the day, a very small and shrinking body of party loyalists and activists, and a public that has become convinced that parties, along with politicians, and indeed government itself, are all part of the problem, party work has become for most a thankless task. For anyone who believes parties are important and a positive force potentially, the present mood about them in Rhode Island is, to say the least, disheartening.

### RESOURCE GUIDE

Providence College and the University of Rhode Island have archival material that would be of interest to anyone doing research on Rhode Island parties. At Providence College are the papers of former Democratic governors Robert E. Quinn (1937–1939), J. Howard McGrath (1941–1945), John O. Pastore (1945–1950), and Dennis J. Roberts (1951–1959). Also of interest at Providence are the papers of Joseph A. Doorley, Jr., mayor of Providence from 1965 to 1975.

At the University of Rhode Island are the papers of Democratic governors Frank Licht (1969–1973), Philip Noel (1973–1977), J. Joseph Garrahy (1977–1985), and Bruce Sundlun

**Table 1**   Rhode Island Resource Guide

|  | Democrats | Republicans |
|---|---|---|
| Archive | Yes | None |
| Location | Rhode Island Democratic Party | — |
|  | P.O. Box 6067 |  |
|  | Providence, RI 02940 |  |
| Dates | 1960–present | — |
| Finding aid | No | — |
| Access | By appointment | — |
| Contents: |  | — |
|   Executive committee minutes | No | — |
|   Correspondence | No | — |
|   Organizational structure | No | — |
|   Budgets | Yes | — |
|   Rules | No | — |

(1991–1995) and the papers of Republican governors William Vanderbilt (1939–1941) and John Chafee (1963–1969).

Both Providence College and the University of Rhode Island have papers of individuals who served in the U.S. Senate and House, but those are somewhat less likely to be useful for state party research.

The Rhode Island Historical Society does not report having many papers that would pertain to state parties. The state committee offices have no formal archives.

The Rhode Island State Archives in Providence has some material on the conduct of elections, including sample ballots and other official material of that sort. The State Board of Elections, also in Providence, will have recent materials, on reported campaign contributions and expenditures in particular.

**NOTES**

1. Steffens (1905, 337–353) provides a detailed discussion of the Republican state machine and its reliance on franchise restrictions and the malapportioned senate.
2. An excellent account of these crucial developments of the 1930s can be found in Levine (1963, ch. 9).
3. Chapter 812 of the Public Laws of 1889; *General Laws of the State of Rhode Island and Providence Plantations, 1896*, title 2, ch. 11.
4. Chapter 1078 of the Public Laws of 1902; *General Laws of the State of Rhode Island, 1909*, title 2, ch. 12.
5. Legislation adopting the direct primary appears in ch. 1886 of the Public Laws of 1947, now title 17, ch. 15 of the *General Laws of Rhode Island, 1956*.
6. *General Laws of Rhode Island, 1956*, title 17, ch. 15, sec. 7(b).
7. *Ibid.*, title 17, ch. 12, secs. 4, 11.
8. *Ibid.*, title 17, ch. 15, sec. 8.
9. Public Laws of 1978, ch. 107, sec. 3; and the *General Laws of Rhode Island, 1956*, title 17, ch. 15, sec. 24.
10. Data from Alpha Research, Providence, R.I., and the Rhode Island Poll, Brown University, Providence, R.I.
11. The term *rotten borough* refers to the grossly depopulated Parliamentary districts before the Reform Act of 1832. In Rhode Island, as long as each city and town was entitled to one senator, the GOP could elect a senate majority based on the votes of very small rural towns.
12. *General Laws of Rhode Island, 1956*, title 17, ch. 12 deals with the composition, powers, duties, and other aspects of the various levels of party committees.

13. *General Laws of Rhode Island, 1956,* title 17, ch. 12, sec. 7.
14. The composition, selection, and other characteristics of state committees and their members are found in the bylaws of the parties.
15. *General Laws of Rhode Island, 1956,* title 17, ch. 12, sec. 13.
16. The law is complex and comprehensive. All candidates and party committees must file a series of reports on contribution receipts and campaign expenditures. (Party committees must file annual reports as well.) Gubernatorial candidates may opt to accept public funding, but if they do, they must raise matching dollars and accept a total expenditure limit. The law regulates political action committee as well as individual contributions. *General Laws of Rhode Island, 1956,* title 17, ch. 25, secs. 1ff.
17. Figures are from the reports filed by the parties with the State Board of Elections.
18. In 1995 the General Assembly changed the date of the Rhode Island presidential primary so that it would match the other New England states (except New Hampshire) and create a regional primary. Rhode Island would hope for more candidate attention as a result. *Public Laws of 1995,* ch. 80.

### REFERENCES

*Asterisks denote the most important publications on Rhode Island party politics.*

Coleman, Peter J. 1969. *The transformation of Rhode Island, 1790–1860.* Providence, R.I.: Brown University Press.

Cunningham, Noble E. 1963. *The Jeffersonian Republicans in power, party operations, 1801–1809.* Chapel Hill: University of North Carolina Press.

Goodwin, George, and Victoria Schuck, eds. 1968. *Party politics in the New England states.* Supplement to *Policy.* Burham, N.H.: New England Center for Continuing Education.

*Kirk, William. 1909. *A modern city, Providence, Rhode Island.* Chicago: University of Chicago Press.

*Levine, Erwin L. 1963. *Theodore Francis Green, the Rhode Island years.* Providence, R.I.: Brown University Press.

*Lockard, Duane. 1959. *New England state politics.* Princeton. N.J.: Princeton University Press.

Lovejoy, David S. 1958. *Rhode Island politics and the American Revolution 1760–1776.* Providence, R.I.: Brown University Press.

*McLoughlin, William G. 1978. *Rhode Island, a history.* New York: W. W. Norton.

*Peirce, Neal R. 1976. *The New England states.* New York: W. W. Norton.

Rhode Island. 1909. *General Laws of Rhode Island, 1909.*

Rhode Island. 1896. *General Laws of the State of Rhode Island and Providence Plantations, 1896.*

Steffens, Lincoln. 1905. *Rhode Island: A state for sale.* McClure's Magazine 24, no. 4 (February): 337–353.

# South Carolina

ROBERT STEED

## PARTY HISTORY

From the 1890s to the 1950s the Democratic Party dominated the South Carolina political and party systems. At the presidential level, for example, Democrats won all but one election between 1900 and 1964; the only exception was in 1948 when Strom Thurmond, a South Carolinian, carried the state as the candidate of the States' Rights Party. Not only did

Democratic presidential candidates normally win, they won impressively, dropping below 90 percent of the vote only once during this period (at 87 percent in 1944). Similarly, prior to the 1960s there were no Republican successes in senatorial, congressional, gubernatorial, or state legislative elections, and frequently Democrats ran virtually unopposed (see Fowler 1966; Bain 1972; Bass and DeVries 1976, ch. 11; Moore 1983; Moreland, Steed, and Baker 1986; Graham 1988; Steed, Moreland, and Baker 1992).

This situation began to change in the 1950s, first at the presidential level and then gradually at the state and local levels. Dramatic economic and social changes, the most important of which were related to the sweeping challenges to the Jim Crow system of race relations, contributed to cracking Democratic solidarity. One of the earliest and clearest manifestations of change in the state's traditional one-partyism came in 1948 when Thurmond launched his third-party candidacy for president. Although the state returned to the Democratic fold in 1952, it was only by a 51 percent to 49 percent margin. In 1956 Adlai Stevenson, the Democratic candidate, carried the state, but only with a plurality, as 55 percent of the vote went to either Republican incumbent Dwight Eisenhower or independent Harry F. Byrd. John F. Kennedy barely carried the state in 1960 with 51 percent of the vote.

In the mid-1960s two events launched a period of Republican growth. The first was the dramatic switch on September 6, 1964, of Senator Thurmond from the Democratic to the Republican Party. The second occurred two months later, when 59 percent of the state's voters cast their presidential votes for the Republican candidate, Barry Goldwater. In a related development, Rep. Albert Watson supported Goldwater and was stripped of his seniority by House Democrats; he resigned, switched parties, and regained his vacated seat in a special election in 1965, thus becoming the first Republican elected to Congress in the state since Reconstruction. Further impetus to the fledgling Republican Party came the next year, when both Thurmond and Watson won reelection to their respective seats and the Republicans actually nominated, for the first time in decades, a gubernatorial candidate, Joseph Rogers. Although Rogers lost, he did gain 42 percent of the vote and carried three counties. Rogers's unexpectedly strong showing was accompanied by Republicans winning sixteen seats in the South Carolina General Assembly. Thus, by the mid-1960s the Republican Party had been reborn in South Carolina (Bain 1972; Steed, Moreland, and Baker 1992; Steed, Moreland, and Baker 1995).

Over the past three decades South Carolina has moved steadily, though slowly, toward a competitive two-party system. This has been most apparent in presidential elections, where Republican candidates carried the state in seven of the eight elections between 1964 and 1992. The only exception was in 1976, when fellow southerner Jimmy Carter won with 56 percent of the vote. Indeed, South Carolina has become one of the staunchest Republican strongholds at this level, frequently ranking as one of the two or three most Republican states in the nation in presidential voting, as measured by percentage of the popular vote. Indeed, South Carolina was George Bush's second-best state in 1992 (Moreland, Steed, and Baker 1986; Moreland, Steed, and Baker 1991; Moreland 1994).

At the state level, Republican successes increased as well. The GOP first won the governorship in 1976 and then ran off a string of three straight gubernatorial victories, in 1986, 1990, and 1994. The state's U.S. Senate seats have been split since Thurmond's party switch in 1964, and the Republicans have consistently held at least one congressional district since 1965. Republicans won three seats (half the state's congressional delegation) in 1982, 1984, and 1992; they held a majority of seats from 1980 to 1982 and returned to majority status in

1994. After two decades of gradual improvement in state legislative elections, Republicans finally passed a significant threshold in 1990 by winning a third of the seats in the lower chamber, enough to sustain a gubernatorial veto (Steed 1994; Steed, Moreland, and Baker 1995). Then, in stunning fashion, they became the majority party in the lower chamber in 1994, a year in which they also won seven of the state's nine constitutional offices, including the governorship (Cook 1994; Charleston *Post and Courier* 1994)

In short, then, the South Carolina party system has undergone a significant realignment in the post–World War II period. Whether Republican growth, especially in 1994, will be sustained is not yet clear, but it is clear that the state's party system has become competitive and is unlikely to return to the solid one-partyism of the past.

## ORGANIZATIONAL DEVELOPMENT

Prior to the 1960s neither party in South Carolina had much in the way of formal organization. Republican organization was virtually nonexistent because Republicans in the state were virtually nonexistent; indeed, the state chair during the 1950s served full time as chair of the Board of Public Welfare in Washington, D.C. The main Republican effort in the 1950s was spearheaded by retired industrialist David Dows, but little progress was made (Moore 1983).

Democratic organization existed, at least on paper, from the precinct through the county to the judicial circuit to the congressional district to the state level; in reality, however, there was little real organization or organizational activity above the county level. During the early 1900s, as the primary became the principal means for making nominations, the judicial circuit and congressional district levels were eliminated (Jordan 1962). Still, formal organizational activity above the county level was rare, in large part because it was unnecessary for Democratic victory (Key 1949).

As the Republican Party became more competitive electorally in the 1960s, both parties responded with greater attention to their respective organizations. As early as 1961 J. Drake Edens, Jr., began to push the organizational development of the state Republican Party with unprecedented vigor. The first fruit of his labor was the election of Charles Boineau as the first Republican in the state legislature this century. Between 1962 and 1965 Edens served as the state chair of the Republican Party and built the state's first genuine party organization (Moore 1983, 46–47; Bass and DeVries 1976, 24). With the party switches of Thurmond and Watson, their subsequent election victories, and the election of a handful of Republicans to the state legislature, the Republican Party had a small but active nucleus interested in organizational development. Of particular importance was the financial support of Roger Milliken, president of the family-owned Milliken-Deering textile corporation, the third largest in the world (Moore 1983). By 1966 the Republicans had established a headquarters divided into four divisions: Administrative, Research, Organization, and Finance. Each division was headed by a full-time salaried director, and an executive director had overall responsibility for headquarters operation *(Standing Operating Procedures of the South Carolina Republican Party Headquarters* 1966).

The Democrats' response was slow, in large part because their dominance of the state's politics was still nearly complete. The focus of the state executive committee was less on interparty combat than on administering the electoral system, especially the party's primaries. Much of the archival materials for the early 1960s are records on candidate filings, primary returns and recounts, and other such details related to conducting primaries and elections. Although the Democrats began to take notice of the emerging Republican threat and moved to become more formally organized and more efficient in such activities as fund raising and candidate support in the mid-1960s, their main concerns were changes occurring within the Democratic Party itself.

Specifically, the South Carolina Democratic Party had to contend with two major changes in the mid- to late 1960s. First, the civil rights movement, as part of its multi-pronged attack on the Jim Crow system, targeted laws denying African Americans the right to vote and rules preventing them from participating in party activities. Second, following the 1968 Democratic National Convention, this broad assault on exclusionary practices became intermingled with the effort to reform the national convention delegate selection process (see, for example, Crotty 1983; Price 1984, ch. 6; Polsby 1983; Steed 1990). In both cases, the South Carolina Democrats found themselves wrestling with a myriad of changes in election law (for example, the 1965 Voting Rights Act) and party rules. At the same time, and in a related matter, they struggled to deal with what many considered to be unwelcome changes in the national party. Thus, the South Carolina Democrats sought ways to remain a part of the national organization while distancing themselves from the increasingly liberal image of the national party and such locally unpopular presidential candidates as Hubert Humphrey and George McGovern.

By the early to mid-1970s both parties had become more organizationally active. Republican efforts to organize at the local level were still concentrated primarily in the state's urban centers, and campaign involvement was still mainly at the presidential level. Although the election of James Edwards to the governorship in 1974 was based in part on a growing Republican organization in South Carolina, it was mainly attributable to a combination of Edwards's own personal appeal and a series of Democratic misfortunes and mistakes (including the late disqualification of the winner of the Democratic primary for fairly narrow technical reasons related to an interpretation of the state's residency requirement; the replacement candidate was tarnished by the widely held belief among many Democrats that he had engineered the disqualification). Even so, Edwards's victory coupled with scattered electoral successes at the state and local levels spurred the party's gradual organizational development over the next two decades. In the late 1970s and early 1980s the Republican Party continued to operate a permanent, well-staffed headquarters in Columbia, succeeded in getting a county chair in almost every county, worked to extend local organizations into at least some precincts in each county of the state, and regularly organized well-attended, efficiently run state conventions.

Once the turmoil associated with adjusting to new national party rules and the entry of African Americans into the party organization had subsided, the Democrats were able to concentrate more of their organizational effort on meeting the new challenge from the Republicans. Understandably, much of this effort went into trying to prevent Republican success at the presidential level from extending into state and local elections while at the same time complying with national party rules. The key to this effort lay in holding together a fragile biracial coalition. African Americans became more heavily involved in party operations, especially at the state level, where by 1988 they had come to comprise a majority of delegates at the state party convention. Although holding a far smaller proportion of official precinct positions as recently as 1992 (less than 15 percent), African Americans constitute a critical component of the Democratic organization. Unfortunately for the Democrats, a large portion of the white party activists do not share the same ideological and issue orientations, and thus the party is faced with the potential for internal conflict regarding platforms, candidates, and election campaign strategy (Steed and McGlennon 1990; Steed, Moreland, and Baker 1995).

## CURRENT PARTY ORGANIZATION

In the mid-1990s both parties in South Carolina have active organizations.[1] Both have a permanent headquarters in Columbia with executive directors and full-time paid staffs, and both are engaged in a variety of electoral and organizational activities. The headquarters are remarkably similar in organization and purpose.

Currently, the Republican headquarters staff consists of an executive director, an administrative director, a finance director, a political director, and supporting clerical staff. In addition, there are normally three or four unpaid interns; in times of extraordinary activity, the staff and interns will be supplemented with volunteers as necessary. Far removed from the days when a skeletal staff operated out of a suite of rooms in a downtown Columbia hotel, the Democratic headquarters staff now consists of an executive director, a communications director, a field director, an administrative assistant/office manager, and clerical support. One or two interns and volunteers supplement the staff. In both parties, the headquarters operate at the behest of the state executive committees and maintain contact with local parties through the county representatives on the executive committees.

Each state party sees its primary purposes as promoting the party's interests throughout the state, providing campaign assistance to the party's candidates for state and national office, and serving as a liaison between the national and local parties. The state parties are, in the words of the Republican administrative director, full-time campaign and party-building organizations; the Democratic field director describes her party's main purpose as electing Democrats at all electoral levels. The development and maintenance of local organizations throughout the state are related activities. In this regard, the state party acts as a general service organization assisting local parties in such matters as fund raising, candidate recruitment, youth outreach, and the development of computer competency and general communications. In each case, the main responsibility rests with the state headquarters staffs, supplemented by volunteers as they are available. For both parties the use of volunteers coupled with relatively frequent turnover in staff positions (including executive director) over the past decade has posed problems of continuity and organizational memory, both of which are important factors in organizational efficiency. However, in both parties these problems have begun to be overcome with more careful attention to recordkeeping (made easier by greater use of computers) and improved staff retention.

Each party's headquarters works with the local party organizations to make sure they are aware of and in compliance with the various national and state laws and party regulations concerning such matters as county, state, and national convention delegate selection procedures, precinct organization, and primaries and elections. In this vein, the state headquarters serve as the repository of all precinct organization forms and county and state convention delegate lists for each county. However, it must be emphasized that the state party has little power over the local organizations, and the records are sometimes incomplete. Still, the parties clearly recognize the importance of local organizations, and both parties work to encourage their development. In this regard, for example, the current Republican executive director points proudly to the establishment at last (in the wake of the electoral successes of 1994) of at least one precinct organization in every county in

South Carolina. Similarly, the Democrats point to county party organizational efforts on training activities as a high priority.

There also is regular interaction between the parties and their national headquarters. The state party headquarters typically serve as liaisons between the national parties and the local parties and work closely with the national parties in party-building activities. For the Democrats cooperation is greater now than in the 1970s and early 1980s and was made even easier by the appointment in 1995 of Donald Fowler, a longtime state party leader, as a cochair of the national committee.

For both state parties, interaction with elected officials is an important component of their activity. The interaction is not routinized so much as it is done ad hoc as a mutual benefit. For example, the Democratic headquarters staff communicates frequently with Sen. Ernest F. Hollings and includes him in any official function, since his participation enhances party building and fund raising. Over the past few years, Republican state officials and headquarters staff have had something of an advantage inasmuch as their party has held the governorship and a number of other offices, including that of the senior senator. Since the 1994 elections, the party leadership and staff have been in an even stronger position to capitalize on their connection with state officials.

The state Republican Party is clearly benefiting from Republican success in recent presidential and gubernatorial elections. Not only does electoral success help in raising money and attracting workers, it contributes to the morale of activists at all levels of the organization. The Republicans' improved morale is clearly reflected in data on local party activists' perceptions of changes in the state's local party organization during the 1980s. For example, 87 percent of the local Republican leaders saw organizational improvement during this period. Similarly, with respect to specific areas of activity, local Republican officials generally saw improved party campaign effectiveness (82 percent), increased ability to raise funds (83 percent), an increased party role in candidate recruitment (76 percent), improved use of the media in campaigns (66 percent), and more effective use of computer technology by the party (65 percent). Only on the question of more effective use of opinion polls did fewer than half (48 percent) of the local party leaders see improvement.[2]

Conversely, the Democratic organization has felt the effect of eroding electoral support and fewer electoral successes. Local Democratic officials have much less optimistic views regarding organizational change in the past decade. For example, in sharp contrast to the Republicans, only 26 percent of Democratic activists polled thought their party's local organizations improved during this period. Similarly low proportions saw improved campaign effectiveness (27 percent), increased ability to raise funds (19 percent), an increased party role in candidate recruitment (23 percent), improved use of the media in campaigns (30 percent), more effective use of opinion polls (23 percent), and more effective use of computer technology (48 percent).

Finally, both parties potentially face some internal divisions. For the Democrats, the key remains holding together a biracial coalition whose members range from slightly conservative to fairly liberal in ideological orientation. For the Republicans, there is some potential for disruption related to increased involvement of the religious right (for example, the Christian Coalition) in party activities. In a few locales religious right activists have openly challenged, sometimes successfully, the long-standing party regulars for control of local organizations. Although this has not posed a serious problem thus far, it could become divisive, especially if such issues as abortion and school prayer become more central to

**Table 1**  South Carolina Resource Guide

| | Democrats | Republicans |
|---|---|---|
| Archive | Yes | Yes |
| Location | State Archives | State Party Headquarters |
| | 1430 Senate St., P.O. Box 11669 | 1508 Lady St. |
| | Columbia, S.C. 29211 | Columbia, S.C. 29201 |
| | (803) 734-8560 | (803) 988-8440 |
| Dates | 1926–1988[1] | 1960–present |
| Finding aid | Yes | No |
| Access | Public | By appointment |
| Contents: | | |
| Executive committee minutes | Yes | Uncertain |
| Correspondence | Yes | Yes |
| Organizational structure | Yes | Uncertain |
| Budgets | Yes | Uncertain |
| Rules | Yes | Yes |

[1] Archival materials for the years since 1988 are located at the state party headquarters in Columbia.

South Carolina politics. For the moment, however, both parties have succeeded in containing and defusing intraorganizational factionalism.

RESOURCE GUIDE

Both parties have collections of documents and records which are available to the public. The Democrats have sent all records prior to 1988 to the state archives, where they are boxed and cataloged; each box has a fairly lengthy listing of its contents. Still, these listings are relatively general and give only partial guidance for research into the records. Of particular interest, beyond the usual organizational materials, are a number of documents relating to the party's efforts to meet the requirements of the national party regarding national convention delegate selection in the 1970s. All materials for the years since 1988 are located at the state party headquarters and are still in boxes and file cabinets without a great deal of systematic organization. The apparent plan is to organize these materials periodically along the lines of those predating 1988, catalog them, and send them to the state archives.

The archival materials of the Republican Party in South Carolina are not so organized or so readily accessible as those of the Democratic Party. For the most part they are boxed and kept in storage at party headquarters with no particular arrangement and with no comprehensive finding aid. Anyone wishing to do research in these materials would surely be able to gain access but would have to work through the storage boxes with little or no guidance. Indeed, the reason for the "uncertain" entries in the summary table is that there is no way of determining whether these materials are in the boxes without a thorough and systematic search of all the storage area. The boxes contain a variety of party records and newspaper clippings but are largely unorganized. The Republican Party noted that Clemson University also has a meticulous set of materials relating to Strom Thurmond's political career (papers, correspondence, and the like), and any person doing research on Republican politics in the state would undoubtedly find these of interest.

For both parties, a large part of their records relate to precinct organizational meetings (and officials elected therein), county convention records, and state convention records.

## NOTES

1. This section draws heavily from interviews with the Republican Party executive director, Trey Walker; the Republican Party administrative director, Marian Meacham; the Democratic Party executive director, Scott Sokol; and the Democratic Party field director, Bonita Holley. The splendid cooperation of these and other party officials made this part of the report possible.
2. These data are from the Southern Grassroots Party Activists Project. The project, directed by Lewis Bowman and Charles D. Hadley and funded by the National Science Foundation under Grant SES-9009846, involved a 1991 survey of party precinct officials and county chairs in all eleven states of the former Confederacy. The particular data reported here are from the South Carolina portion of the survey; the response rates were 55 percent for the Democrats and 51 percent for the Republicans. The government has certain rights to these data. Any research findings, conclusions, or recommendations from this project are those of the author and do not necessarily reflect the views of the National Science Foundation.

## REFERENCES

*Asterisks denote the most important publications on South Carolina party politics.*
*Bain, Chester W. 1972. South Carolina: Partisan prelude. In *The changing politics of the South,* ed. William C. Havard. Baton Rouge: Louisiana State University Press.
Bass, Jack, and Walter DeVries. 1976. *The transformation of southern politics.* New York: Basic Books.
*Charleston Post and Courier.* 1994. Election reports.
*Cohadas, Nadine. 1993. Strom Thurmond and the politics of southern change. Macon, Ga.: Mercer University Press.
Cook, Rhodes. 1994. Dixie voters look away: South shifts to the GOP. *Congressional Quarterly Weekly Report,* November 12, 3230–3231.
Crotty, William. 1983. *Party reform.* New York: Longman.
*Fowler, Donald L. 1966. *Presidential voting in South Carolina, 1948–1964.* Columbia: University of South Carolina, Bureau of Governmental Research and Service.
*Graham, Cole Blease, Jr. 1988. Partisan change in South Carolina. In *The South's new politics: Realignment and dealignment,* ed. Robert H. Swansbrough and David M. Brodsky. Columbia: University of South Carolina Press.
*Graham, Cole Blease, Jr., and William V. Moore. 1994. South Carolina politics and government. Lincoln: University of Nebraska Press.
Jordan, Frank E., Jr. 1962. *The primary state: A history of the Democratic Party in South Carolina, 1876–1962.* Columbia: South Carolina Democratic Party.
Key, V. O., Jr. 1949. *Southern politics in state and nation.* New York: Alfred A. Knopf.
*Moore, William V. 1983. Parties and electoral politics in South Carolina. In *Politics in the Palmetto State,* ed. Luther F. Carter and David S. Mann. Columbia, S.C.: University of South Carolina, Bureau of Governmental Research and Service.
Moreland, Laurence W. 1994. South Carolina: Republican again. In *The 1992 presidential election in the South: Current patterns of southern party and electoral politics,* ed. Robert P. Steed, Laurence W. Moreland, and Tod A. Baker. Westport, Conn.: Praeger.
Moreland, Laurence W., Robert P. Steed, and Tod A. Baker. 1991. South Carolina: Different cast, same drama in the Palmetto State. In *The 1988 presidential election in the South: Continuity amidst change in southern party politics,* ed. Laurence W. Moreland, Robert P. Steed, and Tod A. Baker. Westport, Conn.: Praeger.
———. 1986. South Carolina. In *The 1984 presidential election in the South: Patterns of southern party politics,* ed. Robert P. Steed, Laurence W. Moreland, and Tod A. Baker. Westport, Conn.: Praeger.
Polsby, Nelson W. 1983. *Consequences of party reform.* New York: Oxford University Press.
Price, David E. 1984. *Bringing back the parties.* Washington, D.C.: CQ Press.
*Standard operating procedures of the South Carolina Republican Party State Headquarters.* 1966. Howard H. Bo Calloway Collection, Richard B. Russell Memorial Library, University of Georgia.
Steed, Robert P. 1994. Southern electoral politics as prelude to the 1992 elections. In *The 1992 presidential election in the South: Current patterns of southern party and electoral politics,* ed. Robert P. Steed, Laurence W. Moreland, and Tod A. Baker. Westport, Conn.: Praeger.

————. 1990. Party reform, the nationalization of American politics, and party change in the South. In *Political parties in the southern states: Party activists in partisan coalitions,* ed. Tod A. Baker, Charles D. Hadley, Robert P. Steed, and Laurence W. Moreland. Westport, Conn.: Praeger.

Steed, Robert P., and John McGlennon. 1990. A 1988 postscript: Continuing coalitional diversity. In *Political parties in the southern states: Party activists in partisan coalitions,* ed. Tod A. Baker, Charles D. Hadley, Robert P. Steed, and Laurence W. Moreland. Westport, Conn.: Praeger.

*Steed, Robert P., Laurence W. Moreland, and Tod A. Baker. 1995. South Carolina: Toward a two-party system. In *Southern state party organizations and activists,* ed. Charles D. Hadley and Lewis Bowman. Westport, Conn.: Praeger.

*————. 1992. South Carolina party system: Towards a two-party system. In *Government in the Palmetto State: Toward the 21st century,* ed. Luther F. Carter and David S. Mann. Columbia: University of South Carolina Institute of Public Affairs.

# South Dakota

ALAN CLEM

## PARTY HISTORY

South Dakota's party system, which has long relied on primary elections as the necessary stepping-stone to political power, typifies prairie politics. The people are widely dispersed and comparatively homogeneous, and socioeconomic class struggles are muted. In neither the governmental system nor the parties themselves is power highly concentrated.

South Dakota has given its electoral votes to the Republican presidential nominee in all but five elections since statehood was achieved in 1889; the exceptions were Democrat-Populist William Jennings Bryan in 1896, Progressive Republican Theodore Roosevelt in 1912, Democrat Franklin Delano Roosevelt in 1932 and 1936, and Democrat Lyndon Johnson in 1964. Fifty-four percent of voters even gave their votes to Richard Nixon in 1972 in preference to South Dakotan George McGovern, the Democratic standard-bearer.

The Republican Party has been dominant over the years, winning 78 percent of major elections from 1889 through 1994.[1] Democratic candidates won only occasionally until 1970. Since that time, the Democratic Party has always possessed a major office and has usually possessed at least half of them.

Third parties have played a significant role in South Dakota and in the prairie states generally. The Fusion Party—a short-lived coalition of Populists and traditional Democrats—won several major elections in the 1890s. After World War I the Nonpartisan League constituted a significant third party, and in 1920 it outpolled the Democratic candidate for governor. In 1918, 1922, 1924, and 1926 parties other than the Republican and Democratic attracted over 10 percent of the general-election vote for governor. Two-party competition has been more evident in South Dakota than in its neighboring states of Iowa, Minnesota, Nebraska, and North Dakota, where Populists and the Nonpartisan League were relatively stronger forces for longer periods of time and occasionally displaced one of the two traditional national parties.[2]

Within the Republican Party in the first third of this century, tension existed between progressive and conservative wings. Progressives were generally more successful in major contests, notably in the candidacies of Coe Crawford, Peter Norbeck, and William McMaster (each of whom was in turn elected governor and then U.S. senator), but sometimes the conservative wing was able to carry the primary election, which often resulted in November victories for Democratic candidates.

Since World War II South Dakota Republicans have campaigned and voted in Congress on the conservative side, whereas the state's Democrats, particularly George McGovern and Tom Daschle, have been part of their party's dominant liberal bloc. There was strong support for the presidential candidacies of conservatives Robert Taft and Barry Goldwater among state Republican leaders, though South Dakota voters embraced the more moderate Dwight Eisenhower enthusiastically. Support for Richard Nixon and George Bush was lukewarm as a result of the state's populist and conservative predilections as well as the candidates' lack of color. Both Democratic leaders and rank-and-file Democrats in South Dakota have been drawn to the Kennedys and to leaders from neighboring Minnesota, such as Hubert Humphrey and Walter Mondale.

In recent decades, Democratic officeholders have exhibited greater cohesion and consistency than Republicans despite the fact that ideology takes on different coloration in Pierre, Sioux Falls, and Rapid City than in Washington; congressional Democrats from South Dakota must work hard to make their relatively liberal voting records in Congress acceptable to the generally more conservative state electorate. Daschle, McGovern, Gov. Richard Kneip, Sen. James Abourezk, and Rep. Tim Johnson got along well with each other, each pursuing his goals without colliding with the others. Among Republicans, Sens. Larry Pressler and James Abdnor tolerated each other in spite of personal style differences, and Gov. George Mickelson generally stayed aloof from congressional politics, but Pressler and Gov. William Janklow (1979–1987 and 1995–) have been at each other's throats on several occasions, and Janklow in 1986 unsuccessfully challenged Abdnor for the party's senatorial nomination, which virtually doomed Abdnor's reelection bid. In the subsequent November election, Democrat Daschle beat Abdnor, gathering 51.6 percent of the vote.

Some intraparty cleavage does exist in the Republican Party, but it is based on the relative popularity and campaign effectiveness of individual candidates rather than on any persistent issue or ideological or regional factor. There currently are some signs in the state legislature of disenchantment with confrontational politics that automatically pit Republicans against Democrats. In 1995 several members of the state legislature publicly expressed irritation at Gov. Janklow's attempts to dominate the legislative process and at the intransigence of caucus leaders of both parties (Kranz 1995). This discomfort with pressures to invoke tighter party discipline seems somewhat misplaced in a state where efforts to maintain close party cohesion have been so sporadic and ineffective. Efforts to build bridges between the parties in the legislature could encourage factionalism within South Dakota's parties.

## ORGANIZATIONAL DEVELOPMENT

Political party organizations and their leaders in South Dakota are neither very visible nor very strong. Their actions and decisions seldom receive much press attention. When they do appear, press accounts of party leader activities have to do more often with reactions to external political developments than with actions of the party organization itself. The fact that South Dakota has an early, but widely ignored, presidential primary separate from the "regular" primary in June is a reflection of the domination of state legislators over party officials in making the critical decisions that affect the state's political parties.

Several factors contribute to the relative insignificance of party leaders in South Dakota political decisions and discourse. First, economic class consciousness is not very well developed in the state, and both parties have long appealed to and been composed of business, agricultural, and public service elements. Furthermore, the most important party nominations are made by the thousands of registered party members who take the trouble to vote in the June primary. This means that a candidate seeking the party's nomination for major office can totally ignore the party hierarchy. Indeed, Larry Pressler, in his first race for public office in 1974, exploited the fact that Republican leaders preferred another candidate. Primaries virtually invite competition within the party; primaries are as likely to weaken as to strengthen the party's effort in the subsequent general election campaign (Clem and Meier 1975).[3]

Another factor that diminishes the influence of South Dakota party leaders is that state law governs and regulates the most essential party structures, activities, and decisions. Nor do party leaders or South Dakota political parties have much clout with respect to campaign money. The state's congressional incumbents, because of the rise of political action committees (PACs) as a direct consequence of campaign finance reforms passed by Congress in the 1970s, have amassed large campaign treasuries, and much of the Democratic and Republican largesse has come from outside the state. McGovern, Abdnor, Pressler, Daschle, and Johnson have all collected larger and larger sums from beyond South Dakota's borders and have therefore depended less and less on contributions from individuals or political party elements within the state. The Republican Party at both the federal and state levels has generally been of greater help to its candidates, but PAC contributions to incumbent congressional Democrats have offset this advantage. In recent years, PAC aid to congressional incumbents has been so lavish that incumbents, including Tom Daschle in 1994, have been able to provide considerable help to their party's candidates for the state legislature, further eroding the party organization's position.

Yet another factor limiting the influence of party leaders is that members of Congress have their own staffs of experienced personnel. In several instances these persons have temporarily left the federal payroll to manage election campaigns in the state or have left the congressional scene altogether to take political party or interest group positions in the state (Clem 1981; Jones 1966). Thus, political experience and expertise often come from the outside and from the top, rather than from the grass roots.

## CURRENT PARTY ORGANIZATION

Two political parties, the Democratic and Republican, have long maintained their status as organized political parties eligible under state law to hold primary elections by the simple expedient of having placed a ticket on the ballot at the preceding general election. As long as an organization does that, its status as a party is preserved.

A new political party may be recognized by filing with the secretary of state a written declaration signed by at least 2.5 percent as many voters as cast votes for governor in the preceding general election; the declaration would include the name of the proposed party and a brief statement of its principles.[4] The Libertarian Party was formed in this way in 1991, the first new party in the state since the 1930s, and because its candidate received about 4 percent of the gubernatorial vote in 1994, it remains a viable party in the state. Ross

Perot's Reform Party did not file as a new party in 1996, but it qualified by petition for a position on the November 1996 presidential ballot (and three potential Perot electors will be listed). Third parties were fairly common in the state's first four decades.

In the June primary election, registered party members vote for a precinct committeeman and committeewoman to represent their precinct on the county central committee and for delegates to the state convention. This is the fundamental grassroots action that was intended to undergird party activity in the state. Often, however, there are no candidates for these party positions, in which case the incumbents remain in office or the county central committee appoints successors.

Voter turnout rates in South Dakota primary elections are lower than general election turnout rates and vary widely from year to year and from party to party. In recent contested Republican primaries, turnout rates (total votes cast divided by the number of registered party adherents) have been 52 percent in 1994, 28 percent in 1984, 49 percent in 1980, and 44 percent in 1976. Recent Democratic turnout rates have been 30 percent in 1994, 29 percent in 1984, 22 percent in 1982, 39 percent in 1980, and 33 percent in 1976.

The county central committee includes the precinct committeemen and committeewomen, the state committeeman and committeewoman from the county, and elected public officers who reside in the county. The county central committee elects the county chair, the vice chair, the secretary, the treasurer, and the state committeeman and committeewoman.[5] The county central committee usually does not elect these officers from among its own membership, though it could.

Political parties in South Dakota are governed by two entities. The first is the more powerful and visible state convention, county delegates to which are elected in the June primary; the voting power of county delegates is in direct proportion to their county's share of the statewide vote for the party's gubernatorial candidate in the preceding general election.[6] The convention meets a few weeks after the primary election. The main functions of the state conventions are to draft the party platform, nominate state candidates such as the lieutenant governor and attorney general not voted on in the primary, elect the state party chair, and (in presidential election years) choose the presidential electors and national committeeman and committeewoman.[7]

The work of the other state-level party entity, the state central committee, is to manage party affairs between state conventions, that is, almost all the time. The state central committee is composed of three persons from each county: the county chair and state committeeman and committeewoman. Because the central committee is composed of nearly two-hundred members, both parties have established smaller executive committees to meet at regular intervals to take care of any business that might arise.

Occasionally the state central committee is required by the laws of the state to make an important decision. For example, in 1962, when Sen. Francis Case died after the primary election at which he was nominated for what would have been his third term, the task of naming a new nominee fell to the Republican state central committee. After the committee on the twentieth ballot nominated Joe Bottum, Gov. Archie Gubbrud appointed Bottum to fill the Senate vacancy. In November, Bottum was narrowly defeated by Democrat George McGovern (Clem 1963b).

The state party chair is the vital link in South Dakota political parties. Chosen by the state convention, the party chair manages the convention, the state executive committee, and the state party headquarters; is in contact with the party's national committeeman and committeewoman and with the party's organization in each county; and is expected by candidates for public office to maintain a fair and neutral position in the primary election and an aggressive, supportive posture in the general election.

The state headquarters of the Democratic Party is located in Sioux Falls, the state's population, business, and communications center. The Sioux Falls location results in large part from the dominant position in the party of Senator Daschle and Representative Johnson. In the 1970s, when the state had a Democratic governor, the party maintained its headquarters in the state capital, Pierre. Pierre, despite its central location roughly halfway between Sioux Falls on the state's eastern border and Rapid City in the west, is not the bustling hub that Sioux Falls is. The move to Sioux Falls occurred in 1986 under the state chairmanship of Gene Mahan, a former state legislator who represented a district in the southeastern corner of the state.

The party's executive director, currently Greg Oleson, is responsible to the party chair and manages the day-to-day activities of the state headquarters. The state Demo-cratic Party staff includes four other positions. Working with the executive director in Sioux Falls is an East River field director and a general office worker. A West River field director works from an office in Rapid City. The party also maintains a sort of "political director" in Pierre in the person of Rick Hauffe, a former executive director. Hauffe works with the party's legislative caucuses and handles political research and communications. The Sioux Falls office is shared with members of the staffs of Senator Daschle and Representative Johnson.

As for the Republicans, their state headquarters is located in Pierre, about four blocks from the capitol. Patrick Davis, a native of Huron, became Republican executive secretary in August 1995. Davis had worked in President Bush's 1992 reelection campaign and in 1993 went to work for the Sioux Falls Convention and Visitors Bureau. Davis replaced Lance Russell, who resigned to enter law school. Russell had worked in John Timmer's congressional campaign in 1992 and was executive director of the Pennington County party organization in Rapid City. He had succeeded Georgia Hanson in late March 1995, after she accepted a position on Sen. Phil Gramm's presidential campaign staff.

Davis heads a headquarters that has five staff positions, but not all are filled. In the 1993–1994 biennium there were three full-time and one part-time worker at headquarters, but the plan was to have five persons on board for 1996. There is a finance expert, a field worker who is experienced in communications, a state legislative campaign coordinator, and a clerical person to support the executive secretary.

Of course, a good deal of partisan activity occurs, both theoretically and actually, at the county level. In the larger cities the local party organization usually maintains an office with at least volunteer staff. These offices respond to inquiries about party matters, maintain membership mailing lists, solicit donations, and arrange or coordinate meetings. In many of the smaller counties, the party will arrange temporary headquarters, if no permanent office exists, to serve as a focus of party activity during campaign periods.

### RESOURCE GUIDE

It would require considerable effort to locate, let alone verify, such basic party organizational documents as minutes, rules, budgets, status reports, and lists of officials before 1970. But for the past twenty years, most records are available in the respective party headquarters or the state archives. Recent materials have not been systematically inspected or organized.

Executive Director Jim Pribyl in the 1970s made an effort to systematize Democratic Party records, which in the past had often been taken by outgoing party chairs. There are

**Table 1**  South Dakota Resource Guide

|  | Democrats | Republicans |
|---|---|---|
| Archive | Yes | Yes |
| Location | State Party Headquarters | State Central Committee |
|  | 405 S. 3rd Ave. | 302 Pawnee St. |
|  | Sioux Falls, S.D. 57104 | Pierre, S.D. 57501 |
|  | (605) 335-7337 | (605) 224-7347 |
| Dates | 1972– | 1971– |
| Finding aid | No | No |
| Access | Public | By appointment |
| Contents: |  |  |
| Executive committee minutes | 1972– | 1972– |
| Correspondence | 1972– | 1982– |
| Organizational structure | Nothing systematic | Nothing systematic |
| Budgets | Nothing systematic | 1972– |
| Rules | Nothing systematic | Nothing systematic |

many storage boxes in the party headquarters in Sioux Falls; they are not well sorted but evidently are comprehensive as far back as 1972. There are additional useful materials dating as far back as the early 1950s, when George McGovern was reinvigorating the state party (McGovern 1977, chs. 1–3). McGovern and a former party official have deposited materials in the state archives, and Governor Kneip left many boxes from his eight-year administration (1971–1978) with the University of South Dakota archives in Vermillion.

Republican records, mainly minutes, convention records, correspondence, and budget materials, go back only to about 1970. A party upheaval around 1974 resulted in the loss or disappearance of many older records. Several party officials from earlier in the century gave papers to the state archives. Nothing is known about papers of Republican legislative caucuses or annual reports of the state party.

State law governs many aspects of political party organization and operations in South Dakota, so the *South Dakota Compiled Laws* may be usefully consulted. The daily newspapers of the state's two largest cities—the *Rapid City Journal* and the *Sioux Falls Argus-Leader*—have covered political developments over the decades, and several libraries in the state have maintained the papers over the years. Other dailies attentive to state political developments include the *Aberdeen American-News,* the *Huron Plainsman,* the *Mitchell Daily Republic,* the *Pierre Capital-Journal,* the *Watertown Public Opinion,* and the *Yankton Press and Dakotan.*

## NOTES

1. Major elections are defined here as elections for president, U.S. senator, U.S. representative, and governor.
2. Among the authorities on the political history of South Dakota and the upper Middle West are Hicks 1931; Morlan 1955; Nye 1951; and Schell 1961.
3. For historical materials on the primary laws, debated in the early decades of this century, see the collections of political scientist Clarence Berdahl in the University of South Dakota archives, LR 4 W 5:2.
4. *South Dakota Compiled Laws,* title 12, ch. 5, sec. 1.
5. *South Dakota Compiled Laws,* title 12, ch. 5, sec. 14.
6. *South Dakota Compiled Laws,* title 12, ch. 5, sec. 18.
7. *South Dakota Compiled Laws,* title 12, ch. 5, secs. 17, 19, 21, 23.

**REFERENCES**

*Asterisks denote the most important publications on South Dakota party politics.*

Clem, Alan L. 1981. South Dakota's congressional staffs. *Public Affairs* no. 81 (June). Vermillion: University of South Dakota Governmental Research Bureau.

*———. 1967. *Prairie state politics: Popular democracy in South Dakota.* Washington, D.C.: Public Affairs Press.

———. 1963a. The 1962 election in South Dakota. *Public Affairs* no. 12 (February). Vermillion: University of South Dakota Governmental Research Bureau. (The same author has continued this series of biennial election analyses, 1964 through 1994.)

———. 1963b. *The nomination of Joe Bottum: Analysis of a committee decision to nominate a United States senator.* Vermillion: University of South Dakota Governmental Research Bureau.

Clem, Alan L., and Kenneth J. Meier. 1975. Another look at the effects of divisive party primaries: The South Dakota experience, 1946–1974. *Public Affairs* no. 62 (August). Vermillion: University of South Dakota Governmental Research Bureau.

Hicks, John D. 1931. *The populist revolt: A history of the Farmers Alliance and the People's Party.* Minneapolis: University of Minnesota Press. (Reissued by University of Nebraska Press in 1961.)

Jones, Charles O. 1966. South Dakota in Washington: Profile of a congressional delegation. *Public Affairs* no. 24 (February). Vermillion: University of South Dakota Governmental Research Bureau.

Kranz, David. 1995. Frustrated senators may break away from party caucuses. *Sioux Falls Argus-Leader,* April 20, D1–D2.

*McGovern, George S. 1977. *Grassroots: The autobiography of George McGovern.* New York: Random House.

Morlan, Robert L. 1955. *Political prairie fire: The nonpartisan league, 1915–1922.* Minneapolis: University of Minnesota Press.

*Nye, Russell B. 1951. *Midwestern progressive politics: A historical study of its origins and development, 1870–1950.* East Lansing: Michigan State University Press.

*Schell, Herbert S. 1961. *History of South Dakota.* Lincoln: University of Nebraska Press.

# *Tennessee*

### DAVID M. BRODSKY

Tennessee was one of the first southern states to abandon the Democratic Party in presidential elections, giving its electoral votes to Dwight D. Eisenhower in 1952 and 1956 and to Richard M. Nixon in 1960 and 1968. Tennessee also was one of the first southern states where grassroots support for Republican candidates expanded below the presidential level, electing in 1962 William Brock III to the Third Congressional District House of Representatives seat once held by Democrat Estes Kefauver, sending Howard Baker Jr. to the U.S. Senate in 1966, falling one seat short of controlling the state house of representatives in 1968, and electing in 1970 the first Republican governor since 1920.

## PARTY HISTORY

Present-day Volunteer State politics has its origins in Tennessee's geographic diversity, in the legacies of the Civil War and of Reconstruction, and in the recurring periods of intra-party factional conflict among both Democrats and Republicans.

*Geography, the Civil War, and Reconstruction.* One cannot overestimate the impact of geography and history on contemporary Tennessee politics. Perhaps V. O. Key (1949, 75) best made the point when he wrote:

> Tennessee's Democratic-Republican cleavage stands as a monument to the animosities of Civil War and Reconstruction. Even before the War a sense of separation set off East Tennesseans from their fellow citizens to the west, although partisan divisions did not follow closely geographical lines. The dispute over slavery and secession, however, forged Tennessee partisan alignments into a form that has persisted to this day.

Tennessee, the last state to join the Confederacy, voted twice on secession. In each instance, the slave-holding cotton counties in West Tennessee voted for secession, and the farmers of East Tennessee and six Highland Rim counties in West Tennessee voted to remain in the Union (Swansbrough 1985; Majors 1986). Middle Tennessee divided evenly on the first vote, but on the second vote the predominantly slave-holding counties of the region provided the crucial margin for secession (Key 1949; Bass and DeVries 1976; Majors 1986). These votes and the resulting conflicts between secessionists and unionists during the war and during the Reconstruction and post-Reconstruction periods forged the subsequent contours of Tennessee politics. The counties that had voted for secession became the Democratic Party's base, and the counties that had voted to remain in the Union became the strongholds of Tennessee Republicanism (Key 1949; Majors 1986; Lamis 1990). These differences remain essentially unchanged, although suburbanization and the realignment of whites and the Republican Party have enabled the GOP to move beyond its traditional base in East Tennessee.

*Factionalism.* The Tennessee Democratic and Republican Parties have both felt the effects of statewide factional conflicts. Between 1932 and 1954 Tennessee Democrats routinely divided into two factions. One faction included the Memphis and Shelby County-based machine of Memphis mayor E. H. Crump and his allies elsewhere in the state, whereas the other faction included a relatively stable coalition of anti-Crump Democrats that opposed "machine"-backed candidates in statewide elections. After Crump's death in 1954, the basis of statewide Democratic politics shifted to "personal" factions aligned with the strong individuals (such as Estes Kefauver, Frank Clement, and Buford Ellington) who fought for control of Volunteer State government and politics or to "ideological" factions that united what Parks (1966) identified as "Bourbon" (or conservative) and anti-Bourbon (or progressive) factions.

The contest in 1962 for Kefauver's old seat in the Third Congressional District offers a vivid example of the nature and consequences of post-Crump Democratic factionalism. In the bitter 1962 primary contest, Wilkes Thrasher, a liberal, defeated the incumbent, James B. Frazier, a conservative. The Republican nominee, William E. Brock III, won the general election with the backing of disgruntled Frazier supporters and allies of the Bourbon governor, Frank Clement (Bass and DeVries 1976; Parks 1966). Brock was the first Republican elected to Congress from outside East Tennessee since Reconstruction.

Historically, factionalism among Tennessee Republicans appears to have revolved around such questions as whether or not the party should contest the Democrats at all levels, an effort that would require building a statewide organization, and the party's position toward African Americans. Key (1949) saw a split between a conservative, patronage-oriented organization faction that rarely contested the Democrats in statewide elections and a more populist antiorganization faction that wanted to build a statewide Republican

Party to challenge the Democrats. In contrast, Parks (1966) saw a Republican Party divided between conservatives, led by Barry Goldwater activists from Memphis and other Tennessee cities, and a more moderate anti-Goldwater faction centered in the mountains of East Tennessee. The conservatives gained control of the 1964 state convention and abandoned the party's traditional practice of sending racially integrated delegations to the national convention. Other implications of the conservative victory included the creation of a largely white Republican electorate. Moderates and conservatives have consistently struggled for control of the party; today, for example, former governor Lamar Alexander from East Tennessee represents the more moderate wing of the party, while current governor Don Sundquist from West Tennessee represents the more conservative wing.

*The Parties at the Polls.* During the period between the end of Reconstruction and 1952, Tennessee Republicans found most of their electoral success in the areas that had voted against secession, the mountains of East Tennessee and the Highland Rim counties of West Tennessee. East Tennessee Republicans regularly sent representatives to Congress and to Nashville, but the party's only statewide successes came in the gubernatorial elections of 1910 and 1920 and in the presidential election of 1928, when Herbert Hoover defeated Al Smith, an outcome largely attributed to Smith's religious faith (Roman Catholicism) and his opposition to Prohibition. Between 1952 and 1972, however, the Republicans engineered a series of electoral successes—successes based on recruiting attractive candidates, building effective grassroots organizations, and taking advantage of opportunities presented by factional fights within the Democratic Party. During this period, the Republicans did especially well in national elections, winning six of seven presidential contests (losing only in 1964 to Lyndon B. Johnson), capturing Tennessee's two U.S. Senate seats by electing Howard Baker Jr. in 1966 and William E. Brock III in 1970, and increasing their share of the state congressional delegation from two of nine seats in 1952 to five of eight seats in 1972. The Republicans also made gains in state elections, electing Winfield Dunn, from West Tennessee, as the first Republican governor since 1920, increasing their share of seats in the Tennessee House of Representatives from less than one in five in the 1953–1954 legislative biennium to a working majority in 1969–1970, and expanding their share of seats in the Tennessee Senate from less than one in five to almost two in five.

The national elections between 1976 and 1992 proved less kind to the Republicans. In 1976 presidential candidate Jimmy Carter carried the state, Democratic challenger Jim Sasser upset incumbent Republican senator Bill Brock, and Democrats Marilyn Lloyd and Harold Ford registered unexpected victories in the Third and Eighth Congressional Districts, respectively. In 1984 Albert Gore Jr. captured the U.S. Senate seat left vacant by the retirement of the Republican incumbent, Howard Baker Jr. In 1992 Bill Clinton, aided by the presence of native son Albert Gore on the ticket, became the first Democratic presidential nominee since Jimmy Carter (in 1976) to win Tennessee's electoral votes. Thus in 1992 the Democrats carried Tennessee in the presidential contest, controlled both of Tennessee's seats in the U.S. Senate, and occupied six of the state's nine congressional seats.

Despite the back-to-back gubernatorial victories of Republican Lamar Alexander in 1978 and 1982, the state elections between 1976 and 1992 offered little reason for Republican optimism. Former speaker of the Tennessee House of Representatives Ned McWherter recaptured the governorship for the Democrats in 1986 and then easily won reelection in 1990. The Republican share of seats in the Tennessee House of Representatives fell from near parity in 1972 to just over one in three seats in 1992. During the same period, the Republican proportion of state senate seats hovered around 33 percent.

In 1994 Tennessee Republicans rebounded from earlier disappointments. In the U.S. Senate contests, Bill Frist, a political novice, defeated three-term Democratic incumbent Jim Sasser, and lobbyist and actor Fred Thompson thwarted Fourth District representative Jim Cooper's bid to fill the seat formerly held by Vice President Gore. In the congressional elections, the Republicans retained their three seats in the state's congressional delegation and also gained seats in the Third and Fourth districts, giving them a five-to-four advantage. Finally, the Republicans increased their share of seats in the Tennessee house and, aided by Democratic defectors who switched parties after the election, gained control of the senate.

## ORGANIZATIONAL DEVELOPMENT

Recent analyses of state and local political parties present differing pictures of the Tennessee parties. Jewell and Olson (1988) described Tennessee Republicans as having strong local and state party organizations, whereas Cotter et al. (1989) characterized the Republican organizations at both levels as moderately strong. In contrast to the Republican Party, Jewell and Olson portrayed Tennessee Democrats as having strong local parties but a weak state party, a view similar to that offered by Cotter and his associates, who placed the state Democratic organization among the weakest in the South even though they rated the local parties as moderately strong.

Although Jewell and Olson and Cotter and his associates may have captured the reality of the parties at one point in time, their studies failed to capture the fluid relationship between electoral fortunes and organizational health.

*Republican Party.* Tennessee Republicans long had an organizational presence, but the modern development of the state party organization began in the 1960s. It was sparked by two factors—the leadership vacuum created by the death of First District representative Albert Reece, a formidable opponent of efforts to build an energetic statewide party organization, and the emergence of a cadre of activists, largely Goldwater supporters, who wanted to build a statewide party organization from the grass roots up (Parks 1966). Led by activists from Memphis, Chattanooga, and the state's other urban areas, the insurgents managed by the mid-1960s to staff a party headquarters in Nashville and to establish local organizations in more than three-fourths of Tennessee counties (Bass and DeVries 1976). More important, the state party proved especially effective at raising money, recruiting and training candidates, communicating with its members, and providing the technical assistance (candidate workshops, polling, and mailing lists) essential to winning elections.

By the early 1990s, however, the Republican Party began to feel the cumulative effects of the losses suffered by its candidates for statewide office. In 1992 the party lacked local organizations in twenty-three counties, including five counties in Republican East Tennessee and six counties in increasingly Republican West Tennessee. Also during 1992 the party raised less than one million dollars. Indeed, by January 1993 the Republicans found themselves with $155,000 in debt and delinquent payables, a newsletter circulated to only six hundred people, and a severely eroded major donor base (Mayberry 1995). Then came the victories of 1994. These successes reinvigorated the state party.

By 1995 the Tennessee Republican Party had paid off its debt, carried a staff on payroll, expanded its newsletter circulation to 50,000, and experienced substantial growth in its donor base among both major donors and smaller regular contributors.

*Democratic Party.* It took Tennessee Democrats until the mid-1970s to launch an effective response to the Republican onslaught. With Sasser's 1973 appointment as party chair, the state Democratic Party began the arduous task of repaying its debt and building a party organization where none previously had existed. With the support of legislative leaders, the party increased its efforts to recruit attractive candidates, retired its debt, and began efforts to assist Democratic candidates. By 1992 the party had some form of organization in all ninety-five Tennessee counties and raised, with the help of its legislative caucuses, more than one million dollars.

As the party built an organizational and financial structure, it expanded the services it provided to local party organizations and to candidates. The services provided to the local parties included assistance in identifying Democratic activists and in training local party officials and activists. The services provided to candidates ranged from assistance with direct mailing to efforts to identify Democratic voters.

If January 1993 represented the nadir for Tennessee Republicans, the Tennessee Democratic Party hit bottom in the aftermath of the 1994 electoral debacle. The party experienced a substantial fall in revenues, especially big donations. Consequently, although the party continued to maintain a state headquarters, it virtually eliminated paid staff, relying instead on interns and volunteers to carry out essential functions (Cheek 1995). As the Democrats headed into the 1996 election, the state party decided to focus its efforts on expanding its financial base, especially among very big and very small donors, maximizing the potential for regaining offices lost to the Republicans in 1994 by identifying strong candidates and avoiding divisive primaries, and facilitating communications among the various constituent groups within the Democratic coalition (Clark 1995). The state party also committed itself to continuing its efforts to identify reliably Democratic voters across the Volunteer State and to develop a computerized database for contacting these voters.

## CURRENT PARTY ORGANIZATION

*The State and the Parties.* State laws delimit the role of the political parties in the electoral process and regulate the internal structure of the party organizations. Conlan, Martino, and Dilger (1984) characterize Tennessee as "generally unsupportive" of party involvement in the electoral process and as a "heavy regulator" of party structures and operations. A review of the election laws reveals the basis for their assessment.

In regard to the electoral process, state law mandates primary elections to select the party nominees for governor, public service commissioner, the general assembly, U.S. senators, and U.S. representatives. The election code further weakens the role of the parties in the electoral process through the absence of party registration and straight-ticket voting provisions and the presence of a binding presidential preference primary. In regard to party structure, Tennessee imposes substantial regulation. The Tennessee election laws establish the procedures for electing members to the state executive committees and specify their composition. State law also mandates the meeting dates of state committees, the roles played by county executive committees and county chairs in primary elections, and the procedures the parties must follow if they choose a nonprimary method to nominate candidates.

*Party Structure.* State law requires both parties to have a state executive committee, elected by party voters at the August primary election in gubernatorial election years. Primary voters in each state senatorial district choose one man and one woman to serve four-year terms, resulting in sixty-six-member state executive committees. The bylaws of both parties also provide for nonvoting ex officio members (such as state legislative leaders, national committeemen and national committeewomen, and leaders of such constituent organizations as the Young Democrats, College Republicans, and the Federation of Republican Women).

At the local level, Tennessee Republicans generally employ a multistage process during odd-numbered years to select county executive committee members. In counties with populations of at least 100,000, each precinct first holds a convention to select precinct officers and delegates to a countywide convention that then elects the officers of the county executive committee (including the chair of the county executive committee, a vice chair of the opposite sex of the chair, a secretary, a treasurer and a vice treasurer). Counties with populations of less than 100,000 have the option of electing executive committee officers by means of either the delegated convention process just described or a mass convention. Additionally, the state executive committee members representing each county, the chair of any local Republican Women's Club, and the chair of the County Young Republicans also serve as voting members of the county executive committees.

Tennessee Democrats generally follow a slightly different selection process. Also in odd-numbered years, the Democrats hold countywide conventions to select the county chair and other officers. In addition, many counties include precinct officers (chairs and vice chairs or precinct captains) on their executive committees, with these officials elected in caucuses at the county conventions. Finally, local elected officials also serve as at-large members of some county executive committees.

The bylaws of both parties allow for districtwide party organizations in multicounty congressional districts. Nevertheless, these organizations frequently exist in name only.

*State Party Relationships with National and Local Party Organizations.* Both Tennessee parties have multiple ties with the "institutions" (including national committees, senate campaign committees, and congressional campaign committees) that represent their respective national parties. For both parties, these ties yield benefits that range from substantial financial assistance to technical support for party-building activities and for candidates, although the quality of the technical support frequently depends on the specific services and staff involved.

Several factors influence the relationships between the state parties and the local party organizations. First, state law and state party bylaws mandate how and when the local party organizations select officers and the role of the state parties in this process. For example, the Tennessee Republican Party bylaws allow the state chair to appoint local executive committee members to represent such constituent groups as women and young Republicans if a county does not have a Republican Women's Club or a Young Republicans Club. Second, the electoral fortunes of party candidates across the state frequently influence the relationship between the state and local parties. Finally, the attitudes of local party officials regarding the appropriate relationships between the state and county parties (over such questions as "Should party building efforts flow from the state down or from the county up?") also shape the relationships.

"Variable" best describes the relationships between the state and local parties in Tennessee. The state Democratic and Republican Parties have, in recent years, provided significant technical assistance to their local parties, and over the past few years both state parties have received limited financial support from local party organizations. At the same time, however, both state parties have occasionally experienced problems in working with their constituent parties. For example, during the early 1990s the state Republican Party had difficulty getting some local parties to report the results of the periodic elections mandated in the party bylaws. Similarly, in the aftermath of the 1994 election, the state Democratic Party found some local parties less than enthusiastic about helping with on-going voter identification efforts.

*Institutional Relationships.* The relationships between the state parties on the one hand, and the party organizations in the state legislature and the governor on the other, depend to a great extent on the relative strength of the legislative caucuses and of the governor. In 1973, for example, the leadership of the Democratic majorities in the legislature provided the impetus for the initial efforts to build a state party organization capable of stanching and then reversing the erosion of the party's traditional dominant position in Tennessee politics; in 1994 the state executive committee contributed $75,000 to the legislative caucus. In contrast, the state Republican Party, seeking to expand the Republican presence in the state legislature, spent $375,000 in behalf of the party's 1994 state legislative candidates (Mayberry 1995).

In certain circumstances, differences in goals may lead to conflicts between the legislative parties and the state party committees. In 1994 the Democratic caucus leaders, focused largely on state legislative races, offered less support than they might otherwise have to the state party and its efforts to aid other candidates.

The relationships between the state party organizations and individual campaign organizations vary from campaign to campaign. In some instances, the fund-raising efforts of the candidates undercut similar efforts by the state party organizations (Cheek 1995). In other cases, the statewide candidate organizations funnel money through the state party. For example, in the 1994 election cycle, the Bredesen for Governor campaign contributed substantial resources to the Tennessee Democratic Executive Committee, while the Sundquist for Governor campaign contributed funds to the Republican Party's Victory 94 Legislative Committee.

*Grassroots Party Organization.* Political parties confront the never-ending chore of finding individuals willing to hold party positions and to carry out the tasks necessary to build the party organization, recruit candidates, and mobilize voters. But how do potential activists enter the party organizations? Do they seek party office? Or do party officials, officeholders, or candidates recruit them? A 44 percent plurality of the respondents to a 1991 survey of Tennessee county executive committee members indicated that their own desire to run had the greatest effect on their decision (Brodsky and Brodsky 1995); a somewhat smaller proportion of activists identified recruitment by party officials as the most important motivator. More Republican chairs and county executive committee members than their Democratic counterparts identified the entreaties of a party official as the most salient factor in their decision to seek a position on their party's county executive committee. This pattern fits with what we might expect, given the traditional balance of power between the two parties in the Volunteer state. The Democrats' historic dominance of local government and the state legislature, especially in Middle and West Tennessee, suggests that individuals with political ambitions might select the Democratic Party as the place to start their political careers. Similarly, this traditional dominance would lead the Republican Party to place more effort on recruiting local activists as an important step in the overall process of party building, especially in those areas where the party lacked a tradition of effective local organizations.

After finding people to serve on their county executive committees, the parties then face the challenge of spurring them to perform the various activities essential to organizational maintenance and electoral success. The 1991 survey data indicate widely varying activity levels. Whereas a majority of the activists in each party reported they had recently engaged in such campaign-related activities as organizing campaign events or distributing campaign-related materials, only one in three local activists reported they had recently made efforts to contact or mobilize voters. The Democrats lagged behind the Republicans in most activities.

The activity levels of local party officials serve as one indicator of the vitality of the parties as organizations. The extent of communication among local party leaders and between local activists and state and national party officials represents another. The 1991 survey revealed a pattern of very frequent contact at the local level, but only minimal communication with either state or national party officials. More Republicans than Democrats reported frequent contact with other party officials at each level of the organization.

Taken together, the data describing the activity levels of local party officials and the frequency of communications within the local party organizations and between local activists and leaders of the state and national party organizations indicate that Tennessee Republicans enjoy an organizational advantage over their Democratic counterparts. But what accounts for these differences? Three explanations suggest themselves. First, the variations in activity and contact may result from differences in organizational cultures, with the more hierarchical and centralized Republicans showing more activity than the more decentralized Democrats (Freeman 1986). Second, the differences may reflect the emphasis the Tennessee Republican Party has traditionally (since the 1960s) placed on building local party organizations as an essential step in the process of recruiting and electing candidates. Finally, the differences may reflect the legacy of the Democratic Party's traditional hegemonic position in the state. Simply put, the party's nominees, especially those for state and local offices, regularly would win, even if the local party organizations offered little active support.

## RESOURCE GUIDE

Neither the Democratic nor the Republican Party has an archive of party records. The records that do exist are neither cataloged nor readily accessible. Former and current officials of both parties may have records in their possession, but there is no record of who has what documentation. The parties, however, can provide current bylaws. The papers of some state political leaders are available in the state library and archives in Nashville, and these collections may contain some relevant state party information. Other sources of information include the files of the *Nashville Tennessean* and of newspapers in Memphis, Chattanooga, and Knoxville and various documents and reports available from the Registry of Election Finance.

Two publications produced by the secretary of state may also be helpful. The *Tennessee Blue Book* contains recent primary and general-election returns, descriptions of the party balance in the state legislature, and other statistical information. *Tennessee Election Laws* describes state regulations governing the parties and elections.

## REFERENCES

*Asterisks denote the most important publications on Tennessee party politics.*
Bass, Jack, and Walter DeVries. 1976. *The transformation of southern politics.* New York: Basic Books.
*Brodsky, David M., and Simeon J. Brodsky. 1995. Tennessee: Democratic Party resilience. In *Southern state party organizations and activists,* ed. Charles D. Hadley and Lewis Bowman, 55–72. Westport, Conn.: Praeger.
Brodsky, David M., and Robert H. Swansbrough. 1994. Tennessee: Favorite son brings home the bacon. In *The 1992 presidential election in the South,* ed. Robert P. Steed, Laurence W. Moreland, and Tod A. Baker, 157–168. Westport, Conn.: Praeger.

Cheek, Will. 1995. Chair of the Tennessee Democratic Party. Interview by author, October 24.

Clark, W. Jeff. 1995. Treasurer of the Tennessee Democratic Party. Interview by author, October 24.

Conlan, Timothy, Ann Martino, and Robert Dilger. 1984. State parties in the 1980s. *Intergovernmental Perspective* 10:6–13.

Cotter, Cornelius P., James L. Gibson, John F. Bibby, and Robert J. Huckshorn. 1989. *Party organizations in American politics.* Pittsburgh, Pa.: University of Pittsburgh Press.

Freeman, Jo. 1986. The political culture in the Democratic and Republican Parties. *Political Science Quarterly* 101:327–356.

Jewell, Malcolm E., and David M. Olson. 1988. *Political parties and elections in American states.* 3d ed. Chicago: Dorsey Press.

Key, V. O., Jr. 1949. *Southern politics in state and nation.* New York: Alfred A. Knopf.

Lamis, Alexander P. 1990. *The two-party South.* New York: Oxford University Press.

*Majors, William R. 1986. *Change and continuity: Tennessee politics since the Civil War.* Macon, Ga.: Mercer University Press.

Mayberry, Sherri L. Political director of the Tennessee Republican Party. Correspondence with the author, October 24.

*Parks, Norman L. 1966. Tennessee politics since Kefauver and Reece: A generalist view. *Journal of Politics* 28:144–168.

*Swansbrough, Robert H. 1985. *Political change in Tennessee.* Knoxville: University of Tennessee, Bureau of Public Administration.

# Texas

BRIAN D. POSLER AND DANIEL S. WARD

Party politics in Texas have followed a pattern that is familiar to observers of recent southern history. Nevertheless, there are unique aspects of Texas politics that distinguish the state from its neighbors in important ways.

Like other states in the region, Texas was a one-party dominion for the first half of the twentieth century, ruled by Democrats at all levels of government. And like many other southern states, Texas experienced increased competitiveness in the 1960s and 1970s and has emerged in the 1990s as fully competitive. The causes and consequences of this increased competitiveness are rooted as much in Texas political history as they are in the shared regional experiences of the U.S. South. Certainly, had the Civil Rights Act and Voting Rights Act not fractured the Democratic Party, its dominance would have prevailed in Texas a while longer. Those legal shocks to the system, however, freed nascent Republican forces in the state, inducing a more natural level of competition. Again mirroring many of their southern brethren, Democrats in Texas were organizationally unprepared for competition, providing further opportunity for Republican success.

## PARTY HISTORY

Two factors, common across the South, account for a substantial proportion of the increase in party competition in Texas. First, the native conservatism that characterized many southern voters made them ripe for allegiance to the national Republican Party, especially in the 1960s and 1970s, when liberals held the reins of power in the national Democratic Party. Second, the breakdown of Jim Crow laws and passage of the Voting Rights Act dramatically reconfigured the electorate, bringing African American voters more fully into the political equation. Finding a natural home in the national Democratic Party, African Americans inevitably brought change to the state party.

Coinciding with these southern forces were factors unique to Texas that also provided opportunities for the Republicans. Beginning in the 1950s, the state experienced in-migration of northern voters that exceeded that of any other southern state (though Florida would also sustain a large influx of new citizens). Like many native Texans, many of the newcomers were conservative; unlike the natives, however, the newcomers held no allegiance to the Democratic Party. A second factor that enhanced Republican prospects was the traditional ideological factionalism of the state Democrats, who regularly divided over economic issues and civil rights. V. O. Key was prescient when he noted the potential for Republican exploitation of this traditional Democratic rift (1949, 255). Historically, the conservative wing prevailed in most battles against the moderate/liberal wing. As newly enfranchised African American voters strengthened the liberal wing, however, conservatives not only had to fight for influence in the party but often had to prevent purges of the right (Lamis 1990, 204–205). After years of frustration, the Republicans experienced an unanticipated statewide victory in 1961, when John Tower was elected to the U.S. Senate seat formerly held by Lyndon Johnson. In its euphoria over Lyndon Johnson's ascendancy to national office, the Democratic Party was unprepared for the vigorous campaign fought by the little-known college professor in the special election to fill Johnson's seat in the Senate. Tower's stunning upset provided both a psychological and organizational boost to the Republican Party (Appleton and Ward 1994a).

The increasing competitiveness of the parties in Texas followed a hierarchical pattern, emerging first at the national level, next at the statewide level, and only recently in the local arena.[1] Texas first voted Republican at the presidential level in 1952 and repeated the feat four years later. The state returned to the Democratic column throughout the 1960s (perhaps a testament to the influence of favorite son Lyndon Johnson), but has voted Republican in all but one election since; the state gave Jimmy Carter a narrow victory in 1976.

Competitiveness emerged more slowly at the level of statewide office. In the three elections between 1946 and 1950, Republican gubernatorial candidates averaged 11 percent of the vote. After failing to field a candidate in 1952, Republicans improved their performance only slightly, averaging 16 percent of the vote between 1954 and 1960. In the succeeding three races, Republican candidates averaged 33 percent of the vote, and by the 1968–1974 period they had reached a high level of competitiveness, gaining an average of 41 percent. Increased competition finally yielded an initial Republican victory in 1978, when Bill Clements was elected governor. The office has changed partisan hands regularly since, normally in very close races. Republicans have had less success in obtaining other statewide offices. For example, the Democrats were able to retain the powerful lieutenant governorship and the office of attorney general in the heavily Republican elections of 1994.

The Republicans have made major strides lower on the ballot in recent years, however. As late as 1970, they were able to field candidates in fewer than one-third of the races for the state house of representatives. In 1980 they contested over 50 percent of house races, and they increased their showing to more than 60 percent in 1990. Looking at an alternative measure of competition, Republican candidates for the state house averaged just 20 percent of the vote in 1970, increased their vote share to over 40 percent in 1980, and won 50 percent of the votes in races they contested in 1990. After years of dominating the state legislature, Democrats were faced with historically large Republican minorities in both the house and senate following the 1994 election.

## ORGANIZATIONAL DEVELOPMENT

*Republican Party.* As the electoral fates of the two parties changed in the 1960s, so too did their organizational structures.[2] Prior to John Tower's 1961 victory, the Texas Republican Party was largely a "national patronage dispenser for Republican Presidents" (Weeks 1972, 209). Republicans moved to consolidate their unexpected success in 1961 by building, for the first time, a professional operation that would allow for sustained activity. Democrats were forced to scramble in response to Republican organizing. The Republicans' major task was to construct a party foundation that would work independently of (albeit in cooperation with) the governor. Though over the ensuing three decades there would be periods of success and failure for both Democrats and Republicans, their early motivations for increased organization would continue to shape the parties' behavior.

The Tower victory was an impetus for a number of important changes at the state level in the Republican Party. Most visible was the move of party headquarters from Houston to Austin, where party leaders could work more efficiently with their still-small legislative contingent. Perhaps more important was the greater access to the state's political press that the move afforded. At the same time, the party hired its first full-time executive director and increased funding for travel around the state by the chair and other party officials (Knaggs 1986, 18). A new finance plan was implemented in 1961 providing for county contribution quotas but also for county participation in financial decision making. These efforts were designed explicitly to promote the party as a full-time operation, in both election years and off years (executive committee minutes, RSEC, 6/14/61).

The burst of organizational activity after the Tower victory was not a fleeting impulse of Republican leadership. There was considerable follow-up activity in the ensuing years, even as electoral success came slowly after the ascension of Lyndon Johnson to a position of national power. Most important for the future of the Republican Party was the establishment of a sound base of financial patrons who would serve as a regular source of income. Evidence of this effort can be found in the doubling of administrative budgets from 1962 to 1964 (executive committee minutes, RSEC, 1/18/64). Despite some retrenchment and internal conflict toward the end of the 1960s, stability had been introduced into the Republican Party organization, and the party entered the 1970s with a state headquarters prepared to take advantage of the growing electoral competitiveness in the state.

The party withstood the Watergate scandal and continued to grow coincident with former Democratic governor John Connally's conversion to the Republican Party in 1973 and with Clements' breakthrough victory in 1978. In the 1980s the party enjoyed stability in its leadership and steady growth in its coffers (Feigert and McWilliams 1995, 77).

*Democratic Party.* Because competition for political power in Texas historically had been waged within the Democratic Party, by the early 1960s the state organization was little more than an appendage of the faction in power. The party served its legal function of organizing primaries and certifying nominees, but it had little to say about the conduct of campaigns or public policy. The governor, rather than the state chair, was perceived as party leader, and the governor's office, rather than state headquarters, was the center of attention between

**Table 1**    Democratic Party Expenditures on Salary, 1960–1968

| Year | Election-year salaries | Off-year salaries |
|------|------------------------|-------------------|
| 1960 | $32,521 | — |
| 1961 | — | $10,151 |
| 1962 | 26,644 | — |
| 1963 | — | 24,878 |
| 1964 | 14,280 | — |
| 1965 | — | 9,353 |
| 1966 | Not available | — |
| 1967 | — | 11,401 |
| 1968 | 17,503 | — |

SOURCE: Party budgets, various years. Democratic State Executive Committee archives, housed at the Texas State Library, Archives Division, in Austin, Texas.

NOTE: Figures are in real dollars.

elections. A 1960 memo from a state executive committee member to the state chair makes this case. In proposing working committee assignments for state executive committee members, the memo suggests that those who lack loyalty to the governor be "occupied on the rules or legal committee . . . perhaps avoid[ing] embarrassing 'resolutions activity,'" which would allow the dissidents to promote civil rights issues (DSEC, 10/31/60).

In the absence of competition from the Republicans, there was no need for sustained activity during interelection periods. Hence, when John Tower shocked the Democrats with a statewide victory in 1961, the party was unprepared to respond effectively. In August 1961, shortly after Tower's election, the state Democratic chair had to send a letter to county leaders asking for help "meeting the expenses of maintaining the Democratic Party Headquarters in Texas. Our *funds are depleted,* and we are overdrawn at the bank" (DSEC, 10/31/61, emphasis in original).

As is often the case in politics, victory yielded new vigor for the organization. After rebounding in 1962 from Tower's victory of a year earlier, the Democratic Party held its largest-ever victory dinner early in 1963. Shortly thereafter the party chair proposed hiring two full-time field workers, expanding distribution of the party newsletter, and overhauling the headquarters operation. Apparently, however, the lesson of Tower's victory was lost on the Democratic Party benefactors, who may have viewed it as an aberration. In 1964 the party headquarters reduced staff once again, anticipating "lessened activity during the upcoming primaries" (executive committee minutes, DSEC, 3/9/64). Based on salary information taken from party budgets, it is clear that the party headquarters did not grow throughout the 1960s (see Table 1).

Just as the national Republican Party preceded its Democratic counterpart in the transition to modern campaigning and communications techniques, so too did the Texas Republicans modernize prior to the state Democrats. Part of the explanation for the Democrats' slower innovation at the state level derives from the unequal flow of ideas and resources from the national parties (Appleton and Ward 1994b). The Republicans were fortunate to enjoy the national leadership of two particularly innovative chairs, Ray Bliss and Bill Brock (Frantzich 1989, 91). At the same time that the Republicans were developing direct-mail technologies and engaging in coordinated campaigns, Democrats were struggling nationally with delegate selection and the associated issue of gender and racial quotas. The struggles over representation were transmitted to the state parties. The conflict was acute in Texas because it excited long-standing cleavages in the state party. In fact, a state Democratic Party finance report in 1975 blamed an $86,000 debt on the activism surrounding the delegate selection and presidential nomination debates (finance report, DSEC 4/24/75).

The 1978 election of Republican William Clements as governor was a severe blow to the Democratic Party, which despite its occasional organizational chaos had been able to retain control of the state government. As a result, the Democrats entered the 1980s facing a formidable national Republican Party and an emboldened Republican Party statewide. Like the Republicans, the Democrats enjoyed more stability during the 1980s than they had previously, with a single party chair serving the entire decade. They, too, saw a steady increase in funding over the decade despite the apparent loosening of their stranglehold on Texas electoral politics.

## CURRENT PARTY ORGANIZATION

Based on their study of party organizations in the early 1980s, Cotter et al. (1984) identified the Texas parties as being relatively weakly organized, ranking the Republicans near the middle of the pack (thirty-fifth overall out of the ninety included in their study) and the Democrats much lower (seventy-eighth overall).[3] The wide disparity in organizational strength may have made a significant difference at the polls in the past decade, as Republicans managed a dramatic increase in electoral success rates up and down the ballot. By the mid-1990s, the Republicans approached majorities in both state houses. In 1994, forty-seven of forty-eight judges elected in Harris County (Houston) were Republicans. Texas is no longer dominated by Democrats at all but the highest levels, but is now a legitimate two-party state.

The statutory restrictions on the party organizations are relatively slight; state law allows the parties considerable latitude in writing their bylaws. Whereas the Republicans select their executive committee members through the primary process, the Democrats utilize a more complex hybrid of both primary and convention elements for selection. The Democrats also have a gender equity requirement, which the Republicans do not have.

The state parties play similar roles in their respective organizational hierarchies. The strength of the local organizations is seen as the key to electoral victory. Democrats herald their regional training sessions for local leaders as a vital element of their strategy. The Republicans point to their growth in local organization strength as the key to their recent electoral success. Tom Pauken, the Republican state chair, made priorities of fund raising and building local party organizations, allowing his party to recruit and aid many more local candidates since his election in 1994. The Republicans have also been able to recruit many more candidates than in the past, competing with the Democrats in ever more races. The national parties have a relatively limited role in either party's hierarchy in Texas. Although the national parties help set campaign agendas and issue position papers, it is the state parties that run the campaigns in Texas.

As in any party, factions based an divergent policy and organizing philosophies exist in both parties. The magnitude of the schisms has varied over time for the Texas parties. The Republicans maintain a relatively homogenous party, in general agreement on fiscal matters, but with noticeable rifts occurring on social issues. The conservative wing consistently controls the state party's platform; pro-life planks and other hot-button social issues are constant fixtures in the platform. The struggle for control of local organizations has been intense at times, evidenced by the two groups that each claimed to be the official party organization in Houston in the early 1990s.

The Democrats have become a more homogenous party in recent years, not from resolving factional differences but from the fact that conservatives "cleaved themselves right out of the party," in the words of Ed Martin, the Democratic executive director. The traditional rivalries (urban-rural, liberal-conservative) have also dissipated, but not before some particularly vicious primaries hurt candidates in later contests during the past decade. Martin noted, "We learned our lesson from what we did to ourselves in that Krueger race in 1984," which was a particularly divisive primary season for the Democrats. Thus, as the partisan competition increased, conservative Democrats found a new home in the Republican Party, and the two parties became more homogenous and cohesive as a result.

Both parties in Texas see electoral concerns as their primary focus, generally leaving programmatic policy to the legislative parties. Both parties do create a platform from their respective state conventions, but the platforms are generally used for recruiting candidates and for general guidance to the legislature rather than for influencing day-to-day legislation. State law prohibits elected officials from serving in formal positions on the executive committees, although elected officials do have significant clout, as was made evident in the fall of 1995 when the five statewide Democratic officials successfully called for the resignation of state party chair Robert Slagle.

Recently, Democratic Party leaders have become actively involved in coalition building on key votes, such as on the budget and education bills in the 1995 session; both parties are always quite active on electoral legislation, such as redistricting or election law. Both parties report a good working relationship with the governor's office when they have an official in power, although neither party sees itself as an arm of the governor. The state party organizations and the governor's office are entirely independent of each other but work in tandem on a variety of concerns.

Recent technological changes have made the parties much more sophisticated in their campaign efforts. Republicans employ sophisticated phone bank technologies that enable them to provide important information to candidates, local organizations, and voters at lower cost. The Democrats have new systems on-line that allow them secure communications between all the levels of the party, easing the coordination of multiple campaigns. Extensive voter files are maintained to enable better targeting of campaigns at all levels.

The current party organizations are the product of the historical trends discussed in earlier sections. The last decade has seen a steady demise of Democratic dominance at the local level, as Republican competitiveness has trickled down from the national level to all levels. Thanks as well to a number of recent party defections, the Republicans are at a point where they may control both houses of the state legislature as well as the governorship, which would allow them more power in redistricting the lower levels and help their cause even further. The parties have adapted to their newly competitive environment by adopting new strategies and technologies as they enter a new century of campaigning.

## RESOURCE GUIDE

The records of the Texas Democratic Party, housed at the Texas State Library, Archives Division, provide a comprehensive portrait of the day-to-day operations of the party for a critical period of its history, roughly 1955 through 1985. Essentially, the records consist of office files that appear to have been taken directly from emptied file cabinets. Little organi-

**Table 2**  Texas Resource Guide

|  | Democrats | Republicans |
|---|---|---|
| Archive | Yes | Yes |
| Location | State Library, Archives Division | Party Headquarters |
|  | P.O. Box 12927 | 211 East 7th Street, Suite 620 |
|  | Austin, Texas 78711 | Austin, Texas 78701 |
|  | (512) 463-5480 | (512) 477-9821 |
| Dates | 1955–1985 | 1952–present |
| Finding aid | Yes | No |
| Access | Public | By appointment |
| Contents: |  |  |
|   Executive committee minutes | Yes | Yes |
|   Correspondence | Yes | Yes |
|   Organizational structure | Yes | Yes |
|   Budgets | Yes | Yes |
|   Rules | Yes | Yes |

zation or processing of material is apparent. Despite the lack of organization, a 218-page finding aid does catalog the contents of each file folder in the extensive collection with a good deal of accuracy. The archives appear to be ideal for performing systematic research. Minutes for virtually every state committee meeting were located, providing an excellent resource for tracking changes in party organization. Complete records of state conventions and delegates to those and national conventions are available, as is complete documentation regarding party rules and rule changes.

Because the archives contain a substantial amount of correspondence to and from the state chair, there is an excellent accounting of party functions, in the form of fundraisers, meetings between the chair and county leaders, candidate training sessions, dinners for visiting dignitaries, and the like. Office memos also track the physical changes in party operations; for example, the introduction of computers is covered in detail. By using the committee minutes as a guide to the universe of possible material, we were able to determine that a vast array of significant documents are contained in the party archives.

According to its survey response, the Republican Party of Texas should have records that are among the most complete available. The party claims possession of a full range of materials for the period 1952 to the present. Because the records are housed at the party headquarters, however, the utility of the archives will depend on the individual researcher's success at scheduling a visit and making arrangements for access and photocopying of material. An initial visit to the state headquarters yielded access only to bound copies of all state committee and executive committee meetings from 1957 through the present. According to party staff, many of the original reports and documents referred to in the minutes were not available to be examined. Further inquiry revealed that additional materials may be available for research purposes when party staff are less occupied with campaign concerns. The Texas experience highlights the benefits of archival donations to professional libraries and historical societies.

**NOTES**

1. See Appleton and Ward (1993) for elaboration of the hierarchical model of party change.
2. Some of the information contained in this section was collected at the Republican and Democratic Party archives. The designation "RSEC" refers to items located at the Republican State

Executive Committee archives, housed at party headquarters in Austin, Texas. The designation "DSEC" refers to items located at the Democratic State Executive Committee archives, housed at the Texas State Library, Archives Division, in Austin, Texas.

3. Much of the material in this section derives from telephone interviews with Democratic executive director Ed Martin and Republican executive director Barbara Jackson.

## REFERENCES

*Asterisks denote the most important publications on Texas party politics.*

Appleton, Andrew, and Daniel S. Ward. 1994a. Party organizational response to electoral change: Political upheaval in Texas and Arkansas. *American Review of Politics* 15:191–212.

————. 1994b. Understanding organizational innovation and party-building. In *The state of the parties: The changing role of contemporary American parties,* ed. D. Shea and J. Green. Lanham, Md.: Rowman and Littlefield.

————. 1993. Party transformation in France and the United States: The hierarchical effects of system change in comparative perspective. *Comparative Politics* 26:69–98.

*Casdorph, Paul D. 1965. *A history of the Republican Party in Texas, 1865–1965.* Austin, Texas: Pemberton Press.

Cotter, Cornelius, et al. 1984. *Party organizations in American politics.* Pittsburgh: University of Pittsburgh Press.

*Dallek, Robert. 1991. *Lone star rising: Lyndon Johnson and his times, 1908–1960.* New York: Oxford University Press.

*Davidson, Chandler. 1990. *Race and class in Texas politics.* Princeton: Princeton University Press.

Feigert, Frank B., and Nancy L. McWilliams. 1995. Texas: Yeller dogs and yuppies. In *Southern state party organizations and activists,* ed. Charles D. Hadley and Lewis Bowman. Westport, Conn.: Praeger.

Frantzich, Stephen E. 1989. *Political parties in the technological age.* New York: Longman.

*Jones, Eugene W. 1986. *Practicing Texas politics.* Boston: Houghton Mifflin.

Key, V. O. 1949. *Southern politics in state and nation.* New York: Knopf.

*Knaggs, John R. 1986. *Two-party Texas: The John Tower era, 1961–1984.* Austin, Texas: Eakin Press.

Lamis, Alexander. 1990. *The two-party South.* 2d ed. New York: Oxford University Press.

Weeks, O. Douglas. 1972. Texas: Land of conservative expansiveness. In *The changing politics of the South,* ed. William C. Havard. Baton Rouge: Louisiana State University Press.

# Utah

ROBERT C. BENEDICT

## PARTY HISTORY

Political parties in Utah are the product of a unique mixture of religious, economic, and political factors.[1] After Brigham Young's Mormon pioneers arrived in July 1847, Salt Lake City was divided into nineteen wards, each headed by a church bishop, thereby establishing the Utah Territory as a nonparty theocracy. For twenty years potential opposition groups, which were present due to mining activities and Utah's geographical position astride the overland route to the West, lacked sufficient social or ideological cohesion for a party system. When "new movement" Mormons and non-Mormons formed the People's Party in

1868, it quickly came under church control. The People's Party controlled every seat in the territorial legislature until the 1887 election, and Utah's territorial delegates sat with the Democrats in the U.S. House of Representatives.

National parties were established in Utah as part of a larger effort to achieve statehood (which also required Mormon church leaders to renounce the practice of polygamy). In 1890 the Democratic Party, consisting of Mormons and non-Mormons, was established, followed a year later by the Republican Party (Weaver 1953, 230). Statehood followed in 1896. Democrats retained a prominent political presence, counterbalanced primarily by Republican U.S. senator Reed Smoot (1903–1933), who, according to Utah historian Milton Merrill, firmly believed that "God, the church, the Republican Party and Reed Smoot were all on the same side." [2] Although Democrats swept statewide elective offices after Woodrow Wilson's 1916 election, from 1920 to 1932 the two parties were competitive. With the 1932 election Utah followed the rest of the nation into the Democratic column, and it supplied several prominent New Dealers, including Federal Reserve Board chair Marriner Eccles, Federal Emergency Relief Administration director Robert Hinckley, and Secretary of War George Dern. In 1940, 62 percent of Utah voters cast their vote for FDR.

By the 1960s the state had swung, as part of a gradual realignment of the mountain states, to the GOP (Galderisi et al. 1987; Hrebenar and Benedict 1991). The change was first evident at the presidential level, when in 1964 Barry Goldwater received 46 percent of the vote. In every election from 1972 to 1988 Utah voters gave the GOP presidential candidate over 60 percent of the vote; Utah voters provided the Republican candidate with the highest percentage of the popular vote of any state from 1976 to 1988. Having received only 25 percent of the vote, Bill Clinton finished third in the state in 1992, behind George Bush and Ross Perot.

With the election of U.S. Senators Jake Garn in 1974 and Orrin Hatch in 1976, the Republican Party established hegemony over the state's Senate delegation. The state legislature was next in line to tilt Republican; since 1980 Republicans have controlled from 59 to 83 percent of the seats in both houses. From 1964 to 1984 two Democrats, Calvin Rampton and Scott Matheson, held the governor's office. Their winning electoral formula combined fiscal conservatism and support of state interests against the federal government. At the gubernatorial level, then, the shift to the GOP was not accomplished until the mid-1980s.

State laws and election trends have influenced the parties. The open primary system has been viewed as an impediment to party building and to fund raising. The lack of registration in the open primary system made it difficult to identify partisans who might have assisted in such grassroots activities as get-out-the-vote drives. Although the claim cannot be verified, former Republican representative Dan Marriott (1977–1985) attributed his loss in the open primary of 1984 to "raiding," whereby members of the Democratic Party crossed over, hoping to select the weakest candidate to run in the general election. The degree of independence exercised by voters in the open primary system led one former state Democratic Party chair to exclaim, "What the hell we have a party for, I'm not sure!" Moreover, national party organizations preferred that state parties have voter registration lists before providing financial support, but Utah's open primary provided no record of probable party supporters.

Loss of the governorship in 1984 compounded Democratic frustration. The governorship had been the glue holding the party together by providing statewide visibility, a coherent message, and a platform for fund raising. The party reached a low point in the mid-1980s, when its most visible officeholder was the Salt Lake County sheriff. The lack of statewide visibility persisted in 1996, when the highest elective office held was that of attorney general.

## ORGANIZATIONAL DEVELOPMENT

The two most important developments affecting the parties' organizational capacity have been changes in the state statutes controlling the parties and innovations in campaign fund raising and strategy that have filtered down from the national level.

New laws governing political parties became effective in 1994. Previously, state law had meticulously specified party structure and internal procedures. However, U.S. Supreme Court decisions effectively nullified parts of the law. A bipartisan Election Codification Working Group was formed in April 1991—consisting of the two major parties, several independent parties, and groups such as the League of Women Voters—to recommend changes that would bring state electoral law into compliance with the Supreme Court decisions. Subsequent legislation stated broad principles the parties were to adhere to and left the parties to stipulate the details. For example, party bylaws were to specify party organization and structure, and the party was to designate procedures allowing active participation by party members in selecting party officers and candidates.[3] In addition, the parties agreed to two rules to increase party cohesion. To lessen the chance of divisive primaries, the percentage of state convention votes needed to avoid a party primary was decreased from 70 percent to 60 percent. The second rule change moved the primary election from September to June, to allow primary election divisions to heal and to give more time to publicize candidates before the general election. Although favoring a move to a closed primary system, neither party worked to include this item. Party leaders remembered that when the state had moved to a closed primary system, public dissatisfaction with the change had resulted in a move back to the open system after a two-year period.

Measuring party development and organizational strength in any state is a difficult task. Cotter et al. (1989) identified two dimensions of party organization: programmatic capacity and organizational complexity. This section focuses on programmatic capacity, which is measured by two variables: institutional support and candidate-related activity. Of the five indicators of institutional support, fund raising and electoral mobilization are the most applicable to Utah. Changes in fund-raising techniques reflect the time lag before national trends filter down to the states. By the early 1980s the national parties were placing greater emphasis on small donors, yet the state's parties continued to rely on major donors. In Utah, for a minimum of $1,000, donors became members of the GOP Elephant Club or the Democrats' Chairman's Club. Major donors benefited by being able to talk with national party leaders or officials who visited the state. Moreover, paralleling the "easy payment" plans developed nationally, membership fees could be paid in cash, by credit card, or through payroll deduction. The Democratic Party also followed the national example with a pyramid of clubs, ranging from the Chairman's Club ($1,000 minimum) to the Grass Roots Club ($60 minimum). By 1986 the state parties had begun to raise more funds through telephone and mail solicitation of small donors, asking for sums of $30 or more. For Republicans, although the change in fund-raising strategy created a temporary rift with corporate donors, the party's financial base dramatically expanded due to annual renewals from small donors.

When the Democrats lost the governor's office in 1984, they were deprived of a major source of party funding: the Governor's Ball. With chutzpah rivaling P. T. Barnum, one state legislator suggested a "Legislators' Ball." Surprising even its proponents, the ball in 1985 raised $40,000 for party coffers, and it established a financing method that survives today.

Due to the open primary system, voter identification and mobilization are top campaign priorities for both parties. Republicans began a crude voter identification effort in 1980; currently, both parties combine state data sources with lists sold by private firms. In addition, with assistance from the national party, Republicans have implemented an aggressive absentee ballot program, in large part as insurance for closely contested races.

The second variable used by Cotter et al. to measure a state party's programmatic capacity is candidate-directed activity. The two most important indicators applicable to Utah are recruitment and contributions to candidates. Because of the Democrats' minority-party status, candidate self-recruitment is less common. In March and April of election years the party chair spends most of his or her time recruiting candidates. Compounding the difficulty, the chair must often recruit "sacrificial lambs" to run with minimal party financial support. Self-selection is more common in the Republican Party, and the party often has a surplus of candidates seeking a particular office.

Campaign assistance provides evidence for the innovation-choice model of change developed by Appleton and Ward (1994). Innovations developed initially by national party organizations rapidly diffused to the state. Former state GOP chair Craig Moody credits former House Speaker "Tip" O'Neill's book, *Speaker of the House,* for calling to his attention such techniques as using "comparison pieces" in mass mailings and having state legislators send issue questionnaires to constituents. The state Republican Party initiated the first elements of the coordinated campaign in 1980, and the Democrats followed in 1986. Common resources were provided for state races, and the priority districts were targeted to receive monetary contributions. Among the services were training on how to run a campaign and the printing and distribution of fliers. Democratic chair Randy Horiuichi (1985–1989) initiated coordinated media buys for radio and hired one graphics person for all candidates; however, these two elements were not institutionalized. With fewer financial resources available in 1990, Democrats targeted fewer districts; yet about one-half of the money raised each year (some $35,000) goes to the coordinated campaign. Although recent Republican budget figures are not available to scholars, former chair Bruce Hough (1991–1994) stated that one-third of the party's budget went to the coordinated campaign.

## CURRENT PARTY ORGANIZATION

In revising their party constitutions in the early 1990s, Republicans and Democrats retained the organizational structure previously specified by state law: a chair and vice chair, an executive committee which acts in corporate terms as a board of directors, and a central committee whose role is closer to that of stockholders. In both parties, on most policy issues the chair and the executive committee formulate a general statement, and the policy is routinely confirmed by the central committee. It is on budgetary issues that changes are most likely to be demanded by the central committee.

When Republicans adopted their party constitution in 1994, although they retained the existing organizational structure, they made changes in organizational relationships perceived to be unwieldy in terms of participation and unclear in terms of dividing responsibilities. Previously, central committee membership had averaged 150, and the executive committee had numbered as many as 36. Congressional district chairs and vice chairs had lacked clearly defined roles. The new constitution enlarged the role of the state party chair, who presided over both executive and central committees. All congressional district positions were abolished, and all statewide elected officials were added to the central committee. The membership of the executive committee was reduced to 20. In contrast, Democrats preferred the status quo, keeping an 11-member executive committee consisting of elected party officers. Exhibiting a surfeit of democratic spirit, the 240-member central committee was also retained.

For the Republicans, since 1985 the governor and the two U.S. senators have been the strongest influences on party decision making, but the governor's role depends on that person's priorities. Gov. Norman Bangerter (1985–1993) ran his campaigns without much party input, and his limited role in party affairs was seen in his advice to the party chair: in effect, pay your bills and keep the doors open (Hough 1994). The current governor, Michael Leavitt, plays a very active role in party affairs.

The second dimension of Cotter's framework, organizational complexity, uses such variables as professionalization of leadership, division of labor, and the party budget to evaluate the organization. Indicators of professionalization of leadership are autonomy of the chair, existence of a full-time chair and executive director, and staff tenure.

Chairs of both parties in Utah have at times exercised high levels of autonomy, although for different reasons. In the mid-1980s the Republican chair exercised wide autonomy in decision making, as the executive committee was largely a rubber stamp body and the central committee was not a major force in the party. However, Governor Bangerter made several decisions (such as raising taxes to expand education spending) that angered some executive and central committee members. Given the governor's popularity with the electorate, Republicans who desired more fiscal conservatism in taxing and spending decisions believed a low-cost way to show their displeasure over these policies was to put pressure on the chair. Party rules were changed to allow any decision made by the chair to be brought up for a vote of approval by either the executive committee or the central committee. Party activists forced postponement for a year of a controversial revision to the party constitution to have the chair head both the executive and central committees. At the 1994 state convention, with the congressional delegation and the governor in prominent attendance, the revision was adopted, giving the chair even greater authority than in the mid-1980s.

Among Democrats, since 1984 the autonomy of the chair has depended on three factors: the electoral strength of the party, the chair's personality, and the makeup of the executive committee. After severe election losses in the mid-1980s, Democrats lacked statewide visibility. Chair Randy Horiuichi exerted considerable autonomy in determining campaign strategy. The Democrats dropped national issues, emphasizing such state issues as education and opposition to regulating cable television. Horiuichi, stressing the notion that it is easier to ask forgiveness than permission, undertook projects and then went to the central committee to ratify his deeds. Conversely, Chair Peter Billings (1989–1991), a bankruptcy lawyer by profession, emphasized procedure and thus exercised less autonomy.

Both parties have executive directors who are, as one stated, "full-time, and then some." Democrats employed a full-time chair from 1992 to 1994, but a loss of state legislative seats in 1994 ended the experiment.

There is considerable variation between the parties in terms of staff turnover. Recently, Republicans have experienced a high level of turnover among executive directors—the party had four from 1991 to 1995. The current Democratic executive director, Todd Taylor, who has served since 1992, has by his own account the third-longest tenure of any party executive director west of the Mississippi River. The reasons for the short tenure of executive directors are low pay and use of the position as a political patronage job.

Utah parties maintain minimal staff levels: in addition to an executive director, the Republicans have an accounting person and a secretary, while Democrats employ an all-purpose office administrator. During peak election periods, both parties add up to three temporary staff members.

Both Republicans and Democrats have good working relationships with their national parties. Before providing financial support, however, the national parties require the state parties to draw up a plan detailing what tasks could be better accomplished cooperatively rather than separately. Thus, the national Republican Party provided expertise for fundraisers and telemarketing campaigns and assisted in putting together press releases. In the view of Bruce Hough, Haley Barbour as national chair increased cooperation 100 percent. State relations with the national party had been largely symbolic, consisting of "grip and grin" functions. Under Barbour, some of the changes, such as national and state party officials exchanging lists of financial contributors, have been small but very useful. Other changes, such as more general financial support and a freer flow of political information, are viewed as more significant.

For the Utah Democratic Party the tightrope act has been to maintain good relations with the national party while attempting to distance itself from the national platform to retain an electoral presence. The national party usually becomes involved only in those state races that make the "critical" list, such as the congressional candidacy of Karen Shepherd in 1992.

Both parties are influenced by factions and outside groups. Because the Republican Party is the majority party in a largely homogenous society, coalition building has low priority. Business groups are not involved much in the choice of leadership, but their members exercise influence as delegates at the state convention. The input from other groups has been institutionalized by inclusion on the executive committee (for example, Teenage Republicans, College Republicans, the Women's Federation, and the newly organized Hispanic Republican Assembly). Christian right groups such as the Eagle Forum and single-interest groups such as Utah Right-to-Life exercise influence beyond their numbers. They organized effectively for the 1992 national convention, electing delegates whose knowledge of the political process was slim. They have also been able to elect several supporters to the state legislature. Yet one attempt to elect an advertised pro-life candidate to a party office was not successful.

Groups active in the Democratic Party reflect national trends. Labor's role is reduced from that of the late 1970s, when the AFL-CIO and the Utah Education Association (UEA) had twice the delegates at the state convention as the next largest group. The Democratic Party had all its printing done at one newspaper, the *Salt Lake Tribune,* because it was the only union print shop in the area (Palmer 1981, 71). Union participation is still important both as a source of funds and because retired union members do such tasks as get-out-the-vote telephoning and the screening for lawn signs.

Formerly, both the UEA and the Utah Public Employees Association (UPEA) were key Democratic supporters. In the late 1970s one-quarter of the members of the Century Club (the major fund-raising body for the party) worked for government departments, agencies, or bureaus (Palmer 1981, 62). Although both groups are involved in specific races today, they do not hesitate to cross party lines. Following national trends, both associations put

Table 1 Utah Resource Guide

| Democrats | | Republicans |
|---|---|---|
| Archive | Yes | Yes |
| Location | Marriott Library, Manuscripts Division, Special Collections, University of Utah Salt Lake City, Utah 84112 | Marriott Library, Manuscripts Division, Special Collections, University of Utah Salt Lake City, Utah 84112 |
| Dates | 1960–1990 | 1964–1972 |
| Finding aid | Yes, through 1980 | Yes |
| Access | Public; Archivist permission | Public |
| Contents: | | |
| Executive committee minutes | Yes | Yes |
| Correspondence | Yes | Yes |
| Organizational structure | Yes | Yes |
| Budgets | Yes | No |
| Rules | Yes | Yes |

out legislative "report cards" containing the percentage of "correct voting," a practice that irritates state officials along with their national counterparts. The Women's Caucus exercises greater influence at the state convention than in the executive and central committees. Because the proabortion group Utahns for Choice carries too much ideological baggage for most Democratic candidates, contributions offered by the group are often turned down. Environmentalists are often at odds with the state's culture and only occasionally become active, such as in voter registration drives conducted by the Sierra Club for congressional candidate Wayne Owens in 1988 and 1990.

RESOURCE GUIDE

Records of the Utah Democratic Party from the early 1960s to 1990 are housed at the Marriott Library at the University of Utah.[4] Material through 1980 is cataloged, and a finding aid with name and subject index is available. Although the records through 1980 are listed as "off site," about half the collection is in fact "on site." This collection is contained in thirty-one boxes, organized into four divisions. The first division contains material on committee organization and function, including bylaws, minutes, and membership lists from executive and central committees. The second division concentrates on the election process, with information on mass meetings, delegate selection, and county and state conventions. Financial records form the third division, which includes a fairly complete set of budgets. The fourth division contains miscellaneous material and includes one reminder of a past party role: identification forms for persons seeking patronage positions.

A second data set for the period 1981–1990, given to the library in 1994, is not yet cataloged or computer listed but is available to researchers with the archivist's permission. An afternoon's survey of the six boxes revealed data sets of potential interest to scholars. Party budgets from 1983 to 1990 are broken down into about fifteen categories, allowing comparison of financial priorities over time. If additional detail is needed, copies of all checks written from 1980 to 1990 are available. Within looseleaf folders of district maps and election results from 1980 to 1983 are results of a party survey that asked such questions of party candidates as: "What services or help did the Democratic Party provide?"; "What more could the party have done?"; and "What were the main problems?" Although not every candidate returned the survey, the responses provide candidate assessment of electoral efforts. State convention material is complete over the period, but executive committee minutes and county chair correspondence appear only through 1983. Some opposition research is evident in copies of financial disclosure forms filed by the Republican Party.

For Republicans the data set is far less complete. Records from 1964 to 1972 are in the Marriott Library and are organized into three files.[5] For this collection a finding aid with name and subject index is available. The first file focuses on national politicians prominent from the early 1960s to the early 1970s. A second file has material on the State Republican Central Committee; however, data sets of interest to scholars are scarce. Party budgets, for example, are available only from 1972 to 1974. Most of the material is impersonal and incomplete. The last file is a county file, with election returns, mass meeting forms, and delegate lists from 1962 to 1968.

Republican Party headquarters has files only for the past two years. Party veterans indicated that the earlier records were given to a former party vice chair, who is sorting the records and keeping some files for a future history of the party. Clearly, preserving party records for public or scholarly access lacks the priority it enjoyed in previous years.

**NOTES**

1. The author gratefully acknowledges the assistance of the following individuals: Todd Taylor, executive director of the Democratic Party, 1992–present; Bruce Hough, state Republican Party chair, 1991–1994; Randy Horiuichi, state Democratic Party chair, 1985–1989; Ted Wilson, director of the Hinckley Institute of Politics, University of Utah; Greg Hopkins, executive director of the state Republican Party, 1988–1991; Darcy Dixon Pignanelli, vice chair of the state Democratic Party, 1989–1992; Dave Hansen, executive director of the Republican Party, 1979–1984 and 1991–1993; Craig Moody, state Republican Party chair, 1987–1988; and Dave Jones, state Democratic Party chair, 1992–1994.
2. Milton Merrill, quoted in Jonas (1969, 330).
3. *Utah Code Annotated,* 20A-8–401.
4. Utah State Democratic Committee Papers, Manuscript Accession Number 272, Manuscripts Division, Special Collections, University of Utah, Marriott Library, Salt Lake City, Utah, 84112.
5. Utah State Republican Central Committee Papers, Manuscript Accession Number 171, Manuscript Division, Special Collections, University of Utah, Marriott Library, Salt Lake City, Utah, 84112.

**REFERENCES**

*Asterisks denote the most important publications on Utah party politics.*

Appleton, Andrew, and Daniel S. Ward. 1994. Understanding organizational innovation and party-building. In *The state of the parties: The changing role of contemporary American parties,* ed. Daniel Shea and John Green. Lanham, Md.: Rowman and Littlefield.

Cotter, Cornelius, James Gibson, John Bibby, and Robert Huckshorn. 1989. *Party organization in American politics.* Pittsburgh, Penn.: University of Pittsburgh Press.

*Durham, G. Homer. 1947. The development of political parties in Utah: The first phase. *Utah Humanities* 1 (April):122–133.

Galderisi, Peter F., Michael S. Lyons, Randy T. Simmons, and John G. Francis, eds. 1987. *The politics of realignment: Party change in the mountain West.* Boulder, Colo.: Westview.

*Grow, Stewart. 1963. The development of political parties in Utah. *Western Political Quarterly* 16 (September):35–48.

Hough, Bruce. 1994. Republican Party chair, 1991–1994. Interview by author.

*Hrebenar, Ronald J., and Robert C. Benedict. 1991. Political parties, elections and campaigns II: Evaluation and trends. In *Politics and public policy in the contemporary American West,* ed. Clive S. Thomas, 131–160. Albuquerque: University of New Mexico Press.

Jonas, Frank H. 1969. Utah: The different state. In *Politics in the American West,* ed. Frank H. Jonas, 326–368. Salt Lake City: University of Utah Press.

Palmer, Stanley J. 1981. The economics of political decision making and party platforms: A Utah case study. Ph.D. diss., University of Utah.

Richards, Charles C. 1942. *The organization and growth of the Democratic Party in Utah, 1847–1896.* Salt Lake City: Sagebrush Democratic Club.

*Weaver, Ellsworth. 1953. The evolution of political institutions in Utah. Ph.D. diss., New York University.

# Vermont

## GARRISON NELSON

Wisdom in Vermont politics is often contained in pithy Yankee aphorisms. One of the best known is "If it ain't broke, why fix it?" For more than a century (1854–1958) the state's commitment to the Republican Party was legendary. Republicans won every presidential contest from 1856 through 1960, every contest for federal office between 1854 and 1958, and every gubernatorial election from 1855 through 1960. In addition, all of the lesser statewide offices and the vast majority of the seats in the state legislature were won by the Republican Party. So for Vermont Republicans, the state political system clearly "wasn't broke" for quite some time.

Since 1962 Democratic candidates for governor have won ten elections, to seven for the Republicans. In 1974 Chittenden County States Attorney Patrick J. Leahy became the state's first elected Democratic U.S. senator. In 1992 he captured his fourth successive term. And even more astounding, in 1990 Vermont elected Bernard Sanders, a Brooklyn-born socialist independent, to the state's lone U.S. House seat, which had been held by Republicans for fifty-six of the previous fifty-eight years. Sanders was reelected in 1992 and 1994. For state Republicans, "How come it got fixed?" is clearly the operative question.

As befits a small and historically one-party state, the parties have long been weak organizationally in Vermont. In recent decades the most successful state politicians have created personal organizations, built on years of loyalty and constituent service. U.S. Senators Leahy and James M. Jeffords were both first elected to Congress in 1974, and Sanders, although a relative congressional newcomer, was in 1996 in his fourteenth year of elective service. In a small state like Vermont, with its cozy main streets, town meetings, and county fairs, the "retail politics" of face-to-face campaigning continues to thrive in this era of collapsible party organizations. How long the state can resist more modern and impersonal campaign techniques is the subject of frequent conjecture. But for now, Vermont's uniqueness survives.

## PARTY HISTORY

" Vermont: The Beckoning Country"—it was a simple slogan but an important one, and its influence on the state of Vermont and its politics continues to be felt today. Developed for the Community Affairs and Development Office by William Wheeler during the administration of Democratic governor Phil Hoff in 1965, the slogan was part of a major advertising campaign to lure people to visit and even settle in the state.

There was no question that the growth rate of the state population had fallen relative to the national rate. This was particularly true relative to neighboring New Hampshire. Vermont residents had outnumbered New Hampshire residents as late as the 1870 census, but by the 1960 census, the population of New Hampshire was more than double that of Vermont. In 1810 Vermont contained 3 percent of the nation's population, and the state elected six members to the U. S. House of Representatives. By 1960 that proportion had dropped to two-tenths of 1 percent, and only one House member was elected from the state.

State political and economic leaders determined that something had to be done. The long-term economic survival of the state could not withstand another generation of non-growth and the continuing export of young people to other states with more attractive career opportunities.

So Vermont beckoned, and people came. Motives of the immigrants varied. Some young families came to live in the small towns which had been such a major part of the American ethos but which had been overwhelmed in other states by the urbanization of the postwar years. Other young people with counter-cultural leanings saw Vermont as a relatively hassle-free environment. The newcomers tended to be more liberal philosophically than the natives, and they did much to change the overall political orientation of the state. Another set of urban expatriates were young entrepreneurs who saw that their relatively small amounts of investment capital could go further and yield a greater economic return in Vermont than in Boston or New York City.

Vermont's growth in the 1960s was not remarkable. Its population growth rate of 13.8 percent was slightly higher than the nation's 13.3 percent. What was remarkable was that for the first time since the decade after 1800, the Vermont growth rate exceeded the national rate. The source of the growth was easy to find. Census data revealed that the state had become a net draw for citizens moving from other states (see Table 1).

People were not only coming to Vermont, they were staying. The young urban professional expatriates of the 1960s and 1970s were aging into the "middle-aged rural professionals" of the 1980s. Political consequences were certain to be felt.

*The Decline of Presidential Republicanism.* Vermont's most lasting political impression on outsiders was made on election day 1936, when Vermont was the only state of the forty-seven casting their electoral votes that first Tuesday of November to vote against President Franklin D. Roosevelt and vote instead for Governor Alfred M. Landon of Kansas. (Maine had given Landon its electoral endorsement seven weeks earlier.) The durability of Vermont's commitment to Republican presidential candidates ran to twenty-seven consecutive elections from 1856 through 1960—the longest such streak in the nation's history. Only Arkansas, with twenty-three consecutive Democratic decisions (1876–1964), comes close to Vermont's extraordinary record.

The intensity of Republican sentiment is even more impressive. From 1856 through 1960, Vermont was never below the top five states in the percentage of all voters who cast their ballots for the Republican candidate. In twenty of those contests—including a record eleven in a row between 1868 and 1908—Vermont's percentage was the highest in the nation.

Vermont's long commitment to Republican presidential candidates ended in 1964, when Barry Goldwater had the dubious distinction of being the first Republican presidential nominee not to carry the state. The Republican Party's return to more conventional candi-

**Table 1**  Vermont Population Growth, 1940s–1980s

| Decade | Natural growth | Migration | Net Change | |
|--------|---------------|-----------|-----------|---------|
| | | | Number | Percent |
| 1940s | 18,516 | -17,257 | — | — |
| 1950s | 49,391 | -37,257 | +12,134 | + 3.2 |
| 1960s | 38,340 | +16,511 | +54,851 | +14.0 |
| 1970s | 28,425 | +38,299 | +66,724 | +15.0 |
| 1980s | 37,830 | +16,914 | +54,744 | +10.7 |

SOURCE: Vermont Department of Health, Montpelier, Vermont.

NOTE: Natural growth is the number of births minus the number of deaths. Migration is the number of persons moving in minus the number moving out.

dacies brought Vermont back to the Republican fold, but the strength of the commitment was not the same. Vermont ranked tenth nationally in the percentage of the statewide Republican vote for Richard Nixon in 1968 and twenty-third in his massive landslide in 1972. In 1976 Vermont tied with Colorado for eighth place. This was the closest the state came in a generation to its former home in the top five. Ronald Reagan's two victories in Vermont were not overwhelming. In 1980 Vermont's Republican percentage was 6.2 points below Reagan's national percentage, putting it in forty-fifth place among the states. President Reagan's 1984 showing was a slight improvement—thirty-fifth place—but the days of overwhelming Republican presidential dominance were gone.

Even George Bush, a native New Englander and a long-time summer resident of Maine, had difficulty in Vermont in the 1988 presidential election. Bush captured only 51 percent of the vote against Massachusetts governor Michael Dukakis and a narrow plurality of only 8,556 votes.

The decline of presidential Republicanism in Vermont made it easier for Republican stalwarts such as former U.S. senator Robert Stafford, former U.S. representative (now U.S. senator) Jim Jeffords, and the late five-term governor Richard Snelling to challenge policy initiatives emanating from the Reagan-Bush White House. In Jeffords's case, it would have been difficult to find any Republican member of Congress who bucked the Republican White House more often and was so handsomely rewarded by his or her state's voters for doing so.

Governor Bill Clinton of Arkansas became the second Democrat to capture Vermont's electoral votes when he topped both President George Bush and independent candidate H. Ross Perot in 1992. Clinton's victory, more than Johnson's in 1964, signaled that Vermont had shifted away from the Republican presidential phalanx. As Ronald Reagan and his followers tilted the party's center of ideological gravity toward the South and West, Vermonters no longer felt as connected to it.

## ORGANIZATIONAL DEVELOPMENT

Because the trend lines of population growth and Republican presidential decline converged so dramatically in the 1960s, some believed that there was a clear cause-and-effect relationship between the two. In retrospect, however, they appear to have been dual manifestations of the same phenomenon: that of Vermont's growing linkage to national demographic, social, economic, and political trends. The state's isolation ended.

The convergence of the two trends affected the Vermont parties as well as state politics generally. Among some of the more obvious changes have been split-ticket voting, the disappearance of orderly paths to power, and the uncertainty of incumbency.

From 1856 through 1956, Vermont Republicans held every major statewide office as well as the state's lone U.S. House seat without exception—one full century of total Republican control of Vermont government. It was Bill Meyer, whose upset victory over Harold Arthur, the battered survivor of a fratricidal three-way U.S. House Republican primary, in 1958 who brought the unbroken streak to a halt. Meyer's pioneering advocacy of recognizing "Red" China led to his abrupt departure from Congress in 1960.

In 1962 Burlington's Kennedyesque Phil Hoff captured the governorship, the first Democrat to do so since 1851—before the founding of the Republican Party. Hoff's two reelections, in 1964 and 1966, enabled the Democrats to win nine of the ten contests for the constitutional offices: lieutenant governor, secretary of state, treasurer, attorney general, and auditor of accounts. Hoff's coattails did not extend to control of the state legislature, however. Deane Davis and his Republican "Team for the Times" regained the governorship and the state offices in 1968 and 1970. So it seemed as if the Hoff victories were part of a curious but short-lived abandonment of Vermont's traditional Republicanism.

*Split-Ticket Voting.* Ticket splitting in 1972 made it possible for Democrat Tom Salmon to capture the first of his two gubernatorial terms in the face of the Nixon landslide that same year. Salmon was the beneficiary of an extremely bitter Republican primary between the candidate of the party's "establishment" wing—insurance executive Luther "Fred" Hackett—and the popular but controversial attorney general (and now U.S. senator), Jim Jeffords. Jeffords was considered antibusiness because of his vigorous enforcement of anti-billboard legislation and his willingness to sue International Paper Company for polluting Lake Champlain. His loss in the 1972 primary echoed in Republican circles for many years afterward.

Since then only one election (1982) has been close to the earlier straight-ticket tradition. Vermont now has a new norm, and that is divided control of the statewide offices. Fifteen of the nineteen biennial elections between 1958 and 1994 have seen state voters select candidates of different parties for statewide offices.

Since the end of Republican dominance, the governor's office typically has been out of synch with the other statewide offices. In 1962, 1972, and 1984, Democratic governors were elected to serve when every other state office was held by Republicans. The move to an office-bloc ballot form in 1978 further encouraged split-ticket voting. Grouping candidates together by office and eliminating the party column made it even easier for Vermonters to split their tickets.

Senator Leahy and then-lieutenant governor Madeleine Kunin were the two immediate beneficiaries of the change. In 1980 the new ballot helped Senator Leahy obtain a small measure of protection from the almost total repudiation of his party's presidential incumbent, Jimmy Carter. Leahy ran 11.4 points ahead of the president, and much of the difference was due to the new ballot form, which saved him from the coattail defeats of nine Senate Democratic incumbents nationwide that year. Liberal Republicans along the Connecticut River Valley cast their presidential ballots for John Anderson, whose 15 percent showing tied Vermont with Massachusetts as his best state, and their senatorial ballots for Leahy against his Reaganite foe, Stewart Ledbetter.

The office-bloc ballot also permitted both Republican governor Snelling and Democratic lieutenant governor Kunin to capture landslide votes. No fewer than 43,000 of the state's 210,000 voters in the 1980 election—or one of every five—cast different party votes for these two statewide offices. One of the consequences of the two offices being elected separately is that lieutenant governors often cast covetous eyes toward the governor's chair. The next step for lieutenant governors—emboldened by a statewide electorate that likes them well enough to have elected them—is to challenge for the governorship. It has not been a wise move. Four lieutenant governors who served under governors of a different party all met electoral defeat. Three failed in bids to capture the governorship, and one finished a distant third in a three-way Republican contest for the open U.S. House seat nomination in 1974.

Democrat Howard Dean, a doctor-cum-politician originally from New York City, was elected lieutenant governor in 1986 and reelected in 1988, both times under then-governor (and now U.S. ambassador to Switzerland) Madeleine Kunin. Dean wisely passed on the opportunity to challenge the 1990 comeback bid of former governor Richard A. Snelling and chose to run for reelection. Snelling, who had served four two-year gubernatorial terms earlier (1977–1985), was returned to power in 1990 after a surprisingly close contest with former state senator Peter Welch.

Snelling's death in August 1991, the first Vermont governor to die in office in more than a century, elevated Lt. Governor Dean to the post. Dean overwhelmed Republican opponents John McLaughry in 1992 and David Kelley in 1994, gaining 74 percent of the 1992 vote and 69 percent of the 1994 vote. McLaughry's 23 percent represented a modern low for the Republican Party until Kelley's 19 percent two years later. The Republican statewide base vote of approximately 40 percent was seriously eroded by Governor Dean's moderate-to-conservative fiscal policies and his medical background, which made him atypical of more conventional Democratic candidates. Dean's middle-of-the-road political philosophy infuriated Democratic liberals from Chittenden County (Burlington), but it forced his opponents to challenge him from the political fringes where votes are few.

*The Disappearance of the Career Path.* The plight of many recent lieutenant governors highlights another major postconvergence change: the disappearance of the orderly line of succession which the Republican Party exploited for generations to promote its loyal members from one rung of the ladder to another. Because the Republican Party's control of the state was so total, the offices in the state belonged to the party itself and not to any incumbent. It did not really matter who ran, only that he or she ran under the Republican banner. This enabled Vermont to remain Republican during one stretch of twenty-eight one-term governors (1870–1926).

Total Republican control also enabled the party to alternate the governorship between Republican regional factions—one governor from east of the Green Mountains (Brattleboro, Springfield, and St. Johnsbury), then one from west of the mountains (Burlington, Bennington, Rutland, and St. Albans)—for a century. This control also appeared in the orderly way in which Republicans would serve an apprenticeship in the state legislature, move through the lesser statewide offices, and then gradually move up the ladder to the governorship. If opportunity struck and a seat in the U.S. House or U.S. Senate was available, then the loyalist highest along the trajectory moved into the seat.

Democratic U.S. senator Leahy's route to the Senate defied the traditional Republican ladder. The Senate was only Leahy's second political stop. Whereas it took former senator Stafford twenty-four years to move from Rutland County states attorney to the Senate, Leahy moved directly from the office of Chittenden County prosecutor into the Senate. Leahy's election marked another departure from tradition: the successful use of the broadcast media in campaigns. As broadcast news displaced print media in the 1970s, the importance of Chittenden County, with its television stations and their statewide reach, loomed even larger than before.

U.S. Rep. Dick Mallary (1972–1975), who lost to Leahy in 1974, failed to move from the House to the Senate. Although his loss was a shock at the time, it was just one of fifteen defeats suffered by sitting Vermont politicians in their efforts to "move up" during the postconvergence era. Seven lieutenant governors, four attorneys general, one secretary of state, one treasurer, one governor (Tom Salmon), and U.S. Representative Mallary all met defeat when they chose to use their offices as stepping-stones to higher ones. Stafford's move from the House to the Senate was approved by the state's voters, but the election took place after Stafford had been appointed senator following Senator Prouty's death. U.S. Representative Jeffords's move from the House to the Senate in 1988 was the only other successful example of "progressive ambition" in the postconvergence era.

Candidates who run for higher office after leaving state government appear to be slightly more successful. Madeleine Kunin was more successful running for governor while out of office in 1984 than in 1982 while she served as lieutenant governor. Similarly, Jeffords obtained his House seat in 1974 two years after suffering an agonizing defeat in the gubernatorial primary while serving as attorney general. However, the defeats for the U.S. Senate of former governor Hoff in 1970 and former governor Snelling in 1986, as well as the failure of ex-secretary of state James Guest to move from Montpelier to Washington in the Senate contest of 1982, reaffirm the difficulty confronting Vermont politicians who wish to move up.

*The Uncertainty of Incumbency.* The failures of Hoff, Salmon, Snelling, and Guest may also be attributable to the fact that Vermont's elected senators are never displaced. Vermont is the only state in the Union at the time of the passage of the Seventeenth Amendment that has never voted an elected U.S. senator out of office. An appointed Republican senator, Frank Partridge, failed to be nominated in 1931, but no elected senator has lost a renomination or reelection bid. Since 1914 Vermont's elected senators have faced twenty-one reelections and have won them all.

Although the defeat of an incumbent in Vermont for any office is relatively rare, every statewide office, apart from U.S. senator, suffered at least one defeat in the convergence era of the 1960s and 1970s. Democrat Bill Meyer's loss of a House seat in 1960 and Republican Ray Keyser's loss of the governorship were but a preface for the next seven elections, in which ten incumbents lost including three attorneys general (1964, 1966, and 1974), three treasurers (1964, 1968, and 1974), three secretaries of state (1964, 1968, and 1976), and even one auditor of accounts (1964). Add Lt. Gov. T. Garry Buckley's defeat by Peter Smith in the 1978 Republican primary and the total of incumbent defeats rises to thirteen. The decades before these two tumultuous ones were free of incumbent defeats, and apart from the 1990 loss of U.S. Rep. Peter Smith to Bernard Sanders and the 1994 defeat of one-term secretary of state Don Hooper, the last fifteen years have seen incumbents holding on to office.

*Burlington: "Socialism in One City."* Ironically, the most noted political development in Vermont during the 1980s was decidedly antipartisan. In March 1981, weeks after the nation had inaugurated its most conservative president in fifty years, Burlington elected Bernard Sanders, an avowed socialist, mayor by a scant ten votes. Sanders and his followers ousted a five-term Democratic opponent in a four-way contest. Helped by a revolt among the city's renters, who felt squeezed by landlords eager to displace young families with affluent out-of-state college students attending the University of Vermont, the Sanders campaign generated a huge voter turnout in the city's renter wards.

Burlington, with its mix of Irish and French-Canadian families, had long been the bastion of the state Democratic Party, even during the bad times for the party. Its takeover by the "Sanderistas" was thought to be a fluke that would be corrected at the next election. Sanders went on to victories in 1983, 1985, and 1987, and he was succeeded in 1989 by the development director of his administration, Peter Clavelle, who was reelected in 1991 and in 1995, after a two-year Republican hiatus. Even more striking was the fact that Sanders-backed candidates held a plurality of seats on the city's thirteen-member Board of Aldermen (later changed to the nonsexist fourteen-member City Council) throughout most of the last two decades.

Sanders's initial efforts to take his mayoral message statewide were not as successful. Sanders-style candidates for mayor in Rutland and St. Albans failed, and Sanders lost the gubernatorial race badly in 1986, finishing third with 14.6 percent of the vote behind incumbent Democratic governor Kunin and Republican lieutenant governor Peter P. Smith. In 1988 Sanders finished a surprisingly close second for the U.S. House seat vacated by Jim Jeffords, with 37.5 percent of the vote, trailing the winner, Republican Peter Smith, by only 8,900 votes and 3.7 percentage points. Sanders clearly outdistanced the Democratic candidate, state house floor leader Paul Poirier. Two years later, a rematch between Sanders and Rep. Smith, marred by "Castro-baiting" on Smith's part, led to a major victory by Sanders, 56.0 percent to 39.5 percent. He thus became the first seated independent in the U.S. House since Henry Frazier Reams of Ohio (1951–1955) and the first U.S. representative with socialist leanings since New York's Vito Marcantonio represented the American Labor Party (1939–1951). Sanders has been reelected twice.

With Sanders in the U.S. House and U.S. Senators Leahy, a Democrat, and Jeffords, a Republican, Vermont has congressional representation from three different political parties, but the three are among the most liberal members of their respective chambers. Vermont's delegation to Congress continues to be a liberal counterweight to the conservatism of its neighboring state, New Hampshire.

## CURRENT PARTY ORGANIZATION

As is often the case with states that are both small and dominated electorally by one political party, party organization is difficult to locate in Vermont. For the minority party, there are too few voters to organize, so its structures have little continuity. For the majority party, organizational apparatus is either unnecessary or potentially dangerous; it is unnecessary because the majority party is winning elections regardless of organizational strength, and it is potentially dangerous because the presence of an organizational apparatus opens that structure to capture by one of the party's factions. In states where interparty competition lacks intensity, intraparty competition and factionalism will appear.

Vermont is no exception to this generalization. For many years, the minority Vermont Democrats existed primarily as a "patronage party," receiving rewards for national Democratic Party victories to which they had contributed virtually nothing. It was not until the 1960s, during the three-term governorship of Phil Hoff, that Vermont's Democrats tried to put together a statewide organization. Prior to that time, only the Democratic city strongholds of Burlington, Winooski, and Barre were able to sustain any organizational continuity. But their organizations were local and had great difficulty penetrating the Republican counties along the Massachusetts border and the Upper Connecticut Valley.

Since Hoff's governorship, the Vermont Democrats have tried to maintain some continuous statewide organizational presence. Capable state chairs and less capable ones seemed to follow one another with regularity, and the funds gathered seldom seemed sufficient to pay administrative staff, not to mention defraying the campaign expenses of candidates. The candidate-centered nature of Vermont Democratic candidacies placed party organizational survival in the hands of elected officials, not all of whom believed that the party organization was responsible for their success.

One of the more intriguing organizational efforts of Vermont Democrats in recent years was that undertaken by long-time house speaker Ralph Wright (state representative, 1979–1995; speaker, 1985–1995) of Bennington, a Boston-born high school teacher who understood the importance of recruiting quality candidates for the low visibility offices of state representative. Under Speaker Wright's guidance, the state house Democrats were able to fill slates and to provide financial help and policy definition for their candidates. This effort was instrumental in keeping the Vermont house in the hands of the Democratic Party in the face of Republican control of the Vermont State Senate and the Republican capture of most of the lesser statewide offices

As befits a long-time majority party, the Vermont Republicans' organizational history differs dramatically from that of the Democrats. From 1872 through 1928, the Republicans of Vermont elected twenty-eight one-term governors in a row. It was a clear demonstration of organizational strength. Organization triumphed over personality. The pattern shifted in the 1930s and 1940s as the business-oriented Proctor wing of the Republican Party conflicted with the moderate-liberal Aiken-Gibson wing of the party. During this period, Vermont Democrats regularly crossed in the open primaries in September and voted for Aiken-Gibson Republicans. The cross-over voting made the Vermont Republicans far more liberal than their New Hampshire counterparts across the Connecticut River, who had closed state primaries.

But by the 1960s the Democrats had demonstrated that they could elect their own candidates to statewide office, and mucking around in the Republican primaries held less interest. In an effort to counteract growing Democratic strength, the Vermont Republicans solidified their party organization and hired full-time paid help and provided money for candidate polling, telecommunications, and advertising. "Team campaigning" was a feature of the 1968 election, and Republicans recaptured all of the statewide offices that year. But individual ambition and ideological factionalism were hard to contain, and Republican lieutenant governor Tom Hayes challenged Republican governor Deane Davis in 1970, and two years later the Republican organization denied the party's gubernatorial nomination to Attorney General Jim Jeffords, an independent liberal Republican in the Aiken mold.

The loss of the governorship in 1972 to Democrat Tom Salmon made Republicans more aware than ever that they no longer could afford internecine warfare and that they would have to manage intraparty conflict better if they were to return to their statehouse perches. Business executives such as Richard Snelling of Shelburne Industries brought a hierarchical organizational mentality to Republican affairs. Snelling, with a powerful presence, was able to guide the party toward more organizational coherence, and his capacity to raise substantial sums of money both within the state and nationally gave the Vermont Republican Party the resources to modernize itself.

The irony of the Republican modernization was that the only Republican capable of winning the governorship was Snelling himself. In the thirteen gubernatorial elections between 1972 through 1996, Democrats won eight contests with three different candidates—Thomas Salmon (1972 and 1974); Madeleine Kunin (1984, 1986, and 1988); and Howard Dean (1992, 1994, and 1996)—while Republicans won only five, all of which were won by Dick Snelling (1976, 1978, 1980, 1982, and 1990). Even though Republican organizational strength was demonstrably superior to the Democrats', the party had to be bailed out electorally by the personal popularity of Dick Snelling. So Vermont continues to be a state where party organizational strength is regularly at odds with the personal popularity of the party's candidates. Retail politics continues to determine electability in Vermont.

## RESOURCE GUIDE

Neither party retains archives of historical documents that would be useful for systematic research purposes.

## REFERENCES

*Asterisks denote the most important publications on Vermont party politics.*
*Bensen, Clark H. 1995. *Demographic and political guide to Vermont: Towns, cities and places.* Lake Ridge, Va.: Polidata.
Bryan, Frank M. 1981a. Decline of the party system? The case of Vermont. Paper presented at the annual meeting of the New England Political Science Association.
———. 1981b. *Politics in the rural states: People, parties and processes.* Boulder, Colo.: Westview Press.
*———. 1974. *Yankee politics in rural Vermont.* Hanover, N.H.: University Press of New England.
*Doyle, William. 1992. *The Vermont political tradition: And those who helped make it.* 2d ed. Montpelier, Vt.: William Doyle.
———. 1983. Political parties in Vermont. In *New England political parties,* ed. Josephine F. Milburn and William Doyle. Cambridge, Mass.: Schenkman.
Lockard, Duane. 1959. Vermont: Political paradox. *New England State Politics.* Princeton, N.J.: Princeton University Press.
Nelson, Garrison. 1988. The changing landscape of Vermont politics. *Vermont Quarterly* (August).
*Peirce, Neal R. 1976. Vermont: The beloved state. In *The New England states: People, politics and power in the six New England states.* New York: W. W. Norton.
Thurber, Harris E. 1968. Vermont: The stirrings of change. In *Party politics in the New England states,* ed. George Goodwin and Victoria Schuck. Durham, N.H.: New England Center for Continuing Education.
Wright, Ralph. 1996. *All politics is personal.* Manchester Center, Vt.: Marshall Jones.

# *Virginia*

JOHN MCGLENNON

In the past thirty-five years Virginia has been transformed from a one-party Democratic state, to home of the most successful Republican Party in the nation in major statewide elections, to a closely competitive two-party system. The development of the two-party system is consistent with the history of the commonwealth and foreshadowed the development of party competition throughout the South. Although V. O. Key derided Virginia as a "political museumpiece" in his classic *Southern Politics in State and Nation* (1949, 19–35), even as he wrote, the Old Dominion was becoming a laboratory for understanding the nature of party change in a one-party region. During the past two decades Virginia's Democratic and Republican Party organizations have been held up as examples to the rest of the nation of how parties can be made a more important force in American elections. But Virginia's party history necessarily begins with those who played such a prominent role in the founding of the nation, for from these founders came the roots of the modern Democratic Party, both nationally and in Virginia.

## PARTY HISTORY

Virginia's party history began before the formal establishment of parties in the United States. In the debates over the need for a national government, Virginia leaders such as Thomas Jefferson, James Madison, and James Monroe enthusiastically supported the new Constitution. However, they became leaders of the opposition in the new national government to Alexander Hamilton's push toward the centralization of power (Glass and Glass 1937, 18). The cleavage became persistent in national politics. While secretary of state under President Washington, Jefferson played a key role in organizing the faction that would rise to power with him, the Democratic-Republicans, and that would later become the Democratic Party of Andrew Jackson (Glass and Glass 1937, 23).

The foundations of the Virginia Republican Party are found in the mid-nineteenth century, along the spine of mountains running through the western part of the state, where opposition to secession and antagonism toward the powerful lowland plantation owners provided a natural basis for political opposition. Though never powerful in statewide elections during much of the period from the 1850s to the 1950s, the Republican Party could regularly win local office in some western counties and cities and occasionally win elections for state legislative seats (Key 1949, 280–285).

*The Byrd Era.* Reconstruction jumbled Virginia's party system considerably, with the emergence of significant political factions both within and outside the party structure. The Democratic Party, controlled by eastern Virginia landowners (the "Bourbons"), battled with the populist "Readjusters" over whether to repay the state's Civil War debt, owed largely to supporters of the former faction. However, by the beginning of the twentieth century, like the rest of the South, Virginia began a half century or more of one-party control (Maddex 1970). Aside from the exceptions in the western counties, candidates for state and local offices ran as Democrats. Electoral competition was in the Democratic Party primaries, and control of the primaries was generally in the hands of a statewide network of local political elites. The network maintained control by discouraging participation in elections through both formal methods (poll tax, literacy tests, residency requirements) and informal methods. By the mid-1920s the network had developed into a powerful organization headed by Harry Flood Byrd, who would serve as governor from 1926 to 1930 and as U.S. senator from 1933 to 1965. The Byrd organization would dominate Virginia elections for forty years (Eisenberg 1972, 40–46).

During presidential election years from 1940 until 1964, Byrd refused to let Virginia's Democratic Party make any effort in behalf of the national Democratic ticket. His hostility toward Franklin Roosevelt and succeeding Democratic presidential nominees led Byrd to maintain public neutrality in the national contest; it was referred to as his "golden silence" (Wilkinson 1968, 79). Byrd's refusal to endorse publicly a Democratic presidential ticket prevented the Virginia Democratic Party as an organization from doing any more than the law required for the nominees (choosing electors and filing for a place on the ballot) until 1964, when a coalition of teachers, union members, African Americans, and urban liberals forced an endorsement of Lyndon Johnson and Hubert Humphrey through the state convention (Bass and DeVries 1976, 349).

Since the Byrd organization dominated state offices through control of the Democratic primaries, it was not concerned with general elections. And because two-party competition was geographically isolated, there was no need for a strong party organization (as distinct from Byrd's personal organization). Key began his chapter on party organization in the South by citing five newspaper headlines from 1947 and 1948 declaring Democrats unable to fill party organizational positions (Key 1949, 386). Two of the five were from Virginia. The lack of partisan competition meant that no one had to worry much about maintaining a general-election organization, and holding a party position did not significantly enhance one's ability to influence nomination contests.

In Virginia, the power to determine the method of party nomination has been vested by state law in the political parties. Parties are permitted to decide between direct primaries and nominating conventions. Until 1946 the GOP did not allow primaries, but in that year, Republicans in the Washington, D.C., suburbs convinced their state party to permit the option. Among Democrats, the convention was widely used in nominations for local offices and even some congressional districts, but it was rarely invoked for statewide office. Finally, the law governing party nomination allows incumbent legislators seeking their first renomination and those incumbents who had most recently been renominated by primary to select the primary method.

## ORGANIZATIONAL DEVELOPMENT

In the late 1940s and early 1950s the Byrd organization withstood serious challenges from within the Democratic Party and from a growing Republican Party. Challenges to Byrd candidates by antiorganization forces blocked Senator Byrd's choice for Virginia's other Senate seat in a 1946 convention and nearly upset the Byrd candidate for governor in 1949. The GOP ticket carried the Old Dominion in the 1952 election for president, and Republicans came tantalizingly close to winning the governorship in 1953. However, the Byrd organization's defiant policy of "massive resistance" to integration in the wake of the U.S. Supreme Court's 1954 *Brown v. Board of Education* decision drew overwhelming support among Virginia's white electorate.

The political parties in Virginia were buffeted in the 1960s, as were parties in most other states, by constitutional, legal, social, and demographic developments. Byrd-organization Democrats entered the decade divided between the staunch supporters of segregation and those who advocated peaceful integration after the Court's *Brown* decision. The Republicans were dealt a setback by the resurgence of the Democrats under Byrd's call for "massive resistance" to the federal courts' leadership (Eisenberg 1972, 51–52).

But the movement by the national government to remove restrictions on voting (banning the poll tax by constitutional amendment and then passing the Civil Rights Act of 1964 and the Voting Rights Act of 1965) dramatically increased voter participation. The native, rural population of the state began to decline in influence with the surge of newcomers to northern Virginia, Richmond, and Tidewater and the reapportionment of the General Assembly to reflect the "one man, one vote" principle of the Supreme Court's 1962 decision in *Baker v. Carr* (Eisenberg 1972, 54–63).

*Party Civil Wars: 1964–1972.* During the 1960s, Democratic organizational turmoil occurred as the party's anti-Byrd wing grew with the enfranchisement of African American voters and the expansion of urban populations. In successive state conventions between 1964 and 1972, Democrats first moved firmly away from Byrd's "golden silence" toward support for the Democratic presidential ticket, and finally liberal insurgents seized control of the party from the moderates. In large part, the liberals' success was due to the practice of electing state party officers at the same state conventions at which presidential convention delegates were elected. The McGovern-Fraser Commission reform of the Democratic presidential nominating procedures had opened the party organization to thousands of people who had never attended a party committee meeting, let alone a state convention. In 1972, when local meetings to elect state convention delegates were dominated by anti–Vietnam War activists, the delegation to the Democratic National Convention originally included not a single elected official (Abramowitz, McGlennon, and Rapoport 1981, 10–11).

Republicans were undergoing their own internal turmoil, as young conservatives, attracted by the Barry Goldwater candidacy for president, were drawn into the Virginia GOP. They came in conflict with traditional, more liberal mountain Republicans, who also clashed with a growing number of former Democrats drawn to the Republican Party by the increasingly liberal tilt of the Democrats. The struggle for control of the state Republican Party pitted the moderate, traditional GOP of the mountains against the conservative Goldwater Republicans and their former Byrd Democrat allies. So powerful was the combination of the Goldwater Republicans and former Democrats that it upset Gov. Linwood Holton's choice for state chair in 1972 in a stunning defeat for the state's first Republican governor in one hundred years (Atkinson 1992, 245).

*Republicans Surge While Democrats Start Over: 1973–1980.* The 1970s was a difficult period for party organizations in Virginia, as both parties found themselves distanced from the public officials who nominally were members of their parties. Democrats were so weak organizationally that they were unable to convince their preferred candidate for governor in 1973, Lieutenant Governor Henry Howell, to accept their nomination (he ran as an independent, with Democratic endorsement). The Republicans faced internal disunity over whether to nominate former Democratic governor Mills Godwin that same year, and Godwin only reluctantly accepted the nomination (Atkinson 1992, 262). Between 1969 and 1977, the Democrats lost all three races for governor as well as three U.S. Senate races (two to independent senator Harry F. Byrd Jr.).

Though Republicans were divided over the direction of the party, its electoral success was helping the GOP to gain organizational muscle. In contrast to the Democrats, who nominated their candidates in often bitter and expensive primaries, the Republican Party selected its slate of candidates in conventions, which served an important role in recruiting party membership. In 1978 the GOP held a U.S. Senate nominating convention in Richmond with more than 8,000 delegates registered, making it the largest political nominating convention held to that time. (The 1993 GOP state convention would eclipse the 1978 mark with 13,109 delegates.) The delegates in 1978 selected the most conservative candidate, though when he died in a plane crash during the late summer, one of his more moderate rivals (John Warner) was selected to replace him (Abramowitz, McGlennon, and Rapoport 1981).

Democrats took a lesson from the GOP in 1978 and voted to hold their own nominating convention for U.S. senator, which attracted a lively field of eight candidates and three thousand delegates. In contrast to the general expectation that a convention would likely produce an ideologically extreme candidate, the Democratic delegates (who were in fact much more liberal than the average voter) opted for a moderate candidate (Andrew Miller) who had lost the gubernatorial primary to the more liberal Henry Howell (once again a Democrat) the preceding year.

Though the Democrats lost the 1978 general election for U.S. Senate (by five thousand votes out of 1.25 million cast), they generally were pleased with their ability to confine the damage of the intraparty fight in a convention, and the Democratic State Central Committee has adopted the convention as the nomination method in every statewide contest since, except for the 1994 U.S. Senate nomination. Republicans have continued to utilize the convention with only a few exceptions: in 1989 for governor, and in 1990 and 1996 for a U.S. Senate seat (although in 1990 incumbent senator John Warner was not challenged for renomination, and the primary was canceled). Both parties use primaries and conventions for congressional, state legislative, and local nominations; the northern Virginia suburbs are most likely to use the primary. The GOP has also opted for a 1997 primary for their gubernatorial nomination.

The Democratic Party organization suffered from its neglected grass roots and its estranged relationship with elected officials. The lack of an ongoing state party apparatus made it extremely difficult for the party (as opposed to its candidates) to raise money for operations. The Democrats operated out of a small office suite with one (sometimes) paid employee. Operating expenses came largely from annual assessments on the local party committees and periodic bank loans signed by party leaders. Democratic officeholders were able to raise significant contributions for their own campaigns, and the Democratic caucuses of the General Assembly were also successful at raising funds, with the money generally restricted to the aid of incumbent members.

The Republican Party organization, on the other hand, benefited from its electoral success in the 1970s. The party held successful fund-raising events, built a stable financial base among its thousands of activists, and made profits from its nominating conventions, which charged delegates registration fees to participate. So successful was the GOP in the 1970s that it was even able to purchase a downtown Richmond headquarters building to house the staff (Atkinson 1992, 293). Even though Governor Holton lost control of his party machinery in 1972 to conservative Richard Obenshain, the new chair was able to improve relations with subsequent elected officials, having played a crucial role in converting former governor Godwin to the GOP. Godwin was succeeded as state party chair by former Democratic delegate George McMath Jr., and both worked to expand the Republican ranks with former Byrd Democrats. They also helped to push the Republican Party in the direction of more sophisticated campaign technology and to build the party operation from the grass roots (Atkinson 1992, 297–299).

*Democrats Rebound to Compete with GOP: 1981–1994.* The Democrats had a more optimistic outlook in the 1980s than they had in the 1970s, as the party began to adapt to a highly competitive two-party system. One after another, state party chairs were selected on the basis of their ability to reestablish the link between the party organization and its elected officials and financial contributors (Atkinson 1992, 402). And at the same time, several of the chairs used the party office to launch statewide political campaigns in a system where nominations were won by courting the activists who worked most closely with the party leadership. State Democratic Party chairs in the 1980s were elected lieutenant governor and U.S. representative and sought nominations for governor, U.S. senator, and attorney general.

The thirst of Virginia Democrats for statewide victories led to convention nominations of moderate Democrats in the 1980s, and the nominations paid off in three successive sweeps of the state elections in 1981, 1985, and 1989. Although the candidates were moderate in philosophy, they included the first African American to be elected lieutenant governor of Virginia, L. Douglas Wilder, who would later become the first popularly elected African American governor in the United States; and the first woman elected to statewide office in Virginia, Attorney General Mary Sue Terry. The convention system was critical to the nominations, as liberal delegates opted for more conservative candidates to enhance the prospects of electoral success and as party leaders were able to forestall a challenge to Wilder's nomination for governor in 1989, allowing him to prepare financially for the fall campaign (McGlennon 1990).

During the 1980s Democrats assembled a much more effective state organization, with a full-time executive director running a staff that ranged from a half-dozen to dozens, depending on the year and the offices being contested, and managing budgets ranging between $500,000 and $1 million. Computer technology and direct-mail fund raising were added to the traditional, but now much more successful, annual Jefferson-Jackson Day dinner as means of raising party funds. Convention fees also provided profit for the Democrats, and they began a $10 a month donor plan to provide a stable cash flow for party operations.

Republicans suffered significant setbacks in the 1980s, as their ability to generate funds was hampered by the loss of the governorship. The party had to cut back on staffing, although it was hardly without resources. The White House was in GOP hands throughout the decade, and the GOP was able to raise enough money to keep functioning during its state office drought. More important, the GOP began a period of intense infighting, beginning with the movement of evangelical and born-again Christians into the GOP under the leadership first of Rev. Jerry Falwell's Moral Majority and then Rev. Pat Robertson's Christian Coalition. The economic conservatism of the old-guard Republicans was not always shared by the Christian right, which had a much more ideologically rigid social conservatism than the affluent, suburban GOP base.

Internal dissension also hampered Democratic Party organization during the administration of Governor Wilder (1990–1994), as his hand-picked state chair, Paul Goldman, had strained relations with other Democratic leaders. Goldman resigned in the last year of the Wilder administration and was replaced by northern Virginia business executive Mark Warner, who in 1996 would become the party's U.S. Senate nominee. Warner devoted considerable attention to party revitalization, overseeing a comprehensive strategic planning process, holding statewide hearings on the party, and investing heavily in new campaign technology and expanded staffing. Warner was successful in drawing the operations of the House of Delegates Democratic caucus into the state party headquarters and in convincing the senate Democratic caucus to hire its first executive director, who also was housed in the state party offices. Warner was succeeded as state Democratic chair in June 1995 by Susan Wrenn, the first woman chair of a major Virginia party and a former chair of the Fairfax County Democratic Committee. With about 12 percent of the state's population, Fairfax is the largest local jurisdiction in the state.

Republicans experienced an electoral upsurge in 1993, when they elected a governor for the first time since 1977, but the electoral victory did not end the intraparty tension. Gov. George Allen (1994–) attempted to replace party chair Patrick McSweeney, who had headed the party in its successful statewide effort and had helped the GOP come within three seats of controlling the House of Delegates. McSweeney refused to bow to pressure from Allen to resign, leading to a formal effort to oust him. The motion fell short of the required three-quarters majority of the Republican State Central Committee, and McSweeney retained his position but without the support of the governor.

The decision of Republican U.S. senator John Warner to support the independent candidacy of two-time former Republican gubernatorial candidate J. Marshall Coleman against Republican nominee Oliver North in the 1994 Senate contest exacerbated the internal divisions in the GOP. Warner's own renomination for the U.S. Senate was threatened by opposition among party activists, and McSweeney and Warner battled in 1996 over the method of nomination, with McSweeney calling for a convention and Warner asserting that state law allowed him as the incumbent to choose a primary. Warner won the intraparty battle and the primary, and he was set to face Mark Warner, the Democratic nominee, in the November general election.

Religious and other strongly conservative activists enhanced their position in the GOP during the 1993 and 1994 nominating processes. The 1993 state convention saw nearly 4,500 home-schooling parents among the 13,000 delegates. These parents were drawn to the convention by the candidacy of Michael Farris, the national executive director of the conservative home-schoolers association, for lieutenant governor. Farris was successful in winning the party nomination (he subsequently lost the general election), and his followers largely determined the outcome of the convention contests for governor and attorney general as well. In 1994 Oliver North, the Iran-contra figure who was convicted of lying to Congress (though the conviction was overturned on procedural grounds), won the party nomination for U.S. Senate over former Reagan administration budget director James Miller.

Despite periodic problems for both parties, however, the parties appear to have established an ongoing presence with full-time staff and the development of resources for candidates and elected officials. Party competition in Virginia now means aggressive organizations funded with hundreds of thousands of dollars annually and engaged in the basic activities of modern campaigning.

## CURRENT PARTY ORGANIZATION

Virginia's political parties are organized under provisions of general law for the commonwealth and under a required "Party Plan of Organization" that must be adopted by each party and filed with the State Board of Elections. Both parties choose to elect their state chairs at a quadrennial convention, which is held during presidential election years for the Republicans, who also use the convention to select delegates to the Republican National Convention. Democrats also use a convention to select the presidential convention delegation, but the state party officers are elected at a convention during gubernatorial election years. The Democrats changed the timing of their elections in order to insulate the party offices from presidential politics.

Democrats elect not only their state chair but also the other statewide party officers, including five vice chairs, secretary, and treasurer. Four members of the Democratic National Committee are selected during presidential election years. Republicans defer election of other officers until the first meeting of their state central committee, which elects a first vice chair, four regional vice chairs, secretary, and treasurer. The state convention elects two national committee members.

Each party is governed between conventions by a state central committee. The Republican central committee has a voting membership that can range from sixty-seven to eighty-nine, depending on how many districts supported the GOP in the preceding presidential election and how many elected a Republican to Congress. There is no requirement that local party chairs serve on the central committee, although some do.

The Democratic State Central Committee is a much larger organization; its membership includes all state officers and DNC members, twenty members elected at conventions from each congressional district, one member of the General Assembly per congressional district, one city or county chair per district, plus various other party officials, elected officials, and leaders of constituency groups (such as Young Democrats and the Federation of Democratic Women). In total, more than 260 members serve on the committee.

Both parties empower a subset of the central committee (GOP Executive Committee, Democratic Steering Committee) to meet in place of the larger group, but party rules make its actions subject to review by the larger group. Each party has a congressional district committee for each of the state's eleven U.S. House districts. This committee determines the method for nominating candidates for the House, certifies candidates to the State Board of Elections, and serves as an intermediary between the state party and local party organizations. There is also a legislative district committee for each party for each house and senate district. In both parties, the purpose of this committee is solely to nominate candidates for legislative office, whereas the congressional district committees are mandated by party rules and under state law to meet more frequently and to perform a wider range of functions, including filing campaign finance reports.

The basic organizing unit of each party is the local committee (city or county committee in Democratic parlance, unit committee in GOP terms). Each party requires a biennial election of local committee members and officers, with election by voters at a "mass meeting" or party caucus. Power in the state parties is hierarchical to the extent that decisions made at the local level are subject to appeal first to the congressional district committee and ultimately to the state central committee.

The parties have reversed roles in recent years in regard to who has the most influence on party decisions: elected officials and party leaders or party activists. There has not been a seriously contested race for Democratic state chair since 1978, and usually at state conventions, the person chosen by party leaders is ratified unanimously. More often than not, the Democratic chair has been first formally elected by the central committee, and at least since 1981, the chair has been elected with the endorsement of the Democratic governor or lieutenant governor. Republicans have generally had more spirited contests, most recently in 1992, when McSweeney was elected, and as we have seen, the support of the governor has not been necessary or even sufficient to determine the leader of the party.

The role of the Democratic and Republican Parties in Virginia state politics is paradoxical. Neither party has the power to force policy choices on its elected officials, and both have experienced significant defections in important elections. But candidates have also discovered that the parties can be important sources of support and that the party organizations are capable of making things difficult for candidates who ignore them. The state Republican Party organization is now dominated by conservatives, with the largest single group including those drawn into the GOP by the very conservative social agenda of the Christian Coalition and other organizations of evangelical Christians. They are allied with (and have some overlap with) home-school advocates and other conservative groups, such as antiabortion activists and opponents of gun control. More traditional economic conservatives, who tend to be more moderate on social issues, comprise a significant minority in the GOP, with greater strength in the state's urban areas, especially northern Virginia and Tidewater.

Democrats have a wider spectrum of ideology, and organizationally the Democrats have strong representation from organized labor, educators, African Americans, environmentalists, and women's rights supporters. Democrats have seen the balance of power in their party shift even more toward the populous northern Virginia and Tidewater regions and have recently suffered significant setbacks elsewhere, in southwestern Virginia in particular.

Finally, a word should be said about the comparative position of Virginia's Republicans and Democrats in the formerly one-party South. The Old Dominion experienced Republican success much earlier than most of the rest of the region. Republicans won Virginia's governorship three times between 1969 and 1977, and they held an overwhelming majority of the state's congressional delegation by 1980. Democrats in Virginia came to the realization much earlier than their counterparts in other southern states that they needed to respond to the growth of electoral competition. That may explain why Virginia Democrats and Republicans saw their party organizations differently from their counterparts in the other states of the South in a recent survey of precinct-level party leaders (McGlennon 1993).

Virginia Republicans were much less likely than their counterparts in other states to see their party as having made great strides forward organizationally. That is not likely to be because the Virginia GOP is weaker than the other state parties, but because it has a longer history of electoral effectiveness. Virginia Democrats, on the other hand, were much more likely to see themselves as organizationally improved than were Democrats in other states. Undoubtedly, this is because the Virginia party had to respond two decades ago to the collapse of its once-unassailable position. The lesson for other states rests in the tendency of party organizations to respond to new circumstances, and the tendency of a system that has experienced competition to remain competitive thereafter.

## RESOURCE GUIDE

The Virginia Republican Party does appear to have some archival material available, but although it was used by Frank Atkinson in his book on the modern Virginia Republican Party, his access was largely due to his role as an active Republican (he currently serves as counselor to Gov. George Allen). Access to Republican Party lists and files has been difficult for researchers to obtain. Atkinson's book reflects interviews he conducted with many principals of Virginia politics over the period of about 1980 to 1992. Democratic Party archives are not as well maintained as the Republican and also would not be easily accessible to the scholar.

Libraries at the University of Virginia and the College of William and Mary contain vast collections of papers from prominent state officeholders. In addition, noncurrent records of the Virginia State Board of Elections are available at the State Library of Virginia, but they are not maintained in a readily accessible form.

## REFERENCES

Asterisks denote the most important publications on Virginia party politics.
*Abramowitz, Alan, John McGlennon, and Ronald Rapoport. 1981. *Party activists in Virginia*. Charlottesville: Institute of Government, University of Virginia.
*Atkinson, Frank. 1992. *The dynamic Dominion*. Fairfax, Va.: George Mason University Press.
Bass, Jack, and Walter DeVries. 1976. *The transformation of southern politics*. New York: Basic Books.
*Eisenberg, Ralph. 1972. Virginia: The emergence of two-party politics. In *The changing politics of the South*, ed. William C. Havard. Baton Rouge: Louisiana State University Press.

Glass, Robert C., and Carter Glass Jr. 1937. *Virginia democracy: A history of the achievements of the party and its leaders in the mother of commonwealths, the Old Dominion*. Springfield, Ill.: Democratic Historical Association.

Heard, Alexander. 1952. *A two-party South?* Chapel Hill: University of North Carolina Press.

*Key, V. O. 1949. *Southern politics in state and nation*. New York: Alfred A. Knopf.

Maddex, Jack P. 1970. *The Virginia conservatives, 1867–1879*. Chapel Hill: University of North Carolina Press.

McGlennon, John. 1995. Virginia: Experience with democracy. In *Southern state party organizations and activists*, ed. Charles Hadley and Lewis Bowman. Westport, Conn.: Praeger.

———. 1993. Party activity and party success: Southern precinct leaders and the evaluation of party strength. Paper presented at the annual meeting of the American Political Science Association, Washington, D.C.

———. 1990. New forces in the Old Dominion: Party power in the 1989 gubernatorial election. Paper presented at the Citadel Symposium on Southern Politics, Charleston, S.C.

———. 1988. Virginia's changing party politics, 1976–1986. In *The South's new politics*, ed. Robert Swansbrough and David Brodsky. Columbia: University of South Carolina Press.

*Wilkinson, J. Harvie. 1968. *Harry Byrd and the changing face of Virginia politics, 1945–1966*. Charlottesville: University Press of Virginia.

# Washington

ANDREW M. APPLETON AND
ANNEKA DEPOORTER

## PARTY HISTORY

In Washington, as in other western states, the development of the earliest political party organizations was closely linked to the extension of federal patronage. Before the middle of the nineteenth century, political life was conducted mainly through loosely organized local groups that coalesced around specific issues or interests. In 1853 the Washington Territory was created by the federal government, opening up many administrative positions that would be distributed through patronage from Washington, D.C. This link to the national political system stimulated the emergence of local political party organizations in the Washington Territory that have since formed the backbone of the two-party system. Since the territory was allocated only one delegate to the national legislature, the "elections for that office were as hard and as bitterly fought as were the presidential and congressional elections in the states of the Union" (Johannsen 1951, 5).

The Democrats were the first to organize effectively in the Washington Territory, despite the fact that a Whig president had signed the legislation creating the territory. The Whigs were the major opposition to the Democrats during the first three years of the territory; unlike Whigs in other areas of the country, the Washington Whigs avoided a split over the Kansas-Nebraska Act of 1854 (which they opposed). However, Whig Party organization did not endure for long; by 1856 it was being seriously challenged by the Free Soil movement in local elections (Reed 1968), and in 1857 the latter adopted the label "Republican Party" at a convention in Olympia and began developing strong local organizations. By the end of the decade, the Republican Party had emerged as the main competitor to Democratic control of territorial politics.

During the early years, when power effectively rested with the Democratic Party, the Democrats were not immune to serious factional disputes. Slavery was, of course, the predominant national issue and caused internal disputes within the territorial party organization, but the conduct of Governor Isaac Stevens in the Indian campaigns of 1855–1856 also split the party. Stevens's mobilization of the local militia and his declaration of martial law in Pierce County were ignored by federal judge Edward Lander; Stevens placed Judge Lander under arrest. Freed, Lander again defied the martial law proclamation and was once more arrested. Ultimately the judiciary won, and Stevens was fined for contempt. The case reached the national level when President Franklin Pierce ordered the governor replaced (which did not in fact happen). Both Stevens and Lander sought the Democratic Party nomination for governor in 1857; Stevens won the fight for control of the convention and went on to win the general election. The episode reduced territorial politics for a few years to a pro- and anti-Stevens conflict (Johannsen 1951). The anti-Stevens forces eventually moved to the Republican Party and helped strengthen it in its earliest years of existence.

In fact, the slavery issue was soon to influence the territory. In 1861 fractures within the Oregon Democratic Party over slavery paved the way for a united Republican Party to win the delegateship with less than 50 percent of the vote (Meany 1924). The election was the turning point in the control of territorial politics, for the Republican Party was able to capitalize on its 1861 success and build a strong organizational and electoral base. The Republicans were to retain control of most major political offices until statehood was achieved in 1889.

Republican dominance continued until the New Deal era, with one exception. From 1897 to 1899 the Fusionists controlled the state legislature and every state office, plus they formed a majority of the state congressional delegation. The Fusionists were a conglomeration of Democrats, Populists, and Free-Silver Republicans inspired by the program of William Jennings Bryan, who carried the state by 12,000 votes in the 1896 presidential election (Newell 1975). The collapse of the Fusionist movement heralded an erosion of the organizational base of the Democratic Party, which was reduced to a minority party until the realignment of 1932.

The Democratic Party during the period 1900 to 1932 was so weak that it was unable to present a full slate of candidates for Congress on no fewer than five occasions. The lack of party organization, along with the closed primary in use at the time, led to extremely low primary turnouts. For example, in the U.S. Senate primary elections of 1928, the Democrats mustered just under 34,000 votes in their primary election compared with more than 247,000 for the three Republican hopefuls. However, in the general election, the Democratic incumbent, Clarence Dill (one of only four Democrats to hold high office in this period), gained 261,524 votes to Republican candidate Kenneth Mackintosh's 227,415 (Ogden and Bone 1960, 13). Indeed, the Democratic Party often found itself in third place for state offices behind the Republican Party and either the Progressive Party or the Farm-Labor Party.

The 1930s were a time of change for the Democratic Party as it began to assume more power in the state legislature. In 1932 the Democratic Party gained momentum from the broad support of the general public for the New Deal platform (Ogden and Bone 1960). The progressive and populist tradition within the state electorate facilitated the rejuvenation of the Democratic Party around the New Deal coalition. A concerted effort among the leaders of the state party ensured that the state convention of 1932 would nominate Franklin D. Roosevelt for president unanimously (Krause 1971). So powerful was the Democratic wave that it swept the Republican Party out of all state offices until 1938; only in 1940 did the Republicans begin to compete on an almost equal footing with the Democrats.

The period from 1940 until 1960 was one of vigorous two-party competition (Ogden and Bone 1960). Although the state Republicans were more successful than the Democrats at electing members of the U.S. House, the Democrats retained greater control of the state legislature. Nonetheless, alternation of party control became the rule rather than the exception. "Divided government" began to characterize the Washington State political system in these years. In terms of party organization, the introduction of the "blanket primary" (or, as some have called it, the "wide open primary") in 1935 drastically reduced the leverage that parties had over the nomination of candidates; the 1935 legislation also specifically outlawed preprimary endorsements. Thus the advent of competitive two-party politics in Washington State was accompanied by an atrophying of party organizations; the decentralized party organizations had trouble filling both precinct and county-level posts.

The weakness of the party organizations themselves was highlighted by the defection of eight conservative Democratic state senators from their party in 1951. These senators joined with the Republicans to organize the legislative session, thus allowing control of the upper chamber to pass to the Republican Party. Despite being condemned by the Democratic Party organization at the convention of 1952, several of the renegade state senators sought the party nomination at the next primary. All who sought to be renominated and reelected were successful. While Ogden and Bone (1960) characterized the legislative party organization as perhaps the most important area of party strength, this episode demonstrates the limits even of that.

## ORGANIZATIONAL DEVELOPMENT

By the end of the 1950s the impact of the blanket primary was being felt by the party organizations. Because of the generally weak institutional structures of the state political system and the progressive tradition—indeed, the blanket primary was proposed through voter initiative—political parties in Washington State found themselves in a position of relative disadvantage compared with parties in many other states. In an effort to overcome their environmental difficulties, both parties began the 1960s attempting to develop more professional central organizations. For the first time, both Republicans and Democrats began compensating their staff; the Republicans paid a salary to their executive secretary in 1960, and the Democrats provided their state chair with some monetary compensation. Both parties also hired support staff at this time.

As part of their drive toward more professionalized central party organizations, and perhaps also to some degree as a reflection of it, both parties began to centralize functions at the state-committee level. State law at the time mandated equal representation from the county committees on the state central committee, permitting the rural, less active counties to dominate the body. To circumvent the problem, both parties had developed a state executive committee; these bodies became the vehicle for the professionalization of the party organizations in the early 1960s. Since the parties could no longer serve as the vehicles to nomination, they began to concentrate more on postprimary activities: fund raising, campaign management, and political communication (Bone 1961).

It was not until the 1970s and 1980s, however, that the parties in Washington State became the modern service-vendor institutions they are today. The Republican Party took the lead in the 1970s, owing in large part to the help and guidance provided by the RNC. The state party organization invested time and resources to develop mechanisms for raising and channeling money to candidates, for providing polling and computer data processing, for garnering expert analyses of individual races, and for undertaking demographic studies (Mullen and Pierce 1985). Paradoxically, the lack of partisan voter registration information resulting from the open primary system actually served to make the state party organization more important to individual candidates, because the candidates, even though they had their own campaign organizations, lacked the resources to gather this type of background and contextual data.

Mullen and Pierce (1985) detail the effects of the organizational efforts of the Republicans in this period. In just one state legislative campaign, that of 1978, the state central committee lent its full organizational support to eleven candidates; all of them won their races. By 1980 the party was able to target thirty-five districts and to devote $5,000 to each of the races. The total budget of the Washington Republican Party in 1978 exceeded one million dollars, much of it spent on candidate support. Another $80,000 was spent on polling and opposition research. In addition, the party sponsored a number of training seminars for candidates, campaign managers, and volunteer workers (Mullen and Pierce 1985, 59).

The Democratic Party also underwent organizational change in the 1970s but in a rather different vein from that of the Republicans. A core of reform-oriented activists who joined the party in the wake of reforms initiated by Sen. George McGovern and Rep. Donald M. Fraser were determined to make the party more democratic. The main issue facing the party during the decade was the balance of power within the organization. The statutory prescriptions for representation on the mandatory state central committee of the parties (one man and one woman from each county committee) meant in practice that the populous urban counties could be outvoted by the rural county representatives. As Mullen and Pierce (1985, 59) show, it was theoretically possible that "the twenty smallest counties with a total population of around 265,000 people [could] outvote in the Central Committee the nineteen counties representing more than 3,700,000 people."

The battle of the rural counties and the urban counties exploded into one of the most divisive and fractious episodes in the history of the Washington State Democratic Party. At the 1976 party convention, a temporary platform committee led by reformers from King and Pierce Counties proposed a new charter that would, among other things, add two members to the state central committee from each of the state legislative districts. Because the legislative districts are apportioned according to population, the measure would effectively have increased the representation of the parties in the larger counties. The new charter was passed by the 1976 convention after bitter debate; the state chair, Neal Chaney, resigned from his position. Although the new charter was passed again by the convention in 1978, the majority of the party central committee continued to insist that the committee, not the convention, was the sovereign body of the party; as such, the charter was invalid until ratified by the central committee, which refused to ratify it (Mullen and Pierce 1985).

The fight came down to two essential points of contention: Which body had sovereignty within the party? And, to what extent could the composition of the central committee be altered within the framework of the law? Records contained in the archives of the party at Washington State University provide a fascinating accounting of the evolution of the dispute over the next few years. Chaney was replaced as state chair by Joe Murphy; however, the insurgents, led by Karen Marchioro and the King County Democratic Committee, continued to press their claims in a legal suit. *Marchioro et al. v. Chaney et al.* was heard by the Supreme Court in 1979, having passed through the state supreme court on the way. Both the courts and the DNC ultimately gave favor to the reformers, and Marchioro eventually became state chair. For four years there were virtually two Democratic parties operating in the state, both claiming to be the official organ of the national party.

A second, only slightly less contentious issue facing the Democrats at the same time was the financing of the party. In the late 1970s the state executive committee decided to solve the perennial problem of fund raising in part by getting involved in the gaming industry. Specifically, the party launched a cooperative bingo venture with a commercial operator. For a short period, the initiative produced a dramatic increase in party revenues; although the exact amount cannot be precisely determined from party records, it appears that in one year alone the bingo operation brought more than half a million dollars to the coffers. However, the venture turned sour when an investigation by the state gaming commission revealed irregularities in the operation of the game. In 1979 the central committee's gambling license was revoked by the commission, and the subsequent publicity proved to be an enormous embarrassment for the party organization.

In the 1980s the newly united and expanded Democratic central committee began to implement some of the same reforms that the Republicans had undertaken in the previous decade. Under Marchioro's leadership the state party strengthened its ties to the national party and moved to adopt some of the organizational innovations that had already been introduced by the DNC and other state parties. Evidence of the change is provided by the amount of money the Democrats were giving to state legislative candidates. In 1980 the state party allocated just $9,700. In total, it only gave out $23,000 that year to all election campaigns. Two years later, the figure jumped to $75,000 for legislative candidates (Mullen and Pierce 1985, 60), reflecting the new chair's commitment to rebuilding the party organization as an effective campaign tool. However, comparison with Republican Party expenditures, reported above, shows that the Democrats were lagging far behind in candidate support.

At the dawn of the modern party era, Ogden and Bone (1960) characterized local party organization in the state of Washington as being frequently weak and inactive. The prescriptions of state law and the lack of organizational professionalization meant that the party organizations remained decentralized and generally weak. Survey evidence from the early 1970s showed that state legislators and county party officials thought that Washington State party organizations were somewhat weaker than their counterparts in other states (Mullen and Pierce 1985). However, the Washington State Republican Party ranked as one of the ten strongest in the nation in the late 1970s, and the Democrats were only slightly weaker than the national average. The same study showed that the county party organizations were actually stronger than the national average (Cotter et al. 1989; Nice 1992). Although the measures used in all three studies were different, it would be reasonable to conclude that they reflect rather well the historical effects of the blanket primary, the decentralization imposed by state law, the organizational professionalization of the Republican Party in the 1970s, and the hiatus experienced by the state Democrats during the same decade.

## CURRENT PARTY ORGANIZATION

Most observers agree that Washington State imposes greater legal restraints on party organization than other states. At all levels of party organization, the composition and competence of the party hierarchy are determined by a statute originally adopted in 1925 (RCW 29.42). Although the parties themselves have found formal and informal ways of circumventing the restraints on occasion, the restraints remain one of the fundamental features of party political life in the state. Some of the statutes have been enacted through citizen initiative; for example, the blanket primary was adopted by indirect initiative (a procedure that necessitated the approval of the legislature), whereas others have been passed by the very representatives who sit with party labels in the state legislature.

The three-tier organizational hierarchy codified in law begins at the precinct level. The maximum size of a precinct is mandated, and any registered voter in a precinct can file to be elected a precinct committee officer for a nominal fee (currently one dollar). As there is no partisan registration system in the state, the party organizations can exert no influence on the political preferences of those who file to represent them at the precinct level. Washington State has 5,860 precincts, each with an average of 359 voters; as a result, precinct workers are in short supply, and many of the county committees of both parties expend some effort in trying to recruit precinct workers.

The second tier is that of the county party. Washington State has thirty-nine counties; however, they vary considerably in size. In counties that contain multiple legislative districts, the party may constitute a committee for each district. This provision ensures some redress of the imbalance created by the variance in county size. The county central committees are statutorily composed of all precinct committee members within the county. District committee chairs are appointed by the chairs of county committees. Competencies that are fixed by law include the power to fill vacant slots on the county party ticket and to certify qualified precinct election officials (Mullen and Pierce 1985). The county committees are also endowed with the legal capacity to raise money.

The state central committee is also enshrined in the legal code. Each county committee elects two representatives, one male and one female; thus there are seventy-eight voting members. The state committee selects a chair, who serves for two years. Among the other prescribed duties of the state committee are the filling of vacancies on the party slate for state and federal offices that cross more than one county, the organization of the state convention, the establishment of policies for electing national convention delegates, and the elaboration of regulations governing the selection of presidential electors (Mullen and Pierce 1985).

County and state conventions are held every other year, in even-numbered years. In addition, the Washington State Democrats hold an organizational convention in odd-numbered years, at which the state chair is elected and sworn in. The conventions produce the state party platform and also select national committee members. Both parties, as mentioned above, also have developed state executive committees that are not specifically noted in the laws governing party organizations. In practice, the executive committees have become more powerful at the expense of the state central committees; the latter have seen their nonstatutory role reduced to ratifying the output of the executive committees once per month.

One area of state law actually facilitates the role of party organizations in Washington. There are fewer restrictions on campaign contributions by political parties than in most other states (Nice 1992). In fact, recent legislation has further enhanced the power of state party organizations in the domain of campaign finance. Initiative 134, approved by voter referendum in November 1992, places stringent limitations on the amount that individuals and organizations may contribute to election campaigns; however, political parties escape these provisions. Equally so, there are no restrictions on the contributions that individuals and organizations may make to the state parties themselves. Interviews with party leaders indicate that the parties had an important role in sponsoring this initiative and that they see it as a vital part of the mission of state parties to become the major conduit for money flowing to those running for office.

The lack of partisan voter registration information has also made the state parties important purveyors of voter identification information. The Republican Party has perhaps been more aggressive and more advanced in exploiting the lack of such information to gain influence over candidates. According to the 1994 chair's report, the party had compiled a list of one million voters identified by political persuasion; the information had been culled from a variety of sources, including direct telephone contact. The database was used a reported 270 times by seventy candidates in the 1994 elections, and another twenty-four candidates had direct access to the database on computers in their own campaign headquarters. Candidates' campaigns are required to pay for the service, although at a discounted rate. The goal of the party is eventually to compile partisan preferences and vote histories for all Washington State registered voters.

Both parties now support a paid central staff and permanent headquarters in Seattle. The Democrats employ eight staffers, outside of the state chair; the Republican Party has eleven paid staffers, including three office assistants. In addition, both Democrats and Republicans have paid staff in King County, the largest county in the state. Information technology is an area that many state political parties have begun to invest in; in Washington State the two major parties each maintain a site on the World Wide Web. Some county committees are also on-line: three for the Democrats at the latest count and two for the Republicans.

In the modern era, intraparty division has been somewhat common in Washington State. In the 1960s activists from the John Birch Society mounted a campaign to take control of the Republican Party (Mullen and Pierce 1985), and the travails of the Democrats were recounted above. The split between moderate and conservative Republicans is of long standing; until recent years the moderates generally had retained control over the state party organization. In the early 1990s, however, the conservative faction of the party began to achieve ascendancy and captured many of the important posts in the party organization. The current chair, Ken Eikenberry, a former state attorney general, is identified with the conservative faction. Under his leadership, the state party elaborated a "Contract With Washington" in 1994, emulating the Contract With America. Although the party has been very successful at fund raising in the past few years (having eliminated its budget deficit under Eikenberry's leadership), and although it was very successful in the 1994 election campaign (Washington State experienced the largest swing at the congressional level from Democrats to Republicans), the party remains hampered by internal feuding and ideological divisions.

The Democratic Party has also had to contend with internal disputes in recent years, although not of the same magnitude as those of the late 1970s and early 1980s. The Democratic Party tends to be more socially conservative east of the Cascade Mountains than on the urban west side. The historic defeat of House Speaker Thomas Foley in the midterm elections of 1994, as well as the defeat of many of his fellow Washington State Democrats, had a profound demoralizing effect on the party organization. Finally, the progressive legacy often conflicts with the postmaterialist values of younger Seattle residents, making platform elaboration a sensitive issue for the party.

Thus, in Washington State professional service-vendor parties have developed that have created a niche for raising money and providing candidate services. Like other parties at the state and national levels, they have had to adapt to the changes in their political and legal

**Table 1**  Washington State Resource Guide

|  | Democrats | Republicans |
|---|---|---|
| Archive | Yes | Limited |
| Location | Holland Library Archives | Holland Library Archives |
|  | Washington State University | Washington State University |
|  | Pullman, WA 99164-5610 | Pullman, WA 99164-5610 |
|  | (509) 335-6721 | (509) 335-6721 |
| Dates | 1961–1988 | 1980–1986 |
| Finding aid | Yes | No |
| Access | Public | Public |
| Contents: |  |  |
| Executive committee minutes | Yes | No |
| Correspondence | Yes | Limited |
| Organizational structure | Yes | Limited |
| Budgets | Yes | No |
| Rules | Yes | Limited |

environments. The institutional restraints on the state parties have limited their ability to control their own organizational structures; but those same institutional restraints have paved the way for the parties to exploit their potential to influence campaigns and candidates. To write of "party strength" in the state is to discover a paradox; the parties are by no means organizationally strong by some measures, yet they are indispensable to those running for office.

### RESOURCE GUIDE

The recent records of the Democratic Party of Washington State have been deposited by the state chair in the archives at Washington State University library. The records are extensive; they are contained in thirty-two boxes in thirty-two linear feet of shelf space. There is a finding aid, although some of the files do not necessarily correspond to their labels. The material covers the period 1961–1988, although it is most extensive between 1967 and 1984. Material includes state executive committee minutes, state committee budgets, personnel records, and correspondence. In addition, the Washington State University library archives houses the personal papers of Thomas S. Foley.

The Republican Party also donated some records to the Washington State University library archives; however, these amount to only two containers. There is a limited finding aid. The Republican records contain some minutes and some financial information related to fund raising, although no complete party budgets are available. The party has indicated that the records that were withheld from the archives were placed in storage, although their whereabouts are uncertain.

Various collections of private papers are kept at the University of Washington, and others are located at the state archives. It is believed that neither repository has any records produced by the party organizations themselves in the modern era.

### REFERENCES

*Asterisks denote the most important publications on Washington State party politics.*
Bone, Hugh A. 1961. Washington State: Free style politics. In *Western politics,* ed. Frank H. Jonas, 303–334. Salt Lake City: University of Utah Press.

Cotter, Cornelius, James Gibson, John Bibby, and Robert Huckshorn. 1989. *Party organizations in American politics*. Pittsburgh: University of Pittsburgh Press.

Johannsen, Robert. 1951. National issues and local politics in Washington Territory, 1857–61. *Pacific Northwest Quarterly* 42, no. 1.

Krause, Fayette Florent. 1971. *Democratic Party politics in the state of Washington during the New Deal: 1932–1940*. Ph.D. diss., University of Washington.

Meany, Edmond. 1924. *History of the state of Washington*. New York: Macmillan.

*Mullen, William, and John Pierce. 1985. Political parties. In *The government and politics of Washington State*, ed. William Mullen, et al. Pullman: Washington State University Press.

*Newell, Gorden. 1975. *Rogues, buffoons, and statesmen: The inside story of Washington's capital city and the hilarious history of 120 years of state politics*. Seattle: Superior Press.

*Nice, David. 1992. Political parties in Washington. In *Government and politics in the Evergreen State*, ed. David Nice, John Pierce, and Charles Sheldon. Pullman: Washington State University Press.

*Ogden, Daniel M., and Hugh A. Bone. 1960. *Washington politics*. New York: New York University Press.

Public Disclosure Commission. 1985. *PACs: Their role in campaign finance in Washington State*. Olympia, Wash.: Public Disclosure Commission.

Reed, Sam Sumner. 1968. *An analysis of the factional power struggle in the Republican Party of Washington State from 1962–1967*. Thesis, Washington State University.

# West Virginia

ALLAN HAMMOCK

## PARTY HISTORY

Separated from its southern roots as a result of the Civil War, West Virginia developed a pattern of party politics similar to that of the rest of the nation outside of the South—a two-party system but with long periods of one-party domination. From the time of statehood in 1863 to 1872, West Virginia's politics were controlled by the Unionists/Republicans. Their control was followed by a period of domination by the largely ex-Confederate Democrats, from 1872 to 1896; then, Republicans took control from 1896 to 1932; and finally, the Democrats regained control beginning in 1932. Democratic hegemony has continued since 1932, though occasionally a single Republican or two has won statewide office, thereby justifying Ranney's classification of West Virginia politics as "modified one-party" (Ranney 1971).

The Democratic Party's domination of West Virginia politics is near complete. Since 1932 Republicans have won statewide office (governor, attorney general, secretary of state, auditor, treasurer, commissioner of agriculture, and justice of the supreme court) only seven times. Moreover, three of the seven Republican successes were that of a single person. Arch A. Moore, Jr., a member of the U.S. House from 1957 to 1969, was elected governor three times, largely on the basis of his personality and individual appeal rather than his affiliation with the Republican Party. Democrats have also constituted large majorities in both houses of the state legislature, averaging better than 75 percent of the seats in the one hundred-member House of Delegates and 70 percent of the thirty-four-member Senate.

Perhaps as much as, if not more than, any other state, West Virginia continues a pattern of party politics growing out of the hard times of the depression and the New Deal. The state economy for years depended on extractive industries and heavy manufacturing (coal, chemicals, timber, steel) and experienced periodic economic booms and busts. As a result, West Virginians adopted political attitudes framed by relatively strong class divisions. Essentially, the Democratic Party in the New Deal became the party of the working class, unions, intellectuals, southern "Bourbons," and patronage-seeking opportunists. Republicans were "captains of industry," the wealthy, and traditional Civil War–era Unionists (Williams 1976).

Oddly, West Virginia's strong New Deal heritage in party politics was slow to develop. The state's first two Democratic governors after the inauguration of the New Deal, Herman G. Kump (1933–1937) and Homer Holt (1937–1941), were not classic New Deal "liberals." Rather, they were known principally for their fiscal conservatism and antiunion biases (Morgan 1981, 146, 156). During their tenures, however, each took advantage of a pervasive political patronage system to foster a strong Democratic political machine. By the 1940s a full-blown statehouse Democratic machine was in place, led by a former U.S. senator and governor, Matthew Neely (1941–1945), and his chief lieutenant, Homer Hanna, clerk of the federal court in Charleston (Lanham 1971, ch. 7). Neely, an enormously popular and unabashed liberal, took over the machine and nurtured it by handing out highly prized federal and state patronage jobs. The Neely-Hanna dominated "statehouse machine," though not on the order of other classic political machines—Daley in Chicago or Gump in Tennessee—was nonetheless a formidable political apparatus, controlling tickets, dispensing patronage, and effectively serving as government gatekeeper and agenda setter.

West Virginia's Democratic machine clearly has been a power with which to be reckoned. Yet, its power has not been nearly as complete or effective as its admirers and critics claim. For example, although the political career of the machine's early leader, Neely, spanned a half-century, he still had a mixed record in winning elective office. He lost two of his seven bids for the U.S. Senate and two of his seven bids for the U.S. House of Representatives. He was successful in his only race for governor, in 1940. Neely's defeats are hardly the record of a politician backed by a political organization thought to be invincible. Arch Moore was able to break the hold of the machine in 1968 and then go on to an unprecedented three terms as governor, eventually becoming one of the most popular governors in West Virginia history.

Moore's victories demonstrated the weakness of the statehouse machine. The machine, in reality, was little more than a series of county fiefdoms, with only modest, if any, control at the top. Some degree of statehouse control and influence resulted from centralized control over federal and state patronage jobs. However, each county had its own political "kingpin" who determined whom would be "slated" on the ticket and who dispensed hundreds of jobs to loyal supporters in liquor stores, sheriffs departments, county clerks and assessors offices, county and regional highway departments, and school boards. These county organizations were successfully tapped by John F. Kennedy in his bid for the presidency in 1960. Kennedy's West Virginia primary campaign organization had the cash necessary to get local political leaders to "slate" Kennedy supporters on local primary ballots (Ernst 1962; Flemming 1992). With an organization in place and the money flowing, Kennedy simply overwhelmed his opponent, Hubert Humphrey.

Republicans have lacked the strong institutional base Democrats have enjoyed since 1932. Instead of having well-organized state and county machines, the Republicans have depended on episodic and almost fortuitous events and candidacies to build their party fortunes. The most prominent of these candidate-centered Republican campaigns, and clearly one of the most successful, was that of Moore, who was first elected in 1968, then reelected in 1972, when he upset wealthy Democrat John D. Rockefeller, IV, by far the most dominant politician in West Virginia in the modern age. Moore's political astuteness and undeniable skills, both as a campaigner and as manager of state government, allowed him to co-opt the Democratic machine by taking cash directly to local political kingpins and obtaining their endorsement. Thus, local Democratic politicians, while still maintaining firm control over most other statewide and county offices, came to an "understanding" with Moore in his several elections to the governorship. Though this system worked for Moore personally, it did little for the long-term enhancement of the Republican Party. Moore was ultimately defeated in his bid for a fourth term as governor in 1988. In 1990 he was indicted and found guilty of various federal corruption charges and campaign violations. With Moore's demise, the Republican Party was decapitated and left again to struggle organizationally and electorally.

Given the relative weakness of West Virginia's Republican Party, the "real" election in the state often has been the Democratic primary. Competition by factions within the Democratic Party has often substituted for competition between parties. John Fenton (1957) identified three main factions within the West Virginia Democratic Party in his superb analysis of West Virginia politics in the 1950s. The first was the predominately liberal organized-labor faction, headed by the powerful United Mine Workers of America (UMWA) and geographically located principally in the southern coal-field counties. The second was the traditional Bourbon, or conservative, faction of Kump-Holt origins, located primarily in the more rural areas of the state, but including counties along the Allegheny Highlands and in the Eastern Panhandle. The third faction was the statehouse faction, a group grounded largely on political patronage in the local county courthouses and the statehouse and controlled initially by the Bourbons in the 1930s but taken over by the Neely-Hanna faction in the 1940s.

Though each faction has had its ups and downs, nothing fundamentally has changed in these factional groupings since the time of Fenton's analysis. The liberal organized-labor faction of the party commands about one-third of the vote, as does the conservative Bourbon group. The statehouse faction, the less ideological of the three, thus ends up being a swing group in elections. Successful primary candidates are those who tend to be centrist and who manage to get some or all of the statehouse group on their side. Usually statehouse support is determined by money.

There have been cleavages of a different nature within the Republican Party. In the past, a very personal and sometimes bitter rift existed between the state's leading Republican, Arch Moore, and a former one-term Republican governor, Cecil Underwood (1957–1961). Moore and Underwood squared off against each other on a number of occasions, including in the 1968 Republican primary won by Moore. Although it has never been directly ascertained why the two could not get along—perhaps it was due to Underwood's suggestions of a number of financial improprieties by Moore, or perhaps it was because Moore, almost ego-maniacal in his political and government life, could not broach opposition from anyone—they continued to feud long after leaving office. In Moore's last years in office a rift developed in the party between Moore and anti-Moore factions (the latter led by Morgantown business executive John Raese). The Moore supporters were forced into a lukewarm and sometimes embarrassing defense of their leader, who ultimately was sent to prison by federal prosecutors for conspiracy and obstruction of justice. The rift evolved into a mild, mostly irrelevant cleavage. A new, potentially party-splitting conflict arose in the mid-1990s between the Christian right and mainline Republicans. The Christian right faction has achieved some modest success in recruiting candidates for office and in assuming leadership positions in the party. Its separately organized Republican Legislative Committee is headed by a former Reagan administration official who worked hard and somewhat successfully in 1994 to elect Republican candidates supportive of Christian right positions. The newly emerging Christian right faction has challenged the Republican establishment on a number of issues, including where the party's state headquarters should be located—in Charleston or Wheeling.

## ORGANIZATIONAL DEVELOPMENT

With the ascendancy of the Democrats nationally in 1932, the Democratic Party in West Virginia established itself as the dominant party, relegating the Republican Party to the minority status it suffers to this day. The parties as organizations developed somewhat different modes of operation: the Democratic Party became the party of strong, well-established institutional processes, with considerable financial resources. The Republican Party became a party of episodic fortunes, personalized leadership, and uncertain financial resources.

Capitalizing on the economic recovery programs of the New Deal, the Democratic Party built its organization with political patronage. Thousands of people became permanently allied with the Democratic Party because of the jobs the party controlled—jobs in federal recovery agencies (such as the Civilian Conservation Corps, Works Progress Administration, and the Public Works Administration), in state and county government offices, in the state highway department, in liquor stores, and in local and state agencies charged with school construction and other public works projects. With such economic leverage, the Democratic Party was able to command the loyalty of its adherents year after year, thus assuring itself a permanent, institutionalized position of power.

In this "old style" party atmosphere, the Democratic Party not only controlled patronage but also state contracts. Hardly anyone was awarded a state contract unless they contributed to the Democratic Party. Many of the contracts were perfectly legal and above board; some, however, were clearly illegal in that they involved bribes or kickbacks to high government officials. In 1968 Democratic governor William Wallace "Wally" Barron was convicted of bribery and conspiracy in relation to state contracts (Morgan 1981, ch. 26).

The financial foundation of the Democratic Party apparatus from the 1940s through the 1960s was the so-called flower fund, wherein each state and county employee holding a patronage job had to contribute 2 percent of his or her paycheck to the party (Lanham 1971, 141). Although flowers and other forms of condolences were, in fact, sent to the sick and bereaved, the party used the bulk of the funds to maintain the party machine and to elect candidates to office. The flower fund eventually fell to party reformers in the late 1960s, but even today every appointed or elected officeholder or candidate for office is expected to make a "voluntary" contribution to the state and county party.

The Democratic Party and its various factions, particularly at the local level, also were the frequent recipients of contributions from coal companies or their executives, who sought to maintain influence over local sheriffs, county assessors, and state officials responsible for regulation or taxation of the coal industry (Chafin and Sherwood 1994, 89–91,

146). These contributions, too, helped to guarantee a continuous source of money for the Democratic Party and individual candidates.

The Democratic machine, well-funded and institutionalized in viable county committees and a state committee, with strong, highly visible chairs, maintained itself electorally by satisfying the three main factions within the party. One faction, organized labor, was brought into the party in the 1940s. The earliest labor faction was led by the United Mine Workers of America. Later, leadership of the labor movement passed to the AFL-CIO, whose current president, Joe Powell, is considered one of the most influential leaders in the party. The conservative, southern Bourbon faction, too, must be assured a place at the party table and an occasional office or two at the state level. Finally, the statehouse faction must be satisfied. This faction consists of the various county clerks, judges, commissioners, assessors, sheriffs, magistrates, road supervisors, liquor store managers (before the state went to private liquor stores in 1990), school board members, state agency heads, and various other largely state political appointees beholden to the party or to key leaders. The successful candidate for governor in the Democratic primary needs both the support of one of the ideological factions and the support of most of the statehouse group.

The Republican Party often has lacked the institutionalized base of the Democrats: they have had no long-term patronage, except in a few small counties; they have had very few statewide officeholders, no flower fund to tap, and no state contracts to award. As a result, the Republican Party, with the sole major exception of the Moore years (1969–1977, 1985–1989), has struggled both locally and statewide to raise money for the party and to maintain its state party organization.

The fortunes of the Republican Party improved greatly with the election of Moore, a as governor in 1968. Moore's initial election was due to a combination of factors—corruption in the Democratic Party, a divided Democratic Party, the personality and campaign style of Moore himself, and just plain luck. For example, just two days before the election in 1968, Moore emerged, slightly injured but unflappable, from a helicopter crash, and evoked a huge sympathy vote (Morgan 1981). During Moore's first two terms (1969–1977), the Republican state committee had little difficulty raising money, both for the party and for Moore's reelection. When Moore ran for and won a third term in 1984, the party again raised large sums of money and in much the same institutionalized way as the Democrats—calling in the recipients of patronage and state contracts, coal company contributors, and the like. Almost all the money, however, was focused on the reelection of Moore, the candidate, not on electing other Republicans or solidifying the organization of the Republican Party. As a consequence, Moore's defeat for an unprecedented fourth term in 1988 left the Republican state committee broke. The state committee laid off its executive secretary and closed the state office for a time in the late 1980s and early 1990s.

The machine-like quality of the Democratic Party in the 1940s through the 1960s might make it appear as though the Democratic Executive Committee was a highly structured, organizationally viable vehicle of the party delivering services and votes for the party. In reality, it was little more than a paper organization, with no large sums of money under its direct control and no permanent staff or headquarters. For the most part, the committee chair was a figurehead selected by and loyal to the incumbent governor. Most incoming party money went directly to individual candidates or was controlled by the governor or someone close to the governor who could be considered a patronage and state party kingpin (such as Homer Hanna under Governor Neely, or Curtiss Trent under Governor Barron). In the 1960s through the 1980s, the state committee met occasionally, but only to ratify decisions made earlier by the governor and conveyed to the party through the state chair. Questions of great substance rarely came before the committee. The committee usually decided matters related to who would represent the state on the national committee and how state and national conventions would be organized. The state chair interacted to some degree with county chairs, but there was no coordination of county committees by the state committee and no transfer of funds from the state committee to local committees. Moreover, lacking a permanent staff or a state headquarters in the period 1940–1960, the state committee became an important player only after 1964, when governors were given the opportunity to succeed themselves and the party geared up to raise funds in election years. The one consistent exception to the party's sporadic activity was the annual Jefferson-Jackson Day fund-raising dinner, sponsored by the state committee but planned largely by the party chair (assisted by a permanent staff in the 1960s and thereafter).

The state Democratic committee prior to the 1990s had very little interaction with the national party. The state party received no financial support from the national party and little in the way of organizational support, save the occasional assistance in locating a suitably prominent national Democrat for speaker at the Jefferson-Jackson Day dinner. Even the contracting of campaign consultants was left to individual candidates rather than the state committee.

The operational mode of the Republican state committee between 1940 and 1968 varied depending on whether or not the party occupied the governorship. When the party did not occupy the governorship, the organization was clearly operated hand-to-mouth—with no staff, no headquarters, and no funding to speak of—and did not even hold an annual statewide fund-raising event (such as a Lincoln Day dinner). The Republican state committee did little more than select the national committeeman and committeewoman—both typically old-line Republicans who were elected year after year as a reward for their loyalty to the party.

The Republican state committee during the Moore years, however, was quite different. The committee served as a clearinghouse for patronage, though hiring decisions ultimately were made by the governor. The committee also had a permanent staff and a state headquarters in Charleston. The state committee, in conjunction with the governor, also served as a major fund-raising organization, particularly in election years, and some of the money raised was funneled into county party organizations or to individual candidates. The state office also developed an extensive direct-mail operation, the first of its kind in West Virginia, and direct mail generated a good bit of money for the party. Indeed, as one person close to the party in the Moore years stated, "These were the good times."

Aside from achieving financial solvency, the Republican state committee during the Moore years hired persons to analyze the vote county-by-county (and in some instances, precinct-by-precinct) in order to better estimate future electoral success. The state party also published a newsletter and sponsored "big-name" speakers; both activities, however were only sporadic. Almost all of the activities of the state committee, either during the Moore administration or when the party was out of power, were a function of the chair of the committee, not the committee as a whole. In fact, the committee itself was little more than a ceremonial group, which convened once or twice a year.

An analysis of the rotation and turnover in party chairs reveals some differences between the Democratic and Republican Party committees. The Democrats have had eleven chairs since 1960, whereas the Republicans have had thirteen. The average tenure for the Democratic chairs has been 3.6 years, compared to 2.5 years for the Republicans.

Significantly, although most state chairs have been residents of Charleston (for obvious reasons; it is the capital and the major news center of the state), important regional differences have existed between the parties. Every Democratic chair since 1960, save one, has been from the southern part of the state; six of the thirteen Republican chairs have been from the north. The regional biases of the parties are reflective of antebellum political forces. The Republican Party has always been stronger in a set of counties stretching from the Ohio River (Parkersburg) in the west, across the state's northern border, to the Allegheny Highlands along the Virginia border in the east. The bastion of Democratic power in the state, however, has been the southern counties, or generally, the area local politicians refer to as "south of Route 60," which runs from Huntington in the west through Charleston and along the Kanawaha River to Beckley, terminating in the east at Lewisburg and White Sulphur Springs. This region is composed of eleven of the most heavily Democratic counties in the state, often delivering upward of 70 percent of its votes for the slated Democratic candidates. It is also that portion of the state noted for its political corruption and is the region that Theodore White had in mind when he described West Virginia as having the most "squalid," "corrupt," and "despicable" politics in the nation (White 1961).

Both parties have been affected greatly by changes in state law and by political practices. Passage of the Gubernatorial Succession Amendment in 1964, which allowed the governor to succeed himself, clearly helped the Republicans, since Arch Moore was the first governor to take advantage of the law. But it was no less a boost to the Democrats, who profited by the reinforcement of their tradition of handing out jobs to the party faithful. Passage of the Modern Budget Amendment in 1969, which empowered the governor to submit an executive budget, reinforced the governor's position as the central political figure in the state.

General campaign reforms have also affected the parties, forcing them to focus their efforts on new campaign techniques. One such reform was the 300-foot limit on campaigning at the polls adopted in 1985 (WV Code 3-9-6). The limit virtually eliminated the practice of hiring hundreds of workers to stand at the polls on election day to hand out candidate and party literature. Many campaign workers are still hired, but they do other things (telephoning, driving people to the polls, putting up signs). Campaign workers, however, are now limited to $50 per day per worker, and candidates can only hire a number of workers equal to the number of precincts in a county.

## CURRENT PARTY ORGANIZATION

The single most important actor in the party system in West Virginia is, of course, the governor (or governor-elect). Only in the rarest of circumstances would a state chair not be of the governor's own choosing. When the party is out of power, the party chair is typically an aspiring candidate for high office (such as David McKinley, Republican chair 1992–1995) or someone who has taken the job out of a sense of obligation to the party (such as J. C. Dillon, Democratic chair 1973–1982).

The current (1995) chairs—George Carenbauer in the Democrat Party and Steve LaRose in the Republican—reflect the typical pattern. Carenbauer and his immediate predecessor, Charles Smith, were selected by the sitting governor, Gaston Caperton (1989–1997); LaRose was selected by the Republican committee in part as a "reward" for his long service to the Republican Party and in part because he was acceptable to the various factions of the party.

After the governor, the party chair is the most important actor in the committee, though not necessarily in party politics in general. Both party chairs operate without constraint by the party committee membership. The role of the party chair is paramount. When the party is in power, the party chair or executive director maintains almost daily contact with the governor or a designated staff person of the governor. The current Democratic chair, for example, coordinates the Jefferson-Jackson Day dinner, the state and national conventions, the publication of a periodic newsletter, and candidate and party workshops. He also maintains contact with the Democratic National Committee (at the moment, the party headquarters averages ten facsimiles and three telephone calls to or from the DNC daily), and is in regular contact with the congressional delegation (U.S. Senators Robert C. Byrd and John D. Rockefeller, IV, and Representatives Alan Mollohan, Nick J. Rahall, and Robert Wise). A great deal of the planning, workshop activity, and campaign activity is coordinated with the Democratic Party's principal political allies, the West Virginia Education Association (WVEA), the United Mine Workers of America, and the AFL-CIO.

The fund-raising activities and events of the Democratic committee now consist of a telemarketing operation conducted by the DNC (opted into by the state executive committee), the Jefferson-Jackson Day dinner, a series of cocktail receptions throughout the year, and the solicitation of individual contributions from wealthy contributors, including Senator Rockefeller and Governor Caperton, both of whom are independently wealthy and who in the past have spent millions of their own money in their campaigns. There are also some three thousand state employees who are not in the classified system (see West Virginia Code 29-6-4) and who, though prohibited by law from being solicited for campaign contributions (West Virginia Code 3-8-12), make contributions out of a sense of loyalty or obligation to the party or a particular elected official.

The situation of the Republican committee currently is quite different. Out of power since 1989, the party has had difficulty raising operational funds over the last six or seven years (as of 1995 it was about $125,000 in debt). The party also has been split (the former Moore faction versus the Raese faction) over who should be chair, and some party members have challenged actions taken by former chairs. For example, the party in 1990 moved its headquarters from Charleston to Wheeling, to the home business office of then-chair David McKinley. The move caused such a controversy that a special meeting of the state committee was called in 1993 to address the issue, and the headquarters was moved back to Charleston. Likewise, another former chair, Edgar F. Heiskell, was criticized for spending the committee's money almost exclusively on behalf of Governor Moore's reelection effort in 1988. In response, the bylaws of the state committee were changed in 1989 to circumscribe the chair's ability to spend money (a three-member Financial Resources Allocation Committee must now approve expenditures). The Republicans also have a steering committee to advise the chair. On the other hand, the Republican chair still appoints all committees (including the steering committee), employs the executive secretary, controls the state headquarters, and appoints other officers (vice chairs, secretary, treasurer, and general counsel). The Democratic chair has similar powers and responsibilities.

One interesting Republican bylaw adopted in 1987 that is not shared by the Democrats prohibits any member of the Republican committee from donating to or endorsing a candidate of the other party. This provision was aimed particularly at Edgar Heiskell, who was criticized by the Raese faction for contributing to the "Friends of Jay Rockefeller" committee.

Interviews with numerous state party officials (including four Democratic chairs; four Republican chairs; three executive directors; and several Republican and Democratic state committee members) indicate that one of the most important roles of the party chair today is that of "spokesperson" of the party. Party chairs are constantly appearing in the media,

**Table 1**  West Virginia Resource Guide

|  | Democrats | Republicans |
|---|---|---|
| Archive | Yes | Yes |
| Location | West Virginia Democratic Party | West Virginia Republican Party |
|  | 405 Capitol Street, Suite 501 | P.O. Box A |
|  | Charleston, WV 25301 | Charleston, WV 25362 |
| Dates | 1960–present | 1960–present |
| Finding aid | No | No |
| Access | By appointment | By appointment |
| Contents: |  |  |
| Executive committee minutes | Yes | Yes |
| Correspondence | Yes | No |
| Organizational structure | Yes | No |
| Budgets | Yes | No |
| Rules | Yes | Yes |

issuing press releases, and communicating in various ways with the public. This visibility is in marked contrast to the past, when the communication function was much less apparent. In the Republican Party, the role of party spokesperson has often fallen to a member of the legislature, since many Republican chairs have been members of the state house or senate. In the case of the Democrats, the spokesperson's role has become so important that the state committee has created two new staff positions—research director and communications director. The former deals with research on policy issues (much of which is used to produce political ads); the latter is responsible for getting the party message out to the public through talk radio, facsimiles, and on-line computer. There is no equivalent staff operation projected in the Republican Party.

RESOURCE GUIDE

The two parties make little effort to maintain archives. The records of the Democratic Party (four standard filing cabinets) are located at the party headquarters. In the same building are several boxes of files in storage. The Republican Party has two filing cabinets in its party headquarters. Neither the Republican nor the Democratic material is readily accessible to the public, but researchers can get permission on an individual basis to peruse the files. The Democratic files contain minutes of executive committee meetings, Federal Election Commission (FEC) and state financial reports, records of the state and national conventions, the party platforms, bylaws, general correspondence, and miscellaneous materials, dating back several decades. There are also computer files of party leaders, activists, and donors (mailing lists), but they are not generally available to the public or researchers.

The Republican Party has much less material, though it does have bylaws, minutes, and platforms dating back to the 1960s. Its computer database of donors and party supporters contains some eight thousand names. The party files contain FEC reports but no state financial reports.

One of the best sources of party history in West Virginia through the presidential election of 1960 is the oral history project of the John F. Kennedy Library in Boston. The archival collection contains forty-eight tapes and transcriptions of all major and many minor figures in Kennedy's primary campaign in West Virginia. This oral history is reported on extensively in Young (1982).

The West Virginia State Archives in Charleston has available the papers of the state's governors from 1863 to 1933 and selected papers of governors from 1933 to 1988. The papers of Gov. Hulett Smith, who was state Democratic chair from 1958 to 1962, contain information on party activities. The West Virginia Collection of the West Virginia University Library in Morgantown contains the most extensive holdings of archival data in the state. It holds some, if not all, of the papers of twenty-three of the state's thirty U.S. senators, twenty-four former members of the U.S. House, and twenty-two of the state's thirty governors. The West Virginia Collection also holds the papers of former Republican chairs Walter Hallanan (archival years 1919–1961) and John D. Hoblitzell (archival years 1956–1962), and those of Democratic chair Robert G. Kelly (archival years 1929–1941) and Ernest G. Otey, state executive committee treasurer (archival years 1935–1965).

The *West Virginia Bluebook,* published annually from 1928 to 1987 and biannually from 1989 to the present, lists the chairs, members of the executive committees, other officers (legal counsel, treasurer, vice chair, and secretary), executive secretary (if one is appointed), national committee members, the biographies of chairs and national committee members, the county chairs and county committee members, the officers of the federations of Democratic Women and Republican Women, and officers of the Young Democrats and Young Republicans. It also contains complete election returns (primary and general election), and voter registration and turnout records by county from 1928 to the present.

## REFERENCES

*Asterisks denote the most important publications on West Virginia party politics.*
*Brisbin, Richard, Robert Dilger, Allan Hammock, and Christopher Mooney. 1996. *West Virginia government and politics.* Lincoln: University of Nebraska Press.
Chafin, Truman, and Topper Sherwood. 1994. *Just good politics: The life of Raymond Chafin, Appalachian boss.* Pittsburgh, Pa.: University of Pittsburgh Press.
Ernest, Harry W. 1962. *The primary that made a president: West Virginia 1960.* New Brunswick, N.J.: Eagleton Institution of Politics, Rutgers University.
*Fenton, John H. 1957. *Politics in the border states.* New Orleans: Hawser Press.
*Fleming, Dan B., Jr. 1992. *Kennedy vs. Humphrey, West Virginia, 1960: The pivotal battle for the Democratic presidential nomination.* Jefferson, N.C.: McFarland.
*Johnson, Gerald W. 1970. *Politics, party competition and the county chairman in West Virginia.* Knoxville: Bureau of Public Administration, University of Tennessee.
*Lanham, Robert Eugene. 1971. *The West Virginia statehouse Democratic machine: Structure, function, and process.* Ph.D. diss., Claremont, (Calif.) Graduate School.
*Morgan, John C. 1981. *West Virginia governors 1863–1980.* 2d ed. Charleston, W. Va.: Charleston Newspapers.
Ranney, Austin. 1971. Parties in state politics. In *Politics in the American states,* ed. Herbert Jacob and Kenneth Vines. 2d ed. Boston: Little Brown.
*Ross, William R. 1956. *The West Virginia political almanac.* Morgantown: West Virginia University.
*———. 1971. *The electoral process in West Virginia.* Morgantown: Bureau for Government Research, West Virginia University.
*Clerk of the House of Delegates. 1996. *West Virginia bluebook, 1928–1996.* Charleston, W.Va.: Clerk of the House of Delegates.
White, Theodore. 1961. *The making of the president 1960.* New York: Atheneum Publishers.
Williams, John A. 1976. *West Virginia and the captains of industry.* Morgantown: West Virginia University Library.
Young, William L. 1982. The John F. Kennedy Library Oral History Project, The West Virginia Democratic presidential primary 1960. Ph.D. diss., Ohio State University.

# *Wisconsin*

DAVID G. WEGGE

## PARTY HISTORY

Wisconsin political party organizations have been deeply affected by a high degree of inter- and intraparty competition, legal antiparty bias, and the strong issue orientation and independence of Wisconsin citizens.

Wisconsin became a state in 1848. For the first few years after achieving statehood, until 1855, the Democratic Party was dominant, and the primary opposition came from the Whig Party (Donoghue 1974). For the next century, however, Republicans dominated. The Republican Party of Wisconsin was founded on March 20, 1854, in a small schoolhouse in Ripon when real estate developer Alvan Bovay organized a meeting to protest the Kansas-Nebraska Act, which had been passed by Congress. The meeting consisted of activists from the Whig and Free Soil Parties, which that night disbanded and became the Republican Party. The meeting is also recognized as one of the defining events in the birth of the national Republican Party (Haney 1976, 1).

The central figure in the Wisconsin Republican Party in the early twentieth century was Robert M. La Follette. La Follette was elected governor in 1900 and senator in 1905. He served in the Senate until his death in 1925. During this period the most significant political battles were fought within the Republican Party, between La Follette's more liberal "progressives" and the conservative "stalwarts." It was a time of one-party bifactionalism in Wisconsin.

La Follette broke with the Republican Party in 1924 when he ran for president as a Progressive. His defection from the party broke the hold of the progressive faction over the Wisconsin Republican Party and led to the development of the Republican Voluntary Committee (RVC), made up primarily of stalwart Republicans. William Campbell was the organizer of the RVC and has since been viewed as the father of the Republican Party organization in Wisconsin (Haney 1976, 3). The RVC was successful in electing Walter Kohler governor in 1928.

From the depression of the 1930s until the end of World War II Wisconsin experienced multiparty politics, with control of state offices shifting among Republicans, Progressives, and Democrats. From 1934 to 1938 Wisconsin was dominated by the Wisconsin Progressive Party, founded in 1934 by Robert M. La Follette's sons, Robert Jr., who in 1925 had been elected to his father's seat in the U.S. Senate, and Phillip, who was elected governor in 1934 and reelected in 1936. During this five-year period the Progressive Party also controlled majorities in the state legislature. By 1946, however, the presence of the Progressive Party in the state legislature and governorship had been all but eliminated.

The strength of the Progressive Party during the late 1930s made it nearly impossible for the Wisconsin Democratic Party to build a strong base of support. The demise of the Progressive Party in the early 1940s opened the door for a rebirth of the Democratic Party. The party's rejuvenation began when several liberal political groups met in Fond du Lac in May 1948 and formed the Democratic Organizing Committee (DOC).

The DOC was spearheaded by a group of young liberals including James Doyle, Carl Thompson, Horace Wilkie, Gaylord Nelson, John Reynolds, Henry Reuss, and Patrick Lucey. The DOC was the counterpart to the RVC. Both organizations were to be the "voluntary" organizations of the parties and hence could circumvent statutory limitations placed on the legal party organizations in Wisconsin. The voluntary committees could accept members and campaign contributions, something that the statutory parties were not allowed to do (Haney 1989, 5).

A constitutional convention to organize formally the Democrats was held in November 1949 in Green Bay. Approximately seven hundred delegates from more than fifty counties were present at the convention, which adopted the first constitution of the modern Democratic Party and elected officers, including Jerome Fox as the first chair of the DOC.

In the early 1950s the Republicans continued to dominate state elections. The election of Joseph McCarthy in 1946 and his tumultuous Senate career served as a strong organizing impetus for the Democrats. When McCarthy died in 1957 his seat was won in a special election by a Democrat, William Proxmire. Proxmire had paid his dues to the party by being the Democratic candidate for governor and being defeated in 1952, 1954, and 1956. The election of Proxmire to the Senate marked the beginning of the rise of the Democratic Party in Wisconsin. Democrats controlled the governorship from 1958 to 1964, again from 1970 to 1978, and from 1982 to 1986. Democrats also won control of the state senate in 1974 and continued to control a majority until 1993. Democrats gained a majority of the state assembly in 1970 and held their majority until 1994.

With the election of Tommy Thompson as governor in 1986, the Republican Party began to reemerge as the dominant party. Thompson, a state legislator from Elroy, won a surprising victory over incumbent Democratic governor Tony Earl in 1986. The shift in dominance from the Democratic Party to the Republican Party between 1980 and 1995 is also reflected in survey data of party identification. In the fall of 1980, 42 percent of citizens identified as Democrats, 26 percent as Republicans, and 31 percent as independents. By the spring of 1995 the numbers had changed significantly, with 30 percent saying they were Democrats, 37 percent identifying as Republicans, and 24 percent as independents (St. Norbert College Survey Center 1995). Today the state is a modified one-party Republican state.

## ORGANIZATIONAL DEVELOPMENT

In addition to the varying degree of interparty competition, the strength of the Progressive movement, and the existence of the statutory party, several other factors have significantly influenced the development of party organizations in Wisconsin. Among them are the strong issue orientation and independence of Wisconsin citizens, the open primary, the lack of partisan voter registration, the nonpartisan nature of local elections, campaign finance laws, and national politics. The current organizational arrangement in both parties reflects the pressures of a variety of elements within the broader environment of the Democratic and Republican Parties.

Wisconsin citizens have always been very independent and issue oriented. Hence, it should come as no surprise that political party organizations in Wisconsin tend to be decentralized and issue oriented. The birth of the Wisconsin Republican Party in a small schoolhouse in Ripon and the birth of the RVC both came of issue-based concerns. The intraparty conflict between the progressives and the stalwarts, although it had elements of personality politics, was fundamentally a philosophical conflict (Sorauf 1954). Internal issue-oriented conflict has always ebbed and flowed in the Republican Party; currently, an intraparty battle is emerging between more pragmatic, moderate Republicans and conservatives represented by the Wisconsin Right to Life group and the Christian Coalition.

Likewise, the modern Democratic Party was founded on a very strong issue base. The issue orientation of the Democratic Party has continued through more recent times and has on several occasions been a rallying point as well as a source of significant division within the party. The Democratic Party coalesced in its efforts to defeat Senator McCarthy in the 1950s and in its efforts to bring into the Democratic activist ranks several civil rights leaders from the Milwaukee area in the 1960s. However, the strong issue orientation of Wisconsin party members also caused a significant split in the Democratic Party organization during the Vietnam era. In 1968 Sen. Eugene McCarthy won the Wisconsin primary and garnered forty-nine of the state's fifty-nine delegates to the Democratic National Convention. However, in the district caucuses, party regulars who were more sympathetic to Hubert Humphrey selected pro-Humphrey individuals to serve as McCarthy delegates. McCarthy used his veto power over delegates on the list to eliminate the Humphrey supporters and to replace them with his loyal supporters (Haney 1989).

In the late 1940s through the 1950s the Democratic Party focused on party building at the grassroots level. A great deal of attention was paid to recruiting and training not only party leaders but, more important, viable candidates. Patrick Lucey, during his tenure as state Democratic Party chair (1957–1963), was very insistent that the party run a full slate of candidates for county courthouse races. It was his view that leaving one office unchallenged would cost the party at least one hundred votes for other state and congressional races. The DOC put considerable effort into recruiting and training candidates. One special effort was to host one-day training sessions for potential candidates in local and state elections. About 75 percent of each day-long session was spent educating the candidates on state issues. The remaining 25 percent of the training focused on campaign methods and tactics. In recent years, candidate schools have tended to focus more on the campaign tactics and less on the issues.

The legal structure of the political system—including the open primary, lack of partisan registration, and nonpartisan local elections—is not particularly supportive of political party organizations. In fact, Epstein (1958, 30) argues that in Wisconsin there has been "a strong legal bias against any organized political apparatus." The antiparty attitude grew out of the Progressive era of the early 1900s.

The political parties in Wisconsin have dealt with the open primary in very different ways. The Republicans until 1979 were required by their constitution to endorse a candidate for every statewide constitutional office prior to the September primary. The Democratic Party constitution, on the other hand, forbade the party from endorsing candidates. The Republican constitutional requirement grew out of the stalwarts' desire to influence the nomination process at a time when the progressives were exercising considerable political clout (Bibby 1991). The endorsement procedure, however, had caused some problems and embarrassment for the party organization in more recent times. In 1978, for example, the party endorsed U.S. Representative Robert Kasten over Lee Sherman Dreyfus in the gubernatorial race. In the primary election, Dreyfus defeated Kasten by a comfortable margin. At the 1979 state convention the Republicans amended their constitution to make endorsement optional rather than required. Since 1979, however, the party has not made any preprimary endorsements.

The open primary has also been a source of conflict for the Democrats, but in a different way. The conflict was hierarchical and pitted the state Democratic Party against the national Democratic Party. When the national party changed its presidential delegate selection process for the 1972 convention to require delegate selection either by a closed primary or through a caucus system, the Wisconsin Democratic Party found itself in a bind: state law required an open primary. The conflict continued in 1980 and 1984 before the national party decided to retreat.

The lack of partisan registration has made it very difficult and costly for political parties in Wisconsin to identify their supporters. In states where partisan registration exists, it is a simple task for the parties to purchase the voter registration lists. However, in Wisconsin the parties spend considerable resources attempting to identify their supporters. This has had a significant influence on the staff structure of the Republican Party in that the party now has two staff members who manage a twelve-station computerized telemarketing center. The center is staffed, on an irregular basis, with 35–40 telemarketers. The telemarketing center was founded to broaden the contributor base, to reduce fund-raising overhead, and to increase the revenue from small donations. But it has become an important information-gathering center to assist with all aspects of party building. The center is also shifting the contributing patterns to the Republican Party in that a smaller share of party revenue is coming from large donations ($100 or more).

The Democratic Party has also engaged in a substantial amount of telemarketing to identify its supporters. However, the Democrats do not maintain in-house telemarketing capacity; rather, they contract out for the service. In terms of fund raising, the Democratic Party has directly solicited contributions from large donors, used direct mail, conducted telemarketing to solicit from small donors, and held the annual Jefferson-Jackson Day dinner. In recent years, there has been an increased reliance on telemarketing for fund raising.

Wisconsin has some of the most well developed campaign finance laws among the states, including one of the few public financing systems. The laws have placed some important restrictions on the political party organizations in terms of limiting contributions. One avenue that both interest groups and political parties have used to get around some of the limits is the use of conduits. The Republican Party organization created its own conduit, Majority GOP, in 1992 and has been funneling individual contributions to party members through Majority GOP since that time. The Democratic Party has resisted developing its own conduit largely because of the philosophical opposition to conduits by party leaders.

## CURRENT PARTY ORGANIZATION

In Wisconsin, as in other states, state laws dictate the selection of party members and the organizational structure of a statutory party from the local level through the congressional district level. However, both parties have created their own "voluntary" party structures to carry on most party activities. This section focuses on the structure of the voluntary party organizations.

*Republican Party.* The Republican Party is made up of individuals who are eligible to vote in national and state elections and who are members of the Republican county organization in their county of residence. With the exception of Milwaukee County, the county organization is the basic local unit of the party organization. Milwaukee County is divided into several smaller geographical units called clubs (such as the South Shore Club, West Side Club, North Shore Club). Each county organization has the following officers: a county chair, a vice chair, a secretary, and a treasurer. All officers are elected at the county caucus prior to April 1 in odd-numbered years.

The congressional district organization holds a caucus prior to the state convention. In addition to selecting delegates to the state convention, the caucus also elects two representatives from the congressional district to each state convention committee. In odd-numbered years, the delegates from each congressional district to the state convention meet prior to the state convention to elect the congressional district committee officers, including a chair, vice chair, secretary, and treasurer, and other officers that may be provided for in the district constitution.

At the state level of the organization are the state officers, the executive committee, and the state convention. The state officers consist of a chair, five vice chairs, a secretary, a treasurer, a national committeeman, a national committeewoman, and a state finance chair. Three of the vice chairs represent auxiliary segments of the Republican organization. One is the chair of the organization of county chairs, another is the president of the Wisconsin Federation of Republican Women, and the third is the chair of the Wisconsin Federation of Young Republicans.

The executive committee of the state party consists of all of the officers mentioned above plus the chair and vice chair of each congressional district, the state chair of the Wisconsin College Republicans, the chair of the Wisconsin Black Republican Council, the chair of the Wisconsin Republican Heritage Groups, and the immediate past state chair of the Republican Party. In addition, there are three nonvoting members of the executive committee representing the Republican senate caucus, the Republican assembly caucus, and the Republican delegation to the U.S. Congress.

The Republican Party holds a state convention each year. In even-numbered years the focus of the convention is on adopting a political platform. In years in which there are elections for statewide office, the state convention may decide to endorse one candidate for each of the five statewide constitutional offices. Prior to 1980 the party was constitutionally required to endorse a candidate for each of the state constitutional offices and for the U.S. Senate.

The Republican Party of Wisconsin currently has twelve staff members in its Madison office. In 1995 the party purchased its own building, which is just a few blocks from the state capitol. The staff consists of an executive director; communications and deputy communications directors; a finance director, deputy finance director, and two finance assistants; controller director and controller; telemarketing manager and assistant; and an office manager. As in most state party organizations, the executive director is responsible for running the party on a day-to-day basis. The state party chair is a voluntary, part-time position. The chair serves as a spokesperson for the party and focuses most of his or her time on fund raising and lobbying the state legislature. The chair spends about one or two days a week in the state party office.

The relationship between the state Republican Party organization and the party in government seems to be quite harmonious and cooperative. This appears to be the result of the Republican Party in recent years emerging from minority status in the state. Although the party captured the governorship in 1986, it was not until 1994 that it gained control of the state legislature. During the early 1990s the party was always within reach of capturing the state legislature, and this possibility seems to have increased the cooperation between the state party organization, the governor, and the legislative campaign committees in the state assembly and the state senate.

The state party organization, the governor, and the legislative campaign committees regularly share such tasks and resources as list development, tracking polls, telemarketing efforts, and absentee ballot campaign activities. They also work together with the local parties in candidate recruitment. Typically, the local parties produce lists of possible candidates, which are then provided to the state party organization as well as to the legislative campaign committees. Both of these groups work to encourage high quality candidates to run, and when they need further persuasive assistance, they bring in the governor as the "closer."

In most states the governor is the chief spokesperson for his or her party. This is clearly the case in Wisconsin. The current governor, Republican Tommy Thompson, was elected to his third four-year term in 1994 with 62 percent of the vote and in 1995 enjoyed popularity ratings at the 70 percent level in his ninth year as governor (St. Norbert College Survey Center 1995). Hence, the current governor is clearly the party leader, and the party embraces him. However, since the Republican Party gained control of the state legislature, the assembly and senate party leaders have also increasingly been viewed as spokespersons for the party.

Governors can play very different roles in their party. In some states they may reduce the strength of the party organization, whereas in other states they may play an active role in building the party. Like many other Republican governors, Gov. Thompson has played an active role in building the state Republican Party (Cotter et al. 1984, 111).

*Democratic Party.* Membership in the Democratic Party of Wisconsin is open to any person who is at least fourteen years of age and pays the party dues of $20.00 (Democratic Party of Wisconsin 1995). The regular membership dues are collected by the county organizations and then are shared equally with the state party. The basic organizational unit in the Democratic Party is the county organization. County organizations are allowed to develop subunits if they are based on significant political subdivisions. Currently, Milwaukee County is the only county that has subunits. In Milwaukee County the subunits comprise one or more state assembly districts. Each county or unit party organization elects a chair, vice chair, secretary, and treasurer. The function of the county or unit party organization is basically party building, which involves maximizing party membership, holding regular party meetings, electing delegates to the congressional district and state conventions, recruiting and supporting Democratic Party candidates for elective office, and making recommendations for the party platform.

The congressional district organization is made up of all of the county or unit party organizations that are within its boundaries. Each congressional district organization holds an annual convention. In odd-numbered years the convention elects officers, elects a representative to the state administrative committee, and considers resolutions. In even-numbered years the convention elects two representatives, one male and one female, to the state administrative committee and develops the platform. Each year at the congressional district convention one representative is also elected for a three-year term to the state platform and resolutions committee. Each congressional district organization is allotted three members on the platform and resolutions committee. The organizations are also allowed by the state party to raise funds for their coffers, but in doing so they must follow federal election laws, including filing a finance report with the Federal Election Commission.

The Democratic Party of Wisconsin holds a state convention every year. Delegates to the state convention are elected by the county or unit organizations. Delegates are allotted on the basis of paid membership in the county or unit organization and votes cast in the county for the Democratic Party candidate for governor in the last general election. Automatic delegates include: each county chair and administrative committee member, members of the U.S. House and Senate, state constitutional officers, and state legislators. In odd-numbered years the state convention elects the state party officers and considers resolutions and amendments to the state party constitution. In even-numbered years the focus is on the party platform, and if it is a presidential election year, the convention elects its members of the Democratic National Committee (DNC).

The governing element of the state Democratic Party is the state administrative committee. This body includes the state party officers (chair, the first vice chair of the opposite sex, second vice chair, treasurer, and secretary), the chair of each congressional district, one additional representative of the opposite sex of the congressional district chair from each district, the DNC members, the Milwaukee County chair, one representative of the Young Democrats, the chair of the county chairs' association, the immediate past chair of the state party, a representative from the state senate Democratic caucus, and one representative from the state assembly Democratic caucus. The administrative committee members also can elect a number of at-large representatives to their committee to assure that the state party meets its affirmative action goals under national party rules. Here is evidence that the national policy of affirmative action has had a demonstrable impact on the Democratic Party organization in Wisconsin.

The Democratic Party of Wisconsin currently has six staff members in its Madison office, a rented suite a few blocks from the state capitol. Although the state party does not itself have another office outside of Madison, it financially supports an office in Milwaukee for the Milwaukee County Democrats. The staff members in Madison include the executive director, administrative assistant, finance director, political director, media-communications director, and field coordinator.

The executive director runs the day-to-day activities of the party and serves as a spokesperson for the party, particularly on national issues. The party chair is a voluntary, part-time position, and although the chair is in contact with the Madison office on a regular basis, he or she does not spend much time there. Identifying the chief spokesperson for a minority party is never easy. It appears that the Democratic Party has several spokespersons, depending on the nature of the issue being discussed. On national issues, the executive director is usually the spokesperson because of his or her regular, usually daily, contact with the national Democratic Party and the Clinton White House. On state policy matters, the spokesperson is frequently one of the party's leaders in the state assembly or the state senate. On purely state party organizational matters, the chairperson is usually sought out.

The relationship between the state party organization and the legislative arm of the Democratic Party appears to be somewhat more cyclical than that of the Republicans. During an election year, Democrats mount a coordinated campaign in which the state party organization leaders, the legislative leaders, and the legislative campaign committees meet weekly to develop strategy and discuss their message. However, being in the legislative minority and not controlling the governor's office have made it more difficult for the Democrats to maintain coordinated efforts and a consistent message. Between elections the autonomy of the state legislative campaign committees, in particular, has been a problem for the Democrats in that the state party organization has no control over their activities. With the increased activity of the legislative committees and the lack of a clear spokesperson for the party, there has been a lack of uniformity on the party's message and little control of the agenda.

**Table 1**  Wisconsin Resource Guide

|  | Democrats | Republicans |
| --- | --- | --- |
| Archive | Yes | Yes |
| Location | State Historical Society of Wisconsin | State Historical Society of Wisconsin |
|  | 816 State Street | 816 State Street |
|  | Madison, WI 53706-1488 | Madison, WI 53706-1488 |
|  | Phone: (608) 264-6400 | Phone: (608) 264-6400 |
|  | Fax: (608) 264-6404 | Fax: (608) 264-6404 |
| Dates | 1944–1978 | 1938–1974 |
| Finding aid | Yes | Yes |
| Access | Public | Public |
| Contents: |  |  |
|    Executive committee minutes | Yes | Yes |
|    Correspondence | Yes | Yes |
|    Organizational structure | Yes | Yes |
|    Budgets | Very limited | Very limited |
|    Rules | Yes | Yes |

## RESOURCE GUIDE

The records of the Democratic Party of Wisconsin are housed primarily at the State Historical Society of Wisconsin in Madison. The archive is quite good for the early period of the modern Democratic Party (1948 through 1950s). Some systematic research may be possible for this early period. The files from the 1960s to the present are very fragmentary. The materials available for these later years are so spotty that it would be very difficult to get a complete picture of party operations from the files. There is a finding aid to assist the researcher. In addition, all of the state historical society's files are cataloged on computer, so that a computer search by key word is possible. The search feature allows the researcher to access information that may not be in party files per se, but that may be useful to the researcher of party organizations (such as personal papers of state political leaders). The Democratic Party also engaged in an oral history project in 1985 that will be of use to some scholars. Interviews were conducted with thirty-seven party activists who were influential in the Democratic Party from the end of World War II through the 1950s.

The records of the Republican Party of Wisconsin are of similar quality. The records are fairly good for the late 1940s to about 1970. After 1970 the records are quite fragmentary. State convention records are good from 1946 to 1963. Some materials from 1964 to the present are available from the state party headquarters. George Greeley, who was executive director from 1960 through 1970, has deposited his papers at the state historical society. They consist of a smattering of correspondence, clippings, financial reports, and press releases.

Ody Fish, party chair from 1966 to 1970, is the only chair who has deposited a significant collection of materials. His collection of papers covers the period from 1961 to 1985 and is located at the University of Wisconsin-Milwaukee Area Research Center.

## REFERENCES

*Asterisks denote the most important publications on Wisconsin party politics.*
Adamany, David. 1976. Cross-over voting and the Democratic Party's reform rules. *American Political Science Review* 70:536–541.
*Bibby, John F. 1991. Political parties and elections. In *Wisconsin government and politics.* 5th ed., ed. Wilder Crane et al. Milwaukee: University of Wisconsin Board of Trustees.

Cotter, Cornelius P., James L. Gibson, John F. Bibby, and Robert J. Huckshorn. 1984. *Party organizations in American politics.* New York: Praeger.

Democratic Party of Wisconsin. 1995. *Democratic Party of Wisconsin leadership manual.* Madison: Democratic Party of Wisconsin.

*Donoghue, James R. 1974. *How Wisconsin voted 1848–1972.* Madison: Department of Government Affairs, University of Wisconsin-Extension.

Epstein, Leon D. 1958. *Politics in Wisconsin.* Madison: University of Wisconsin Press.

*———. 1956a. A two-party Wisconsin? *Journal of Politics* 18:427–458.

———. 1956b. American parties: A Wisconsin case-study. *Political Studies* 4:30–45.

*Haney, Richard C. 1989. *A history of the Democratic Party of Wisconsin 1949–1989.* Madison: Democratic Party of Wisconsin.

*———. 1976. *A concise history of the modern Republican Party of Wisconsin 1925–1975.* Madison: Republican Party of Wisconsin.

Johnson, Roger T. 1964. *Robert M. La Follette, Jr. and the decline of the Progressive Party in Wisconsin.* New Haven: Shoe String Publishers.

La Follette, Robert M. 1913. *La Follette's autobiography: A personal narrative of political experience.* Madison: University of Wisconsin Press.

*Loftus, Tom. 1994. *The art of legislative politics.* Washington D.C.: CQ Press.

Margulies, Herbert F. 1968. The decline of the Progressive Movement. In *Wisconsin: 1890–1920.* Madison: State History Society of Wisconsin.

*Nesbit, Roger C. 1973. *Wisconsin, a history.* Madison: University of Wisconsin Press.

Ranney, Austin, and Leon D. Epstein. 1966. The two electorates: Voters and non-voters in a Wisconsin primary. *Journal of Politics* 28: 598–616.

Reeves, Thomas C. 1982. *The life and times of Joe McCarthy.* Lanham, Md.: University Press of America.

Sorauf, Frank J. 1954. Extra-legal parties in Wisconsin. *American Political Science Review* 48 (September): 692–704.

*St. Norbert College Survey Center. 1995. Wisconsin survey 1984–1995. De Pere, Wis.: St. Norbert College Survey Center.

State of Wisconsin. Political party organization in Wisconsin. *State of Wisconsin blue book. 1993–1994.* Madison: State of Wisconsin, Legislative Reference Bureau.

Wegge, David G., and Amy Pottner. 1993. Party competition and identification in Wisconsin, 1980–1992: The emergence of a more competitive state. *Wisconsin Political Scientist* 7 (spring): 13–17.

*Wekkin, Gary D. 1984. *Democrat versus Democrat: The national party's campaign to close the Wisconsin primary.* Columbia: University of Missouri Press.

# *Wyoming*

OLIVER WALTER

## PARTY HISTORY

The history of Wyoming political parties is marked by the dominance of the Republican Party. Wyoming achieved statehood in 1890, and in the elections of that year Republicans won all state offices and majorities in the two houses of the legislature. The results of the 1994 state elections were identical: Republicans won all five state government offices, carried the legislature, and won the lone congressional seat. In addition, Republican Craig Thomas won the U.S. Senate seat vacated by Republican Malcolm Wallop.

Historically, Republicans have won majorities in the state senate 96 percent of the time and majorities in the house 85 percent of the time. With the exception of the governor's office, Republicans have won all executive offices at least seven times out of ten. Only once in history has a Democrat been elected as state treasurer. On the other hand, Democratic candidates have won nearly one-half of the elections for governor. And until Republican Jim Geringer won the governorship in 1994, Democrats had held the state's highest executive office continuously since 1974.

In 1996 nearly 60 percent of registered Wyoming voters designated themselves as Republicans, whereas only 33 percent called themselves Democrats, a percentage that has been decreasing rather steadily for a quarter-century. In terms of party identification, only one in five Wyomingites identifies as a Democrat. Four in ten identify as a Republican (Wyoming Election Survey 1994).

Without doubt the dominant political figure in the early political history of the state was Francis E. Warren. Warren was the first governor of Wyoming, but he served only a few months before moving to the U.S. Senate. He served in the Senate for thirty-seven years, and from 1921 until his death in 1929 he chaired the Senate Appropriations Committee. With brief exceptions, the "Warren machine" dominated Wyoming politics, and the early history of the Republican Party is very much the history of Francis E. Warren. His political power was based on strong personal and economic ties to the state's political elite, most importantly, Wyoming cattlemen. Even in the face of Republican dominance, the Democrats won the governorship on several occasions during the Warren era, but few other offices.

As in the nation as a whole, Democrats in Wyoming were considerably more successful during the Great Depression years. Democrat Joseph O'Mahoney was elected U.S. senator in 1934 and, with the exception of a brief period, served until his retirement in 1961. Although popular, O'Mahoney never built the organizational support that was the hallmark of the Warren years, nor did any Wyoming politician, Republican or Democrat, demonstrate substantial influence beyond personal political popularity.

## ORGANIZATIONAL DEVELOPMENT

A myth long espoused by Wyoming politicians is that Wyoming is somehow much different from the rest of the nation. Perhaps there is some validity in the assertion, but Wyoming clearly is not immune to national political trends. Wyoming Democrats have fared best when the national party has done well. Democratic gains in the 1958, 1964, and 1974 elections were followed by considerable fall-offs in party support in subsequent elections.

Democrat Ed Herschler won election to the governorship in 1974 and again in 1978 and 1982, becoming the only governor in Wyoming history to serve three terms. Subsequently, Democrat Mike Sullivan won gubernatorial election twice before the Republicans regained the chief executive position in 1994.

In the past quarter-century, the Wyoming politician with the highest profile both within the state and nationally has been Sen. Alan Simpson, who first won election to the Senate in 1978. Simpson's father, Milward, had served as both governor and U.S. senator. Herschler, Sullivan, and particularly Simpson were popular, but their popularity seldom translated into support for other would-be officeholders of their respective parties. Not even their political enemies accused them of building a political machine.

For Wyomingites in recent times, Ronald Reagan was by far the most popular president. Not only did he carry the state by huge margins, but his job approval rating among Wyoming citizens was the highest of any politician during the past quarter-century. George Bush, although he carried Wyoming twice, was not particularly popular. During the last two years of his term in office, Bush's job performance rating among Wyomingites fell from about 50 percent to under 30 percent. Concurrently, Wyoming citizens' "trust" in the federal government suffered a precipitant fall. In 1988, 31 percent of Wyoming citizens indicated that they trusted the federal government all or most of the time. By 1992 only 16 percent expressed the same degree of trust for the federal government, and by 1994 just over 10 percent of Wyomingites said they trusted the federal government all or most of the time. Twenty-two percent declared no trust in the federal government. Wyoming's alienation from the national government has several causes, among them a stagnant economy that has not recovered from the energy boom years of the early 1980s and a long tradition of suspicion of the government resulting, at least in part, from the fact that the federal government owns much of the state's land base. Not surprisingly, Ross Perot won nearly 26 percent of the vote in the 1992 presidential election (Wyoming Election Survey 1994).

## CURRENT PARTY ORGANIZATION

The structure of Wyoming political parties is not unlike that of parties in most western states. A state law passed in 1957 sets the basic structure of the two major parties from the precinct level to the state convention. A committeeman and committeewoman are elected from each precinct. (Many precincts, however, elect neither a committeeman nor committeewoman because no one files for election.) These individuals make up the county central committee.

By law each party is required to hold a convention every two years. The state central committees are composed of county party chairs plus a state committeeman and committeewoman elected from each county. The state central committees elect chairs and organize the state conventions, which are held in even-numbered years. Party organizations play a direct role in nominating members of their party for county and state offices only when the offices become vacant between elections. All other county and statewide candidates are nominated in primary elections. On the other hand, the Wyoming state conventions select candidates to the national presidential conventions.

State law specifies that county and state conventions approve party platforms. When there is controversy within one party or the other, in most instances it revolves around the platform.

As might be expected in a state with a small population and political parties that have very few patronage favors to dispense and little influence on the nomination process, Wyoming political parties have seldom displayed political power independent of the state's leading politicians. For the Democrats, the greater concern has been to identify candidates who are willing to run for office. Even for the major state offices, the Democratic Party frequently fields candidates who have no chance of seriously challenging Republican candidates. Governors Herschler and Sullivan owed their initial elections in part to bitter primary fights among the Republican aspirants for governor. In 1994 Republican Party chair Diemer True demonstrated considerable leadership by convincing the major competitors in the gubernatorial primary to lend their verbal support to the winner of the primary.

Neither party began hiring a permanent staff at the state level until the 1950s. As would be expected, the dominant Republican Party has consistently outdistanced the Democratic Party in professionalizing its party organization. Even today, the permanent staff of the Democratic Party consists of only one or two persons. Before the 1950s, Wyoming political party organization all but disappeared between elections. Today it is skeletal.

Traditionally, political campaigning in Wyoming centered on direct contact between the candidate and the voter. Even today, Wyoming's most capable politicians, such as Senator Simpson and former governor Mike Sullivan, are on a first-name basis with a huge percentage of the state's population. But Malcolm Wallop's 1976 senatorial victory over incumbent Gale McGee was attributed largely to Wallop's skillful media campaign. With few exceptions, the candidates for major political office, particularly governor and the U.S. Congress, have relied on out-of-state media consultants and producers. Simultaneously, the major candidates began using extensive polling, virtually all of which was conducted by out-of-state firms. In many, if not most, instances, the national party organizations provided Wyoming candidates with links to their polling and campaign consultants as well as some funding.

Clearly, for both Wyoming political parties, the national parties have become increasingly important in providing campaign expertise and campaign funds and in providing the links between candidates and groups or individuals who will provide campaign support. For instance, the "Dollars for Democrats" fund-raising effort undertaken by Wyoming Democrats was initiated and administered at the national level. Certainly, the Wyoming Democratic Party did not and does not have the capacity to mount such an effort on its own. The McGovern reforms, which had a significant effect on the composition of party conventions, are another example of a national party initiative.

Perhaps the most noticeable change in the relationship between the state and national parties is the amount of information provided by the national party organizations to the state parties. Technical advice on campaign strategies, as well as information concerning the political strategies of national party leaders, is abundantly available to state party organizations.

### RESOURCE GUIDE

One of the major problems with researching Wyoming political parties is that, until recently, little attempt had been made to archive party records. When a party chair left office, he or she either kept the records or disposed of them. The Republican Party headquarters currently has reasonably good records of central committee and convention proceedings for the past couple of decades.

The Democrats have much less complete records, but these have recently been donated to the University of Wyoming American Heritage Center. The Republican Party has more extensive records, but they are maintained by the party.

The American Heritage Center also has extensive collections of the papers of Wyoming political leaders. These include the papers of Frank Barrett (U.S. representative, 1943–1950; governor, 1951–1953; U.S. senator, 1953–1959); Bryant Brooks (governor, 1905–1911); Joseph Carey (U.S. senator, 1890–1895; governor, 1911–1915); Robert Carey (governor, 1919–1923; U.S. senator, 1930–1937); Fenimore Chatterton (governor, 1903–1905); Richard Cheney (U.S. representative, 1979–1989); Jack Gage (governor, 1961–1963); Clifford Hansen (governor, 1963–1967; U.S. senator, 1967–1979); William Henry Harrison (U.S. representative,

1951–1955, 1961–1965, 1967–1969); Joseph Hickey (governor, 1959–1961; U.S. senator, 1961–1962); Lester Hunt (governor, 1943–1949; U.S. senator, 1949–1954); John Kendrick (governor, 1915–1917; U.S. senator, 1917–1933); Gale McGee (U.S. senator, 1959–1977); Joseph C. O'Mahoney (U.S. senator, 1934–1953, 1954–1961); Frank W. Mondell (U.S. representative, 1895–1897, 1899–1923); W. A. Richards (governor, 1895–1899); Teno Roncalio (U.S. representative, 1965–1967, 1971–1978); Milward Simpson (governor, 1955–1959; U.S. senator, 1962–1967); Nels Smith (governor, 1939–1943); Mike Sullivan (governor, 1987–1995); Nellie Tayloe Ross (governor, 1925–1927); Keith Thomson (U.S. representative, 1955–1960); Thyra Thomson (secretary of state, 1963–1987); Malcolm Wallop (U.S. senator, 1977–1995); F. E. Warren (governor, 1890; U.S. senator, 1890–1893, 1895–1929).

## REFERENCES

Cawley, Gregg, et al. 1991. *The equality state: Governmental politics in Wyoming.* Dubuque, Iowa: Eddie Bowers Publishing.

Larson, T. A. *History of Wyoming.* 1965. Lincoln: University of Nebraska Press.

Wyoming Election Survey. 1994. Survey Research Center. University of Wyoming. October.

# Appendix
# The Legal Environment of State Parties

As quasi-governmental organizations, political parties often are responsible for overseeing the conduct of election campaigns, including voting procedures, and thus face regulation by the government. As quasi-private organizations, however, they historically have been granted considerable autonomy by the U.S. Supreme Court. The Court's decision in 1989 in *Eu v. San Francisco County Democratic Central Committee* (489 U.S. 214) was particularly unburdening for the parties. That decision struck down California statutes that prevented preprimary endorsements by parties and that set the length of term for state party chairs, among other regulations. More than half a decade after that decision, however, state parties are still weighing its impact and considering internal reforms. There has been no rush to change as a result of the *Eu* decision.

The degree of regulation has varied considerably across states and has changed within states over time as well. One of the recurring difficulties for students of state parties has been to identify the existing legal environment for particular states and to compare them across states. This appendix is designed to provide a clear contemporary snapshot of state party regulations. With the uncertainty caused by the *Eu* case in mind, we asked contributors to this volume to complete a checklist of statutory regulations that face state parties in their states. Although some, if not most, of these regulations might be called into question by the *Eu* decision, most state parties continue to operate under statutory guidelines. Despite the complexity of some state laws, with the assistance of the contributors, we have been able to present this information in a tractable manner. A series of twelve questions regarding state party laws have been pared down to "yes" and "no" responses. For each question, a proparty—or antiregulatory—response has been designated, and that response is shaded in the table that follows the questions.

## QUESTIONS REGARDING STATE PARTY LAWS

1. Does state law mandate the manner of selecting members of the parties' state central committee?

2. Does state law mandate the timing of central committee meetings?

3. Does state law mandate the composition of central committees?

4. Does state law regulate leadership of party organizations?

5. Does state law forbid nominating conventions for statewide office?

6. Does state law forbid preprimary endorsements by the party?

7. Does state law require an open primary for statewide office?

8. Does state law prevent primary losers from running in the general election as an independent or third-party candidate (that is, include "sore loser" provision)?

9. Does the state ballot allow for a single straight-party vote?

10. Were presidential primaries held on the same day as primaries for statewide office in 1992?

11. Were presidential primaries held on the same day as primaries for statewide office in 1996?

12. May a voter participate in different party primaries for president and statewide offices?

| | 1. Mandate selection of state central committee? | 2. Mandate central committee meetings? | 3. Mandate composition of central committees? | 4. Regulate leadership of party organizations? | 5. Forbid party nominating conventions? | 6. Forbid preprimary endorsements? | 7. Mandate open primary? | 8. Include "sore loser" provision? | 9. Allow straight party vote? | 10. Hold simultaneous primaries, 1992? | 11. Hold simultaneous primaries, 1996? | 12. Allow crossover party primary voting? |
|---|---|---|---|---|---|---|---|---|---|---|---|---|
| Alabama | N | N | N | N | N | N | N | N | Y | Y | Y | N |
| Alaska | N | N | N | N | Y | N | N | N | N | N/A | N/A | N/A |
| Arizona | Y | Y | Y | Y | Y | N | Y | Y | N | N | N | N |
| Arkansas | Y | N | N | N | Y | N | N[1] | Y | Y[2] | Y | Y | N |
| California | Y | N | Y[3] | Y | Y | N | Y[4] | N | N | Y | Y | Y |
| Colorado | Y | Y | Y | Y | Y[5] | N | Y | N | N | N | N | N |
| Connecticut | N | N | N | N | Y[6] | N | Y[7] | N | N | N | N | N |
| Delaware | N | N | N | N | Y | N | N | N | N | N/A | N | N |
| Florida | N | N | N | N | Y | Y | Y | N | N | N | N | N |
| Georgia | N | N | N | N | Y | N | N | N | N | N | N | Y |
| Hawaii | N | N | N | Y | Y | N | N | N | N | N/A | N/A | N/A |
| Idaho | Y | Y | Y | N | Y | N | N | Y | Y | Y | Y | N |
| Illinois | Y | Y | Y[8] | Y | N | N | N | Y | Y | Y | Y | N |
| Indiana | Y | Y | Y[9] | Y | Y[10] | N | N[11] | Y | Y | Y | Y | N |
| Iowa | Y | N | Y | N | Y | N | Y[12] | N | Y[13] | N/A | N/A | N/A |
| Kansas | N | N | N | N | Y[14] | N | N[15] | N | N | N | N | N/A |
| Kentucky | N | N | N | N | Y | N | Y | Y | Y | N | N | N |
| Louisiana[16] | Y | Y | Y | Y | Y | N | Y | N | N | N/A | N/A | N |
| Maine | Y | N | N | Y | Y | N | Y[17] | N[18] | N | N/A | N | Y |
| Maryland | Y | Y | N | Y | Y[19] | N | N[20] | Y | N | N | N | N |
| Massachusetts | Y | N | Y[9] | Y | Y[19] | N | N | Y | N | N | N | Y |
| Michigan | Y | N | Y[9] | Y | Y[21] | N | N | Y | Y | N/A | N/A | Y |

| State | 1 | 2 | 3 | 4 | 5 | 6 | 7 | 8 | 9 | 10 | 11 | 12 |
|---|---|---|---|---|---|---|---|---|---|---|---|---|
| Minnesota | N | N | N | N | N | Y | N | N | Y | N | N | N |
| Mississippi | Y | N | N | Y | Y | N | N | N[22] | N[23] | N/A | N/A | N/A |
| Missouri | Y | Y | Y[9] | Y | Y | N | N | N | Y | Y | Y | N/A |
| Montana | Y | Y | Y[9] | N | N | N | Y | Y | Y | Y | Y | N |
| Nebraska | N | Y | N | N | Y | N | Y | N | N | N | Y | Y |
| Nevada | Y | N | Y | Y | Y | N | Y | Y | N | N/A | N/A | N/A |
| New Hampshire | Y | N | Y | Y | Y | N | N[24] | N | Y | N | N | Y[25] |
| New Jersey[26] | Y | Y | Y[9] | Y | Y | Y | Y | Y | N | Y | Y | N |
| New Mexico | Y | N | N | Y | N | N | Y | Y | N | Y | Y | N |
| New York | Y | N | N | Y | N | Y | Y | N | N | N/A | N/A | N/A |
| North Carolina | N | N | N | N | Y | N | Y | Y | Y | Y | Y | Y |
| North Dakota | Y | Y | Y | Y | Y | Y | N | Y | N | N | N | Y |
| Ohio | Y | Y | Y[9] | Y | Y | Y | N | N | N | N/A | N/A | N/A |
| Oklahoma | N | N | N | N | Y | N | N | N | Y | N | N | N |
| Oregon | Y | Y | N | Y | Y | N | Y | Y | Y | Y | Y | N |
| Pennsylvania | Y | N | N | N | Y | N | N | Y | Y | Y | Y | Y |
| Rhode Island | N | N | N | Y | Y | Y | Y | N | N | Y | N | Y |
| South Carolina | Y | N | Y | Y | N | N | N | N | Y | N/A | N/A | N/A |
| South Dakota | Y | Y | Y[9] | Y | Y[27] | N | Y | N | Y | N | Y | Y |
| Tennessee | Y | N | Y[9] | Y | Y[28] | N | N | Y | N | N | Y | Y |
| Texas | Y | N | Y | Y | Y | N | N[29] | Y | Y | Y | Y | N |
| Utah | N | N | N | Y | N | N | N | N | Y | N/A | N/A | N/A |
| Vermont | Y | Y | Y[9] | Y | Y | N | N | N | Y | N | Y | Y |
| Virginia | N | N | N | N | N | N | Y | Y | N | N/A | N/A | N/A |
| Washington | Y | Y | Y[9] | Y | Y | N | Y | N | Y | Y | Y | Y |
| West Virginia | Y | N | Y[9] | Y | Y | N | N | N | Y[30] | N | Y | N |
| Wisconsin | N | N | Y | N | Y | N | N | N | Y | N/A | N/A | N/A |
| Wyoming | Y | N | Y | Y | N | N | N | N | N | N | N | N |

Y = yes; N = no; N/A = not applicable.
*Note:* Shaded letters indicate a "proparty" or nonregulatory response.

Notes continue.

1 Voters in Arkansas declare their party on primary election day. In runoffs participation is restricted to the party declared at the primary.

2 County election commissions in Arkansas set the ballot for the general election. A vast majority do not give voters a straight party option.

3 Section 7162 of the California elections code mandates gender balance "to the extent possible," but the provision applies only to the Democratic Party. The Republican Party is mandated only to select members on the basis of nondiscrimination.

4 California's Proposition 198, passed by voters in March 1996, establishes an open primary, but the proposition is under court challenge.

5 In Colorado a candidate must receive 30 percent of the convention vote to be listed on the primary ballot, or a candidate may petition to be listed on the primary ballot.

6 In Connecticut party conventions can nominate candidates for statewide office, subject to a "challenge primary," whereby a candidate receiving 15 percent of the vote at the convention may call for a primary.

7 In Connecticut parties may choose to allow unaffiliated voters to participate, though this is not the current practice of either major party.

8 In Illinois gender balance is required for Democrats.

9 Gender balance is a requirement in Indiana, Massachusetts, Michigan, Missouri, Montana, New Jersey, Ohio, South Dakota, Tennessee, Vermont, Washington, and West Virginia.

10 In Indiana a primary is required for gubernatorial and U.S. Senate elections; conventions are required for other statewide offices.

11 Although there is no party registration in Indiana, voters can be challenged. Voters must affirm that they voted for or will vote for a majority of the party's candidates in the previous or next general election.

12 Voters in Iowa may change party affiliation on election day.

13 In Iowa party column ballots are permitted by state law. Choice of ballot form is made by the county boards of supervisors.

14 The restriction on nominating conventions holds in Kansas except for parties that received less than 5 percent of the vote cast for governor in the preceding election.

15 Voters in Kansas must be declared for a party in order to vote in the party's primary. Unaffiliated voters may declare on primary election day.

16 Louisiana law has separate provisions for major (greater than 25 percent of registered voters) and minor parties. These provisions apply to major parties only.

17 Unaffiliated voters in Maine may declare for a party on primary election day. Voters wishing to change parties must do so sixteen days before the election.

18 Filing dates in Maine make it impossible for a primary loser to qualify for the general election as an independent.

19 In Massachusetts a threshold is required at the convention for a place on the primary ballot.

20 Unaffiliated voters in Massachusetts may register on primary election day and participate in a party primary. They may switch back to unaffiliated status immediately after voting.

21 In Michigan the primary is for governor only; other statewide offices are nominated at convention.

22 In Mississippi the first primary is open. Voters in the first primary may vote only in the same party's runoff.

23 Filing dates in Mississippi make it impossible for a primary loser to qualify for the general election as an independent.

24 Independents in New Hampshire may declare party preference at the polls by changing registration.

25 Voters in New Hampshire may change registration between primaries.

26 In New Jersey provisions of state law that affect party structure and party involvement in primaries (questions 1–6) are now considered unenforceable because of the Supreme Court's decision in *Eu v. San Francisco*, in which the Court held that laws regulating political parties must further a "compelling state interest." Both parties have made changes in their structure and functioning that deviate from provisions of state law.

27 In South Dakota the primary is for governor and federal offices; others are nominated by convention.

28 In Tennessee the provision applies to the governor, public service commission, general assembly, and U.S. House and Senate seats.

29 Voters in Texas may select their party on primary election day. Registration is then retained for two years.

30 In Wisconsin the president and vice president are excluded from a straight ticket vote.

# Index